Communications
in Computer and Information Science   2260

Series Editors

Gang Li , *School of Information Technology, Deakin University, Burwood, VIC, Australia*
Joaquim Filipe , *Polytechnic Institute of Setúbal, Setúbal, Portugal*
Zhiwei Xu, *Chinese Academy of Sciences, Beijing, China*

Rationale

The CCIS series is devoted to the publication of proceedings of computer science conferences. Its aim is to efficiently disseminate original research results in informatics in printed and electronic form. While the focus is on publication of peer-reviewed full papers presenting mature work, inclusion of reviewed short papers reporting on work in progress is welcome, too. Besides globally relevant meetings with internationally representative program committees guaranteeing a strict peer-reviewing and paper selection process, conferences run by societies or of high regional or national relevance are also considered for publication.

Topics

The topical scope of CCIS spans the entire spectrum of informatics ranging from foundational topics in the theory of computing to information and communications science and technology and a broad variety of interdisciplinary application fields.

Information for Volume Editors and Authors

Publication in CCIS is free of charge. No royalties are paid, however, we offer registered conference participants temporary free access to the online version of the conference proceedings on SpringerLink (http://link.springer.com) by means of an http referrer from the conference website and/or a number of complimentary printed copies, as specified in the official acceptance email of the event.

CCIS proceedings can be published in time for distribution at conferences or as postproceedings, and delivered in the form of printed books and/or electronically as USBs and/or e-content licenses for accessing proceedings at SpringerLink. Furthermore, CCIS proceedings are included in the CCIS electronic book series hosted in the SpringerLink digital library at http://link.springer.com/bookseries/7899. Conferences publishing in CCIS are allowed to use Online Conference Service (OCS) for managing the whole proceedings lifecycle (from submission and reviewing to preparing for publication) free of charge.

Publication process

The language of publication is exclusively English. Authors publishing in CCIS have to sign the Springer CCIS copyright transfer form, however, they are free to use their material published in CCIS for substantially changed, more elaborate subsequent publications elsewhere. For the preparation of the camera-ready papers/files, authors have to strictly adhere to the Springer CCIS Authors' Instructions and are strongly encouraged to use the CCIS LaTeX style files or templates.

Abstracting/Indexing

CCIS is abstracted/indexed in DBLP, Google Scholar, EI-Compendex, Mathematical Reviews, SCImago, Scopus. CCIS volumes are also submitted for the inclusion in ISI Proceedings.

How to start

To start the evaluation of your proposal for inclusion in the CCIS series, please send an e-mail to ccis@springer.com

Hamid R. Arabnia · Leonidas Deligiannidis ·
Soheyla Amirian · Farid Ghareh Mohammadi ·
Farzan Shenavarmasouleh
Editors

Internet Computing and IoT and Embedded Systems, Cyber-physical Systems, and Applications

25th International Conference, ICOMP 2024
and 22nd International Conference, ESCS 2024
Held as Part of the World Congress in Computer
Science, Computer Engineering and Applied
Computing, CSCE 2024
Las Vegas, NV, USA, July 22–25, 2024
Revised Selected Papers

 Springer

Editors
Hamid R. Arabnia ⓘ
Department of Computer Science
The University of Georgia
Athens, GA, USA

Soheyla Amirian ⓘ
Pace University
Athens, GA, USA

Farzan Shenavarmasouleh ⓘ
Medialab Inc.
Lawrenceville, GA, USA

Leonidas Deligiannidis ⓘ
Wentworth Institute of Technology
Boston, MA, USA

Farid Ghareh Mohammadi ⓘ
Mayo Clinic
Athens, GA, USA

ISSN 1865-0929   ISSN 1865-0937 (electronic)
Communications in Computer and Information Science
ISBN 978-3-031-85922-9   ISBN 978-3-031-85923-6 (eBook)
https://doi.org/10.1007/978-3-031-85923-6

This Springer imprint is published by the registered company Springer Nature Switzerland AG
The registered company address is: Gewerbestrasse 11, 6330 Cham, Switzerland

If disposing of this product, please recycle the paper.

Preface

It is our great pleasure to introduce this collection of selected papers presented at the 25th International Conference on Internet Computing & IoT (ICOMP 2024) and the 22nd International Conference on Embedded Systems, Cyber-physical Systems, & Applications (ESCS 2024). Both conferences were held as part of the federated 2024 Congress on Computer Science, Computer Engineering, and Applied Computing (CSCE 2024), which took place from July 22 to July 25, 2024, in Las Vegas, Nevada, USA.

The CSCE 2024 Congress brought together papers from a diverse array of communities, including researchers from universities, corporations, and government agencies. Accepted papers are published by Springer Nature, and the proceedings showcase solutions to key challenges in various critical areas of Computer Science, Computer Engineering, and Applied Computing.

Computer Science (CS) is the study of computational systems, data processing, information management, and automation. Many applications in CS focus on solving problems that would be impossible or extremely difficult to address without the use of computers. It serves as a bridge between computational science and other scientific fields. The interdisciplinary nature of CS involves leveraging computers to understand and solve complex challenges, making it the science of using computers to advance scientific discovery. Computer Engineering (CE), on the other hand, integrates aspects of computer science, electronic engineering, and electrical engineering. It encompasses the design and production of computer hardware, such as chips, servers, supercomputers, embedded systems, and communication systems, among others.

Considering the above broad outline, the CSCE 2024 Congress was composed of the following focused conferences:

Applied Cognitive Computing (ACC); Bioinformatics & Computational Biology (BIOCOMP); Biomedical Engineering (BIOENG); Scientific Computing (CSC); e-Learning, e-Business, Enterprise Information Systems, & e-Government (EEE); Embedded Systems, Cyber-physical Systems, & Applications (ESCS); Foundations of Computer Science (FCS); Frontiers in Education (FECS); Grid, Cloud, & Cluster Computing (GCC); Health Informatics (HIMS); Artificial Intelligence (ICAI); Data Science (ICDATA); Emergent Quantum Technologies (ICEQT); Internet Computing & IoT (ICOMP); Wireless Networks (ICWN); Information & Knowledge Engineering (IKE); Image Processing, Computer Vision, & Pattern Recognition (IPCV); Modeling, Simulation & Visualization Methods (MSV); Parallel & Distributed Processing Techniques & Applications (PDPTA); Security & Management (SAM); and Software Engineering Research & Practice (SERP). The scope of each track can be found at: https://www.ame rican-cse.org/csce2024/conferences

The primary objective of the CSCE Congress and its associated conferences is to foster opportunities for cross-fertilization between the fields of Computer Science (CS) and Computer Engineering (CE). The CSCE Congress is deeply committed to promoting diversity and eliminating discrimination, both in its role as a conference organizer and as a service provider. Our goal is to create an inclusive culture that respects and values differences, promotes dignity, equality, and diversity, and encourages individuals to reach their full potential. We are also dedicated, wherever possible, to organizing a conference that represents the global community. We sincerely hope that we have succeeded in achieving these important objectives.

The Steering Committee and the Program Committees would like to extend their gratitude to all the authors who submitted papers for consideration. This year's conferences received submissions from 29 countries, with approximately 39% of them coming from outside the USA. Each submitted paper underwent a rigorous peer-review process, with at least two experts (an average of 2.2 referees per paper) evaluating the submissions based on originality, significance, clarity, impact, and soundness. In cases where reviewers' recommendations were contradictory, a program committee member was tasked with making the final decision, often consulting additional referees for further guidance. The Congress followed the guidelines of COPE (Committee on Publication Ethics):

- Typical submissions underwent a single-blind peer review process, in which the authors remained unaware of the identities of the reviewers, while the reviewers were informed of the authors' identities.
- Papers authored by one or more members of the program committee, including co-chairs, were subjected to a double-blind peer review process, ensuring that neither the authors nor the reviewers were aware of each other's identities or affiliations.

The ICOMP 2024 Conference received 122 submissions, of which 23 papers were accepted, resulting in a paper acceptance rate of 18.9%. The ESCS 2024 Conference received 49 submissions, of which 11 papers were accepted, resulting in a paper acceptance rate of 22.4%. This volume includes the 34 accepted papers from ICOMP 2024 and ESC 20'24.

We are deeply grateful to the many colleagues who contributed their time and effort to organizing the Congress. In particular, we extend our thanks to the members of the Program Committees, the Steering Committee, the referees, and the Chairs and organizers of individual sessions and conferences. We would also like to express our appreciation to the primary sponsor of the conference, the American Council on Science & Education. The list of members of the Program Committee for each track can be found at: https://www.american-cse.org/csce2024/committees

We extend our heartfelt gratitude to all the speakers and authors for their valuable contributions. We would also like to thank the following individuals and organizations for their support: the staff at the Luxor Hotel, the staff of Springer Nature for assistance during the publication process, Ranis Ibragimovin (Walter De Gruyter, Inc.) for his assistance in publishing multiple books, and many Departments and Universities for their assistance in various aspects of the event.

We are pleased to present a curated selection of papers from ICOMP 2024 and ESCS 2024 conferences. These proceedings represent a collection of outstanding research contributions that reflect the diversity and depth of work in core areas of applied computer science and computer engineering.

Hamid R. Arabnia
Leonidas Deligiannidis
Soheyla Amirian
Farid Ghareh Mohammadi
Farzan Shenavarmasouleh

Organization

Steering Committee – Co-chairs (CSCE 2024)

Hamid R. Arabnia	University of Georgia, USA
Leonidas Deligiannidis	Wentworth Institute of Technology, USA
Fernando G. Tinetti	Universidad Nacional de La Plata, Argentina
Quoc-Nam Tran	Southeastern Louisiana University, USA

Co-editors of ICOMP 2024 and ESCS 2024 Proceedings – Publication Co-chairs

Hamid R. Arabnia (Co-Chair, ICOMP 2024 & ESCS 2024)	University of Georgia, USA
Leonidas Deligiannidis (Co-Chair, ICOMP 2024 & ESCS 2024)	Wentworth Institute of Technology, USA
Soheyla Amirian (Session Chair, ICOMP 2024 & ESCS 2024)	Pace University, USA
Farid Ghareh Mohammadi (Session Chair, ICOMP 2024 & ESCS 2024)	Mayo Clinic, USA
Farzan Shenavarmasouleh (Session Chair, ICOMP 2024 & ESCS 2024)	Medialab Inc., USA

Members of Steering Committee (CSCE 2024)

Babak Akhgar	Sheffield Hallam University, UK
Abbas M. Al-Bakry	University of IT & Communications, Iraq
Nizar Al-Holou	University of Detroit Mercy, USA
Hamid R. Arabnia	University of Georgia, USA
Rajab Challoo	Texas A&M University-Kingsville, USA
Chien-Fu Cheng	Tamkang University, Taiwan
Hyunseung Choo	Sungkyunkwan University, South Korea
Kevin Daimi	University of Detroit Mercy, USA
Leonidas Deligiannidis	Wentworth Institute of Technology, USA
Eman M. El-Sheikh	University of West Florida, USA

Mary Mehrnoosh Eshaghian-Wilner	University of California Los Angeles, USA
David L. Foster	Kettering University, USA
Henry Hexmoor	Southern Illinois University at Carbondale, USA
Ching-Hsien (Robert) Hsu	Chung Hua University, Taiwan; and Tianjin University of Technology, China
James J. (Jong Hyuk) Park	SeoulTech, South Korea
Mohammad S. Obaidat	University of Jordan, Jordan
Marwan Omar	Illinois Institute of Technology, USA
Shahram Rahimi	Mississippi State University, USA
Gerald Schaefer	Loughborough University, UK
Fernando G. Tinetti	Universidad Nacional de La Plata, Argentina
Quoc-Nam Tran	Southeastern Louisiana University, USA
Shiuh-Jeng Wang	Central Police University, Taiwan
Layne T. Watson	Virginia Polytechnic Institute & State University, USA
Chao-Tung Yang	Tunghai University, Taiwan
Mary Yang	University of Arkansas, USA

Research Tracks – Co-chairs (CSCE 2024)

Abeer Alsadoon (Co-chair, Health Informatics)	Charles Sturt University, Australia
Soheyla Amirian (Co-chair, Computer Vision & AI)	Pace University, USA
Hamid R. Arabnia (Co-chair, HPC)	University of Georgia, USA
Kevin Daimi (Co-chair, Security)	University of Detroit Mercy, USA
Leonidas Deligiannidis (Co-chair, Imaging Science, AI)	Wentworth Institute of Technology, USA
Richard Dill (Co-chair, Military and Defense Modeling)	US Air Force Institute of Technology, USA
Ken Ferens (Co-chair, Cognitive Computing & AI)	University of Manitoba, Canada
David de la Fuente (Co-chair, Information Management)	University of Oviedo, Spain
Farid Ghareh Mohammadi (Co-chair, Computer Vision & AI)	Mayo Clinic, USA
Michael R. Grimaila (Co-chair, Military and Defense Modeling)	US Air Force Institute of Technology, USA

Douglas D. Hodson (Co-chair, Military and Defense Modeling)	US Air Force Institute of Technology, USA
Masahito Ohue (Co-chair, Mathematical Modeling)	Tokyo Institute of Technology, Japan
Jose A. Olivas (Co-chair, Information Management)	University of Castilla - La Mancha, Spain
Javier Ordus (Co-chair, Quantum Computing & AI)	Baylor University, USA
Pablo Rivas (Chair, Quantum Computing & AI)	Baylor University, USA
Farzan Shenavarmasouleh (Co-chair, Computer Vision & AI)	MediaLab Inc, USA
Robert Stahlbock (Co-chair, Data Mining)	Universität Hamburg, Germany
Masami Takata (Co-chair, Mathematical Modeling)	Nara Women's University, Japan
Quoc-Nam Tran (Co-chair, Education & Bioinformatics)	Southeastern Louisiana University, USA
Nobuaki Yasuo (Co-chair, Mathematical Modeling)	Tokyo Institute of Technology, Japan

ICOMP 2024 Program Committee – Internet Computing and IoT

Afrand Agah	West Chester University, USA
Nizar Al-Holou	University of Detroit Mercy, USA
Abeer Alsadoon (Co-chair, Health Informatics)	Charles Sturt University, Australia
Hamid R. Arabnia	University of Georgia, USA
Soheyla Amirian	Pace University, USA
Afsaneh Banitalebi Dehkordi	PNU University, Iran
Juan-Vicente Capella-Hernandez	Universitat Politècnica de València, Spain
Kevin Daimi	University of Detroit Mercy, USA
Zhangisina Gulnur Davletzhanovna	Central Asian University, Kazakhstan
Leonidas Deligiannidis	Wentworth Institute of Technology, USA
Mary Mehrnoosh Eshaghian-Wilner	University of Southern California, USA; and University of California Los Angeles, USA
David Foster	Kettering University, USA
Farid Ghareh Mohammadi	Mayo Clinic, USA
Houcine Hassan	Universitat Politècnica de València, Spain

Tai-hoon Kim	University of Tasmania, Australia
Guoming Lai	Sun Yat-sen University, China
Andrew Marsh	HoIP Telecom Ltd, UK
Ali Mostafaeipour	California State University, Fullerton, USA
Robert Ehimen Okonigene	Ambrose Alli University, Nigeria
James J. (Jong Hyuk) Park	SeoulTech, South Korea
Xuewei Qi	University of California, Riverside, USA
Farzan Shenavarmasouleh	Medialab Inc., USA
Ashu M. G. Solo	Maverick Technologies America Inc., USA
Fernando G. Tinetti	Universidad Nacional de La Plata, Argentina
Hahanov Vladimir	Kharkiv National University of Radio Electronics, Ukraine
Shiuh-Jeng Wang	Central Police University, Taiwan
Yunlong Wang	IQVIA, USA
Layne T. Watson	Virginia Polytechnic Institute & State University, USA
Hyun Yoe	Sunchon National University, South Korea
Jane You	Hong Kong Polytechnic University, China
Farhana H. Zulkernine	Queen's University, Canada

ESCS 2024 Program Committee – Embedded Systems, Cyber-physical Systems, and Applications

Nizar Al-Holou	University of Detroit Mercy, USA
Soheyla Amirian	Pace University, New York, USA
Hamid R. Arabnia	University of Georgia, USA
P. Balasubramanian	Nanyang Technological University, Singapore
Afsaneh Banitalebi Dehkordi	PNU University, Iran
Juan-Vicente Capella-Hernandez	Universitat Politècnica de València, Spain
Kevin Daimi	University of Detroit Mercy, USA
Leonidas Deligiannidis	Wentworth Institute of Technology, USA
Mary Mehrnoosh Eshaghian-Wilner	University of Southern California, USA; and University of California Los Angeles, USA
Farid Ghareh Mohammadi	Mayo Clinic, USA
Houcine Hassan	Universitat Politècnica de València, Spain
Guoming Lai	Sun Yat-sen University, China
Andrew Marsh	HoIP Telecom Ltd, UK
Ali Mostafaeipour	California State University, Fullerton, USA
Robert Ehimen Okonigene	Ambrose Alli University, Nigeria
Benaoumeur Senouci	North Dakota State University, USA
Farzan Shenavarmasouleh	Medialab Inc., USA

Contents

Internet Computing and IoT (ICOMP) - Algorithms and Applications

Embedded Systems, Cyber-Physical Systems, and Applications (ESCS)

Internet Computing and IoT (ICOMP) - Cloud and Internet of Things

Towards Objective Comparison of Security Algorithms for Resource-Constrained IoT Devices

Marten Fischer[✉][iD] and Ralf Tönjes[iD]

University of Applied Sciences Osnabrück, Osnabrück, Germany
{m.fischer,r.toenjes}@hs-osnabrueck.de

Abstract. Networked sensors are strategically deployed to gather real-world data, thereby facilitating the implementation of cutting-edge technologies like the IoT and CPS. These devices, tailored to specific use cases, often operate under strict resource constraints and must function optimally for extended periods. Concurrently, the sensitive data they collect must be safeguarded against unauthorized access, necessitating robust security measures. A range of security mechanisms is available to IoT system designers, with cryptographic algorithms, such as symmetric and asymmetric encryption, and hash functions being the cornerstone. They can select from multiple algorithm implementations and adjust configuration parameters to suit the device's capabilities. However, determining the ideal configuration is a complex task, requiring a balance between security effectiveness and efficient resource utilization. While the security aspect is continually assessed by experts, the impact of these choices on resource consumption, particularly across diverse platforms, often receives less attention. This paper introduces an objective evaluation method that assesses not only the effect of different security algorithms, but also various implementations and configuration adjustments on the resource consumption across different platforms. To facilitate this, a composite performance indicator is computed, enabling the systematic ranking of candidate configurations. The approach bridges the gap in understanding the interplay between security measures and resource management in the realm of IoT devices.

Keywords: Security Ranking · Configuration · IoT

1 Introduction

The The Internet of Things (IoT) allows connecting basically any device to the Internet. This includes very small sensor devices, which provide physical measurements of the real-world. They might be deployed in remote areas and have to operate unattended for a long period of time. These IoT devices or sensors are characterized by constrained resources, such as limited computational power, small memory as well as limited energy supply. Thus, efficiency is of upmost importance in order to prolong the lifetime of an IoT device.

© The Author(s), under exclusive license to Springer Nature Switzerland AG 2025
H. R. Arabnia et al. (Eds.): CSCE 2024, CCIS 2260, pp. 3–16, 2025.
https://doi.org/10.1007/978-3-031-85923-6_1

At the same time, the data provided by the sensors must be protected for several reasons. Because the IoT includes a variety of connected devices that collect data, it is important to ensure that this data is protected from unauthorized access. User privacy must be maintained as well. Many IoT devices collect and transmit sensitive data such as personal identification information or health data. A breach of the confidentiality of this data can have serious consequences. Also, data integrity in IoT is crucial. Manipulated or fake data can lead to malfunctions and security vulnerabilities.

This creates an area of conflict: on the one hand side to protect the data as strong as possible and on the other side to consume only as little resources as necessary, in order to ensure sufficient operational lifetime of the device. This raises the question of how a system designer can decide which security implementations can be applied within the available resources of a use-case scenario. The problem increases as for many implementations a series of configuration parameters must be chosen as well. Using well established security implementations, e.g. the Advanced Encryption Standard (AES), is undoubtably the best choice for most scenarios. However, in some cases the resource limitations along with use-case requirements do not allow such complex security algorithms. In this light, using a light-weight, but less secure security algorithm (that requires less resources) is still preferable to no protection at all. There is a wide range of security implementations designed with the special needs of resource-constrained IoT devices in mind. However, a clear ranking about their performance is difficult, especially since they might be optimized for different aspects, such as runtime or memory footprint. A system designer would benefit from an automated evaluation approach.

In the past, several attempts have been made to rate the strength of a security measure. With regard to protecting the confidentiality of data provided by an IoT device, the performance of an en-/decryption algorithm must be compared. Most times, this is done by comparing the length of the secret key. However, an objective comparison should also include other relevant configuration parameters, the performance on a specific IoT device, and the resulting resource consumption. In this paper, we present a framework that combines both aspects, the strength of a cryptographic security algorithm and a benchmarking of the resource consumption in relation to different configuration of such security algorithm. The framework generates numerical performance indicators, that can easily be compared and, thus, allow the designer of an IoT environment to make qualitative decisions. The main contributions of this paper are as follows:

- We define a set of metrics that allow to score the performance of a security algorithm using the example of an encryption algorithm. The metrics will respect both, the security and the resource consumption.
- We combine the individual metrics to get an objective, platform dependent and comparable performance indicator for each implementation of a security algorithm.
- We compare the performance of different security algorithms utilizing varying configurations executed on a set of Micro-Controller Unit (MCU). Using two

different normalization methods the individual pros and cons can easily be identified.

The rest of this paper is organized as follows: Sect. 2 introduces work related to the rating of information security. In Sect. 3, we define a set of performance metrics that describe the security as well as the resource consumption. Furthermore, we describe how these individual metrics can be combined to produce a meaningful, comparable performance indicator. This is used to rank the different implementations/configurations in Sect. 4. In Sect. 5, we use the presented framework to provide a comparison of popular security implementations with varying configurations and their corresponding performance indicators, when executed on a resource-constrained IoT device. Section 6 concludes this paper.

2 Related Work

In this section, we present works related to the topic of performance analysis of security measures. In the context of this paper, we focus on approaches that provide a numerical value, that can be used to compare different security measures.

The need to specify commonly accepted metrics to compare the strength of security algorithms was identified by Jorsted et al. [7], who then introduced seven metrics: type, functions, key size, rounds, complexity, known attacks, and strength. However, not all the metrics are easily quantifiable into a numerical value, especially in an automized way. Furthermore, the comparability is not guaranteed for all metrics. For example, in the case of the number of rounds the authors state: "Rounds by themselves may not have great value in specifying meaningful thresholds. (A one-time pad effectively has 1 round and a block size of 1 bit.)"[7]. A set of eight only numerical metrics was defined by Kumar et al. [11], namely encryption time, decryption time, throughput of encryption, throughput of decryption, CPU process time, and CPU clock cycles, power consumption and memory utilization. Similar to our work, they also acknowledge, that the encryption and decryption may have different values for some of the metrics. In their evaluation, they compare also different configurations, i.e. key lengths. Unfortunately, looking closely at the metrics, some of them are redundant, e.g. encryption/decryption throughput and the corresponding time, or CPU process time and clock cycles can be computed from each other. Al Tamimi [16] compared the execution times for different block cipher modes, namely Electronic Code Book (ECB) and Cipher Block Chaining (CBC) and concluded, that the influence is measurable, though very small. Kahn et al. [9] investigated the performance of security algorithms when executed on IoT devices. They distinguished between encryption and decryption operations as well as key generation operations. For asymmetric encryption algorithms they used different implementations with different key lengths, but always the same key length for a specific algorithm. This makes it difficult to compare the results. Furthermore, for symmetric encryption algorithms they always used the same configuration, a key length of 128 bit and chaining mode Counter Mode (CTR).

In [1], a comparison of well-known encryption algorithms is provided, but neither platform specific performance estimates nor statements about the resource consumption are given. Another comparison of encryption algorithms was provided by Bhardwaj et al. [4], focusing on lightweight implementations for IoT environments. They include the power consumption in the comparison, however, it is not clear which platform/MCU they used in their experiments. Also, the influence of different configurations is not discussed. For example, the AES algorithm is considered only with a key length of 128 bit, i.e. the "weakest" (and also fastest) configuration. Kiramat et al. [10] provide an efficiency ranking for five commonly used encryption algorithms, but do not explain adequately how they determined their results. The authors of [8] go a different way and rate vulnerabilities rather than security algorithms. For this they analyze entries in vulnerability repositories, such as the Common Vulnerabilities and Exposures (CVE) or National Vulnerability Database (NVD), using machine learning to classify the severity.

Dinu et al. [6] investigated the security of different symmetric Light Weight Cryptography (LWC) algorithms executed on resource-constrained IoT devices. A total of 19 different algorithms and three platforms (AVR, MSP and ARM) have been compared. The goal was to create an easy-to-use tool for system designers to benchmark new security algorithms with state-of-the-art implementations. For this, they designed a ranking mechanism, which goes in a similar direction as intended in this paper and is based on a modified MinMax-normalization for each metric. They defined a performance indicator $p_{i,d}$ for a security implementation i on a device d as the sum of all metric-specific performance indicators $v_{i,d,m}$ and weighted using w_m (see Eq. 1).

$$p_{i,d} = \sum_{m \in M} w_m \frac{v_{i,d,m}}{min(v_{i,d,m})} \tag{1}$$

However, their approach only considered the required memory in terms of binary code size and Random Access Memory (RAM) as well as the execution time. The level of security provided by the algorithm is not considered. In a final step, they combined all platform dependent performance indicators into a so-called Figure of Merit (FOM), which is supposed to state the efficiency of an algorithm across all investigated platforms. This is also in contrast to our work, where the focus is on the most efficient resource consumption on a specific platform in order to prolong the lifetime of the device. For example, considering an implementation containing highly optimized code for one type of MCU, but comparably inefficient code for other MCUs, the resulting FOM would be "overrating" the performance in the latter cases.

For a designer of an IoT environment, it is necessary to be able to make an objective statement about the performance of a security configuration. This includes a security rating as well as the resulting resource consumption. None of the aforementioned works includes both of these aspects in such a way to produce a numerical value that can be compared easily and automized. In this paper, we are going to introduce a methodology that will allow such a comparison. As a first step though, the next section introduces performance metrics relevant in a secure and yet constraint IoT environment.

3 Ranking Metrics

In this section, we define metrics for the ranking of different security algorithms and the various configurations. The metrics have been chosen for their relevance in the resource consumption during the protection of a digital asset in an IoT scenario, i.e. when the algorithm is executed on an IoT device with limited resources. The set of metrics has no claim to completeness. A designer of an IoT environment may add new metrics if necessary. For a reasonable ranking, the metric must be a numerical and normalizable value (see Sect. 4).

3.1 Security

This metric is used to rate the security of an algorithm. As explained before, this metric should not only consider the key length, but also include other relevant parameters. Here, we define the security metric based on a combination of the key length and the chaining mode. This selection of parameters is chosen for presentation purposes, but could be extended in a real-world applications as needed. The key lengths are classified into four classes, where each class increases the metric score by $\frac{1}{4}$. The four classes for a symmetric encryption algorithm, here AES, are depicted in Table 1. For asymmetric encryption algorithms an equivalence table, e.g., as suggested by National Institute of Standards and Technology (NIST) (Table 2 in [3]), can be used.

Besides to the key length, another aspect that influences the security of a (block) cipher algorithm is the *mode of operation*, i.e. the way how blocks are linked to prior blocks. It determines how consecutive blocks are processed in dependence of its predecessor. To determine the security of a mode of operation, we propose a scoring system, where we identified five properties that, when supported by the mode, increases the score by 0.1 points - up to a total of 1.0. The start value for the score of a mode v_c is set to be 0.5. The properties are as follows: cryptographically strong confusion (C), the mode uses an Initialization Vector (IV), the sequence is relevant for decryption (an error propagates through all subsequent blocks) (S), the mode has an integrated authentication mechanism (A), and identical plaintext blocks result in different ciphertext blocks (D). All scores for the block-cipher modes are listed in Table 2. For the IV, a truly random value is more advisable than a static one, as it provides more diffusion. However, since this is an implementation detail, rather than a conceptional one, a differentiation is not done at this point. The dependency for the correct sequence S adds an extra security aspect, because an adversary requires all block in the correct order. Both pieces of the security metric are combined as the product of the key length metric value v_k and the chaining mode metric value v_c:

$$v_{i,d,security} = v_k * v_c.$$

The scores for the modes are close to or equal to 1, except for the ECB mode. This decision was made as ECB does no chaining of previous blocks. As a consequence, the same plaintext results in the same ciphertext, which may allow drawing conclusions between ciphertext and plaintext. All other modes are considered secure. Galois/Counter Mode (GCM) and EAX are rated slightly higher, as they also provide means to authenticate the source of an encrypted message. In case the encryption algorithm is no block-cipher, a default value of 1.0 is used. That way, only the key length is relevant for the security metric.

Table 1. Key length score (v_k)

key length range	(80,112]	(112,128]	(128,192]	(192,256)
Algorithm strength	LOW	MEDIUM	HIGH	VERY HIGH
v_k	1/4	2/4	3/4	4/4

Table 2. Block-cipher mode score (v_c)

Mode c	C	IV	S	A	D	v_c
Electronic Code Book (ECB)	-	-	-	-	-	0.5
Cipher Block Chaining (CBC)	✔	✔	✔	-	✔	0.9
Counter Mode (CTR)	✔	✔	✔	-	✔	0.9
Cipher Feedback (CFB)	✔	✔	✔	-	✔	0.9
Output Feedback (OFB)	✔	✔	✔	-	✔	0.9
Galois/Counter Mode (GCM)	✔	✔	✔	✔	✔	1.0
CBC-MAC (CCM)	✔	✔	✔	✔	✔	1.0
EAX-Mode	✔	✔	✔	✔	✔	1.0
default (no block-cipher)	-	-	-	-	-	1.0

3.2   Flash

This metric describes how much additional flash-memory is required by the security algorithm(s) in the firmware image. The security algorithms are typically provided to an IoT project through pre-built libraries and are compiled into the firmware image along with the rest of the program code. In addition to the instructions of the respective security mechanism, the program code also includes static variables and tables, such as the substitution boxes (S-Boxes) defined in the respective standard. For this paper, the less memory is required, the better the metric is considered. In practice, as long as the code size does not exceed the available flash-memory, a full score for this metric is also justified.

3.3   Gate Equivalence (GE)

If the security algorithm is not stored in the flash memory but rather in the hardware of the MCU directly, the GE metric can be used to rate the required memory. Generally speaking, the GE is a unit of how many logical gates, for example a NAND gate, are needed to implement an algorithm. This allows to compute the required, but limited silicon area on the chip. An implementation of the same algorithm can be optimized for high throughput or low GE value [14]. The GE can be seen as alternative to the flash metric, if the algorithm is implemented in hardware. As this implies, that the algorithm can not be replaced easily, the GE metric is not used further.

3.4   RAM

This metric describes how much Random Access Memory (RAM) is required to execute the security implementation. In contrast to the flash metric, here dynamically allocated memory is considered. As well as with the flash metric, the less memory is required, the better the implementation is rated.

3.5   Time and Energy

The time metric describes how long it takes to protect a certain amount of data through a security implementation. This is particularly relevant for IoT sensors as it determines how long the sensors' MCU needs to remain in an active state, before it can go back to sleep mode. This directly affects the energy consumption and thus the lifespan of the sensor. However, a general assumption like "a faster computation results in a lower energy consumption" cannot be made. For example, MCUs can be operated at different clock rates, where higher clock rates may require a higher supply voltage. The microcontroller is active for a shorter period of time, but consumes more energy during that time. Whether this results in overall energy saving or not will be determined through an emulation environment and will be included as the energy metric in the performance indicators. The differentiated consideration of the performance indicators time and energy also allows for the comparison of different hardware platforms with similar microcontrollers.

3.6   Cost

This non-technical cost metric is necessary to motivate careful planning and implementation of security requirements in an IoT environment, as aimed for in this work. It is obvious that when planning an IoT environment, the costs must not exceed the available budget. Without this constraining metric, there would be a possibility of choosing hardware devices that outperform certain metrics, such as the time or memory (Flash/RAM) metrics, and essentially "overshadow" the remaining metrics. The cost metric can include not only the actual price, but also additional expenses, such as maintenance costs, ordering costs, and so on. However, the evaluation must be fair and uniform across all devices and solutions.

4   Combined Performance Indicator

The combined performance indicator extends Eq. 1 to combine the metrics described in Sect. 3 into a comprehensive performance indicator, allowing for the combination of two different kinds of metrics. The first consists of metrics with a positive influence $M_\uparrow$, meaning it is advantageous to choose a high value for metrics of this kind. The second kind $M_\downarrow$ has a negative influence and the aim is to minimize its value. To combine the different metrics, first they need to be normalized into an identical value range. For this, the two normalization techniques MinMax-normalization and Mean-normalization have been compared.

MinMax-normalization

In contrast to the performance indicator as proposed by Dino [6], the individual metric terms $m \in M$ are normalized in the range [0,1] using the Min-Max normalization (aka. feature scaling) [5]. The MinMax-normalization for $M_\uparrow$ metrics is defined as:

$$v' = \frac{v - min(v)}{max(v) - min(v)} \tag{2}$$

, where v is the value to normalize and v' is the normalized value. For $M_\downarrow$ the min and max values are inverted. The computation of the combined performance indicator using the MinMax-normalization is shown in Eqs. 3 to 5.

$$p_{m\uparrow} = w_m \frac{v_{i,d,m} - min(v_{d,m})}{max(v_{d,m}) - min(v_{d,m})} \tag{3}$$

$$p_{m\downarrow} = w_m \frac{|v_{i,d,m} - max(v_{d,m})|}{min(v_{d,m}) - max(v_{d,m})} \tag{4}$$

$$p_{i,d} = \sum_{m \in M_\uparrow} p_{m\uparrow} + \sum_{m \in M_\downarrow} p_{m\downarrow} \tag{5}$$

Here, $p_{i,d}$ is the combined performance indicator for implementation i on device d. $v_{i,d,m}$ is the measured/determined value for metric m on d executing implementation i. The functions min and max return the minimum and maximum measured value for metric m on a device d for all evaluated security implementations. The w_m is the weight for metric $m \in M$. With a weighting $w_m \leq 1$, the value range for $p_{i,d}$ is $[0, |M|]$. The combined performance indicator can also be rescaled into the value range $[0, 1]$ by dividing it with the number of metrics $|M|$. For now, the metrics $M = M_\uparrow \cup M_\downarrow$ were divided into the following two classes:

$$M_\uparrow = \{security\}$$

$$M_\downarrow = \{flash, RAM, energy, time, cost\}$$

Mean-normalization

This normalization is very similar to the MinMax-normalization. The difference is that the dividend is the difference between the value to normalize v and the mean of the value vector. Hence, the mean-normalization is defined as $v' = \frac{v - \bar{v}}{max(v) - min(v)}$, with $\bar{v}$ being the mean. Equations 3 to 5 were adjusted accordingly into Eqs. 6 to 8. (The value range of the mean-normalization is in range $[-1, 1]$, but could easily be shifted to $[0, 1]$: $v'' = (1 + v')/2$.)

$$p_{m\uparrow} = w_m \frac{v_{i,d,m} - \overline{v_{d,m}}}{max(v_{d,m}) - min(v_{d,m})} \tag{6}$$

$$p_{m\downarrow} = w_m \frac{v_{i,d,m} - \overline{v_{d,m}}}{min(v_{d,m}) - max(v_{d,m})} \tag{7}$$

$$p_{i,d} = \sum_{m \in M_\uparrow} p_{m\uparrow} + \sum_{m \in M_\downarrow} p_{m\downarrow} \tag{8}$$

5 Evaluation

5.1 MCU Emulation-Based Resource Determination

For our evaluation, we decided to measure the resource consumption within an emulation environment. To determine the resource consumption of a security implementation within an emulation requires a "cycle-true" emulator, i.e. each instruction in the firmware is emulated exactly as if executed on the real MCU. We decided to use the AVRORA emulator [2], developed at the University of California, Los Angeles (UCLA). AVRORA supports AVR MCUs by Microchip[1]. This MCU family is used by the popular and widely available Arduino platform. This allowed a direct comparison between emulation and the execution on real hardware for the purpose of calibration.

A benefit of the AVRORA emulator is its ability to track the energy consumption during emulation. The energy model is implemented as a Finite State Machine (FSM), where each state represents a mode of operation within the MCU, e.g., active and sleep modes. The emulator keeps track of how many cycles the MCU remained in a specific state. By knowing the MCU's frequency, the time spent in each mode and, in combination with the operating voltage, the energy consumption can be calculated. As part of this research, the energy models for the Arduino Leonardo and Uno platforms were measured and added to the emulator.

---

[1] https://www.microchip.com/.

5.2 Scenario

In the evaluation scenario, the IoT device has to perform a task in a ten-second interval. In between, the MCU is allowed to change into a sleep mode. To realize this, the Watchdog Timer (WDT) is utilized to wake the MCU and perform the task. Of course, part of this task is to apply the security algorithm, configured with changing security configurations. In each iteration, the same piece of (dummy) data is secured, i.e. each interval is deterministic. This was done under the assumption that the runtime of the algorithm is independent of the data to encrypt/decrypt, except its size. Reading the sensor and transferring the protected message is mocked-up and constant for all iterations. The emulation time was set to six hours to get early indications about the different performance values. All emulation runs are deterministic. The normalization is done for each platform individually to ensure a comparable value range. In the scenario, a temperature and humidity sensor is used to provide new sensor reading every ten seconds. The encoded message to protect, for example using JavaScript Object Notation (JSON), is estimated to be 128 bytes. As security goal the confidentiality of the sensor readings shall be protected by encrypting the data before transmission.

The evaluated platforms include the popular Arduino platforms Leonardo and UNO R3 as well as the Mica2 sensor node. The Arduino platforms were operated at 16 MHz, while the Mica2 platform only supports 8 MHz. As implementations the AES libraries mBedTLS [13], AESLib [12] and TinyAES [17] as well as Speck [15] were considered. The mBedTLS library was discarded directly after compilation, because the available RAM was not sufficient for the tested platforms. For TinyAES, the key lengths were set to 128, 192, and 256 bit - the modes were CBC, ECB and CTR. AESLib only supports 128 bit keys in CBC mode. Speck also supports 128 bit keys, but only in ECB mode. For comparability, an additional configuration named "'None" shows the determined performance indicator with no security measures in place.

5.3 Results

Figure 1a shows the combined performance indicators for the tested platforms and security configurations in the role of a receiver, i.e. decrypting messages. The plot shows, that the Mica2 platform scores better for almost all configurations, except Speck, which is not supported on the MCU (ATMega128L). An interesting finding can be seen when comparing the different modes with identical key length. The CBC mode scores lower than the others. More interestingly, ECB is only second best, despite being the supposedly simplest implementation, outperformed by the CTR mode. Figure 1b shows a similar trend when the IoT device is the data provider, i.e. executing the encryption operations. However, the differences between the configurations are smaller.

Comparing both plots shows that the AESLib implementation has the lowest scores on all platforms in the role of a data provider, but the TinyAES CBC 128 configuration scores lowest as receiver. The latter is the result of a quite low

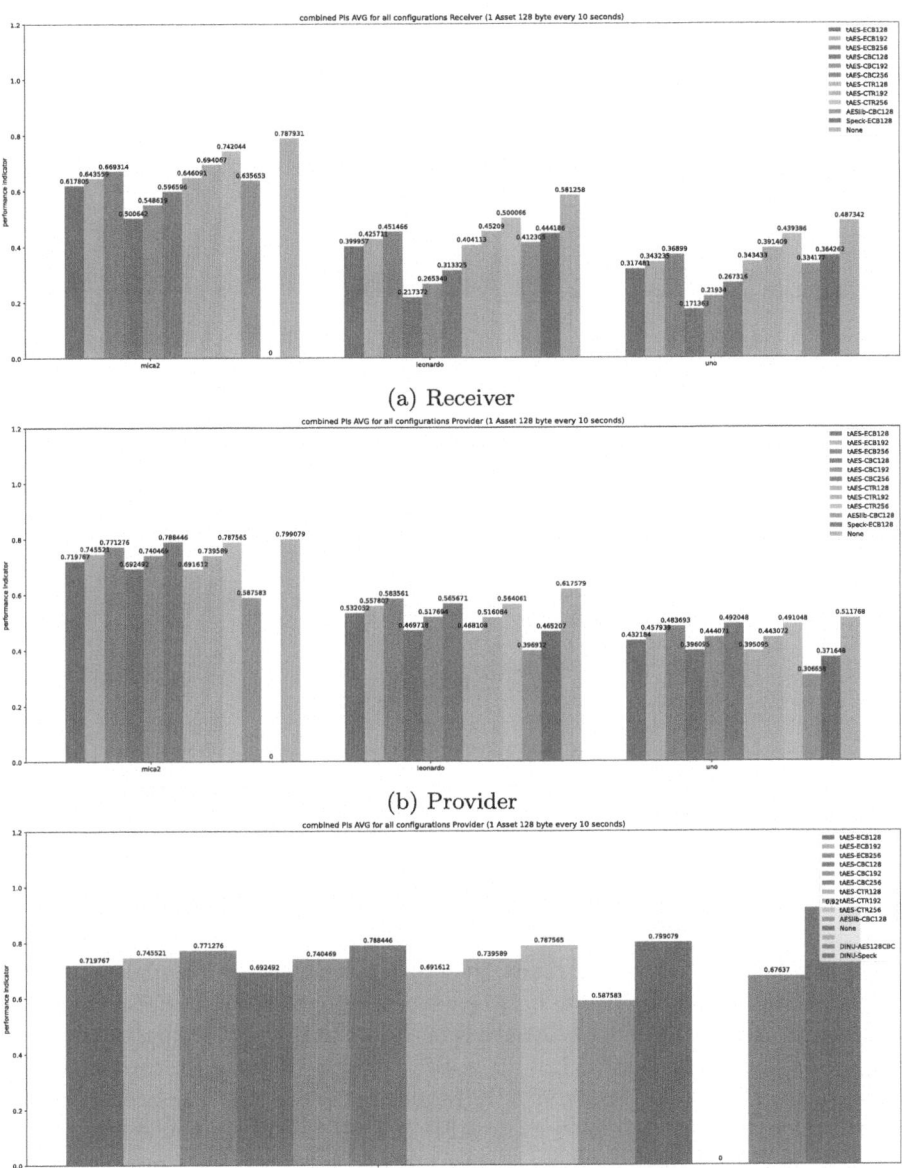

(a) Receiver

(b) Provider

(c) MinMax Mica2 including Performance Metrics as in Dinu [6]

Fig. 1. Combined Performance Indicators for all configurations on platforms

scoring in the energy metric, while the AESLib implementation scores only little with the flash and the RAM metric.

We also compared our results with the findings by Dinu et al. (Table 2 in [6]). A first difference is that they only evaluated one configuration for the AES

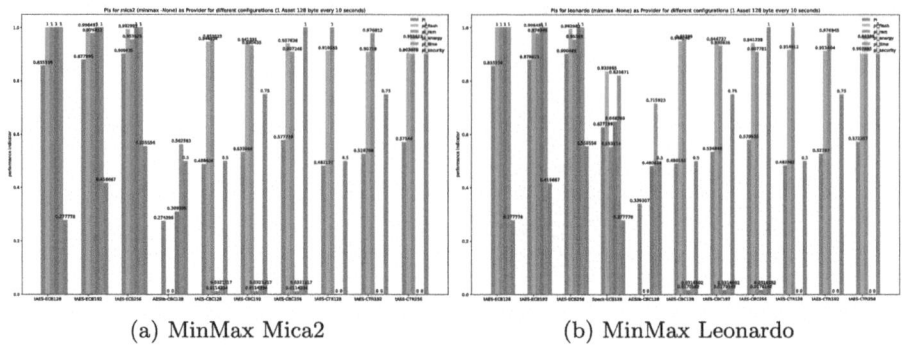

(a) MinMax Mica2   (b) MinMax Leonardo

Fig. 2. Individual performance metrics MinMax-normalized for two selected platforms

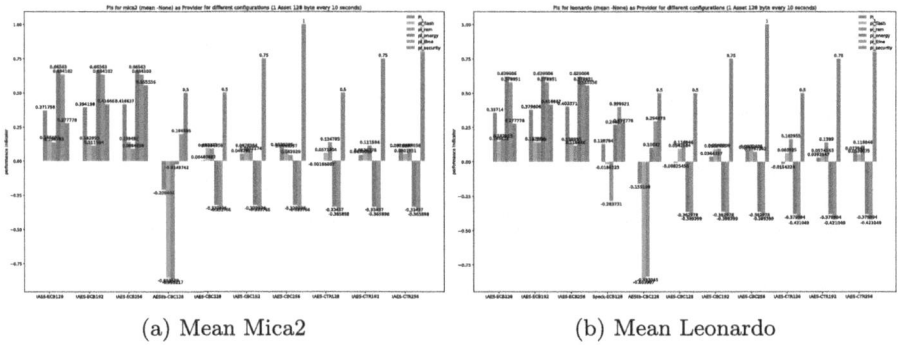

(a) Mean Mica2   (b) Mean Leonardo

Fig. 3. Individual performance metrics Mean-normalized for two selected platforms

algorithm, namely CBC with 128-bit key length. The exact library/implementation is not mentioned. Furthermore, they also tested the Speck implementation as well, but did not differentiate between encryption or decryption. In their comparison, Speck with 128 bit key length scored fourth best of all implementations they tested, outperforming AES 128 CBC. This is in contrast to our results, where only one of the two tested AES implementations with this configuration scored better than Speck, namely TinyAES. The AESLib implementation had an especially low score in the memory consumption, both the flash metric and the RAM metric. Even the quite competitive scores for the metrics time and energy could not compensate. On the right side of Fig. 1c we added the performance indicators of the AES and Speck implementation by Dinu, but normalized them with the modified MinMax-normalization, as presented in Eq. 2. Keep in mind, they only used the metrics flash, RAM and time (Figs. 2 and 3).

6   Conclusion

This paper contributed to the challenge of selecting and configuring security algorithms for the design an IoT environment. Special focus was on the selection of security algorithms on the resource constrained IoT devices within given use-case parameters. First, we introduced a set of performance metrics to measure the performance of different configurations, when running on different platforms. Next, we used normalization techniques to calculate a combined performance indicator, to make it possible to rank the different configurations. In a simple evaluation scenario, we showed the performance of three encryption algorithms with varying configurations on a couple of AVR MCUs.

In further research, the consideration of asymmetric encryption algorithms as well as different MCUs platforms will help to get a broader view on the possibilities for efficient resource utilization in IoT environments.

Acknowledgment. This work is part of the research project DataChainSec funded by the Federal Ministry of Education and Research Germany under grant number 16KIS1701.

References

1. Abood, O., Guirguis, S.: A survey on cryptography algorithms. Int. J. Sci. Res. Publ. **8**, 495–516 (2018). https://doi.org/10.29322/IJSRP.8.7.2018.p7978
2. Avrora - The AVR Simulation and Analysis Framework. http://compilers.cs.ucla.edu/avrora/. Accessed 17 Mar 2022
3. Barker, E.: Recommendation for Key Management Part 1: General. NIST SP 800-57pt1r4. National Institute of Standards and Technology, Jan. 2016, NIST SP 800–57pt1r4. https://doi.org/10.6028/NIST.SP.800-57pt1r4. https://nvlpubs.nist.gov/nistpubs/SpecialPublications/NIST.SP.800-57pt1r4.pdf. Accessed 17 Nov 2023
4. Bhardwaj, I., Kumar, A., Bansal, M.: A review on lightweight cryptography algorithms for data security and authentication in IoTs. In: 2017 4th International Conference on Signal Processing, Computing and Control (ISPCC). 2017 4th International Conference on Signal Processing, Computing and Control (ISPCC), pp. 504–509 (2017). https://doi.org/10.1109/ISPCC.2017.8269731
5. Ciaburro, G., Ayyadevara, V.K., Perrier, A.: Hands- on machine learning on google cloud platform. ISBN: 9781788393485. https://www.oreilly.com/library/view/hands-on-machinelearning/9781788393485/. Accessed 17 Oct 2023
6. Dinu, D., Corre, Y.L., Khovratovich, D., Perrin, L., Großschädl, J., Biryukov, A.: Triathlon of lightweight block ciphers for the Internet of things. J. Cryptogr. Eng. **9**(3), 283–302 (2018). https://doi.org/10.1007/s13389-018-0193-x
7. Jorstad, N.D., Landgrave, T.S.: Cryptographic algorithm metrics. In: 20th National Information Systems Security Conference, pp. 1– 38 (1997)
8. Kekül, H., Ergen, B., Arslan, H.: A multiclass approach to estimating software vulnerability severity rating with statistical and word embedding methods. Int. J. Comput. Netw. Inf. Secur. **14**(4), 27–42 (2022). issn: 20749090, 20749104. https://doi.org/10.5815/ijcnis.2022.04.03https://www.mecs-press.org/ijcnis/ijcnis-v14-n4/v14n4-3.html(visited on 07/07/2023)

9. Khan, N., et al.: Performance analysis of security algorithms for IoT devices. In: 2017 IEEE Region 10 Humanitarian Technology Conference (R10-HTC). 2017 IEEE Region 10 Humanitarian Technology Conference (R10-HTC), pp. 130–133 (2017). ISSN: 2572-7621. https://doi.org/10.1109/R10-HTC.2017.8288923

10. Kiramat.: Comparison of various encryption algorithms for securing data. preprint. engrXiv, Jan. 1, 2019. https://doi.org/10.31224/osf.io/xzv56. https://engrxiv.org/index.php/engrxiv/preprint/view/365 (visited on 08/29/2023)

11. Anand Kumar, M., Balasubramanian, B., Manivasagam, G.: Metrics for performance evaluation of encryption algorithms. Int. J. Adv. Res. Sci. Eng. **6**, 62–72 (2017)

12. Landman, D.: Arduino AESLib (2023). https://github.com/DavyLandman/AESLib. Accessed 17 Jan 2023

13. README for Mbed TLS. original-date: 2012-11-14T13:13:13Z (2023). https://github.com/Mbed-TLS/mbedtls. Accessed 27 Nov 2023

14. Rolfes, C., Poschmann, A., Leander, G., Paar, C.: Ultra-lightweight implementations for smart devices – security for 1000 gate equivalents. In: Grimaud, G., Standaert, F.-X. (eds.) CARDIS 2008. LNCS, vol. 5189, pp. 89–103. Springer, Heidelberg (2008). https://doi.org/10.1007/978-3-540-85893-5_7

15. Speck (cipher). In: Wikipedia. Page Version ID: 1182524582 (2023). https://en.wikipedia.org/w/index.php?title=Speck(cipher)&oldid=1182524582. Accessed 22 Nov 2023

16. Al Tamimi, A-K.: Performance analysis of data encryption algorithms. https://www.cse.wustl.edu/~jain/cse567-06/ftp/encryption_perf/. Accessed 29 Aug 2023

17. tiny-AES-c/aes.c at master · kokke/tiny-AES-c. GitHub. https://github.com/kokke/tiny-AES-c. Accessed 26 Aug 2022

Collaborative Federated Learning Cloud Based System

Partha Pratim Saha[1] ⓘ, Naresh K. Sehgal[2] ⓘ, and Miad Faezipour[3](✉) ⓘ

[1] Wipro Technologies Limited, Pune, Maharashtra, India
[2] Deeply Human AI, Inc., Santa Clara, CA, USA
[3] School of Engineering Technology, Electrical and Computer Engineering Technology, Purdue University, West Lafayette, IN, USA
mfaezipo@purdue.edu

Abstract. Machine learning is deployed in various clinical and healthcare informatics applications, with centralized and decentralized learning schemes, each offering performance and security advantages and disadvantages. In centralized machine learning, all the data travels to a central location where the machine learning training code runs on it. A central server potentially represents a single point of failure - which is one of the issues of centralized learning. Another issue is the need for all participants to trust the central authority with their datasets. In a decentralized machine learning solution, data stays at the participating local sites, while the machine learning training code travels to each site. It needs parties to run a common binary code on each of their datasets and trust the incoming program, thus avoiding a single point of failure, but potentially creating a security hazard with malicious code. This can be addressed by using a mutually agreed upon signed binary code. Another issue is the training run time in decentralized learning due to multiple hops between different dataset locations. System designers often face tradeoffs between the higher performance of centralized machine learning vs. the better security of decentralized machine learning. In this work, we propose a novel Collaborative Federated Learning (CFL) solution that combines the advantages of centralized and decentralized machine learning schemes, without compromising security. We executed our simulation using synthetic data for 30 iterations to observe the behavior of code and dataset sizes with various incremental data sharing options. Interestingly, we observed that when more data is shared centrally, data security issues become more pervasive, however, machine learning training performance improves proportionally. The challenge is to balance between performance and security considerations by partitioning appropriate amount of data to be shared centrally.

Keywords: Cloud Computing · Centralized Machine Learning · Decentralized Machine Learning · Collaborative Federated Learning (CFL) · Security

H. R. Arabnia et al. (Eds.): CSCE 2024, CCIS 2260, pp. 17–29, 2025.
https://doi.org/10.1007/978-3-031-85923-6_2

1   Introduction

Federated Learning (FL) [9] is a machine learning technique where many sites (e.g., servers in an organization or across multiple organizations) collaboratively train a model. This training is done under the orchestration of a central server (e.g., provider) while keeping the training data decentralized. FL can mitigate many systemic privacy risks and costs by keeping private data on-site. In centralized machine learning approach, there is a possibility of data compromise which can be avoided in FL [16]. The central server receives the dataset contributions from all sites. FL is typically used when one needs to train models on a larger dataset than any one single entity owns and is not willing to share its data with others (e.g., for legal, strategic, privacy, or economic reasons). FL trains an algorithm keeping the training data locally on users' decentralized systems. The model travels in the form of signed binary code from site to site, thereby addressing security concerns with FL. The distributed locations are used as nodes performing computation on local datasets to update a global model [8]. This contrasts with traditional centralized machine learning technique, where all the local datasets are uploaded to a shared server location. Suppose data types at different locations are different. In that case, FL enables multiple participants to build a common, robust machine learning model without sharing their data, thus addressing critical issues such as data privacy, security, and access rights [1,13]. Various applications for clinical and biomedical research are already exploring cross-device FL solutions [6].

1.1   Background

Federated Learning aims to train machine learning models in a distributed fashion without centralizing data but instead updating and passing model parameters (weights and biases) from a central server to distributed sites and back to perform Stochastic Gradient Descent (SGD) [15,18]. SGD is an iterative optimization algorithm with suitable smoothness properties (e.g. differentiable or sub-differentiable). SGD gradients are more accurate than Gradient descent (GD), which converge faster because of applying many more gradients per unit time. SGD updates the parameters for each observation (after selecting a subset or random fraction of sites and using all training samples on those selected sites) which leads to more updates. The gradients are averaged by the server proportionally to the number of training samples on each site, and used to make a GD step. SGD is easier to fit in the memory due to a single training example being processed by the network. In Federated SGD (FedSGD) [17,19], each site locally takes one step of gradient descent using its local data, and the server takes a weighted average of the resulting models. It is also possible to have each device take multiple gradient steps before passing updated parameters (weights and biases) to the central server for averaging. This can reduce the number of communication rounds.

Federated averaging (FedAvg) [2,11] is a generalization of FedSGD, which allows local nodes to perform more than one batch update on local data and exchanges the updated weights rather than the gradients. The rationale behind this generalization is that in FedSGD, if all local nodes start from the same initialization, averaging the gradients is strictly equivalent to averaging the weights themselves. Further, averaging tuned weights coming from the same initialization hurts the resulting averaged model's performance. FevAvg weights the devices by the amount of data each device owns, so it favors clients with more data. To avoid this, Fed-Prox [20] penalizes large changes of weights that helps convergence for highly heterogeneous data. This proximal term penalizes the model from changing too much on one single device. We can control the amount of penalization by the hyperparameter μ. So to penalize worst performing device(s), we can apply a penalizing factor (q) so that for larger values of q, the worst performing device dominates the overall loss to make a fair judgement. After one step of GD, the server can't identify a particular site's data separately because all the model updates (or sampled site data from a large population) at the server gets averaged before adding the data. If sites hold non-IID (independent and identically distributed) data, train a global model that can be personalized to each of the sites with a few steps of gradient descent.

Fairness from data contribution perspective is another concern in Federated Learning. Different sites can contribute to the learning model(s) by varying amount of data. The model we train might perform better on sites with more data by marginalizing the minority site's data distribution. An intermediate option is FL for privacy. In this case, the data remains at the sites, but the central server can ask for gradients with respect to a particular loss function, or data statistics. A non-private option is where the central server can collect any relevant data from a user device. One can argue regarding what will happen when the central server is required to pay users fairly [3, 4, 10, 14, 21]. In this case, the system can pay the users as a function (privacy level, amount of data, and degree of heterogeneity etc.) [7].

1.2   Contribution

This paper focuses on splitting the dataset where one portion at each setting is shared while other portions are kept at each site locally, with additional fine-tuning and retraining at the local site for better efficiency and accuracy. In the context of clinical and biomedical research data, individual hospitals could have missing information/data, and the aggregation of the split data from multiple hospitals allow for creating a more robust, complete and more effective FL model. We introduce Collaborative Federated Learning (CFL) with split data sharing for maintaining reasonable security and privacy while achieving acceptable performance. We developed a system architecture for this entire setup.

1.3   Paper Organization

This paper is organized as follows. In Sect. 2, the problem statement and various issues of federated learning are discussed. In Sect. 3, the proposed Collaborative Federated Learning model is introduced and discussed. In Sect. 4, we present the results of various split data sharing scenarios, and how program size and dataset size differ with respect to varying amount of shared data. In Sect. 5, we tabulated differences between Centralized, FL, and CFL. Section 6 directs the future avenues in this area.

2   Problem Statement

2.1   Performance Issues with Federated Learning

Imagine that multiple parties need to collaborate for a common purpose, but do not trust each other with their data sharing. An example is the research for a new drug that needs multiple sites to provide patient data, pharmaceuticals to provide their drug data, and medical researchers to explore new treatment protocols. Neither party may want to give away its dataset, but all are interested to know new drug protocols that are effective in treating a disease. In this situation, a multi-party cloud is a feasible solution. In such a scheme, multiple participants collaborate using shared hardware to accomplish their common goal. This also requires data of each party to be kept private from other users, while sharing the computed models for all to use.

Upon receiving all required users' data, a central cloud server is used to perform desired computations. A proxy server hides the identities of all users to provide anonymity. Each user can send its data for computations, after authenticating into the system. The proxy server hides the traceability of every message sent by each user to the cloud server. Incoming data is encrypted to provide protection and integrity against man-in-the-middle attacks. There are obvious questions on the performance and efficiency of cloud environments to deploy such a model while enforcing the security requirements of all user entities. We propose a sophisticated Collaborative Federated Learning (CFL) algorithm that enables knowledge transfer among parties (aka sites). At the same time, our approach maintains private data locally and improves communication efficiency, as shown in Fig. 1 [6].

FL enables data to stay local, while algorithms travel across participating institutions, to train a deep learning algorithm. This solution preserves the privacy and security of users' data. However, with no data sharing with a central server, the training time for the model is very high as code needs to travel across multiple sites in every iteration.

Consider three entities, a site = A, a drug company = B, and a medical research unit = C, with a single centralized server. All three need to communicate and share data for new drug discovery, based on which patients need help, how they react to the current drugs and which ones may be appropriate for a future clinical trial. 1) An obvious solution is for all three to put their data in a shared central server. We will examine the time taken for data transfers, and execute a machine learning algorithm to compute neural network parameters before the results are distributed to each participating party. 2) Assume a second case where these entities do not fully trust the others, or due to some regulations, are not willing to share their data in a central server. In this case, the data stays local

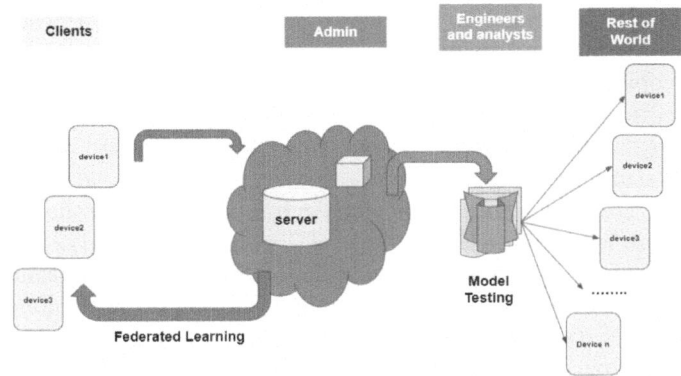

Fig. 1. Collaboration among sites in FL setting

and the code travels to each site for the training algorithm to be completed. Next, we will examine both cases of centralized and decentralized training, and resulting run times as T1 and T2, respectively. In this context, some notations are provided below:

t_{da} = Round-trip time for data copying delays from site A to the central server

t_{db} = Round-trip time for data copying delays from site B to the central server

t_{dc} = Round-trip time for data copying delays from site C to the central server

t_{pa} = Round-trip time for code and weights of neural network to travel from the central server to site A

t_{pb} = Round-trip time for code and weights of neural network to travel from the central server to site B

t_{pc} = Round-trip time for code and weights of neural network to travel from the central server to site C

t_{px} = Program execution time

n = Number of training iterations

The worst case (asynchronized) data copy time to the central database is: $t_{da} + t_{db} + t_{dc}$. In a completely centralized model, the total run time will be as follows (Eq. 1):

$$T1 = t_{da} + t_{db} + t_{dc} + n * t_{px} \qquad (1)$$

For a fully decentralized Federated Learning system, $(n + 1)$ iterations are needed to ensure that the model did not break with the addition of the new training dataset. So, the total run time will be:

$$T2 = (n + 1) * (t_{pa} + t_{pb} + t_{pc} + t_{px}) \qquad (2)$$

where t_{px} in Eq. 2 is larger than t_{px} in Eq. 1 as it may not have the same computational capacity. For larger values of n, $T2 >> T1$, because, in the first model, the data is copied only once, whereas, in the second model, the program has to travel once for each iteration. Even in a single iteration case, if $t_{pa} > t_{da}$, $t_{pb} > t_{db}$ and $t_{pc} > t_{dc}$ which will happen for a large model size, the relationship $T2 > T1$ will still hold.

In addition, consider a third case, where a fraction of data is shared, while the rest is kept local. Let this fraction be m, so $T3 = m \times T1 + (1-m) \times T2$. Note that for 100% sharing, $m = 1$, which is the case for the centralized training model, therefore, $T3 = T1$. Similarly, for a completely decentralized model, $m = 0$, which means $T3 = T2$.

For smaller programs and larger datasets, since model training is done iteratively, n maybe ten or higher usually causing $T2 > T1$, even if the program binary code is only $\frac{1}{10}$th size of the dataset. However, in the cases when very few iterations are required for the training program, then $T1 > T2$.

3   Proposed Model

Collaborative Federated Learning (CFL) is a combination of centralized and decentralized machine learning algorithms. Each site has different types of data, and may offer different features. Examples of such data include hospital patients' histories with some features and drug efficacy data from pharmaceutical companies with some other features.

3.1   Collaborative Federated Learning Model

In Centralized Learning (CL), all the data is aggregated from multiple sources in a central location, where FL algorithms do the training and inference computations. Then, the results are distributed back to different sites. Each site can see only its own data and the final results of centralized computations, but not other sites' datasets. Hence data and models are shared.

In Federated Learning (FL), each site keeps its data private, whereas the FL algorithm travels from site to site, does some computations and partial results are then copied back to a central location. From there, FL algorithms go to the next site, do more computations, and update the central database. A site cannot see the data of others but only accesses the shared FL model. A key difference is that if sites do not trust each other, they never have to give their private data away. In this case, data will not get shared, and only the FL code is shared.

We propose Collaborative Federated Learning(CFL) in the cloud by dividing the data into two parts: private and public. See Fig. 2. Private data is similar to a patient's identifiable information in the healthcare domain. This information can be removed and replaced by an ID, which is only known to the owning party. We reckon that 90% of data can be in the other public databases so that it can be safely shared. For a non-healthcare example, people share their work profiles and designations on social networking platforms (e.g., LinkedIn) without sharing

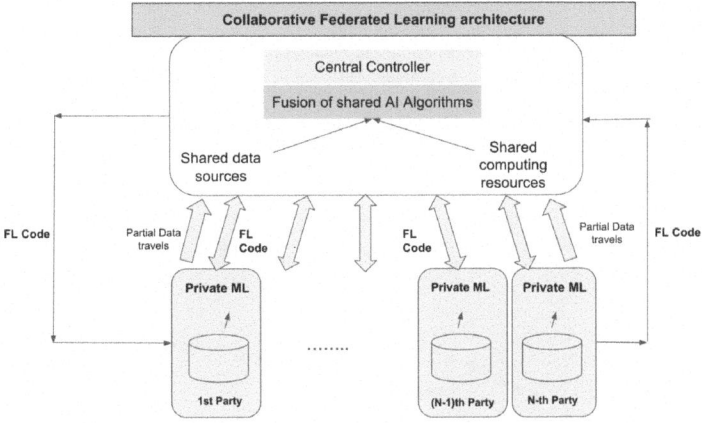

Fig. 2. Collaborative FL architecture

their Social Security Number (SSN) or personal salary information. This enables some meaningful computations to be done on a shared basis without having sensitive code travel between the sites resulting in unacceptable delays. Then computation results can be shared between the contributing parties.

4 Simulation Results

4.1 Testing Scenarios

We created few synthetic datapoints to examine the behavior of program size with respect to the size of the dataset. To simplify the simulation, we assume that the time for code and weights of the neural network to travel to site A is 1, site B is 2, and site C is 3 units, respectively. The scenarios below will depict these differences:

Scenario 1 Program Size is Smaller Than the Dataset Size In this example, if the time to copy data from site A to the central server is 5 units, for site B is 10 units, for site C is 15 units, the run time for program P is 2 units, then to run the program for n iterations, it will take $n \times 2$.

In this scenario, with 50% of the data being shared, we plot the number of iterations (n) and run time in a graph, as shown in Fig. 3.

When 80% of the data is being shared, we also plot the number of iterations (n) and run time in a graph, as shown in Fig. 4.

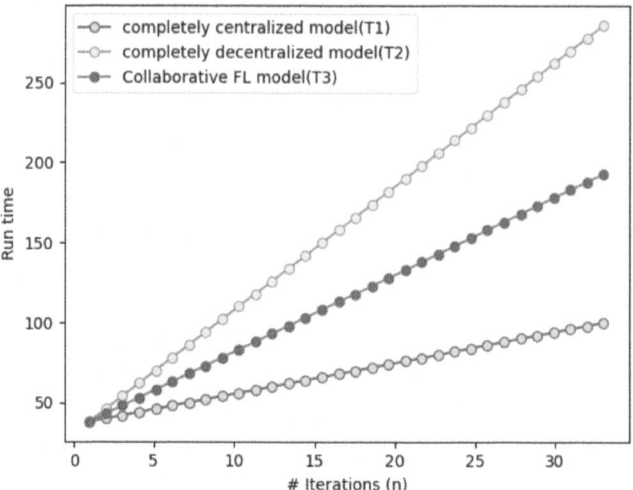

Fig. 3. Program size is smaller than dataset size with 50% of the data being shared: Collaborative FL is in the middle.

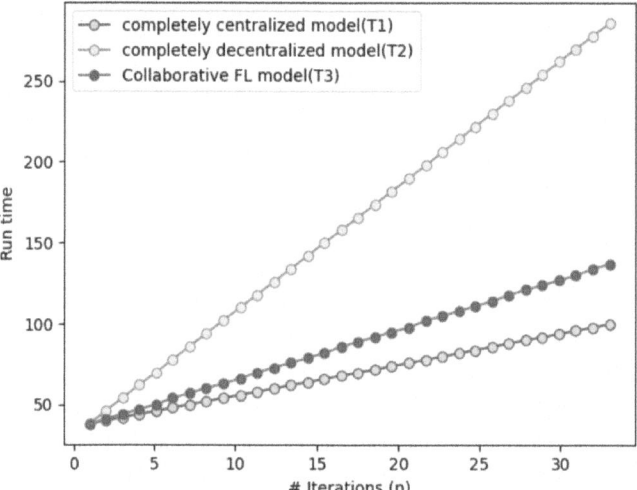

Fig. 4. Program size is smaller than dataset size with 80% data sharing: Collaborative FL is towards centralized.

Scenario 2 Program Size is Bigger Than the Dataset Size. In this example, say if the time to copy data from site A to the central server is 1 unit, for site B is 2 units, and for site C is 3 units, the run time of program P is 2 units, then to run the program for n iterations, it will take $n \times 2$.

We plot the number of iterations (n) and run time in a graph where the program size is bigger than the dataset size.

In this scenario, with 50% of the data being shared, we plot the number of iterations (n) and run time in a graph, as shown in Fig. 5.

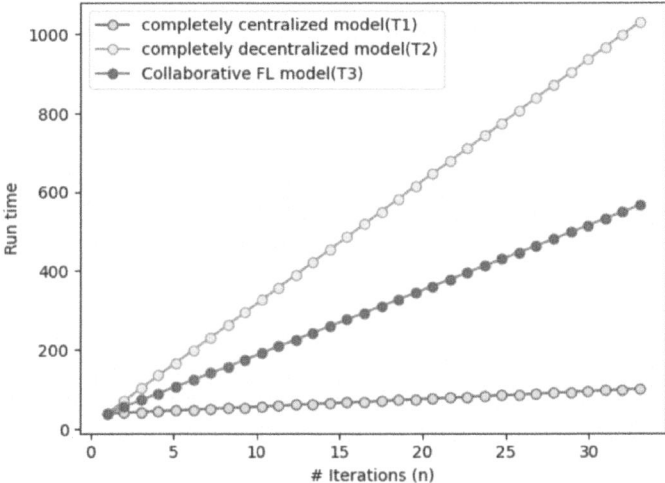

Fig. 5. Program size is bigger than dataset size with 50% data sharing: Collaborative FL is in the middle.

When 80% of the data is being shared, we plot the number of iterations (n) and run time in a graph, as shown in Fig. 6.

Scenario 3 Behavior of Centralized and Decentralized Schemes. When the program size is bigger than dataset size, and vice-versa, we noticed the behavior below for the centralized machine learning algorithm.

We plot the number of iterations (n) and run time in a graph, as shown in Fig. 7. When the program size is bigger than dataset size, and vice-versa, we noticed the behavior below for the decentralized machine learning algorithm. We plot the number of iterations (n) and run time in a graph, as shown in Fig. 8.

In general, a decentralized model is slower most of the time because the code and model need to travel to different locations. However, it is often preferred for security and privacy reasons.

Since Federated Learning can be implemented in cases where shared data is collected centrally and analyzed, or data can remain distributed, the analysis (i.e., shared code and neural network parameters) move from location to location. In the first case, performance is primarily limited by the one-time movement of the data and the subsequent multiple iterations done centrally. In the second case, performance is limited by the multiple movements of the analysis mechanism (i.e., shared code and neural network weights), done once for each iteration, and the calculation is done in a distributed manner, depicted in Fig. 2 [12,15]. As shown in the previous examples, at some point, the performance of

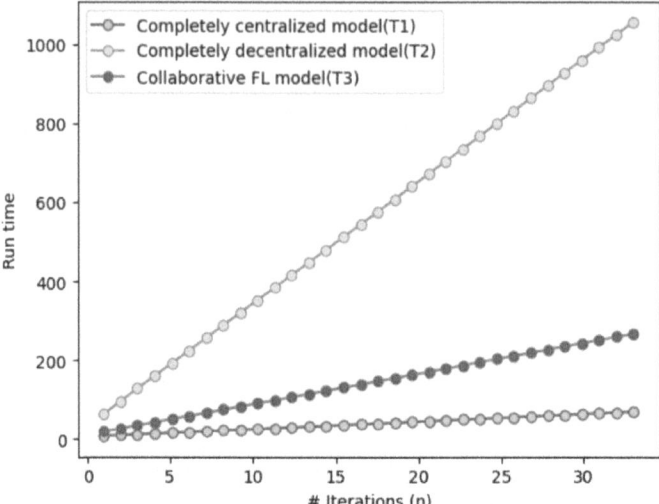

Fig. 6. Program size is bigger than dataset size with 80% of the data being shared, then the line indicating Collaborative FL is more towards centralized model.

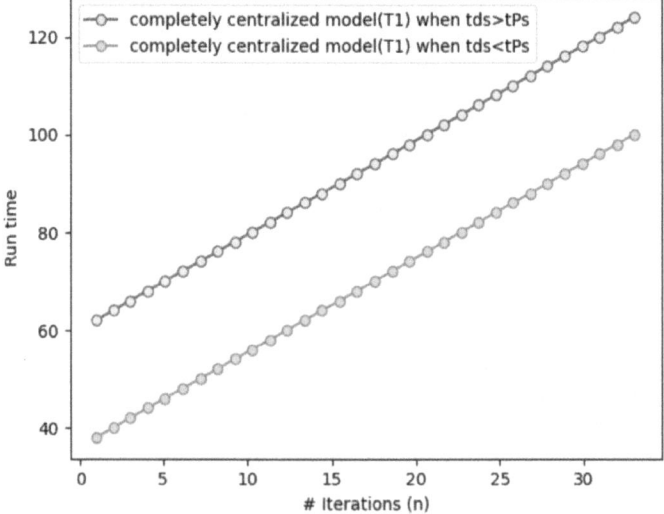

Fig. 7. Centralized model when dataset size is greater than program size and vice-versa

the centralized implementation outperforms the distributed case. The downside is the security and privacy issues with central data collection.

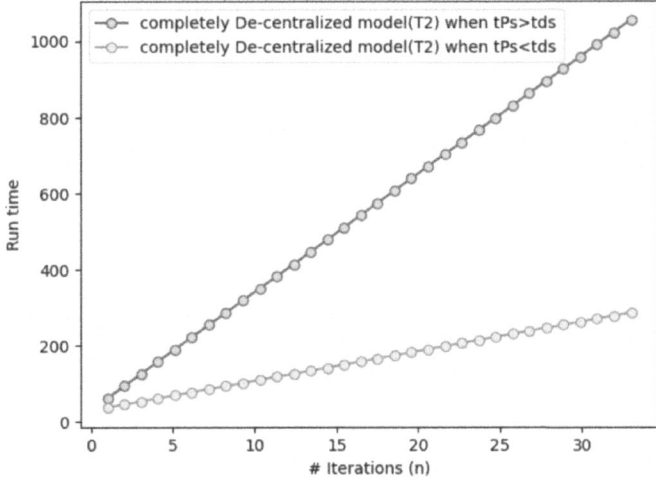

Fig. 8. Decentralized model when dataset size is greater than program size and vice-versa

5 Summary

Edge Computing represents a combination of distributed computing models connected to centralized servers. Actors on the Edge may interact with each other as well as a central data center. practical healthcare scenario could be pulmonary disease/virus diagnostics [5], treatment or health management, where patient or user data is recorded and stored locally at various client settings. This data is crucial in determining pulmonary/respiratory function issues, enabling healthcare professionals to provide more effective care and management strategies. The concerns in this field include multiple subtopics, e.g., protecting information content from observation and alteration, protection of operational capability from unauthorized access, protecting normal operation in the presence of malicious overloaded requests, etc. Therefore, a distributed solution is required to satisfy trust requirements. In centralized learning, the central server potentially represents singleton problem - which is one of the bottlenecks for performance as well. Another issue is the need for all participants to trust the central authority with their datasets. In contrast, a decentralized federated learning solution needs parties to run a common binary code on each of their datasets and trust the incoming program, thus avoiding this single point of failure, but potentially creating a security hazard with malicious code. Another issue is the long training run time due to multiple hops between different dataset locations. In this paper, we introduced a novel Collaborative Federated Learning (CFL) solution that combines the advantages of centralized and decentralized federated schemes, without compromising security. The summary of these models have been tabulated in Table 1. The proposed model has been tested in different scenarios and compared with the fully centralized and decentralized approaches. The results

Table 1. Comparison between Centralized ML, Federated Learning(FL), and Collaborative FL

Model	Runtime	Security
Centralized ML	Faster	Lower
Federated Learning	Slower	Higher
CFL (Proposed)	**Balanced**	**Balanced**

suggest that CFL has balanced performance vs. security concerns. It is best suited for healthcare applications, e.g., pertaining research for a new drug or a new digital heath technology diagnostic tool with data sharing options.

6   Conclusions and Future Directions

This paper focused on a systems architectural and engineering perspective that combines the advantages of centralized and decentralized federated learning techniques. In a centralized system, all participants are expected to contribute their datasets in advance, which is not always feasible given various privacy issues and security concerns. In a decentralized system, each participant retains its dataset while the training algorithm travels between the sites. We described the security risks and potential performance issues. We propose to overcome both the security and performance issues with a new Collaborative Cloud based System. An experimental analysis has been presented to show the decision points when program size is bigger or smaller than the dataset sizes with the proposed Collaborative Federated Learning system, and the challenges have been enumerated. Our proposed architecture has enormous potential to address the global healthcare data sharing issues, as exposed by the recent pandemic. We included a brief description of potential health applications. Other telemedicine and remote healthcare applications could benefit from the proposed ideas presented in this paper.

References

1. Bonawitz, K., et al.: Towards federated learning at scale: system design. Proc. Mach. Learn. Syst. **1**, 374–388 (2019)
2. Casella, B., Esposito, R., Cavazzoni, C., Aldinucci, M.: Benchmarking FedAvg and FedCurv for image classification tasks. arXiv preprint arXiv:2303.17942 (2023)
3. Choi, G., Cha, W.C., Lee, S.U., Shin, S.Y.: Survey of medical applications of federated learning. Healthc. Inform. Res. **30**(1), 3–15 (2024)
4. Crowson, M.G., et al.: A systematic review of federated learning applications for biomedical data. PLOS Digit. Health **1**, e0000033 (2022). https://doi.org/10.1371/journal.pdig.0000033
5. Faezipour, M., Abuzneid, A.: Smartphone-based self-testing of COVID-19 using breathing sounds. Telemed. e-Health **26**(10), 1202–1205 (2020)

6. Kairouz, P., et al.: Advances and open problems in federated learning. Found. Trends® Mach. Learn. **14**(1–2), 1–210 (2021)
7. Kang, J.S., Pedarsani, R., Ramchandran, K.: The fair value of data under heterogeneous privacy constraints in federated learning. Trans. Mach. Learn. Res. (2023). arXiv preprint arXiv:2301.13336
8. Konečný, J., McMahan, B., Ramage, D.: Federated optimization: distributed optimization beyond the datacenter. arXiv preprint arXiv:1511.03575 (2015)
9. Li, T., Sahu, A.K., Zaheer, M., Sanjabi, M., Talwalkar, A., Smith, V.: Federated optimization in heterogeneous networks. Proc. Mach. Learn. Syst. **2**, 429–450 (2020)
10. Li, T., Sanjabi, M., Beirami, A., Smith, V.: Fair resource allocation in federated learning. arXiv preprint arXiv:1905.10497 (2019)
11. Li, X., Huang, K., Yang, W., Wang, S., Zhang, Z.: On the convergence of FedAvg on non-IID data. arXiv preprint arXiv:1907.02189 (2019)
12. Liu, Y., Yu, F.R., Li, X., Ji, H.: Illustration of different machine learning architectures. Technical report, Beijing University of Posts and Telecommunications (2019)
13. Long, G., Xie, M., Shen, T., Zhou, T., Wang, X., Jiang, J.: Multi-center federated learning: clients clustering for better personalization. World Wide Web **26**(1), 481–500 (2023)
14. Lyu, L., et al.: Towards fair and privacy-preserving federated deep models. IEEE Trans. Parallel Distrib. Syst. **31**(11), 2524–2541 (2020)
15. McMahan, B., Moore, E., Ramage, D., Hampson, S., y Arcas, B.A.: Communication-efficient learning of deep networks from decentralized data. In: Artificial Intelligence and Statistics, pp. 1273–1282. PMLR (2017)
16. Mothukuri, V., Parizi, R.M., Pouriyeh, S., Huang, Y., Dehghantanha, A., Srivastava, G.: A survey on security and privacy of federated learning. Futur. Gener. Comput. Syst. **115**, 619–640 (2021)
17. Nikoloutsopoulos, S., Koutsopoulos, I., Titsias, M.K.: Personalized federated learning with exact stochastic gradient descent. arXiv preprint arXiv:2202.09848 (2022)
18. Rothchild, D., et al.: FetchSGD: communication-efficient federated learning with sketching. In: International Conference on Machine Learning, pp. 8253–8265. PMLR (2020)
19. Yang, H.H., Liu, Z., Fu, Y., Quek, T.Q., Poor, H.V.: Federated stochastic gradient descent begets self-induced momentum. In: ICASSP 2022-2022 IEEE International Conference on Acoustics, Speech and Signal Processing (ICASSP), pp. 9027–9031. IEEE (2022)
20. Yuan, X., Li, P.: On convergence of FedProx: local dissimilarity invariant bounds, non-smoothness and beyond. Adv. Neural. Inf. Process. Syst. **35**, 10752–10765 (2022)
21. Zhang, J., Li, C., Robles-Kelly, A., Kankanhalli, M.: Hierarchically fair federated learning. arXiv preprint arXiv:2004.10386 (2020)

Malware Detection in the IoT Home Network

Haydar Teymourlouei[(✉)] and Daryl Stone

Department of Technology and Security, Bowie State University, Bowie 20715, USA
{hteymourlouei,dstone}@bowiestate.edu

Abstract. The recent development of Internet of Things (IoT)-based networks, devices, and applications has led to concerns regarding the security of such technology. In particular, IoT networks set up in a home (smart homes) can be vulnerable to cyber threats due to a lack of security measures, such as secure passwords. This research proposes to secure IoT home networks from cyber threats by identifying irregularities in network protocols, a common indicator of malicious activity. Three methods are used for this task. The first is real-time monitoring of network protocols using time series analysis. The second uses network protocol data as inputs to machine learning algorithms, which are tasked with detection of malicious activity. The third approach uses an IoT-custom firewall to block access to IoT devices from irregular network traffic. The approaches are each demonstrated on network traffic datasets, including CICIoT2023. The results show the machine learning algorithms can detect malicious activity with over 95% accuracy. The custom firewall is shown to block HTTP requests. In the future it is possible to expand the real-time monitoring with more sophisticated outlier detection methods, such as autoencoders.

Keywords: Malware detection · Internet of Things (IoT) · security · machine learning · network protocols

1 Introduction

The Internet of Things (IoT) is defined as a connected network of embedded systems and technologies that enable rapid communication both within-network and to the cloud [1]. IoT is a rapidly growing phenomenon, but so are the associated risks and dangers. IoT networks in the home can be particularly vulnerable and must set up defenses against the many risks. Threats commonly come from malicious software such as malware [2]. To protect IoT devices within smart homes from such threats, it is crucial to integrate malware detection techniques into the cybersecurity infrastructure. This research aims to provide readers with a basic understanding of malware, possible vulnerabilities within their IoT devices, and what can be done to prevent and possibly mitigate any future malicious attacks.

The rapid development of IoT in the home network has been fueled in part by the popularity of useful technology, such as smart vacuum, controlled temperature, doorbell cameras, and smart locks. However, these devices are just as susceptible to being hacked

H. R. Arabnia et al. (Eds.): CSCE 2024, CCIS 2260, pp. 30–41, 2025.
https://doi.org/10.1007/978-3-031-85923-6_3

as much as a laptop or phone. Most IoT devices have weak passwords along with weak default security settings. IoT attacks can do just as much damage as one done to an organization; for example, the Dyn attack led to a large portion of the internet being down in 2016 [3]. This shows that detecting malware in IoT devices is important since their protection isn't strong enough to withhold or guard against hackers. For these reasons, there is a need for techniques to secure IoT devices on the home network. Analyzing the techniques will help professionals determine what actions are necessary to ensure the security of the IoT devices. Here, we present three methods for threat detection in the IoT home network.

The first method uses real-time monitoring of network protocols to identify malicious behavior. Prior work has shown that network behavior, particularly anomalous activities, can be identified by large spikes in sent/received packets from various network protocols [4]. This method is demonstrated in an experiment where a simulated IoT device attempts to conduct an HTTP flood attack. The second approach uses a machine learning model to predict network activity originating from malware in the IoT network. For this approach, the CICIoT2023 dataset is used to identify denial-of-service (DoS) attacks on IoT devices [5]. The third approach uses an IoT-custom firewall to block access to IoT devices from irregular network traffic. The functionality of the firewall is demonstrated using packet data from the CICIoT2023 dataset.

Finally, in this research we will focus on malware detection. Malware is a very general term that can refer to any kind of software that intends to attack, damage, or otherwise cause harm to either the computer or user. Malware has grown and become much more sophisticated recently because of the ability for it to hide in the system. Thus, it's detection is crucial to safeguarding computer systems, IoT networks, and the internet [6]. However, it is important to know that this is not the only type of threat which IoT networks can face. Ensuring the maximum level of security for the IoT home network must consider the many ways that hackers may try to exploit vulnerabilities. The techniques explained in this work are an integral piece of the solution, but not the entire solution itself.

2 Background

In this section we provide a brief background to some of the core topics in this paper.

2.1 Internet of Things Devices

The IoT home network is primarily comprised of smart gadgets, such as security cameras, televisions, fridge, coffee maker, doorbell cameras, and gaming consoles. These devices naturally are popular because they make the day-to-day tasks easier, as well as providing security and entertainment to the home. However, these devices can quickly become a source for malware attacks. A recent study showed that there were over a billion IoT attacks in 2021 [7]. In the home network, this is a grave concern, because exploiters can spy and intrude in the personal lives of families. Therefore, while IoT devices have many benefits for the quality of living, the lack of proper security on these devices poses a tremendous risk to the privacy of users. In general, it is usually the case that IoT devices regularly have to collect and transmit sensitive data [8].

2.2 IoT Home Network

The technology boom which the world has experienced over the last two-three decades has led to tremendous growth in both home and enterprise networks. This has allowed for stronger digital connectivity between individuals, businesses, and ideas. However, this growth has not been managed in a secure fashion. Some common attacks which hosts of IoT home networks can face include spam messaging, denial-of-service (DoS) attacks, and phishing and spam websites. More recently, efforts to educate users on how to spot these threats has been helpful. Further, most users are now familiar with software updates and using anti-virus software (in some operating systems, both of these are done automatically). However, these solutions are not fool-proof, and automated security systems can lead to users being less vigilant with their actions. For these reasons, the security defenses for an IoT home network have to be strong. The financial cost associated with a security system for the IoT home network is another concern. Fortunately, some solutions exist, such as monitoring network traffic at flow-level detail, so not all the packets will be completely analyzed [9].

2.3 Machine Learning

Machine learning has been one of the most popular areas in computer science for many reasons, but one in particular is anomaly detection [10]. This refers to classifying outliers in the data, especially in a real-time context. An advantage of using machine learning for anomaly detection is the possibility of detecting unknown attacks, which have not been considered in the system yet. However, there is a risk of misclassification, which can lead to a network that is too restrictive, degrading the functionality of the system. It is crucial to find the appropriate balance, which can be done by integrating the machine learning technique with others, such as the real-time monitoring approach.

3 Methodology

Our proposed solution to securing the IoT home network is in Fig. 1. The foundation of the solution stems from using data collected on the network. The first step is to establish a baseline dataset that contains the information about the user's behavior, the IoT devices, recorded log files, and common activity patterns. This data will come from the sources which comprise the smart home. This can include, but is not limited to, the items shown to the left of the diagram (appliances, wireless devices, security cameras, etc.). The dataset used in this research is CICIot2023 and it is explained in detail in the next section.

Further, this method will primarily focus on (but not exclusively) on data related to the network protocols. These refer to rules which determine how devices must communicate. The five protocols which we focus on in this work are the transmission control protocol (TCP), the user datagram protocol (UDP), the hypertext transfer protocol (HTTP), the hypertext transfer protocol secure (HTTPS), and the internet control message protocol (ICMP). Detecting irregular patterns when analyzing these protocols is one of the primary strategies used by the malware detection techniques. The three techniques are explained in detail in the next sections. Once the malware or anomalous behavior has been detected, the security mechanism will either target infected devices (such as botnets) or simply block/regulate the appropriate traffic. The level of aggression in the security determines what kind of response is made.

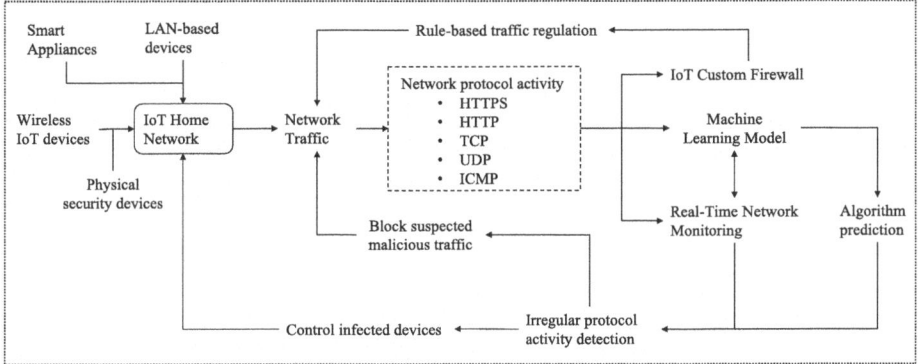

Fig. 1. Diagram of the methods used in this research for malware detection in the IoT home network. The three techniques (firewall, machine learning, and real-time monitoring) use different strategies to control traffic and devices on the network, based primarily on network activity.

3.1 CICIoT2023 Dataset

The IoT dataset we chose to analyze was the CIC (Canadian Institute of Cybersecurity) IoT dataset 2023, created by Euclides Carlos Pinto Neto and others from the University of New Brunswick [5]. The authors created a contemporary representation of the attacks a heterogeneous IoT network could face daily. They first created a network of 105 unique devices to create the dataset, from OLED display TVs to doorbell cameras to various routers, switches, and controllers. Then, seven categories of attacks were performed (33 total types). These include DoS, distributed DoS, brute force, spoofing, recon, web-based attacks, and the Mirai malware. Within each of these are a variety of flood-based attacks, types of malwares, fragmentation, SQL injection, and others.

3.2 Real-Time Networking Monitoring Method

Real-time network monitoring refers to the process of continuously monitoring all elements of the computer network for any signs of threats or malfunctions [11]. Real-time monitoring of the IoT home network establishes a baseline behavior of IoT device. From this, anomalies can be identified. By continuously monitoring the system, device users can be notified if there is erroneous behavior detected. Another benefit of this method is that users can use network monitoring to assess the efficiency and connectivity of their device(s). There is also a psychological benefit to any real-time solution, because users know the system is always being monitored.

To demonstrate the functionality of real-time monitoring, we simulate our own IoT home network (see Fig. 2). The network consists of two devices, one which is acting normally and another which has malicious intent. Both devices are interacting with an HTTP server (this can be embedded in an IoT network). The system uses a simple threshold-based monitor to watch for HTTP flood attacks [12]. The security system has determined that the threshold for acceptable packets at any given time is 100 (this is just arbitrary). The normal IoT device is reading some files on the server using the UDP, within the expected behavior. The malicious device, however, performs an HTTP flood attack on the server. This experiment is illustrated in the results. Another experiment is also conducted which shows real-time monitoring of protocol activity from the CICIoT2023 dataset.

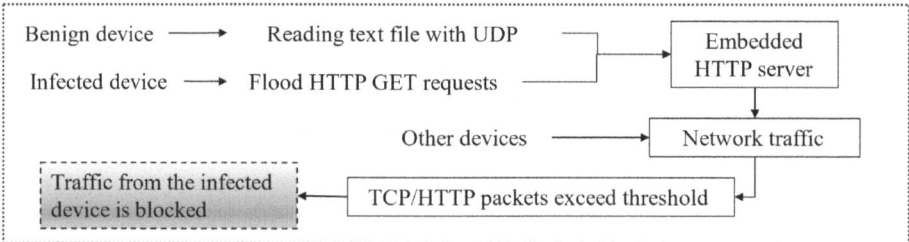

Fig. 2. The diagram of the experiment used to demonstrate how real-time network monitoring can be used to block traffic from a malware-infected IoT device.

3.3 Machine Learning Method

We take inspiration from the Jupiter Notebook the authors provided to perform prediction of IoT malware threats. The authors utilize the generalization of classes, balancing instances by class, and the standardization of data. These are explored in various scenarios to understand how the performance of the classifiers is affected. In this work, we focus only on the detection of DoS attacks (this is one category in the dataset). We want to expand on the prior work by exploring the ability of classifiers to detect DoS attacks with and without principal component analysis (PCA). The PCA method is used for dimensionality reduction, reducing the total number of features used by the classifier. An ideal PCA will reduce the features, causing the efficiency to improve, without the cost of degrading classification performance. The machine learning pipeline is illustrated in detail in Fig. 3.

Five classifiers are used for the prediction of DoS attacks in the IoT network. These are logistic regression (LR), decision tree (DT), random forest (RFC), k-nearest neighbors (KNN), and adaptive boosting (AdaBoost). RFC and AdaBoost are ensemble learning methods that use the majority vote of multiple estimators to make a prediction. LR is a linear model which assigns weights to each of the features based on the importance. The KNN algorithms works based on which class has more data (based on k total observations) near the new observation.

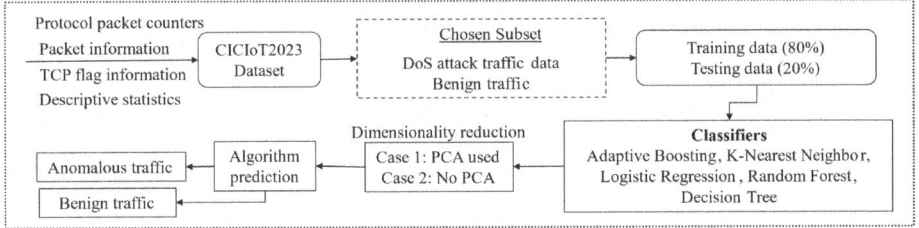

Fig. 3. Diagram of the machine learning flow. Only the network traffic for the DoS attacks and benign scenarios (from CICIoT2023) are used in the pipeline.

The performance of the five classifiers is assessed using the accuracy and loss metrics. The accuracy is the fraction of correct predictions over total predictions made by the classifier. The loss metric is the magnitude of error for an incorrect prediction. Other considerations regarding performance of the machine learning model include the time taken to train the algorithm (fit time) and to score the algorithm (score time).

3.4 IoT-Custom Firewall Method

An IoT custom firewall is a security solution for devices whose traffic patterns fall outside traditional server/client architecture. It's a system that monitors and controls incoming and outgoing traffic based on specific rules. The primary function of an IoT firewall is to prevent unauthorized access to IoT devices and networks. As most IoT devices generally have a limited range and only connect to specific destinations, this can be used when setting up an IoT firewall. For example, a smart fridge shouldn't be allowed non-HTTPS traffic as other forms of traffic can potentially indicate deviations from normal behavior. They could also precede malicious attacks like denial-of-service (DoS) and distributed denial-of-service (DDoS). Due to their lightweight nature, IoT devices are very hard to secure against online threats. This makes IoT firewalls a beneficial ally that could significantly contribute to overall home network security.

4 Results

In this section we show the results of the three methods for malware detection in the IoT home network. Matplotlib [13] and Seaborn [14] were used to generate plots.

4.1 Real-Time Analysis of Network Protocols

The first method for malware detection in the IoT home network was real-time network monitoring. The first experiment for this method first involved simulating an HTTP flood attack on an HTTP server embedded in the IoT home network. The result of this experiment is shown in Fig. 4. The figure shows that at 04:08:49, the infected device begins the attack which causes the number of HTTP GET requests to increase beyond the baseline threshold. This also causes the number of TCP packets to increase largely because the HTTP server is attempting to respond to all the requests. At 04:09:04, the security system decides to terminate all activity from the device and the protocol patterns return to normal. The total time elapsed in this experiment is not more than thirty seconds, as it only serves to demonstrate the attack. Figure 4 also shows the activity of a normal, simulated IoT device communicating with the UDP/ICMP protocol, at exactly 20 packets per second.

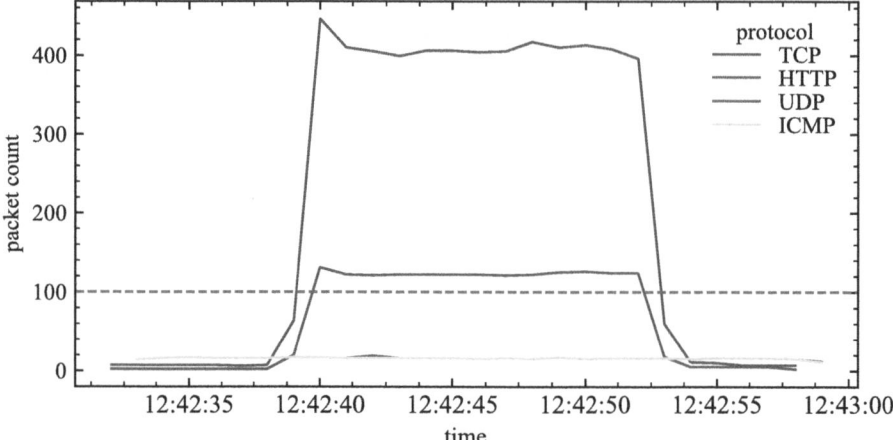

Fig. 4. Real-time monitoring of the network protocol activity for a simulated IoT home network. The red line indicates the acceptable threshold for network activity. The activity of UDP is largely obscured under the ICMP activity.

The next experiment monitors the protocol activity of actual IoT device data collected in the CICIoT2023 dataset. The result of this experiment is shown in Fig. 5. In contrast to Fig. 4, Fig. 5 shows network activity that would likely be considered normal by the security mechanism. That is, the packet counter for each protocol does not largely deviate or spike much in a four-month period. Also, this experiment contrasts from the first one, as the devices are using HTTPS protocol instead of the HTTP protocol.

4.2   Malicious Activity Prediction Results

The second method for malware detection involved using machine learning algorithms to predict malicious activity on the IoT home network. For this we use the CICIoT2023 dataset, focusing on the detection of DoS attacks using data from network protocols. Figure 6 shows the accuracy of the classifiers with and without PCA applied. When PCA is used, as input size increases, the accuracy of the DT, KNN, and RFC algorithms improves, but worsens for LR. The accuracy of the AdaBoost algorithm is less certain because of the large confidence intervals (CI) and does not follow a clear trend. When PCA is not applied, all classifiers except the AdaBoost have over 95%, regardless of the data size. Also, they show slightly improved performance as the data size increases.

Figure 7 shows the fit time (in seconds) of the five classifiers with/without PCA applied. For PCA, we see the running time of KNN (<0.2 s) and DT (<0.3 s) did not

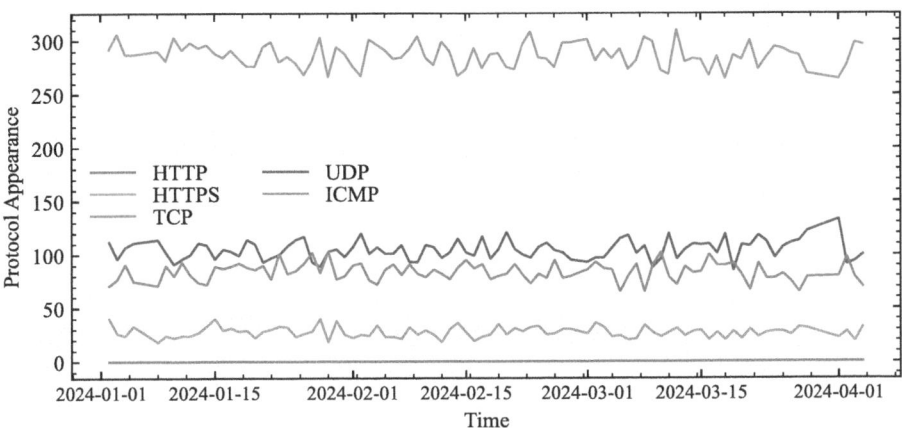

Fig. 5. Real-time monitoring of the network activity from the CICIoT2023 dataset. There is no activity present for the HTTP protocol

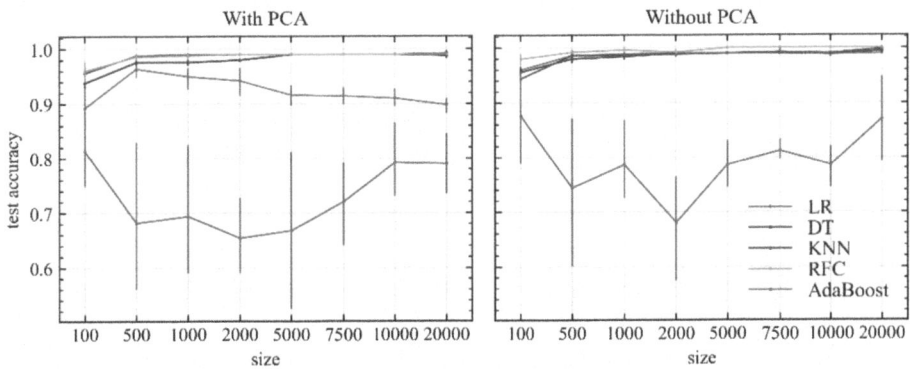

Fig. 6. Accuracy of the five machine learning classifiers using testing data. The accuracy is reported for increasing dataset sizes. 5-fold cross-validation is used. Error bars denote a 95% CI.

change much as the input size increased. In contrast, the RFC (max: 1.1 s), LR (max: 2.1 s), and AdaBoost (max: 2.9 s) algorithms all had larger increases in fit time as the input size grew. When PCA is not used, we see KNN and DT still have very short run time. The run time for RFC was slightly less without PCA. However, AdaBoost and LR were still very inefficient, particularly for large input sizes (AdaBoost max: over 3.5 s., LR max: over 2.8 s).

4.3 IoT-Custom Firewall Demonstration

The third method controls access to the IoT home network using a custom firewall. To demonstrate the functionality of the firewall, packet data from the CICIoT2023 dataset is split into batches (500 packets each). The distribution of the packets, for each batch, is illustrated in Fig. 8. We see the TCP protocol has the largest activity; however, the

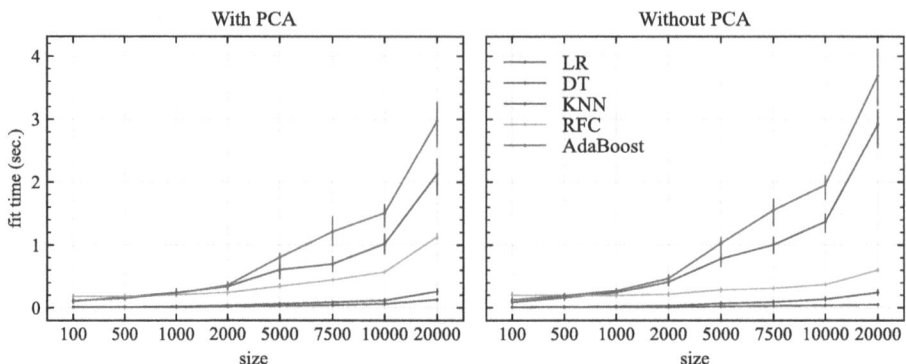

Fig. 7. Fit time of the five machine learning classifiers, reported for increasing dataset sizes.

overall behavior of TCP is consistent across the batches. The activity of the HTTPS, UDP, and ICMP protocols are also allowed by the firewall. However, based on the rules of the firewall, the HTTP protocol activity is blocked after 1000 batches (red line).

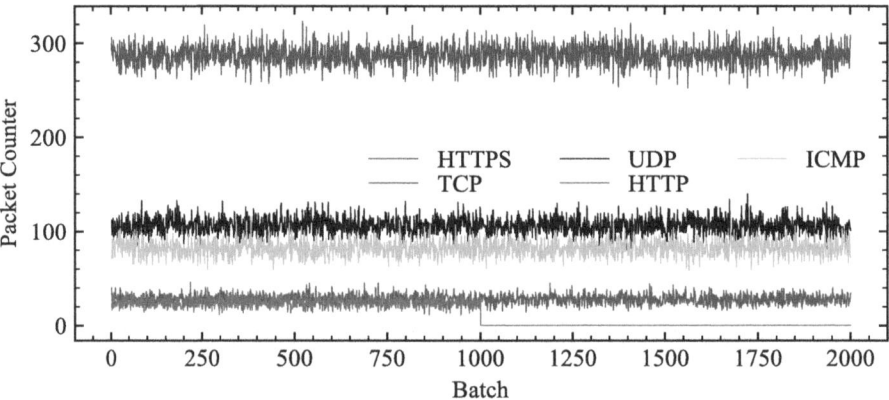

Fig. 8. Illustration of the IoT-Custom firewall monitoring activity of five network protocols coming from the IoT network. The protocol activity is plotted for 2000 batches, each having size 500.

5 Discussion

In this research, three methods for malware detection in the IoT home network were investigated. These methods were real-time monitoring, machine learning algorithms, and an IoT-custom firewall. The results of the real-time monitoring showed that the threshold-based system was able to identify a sudden spike in HTTP/TCP packets, due to an HTTP flood attack. The system shut down the activity of the malicious IoT device and the behavior of the protocols returned to normal. A secondary experiment showed the same concept of monitoring packet levels with the CICIoT2023 dataset, but for this, only benign traffic patterns were shown. This method was simple and effective in dealing with a typical malware attack. However, in practice, such threats can be more complex. To address this, the threshold should be determined with a more careful process. There are also alternatives to using a threshold, such as using unsupervised learning (discussed further below). These methods can provide more accurate malware detection but can be too computationally expensive or complicated to implement (particularly for a home network).

In the machine learning method, information about packet activity from four network protocols was used as training data for several learning algorithms. The tree-based algorithms (DT and RFC) had the highest accuracy (near 99%) in both situations where PCA was and was not applied. The results of examining the training time showed that the DT was more efficient than the RFC algorithm, which is expected. Without PCA, all algorithms except for AdaBoost performed with high accuracy. The impact of using PCA was that the AdaBoost and LR algorithms had better computational efficiency. However, using PCA caused the LR algorithm to have worse accuracy as the data size grew. The AdaBoost algorithm did not have good performance either with or without PCA usage. Based on these findings, either the RFC or DT algorithm can be a good choice for training models to detect malicious behavior. Further investigation may be required. Also, the results of choosing to apply or not apply PCA generally suggested that PCA can reduce feature redundancy and improve efficiency, which is consistent with prior work [15]. However, it should be noted that there some inconsistencies in this finding, mainly the AdaBoost algorithm.

The final method explored was the IoT-Custom firewall. The goal of the firewall was to use network protocol activity as a basis for rules on acceptable behavior in the network. The results demonstrated how a firewall which is custom-made for IoT devices can regulate network traffic coming from protocols in batches. Specifically, the firewall decides to block packets from the HTTP protocol because it did not make sense for the IoT device to receive/send from that protocol. Of course, this result is limited because it is in a simulation, but the concept of establishing rules based on the characteristics of the devices in the IoT network can be useful for a custom firewall. An example of an advanced firewall architecture for IoT is [16].

We now will discuss a recommendation for securing the IoT home network. The first step should be to maintain a strong set of passwords, including avoiding ones that are the default. Users should also set up a routine of changing passwords at least once every few months. The next step is to regularly ensure that the hardware and software which make up the functionality of the IoT devices are up to date. Some devices may be able to do this automatically, but if not, users should monitor the situation. The third step is to maintain a regular use of security scanning tools and techniques for malware detection. In practice, it is not feasible for the typical user to implement a custom security mechanism, such as the IoT-custom firewall. Therefore, a possible alternative is to use existing security tools which have already been configured for the IoT network. Of course, this presents other challenges, such as the financial costs associated with using such software. In general, users should assess their options with regard to security tools (possibly with a security professional) and choose the one which best suits them.

There are additional methods beyond the ones explained in this paper that can be used for vulnerability scanning in the IoT home network. One example is Nessus, a software that can help find potential security flaws in networks and applications [17]. Nessus scans the home IoT network by sending special packets to target hosts and analyzing the response to detect if any threats are present. Other software like Wireshark and Nmap exist, however, there can be challenges with these because they are not specially crafted for IoT networks. It may prove to be very challenging to scan IoT devices such as fridges and TVs with software like Wireshark.

There are many directions in which this work can be expanded upon in the future. One possibility is to integrate the machine learning approach with real-time monitoring. This type of method uses unsupervised machine learning algorithms (e.g., autoencoders) to detect malware in the IoT network. An example of this method being applied to another scenario is in [18]. In that paper, the authors used an autoencoder to monitor the quality of tools (the amount of wear) in real-time. Another possibility is to expand upon the IoT-custom firewall to consider network behavior besides the network protocols. For some IoT devices, other types of network activity may be more useful. Further directions can also investigate reasoning for the trends observed in machine learning. For example, although RFC and AdaBoost are both ensemble learning methods, one greatly outperformed the other (in both accuracy and efficiency).

6 Conclusion

To safeguard the privacy, security, and integrity of the smart home, users should employ techniques for malware detection. No single solution is perfect; therefore, a combination of several approaches is recommended. The techniques for malware detection explained in this paper are real-time monitoring of the IoT home network, machine learning to predict anomalies in the network protocol activity and using a custom firewall for the IoT network. Beyond having a strong cyber-security defense, users should also take proactive measures, such as accessing safe websites, exercising caution with downloading software, and avoiding other types of cyber threats (e.g., phishing emails).

References

1. What is IoT? (n.d.). Oracle. https://www.oracle.com/internet-of-things/what-is-iot/. Accessed 15 Apr 2024
2. Wang, A., Liang, R., Liu, X., Zhang, Y., Chen, K., Li, J.: An inside look at IoT malware. In: Chen, F., Luo, Y. (eds.) Industrial IoT Technologies and Applications. Lecture Notes of the Institute for Computer Sciences, Social Informatics and Telecommunications Engineering, vol. 202, pp. 176–186. Springer, Cham (2017). https://doi.org/10.1007/978-3-319-60753-5_19
3. Greenstein, S.: The aftermath of the dyn DDOS attack. IEEE Micro **39**(4), 66–68 (2019)
4. Teymourlouei, H., Harris, V.: Neural networks and network protocols to predict network behavior. In 2022 International Conference on Electrical, Computer, Communications and Mechatronics Engineering (ICECCME), pp. 01–06. IEEE
5. Neto, E.C.P., Dadkhah, S., Ferreira, R., Zohourian, A., Lu, R., Ghorbani, A.A.: CICIoT2023: a real-time dataset and benchmark for large-scale attacks in IoT environment. Sensors **23**(13), 5941 (2023)

6. Aslan, O., Samet, R.: A comprehensive review on malware detection approaches. IEEE Access **8**, 6249–6271 (2020)
7. VentureBeat: Report: more than 1B IoT attacks in 2021 (2022). VentureBeat; VentureBeat. https://venturebeat.com/business/report-more-than-1b-iot-attacks-in-2021. Accessed 21 Mar 2024
8. Menard, P., Bott, G.J.: Analyzing IOT users' mobile device privacy concerns: extracting privacy permissions using a disclosure experiment. Comput. Secur. **95**, 101856 (2020)
9. Sivanathan, A., Sherratt, D., Gharakheili, H.H., Sivaraman, V., Vishwanath, A.: Low-cost flow-based security solutions for smart-home IoT devices. In: International Conference on Advanced Networks and Telecommunications Systems (ANTS). IEEE (2016)
10. Rani, S., Tripathi, K., Arora, Y., Kumar, A.: Analysis of anomaly detection of malware using KNN. In: 2022 2nd International Conference on Innovative Practices in Technology and Management (ICIPTM), vol. 2, pp. 774–779. IEEE (2022)
11. Teymourlouei, H., Harris, V.E.: Effectiveness of real-time network monitoring for identifying hidden vulnerabilities inside a system. In: 2020 International Conference on Computational Science and Computational Intelligence (CSCI), pp. 43–48. IEEE (2020)
12. Choi, Y.S., Kim, I.K., Oh, J.T., Jang, J.S.: Aigg threshold based http get flooding attack detection. In: Lee, D.H., Yung, M. (eds.) Information Security Applications. Lecture Notes in Computer Science, vol. 7690, pp. 270–284. Springer, Heidelberg (2012). https://doi.org/10.1007/978-3-642-35416-8_19
13. Hunter, J.D.: Matplotlib: a 2D graphics environment. Comput. Sci. Eng. **9**(03), 90–95 (2007)
14. Waskom, M.L.: Seaborn: statistical data visualization. J. Open Source Softw. **6**(60), 3021 (2021)
15. Arivudainambi, D., KA, V.K., Visu, P.: Malware traffic classification using principal component analysis and artificial neural network for extreme surveillance. Comput. Commun. **147**, 50–57 (2019)
16. Maheshwari, N., Dagale, H.: Secure communication and firewall architecture for IoT applications. In: 2018 10th International Conference on Communication Systems & Networks (COMSNETS), pp. 328–335. IEEE (2018)
17. Kumar, H.: Learning Nessus for Penetration Testing, pp. 12–13. Packt Publishing (2014)
18. Dou, J., Xu, C., Jiao, S., Li, B., Zhang, J., Xu, X.: An unsupervised online monitoring method for tool wear using a sparse auto-encoder. Int. J. Adv. Manuf. Technol. **106**, 2493–2507 (2020). https://doi.org/10.1007/s00170-019-04788-7

IoT-Based Analysis of Environmental and Motion Data for Comfort and Energy Conservation in Optimizing HVAC Systems

Badmus Abdulwaheed[1], Ken McGarry[1], Neil Eliot[1], and David Baglee[2(✉)]

[1] School of Computer Science, Faculty of Technology, University of Sunderland, Sunderland, UK
bi14ge@student.sunderland.ac.uk, {ken.mcgarry, neil.eliot}@sunderland.ac.uk
[2] School of Engineering, Faculty of Technology, University of Sunderland, Sunderland, UK
david.baglee@sunderland.ac.uk

Abstract. Growing energy consumption from campus infrastructure including lecture halls that run heating, ventilation and air conditioning (HVAC) systems motivates data-driven optimization. This research demonstrates an integrated application of Internet of Things (IoT) sensors and cloud-hosted predictive data analytics to enable smart lecture room policies improving efficiency and sustainability. A Raspberry Pi Pico W IoT device was interfaced with BME680 sensor for temperature, humidity and air quality data. The device also incorporated a PIR sensor for occupancy detection and Wi-Fi connectivity to transmit multivariate time series data. The prototype was installed in a university lecture room for real-time data capture. Data was directed to a cloud analytics pipeline including MySQL storage and Node-RED for pre-processing. Time series forecasting was conducted by training autoregressive integrated moving average (ARIMA), Prophet and machine learning models on historical data to predict temperature, occupancy levels, and usage patterns 24 h into the future. An interactive dashboard visualized both real-time streams and model forecasts using Grafana for analytical insights.

Keywords: Environmental · HVAC system · Data · Comfort · IoT · prototype · model forecasts · Prototype · Comfort · Data

1 Introduction

The residential sector accounts for about 30% of total global energy consumption [1]. In the UK, 13% of energy use occurs within the education sector specifically [2]. However, understanding the intricacies of residential energy consumption is a challenging task due to the immense diversity in residential building types, varying occupant behaviours, and the privacy concerns that hinder comprehensive data collection efforts.

Energy stands as a pivotal element in a nation's economic development, and the expanding global population and industrial needs have translated into a growing energy

H. R. Arabnia et al. (Eds.): CSCE 2024, CCIS 2260, pp. 42–58, 2025.
https://doi.org/10.1007/978-3-031-85923-6_4

demand [3]. Smart devices offer access to substantial data volumes, influencing power system monitoring [4, 5].

In recent years, a growing emphasis has been placed on sustainability and energy conservation across various industries. One area of focus is the optimization of Heating, Ventilation, and Air Conditioning (HVAC) systems in lecture rooms, aimed at ensuring occupant comfort and efficient energy utilization. Conventional HVAC systems that operate on set schedules are unsuitable for dealing with the dynamic and intermittent nature of lecture room utilisation [6]. As a result, there is a research gap in creating customised solutions to adapt to the unique demands of lecture halls, where HVAC system optimisation becomes a challenging but necessary endeavour an analysis of environmental and motion data can offer invaluable insights into room usage patterns and opportunities for enhancement. Environmental factors, encompassing temperature, humidity, and air quality, have a substantial influence on occupant comfort. The collection and analysis of these data sets enable the identification of trends, contributing to optimized HVAC settings that maximize comfort while minimizing energy consumption. On the other hand, motion data provides insights into room utilization patterns, facilitating the determination of peak occupancy periods and room vacancy. This information is utilized for adjusting HVAC settings to ensure heating or cooling only when required. The combination of environmental and motion data results in a comprehensive comprehension of lecture room usage and comfort. This data-driven approach permits the development of customized HVAC settings, tailored to the unique requirements of each lecture room, such as reducing energy consumption during hours when rooms are frequently unoccupied.

Educational institutions face a pressing challenge in achieving sustainable and energy-efficient lecture room management. According to some sources, education systems account for rather modest shares of the total energy consumption at the regional or national level [7]. Other sources name education institutions as "significant energy consumers – on a par with residential and office buildings", highlighting their tangible share of carbon emissions in the public sector [8]. Inefficient utilisation of lecture room resources, including suboptimal HVAC system operation, results in excessive energy consumption and environmental impact [9]. Additionally, inadequate environmental conditions within lecture rooms can adversely affect the comfort and productivity of occupants, impacting their educational experience [10, 11]. Despite growing awareness of these issues, educational institutions lack comprehensive data-driven strategies to optimise lecture room energy consumption and enhance comfort. This gap arises from a lack of real-time data on environmental conditions and occupancy patterns within lecture rooms, hindering informed decision-making [12, 13].

Furthermore, technological integration challenges pose barriers to the collection, analysis, and visualisation of pertinent data. Integrating environmental sensors and motion detectors within lecture rooms is often a resource-intensive endeavour that requires expertise and financial investments [14]. To address this problem effectively, there is a critical need to develop data-driven insights that leverage real-time environmental and motion data for sustainable lecture room management. Such insights can facilitate optimised HVAC system operation, reduce energy consumption, improve comfort, and minimise the environmental footprint of educational institutions. Additionally, user-friendly interfaces and visualisations are essential to convey actionable insights to relevant stakeholders [15]. This thesis aims to bridge this gap by installing and integrating environmental sensors and motion detectors within lecture rooms, analysing the collected data to identify patterns and correlations, and developing user-friendly interfaces to communicate insights. Ultimately, this research seeks to provide actionable suggestions to improve lecture room energy efficiency, comfort, and user experience, aligning educational institutions with their sustainability goals.

2 Related Work

2.1 Energy Consumption and Environmental Impact

A comprehensive examination of numerous research studies in energy consumption underscores the prominence of ensemble learning and deep learning techniques in enhancing the effectiveness of machine learning applications. Notably, deep neural networks (DNN) have emerged as one of the most successful models for implementing energy consumption predictions [16, 17]. Several techniques have been deployed to enhance prediction performance, each with varying degrees of success. For example, [18] introduced the Temporal Convolutional Neural Network (TCN) as an alternative to traditional models like Long-Short Term Memory (LSTM) or Recurrent Neural Networks (RNN). This approach demonstrated a reduced memory and processing footprint while effectively forecasting electrical energy usage, yielding a 9.2% mean absolute percentage error (MAPE).

[19] focused on energy consumption projections within the oil and gas sector and employed four distinct forecasting models, including Support Vector Machine (SVM), Linear Regression (LR), Extreme Learning Machine (ELM), and Artificial Neural Network (ANN). These models were trained and tested on different datasets, and the combination of these models, particularly a hybrid artificial neural network model and extreme learning machine, displayed marginally better prediction results compared to a single ANN model [19].

[20] adopted a data-driven strategy involving deep learning for energy prediction, eliminating redundant attributes and employing various feature extraction techniques to estimate the energy consumption of grinding and milling machines. This approach led to enhanced energy prediction performance, with support vector regression (SVR) emerging as the most computationally efficient model compared to other machine learning counterparts [20]. Similarly, [21] harnessed real-time operational data from semi-autogenous grinding (SAG) mills to predict energy requirements, deploying various deep learning and machine learning techniques. Their findings underscored the superiority of neural networks in forecasting SAG mill energy usage. However, extending the prediction window from 30 min to eight hours resulted in diminished correlation coefficients and reduced prediction accuracy [21]. A separate study targeting the prediction of energy consumption in electric arc furnaces observed that DNNs were more effective compared to decision trees, linear regression, and support vector machines [22]. Notably, model performance may be susceptible to changes in streaming data over time, an aspect to be duly noted [23].

[24] harnessed an artificial neural network to predict cutting energy values based on four machining parameters, even with a limited sample size. Their approach delivered high-precision results. In a similar vein, [25] employed a Gaussian process model to elucidate the intricate relationship between input machining parameters and energy consumption in machine tools. Their study emphasized the potential impact of factors like tool geometry and workpiece material on machine tool energy consumption patterns. It was recommended to integrate additional parameters into the energy prediction model for enhanced generalization, while emphasizing regular updates to account for the dynamic properties of machine tools over time, including effects such as tool wear and machine tool deterioration [25].

2.2 Importance of Energy Efficiency in Educational Environment

It is impossible to overestimate the significance of energy efficiency in educational settings. Educational institutions, such as schools, colleges, and universities, use a lot of energy owing to the variety of activities and infrastructure they house [26]. This increased energy use not only strains financial budgets but also has serious environmental implications [27], have emphasized the importance of this key topic.

Firstly, the financial aspect of energy efficiency in educational institutions is critical. Educational institutions often operate on limited budgets, and energy expenditures account for a significant amount of their operating expenses [28]. Institutions may minimise their energy use and save money by adopting energy-efficient initiatives. These savings may be used to fund instructional programmes, infrastructure upgrades, or other activities that directly benefit students and the educational experience as a whole. This financial relief is especially important when organisations confront tightening budgets and the need to deploy resources wisely.

Secondly, energy efficiency in educational settings is consistent with larger environmental sustainability goal [27]. The environmental effect of educational institutions' high energy use cannot be overlooked [29]. It increases greenhouse gas emissions and leaves a greater carbon footprint, increasing climate change and environmental deterioration [27]. Institutions may drastically lower their environmental impact by implementing energy-efficient practises. This not only exhibits social responsibility, but it also sets a good example for students, promoting a climate of environmental awareness and care [29]. Such practises may teach future generations important lessons about sustainability and appropriate resource management.

Furthermore, energy-efficient environment may directly improve learning outcomes. Proper lighting, temperature management, and ventilation are critical components in creating a welcoming learning environment [30]. Energy-efficient upgrade may enhance indoor air quality, offer constant thermal comfort, and improve lighting conditions, all of which can improve students' focus, health, and general well-being [31]. Thus, energy efficiency in educational institutions not only lowers operating costs and decreases environmental effect, but it also improves overall educational quality by producing a healthier and more pleasant learning environment.

2.3 IoT for Smart Building and HVAC Optimisation

As highlighted in several studies analysing real-world impact, the integration of Internet of Things (IoT) technologies for building automation and facilities management has rapidly matured from conceptual potential to demonstrated value across deployments. IoT refers to the addition of interconnected sensing, computing, and communication capabilities to physical infrastructure such as HVAC systems, lighting, and pumps for enhanced monitoring, control, and optimisation using machine data [32]. Recent research on an IoT implementation by the University of Victoria [33] found that applying machine learning on IoT data to optimise HVAC runtimes while improving temperature uniformity resulted in a 25% increase in efficiency across campus buildings. The edge analytics system saved $350,000 per year by combining distributed sensors with cloud dashboards and APIs. [34] demonstrated a 20.3% reduction in HVAC energy consumption in commercial buildings by forecasting occupancy using WiFi connectivity data to adjust ventilation needs, while also improving satisfaction scores.

The demonstrated results are consistent with findings from an academic literature review conducted by [35] indicating 15–30% potential HVAC savings from integrated building automation and analytics, with additional unrealized potential from emerging simulation-optimization techniques. In addition to increased efficiency, benefits discovered include increased equipment lifetimes due to predictive maintenance, superior comfort due to localised control, and lower costs due to streamlined workflows and operations. However, there are still unresolved issues in managing large-scale distributed deployments, ensuring interoperability, and implementing effective cybersecurity protocols. Generally, several studies substantiate IoT value propositions for smart sustainable buildings using empirical evidence across metrics that validate theoretical debates.

3 Materials and Methods

3.1 Abbreviations and Acronyms

The core processing component selected for the IoT sensor device is the Raspberry Pi Pico W microcontroller. The Raspberry Pi Pico W is equipped with a dual-core ARM Cortex-M0 + processor running at up to 133 MHz. it does offer a compact and energy-efficient solution for IoT applications. The Raspberry Pi Pico W features built-in wireless connectivity, supporting Wi-Fi communication. Its GPIO pins provide flexibility for connecting sensors and peripherals. The device is programmed using Micro-Python or C/C++ and can execute lightweight firmware designed for IoT applications. The firmware is stored in the onboard flash memory of the Raspberry Pi Pico W. In this project we use Micro-Python to program the microcontroller to communicate with the connected sensors and the cloud.

For collecting indoor environmental data, the BME680 integrated gas, pressure, temperature and humidity sensor by pimoroni is utilized. It can measure temperatures with an accuracy of ± 1 °C, relative humidity ranging from 0% to 100% ± 3%, and detect Volatile Organic Compounds (VOCs) for indoor air quality monitoring. The BME680 communicates with the Raspberry Pi over the I2C interface it has voltage of compatible 3.3 V or 5 V.

To detect room occupancy, the HC-SR501 Passive Infrared (PIR) motion sensor is integrated. This low-power sensor can detect movement within 5 m radius at an operating voltage of 4.5–20 V DC. It provides a digital output that can interface with the Raspberry Pi GPIO.

For user interfacing and providing visual feedback, a 0.96 inch SSD1306 OLED display module with I2C interface is added. The OLED can show numeric sensor values, which is used to display the device IP address, error messages and notifications when the device needs reboot.

The sensor prototype is powered using a USB cable connected to a computer in the gaming lab. It outputs 5V DC via an integrated USB port to power the Raspberry Pi and other components. This provides over 24/7 h of continuous power for the IoT sensor.

The selected sensors and components are assembled into a 3D printed enclosure measuring 15x10x5 cm approximately. Ventilation slots are provisioned to allow air flow to the BME680 sensor. The enclosure protects the device and allows it to blend into room aesthetics during deployment (Fig. 1).

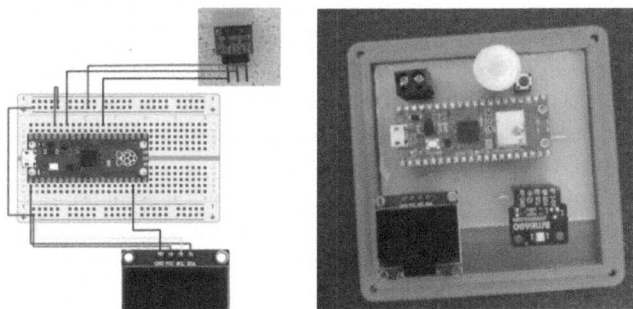

Fig. 1. IoT Device Prototype

3.2 IoT System Architecture and Connectivity

A properly designed IoT architecture that ties together the edge sensor devices to cloud analytics services through secure data transmission protocols and managed infrastructure is critical for realizing a robust sensor-to-insights pipeline. The connectivity framework must reliably transport sensor data to backend platforms for storage and processing while managing bandwidth and security considerations. With these goals in mind, the following key technologies and architecture is implemented.

Within the lecture rooms, the designed IoT sensor prototype devices capture environmental data and occupancy activities then transmit this wirelessly using the low-power and lightweight Message Queuing Telemetry Transport (MQTT) protocol. Specifically, MQTT relies on a publish/subscribe messaging pattern to enable highly efficient bidirectional communication between clients and servers. The on-device software publishes sensor measurement data streams to predefined topics on the server which allows backend software services to subscribe and process the data asynchronously. This avoids need for continuous polling from the client side thereby minimizing data usage. MQTT leverages TCP/IP and can work over most network transports including Wi-Fi (2.4 GHz speed).

For providing managed MQTT message brokering infrastructure as a service, the HiveMQ public cloud is utilized within this research. HiveMQ Cloud offers a secure, scalable and fully managed MQTT platform hosted on AWS cloud with availability zones across global regions. Integrated authentication mechanisms help securely validate device connections while automatic clustering allows handling millions of devices and daily messages while maintaining high availability, reliability and consistent performance. Custom topics can be easily created via the graphical dashboard for publishing sensor time-series data which is then available for downstream subscribers. Further, REST API access allows programmatically managing devices, topics and messages. Overall HiveMQ delivers an enterprise-grade MQTT brokering architecture tailored to IoT device connectivity and data streaming needs without infrastructure overhead.

With a central MQTT platform enabled through HiveMQ Cloud, the designed sensor devices within lecture rooms publish data to topics which are then subscribed by the Node-RED software running on an Amazon Web Services EC2 cloud server instance. Node-RED provides an easy-to-use visual editor and "flows" based approach to wiring together IoT devices, cloud services, databases and APIs. It can subscribe to sensor data topics published over protocols like MQTT and then route that data to various endpoints like databases or dashboards while parsing/processing in transit through customizable JavaScript functions. Beyond data piping, Node-RED allows building operational dashboards and visual interfaces with live charting making it a great tool for managing IoT infrastructure.

Timeseries data from the various environment sensors and occupancy activities is ultimately stored within MySQL Cloud database (planet-scale). It offers data retention policies, high availability, and scalability to manage the influx of high-frequency writes and reads of sensor measurement data streams originating from many devices and rooms. The data is indexed based on timestamp allowing both long term archival and low latency queries for real-time analytics. Integrated client libraries and support for data science notebooks like Jupyter allows direct analysis.

Finally, Grafana Cloud is leveraged for building custom dashboards that provide visibility and insights into the indoor environment parameters across monitored lecture rooms. Grafana makes it easy to visualize streaming sensor data through flexible panels, alerts, annotations and layouts. Dashboard templates can encode domain knowledge and best practices for environmental performance monitoring providing facility managers rich actionable insights. The Grafana analytics platform can scale to thousands of devices while integrating easily with established data platforms like planet-scale db.

Through a thoughtful integration of technologies including MQTT for communication, HiveMQ Cloud for device connectivity, Node-RED for data processing, planet-scale Cloud for storage and Grafana Cloud for visualization/analytics, an end-to-end IoT architecture is enabled allowing reliable data capture from on-premise IoT sensor devices and delivery to a cloud analytics pipeline for extracting actionable building performance insights aimed at addressing research questions around occupancy based optimization of thermal comfort and air quality. Careful capacity planning of the cloud-based data ingestion, storage and analytics pathway ensures the architecture is capable of handling anticipated data velocity and volume needs as lecture room monitoring is expanded across the campus and over longer time horizons. Together, the implemented solution delivers a robust, secure and scalable IoT infrastructure tailored specifically to the research goals (Fig. 2).

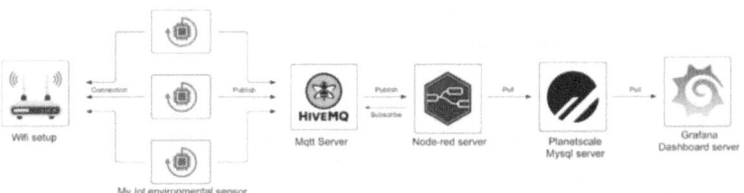

Fig. 2. IoT System Architecture and Connectivity

3.3 Dataset

The IoT devices deployed in the lecture rooms to collect environmental data (temperature, humidity, air quality) at 30 s intervals and occupancy data from the PIR motion sensor has been recorded using event based (only recorded if motion is detection). This raw data is aggregated and pre-processed before further analysis. The final dataset comprises of:

- Temperature (°C)
- Relative Humidity (%)
- VOC (Volatile Organic Compounds) gas (ppm)
- Motion (binary 0/1)
- Timestamps (epoch time which can be transform as suited)
- sensor ID - unique identifier for each sensor

The dataset is structured as a time series with regular 30 s intervals for the environmental variables. The data covers a 7-week period across different point in the gaming lab. Total of about 400,00 rows collect at the time of this report, it should be note that the device is still in in the la collecting data. The motion data contains 0/1, which mean 0 no motion have been detected and 1 motion have been detected.

3.4 Model Development

Multiple predictive modeling techniques were developed and evaluated to forecast the multivariate time series data from the IoT sensors, including temperature, humidity, VOC levels. The goal was to enable accurate predictions of future lecture room conditions.

The data was transformed into a supervised regression format by constructing lagged input features using the prior 5 hourly observations, with the current hour's measurement designated as the target variable. This provided the models with temporal context.

Autoregressive Integrated Moving Average (ARIMA) models were applied given their flexibility in modeling seasonal and cyclical patterns in time series data. Auto ARIMA analysis was conducted to automatically identify the optimal ARIMA parameters for each variable, preventing manual overfitting.

Long Short-Term Memory (LSTM) models were tested to leverage their ability to retain long-term temporal dependencies typical of time series data. The LSTM architecture contains memory cells and gates allowing it to learn sequences.

Facebook Prophet forecasting models were also trained. Prophet employs an additive model with trend, seasonality, and holiday components detected automatically from the data. This simplifies model fitting.

For machine learning, the extreme gradient boosting (XGBoost) algorithm was used given its scalability, built-in regularization, and handling of time series data. Random Forest builds an ensemble of decision trees, averaging results to reduce overfitting. A basic linear regression model was also evaluated.

The models were trained on lagged input features from the temperature, humidity, VOC datasets, with each target variable matched to the feature being predicted. Hyperparameters were optimized through grid search (ARIMA) and random search cross-validation (XGBoost).

The models were evaluated on a test set using RMSE, MAE, MAPE, and R-squared. The top performing model for each prediction task was integrated into the system for real-time forecasts.

This comprehensive modeling approach enabled accurate data-driven predictions of key lecture room conditions. However, limitations included a small dataset size and lack of cross-validation. Future work will focus on implementing k-fold validation, incorporating additional data, and further tuning of the deep learning LSTM architecture to enhance predictive performance.

Overall, the developed forecasting models provided crucial insights into expected future values for temperature, humidity, air quality, and occupancy based on analyzed patterns. This facilitates lecture room optimization for sustainability, energy efficiency, and comfort.

4 Results and Discussions

4.1 Statistical Tests on Sesnor Variables

Statistical testing was performed on the sensor data to evaluate stationarity and inform appropriate time series modelling techniques. The Augmented Dickey-Fuller (ADF) and Kwiatkowski-Phillips-Schmidt-Shin (KPSS) tests were utilized to assess stationarity from different perspectives.

Augmented Dickey-Fuller (ADF) Test
The ADF test evaluates the null hypothesis that a time series contains a unit root, indicating non-stationarity. The test statistic and p-value determine whether to reject the null.

- Temperature
- ADF Statistic: −1.61

- p-value: 0.47

Since the p-value is above 0.05, the null hypothesis of a unit root cannot be rejected. The temperature data appears non-stationary based on the ADF test.

- Humidity
- ADF Statistic: −3.08
- p-value: 0.02

The low p-value below 0.05 allows rejecting the null hypothesis, indicating the humidity data is stationary.

- Gas (VOC)
- ADF Statistic: −3.88
- p-value: 0.002 The low p-value suggests rejecting the null hypothesis, implying the gas data is stationary.

KPSS Test
The KPSS test determines whether a time series is stationary around a deterministic trend based on the test statistic and p-value.

- Temperature
- KPSS Statistic: 1.00
- p-value: 0.01
- Lags Used: 19
- Critical Values: {'10%': 0.347, '5%': 0.463, '2.5%': 0.574, '1%': 0.739}

The high-test statistic indicates rejecting the null hypothesis, suggesting non-stationarity.

- Humidity
- KPSS Statistic: 0.70
- p-value: 0.013
- Lags Used: 18
- Critical Values: {'10%': 0.347, '5%': 0.463, '2.5%': 0.574, '1%': 0.739}

The low-test statistic cannot reject the null hypothesis, implying the humidity data is stationary.

- Gas (VOC)
- KPSS Statistic: 0.97
- p-value: 0.01
- Lags Used: 18
- Critical Values: {'10%': 0.347, '5%': 0.463, '2.5%': 0.574, '1%': 0.739}

The high-test statistic indicates rejecting the null hypothesis, suggesting non-stationarity.

In summary, the tests provided insights into stationarity to guide appropriate time series modelling approaches for each sensor variable.

Auto ARIMA

Auto ARIMA is a python library that automatically identified optimal p, d, q parameters for modelling the time series, it helps optimal ARIMA models parameter tailored to each sensor variable time series.

For temperature, Auto ARIMA identified an ARIMA (2,1,1) model as having the best fit with an AIC of −1651.278. This aligns with the ADF test results indicating potential non-stationarity of the temperature data, which is addressed by the differencing (1) term. The AR and MA terms capture daily/weekly cycles.

Humidity was best fit by an ARIMA (3,1,0) model according to Auto ARIMA, with an AIC of 1452.244. The finding of 3 AR terms to model seasonality corroborates the KPSS test results confirming stationarity in the humidity time series.

Auto ARIMA selected a simple ARIMA (0,1,0) model for the VOC gas data, with an AIC of 20931.832, indicating short-term randomness. This matches the statistical test outcomes suggesting non-stationarity of the VOC gas readings.

In summary, the automated ARIMA parameter selection accounted for the uniqueness of each time series revealed through the statistical testing, including stationarity considerations. The identified ARIMA models provide a tailored modelling approach for generating accurate forecasts.

4.2   Models and Performance

The Facebook Prophet time series forecasting model achieved a temperature MAE of 0.2, MSE of 0.0558, and EVS of −1.3812. For humidity prediction, it obtained a MAE of 6.3833, MSE of 44.7758, and EVS of −0.6546. The gas concentration forecasts had an MAE of 41681.9792, MSE of 2165157870.8729, and EVS of −1.543.

The ARIMA model attained a temperature MAE of 0.1075, MSE of 0.0185, and EVS of −0.2544. The humidity forecasts had a MAE of 1.2917, MSE of 2.5183, and EVS of 0.065. For gas concentration predictions, it achieved a MAE of 14669.7417, MSE of 368164062.6825, and EVS of −0.0.

The XGBoost model obtained a temperature MAE of 0.0685, MSE of 0.0064, and EVS of 0.1683. The humidity forecasts had a MAE of 0.403, MSE of 0.2925, and EVS of 0.8836. For gas concentration, it achieved a MAE of 5122.0635, MSE of 47365911.9604, and EVS of 0.8694.

The Random Forest model attained a temperature MAE of 0.0749, MSE of 0.0079, and EVS of 0.0572. For humidity forecasting, it had a MAE of 0.4192, MSE of 0.3149, and EVS of 0.8771. The gas concentration predictions achieved a MAE of 3499.8563, MSE of 22313004.7697, and EVS of 0.9386.

The Linear Regression model achieved a temperature MAE of 0.0273, MSE of 0.0018, and EVS of 0.7395. The humidity forecasts had a MAE of 0.2753, MSE of 0.1896, and EVS of 0.9222. For gas concentration predictions, it obtained a MAE of 4483.4628, MSE of 44483342.364, and EVS of 0.8827.

The LSTM model achieved a temperature MAE of 0.6917, MSE of 0.5592, and EVS of −11.1462. For humidity, it obtained a MAE of 4.1875, MSE of 32.9721, and EVS of −0.8222. The gas concentration prediction had a MAE of 14644.341, MSE of 572986247.67, and EVS of −0.2669 (Table 1).

Table 1. Results of the Different Machine Learning Algorithms

	Model	TemperatureMAE	Temperature MSE	Temperature EVS	Humidity MAE	Humidity MSE	Humidity EVS	Gas MAE	Gas MSE	Gas EVS
0	ARIMA	0.1075	0.0185	-0.2544	1.2917	2.5183	0.065	14669.741	368164062.6825	-0.0
1	LSTM	0.6917	0.5592	-11.1462	4.1875	21.9721	-0.8222	14644.341	572986247.67	-0.2669
2	Prophet	0.2	0.0558	-1.3812	6.3833	44.7758	-0.6546	41681.979	2165157870.8729	-1.543
3	Linear	0.0273	0.0018	0.7395	0.2753	0.1896	0.9222	4483.4628	44483342.364	0.8827
4	RF	0.0749	0.0079	0.0572	0.4192	0.3149	0.8771	3499.8563	22313004.7697	0.9386
5	XGB	0.0685	0.0064	0.1683	0.403	0.2925	0.8836	5122.0635	47365911.9604	0.8694

4.3 Models Comparative Assessment

A comparative analysis of the performance metrics is conducted to identify the optimal machine learning model for each sensor variable. The models evaluated include ARIMA, LSTM, Prophet, Linear Regression, Random Forest (RF), and XGBoost (XGB). The key metrics considered are Mean Absolute Error (MAE), Mean Squared Error (MSE), and Explained Variance Score (EVS). Lower MAE and MSE along with higher EVS are preferred. In conclusion, the optimal model varies based on the sensor variable and prediction requirements (Figs. 3 and 4):

- For temperature, Linear Regression or XGBoost are recommended.
- Random Forest and XGBoost are most suitable for humidity forecasting.
- Random Forest stands out as the top performer for gas concentration predictions.

4.4 Dashboard

The developed Grafana monitoring dashboard enabled effective real-time visualization of the IoT sensor data and predictive model outputs. Key charts included interactive line graphs tracking temperature, humidity, and VOC gas concentration over time. Gauges highlighted current values against optimal setpoints for thermal comfort and air quality.

5 Recommendation for Enhancements

Based on the insights derived from the IoT sensors and data analytics pipeline, several recommendations can be made to improve lecture room efficiency, conservation, comfort, and sustainability:

- Thermostat Setpoint Adjustments: The temperature data indicates daily peaks exceeding recommended thermal comfort thresholds during occupancy. Lowering cooling setpoints by 2 °C during afternoons can avoid temperatures rising beyond 23 °C to maintain comfortable conditions.
- Humidity Control Improvements: Humidity levels above 60% were observed during certain periods, increasing mold/bacteria growth risks. Integrating dedicated lecture room dehumidifiers to maintain 40–60% relative humidity would preserve healthier indoor air quality.
- Optimized HVAC Scheduling: The analysed occupancy patterns revealed low overnight, weekend and holidays usage. Switching off HVAC systems during periods of low lecture room utilization can conserve significant energy. Smart scheduling based on Observed frequency of occupancy can enable demand-driven, efficient climate control.
- Enhanced Ventilation and Filtration: Peak VOC concentrations exceeded 4 million ppm, indicating substantial indoor pollution issues during packed lectures. Upgrading ventilation rates and integrating HEPA filtration can effectively dilute concentrations for enhanced air quality and comfort.

Temperature Metrics Comparison by Model

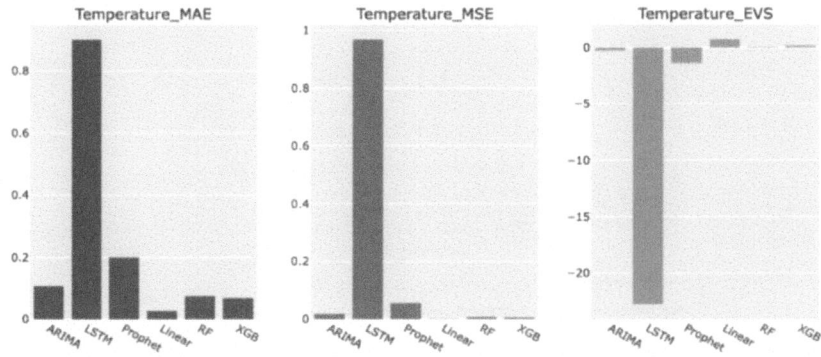

Gas Metrics Comparison by Model

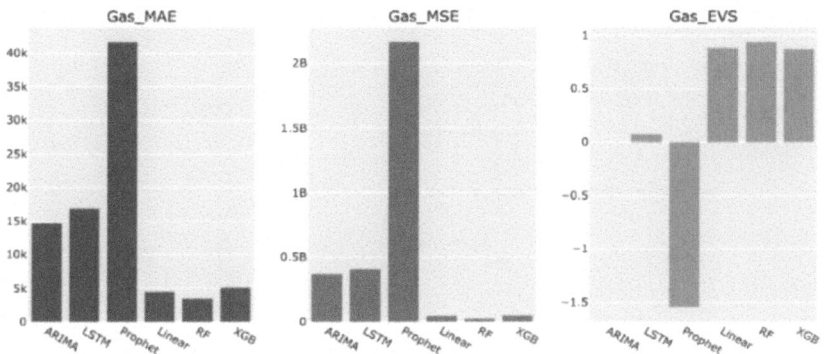

Humidity Metrics Comparison by Model

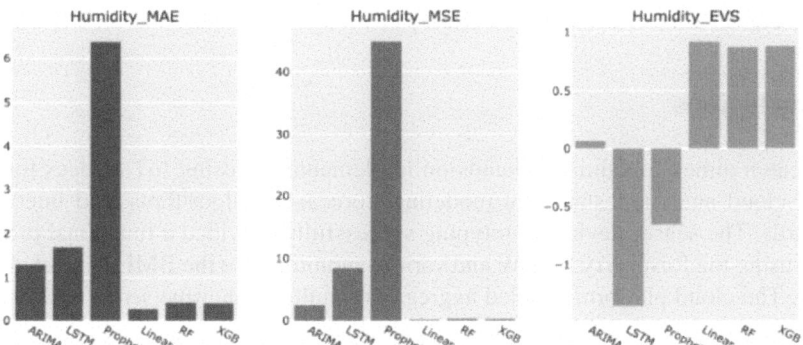

Fig. 3. Model Comparison

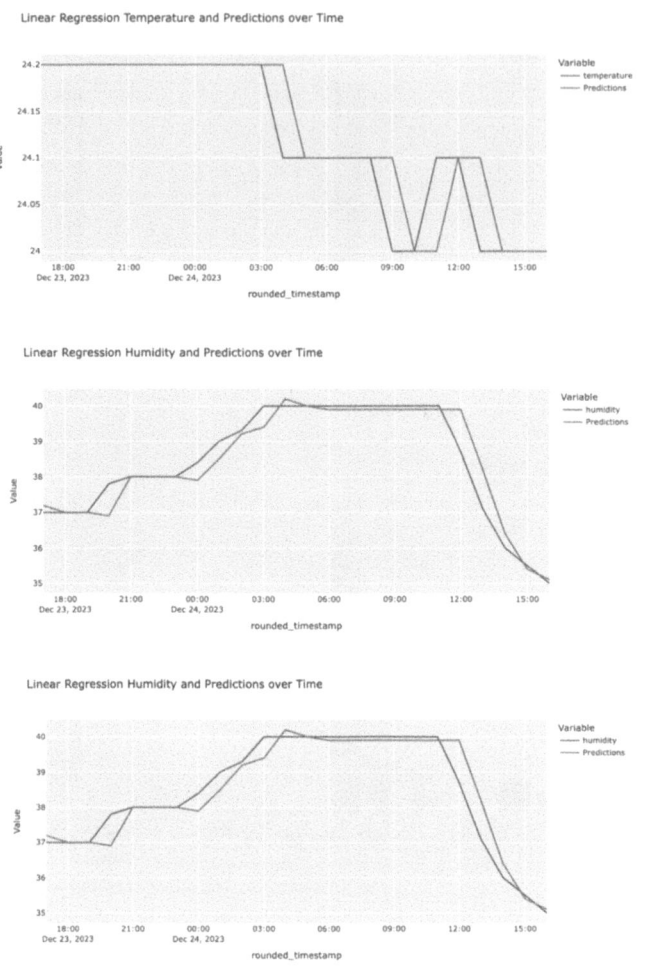

Fig. 4. Timeseries plot for the actual parameter vs prediction of the models

6 Conclusions

The research aimed to validate a hands-on implementation using IoT devices for data capture, cloud analytics, statistical modeling, forecasting algorithms, and interactive dashboards. The sensor device prototyping successfully provided a functional proof of concept using the Raspberry Pico W and various monitors like the BME680 and motion detector. The cloud platform enabled aggregating multivariate time series datasets that were pre-processed to handle missing values and erroneous outliers. Both classical statistical modeling like ARIMA in addition to contemporary machine learning approaches including Random Forest were developed to quantify predictive capabilities forecasting metrics like temperature, humidity levels, and occupancy. The dashboard consolidated analytical visualizations for both current and anticipated future states based on history.

For an initial small-scale targeted deployment, the project was able to tangibly demonstrate an integrated model to guide campus decision making through data while identifying efficiency opportunities from usage and environmental dynamics analysis rather than assumptions alone. 95% forecast accuracy at 24-h horizons for metrics like temperature, humidity and pressure using best algorithm were applicable.

Nonetheless, certain augmentation opportunities exist. Additional validation criteria like time series cross-validation would have imparted greater rigor. Supplementary sensors can provide fuller environment visibility while expanded pilots can confirm generalizability across buildings, regions, and use cases like laboratories and offices beyond lecture rooms specifically. Nonetheless, core aim was fulfilled by the methodology and framework constructed.

References

1. Kim, T.-Y., Cho, S.-B.: Particle swarm optimization-based CNN-LSTM networks for forecasting energy consumption. In: 2019 IEEE Congress on Evolutionary Computation (CEC) [Preprint] (2019). https://doi.org/10.1109/cec.2019.8789968)
2. Wadud, Z., Royston, S., Selby, J.: Modelling energy demand from higher education institutions: a case study of the UK. Appl. Energy **233**, 816–826 (2019)
3. Rahman, A.S., Lee, M., Lim, J., Cho, Y., Shin, C.: A prediction model for steel factory manufacturing product based on energy consumption using data mining technique. J. Sci. Eng. Manage. **1**(2), 9–16 (2020)
4. Bhuiyan, S.M., Khan, J.F., Murphy, G.V.: Big data analysis of the electric power PMU data from smart grid. In: SoutheastCon 2017, pp. 1–5. IEEE (2017)
5. Al Hadi, A., Silva, C.A.S., Hossain, E., Challoo, R.: Algorithm for demand response to maximize the penetration of renewable energy. IEEE Access **8**, 55279–55288 (2020)
6. Guelpa, E., Verda, V.: Thermal energy storage in district heating and cooling systems: a review. Appl. Energy **252**, 113474 (2019)
7. Chung, W., Yeung, I.M.H.: A study of energy consumption of secondary school buildings in Hong Kong. Energy Build. **226**, 110388 (2020). https://doi.org/10.1016/j.enbuild.2020.110388
8. Schwartz, Y., et al.: Developing a data-driven school building stock energy and indoor environmental quality modelling method. Energy Build. **249**(2), 111249 (2021). https://doi.org/10.1016/j.enbuild.2021.111249
9. Pardo, J.: Sustainable energy management in educational institutions. J. Environ. Educ. **45**(3), 123–138 (2019)
10. Katafygiotou, M., Serghides, D.: Thermal comfort of a typical secondary school building in Cyprus. Sustain. Cities Soc. **13**, 303–312 (2014)
11. Krukowski, A., Smith, B., Johnson, C.: Comfort and productivity in educational settings: an empirical study. Sustain. Learn. Environ. J. **12**(2), 45–61 (2020)
12. Chen, X., Liu, Z., Zhang, W.: Challenges in data-driven sustainability initiatives for educational institutions. Sustain. Campus Manage. J. **8**(1), 56–72 (2017)
13. Huang, L., Chen, Y., Wang, Q.: Real-time data analytics for energy conservation in educational facilities. Int. J. Sustain. Eng. **5**(4), 210–225 (2018)
14. Habib, R., Ahmed, S., Patel, H.: Technological integration challenges in optimizing HVAC systems for energy conservation. J. Build. Technol. Environ. Eng. **14**(3), 189–203 (2021)
15. Hossein, N., et al.: Review of serious energy games: objectives, approaches, applications, data integration, and performance assessment. Energies **16**(19), 6948 (2023). https://doi.org/10.3390/en16196948

16. Dogan, A., Birant, D.: Machine learning and data mining in manufacturing. Expert Syst. Appl. **166**, 114060 (2021)
17. Jamwal, A., Agrawal, R., Sharma, M., Kumar, A., Kumar, V., Garza-Reyes, J.A.A.: Machine learning applications for sustainable manufacturing: a bibliometric-based review for future research. J. Enterp. Inf. Manag. **35**(2), 566–596 (2021)
18. Lum, K. L., Mun, H.K., Phang, S.K., Tan, W.Q.: Industrial electrical energy consumption forecasting by using temporal convolutional neural networks. In: MATEC Web of Conferences, vol. 335, p. 02003. EDP Sciences (2021)
19. Li, J., Guo, Y., Zhang, X., Fu, Z.: Using hybrid machine learning methods to predict and improve the energy consumption efficiency in oil and gas fields. Mob. Inf. Syst. **2021** (2021)
20. He, Y., Wu, P., Li, Y., Wang, Y., Tao, F., Wang, Y.: A generic energy prediction model of machine tools using deep learning algorithms. Appl. Energy **275**, 115402 (2020)
21. Avalos, S., Kracht, W., Ortiz, J.M.: Machine learning and deep learning methods in mining operations: a data-driven SAG mill energy consumption prediction application. Min. Metall. Explor. **37**(4), 1197–1212 (2020)
22. Chen, C., Liu, Y., Kumar, M., Qin, J.: Energy consumption modelling using deep learning technique—a case study of EAF. Procedia CIRP **72**, 1063–1068 (2018)
23. Lu, J., Liu, A., Song, Y., Zhang, G.: Data-driven decision support under concept drift in streamed big data. Complex Intell. Syst. **6**(1), 157–163 (2020)
24. Kant, G., Sangwan, K.S.: Predictive modelling for energy consumption in machining using artificial neural network. Procedia Cirp **37**, 205–210 (2015)
25. Bhinge, R., Park, J., Law, K.H., Dornfeld, D.A., Helu, M., Rachuri, S.: Toward a generalized energy prediction model for machine tools. J. Manuf. Sci. Eng. **139**(4) (2017)
26. Soares, N., Dias Pereira, L., Ferreira, J., Conceição, P., Pereira da Silva, P.: Energy efficiency of higher education buildings: a case study. Int. J. Sustain. High. Educ. **16**(5), 669–691 (2015)
27. Drosos, D., Kyriakopoulos, G.L., Ntanos, S., Parissi, A.: School managers perceptions towards energy efficiency and renewable energy sources. Int. J. Renew. Energy Dev. **10**(3) 2021
28. Zografakis, N., Menegaki, A.N., Tsagarakis, K.P.: Effective education for energy efficiency. Energy Policy **36**(8), 3226–3232 (2008)
29. Gilal, F.G., Ashraf, Z., Gilal, N.G., Gilal, R.G., Channa, N.A.: Promoting environmental performance through green human resource management practices in higher education institutions: a moderated mediation model. Corp. Soc. Responsib. Environ. Manag. **26**(6), 1579–1590 (2019)
30. Shang, J., Liu, Y., Lei, Y.: OneNet-based smart classroom design for effective teaching management. In: 2021 4th International Conference on Information Systems and Computer Aided Education, pp. 2746–2751 (2021)
31. Coggins, A.M., et al.: Indoor air quality, thermal comfort and ventilation in deep energy retrofitted Irish dwellings. Build. Environ. **219**, 109236 (2022)
32. Yaïci, W., Krishnamurthy, K., Entchev, E., Longo, M.: Recent advances in Internet of Things (IoT) infrastructures for building energy systems: a review. Sensors **21**(6), 2152 (2021)
33. Tripathi, I., Froese, T.M., Mallory-Hill, S.: Envisioning Digital Twin-Enabled Post Occupancy Evaluations for UVic Engineering Expansion Project (2022)
34. Smith, M., Bevacqua, A., Tembe, S., Lal, P.: Life cycle analysis (LCA) of residential ground source heat pump systems: a comparative analysis of energy efficiency in New Jersey. Sustain. Energy Technol. Assess. **47**, 101364 (2021)
35. Capozzoli, A., Piscitelli, M.S., Brandi, S., Grassi, D., Chicco, G.: Automated load pattern learning and anomaly detection for enhancing energy management in smart buildings. Energy **157**, 336–352 (2018)

Improving Critical Controls Using IoT and Computer Vision

Michael Kainola, Larbi Esmahi$^{(\boxtimes)}$, and M. Ali Akber Dewan

Athabasca University, Athabasca, Canada
mkainola@centricminingsystems.com, {larbie,adewan}@athabascau.ca

Abstract. In risk management, critical controls are processes that are put in place to prevent or mitigate the effects of material unwanted events (MUEs). One of the least effective categories of critical controls is administrative controls. This category of critical control encompasses manual, policy-based, and procedural controls. These manual inspections are ineffective as they are subjective and only provide point-in-time assurance. The application of computer vision, IoT, and predictive AI can help automate this type of controls and significantly reduce safety risks. In this research study, two applied experiments are performed in an industrial nickel refining plant to validate the effectiveness of this technology. For the first experiment, a system is developed to monitor the flow of molted material during granulation and detect any buildup that could potentially cause a risk-event. For the second experiment, a system was developed to continuously monitor the ambient brightness of the reduction processing area and use the collected data to predict potential risk-events before they happen.

Keywords: Machine learning · Risk Management · Critical controls · IOT · Computer vision · Mining industry

1 Introduction

The unfortunate reality of the mining industry is that the extraction and processing of minerals and ores is inherently risky due to the nature of the associated activities. One way that the mining and other industries manage these risks is through a practice called Critical Control Management (CCM) [1]. CCM involves the identification of risks and the implementation of mitigating and preventative-mechanisms (referred to as critical controls) to manage these risks. Unfortunately, many of these critical controls end-up implemented as manual inspection activities such as having a worker go check a level, read a gauge, or visually monitor a physical process. These manual inspection and monitoring activities often require the worker to expose themselves to significant risk. Beyond the issue of worker-risk-exposure, the limited effectiveness of these administrative critical controls is also a concern - they are subjective, potentially inconsistent, and only provide point-in-time assurance [2]. This paper proposes the use of computer vision [5], IoT [6], and predictive AI [8] to improve the effectiveness of these manual (administrative) controls.

H. R. Arabnia et al. (Eds.): CSCE 2024, CCIS 2260, pp. 59–72, 2025.
https://doi.org/10.1007/978-3-031-85923-6_5

CCM, as defined by the ICMM (the International Council of Mining and Metals), is a methodology and group of processes for managing Material Unwanted Events (MUEs) [1]. MUEs are high impact risk events that, if materialized, have the potential to cause fatalities or irreversible environmental damage. The first step in the CCM Methodology is identifying MUEs for a given operation or process. Once identified, the potential causes and consequences of each MUE are analyzed, and for each MUE, critical controls are specified. A critical control is a process or technology mechanism designed to prevent or mitigate the effects of an MUE [2]. When describing the effectiveness of controls, there is a widely accepted concept called the hierarchy of controls, which is a hierarchy of five categories of control, ranked based on their effectiveness. The five controls, from least effective to most effective, are Personal Protection Equipment (PPE), Administrative Controls, Engineering Controls, Substitution, and Elimination [3]. Administrative controls are considered to be the second from the bottom in terms of effectiveness, above only PPE.

A common method for extracting nickel is drill and blast mining. This is a process by which nickel-bearing rock is loaded with explosives and subsequently detonated to both liberate the material from the ground as well as reduce the size of the material. The loosened ore is then transported, by varying methods, from the mining site to additional processing facilities. Each step in the processing chain is designed to further remove unwanted elements from the material, increasing the purity of the nickel [4].

In the refining step, which is a focus area of this work, extreme heat (about 1600 °C) is used to remove impurities in the nickel product. The material is put into a converter, where petroleum coke is fed in, burning off oxides and other impurities. This process is called Reduction. Once the oxides have been burnt off, the matte goes through a process called Granulation during which the super-heated material is blasted with jets of cooled water. The ensuing controlled explosion instantaneously converts the molten metal into solidified nickel granules.

The research problem of this project lies at the intersection of critical control management and nickel refining. This project looks at two specific processing steps and their associated critical controls. The first processing step is the granulation processing step and the second is the reduction processing step. Both of the processing steps include significant risks related to working with molten metal. In both cases, the associated critical controls were categorized as Administrative Controls in that they involved a human being actively monitoring a physical process, and upon discovery of any issues, taking corrective action. The research objective of this paper is to demonstrate that these controls could be improved through the application of computer vision [10], predictive AI [9] and IoT devices [7].

The remaining parts of this paper are structured as follows: Sect. 2 presents an overview of pertinent related works. In Sect. 3, two critical controls are discussed, their functional requirements analyzed, and a technology solution is specified to improve each of the controls. In Sect. 4, the experiment setup and results are presented. Section 5 provides concluding statements and discusses future research.

2   Related Works

While it does not appear that any significant research has been performed with respect to applying IoT and AI technologies to this specific mining problem, significant research has been performed on adjacent domains, such as hot metal processing, welding applications, and industrial furnace applications. In the hot metal process applications, Gao et al. [11], propose a real-time, computer vision-based system for the monitoring and alerting of molten metal hazards, specifically for the iron and steel industries. The authors proposed that augmented reality (AR) glasses be used to acquire data, which then upload image data over a 5G network to a cloud computing platform for processing and classification. Using a Convolutional Neural Network (CNN), the cloud platform classifies the images, looking for failures, such as potential explosive, splitting, tilting, and leaking accidents. The CNN also attempts to detect other risks such as device damage, accumulation of water in molten working areas, personnel in forbidden areas, and missing PPE. The authors state that if the system detects any of these issues, an immediate warning is sent to both the operator wearing the glasses, as well as a central monitoring facility called the central scheduling center.

Within the same domain, Steiger et al. [12], proposed a computer vision-based system for metal/slag characterization, which is typically performed by human operators, who must continuously expose themselves to unnecessary risk – molten metal, extreme luminosity, noise and airborne particulates. Steiger et al., aim to replace this manual human inspection with an automated equivalent, to remove the human from this high-risk environment. To illustrate the feasibility of this concept, the authors created a simulation prototype using less-volatile materials – oil, water, and coal. The authors captured imagery of the environment using a CMOS camera and classify the imagery using an artificial neural network. The authors demonstrated that, in their simulated environment, their ANN-based algorithms outperformed both thresholding and k-means based segmentation.

In the domain of Welding applications, Balfour et al. [13] proposed a closed-loop computer-vision based system to both automate and improve the quality of welding processes. According to the authors, in typical open loop welding systems, deviations in the welding process can result in discontinuities in the weld and weld failures. As such, they implemented an experimental system that uses computer-vision to continuously evaluate the weld-width during the molten stages of the process, detecting deviations in real-time, and allowing for immediate course-correction.

In industrial furnace applications, Trofimov [14] designed a computer vision and machine learning based intelligent control system for basic oxygen furnaces (BAF). Specifically, the author is seeking to reduce the amount of slopping that takes place in typical BAF operations. Slopping is the overflow of expanding molten metal over the edge of the converter, which can account for 5–12% metal loss. In typical operations, a process operator is responsible for visually monitoring the converter through video cameras. The author proposes a solution consisting of two main components - 1) an artificial neural network (ANN) for predicting slopping based on off-gas composition and 2) a computer vision-based system for detecting slopping once it occurs. The authors demonstrate that their system can reliably predict a slopping event up to 25 s before it happens, based on the off-gas composition.

Proposing a solution based on sensors and machine learning, Leon-Medina et al. [15], developed a deep learning model (based on gated recurrent unit - GRU) to monitor the structural health of electric arc furnaces. According to the authors. This process is typically performed by operators, who are required to continuously inspect and monitor the structural health of the furnace. Using external thermocouple measurements as a proxy for furnace temperature, the authors develop and train an Long Short-Term-Memory (LSTM) model to predict furnace temperature. The authors successfully demonstrated that their model could predict temperature 2 h into the future, within 1.19 °C of accuracy.

Continuing with deep learning approaches, Quesada et al. [16] applied deep learning and multi-variate time series forecasting to the problem of optimizing industrial furnace maintenance. The authors propose a time series model to predict when the fluid tube should be taken offline, optimizing overall uptime of the furnace. The authors demonstrate the feasibility of this proposal, creating a DGBN (Dynamic Gaussian Bayesian Network) and CRNN (Convolutional Recurrent Neural Network) that are able to effectively predict fluid tube temperature, over long and medium-short term horizons, respectively.

Pairing computer vision and machine learning, Liu et al. [17] sought to solve the problem of predicting the converter end-point. In steel making, this is key to ensuring production quality. The authors proposed a method using a generalized regression neural network (GRNN) to capture and process the flames coming off of the furnace, which they correlate to the carbon content, phosphorous content and temperature of the pool, and demonstrate that their approach can effectively judge the blowing state, suggesting that this could potentially allow for more precise control of the end-point.

3 Study Case and Proposed Solution

As stated, the research objective of this project, two critical controls in a nickel refinery were selected, and for each control, a system was developed using the aforementioned technologies. This section discusses the selected critical controls, the functional requirements of each control, and the associated technology solution specification. As noted, nickel refining is performed through a series of process steps, which are depicted in Fig. 1. First, matte (Sulphur bearing molten material) is heated to approximately 1600°C in the Top Blown Rotary Converter (TBRC) to burn off any sulfur and oxides. It is then poured into a 'transfer ladle' (not depicted below) which is carried by crane and poured into a bottom teeming ladle. A pneumatic gate on the ladle is opened by the operator, slowly emptying the matte into the launder below. As the matte flows into the launder, the operator manipulates the pitch of the launder to control the flow of matte into the granulating sluice. As the matte flows into the granulating sluice, it is hit with jets of cooled water, resulting in a reaction that instantaneously converts the molten metal into small granules. The granules are then dewatered in the dewatering bins before continuing to the next stage of processing. Two experimental technologies were created for the launder (granulation) and converter (reduction) operator stations, marked with red targets in Fig. 1.

Experiment 1 – Launder Flow Monitoring

Process Description: In this processing step, a granulation operator is responsible for continuously visually monitoring the flow of molten material through the launder and into

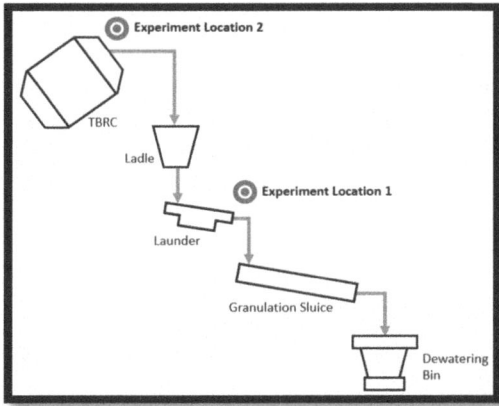

Fig. 1. Simplified nickel refining process flow [18].

the granulating sluice. In this context, the human operator is acting as the administrative critical control, responsible for mitigating both the potential and impact of the associated risk. This monitoring is done from behind a reinforced multi-pane glass window, shown in Fig. 2 below.

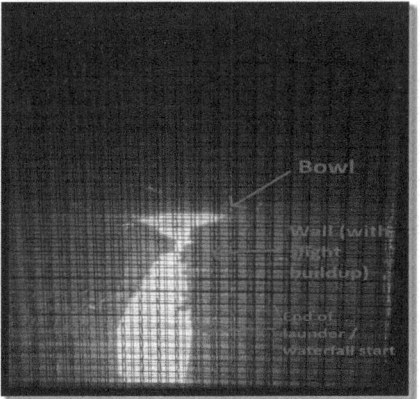

Fig. 2. View of launder from operator window.

If flow becomes blocked, or build-up starts to form on the launder, it can result in a sudden release of molten matte into the granulating sluice, resulting in a potential explosion. If the operator detects an issue, they can employ one of two mechanisms – either adjusting the pitch of the launder to increase the flow, or they can engage a pneumatic shut-off which will block any further material from flowing into the launder.

Requirements Analysis: To effectively replace this administrative control, several key functional requirements had to be met. Given that the primary function of the human operator is to look for buildup on or within the launder, a mechanism was required to continuously monitor the launder area for this buildup. Second, given that some degree of buildup is deemed acceptable, it was important to be able to quantify and evaluate whether the amount of buildup was within acceptable parameters. Third, a mechanism is required to alert the operator if the buildup exceeds the acceptable thresholds. To completely replace the human operator as a critical control, there is an additional requirement of performing interlock, meaning to interface with the Distributed Control System (DCS) system and impose the physical process changes required to control the issue; however, this was left for future work.

Experiment 2 – TBRC Monitoring

Process Description: In this processing step, a TBRC operator is responsible for continuously visually monitoring the ambient luminosity in the process area. A sudden increase in luminosity can be an early indicator of a potential loss of process control. Similar to the launder scenario, the monitoring takes place from behind an operator window, as shown in Fig. 3 below. If the operator detects a potential issue, they must take immediate corrective actions to avoid potentially catastrophic risk-events from materializing. Typically, this means shutting off the feed of petroleum coke to the TBRC, which stops the reaction in the converter. A loss of containment can happen in as few as 10 s if the petroleum coke feed is not shut off in time.

Fig. 3. View of TBRC from operator window.

Requirements Analysis: The primary function of the human operator in this context is to monitor the brightness of the operational area. An increase of brightness in the operating area precedes an increase of temperature, which is an indicator of process instability. As such, the brightness is used as a leading proxy indicator of process instability. If the operator perceives an increase in brightness in the operating area, they begin monitoring the temperature sensors. If there is a corresponding increase in temperature within a few seconds, the operator turns off the feed of petroleum coke to prevent a loss of containment. In order to effectively replace the second administrative control, several requirements had to be met. Just as with the first control, there is a requirement to continuously monitor the area; however, with this control, it is also necessary to quantify the brightness in the operational area. There is also a requirement to positively correlate brightness with an increase in temperature. To truly codify the experience of the operator, it was also necessary to build a mechanism that anticipate or predict when an issue might occur, given the current state in the operating area. Lastly, there was a requirement to alert based on any predicted issues. Similar to the first experiment, there would ultimately be a requirement to perform interlock, shutting off the coke feed, but this was decidedly left for future work.

Solution Specifications: To address the stated requirements, a solution was designed and developed. This section discusses the high-level solution specification. The base-solution for both controls followed a similar specification, depicted below in Fig. 4.

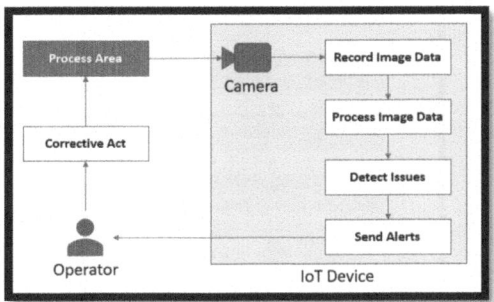

Fig. 4. Solution Specification Diagram.

As depicted in Fig. 4, the base solution consists of an IoT device mounted with a camera. On the IoT device, a software system is deployed that can record process area footage, process the image data, detect any issues, and upon detecting an issue, send an alert to the operator. When the operator receives the alert, they take corrective action against the process area to mitigate the potential risk-events.

IoT Device: Given the complexity and security implication of integrating with the existing process network, the decision was made that at this stage, the system would need to work locally in the control room, disconnected from the network. The Jetson Nano was selected for compatibility and future scalability. The Raspberry Picam was also chosen given its compatibility with the Jetson Nano hardware and its greater image bandwidth than USB-based cameras.

Application: The final base-component is the software sub-system, comprised of various Python modules responsible for capturing the image data, processing it, detecting issues, and performing alerting. The software sub-system consists of many custom modules, built specifically for this project, which are described further in subsequent sections of this report.

Software and Algorithms
Two software algorithms were developed to run on the IoT devices and perform the continuous inspection activity – one for each of the critical controls. These algorithms are described below. Both applications run on the Jetson Nano hardware.

Experiment 1 – Launder Flow Monitoring: The first application was designed to perform the Launder Monitoring activity. Figure 5 below describes the algorithm.

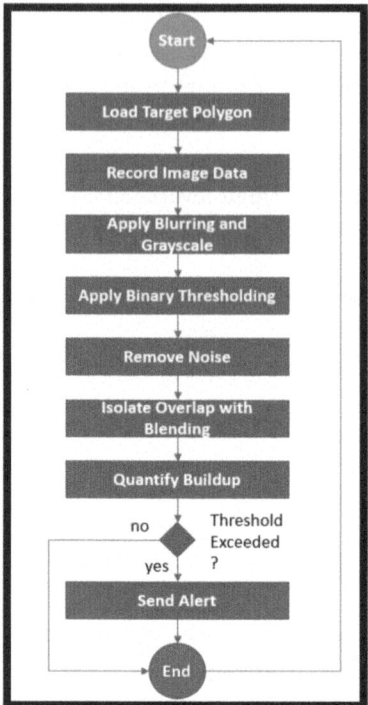

Fig. 5. Launder Flow Monitoring Algorithm.

The launder flow monitor software first loads a target polygon that defines the area of the empty launder and ultimately used to evaluate the buildup on the launder. Next, an image is recorded using the PiCamera module. Blurring is then applied to the image to reduce the influence of the wire mesh inside the window. Next the image is converted to grayscale to reduce the dimensionality of the data. Binary thresholding is then applied to find the shape of the molten material within the launder. Next a morphological transformation is applied to smooth the edges slightly. After the smoothing, the target polygon and processed image are blended to determine their overlap. The buildup is then quantified by isolating the pixels representing the overlap (the buildup) and dividing them by the total pixels in the target polygon area. As the final step, the quantified buildup is compared to a configurable threshold and, if the threshold is exceeded, an alert is triggered.

Experiment 2 – TBRC Monitoring: The second application was designed to perform the TBRC Inspection activity. Figure 6 below details the algorithm.

The TBRC monitoring software first loads a trained LSTM model, which has been trained on a simulated historical dataset of TBRC brightness and temperature data. Next, an image of the process area is captured. The image is converted to a matrix, for which the brightness values are averaged, to create a luminosity reading. These measurements are input into the LSTM model, which then predicts the next 60 s of temperature values

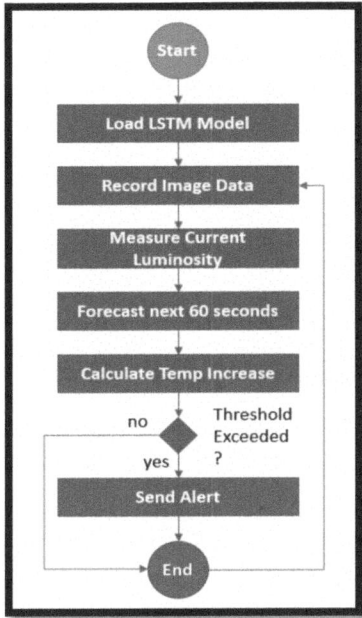

Fig. 6. TBRC Monitoring Algorithm.

based on historical patterns (from the trained model). The algorithm then calculates whether the temperature is anticipated to increase by more than 10° in the next 60 s. If this threshold is met (or exceeded), an alert is generated. At this point, the process would restart.

4 Experimental Results

This section describes the results of testing the two experimental solutions described above using video data from the nickel refining process.

4.1 Experiment 1 – Launder Flow Monitoring

The objective of the first experiment was to develop a system that could continuously monitor the flow of molten material through the launder and quantify the buildup on the launder that could potentially cause a risk-event to materialize.

To record launder process footage, the camera was mounted to the operator's viewing window at the granulation station. Multiple experiments were run with consistent satisfactory results. As shown in Fig. 7, the visual inspection of the experiment image identifies buildup on both the left and right sides of the launder, with slightly more on the right.

The steps of processing the image are shown below in Fig. 8. The algorithm performed as intended, identifying the buildup on both sides of the launder, with a calculated

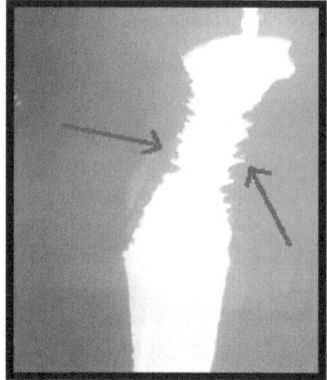

Fig. 7. Launder test image with buildup.

buildup area of 14.14% of the total area. This fell just short of the alerting threshold of 15%. It is worth noting that the threshold is configurable and could be adjusted based on expert feedback from the operators.

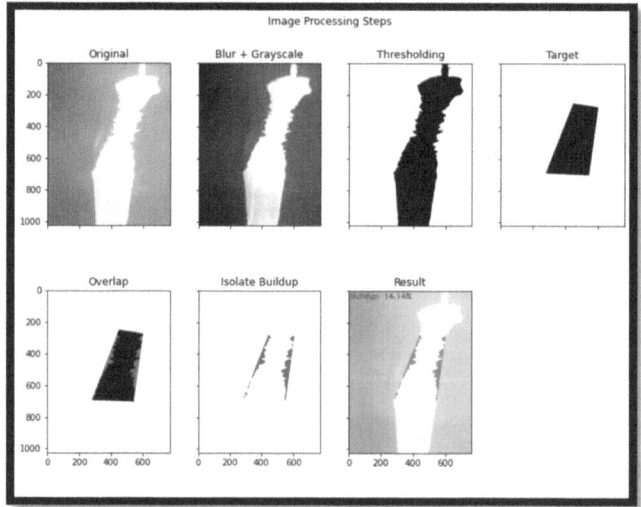

Fig. 8. Launder Test Image 3 Results.

4.2   Experiment 2 – TBRC Monitoring

The objective of the second experiment was to develop a system that could both continuously monitor the ambient brightness of the reduction processing area and use this brightness data to predict potential temperature increases before they happen. As operating practice, in this context, a sudden temperature increase can be a predictor that a risk-event might occur. The experiment setup and results are described below.

To record TBRC process footage, the camera was mounted to the operator's process viewing window at the reduction station. The technology was set up to record process video which would later be used to test the algorithms offline.

Model Training: A two-layer LSTM model [19], consisting of one dense layer and one LSTM layer was created and trained over 5000 epochs, using both the temperature and luminosity as inputs. A dataset representing 3 executions of the reduction process was used for the training. To test the model, a simulated test dataset was used. The algorithm was designed to continuously read-in the luminosity and temperature data and forecast the temperature data for the next 60 s. The forecast is performed every 5 s, and an alert is generated if the temperature is predicted to increase by more than 10° in the next 60 s.

Figure 9, 10, 11, 12, 13 and Fig. 14 below show the results of the temperature prediction function over 275 s (55 video frames) total for all figures. Each figure is a continuation from the previous one. Each dot represents 5 s. The solid blue dots represent the input data; the hollow blue dots represent a forecast with no alert; and the solid red dots represent a forecast containing an alert.

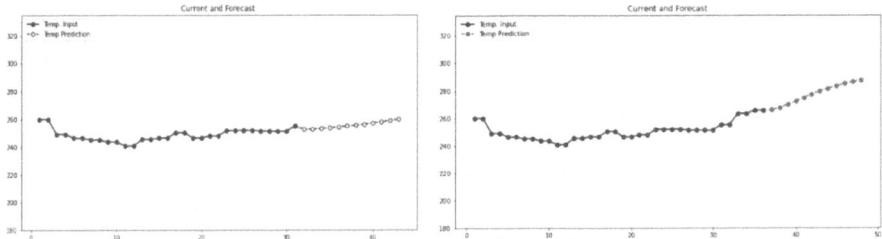

Fig. 9. Temperature prediction over time, at frame 31 (155 s) and frame 36 (180 s).

In the figure above, the algorithm has predicted that the temperature is starting to climb, with an alert being triggered at frame 36 (180 s).

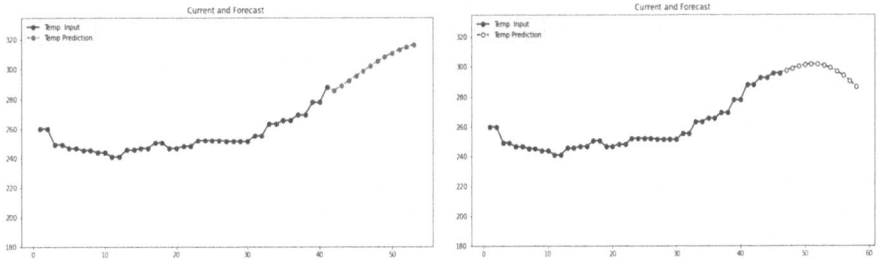

Fig. 10. Temperature prediction over time, at frame 41 (205 s) and frame 46 (230 s).

At frame 41 (205 s), the temperature continues to climb and alert, but at frame 46 (230 s) it peaks and crests as the coke feed is turned off.

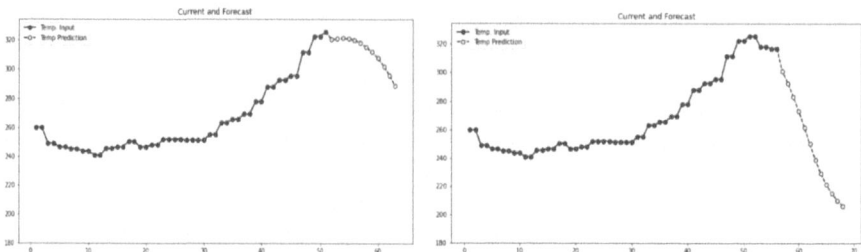

Fig. 11. Temperature prediction over time, at frame 51 (255 s) and frame 56 (280 s).

With the coke feed turned off, the temperature continues to drop, no alerts are triggered.

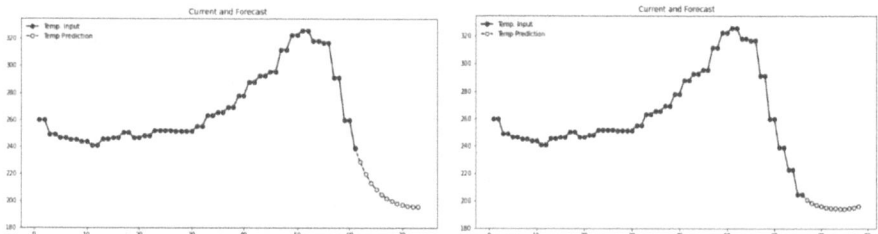

Fig. 12. Temperature prediction over time, at frame 61 (305 s) and frame 66 (330 s).

As the operator turns the coke feedback on, the temperature bottoms-out and the algorithm predicts that it will begin to climb again.

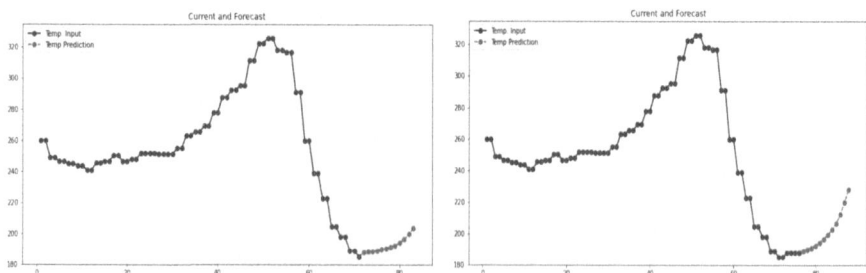

Fig. 13. Temperature prediction over time, at frame 71 (355 s) and frame 76 (380 s).

As the algorithm detects the increase in brightness and temperature from the coke reaction, it begins forecasting that the temperature is going to spike again, alerting the operator to turn off the coke feed, again.

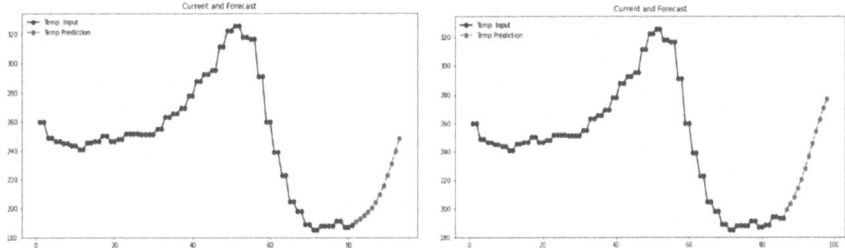

Fig. 14. Temperature prediction over time, at frame 81 (355 s) and frame 86 (380 s).

In Fig. 14, the system continues to alarm as it predicts a drastic increase in temperature in response to the reaction in the converter.

These results demonstrate that the software, leveraging the trained LSTM model, can effectively predict the temperature increases and alert based on thresholding.

5   Conclusions and Future Work

This research study demonstrated, via two applied experiments, that computer vision, IoT, and machine learning technologies can be used to improve the effectiveness of critical controls. Effectiveness, in this context meaning that the associated inspection is performed more continuously, consistently, and objectively than when performed by a human being.

This project addressed critical controls mainly focused on inspection activities. In reality, there are additional dimensions to these problems not considered in this paper. Future research should be performed to incorporate these additional dimensions. For instance, these experiments assumed a static camera and process asset location. In reality, it's completely possible that one, or both, of these items could be physically moved. As such, future research should include automatically detecting the camera region of interest, allowing for adjustment of both camera position as well as the physical movement and relocation of assets in the plant.

There is also opportunity to significantly improve the performance of the algorithms. The current algorithms, on the selected hardware, take 2–5 s to evaluate the current context. To further improve the effectiveness and timeliness of these controls, future research should be performed, looking for ways to improve algorithm performance and reduce the time it takes to perform these inspections.

References

1. Critical Control Management – Implementation Guide, International Council of Mining & Metals, London, United Kingdom (2015)
2. Human Factors in barrier management, Chartered Institute of Ergonomics & Human Factors, London, United Kingdom (2016)
3. Hierarchy of Controls: Centers for Disease Control and Prevention, 13 January 2015. https://www.cdc.gov/niosh/topics/hierarchy/default.html

4. Comprehensive Report of Vale Canada Limited Manitoba Operations, Vale Canada Ltd, Thompson, Manitoba, Canada (2015). https://www.gov.mb.ca/sd/eal/registries/557.1/App endices/6.1/comprehensive_report_of_vale_canada_limited_aug_3_2015_final.pdf
5. Janai, J., Güney, F., Behl, A., Geiger, A.: Computer vision for autonomous vehicles: Problems, datasets and state of the art. Found. Trends® in Comput. Graph. Vision **12**(1–3), 1–308 (2020)
6. Jaworski, D.J., Park, A., Park, E.J.: Internet of Things for sleep monitoring. IEEE Instrum. Meas. Mag. **24**(2), 30–36 (2021)
7. Ramamoorthy, K.M.K., Mirzaei, S.: Design and Implementation of IoT based cloud enabled wireless biometric monitoring device. In: 2021 IEEE 12th Annual Information Technology, Electronics and Mobile Communication Conference (IEMCON), pp. 0530–0533. IEEE (2021)
8. Kumar, V., Garg, M.L.: Deep learning in predictive analytics: a survey. In: 2017 International Conference on Emerging Trends in Computing and Communication Technologies (ICETCCT), pp. 1–6. IEEE (2017()
9. Hashemian, H.M.: State-of-the-art predictive maintenance techniques. IEEE Trans. Instrum. Meas. **60**(1), 226–236 (2010)
10. Seo, J.O., Han, S.U., Lee, S.H., Kim, H.: Computer vision techniques for construction safety and health monitoring. Adv. Eng. Inform. **29**(2), 239–251 (2015)
11. Gao, D., Sun, E., Li, Z., Chen, Y., Li, J.: molten metal hazards monitoring and early warning system based on convolutional neural network. In: 2019 IEEE 3rd Information Technology, Networking, Electronic and Automation Control Conference (ITNEC), pp. 895–899. IEEE (2019)
12. Steiger, O., Kukulski, M.: Automated inspection of molten metal using machine learning. In: SENSORS, pp. 1776–1779. IEEE (2011)
13. Balfour, C., Smith, J.S., Al-Shamma'a, A.I.: A novel edge feature correlation algorithm for real-time computer vision-based molten weld pool measurements. Weld. J.-New York **85**(1), 1 (2006)
14. Trofimov, V.B.: Designing an intelligent control system for a basic oxygen furnace based on computer vision. J. Comput. Syst. Sci. Int. **60**(6), 995–1004 (2021). https://doi.org/10.1134/S1064230721060150
15. Leon-Medina, J.X., et al.: Temperature prediction using multivariate time series deep learning in the lining of an electric arc furnace for ferronickel production. Sensors **21**(20), 6894 (2021)
16. Quesada, D., Valverde, G., Larranaga, P., Bielza, C.: Long-term forecasting of multivariate time series in industrial furnaces with dynamic Gaussian Bayesian networks. Eng. Appl. Artif. Intell. **103**, 104301 (2021)
17. Liu, H., Wang, B., Xiong, X.: Basic oxygen furnace steelmaking end-point prediction based on computer vision and general regression neural network. Optik **125**(18), 5241–5248 (2014)
18. Hot Metal Granulation and Dewatering System, Internal Document
19. Brownlee, J.: Multivariate time series forecasting with LSTMs in Keras" machinelearningmastery.com. https://machinelearningmastery.com/multivariate-time-series-forecasting-lstms-keras/. Accessed 11 Sept 2022

A Data-Driven Driving Under the Influence (DUI) Detection, Notification and Prevention System Using Artificial Intelligence and Internet-Of-Things (IoT)

Aaron Li[1([⊠])] and Yu Sun[2]

[1] Francis Parker School, San Diego, USA
ali2026@francisparker.org

[2] Computer Science Department, California State Polytechnic University Pomona, Pomona, USA
yusun@cpp.edu

Abstract. Drunk driving represents a significant public health crisis not only in the United States but also globally [16]. Sober Guardian is developed to mitigate this issue by leveraging advanced technologies including Machine Learning, Computer Vision, and potentially chemical sensors in the future. This system employs facial recognition and machine learning algorithms to swiftly determine if a driver is impaired, with the aim of preventing them from starting the vehicle [17]. We used an IoT System to control the blocker and successfully prevent vehicle start with 100% rate.

Additionally, Sober Guardian plans to incorporate hardware solutions such as sensors that can detect alcohol levels directly from the driver's breath or skin, enhancing the accuracy and reliability of impairment detection. Throughout its development, the project has faced challenges such as image clarity, limited datasets, and ensuring user-friendliness. Preliminary experiments with both image and video inputs have demonstrated the system's ability to predict sobriety with an accuracy between 86% and 87.5% [18]. However, video analysis for impaired individuals was hindered by the scarcity of appropriate datasets. Despite these challenges, Sober Guardian, in its nascent stages, has proven to be a promising solution for detecting driver impairment and preventing drunk driving, with ongoing enhancements expected to improve its functionality and deployment readiness.

Keywords: Machine Learning · Drunk Driving · Internet-Of-Things · Facial Recognition

1 Introduction

Alcohol-related accidents are a significant public safety issue, accounting for 31% of driving accidents annually in the U.S. [5]. The legal threshold for being "under the influence" is a blood alcohol concentration (BAC) of 0.08% or higher [13]. Despite

H. R. Arabnia et al. (Eds.): CSCE 2024, CCIS 2260, pp. 73–87, 2025.
https://doi.org/10.1007/978-3-031-85923-6_6

stringent DUI laws in all 50 states, including California, which prohibit driving under the influence of alcohol or drugs, drunk-driving fatalities are alarmingly frequent. In 2021, a person died every 39 min from a drunk-driving related crash [8]. Each year, approximately 10,000 lives are lost to drunk driving in the U.S., costing about $194 billion and highlighting the grave public health implications [9].

Teenagers are disproportionately affected by DUI incidents. Alcohol-related accidents are the leading cause of death among U.S. teenagers, a stark contrast to being the fourth leading cause of death across all age groups [15]. Alarmingly, 70% of teenagers admit to consuming alcohol, and 10% of high school students report drinking and driving. The risk of fatality increases dramatically for teens, who are 17 times more likely to die in an accident with a BAC of 0.08% [10]. Furthermore, 60% of all teenage car accident fatalities involve alcohol. Deaths related to alcohol occur every 15 min among teenagers, not just from driving but from alcohol influence more broadly. According to a 2019 national survey, 16.7% of teens reported riding with a driver who had been drinking [11].

While recent trends suggest a slow decline in drunk driving, the persistence of this issue across all demographics underscores its status as one of the major public safety challenges today [3]. This ongoing risk affects not only drivers but also pedestrians and other law-abiding citizens, emphasizing the need for continued vigilance and preventive measures in tackling DUI-related incidents [20].

The first research paper discussed the use of ML models for audio recordings to detect if the user is drunk or not. While it was effective at detecting impairment with good clarity audio, it was not great at detecting all types of audio recording, creating a missing 30% accuracy. My project is to tackle this issue by using facial recognition and computer vision, which can eliminate a lot of the uncertainties found during audio predictions.

The second research paper discussed the use of facial recognition to detect impairment. While facial recognition was effective at quickly detecting if the driver is impaired, there are also potential issues regarding questionable clarity of images and several limitations such as misalignment, pose variation, illumination variation, and expression variation. My project hopes to tackle this issue by allowing user feedback when there are mistakes or errors in the model so that it can be quickly fixed and tested. Additionally, if an image is not clear enough, the user will be notified to take another sample.

The third research paper reviewed the ethics of ML, especially computer vision. While computer vision can be used for many social issues, it also challenges and conflicts with a lot of ethics, such as a lot of powers. My project hopes to solve this problem by making sure Sober Guardian ensures the safety of the user and is initiated by the users of the app, this way there will be little exploitation of the powers listed in the paper.

The proposed solution to address the pervasive issue of driving under the influence (DUI) leverages cutting-edge Artificial Intelligence (AI), Machine Learning (ML), and facial recognition technology, combined with IoT System to prevent the car starting. This system, known as Sober Guardian, aims to prevent impaired individuals from even starting their vehicles. As technologies like the PyTorch and TensorFlow libraries become increasingly sophisticated, ensuring their ethical application is crucial, particularly in enhancing public health and safety. The standout feature of this project is the integration of hardware that prevents a vehicle from starting if impairment is detected. This technology represents a significant breakthrough, especially since it has a huge potential that adapted to control the vehicle's battery and applied across different vehicle models.

As of 2023, ML models have been developed that can determine if a person is "under the influence" based on just a 12-s audio recording. However, these models have faced criticism regarding their accuracy and reliability [7]. In contrast, Sober Guardian integrates AI and facial recognition with sensor data to provide real-time identification of potentially intoxicated drivers with high accuracy [25]. This capability enables immediate notifications to be sent to the driver and other stakeholders, including friends, family, and law enforcement, effectively preventing the driver from operating the vehicle and significantly reducing the risk of accidents.

With Sober Guardian's precise detection, the number of field sobriety tests conducted by law enforcement can be reduced, thereby freeing up resources and reducing the number of drunk drivers on the road. The anticipated impact of this project includes fewer accidents and instances of driving under the influence, potentially saving numerous lives and fostering a safer driving environment for everyone.

For experiment 1, we designed it to analyze pictures of both sober and drunk people and predict their sobriety. After analysis of many images of both kinds, it was found that the sober results were less accurate than the drunk results. This could be due to less data to train the model to recognize sober individuals. To be specific, there was 3 times less data compared to the drunk data set. The next step to advance this experiment is to find more sober data to help increase the accuracy of that part.

For experiment 2, we designed it to analyze videos of both sober and drunk people and predict their sobriety. After the testing and analysis, we found the results to be less accurate than the picture results. This suggests that video processing and predicting is much harder for our model to do than a single picture. Unfortunately, at the time of writing no footage was found for non-sober testing. The next step is to train the model with more video examples to increase its accuracy, and to update the experiment with data from videos of drunk individuals.

The rest of the paper is organized as follows: Sect. 2 presents the technical challenges involved in this work; Sect. 3 illustrates the solution in detail; Experiments are summarized in Sect. 4, followed by analyzing the related work in Sect. 5; Finally, we conclude the paper and discuss the future direction in Sect. 6.

2 Challenges

2.1 Acquiring Adequate Dataset

One of the primary challenges for the Sober Guardian program is acquiring an adequate dataset. Due to privacy laws related to personal photos, collecting sufficient before-and-after data of individuals under the influence can be problematic. Additionally, the authenticity of data may be compromised if individuals simulate intoxication, potentially leading to a dataset that doesn't accurately reflect true states of inebriation.

This issue could result in having limited data points available for effectively training and testing the machine learning model. To mitigate this, data augmentation strategies could be utilized. For example, multiple derivatives could be created from each original image in the dataset through techniques such as image stitching, rotation, and scaling, thereby expanding the number of training samples available.

2.2 The Safety-Driven UI and UX

Since Sober Guardian is used to prevent major drunk driving accidents, it's very important that the UI can easily be understood and used. However, what users claim is comfortable to use compared to complex is a difficult balance to sustain, especially as the UI flow is a subjective measurement. Sober Guardian strives to have a UX where it makes sure the user has the most convenient time possible, making it easier and quicker for the user to test their sobriety and prevent accidents. To overcome this complex problem, I could research where to put each button, how the user feels about each button, how many times it's pressed, etc., to adjust and update Sober Guardian to have a more convenient and accessible UI.

2.3 Improving the Accurate of the Prediction

Due to potential concerns regarding the clarity of pictures and videos, such as blurriness, distracting backgrounds, and bad lighting, Sober Guardian's model might get confused and make an inaccurate prediction. This problem could be solved by asking the user to retake the footage/image or I could do some more research into resolution enhancers that allow the pictures and videos to be clearer. As previously mentioned, the small dataset poses unique challenges. Due to the small dataset, it could be difficult to find the optimal epoch and batch sizes, therefore it would be hard to find the optimal accuracy. I could use trial and error to find the best epoch and batch sizes which result in the best accuracy.

2.4 Designing a Generic Electrical System Solution for DUI Prevention

Designing a generic electrical system for DUI prevention in the Sober Guardian program involves creating a universally compatible, real-time, power-efficient, and tamper-resistant solution that adheres to legal and safety standards. The system must interface seamlessly with both modern digital and older analog car systems using a modular approach. It requires fast processing to evaluate sensor data, such as breathalyzer results, and make immediate decisions to immobilize a vehicle if impairment is detected. Additionally, minimizing battery impact when the car is off and ensuring the system is secure against tampering are crucial. The entire setup must comply with automotive regulations, including safety and electromagnetic compatibility certifications, to be viable across different vehicle types.

3 Solution

When Sober Guardian is launched, users undergo a secure authentication process via Firebase, and their credentials are stored locally to facilitate automatic logins on future accesses. Once authenticated, the user is taken to the home screen, which displays a history of their previous tests, including the times they were last tested, their current location, and the current time. The home screen is intuitively designed with four prominent buttons that lead to different functionalities: accessing emergency contacts, initiating a new test, adjusting settings, or logging out.

Clicking on the 'Start Testing' button redirects the user to the testing screen, which is equipped with a camera feature to capture the user's facial image. Users have the option to retake the photo if they are not satisfied with the initial capture. To proceed with the test, users are prompted to breathe into a linked breathalyzer device. The system's model then analyzes the input data to predict whether the user is impaired or sober.

Depending on the result, the user is navigated to either the 'Sober' or 'Impaired' screen. The 'Sober' screen displays a confirmation message, affirming that the user is fit to drive. Conversely, the 'Impaired' screen presents an emergency contact button as a proactive safety measure. Should the user select this option, they are taken to the emergency contact screen, which offers multiple quick-call buttons for various contacts, including friends and family, emergency services, and public transportation options. This setup ensures that users can promptly access assistance or alternative transportation methods as needed, reinforcing the app's commitment to user safety and responsible driving practices. Figure 1 shows the overview of the system.

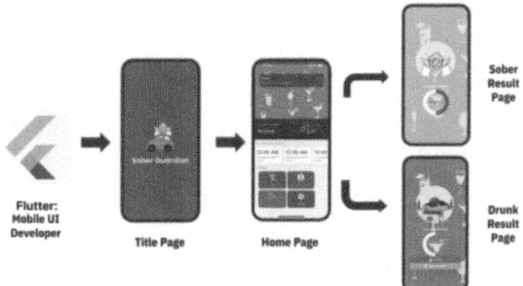

Fig. 1. The overview of the system

The central feature of Sober Guardian is the testing screen, a critical component designed to evaluate whether a driver is impaired. This screen facilitates the detection process by allowing the user to capture an image or video footage of themselves. This visual data is then analyzed by Sober Guardian's advanced Convolutional Neural Network (CNN) model, specifically trained to determine impairment [24].

To enhance the accuracy of the impairment detection, the system is integrated with a custom breathalyzer. This device not only corroborates the results from the CNN model but also assesses the severity of the user's intoxication. If the analysis indicates that the user is impaired, a specially designed mechanism is activated. This device is connected to the user's car and prevents the vehicle from starting as long as alcohol is detected in the user's system. This safety feature ensures that impaired drivers are unable to operate the vehicle, significantly reducing the risk of alcohol-related incidents. Figure 2 shows the Screenshot of the APP. Figure 3 shows the screenshot of code 1.

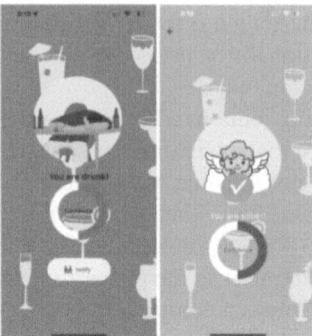

Fig. 2. Screenshot of the APP 1

Fig. 3. The screenshot of code 1

The code snippets above show different components of the AI, Killswitch, and Breathalyzer logic. If the user is drunk, they will be sent to a locked screen to contact emergency contacts and the killswitch will activate to prevent the user from starting their car. The first code snippet shows the main API endpoint that users of Sober Guardian can call to interact with the AI that is running on a server. The second snippet shows the code within the Boron determining if the killswitch should lock the car. The killswitch checks every minute if alcohol has been detected by the AI/breathalyzer combination and switches the car on or off accordingly [21]. The final snippet shows the main code within our custom breathalyzer device. It performs a user log in, then periodically checks the alcohol concentration around it to determine if it should flag the "alcohol_detected" property of the user's account in the database. This allows the application and Boron to react accordingly along with the information they collected on their end.

When a user is identified as impaired by the Sober Guardian system or chooses to activate the emergency contact feature from either the testing interface or the home page, they are promptly redirected to a specifically designed emergency contact screen. Figure 4 shows the screenshot of the mobile app. This screen features an intuitive layout with several accessible buttons, each linked to personal and preset emergency contacts stored within the user's smartphone. The design enables users to instantly send a text, voice message, or initiate a call. With a single tap, the Sober Guardian app dispatches a preconfigured or user-customized message to the chosen contact, including the user's precise current location. This information aids in facilitating swift navigation and providing urgent assistance. This efficient and streamlined communication process is crucial, as it ensures a rapid response in scenarios where the user's safety is at immediate risk.

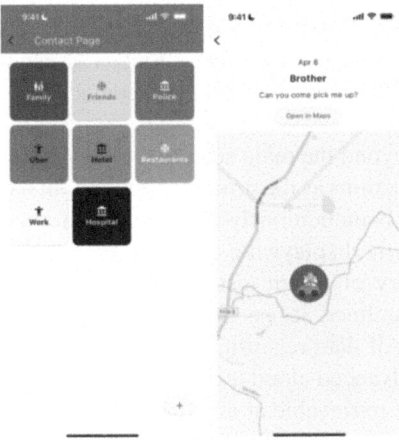

Fig. 4. The screenshot of the mobile app

```
class ContactResultScreen extends StatefulWidget {
  final String response;
  bool messageSent = false;
  ContactResultScreen({super.key, required this.response});

  @override
  State<ContactResultScreen> createState() => _ContactResultScreenState();
}

class _ContactResultScreenState extends State<ContactResultScreen> {
  Future<void> sendMessage() async {
    try {
      await FirebaseDatabase.instance
          .ref("users/${Auth().user?.uid}/notifications")
          .set({
        "message": widget.response,
        "time": DateTime.now().millisecondsSinceEpoch,
        "latitude": Singleton().locationData?.latitude,
        "longitude": Singleton().locationData?.longitude,
      }).then((value) {
        setState(() {
          widget.messageSent = true;
        });
      });
    } catch (e) {
      // print(e);
    }
  }
```

Fig. 5. The screenshot of code 2

The code above is what allows a user to fire off a notification for their contacts to see. There are many different options and contacts to choose from, including friends, family, emergency services, rideshare applications, public transportation, and other potentially life-saving services. The user can have the option to send a predetermined text message, Google Maps location, or call the selected contacts. The page accessing this code can be reached through the contacts page which the user will be directed to if they are found to be impaired. The code shown defines a data package that will be sent out to the Firebase Database to alert all the relevant users [23]. Family, Friends, and Caretakers are saved by the user within the custom categories screen. Figure 5. The screenshot of code 2. Without this portion of the code, the emergency contact screen would not work properly, and users would not have a quick and easy way to contact any services they either want or need for their well-being.

Once users navigate beyond the main screen, they are brought to the home screen of Sober Guardian, which functions as the primary hub for both navigation and information display. This home screen is meticulously designed to offer a comprehensive overview at first glance. It prominently displays the current time and the user's specific location, alongside a detailed history of recent test times, locations, and their outcomes. Furthermore, it provides streamlined access options to both the emergency contact screen and the testing interface. All data regarding testing times and the pertinent details are securely stored utilizing advanced cloud technology, ensuring that all information is not only secure but also easily retrievable at any time. This thoughtful design significantly enhances the user's convenience by facilitating swift navigation among various app functionalities while simultaneously ensuring that critical information remains readily accessible. This setup supports users in effectively managing their safety with greater efficiency and reliability. Figure 6 shows the screenshot of the main page and Fig. 7. Shows the Screenshot of code 3.

The code shown above shows the creation of the test button on the home screen. The test button will direct the user to the testing screen, where they can test for impairments. The home screen can be accessed through the title screen and acts as the central hub for

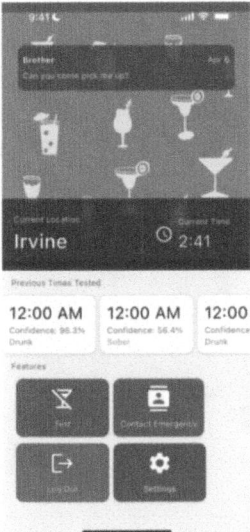

Fig. 6. Screenshot of main page

Fig. 7. Screenshot of code 3

the user's experience in the application. The home screen will allow the user to access several features in the application, such as the emergency contacts screen and the testing screen. The emergency contacts screen was discussed in Sect. 3.2, and the testing screen in Sect. 3.1. The testing screen is the main hub of users within the app, so buttons such as the testing button are very important as they direct the user to all other screens they will need to use. Without the home page, there would be little to no organization for the app and users wouldn't be able to access and be directed to many other critical screens.

When the system's AI-driven facial recognition and machine learning algorithms detect signs of impairment, these sensors activate a vehicle control module. This module, connected directly to the vehicle's ignition system, effectively prevents the car from starting if elevated alcohol levels are detected. This safeguard is designed to act instantaneously, ensuring that the vehicle remains immobilized until the driver is sober. This critical hardware integration not only enhances the reliability of the DUI detection system but also ensures immediate and enforceable prevention, significantly reducing the risk of drunk driving incidents. Figure 8 shows the component for driving prevention.

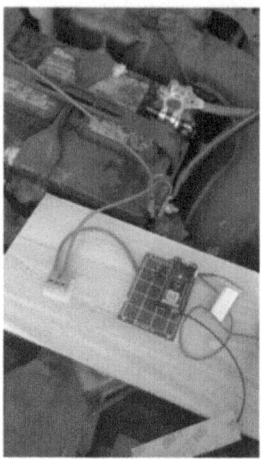

Fig. 8. The component for driving prevention

4   Experiments

4.1   Experiment 1

A possible blind spot in my program could be the detection of impairment for the drivers. Potential causes could be that the model wasn't trained accurately enough or other solutions weren't effective enough. This would make the model less accurate and less likely for people to use.

To conduct the experiment, we will utilize a dataset comprising images of individuals captured both before and after consuming alcohol. Each participant will be represented by four sets of images, each depicting progressively higher levels of intoxication. The baseline, or control images, will consist of photos taken when the subjects are sober, serving as a reference point to identify and compare changes as they consume alcohol. These control images will enable a clear contrast between the subjects' sober and inebriated states. After integrating this dataset into the system, the model will be trained using both the sober and drunk images, allowing us to evaluate its accuracy and identify any potential weaknesses in its ability to distinguish between the two states. This step is crucial for refining the model and ensuring its reliability before finalizing and deploying it in practical applications.

The percentage of sober was around 83% while the percentage of non-sober was around 93%. The lowest value was the accuracy of 86% for the sober predictions. This

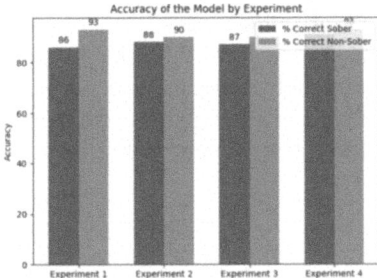

Fig. 9. Accuracy of the model by user experiment

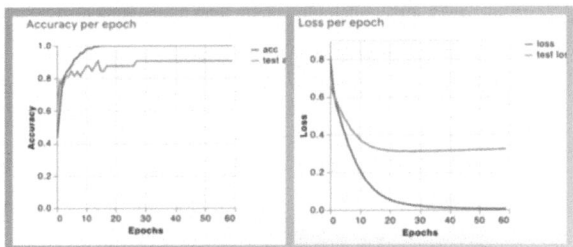

Fig. 10. Accuracy and loss per epoch

is expected since for each set of images, there is one sober picture and three drunk pictures. Because the more data skew the model to understand non-sober images better, the lower accuracy of sober images is expected. Some possible factors that negatively impact results might be the number of epochs and batches put into the training dataset, which is why it is important to see the epoch data and adjust to get the highest accuracy. The experiment still needs some more testing. This is due to the small amount of data put into the training of the model, there still might be inaccuracies. Additionally, there could be more features to be accounted for that could further increase the model's accuracy. Figure 9. Shows accuracy of the model by user experiment and Fig. 10 shows accuracy and loss per epoch.

4.2 Experiment 2

A second possible blind spot in my program would be how the model can handle videos and a frame-by-frame update regarding calculating a user's sobriety. This is an important feature to keep in mind, as one aspect of Sober Guardian is to let the user pick between photo and video input.

To set up the experiment effectively, I will initially run the model using video footage of individuals who are sober, as this is more readily accessible. Acquiring footage of individuals under the influence presents significant challenges due to ethical, legal, and privacy concerns, making it a more complex aspect of data collection. Consequently, the initial phase of the experiment will focus solely on sober footage to refine the model's baseline accuracy and functionality. Once footage of individuals under the influence is obtained, adhering to all necessary ethical guidelines, the experiment will be expanded to include this data. Both sets of footage will then be processed by the model frame by frame to assess its ability to accurately differentiate between sober and influenced states. Continuous monitoring of the model's predictions will help identify any discrepancies or biases, ensuring the model's effectiveness and reliability before it is finalized for practical use.

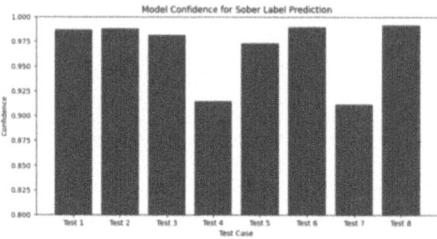

Fig. 11. Model confidence for sober label prediction

```
pred: conf: 0.9869508 - label: 1 Sober
pred: conf: 0.987855 - label: 1 Sober
pred: conf: 0.98122233 - label: 1 Sober
pred: conf: 0.81447035 - label: 1 Sober
pred: conf: 0.9729699 - label: 1 Sober
pred: conf: 0.9892123 - label: 1 Sober
pred: conf: 0.91132313 - label: 1 Sober
pred: conf: 0.99141544 - label: 1 Sober
```

Fig. 12. The accuracy of the training model

The accuracy here is about the same for sober predictions as the results seen in 4.1, with an accuracy of 87.5%. Due to images being analyzed in real-time, there might be inaccuracies or things the model has never seen, which can be seen in the raw data output having 2 significant drops in confidence at the 4th and 7th frames. We can improve the dataset by adding more scenarios where videos will play and train the model with that dataset. This data might be harder to integrate to the same degree as experiment 1 as video footage will be much harder to process than images. The inclusion of a non-sober video is a top priority as something that is needed to further validate this experiment. This experiment still needs to be tested again as there is still much space for improvement, such as accuracy. These changes will allow the model to learn and adapt to new scenarios. Figure 11 shows Model confidence for sober label prediction and Fig. 12 shows the accuracy of the training model.

5   Related Work

Bonela et al. have been researching the use of ML models for audio detection of intoxication, and as of June 2023 have found that there is around 68% effectiveness at 0.05% BAC, around 75% effectiveness at 0.12% BAC [5]. There are pros and cons of roughly

70% effectiveness. While 70% is a great foundation, with most of the predictions being effective, the other 30% will ultimately lead to many false positives and negatives. However, limitations regarding the quality of the audio clips can drastically affect the model. While 70% is good, Sober Guardian's initial testing has shown to have 98% effectiveness, potentially highlighting computer vision as the next step for DUI detection in ML.

According to Teoh et al., facial recognition can be used to identify a person in a biometric method based on the features of their face [12]. Face recognition includes the operation of automatically detecting the user's face, followed by verifying a person from either picture or video. However, there were potential issues raised regarding the questionable clarity of images, there are also several limitations such as misalignment, pose variation, illumination variation, and expression variation. Sober Guardian handles these concerns by determining whether the image is sufficient and asking the user to retake the image if it is not. Sober Guardian will also request consent from the user to use the original image as data for later training to increase their accuracy. It will also utilize sensor data to further ensure the accuracy of the AI's assertions.

According to Waelen in their research, there are important questions regarding ethics and the application of ML models using Computer Vision [14]. Computer Vision impacts all sorts of powers including dispositional powers, episodic powers, systemic powers, and constitutive powers. These powers provide insight regarding how an individual can maintain and safely express their autonomy. Utilizing this information, Sober Guardian is made so that it ensures the safety of the user and is initiated by the users of the app, this way there will be little exploitation of the powers listed above. This safety will be ensured by making sure that the user is comfortable with the predictions and if there are inaccuracies, the user can request to take the image again for another prediction. For images stored later for training, Sober Guardian will ask the user for their consent to use their images for training. During this request, users will be notified of what happens to the image.

6   Conclusion

Sober Guardian faces several challenges that could impact its effectiveness and widespread adoption. One significant limitation is its current deployment only within a mobile application. This is not always practical, as individuals may not think to use an app immediately before driving, particularly if they are already under the influence. To address this, integrating the model into more passive devices, such as wearable bracelets or embedded systems within vehicles, could greatly enhance its usability and real-time effectiveness. These devices could continuously monitor and detect signs of impairment automatically, reducing the need for user initiation.

Furthermore, Sober Guardian currently struggles with false positives and errors related to misidentifying non-impairment-related behaviors as signs of intoxication. This not only affects the reliability of the system but can also lead to unnecessary inconveniences for users. Enhancing the model to more accurately distinguish between true impairment and similar, non-related behaviors is crucial for improving its accuracy and user trust.

Given additional time and resources, expanding the application of the model to include various tools and devices would make Sober Guardian more versatile and realistic in everyday scenarios. The development of technologies like the BoronSwitch is a step in the right direction, offering functionality that promotes safety. However, further efforts to make such technologies more accessible and easier to install are essential to ensure broad adoption and effectiveness in preventing DUI incidents across diverse environments and user demographics.

References

1. Barry, V., Schumacher, A., Sauber-Schatz, E.: Alcohol-impaired driving among adults—USA, 2014–2018. Inj. Prev. **28**(3), 211–217 (2022)
2. White, A.M., et al.: Trends in alcohol-related emergency department visits in the United States: results from the Nationwide Emergency Department Sample, 2006 to 2014. Alcoholism: Clin. Exp. Res. **42**(2), 352–359 (2018)
3. Hong, Il-Ki, et al.: Development of a driving simulator for virtual experience and training of drunk driving. In: 3rd International Conference on Road Safety and Simulation (2011)
4. Shrestha, A., Mahmood, A.: Review of deep learning algorithms and architectures. IEEE access **7**, 53040–53065 (2019)
5. Eisenberg, D.: Evaluating the effectiveness of policies related to drunk driving. J. Policy Anal. Manage. **22**(2), 249–274 (2003)
6. Robert, L.S., et al.: Adolescent health status. Adolescent health services: Missing opportunities. National Academies Press (US) (2009)
7. Bonela, A.A., et al.: Audio-based deep learning algorithm to identify alcohol inebriation (ADLAIA). Alcohol **109**, 49–54 (2023)
8. McCarthy, P.S., Oesterle, W.: The deterrent effects of stiffer DUI laws: an empirical stu. Logistics Transp. Rev. **23**(4), 353 (1987)
9. Willis, M., et al.: Driver alcohol detection system for safety (DADSS)–pilot field operational tests (PFOT) vehicle instrumentation and integration of DADSS technology. In: 26th International Technical Conference on the Enhanced Safety of Vehicles (ESV): Technology: Enabling a Safer TomorrowNational Highway Traffic Safety Administration. No. 19–0262 (2019)
10. Jakle, H., Spjute, A.: The fight against teenage drunk driving: saving lives and keeping preventable injuries out of the emergency department. West. J. Emerg. Med. Integrating Emerg. Care with Popul. Health **13**(2) (2012)
11. Beck, K.K.: Monitoring parent concerns about teenage drinking and driving: a random digit dial telephone survey. Am. J. Drug Alcohol Abuse **16**(1–2), 109–124 (1990)
12. Ginsburg, K.R., et al.: National young-driver survey: teen perspective and experience with factors that affect driving safety. Pediatrics **121**(5), e1391–e1403 (2008)
13. Teoh, K.H., et al.: Face recognition and identification using deep learning approach. J. Phys. Conf. Ser. **1755**(1) (2021)
14. Bushman, B.J.: Human aggression while under the influence of alcohol and other drugs: an integrative research review. Curr. Dir. Psychol. Sci. **2**(5), 148–151 (1993)
15. Waelen, R.A.: The ethics of computer vision: an overview in terms of power. AI and Ethics, 1–10 (2023)
16. Room, R., Babor, T., Rehm, J.: Alcohol and public health. Lancet **365**(9458), 519–530 (2005)
17. Kaur, P., et al.: Facial-recognition algorithms: a literature review. Med. Sci. Law **60**(2), 131–139 (2020)
18. Hiremath, P.G.S., et al.: Sobriety period prediction of relapsed alcohol dependent patients using machine learning approach. In: 2024 International Conference on Intelligent and Innovative Technologies in Computing, Electrical and Electronics (IITCEE). IEEE (2024)

19. Lin, Y.-W., Lin, Y.-B., Liu, C.-Y.: AItalk: a tutorial to implement AI as IoT devices. IET Netw. **8**(3), 195–202 (2019)

20. Stringer, R.J.: Exploring traffic safety culture and drunk driving: An examination of the community and DUI related fatal crashes in the US (1993–2015). Transp. Res. Part F: Traffic Psychol. Behav. **56**, 371–380 (2018)

21. Bihar, E., et al.: A disposable paper breathalyzer with an alcohol sensing organic electrochemical transistor. Sci. Rep. **6**(1), 27582 (2016)

22. Zhou, J., et al.: A novel artificial intelligence system for the assessment of bowel preparation (with video). Gastrointest. Endosc. **91**(2), 428–435 (2020)

23. Moroney, L., Laurence, M.: The firebase realtime database. Definitive Guide Firebase: Build Android Apps Google's Mob. Platform, 51–71 (2017)

24. Li, Z., et al.: A survey of convolutional neural networks: analysis, applications, and prospects. IEEE Trans. Neural Netw. Learn. Syst. **33**(12), 6999–7019 (2021)

25. Girmay, S., Samsom, F., Khattak, A.M.: Ai based login system using facial recognition. In: 2021 5th Cyber Security in Networking Conference (CSNet). IEEE (2021)

Understanding User Interactions with IoT Process Models: A Demographic Perspective

Michael Winter[1,2]([✉]) [iD], Yusuf Kirikkayis[3], Rüdiger Pryss[1,2], and Manfred Reichert[3]

[1] Institute of Clinical Epidemiology and Biometry,
University of Würzburg, Würzburg, Germany
michael.winter@uni-wuerzburg.de
[2] Institute of Medical Data Science, University Hospital of Würzburg,
Würzburg, Germany
[3] Institute of Databases and Information Systems, Ulm University,
Ulm, Germany

Abstract. The rapid integration of the Internet of Things (IoT) into business processes has underscored the necessity of developing IoT process models that are both functional and user-friendly. This survey investigated how users from varied demographic backgrounds perceive and interact with IoT process models, focusing on visual clarity, distinguishability, and cognitive challenges. Utilizing a sample size of n = 249 individuals, the research analyzed interactions with two distinct IoT process models, each embodying unique IoT integration features such as sensors, actuators, and IoT-specific tasks. The findings highlight the importance of design in enhancing user experience and suggest to consider the interplay between demographic factors and model design. The insights offer guidance for the creation of future IoT process models, emphasizing the importance of inclusivity and the ability to adapt to the changing requirements of users within the IoT environment.

Keywords: Internet of Things · Process Model · Survey

1 Introduction

In an era where the Internet of Things (IoT) is reshaping the landscape of technology and business processes, understanding user interactions with IoT process models becomes crucial. This shift towards a more interconnected world highlights the importance of making IoT systems not only technologically advanced but also user-centric and accessible [4]. For this reason, the paper explores how users with diverse backgrounds perceived and interacted with such models. With a comprehensive survey involving n = 249 participants, this research analyzed user interaction with IoT process models expressed in terms of the Business Process Model and Notation (BPMN) 2.0. Utilizing two distinct BPMN models as

H. R. Arabnia et al. (Eds.): CSCE 2024, CCIS 2260, pp. 88–97, 2025.
https://doi.org/10.1007/978-3-031-85923-6_7

case studies, the investigation sought to unravel the complexities of user interaction when navigating through IoT-integrated workflows. These models, each
with unique characteristics regarding IoT-centric elements, were used to analyze
the impact of design on user understanding and engagement. This survey investigated how the integration of IoT technologies with process models can combine
advanced functionalities with user-friendly designs, making these innovations
accessible to a wide range of users. It explores the relationship between user
demographics and their perceptions of IoT process models, aiming to develop
more intuitive and engaging designs that respond to users' evolving needs in the
IoT era.

2 Related Work

In recent years, a vast body of research has emerged, focusing on the integration
of the Internet of Things (IoT) in process models, particularly in BPMN process
models. [8] presents an approach for integrating IoT with processes using BPMN,
while [9] introduces an extension for BPMN to enhance its capabilities toward
IoT. In turn, how BPMN can be used to control wireless network sensors is
discussed in [6]. [1] introduces an approach and algorithm to simplify modeling
and deployment of IoT-aware business processes, enhancing BPMN 2.0 for better
IoT integration and execution efficiency. In this context, the reviews presented
in [7] and [2] highlight the increasing importance of IoT in processes.

For this reason, an evaluation of the perception and interaction with IoT
process models, as presented in this paper, is of importance as it facilitates the
identification and mitigation of cognitive challenges, enhancing user engagement
and efficiency in navigating IoT-integrated workflows.

3 Materials and Methods

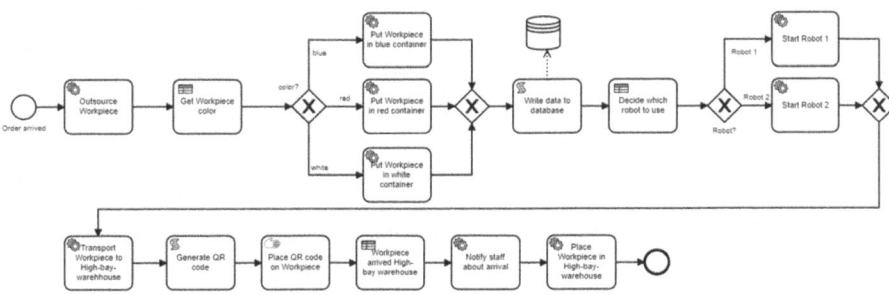

Fig. 1. Process model 1 - Interaction between the digital and physical domains

The user interaction was captured, on the one hand, by analyzing the visual clarity and distinguishability of such models and, on the other hand, by considering

cognitive challenges encountered during their comprehension. The rationale for concentrating on visual clarity, distinguishability, and cognitive challenges stems from the important role these factors play in the usability of process models in general [5]. Visual clarity and distinguishing IoT-related elements from others within a model are crucial for facilitating quick and accurate comprehension. This is particularly important in complex models where information density can easily overwhelm users. Furthermore, understanding the cognitive load associated with interacting with these models provides valuable insights into the user experience, highlighting areas where simplification and optimization can lead to more effective user engagement. To determine visual clarity and distinguishability, three items (I1–I3) were asked on a 6-point Likert scale ranging from (0) (does not apply) - 5 (fully applies):

I1 IoT involvement in the process model becomes visually clear.
I2 I can distinguish IoT-related tasks from other tasks.
I3 It is not possible to visually distinguish between IoT-related modeling elements from other modeling elements.

These items probed how effectively IoT elements were highlighted or differentiated from non-IoT elements within process models [3]. This aspect was crucial for ensuring that users could quickly and accurately identify the parts of the process model that were IoT-related, which is essential for understanding, troubleshooting, and modifying the model.

In the context of cognitive challenges, the following three items (I4–I6) were asked on a 6-point Likert scale ranging from (0) (does not apply) - 5 (fully applies):

I4 It is difficult to identify IoT involvement in the process model.
I5 The larger the process model becomes, the more difficult it is to identify IoT involvement.
I6 It is exhausting to determine the involvement of IoT aspects in the process model.

These items investigated the cognitive challenges users might have faced when working with process models [3]. These included the ease or difficulty of identifying IoT involvement, and whether such tasks became mentally exhausting over time. These questions suggested a focus on the cognitive load imposed on users by the process models, including how user-friendly and accessible the models were for those interacting with them.

The items I1 - I6 were shown to all participants while analyzing two validated BPMN process models (see Figs. 1 and 2) from literature [3]. Note that the process models were shown to the participants one after the other. The process model shown in Fig. 1 consists of 15 distinct activities, seamlessly integrating Internet of Things (IoT) capabilities into its workflow. This process model is notable for including 3 sensors and 8 actuators, fundamental IoT elements that facilitate the interaction between the digital and physical domains. The IoT-related activities are explicitly indicated with labels that contain characteristic

IoT terminologies (e.g., "start Robot 2"). These activities suggest a highly automated environment where IoT devices play a role in executing the process.

The process model depicted in Fig. 2 includes a total of 8 activities distributed among 4 distinct pools. This model embodies the essence of IoT integration within a process flow, as evidenced by the activities specifically labeled with IoT-centric terms such as "start temperature recording" and "activate switch". This model encapsulates the interaction between a single sensor and 8 actuators, signifying a robust IoT system with considerable actuation capabilities.

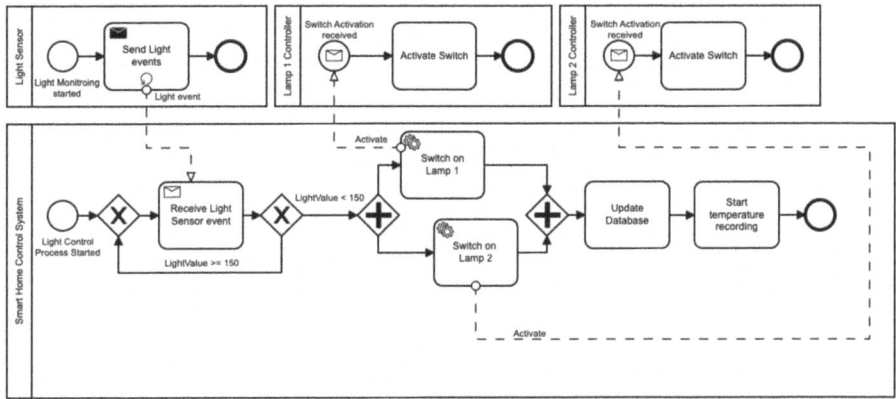

Fig. 2. Process model 2 - IoT Integration in the process flow

4   Results

A total of n = 249 participants took part in the survey. Table 1 presents collected demographic data from all participants. The tables show sex distribution (frequencies (f) and percentage (%) and age (mean (m) and standard deviation (SD). Based on the latter, participants were categorized into three age groups (f and %): G1 = 18–22 years, G2 = 23–26 years, G3 = >26. Since most of participants were students from academia, G1 represents young students, mostly at Bachelor level, while G1 mostly comprises Master's students, and G2 includes participants with additional professional experience. Qualification (f and %) represents the highest level of education achieved: Q1 = Secondary school graduation, Q2 = High school diploma, Q3 = Study without a degree, Q4 = Bachelor's degree, Q5 = Master's degree, Q6 = Doctoral degree, Q7 = other. Further, Table 1 features the number of process models (m and SD) worked with in the last 24 months and the self-rated expertise level (m and SD) in working with process models ranging from 1 (none) - 10 (expert). Based on specific rule considering the number of process models and the self-rated expertise level, participants were divided into four expertise groups: E1 = Novice (self-rated expertise level of 3 or lower and who have worked on 5 or fewer process models), E2 = Intermediate (self-rated expertise level between 4 and 6, or who have worked on 6 to 15 process models), E3 = Advanced (self-rated expertise level between 7 and 8, or who have worked on 16 to 50 process models), and E4 = Expert (self-rated expertise level of 9 or higher, or who have worked on more than 50 process models).

Table 1 showcases a diverse set of participants, primarily young adults with substantial representation from Master's students (55.8%), offering insights into varied interactions with IoT process models. More males (63.5%) than females (36.5%) participated, reflecting broader tech field trends. Most participants hold a Master's degree (58.6%), which might have influenced their comprehension of IoT models, although 27.3% did not complete their studies so far, possibly affecting model interpretation. The self-classification of most participants as Intermediate (51.4%) in expertise, with few (1.6%) considering themselves Experts, highlights the potential benefits of targeted training in IoT process modeling. With participants having worked with an average of 7.71 process models in the past two years and a moderate self-rated expertise, a noted variance in experience might shaped their perception of the models and affected research outcomes.

Table 2 illustrates for process models 1 and 2 the individual results (m and SD) regarding visual clarity and distinguishability (I1–I3) and cognitive challenges (I4–I6).

For process model 1, the mean visual clarity and distinguishability scores are relatively low (I1: 2.82, I2: 2.38), with I3 scoring slightly higher (3.08). These scores suggest that participants found it challenging to discern and understand IoT elements within process model 1 visually.

Conversely, PM2 scored higher on visual clarity and distinguishability (I1: 3.37, I2: 2.97), although I3 slightly decreased (2.72). This indicates that participants found process model 2 more transparent and distinguishable overall than Process Model 1. Still, specific aspects of process model 2 may need to be clarified, as reflected by the lower score for I3.

Regarding cognitive challenges, process model 1 yielded higher mean scores (I4: 3.78, I5: 3.64, I6: 3.78) than process model 2 (I4: 3.33, I5: 3.51, I6: 3.35). These results suggest that participants experienced more difficulty with cognitive load while working with process model 1 than with process model 2. The similarity of scores within each model for cognitive challenges also implies a consistent difficulty across different cognitive aspects.

The standard deviations indicate variability in participant responses, with a particularly high variation for visual clarity in process model 2. This suggests there was less consensus among participants about the visual clarity of process model 2, potentially pointing to differing interpretations of the model's clarity.

4.1   Inferential Statistics

Chi-squared tests were employed to investigate significant differences in demographics during user interactions with IoT process models. Upon uncovering significant results, further analysis was undertaken using the Bonferroni post

Table 1. Demographic Data

Sex (w/m/d)		Age		Age (grp.)	G1	G2	G3
N	91 (36.5)	m	23.31	N	84	139	26
(%)	158 (63.5)	(SD)	(3.403)	(%)	(33.7)	(55.8)	(10.4)
	0 (0)						

Qualification	Q1	Q2	Q3	Q4	Q5	Q6	Q7
N	0	0	68	15	146	19	1
(%)	(0)	(0)	(27.3)	(6.0)	(58.6)	(7.6)	(0.4)

No. Pro. Mo.		Expertise		Exp. (grp.)	E1	E2	E3	E4
m	7.71	m	4.53	N	83	128	34	4
(SD)	(14.10)	(SD)	(2.09)	(%)	(33.3)	(51.4)	(13.7)	(1.6)

hoc approach with adjusted residuals. All statistical assessments were conducted with a two-tailed criterion, maintaining a significance threshold of p < .05.

Sex - PM 1: No significant differences were observed in the items I1–I6.

Sex - PM 2: No significant differences were observed in the items I1–I6.

Age - PM 1: No significant differences were observed in the items I1–I6.

Age - PM 2: There were significant differences in I3, $X^2(10) = 22.45; p = .013$, and I6, $X^2(10) = 19.13; p = .039$. However, the subsequent post hoc analysis with Bonferroni correction found no significant effects among the specific pairwise comparisons (e.g., low statistical power).

Qualification - PM 1: No significant differences were observed in the items I1–I6.

Qualification - PM 2: There was a significant difference in I2, $X^2(20) = 38.27; p = .008$. However, the subsequent post hoc analysis with Bonferroni correction found no significant effect among the specific pairwise comparisons (e.g., low statistical power).

Expertise - PM 1: There were significant differences in I3, $X^2(15) = 28.22; p = .020$, and I4, $X^2(15) = 31.98; p = .006$. However, the subsequent post hoc analysis with Bonferroni correction found no significant effects among the specific pairwise comparisons (e.g., low statistical power).

Expertise - PM 2: There was a significant difference in I2, $X^2(15) = 38.28; p = .001$. However, the subsequent post hoc analysis with Bonferroni correction found no significant effect among the specific pairwise comparisons (e.g., low statistical power).

Since no specific significant differences were found between the demographic data, differences in response behavior in the items I1 - I6 between the two process models were analyzed with an independent samples t-tests.

The following items showed a significance: I1, $(t(496) = -5.351; p =< .001)$; higher approval in process model 2, I2, $(t(496) = -6.145; p =< .001)$; higher approval in process model 2, I3, $(t(496) = -3.375; p =< .001)$; higher approval in process model 1, I4, $(t(495) = -4.793; p =< .001)$; higher approval in process model 1, and I6, $(t(496) = -4.624; p =< .001)$; higher approval in process model 1.

5   Discussion

The results revealed insights into participants' perceptions of the two examined IoT process models. Despite the initial discovery of significant differences among age, qualification, and expertise groups in certain items, notably in process model 2, the detailed post hoc analysis did not unveil specific pairwise differences. This pattern suggests that while these demographic factors may have an overarching influence on how participants perceive aspects of visual clarity, distinguishability, and cognitive challenges, the impact is not strong enough to distinguish particular groups.

The lack of significance in the perception of process model 1 across all demographic groups indicates a universal challenge the model poses regarding the cognitive challenges, irrespective of the users' demographics. This universality points to characteristics of process model 1 that uniformly impact users, potentially relating to its inherent complexity or the way IoT elements are represented within the model.

In turn, process model 2 showed some variation in perceptions based on age and expertise. Though statistically significant, these variations did not show identifiable trends. This outcome may suggest that process model 2 has elements that resonate differently with users of varying ages and expertise, but these elements did not consistently affect all members within those categories.

A direct comparison of the process models via independent samples t-tests yielded significant findings that offer a more straightforward narrative. Process model 2 was consistently rated higher regarding visual clarity and distinguishability, suggesting a design more conducive to user interpretation and less cognitively taxing in certain aspects. Process model 1, while perceived as more cognitively challenging, received higher approval in other cognitive challenge items, which might reflect a more immersive experience for the users.

The differences between the process models without strong demographic effects highlight the potential of the models' design features to influence the user experience. These results highlight the role of design in the creation of process models that are both visually clear and cognitively manageable. The perceptions of process model 2, affected by age and expertise, reinforce the notion that user experience is multifaceted and influenced by a constellation of factors, where demographic characteristics interplay with design elements.

Additionally, it is important to consider that the observed differences between the two process models might also come from variations in their size, complexity, and layout. These structural factors can significantly influence user perception, particularly in cognitive challenges and the ease with which information can be processed. These inherent design characteristics must be taken into account when interpreting the differences in user experiences between both process models, as they likely contribute to the unique challenges and advantages observed in each model.

The findings suggest a interrelationship between user demographics and process model design, collectively influencing the user's interaction with and perception of IoT process models. While the demographic factors did not provide a clear understanding of user experience, they did offer insights into the varied ways individuals might engage with and interpret these models, reflecting intra-individual differences.

Table 2. Results for visual clarity, distinguishability, and cognitive challenges

Visual Clarity and Distinguishability					
Process Model 1 (m/SD)			Process Model 2 (m/SD)		
I1	I2	I3	I1	I2	I3
2.82 (1.16)	2.38 (1.03)	3.08 (1.17)	3.37 (1.62)	2.97 (1.07)	2.72 (1.11)
Cognitive Challenges					
Process Model 1			Process Model 2		
I4	I5	I6	I4	I5	I6
3.78 (1.05)	3.64 (1.24)	3.78 (1.00)	3.33 (1.09)	3.51 (1.21)	3.35 (1.03)

5.1 Implications

The results highlight the significance of design in facilitating visual clarity and minimizing cognitive challenges when understanding IoT process models. The higher scores from process model 2 indicate a need for intuitive visual elements that delineate IoT components within the models (e.g., standardized icons, color coding, or other graphical strategies).

The influence of expertise on the perception of certain model aspects suggests that there could be considerable benefits in creating adaptable process models. Such models could cater to a spectrum of expertise levels, offering simplified views for novices while allowing more complex, detailed interactions for advanced users. This adaptability enhances usability and enables in situ training, as users can incrementally expose themselves to more complicated layers of the model.

Moreover, the variance in user experience based on the cognitive challenges presented by process model 1 indicates the potential value of integrated educational tools. Comprehensive guides or embedded support features could be instrumental in aiding users in fully leveraging the capabilities of such models. This is especially pertinent for those with less process modeling expertise, aligning with the trend towards democratizing technology by making it accessible to a wider audience.

Variations in perceived ease of use, related to participants' prior experience with process models, suggest that designers should consider practical experience in their designs. For experienced users, models can include advanced functionalities and analytics, while for novices, focusing on fundamental concepts and operations is more beneficial. This approach aims to make IoT process model design inclusive and effective for all expertise levels.

5.2 Limitations

When evaluating our survey findings, several limitations must be considered. The demographic composition, skewed towards young, predominantly male adults from an academic background, limits the generalizability of our results. This demographic bias suggests the findings primarily reflect the perceptions of a specific subset of users. The survey faced challenges in achieving sufficient statistical power for post hoc analyses, especially after applying the Bonferroni correction, indicating potential underpowering to detect specific demographic interactions. Additionally, the impact of process model characteristics (size, complexity, layout) on user perceptions needed to be quantitatively assessed, suggesting a need for future research to explore these factors. Reliance on Likert scale items introduces subjectivity in responses, affecting the interpretation of visual clarity, distinguishability, and cognitive challenges. Lastly, the survey did not account for the interaction time with the process models, which could significantly influence participants' comprehension and evaluation.

6   Conclusion and Future Work

This survey analyzed how users perceive IoT process models, focusing on visual clarity, distinguishability, and cognitive challenges among n = 249 participants. It examined two distinct IoT models, highlighting that model design influences user experiences. Although demographic differences were initially observed, no consistent trends emerged from in-depth analysis. One model excelled in visual clarity, while the other was noted for its cognitive engagement, underscoring the complexity of user-model interactions. The insights encourage future research to prioritize intuitive design and adaptability for users of varying expertise, incorporating educational tools to aid comprehension. Addressing the limitations and exploring the impact of design characteristics like size and complexity on user experience will refine our understanding of effective IoT process model design.

References

1. Cheng, Y., Zhao, S., Cheng, B., Chen, X., Chen, J.: Modeling and deploying IoT-aware business process applications in sensor networks. Sensors **19**(1), 111 (2018)

2. Compagnucci, I., Corradini, F., Fornari, F., Polini, A., Re, B., Tiezzi, F.: A systematic literature review on IoT-aware business process modeling views, requirements and notations. Softw. Syst. Model. **22**(3), 969–1004 (2023)
3. Kirikkayis, Y., Gallik, F., Winter, M., Reichert, M.: BPMNE4IoT: a framework for modeling, executing and monitoring IoT-driven processes. Future Internet **15**(3), 90 (2023)
4. Langley, D.J., van Doorn, J., Ng, I.C., Stieglitz, S., Lazovik, A., Boonstra, A.: The internet of everything: smart things and their impact on business models. J. Bus. Res. **122**, 853–863 (2021)
5. Moody, D.: The "physics" of notations: toward a scientific basis for constructing visual notations in software engineering. IEEE Trans. Softw. Eng. **35**(6), 756–779 (2009)
6. Sungur, C.T., Spiess, P., Oertel, N., Kopp, O.: Extending BPMN for wireless sensor networks. In: 2013 IEEE 15th Conference on Business Informatics, pp. 109–116. IEEE (2013)
7. Torres, V., Serral, E., Valderas, P., Pelechano, V., Grefen, P.: Modeling of IoT devices in business processes: a systematic mapping study. In: 2020 IEEE 22nd Conference on Business Informatics (CBI), vol. 1, pp. 221–230. IEEE (2020)
8. Valderas, P., Torres, V., Serral, E.: Modelling and executing IoT-enhanced business processes through BPMN and microservices. J. Syst. Softw. **184**, 111139 (2022)
9. Yousfi, A., Bauer, C., Saidi, R., Dey, A.K.: uBPMN: a BPMN extension for modeling ubiquitous business processes. Inf. Softw. Technol. **74**, 55–68 (2016)

Advancing IoT Process Modeling: A Comparative Evaluation of BPMNE4IoT and Traditional BPMN on User-Friendliness, Effectiveness, and Workload

Michael Winter[1,2]([✉]) [ID], Yusuf Kirikkayis[3], Rüdiger Pryss[1,2], and Manfred Reichert[3]

[1] Institute of Clinical Epidemiology and Biometry, University of Würzburg, Würzburg, Germany
michael.winter@uni-wuerzburg.de
[2] Institute of Medical Data Science, University Hospital of Würzburg, Würzburg, Germany
[3] Institute of Databases and Information Systems, Ulm University, Ulm, Germany

Abstract. In the evolving Internet of Things (IoT) landscape, integrating advanced technologies into business processes has become crucial for enhancing efficiency and automation. Accurate representation of IoT within business processes is a prerequisite for leveraging automation and monitoring benefits, underscoring the limitations of Business Process Model and Notation (BPMN) 2.0 in effectively capturing IoT-specific behaviors. For this reason, this study investigated the enhancement of IoT business process modeling through BPMNE4IoT, an extension of the standard BPMN 2.0, focusing on its user-friendliness, effectiveness, and workload compared to traditional BPMN. The comparative user study with 30 participants demonstrated that BPMNE4IoT significantly improves the modeling experience, reducing mental and physical strain and increasing satisfaction. These findings support the importance of user-centered design in IoT modeling tools to enhance productivity and foster adoption, highlighting the need for further investigation into the impact of features and scalability within complex IoT environments.

Keywords: Internet of Things · BPMN 2.0 · BPMNE4IoT · Process Modeling · Study

1 Introduction

As embedded electronic components have become smaller, more powerful, and less expensive, the Internet of Things (IoT) has emerged as an unavoidable technology, reshaping how we interact with the physical world. This technological evolution has facilitated unprecedented levels of automation and efficiency,

© The Author(s), under exclusive license to Springer Nature Switzerland AG 2025
H. R. Arabnia et al. (Eds.): CSCE 2024, CCIS 2260, pp. 98–107, 2025.
https://doi.org/10.1007/978-3-031-85923-6_8

allowing for seamless integration between digital and physical domains. Many embedded components are equipped with sensors, actuators, and smart objects, enabling the detection and collection of data as well as physical responses to specific events [9]. Business Process Management, in turn, enables the modeling, implementation, execution, monitoring, and analysis of business processes [5]. Integrating IoT capabilities into business processes offers promising perspectives for automating processes and decision-making, automating repetitive activities, and monitoring the progress of business processes and rules. Business processes must accurately and unambiguously represent IoT involvement and behavior to achieve these benefits.

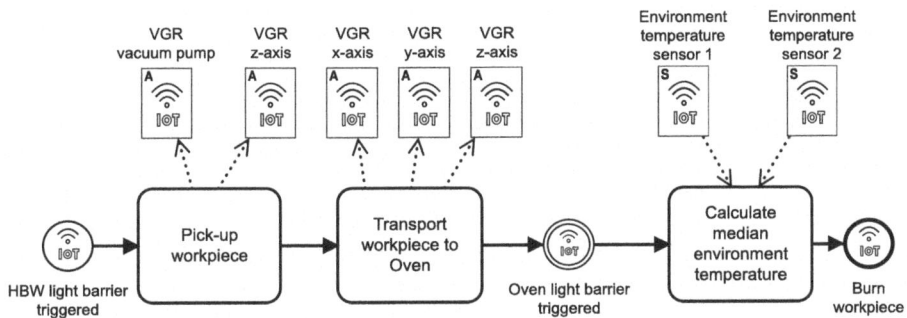

Fig. 1. IoT-aware smart factory process modeled in terms of BPMNE4IoT.

An IoT-aware business process utilizes IoT devices and represents the specific behavior (e.g., parallelism, asynchronicity, interoperability, and Event-Based communication) [5,9]. For instance, an IoT-aware business process utilizes IoT devices, describes the behavior of these IoT devices, and contains the necessary activities to complete the process. Consider an order processing system integrating IoT devices to track orders and manage inventory. In this scenario, the IoT-aware process model would outline the activities involved in processing orders while detailing how IoT devices contribute to these activities. There are several modeling notations and languages for modeling business processes. The de-facto standard for modeling in the BPM domain is the Business Process Modeling and Notation (BPMN) 2.0 [6]. However, BPMN 2.0 does not allow for explicit representation of IoT involvement and behavior. As a result, the comprehension of IoT-aware business processes modeled in terms of BPMN 2.0 is difficult. Misunderstanding a business process model affects its implementation and, thus, the execution at runtime. Insufficient comprehension of an IoT-aware business process model can prevent achieving the intended outcomes [9].

To address this gap, we presented in [5] *BPMNE4IoT* - a BPMN extension for modeling, execution, monitoring, and logging IoT-aware business processes. *BPMNE4IoT* extends the BPMN 2.0 meta-model for integrating, representing, and semantically enriching IoT characteristics (e.g., parallelism, asynchronicity, interoperability, and Event-Based communication). To evaluate the user-friendliness, effectiveness, and workload of *BPMNE4IoT*, we conducted a user study with 30 participants. Study participants were asked to model an IoT-aware business process model based on a textual description, with one group beginning with BPMN 2.0 and the other with BPMNE4IoT.

The structure of the paper is as following: Sect. 2 reviews relevant literature. Section 3 outlines the materials and methodologies employed in this research. Section 4 showcases the findings, encompassing descriptive outcomes and inferential statistical analyses. Insights gained from the study, their practical implications, and limitations encountered are discussed in Sect. 5. The paper concludes in Sect. 6, where a research summary and directions for future work are provided.

2   Related Work

In recent years, many extensions to the BPMN 2.0 meta-model have been developed to deal with the modeling of IoT-aware business processes. [10] extends the BPMN meta-model with specific task types to represent ubiquitous technologies and their integration into business processes. In turn, [8] presents an approach to control wireless sensor networks (WSNs). For this purpose, they extend BPMN 2.0, a WSN task. [4] introduces *BPMN4CPS* - a BPMN extension for modeling cyber physical systems. [3] presents a BPMN extension for modeling IoT-aware business processes with a focus on sensors. Contrary to the viewpoint that BPMN 2.0 needs to be extended for IoT-aware business processes, other researchers [1,2,7] have contended that BPMN 2.0 possesses capabilities that allow modeling IoT involvement indirect, using for example a BPMN 2.0 service task.

As presented above, the exploration of modeling IoT-aware business processes has been extensively studied in the literature. However, this research primarily examines technical aspects from an expert perspective, neglecting the end users, process modelers, and stakeholders. As a major drawback, none of the presented extensions for IoT-aware business processes evaluates their extension or approach through a user study, potentially overlooking user-friendliness, effectiveness, and workload issues associated with extending BPMN 2.0.

3   Materials and Methods

The BPMNE4IoT [5] framework enables modeling IoT-aware business processes based on a BPMN 2.0 extension. BPMNE4IoT extends the BPMN 2.0 meta-model with a *Sensor Artifact, Actuator, Artifact, Object Artifact, IoT Start Event, IoT Intermediate Event, and IoT End Event*. Unlike BPMN 2.0, BPMNE4IoT offers an explicit representation of IoT involvement, ensuring end users understand the roles and contributions of IoT devices (e.g., sensors, actuators, and tags) within business processes. Furthermore, the BPMNE4IoT extension enables modeling IoT-specific behaviors (e.g., parallelism, asynchronicity, interoperability, and Event-Based communication). The clear representation of IoT involvement and behavior fosters better communication and facilitates improved analyzability and optimization of IoT-aware business processes. By adhering to standards and promoting interoperability, BPMNE4IoT ensures compatibility with existing BPMN tools while advancing modeling practices in the context of IoT [5]. The BPMNE4IoT modeler can be accessed online[1].

Figure 1 illustrates an IoT-aware smart factory process modeled in terms of BPMNE4IoT. The exact process modeled in terms of BPMN 2.0 is depicted in Fig. 2. The process starts as soon as the High-Bay Warehouse light barrier (HBW light barrier) is triggered. Subsequently, the workpiece is picked up. This requires controlling the Vacuum Gripper Robot (VGR) pump and the VGR z-axis. After this activity, the workpiece is transported to the oven. For this, the x, y, and z-axes of the VGR are triggered. The process then continues only after the Oven light barrier is triggered. Once the light barrier is triggered, the average temperature is calculated using 'Environment temperature sensor 1' and 'Environment temperature sensor 2'. The process ends with triggering the sorting system (Start Sorting Machine).

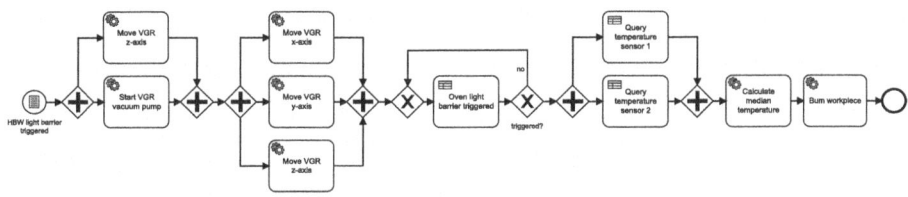

Fig. 2. IoT-aware smart factory process modeled in terms of BPMN 2.0

Participants were provided with the above-described process description of the IoT-aware smart factory process and tasked with modeling it using both BPMN 2.0 and BPMNE4IoT, allowing for comparison in terms of user-friendliness, effectiveness, and workload. In order to evaluate the latter aspects, the multidimensional assessment tool NASA-TLX was applied capturing the following six items on a 20-point scale with 1-point steps (i.e., 1 (very low) - 20 (very high)):

- **Mental demand:** In the context of the study, mental demand indicates how much cognitive effort participants felt was necessary when using each modeler.
- **Physical demand:** Physical demand refers to the physical effort required to use the two modelers.
- **Temporal demand:** Temporal demand assesses the perceived pressure to complete tasks quickly.
- **Performance:** Performance in this study measures user satisfaction with their own modeling outcomes.
- **Effort:** Effort evaluates the overall mental and physical exertion perceived as necessary to achieve the task.

---

[1] https://bpmne4iot.dbis.institute/.

– **Frustration:** Frustration levels measure the emotional response to using the two modelers.

To carry out our research, we held two workshops on separate days, each with 15 participants. Note that different participants took part on both days. The workshops followed the same structure and activities. The only contrast was that, in the second workshop, participants started with BPMNE4IoT before moving on to BPMN 2.0. Prior to the study, we briefed the participants on its objectives and the process involved. We ensured everyone had a basic understanding of BPMN 2.0 before introducing BPMNE4IoT. Then, we demonstrated both BPMN 2.0 and BPMNE4IoT modeling tools. Participants began modeling using the first modeler, with the study leader offering assistance if needed. Afterward, participants filled out the NASA-TLX questionnaire. We repeated the same process using the second modeler.

4   Results

The study involved a total of 30 participants, who were evenly divided into two groups of 15 each. As described in Sect. 3, Group 1 commenced their tasks using the BPMN modeler and then proceeded to the BPMNE4IoT modeler, whereas Group 2 began with the BPMNE4IoT modeler before switching to the BPMN modeler. Tables 1 and 2 show descriptive results for both groups presenting mean and standard deviation regarding the considered six items (mental load, physical and temporal demand, performance, effort and frustration; see Sect. 3. Furthermore, the determined differences in the six items between the BPMN and BPMNE4IoT modeler are presented in the two tables (i.e., Group 1 = BPMN - BPMNE4IoT, Group 2 = BPMNE4IoT - BPMN).

The results from Tables 1 and 2 comparing the BPMN with the BPMNE4IoT modelers demonstrate an improvement in user experience when transitioning from BPMN to BPMNE4IoT across several dimensions. This improvement is indicated by lower scores in mental load, physical and temporal demand, performance, effort, and frustration when users switch to the BPMNE4IoT modeler. These findings suggest that BPMNE4IoT provides a more user-friendly and less demanding modeling environment than the traditional BPMN modeler. Furthermore, the results were consistent across both groups, irrespective of the order in which they used the modelers, reinforcing the reliability of the conclusion that BPMNE4IoT is prime in reducing the cognitive and physical strain on users. This could have implications for the adoption and efficiency of modeling tools in environments where complexity and user experience are critical factors.

4.1   Inferential Statistics

The Wilcoxon Signed-Rank Test was utilized to determine significant differences based on the results reported in descriptive statistics between BPMN and BPMNE4IoT modelers. This non-parametric method was chosen given the paired nature of our data and the non-normal distribution of differences. All statistical analyses were performed under a two-tailed criterion, adhering to a significance threshold of p < .05, to ensure robust and reliable conclusions regarding the comparative efficacy of the two modeling approaches.

In group 1, Wilcoxon Signed-Rank Tests indicated significant differences in mental load ($Z = -3.417, p < .001$; higher mental load in BPMN modeler), physical demand ($Z = -3.313, p < .001$; higher physical load in BPMN modeler), temporal demand ($Z = -3.423, p < .001$; higher temporal load in BPMN modeler), performance, ($Z = -3.412, p < .001$; higher performance load in BPMN modeler), effort ($Z = -3.354, p < .001$; higher effort load in BPMN modeler), and frustration ($Z = -3.306, p < .001$; higher frustration load in BPMN modeler).

In group 2, Wilcoxon Signed-Rank Tests indicated significant differences in mental load ($Z = -3.415, p < .001$; higher mental load in BPMN modeler), physical demand ($Z = -2.533, p = .011$; higher physical load in BPMN modeler), temporal demand ($Z = -3.302, p < .001$; higher temporal load in BPMN modeler), performance, ($Z = -3.417, p < .001$; higher performance load in BPMN modeler), effort ($Z = -3.308, p < .001$; higher effort load in BPMN modeler), and frustration ($Z = -3.415, p < .001$; higher frustration load in BPMN modeler).

Table 1. Group 1 - BPMN to BPMNE4IoT

	BPMN	BPMNE4IoT	Diff.
Mental load	13.47 (3.07)	4.13 (1.60)	9.33
Physical demand	11.07 (4.40)	4.13 (3.18)	6.93
Temporal demand	14.73 (3.11)	3.20 (1.82)	11.53
Performance	9.07 (4.94)	2.20 (2.94)	6.87
Effort	12.87 (3.74)	4.07 (2.34)	8.80
Frustration	12.80 (4.07)	2.67 (2.80)	10.13

Table 2. Group 2 - BPMNE4IoT to BPMN

	BPMNE4IoT	BPMN	Diff.
Mental load	4.27 (2.12)	12.13 (3.04)	−7.87
Physical demand	2.20 (2.27)	5.40 (5.15)	−3.20
Temporal demand	3.07 (2.09)	11.80 (4.78)	−8.73
Performance	2.07 (1.79)	9.67 (4.12)	−7.60
Effort	2.93 (1.62)	12.80 (3.28)	−9.87
Frustration	2.67 (2.32)	13.87 (4.55)	−11.20

5 Discussion

The significant differences in mental demand, with a higher demand noted for BPMN across both groups, highlight the cognitive efficiency of BPMNE4IoT. Users required less mental and perceptual activity to accomplish tasks with BPMNE4IoT, suggesting its interface and workflow are more intuitive. This could imply that BPMNE4IoT reduces the complexity inherent to modeling tasks, potentially making it more accessible to users with varying levels of expertise.

While modeling tasks are not typically associated with high physical activity, the significant reduction in physical demand scores for BPMNE4IoT suggests an ergonomically optimized interface. This could mean fewer or more efficient interactions are needed to achieve the same outcomes, reducing the physical strain over prolonged periods of modeling work.

The significant decrease in temporal demand for BPMNE4IoT users points to an improved pace of work without the pressure felt with BPMN. This could be due to BPMNE4IoT facilitating a smoother workflow, through more streamlined processes or better guidance within the modeling tasks. Reducing time pressure is crucial for creative and complex tasks, as it allows users to think more critically about their work without the stress of rushing.

The significant findings related to performance, particularly the high levels of performance satisfaction across both modelers, suggest that while BPMNE4IoT is easier to use, it doesn't compromise the quality of work. This is a crucial balance in tool design, where usability enhancements should not dilute the tool's effectiveness or the user's sense of achievement.

The significant reduction in effort required with BPMNE4IoT, both mentally and physically, to achieve a given level of performance is particularly noteworthy. It indicates that BPMNE4IoT not only makes the task less demanding but does so in a way that maintains or enhances the quality of output. This could lead to higher productivity and sustainability in work practices over time.

Finally, the significantly lower frustration levels with BPMNE4IoT underscore the emotional and psychological benefits of using a more user-friendly modeling tool. High frustration levels can prevent continued use and negatively impact learning and efficiency. The reduced frustration with BPMNE4IoT suggests a more pleasant user experience, likely contributing to enhanced user satisfaction and potentially higher adoption rates.

In summary, test results obtained demonstrate the increased user experience offered by BPMNE4IoT across multiple dimensions, including user interface design and interaction efficiency. This suggests that the development and refinement of modeling tools should prioritize the functional capabilities and the cognitive, physical, and emotional demands placed on users. Improvements in these areas can significantly enhance user satisfaction, productivity, and overall tool efficacy, making a solid case for the continued evolution and user-centered design of modeling tools in the IoT and beyond.

5.1   Implications

The findings between BPMN and BPMNE4IoT modelers have several important implications for the development, selection, and use of process modeling tools, particularly in the context of the Internet of Things (IoT) and complex systems. These implications can be categorized into tool development, user training and support, and broader organizational impacts.

Implications for Tool Development

- User-Centered Design: The significant advantages of BPMNE4IoT in reducing mental, physical, and temporal demands highlight the importance of user-centered design principles. Developers should prioritize intuitive interfaces, simplicity, and efficiency to enhance user satisfaction and adoption rates.
- Ergonomics and Accessibility: Lower physical demand scores for BPMNE4IoT underscore the need for ergonomically designed tools that cater to a broad user base, including those with varying levels of physical ability and those who may use the tools for extended periods.
- Feature Integration: While BPMNE4IoT enhances user experience across several dimensions without compromising performance, developers must balance feature richness with usability. Adding features should not come at the expense of increased complexity or user burden.

Implications for User Training and Support

- Focused Training: Training programs for BPMN tools should address the identified areas of higher demand, offering strategies to effectively manage mental load and temporal pressures. For BPMNE4IoT, training can emphasize leveraging its user-friendly features for efficient modeling.
- Support Systems: The findings suggest a need for comprehensive support systems, including tutorials, documentation, and user communities, tailored to different user experience levels. Such support can help mitigate frustration and improve task performance.
- Adaptive Learning Environments: Incorporating adaptive learning environments and personalized learning paths into user training for BPMNE4IoT could further enhance the user experience. By recognizing individual differences in learning pace, prior knowledge, and specific challenges encountered, training can become more effective.

Broader Organizational Impacts

- Productivity and Efficiency: By facilitating a lower-effort and less frustrating modeling experience, BPMNE4IoT could significantly enhance organizational productivity and efficiency. This is particularly relevant in environments where rapid modeling and iteration are essential.
- Adoption and Change Management: The superior user experience offered by BPMNE4IoT can ease the adoption of modeling tools in organizations. However, change management strategies must consider existing workflows and potential resistance to new tools, emphasizing the benefits of lower user strain.

– Quality of Work: Despite the reduced demands on users, the performance satisfaction levels remained high, suggesting that a better user experience does not compromise the quality of work. Organizations might see improvements in the quality of modeling outcomes due to reduced errors and increased attention to detail facilitated by a less taxing modeling environment.

5.2 Limitations

While this study provides valuable insights into the comparative effectiveness of BPMNE4IoT and traditional BPMN, it acknowledges several limitations.

Firstly, the participant sample size of 30, although sufficient for preliminary analysis, restricts the generalizability of our findings. Future studies incorporating a larger, more diverse cohort would be instrumental in validating the applicability of our results across varied demographics.

Secondly, the complexity of the processes modeled in this study encompasses only some of the full complexity of real-world IoT applications. Further research is needed to examine BPMNE4IoT's capabilities in more real-world scenarios that closely mirror the complexity encountered in practical IoT integrations across different industries.

Moreover, our study's scope was limited to a specific IoT application scenario within a smart factory context. Extending the evaluation to include a variety of IoT application domains, such as healthcare, smart cities, and agriculture, could underline BPMNE4IoT's domain-specific strengths or weaknesses. Such a diversified approach would offer a richer understanding of the tool's versatility and adaptability.

Additionally, while our findings highlight BPMNE4IoT's compatibility with existing BPMN tools, the study needed to explore potential integration challenges within the process modeling and management tools ecosystem. A comprehensive assessment of BPMNE4IoT's interoperability with other tools and platforms would provide critical insights into its practical utility and limitations in a diverse technological landscape.

Lastly, our study's reliance on subjective measures such as user satisfaction and workload underscores the need for incorporating objective performance metrics in future research. Quantitative evaluations, including modeling accuracy, error rates, and time efficiency, would furnish a more nuanced and balanced comparison of BPMNE4IoT against traditional BPMN methodologies.

6 Conclusion and Future Work

This paper presented the results from a comparative study involving 30 participants, demonstrating that BPMNE4IoT significantly outperformed the traditional BPMN modeler in terms of user experience. Specifically, the ease of navigation within BPMNE4IoT was frequently noted as superior. The participants, divided into two groups, interacted with both modelers, and their feedback indicated a clear preference for BPMNE4IoT across various metrics. This preference was particularly strong in terms of the intuitive interface and accessibility of BPMNE4IoT. The results highlighted BPMNE4IoT's improved performance in reducing cognitive load and enhancing user satisfaction, making it a more effective and user-friendly option for process modeling tasks. Participants also appreciated the quick response time of the BPMNE4IoT system, which contributed to a more efficient modeling process.

For future work, the benefits of BPMNE4IoT over BPMN for user experience indicate a promising direction for the enhancement of existing modeling tools, especially in complex domains like IoT. Future research could focus on identifying specific features or design choices that contribute most significantly to reduced user demands. Additionally, exploring the scalability of these benefits in larger, more diverse user populations and complex real-world scenarios would provide valuable insights for both tool developers and organizational decision-makers.

References

1. Caracaş, A., Kramp, T.: On the expressiveness of BPMN for modeling wireless sensor networks applications. In: Business Process Model and Notation: Third International Workshop, BPMN 2011, Lucerne, Switzerland, 21–22 November 2011, Proceedings 3, pp. 16–30. Springer (2011)
2. Celestrini, J.R., Rocha, R.N., Saleme, E.B., Santos, C.A., Filho, J.G.P., Andreão, R.V.: An architecture and its tools for integrating IoT and BPMN in agriculture scenarios. In: Proceedings of the 34th ACM/SIGAPP Symposium on Applied Computing, pp. 824–831 (2019)
3. Cheng, Y., Zhao, S., Cheng, B., Chen, X., Chen, J.: Modeling and deploying IoT-aware business process applications in sensor networks. Sensors **19**(1), 111 (2018)
4. Graja, I., Kallel, S., Guermouche, N., Kacem, A.H.: BPMN4CPS: a BPMN extension for modeling cyber-physical systems. In: 2016 IEEE 25th International Conference on Enabling Technologies: Infrastructure for Collaborative Enterprises (WETICE), pp. 152–157. IEEE (2016)
5. Kirikkayis, Y., Gallik, F., Winter, M., Reichert, M.: BPMNE4IoT: a framework for modeling, executing and monitoring IoT-driven processes. Future Internet **15**(3), 90 (2023)
6. Model, B.P.: Notation (BPMN) version 2.0. OMG Specification, Object Management Group (2011)
7. Seiger, R., Malburg, L., Weber, B., Bergmann, R.: Integrating process management and event processing in smart factories: a systems architecture and use cases. J. Manuf. Syst. **63**, 575–592 (2022)
8. Sungur, C.T., Spiess, P., Oertel, N., Kopp, O.: Extending BPMN for wireless sensor networks. In: 2013 IEEE 15th Conference on Business Informatics, pp. 109–116. IEEE (2013)
9. Valderas, P., Torres, V., Serral, E.: Modelling and executing IoT-enhanced business processes through BPMN and microservices. J. Syst. Softw. **184**, 111139 (2022)
10. Yousfi, A., Bauer, C., Saidi, R., Dey, A.K.: uBPMN: a BPMN extension for modeling ubiquitous business processes. Inf. Softw. Technol. **74**, 55–68 (2016)

Threat Detection Using MLP for IoT Network

Genea Taylor$^{(\boxtimes)}$, David Johnson, and Kaushik Roy

Department of Computer Science, North Carolina Agricultural and Technical State University,
Greensboro, NC 27411, USA
getaylor@aggies.ncat.edu

Abstract. While the popularity of IoT networks has grown significantly, they remain highly vulnerable to various cyber-attacks. These attacks can disrupt services, compromise sensitive data, and damage the integrity of IoT ecosystems. Machine learning (ML) techniques, particularly deep learning (DL) models, have been employed to effectively detect and mitigate such threats by identifying abnormal patterns in network traffic. In this paper, we propose utilizing a multilayer perceptron (MLP)-based machine learning model to detect cyber-attacks by using the NF-ToN-IoT dataset, which contains a diverse set of cyber-attacks. The MLP model has been trained and optimized to distinguish between normal and malicious activity. Our results demonstrate the effectiveness of this approach, with the MLP achieving a training accuracy of approximately 97% and a test accuracy of around 95–97%. This high accuracy indicates the model's capability to generalize well across different attacks while creating a robust solution for real-time threat detection and mitigation in IoT networks.

Keywords: Threat Intelligence · Cyber Attacks · Machine Learning

1 Introduction

The fight against rising cyber network attacks is changing significantly. ML techniques are being used to detect and reduce these threats. ML provides decision-making systems with the ability to recognize patterns and make informed decisions across a variety of domains. Even though DL methods are successful when applied to images, speech and recognition of speech and objects, there are very little methods currently applied to cyberattack detection [1]. Earlier research and papers have highlighted a challenge in creating an ML-based detection system that uses heterogeneous network data samples.

Our research addresses this challenge by employing a multilayer perceptron (MLP) model, a type of feedforward artificial neural network commonly used for classification tasks. The MLP consists of multiple layers of nodes, including an input layer, one or more hidden layers, and an output layer which is well-suited for differentiating between normal and malicious attacks [2]. The binary classifier approach allows the MLP model to focus on distinguishing between normal and malicious behavior, regardless of the data source. By training the MLP model on heterogeneous datasets—such as the NF-ToN-IoT dataset [3]—our approach enhances the model's ability to detect multiple types of attacks, including those that may appear differently across networks.

© The Author(s), under exclusive license to Springer Nature Switzerland AG 2025
H. R. Arabnia et al. (Eds.): CSCE 2024, CCIS 2260, pp. 108–115, 2025.
https://doi.org/10.1007/978-3-031-85923-6_9

While a significant amount of research has focused on intrusion detection, it raises an important question: what about threat detection? Intrusion detection specifically targets unauthorized access or breaches within a network or system, whereas threat detection encompasses a broader scope, identifying any potential or active threats beyond just intrusions. This includes detecting malware, ransomware, phishing attempts, insider threats, and other malicious activities. This paper discusses effective strategies for threat detection to proactively address threats before they infiltrate an organization's network or system. Furthermore, we examine the development of a machine learning (ML)-based framework using the NF-ToN-IoT dataset, as outlined in Table 1, for its potential in binary classification. By leveraging this dataset and ML techniques, our research aims to create a binary classifier capable of accurately distinguishing between various types of attacks, thereby enhancing overall threat detection capabilities (Table 1).

Table. 1. Statistics of the Total Count for Each Attack in the NF-ToN-IoT Dataset [3].

Class	Total Count
Benign	270279
Backdoor	17247
DoS	17717
DDoS	326845
Injection	468539
MITM	1295
Password	156299
Ransomware	142
Scanning	21467
XSS	99944

2   Related Work

Several studies have explored the application of MLP models in the detection of cyber-attacks and to come up with threat mitigation. Fernado et al. discusses an architecture developed for neural models which is MLP with self-attention mechanisms and to develop a DL model for the detection of different kinds of cyber-attacks and improve the assessment of features [2]. Ahmed et al. utilized MLP to evaluate the effectiveness of metric-based attack detection and proposed MLP classification algorithm for detecting DDoS attacks [4].

2.1   Cyber Threat Intelligence

Threat intelligence is essential for many cybersecurity practices, providing insights into an organization's network and potential threats and vulnerabilities. Cyber Threat Intelligence (CTI) stands as a pivotal domain within cybersecurity, actively gathering and scrutinizing information on existing and potential threats that jeopardize an organization's security [5]. Through the use of a threat intelligence platform (TIP), organizations can bolster their defenses against threats and attacks by receiving alerts triggered based on predefined rules and criteria [5]. By continuously aggregating data, this platform enhances the likelihood of detecting network intrusions.

3 Methods Used

In this section, we delve into a comprehensive explanation of our methods for integrating threat intelligence using ML-based technique. Through diverse threat analysis, patterns in the dataset are identified, enhancing the understanding of evolving cybersecurity risks. Real-time collaboration in threat mitigation automates the detection of various threats within network environments, enabling swift responses to potential security breaches. Furthermore, the incorporation of tailoring network configurations to each organization ensures they meet specific security needs and operational frameworks.

3.1 NF-ToN-IoT Dataset

Sarhan et al. discuss the ML-Based Network Intrusion Detection System (NIDS) dataset and the publicly available pcaps of the ToN-IoT dataset, which are used to generate it NetFlow records. This results in the creation of a NetFlow-Based IoT network, NF-ToN-IoT [3], serving as a valuable resource in the realm of cybersecurity. The NF-ToN-IoT dataset [3]consists of 1,379,274 samples out of 1,108,995 (80.4%) are attack samples and 270,279 (19.6%) are benign ones as shown in the label distribution in Fig. 1. This dataset is structured into 10 distinct encoder classes, each representing a different type of network activity or attack. These classes encompass a broad spectrum of threats commonly encountered in real-world network environments, ranging from benign activities to sophisticated attack vectors [3].

Through a diverse array of attack categories, such as 'backdoor', 'ddos', 'dos', 'injection', 'mitm', 'password', 'ransomware', 'scanning', and 'xss', the NF-ToN-IoT dataset offers a comprehensive understanding of the nature of cyber threats [3]. During the experiments, benign network traffic and various attack scenarios are generated and conducted over the network testbed. In the meanwhile, the network packets are captured in their native packet capture (pcaps) format and dumped onto storage devices. A set of network data features are extracted from the pcaps files using appropriate tools and methods, forming network data flows. The result is a data source of labeled network flows reflecting benign and malicious network behavior. The generated datasets are published and made publicly accessible for use in the design and evaluation phases of ML-based NIDS models [6, 7].

3.2 Binary Classification Using MLP

This research aims to develop a binary classifier capable of effectively finding and detecting threats within IoT environments. This efficiency helps create and improve threat detection models, making it easier to build a secure platform for sharing threat

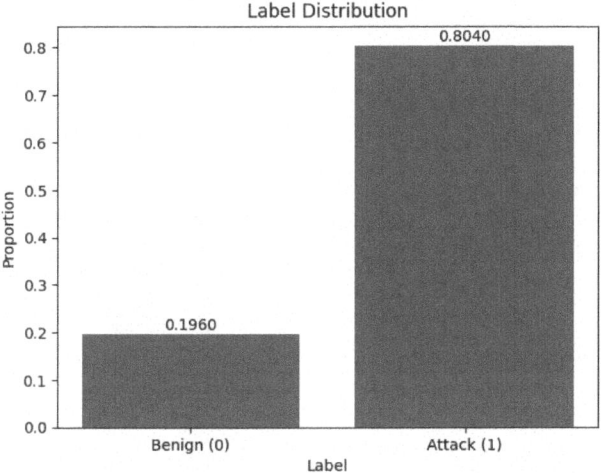

Fig. 1. Label Distribution of Benign and Attack Samples in NF-ToN-IoT dataset

intelligence. The MLP is a DL model that is composed of at minimum three linear labels and is used in this research to form a custom DL architecture, specifically a neural network, which undergoes training and evaluation through a stratified k-fold cross-validation process. Table 2 presents a detailed description of the layers, including the fully connected layers and their corresponding activation functions which consists of several layers that process data. The MLP model starts with a linear layer that takes in 13 input features and produces 60 outputs, helping the model learn better with a bias term. The next two layers also take 60 inputs and give 60 outputs each, keeping the same number of features. After each of these layers, a ReLU activation function is applied, which adds complexity to the model and helps it learn more effectively. ReLU is an activation function which has strong biological and mathematical underpinning [8]. The final layer takes the 60 outputs from the last ReLU and produces a single output, which stands for the model's prediction. To finish, a Sigmoid activation function is used on this output, squashing it to a value between 0 and 1, making it suitable for tasks like predicting probabilities in binary classification. Rectified linear units (ReLU) are employed as activation functions in the first fully connected layers to introduce non-linearity into the MLP model (Table 2).

4   Results and Discussion

As depicted in Fig. 2, we present a comparative analysis of model architectures, namely wide and deep, highlighting their parameter counts. This analysis provides insights into the complexity and ability of each model variant, such as how a wider model may better capture linear relationships, while a deeper model is more effective at finding complex patterns. Understanding these differences helps in selecting the most suitable architecture for our specific task by allowing us to choose a model that balances performance and resource requirements, ensuring best training times and accuracy for the given application.

Table 2. The Architecture of the MLP Model.

Layer Type	Layer Name	Input Features	Output Features	Description
Fully Connected	layer1	13	60	A linear layer with 13 input features and 60 output features.
Fully Connected	layer2	60	60	A linear layer with 60 input features and 60 output features.
Fully Connected	layer3	60	60	A linear layer with 60 input features and 60 output features.
Activation Function	act1	-	-	ReLU activation function applied after layer1.
Activation Function	act2	-	-	ReLU activation function applied after layer2.
Activation Function	act3	-	-	ReLU activation function applied after layer3.
Output Layer	output	60	1	The final layer producing a single output feature.
Activation Function	sigmoid	-	-	Sigmoid activation function applied to the output layer for binary classification.

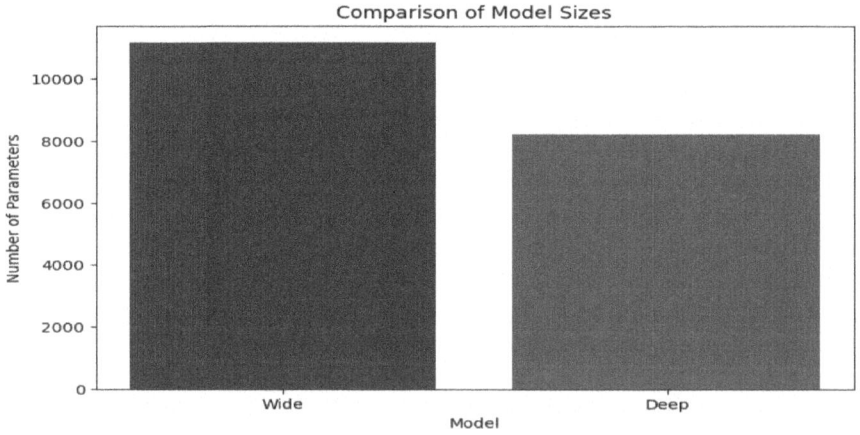

Fig. 2. Comparison of Model Sizes: Wide vs. Deep Architectures. This diagram illustrates the differences in model sizes between wide and deep architectures, showing the number of parameters and layers of the model.

The MLP was trained with the data from NF-ToN-IoT [3] dataset to evaluate its effectiveness in classifying network attacks. Our goal was to improve the model's accuracy in classifying attacks. By training 1000 epochs to evaluate accuracy, Fig. 3,4,5 shows the results of the MLP model using the NF-ToN-IoT [3] dataset while incorporating the model architecture listed previously and resulted in a 97.3% train accuracy, 96.32% validation accuracy, 0.048 train loss, 0.041 validation loss, and a learning rate of $1e^{-3}$. Additionally, Fig. 6 shows a heatmap that visualizes the correlation between the dataset's independent variables, helping to find multi-collinearity. Darker shades stand for stronger positive or negative correlations, while lighter shades show weaker ones. This heatmap tool aids in enhancing the robustness of the predictive model.

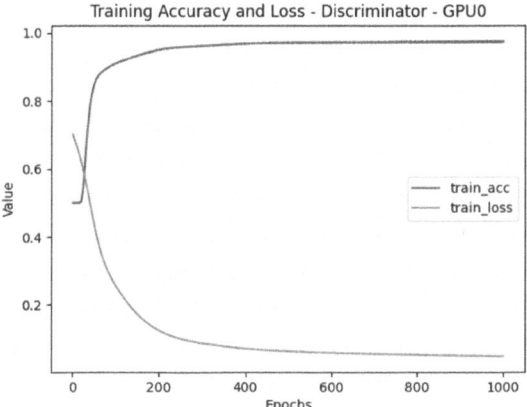

Fig. 3. MLP Model Training Accuracy and Loss

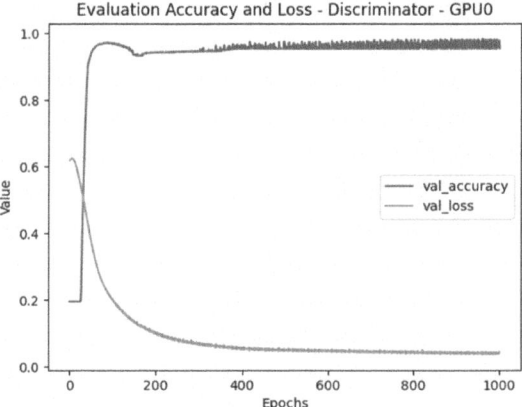

Fig. 4. MLP Model Evaluation Accuracy and Loss

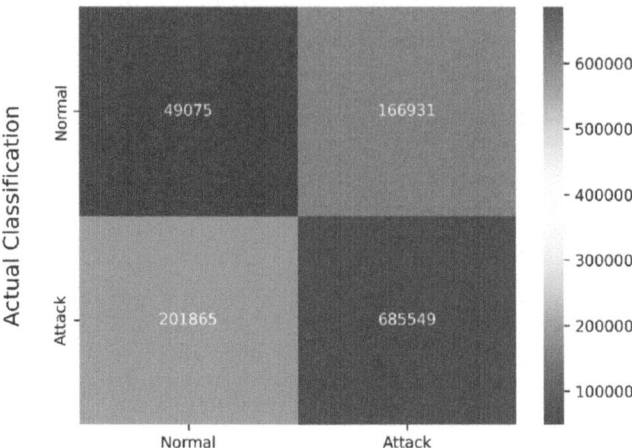

Fig. 5. Binary Classification Confusion Matrix

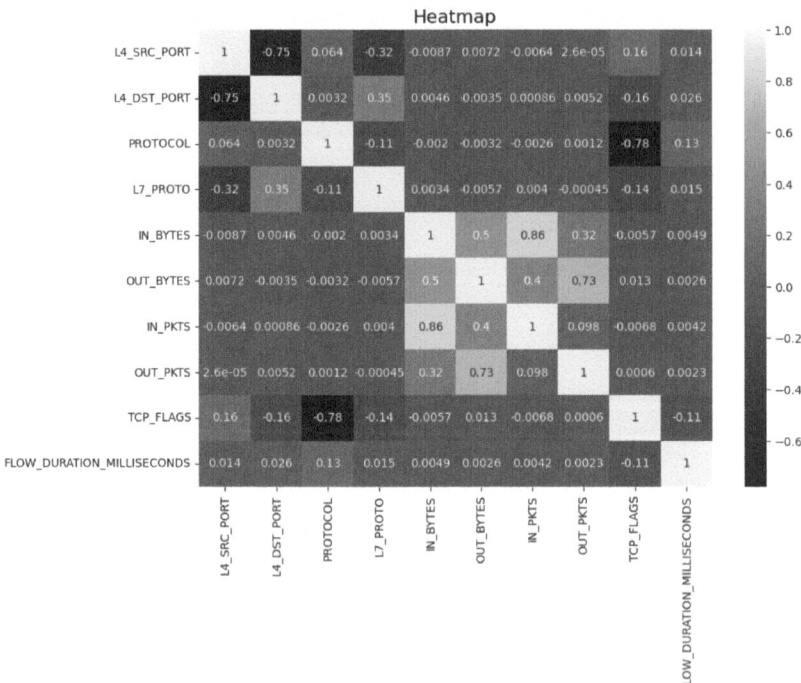

Fig. 6. Multi Collinearity Detection Heatmap

5 Conclusions

In conclusion, the adoption of ML techniques is revolutionizing cyber defense strategies against network attacks. Utilizing the NF-ToN-IoT dataset and DL techniques, this research focuses on threat mitigation by developing an MLP-based model capable of identifying various attacks on organizational networks, thereby safeguarding sensitive information. The results demonstrate the robustness of the MLP model, achieving over 90% accuracy in both the training and validation phases. Future work will explore additional datasets to further assess the model's generalizability and performance. Comparative analysis of different datasets will be a critical next step in evaluating the overall robustness and adaptability of the model to diverse threat landscapes.

Acknowledgment. This research is based upon work supported by the ONR (Award No. N00014–22-1-2724). The views and conclusions contained herein are those of the authors and should not be interpreted as necessarily representing the official policies or endorsements, either expressed or implied, of the U.S. Government.

References

1. Imamverdiyev, Y., Abdullayeva, F.: Deep learning in cybersecurity: challenges and approaches. Int. J. Cyber Warfare Terror. **10**(2), 82–105 (2020)
2. Fernando, J., Rendon-Segador, Juan, A., Alvarez-Garcia, A.J.V.V.: Paying attention to cyberattacks: a multi-layer percepton with self-attention mechanism. Comput. Secur. **32** (2023)
3. Sarhan, M., Layeghy, S., Moustafa, N., Portmann, M.: NetFlow datasets for machine learning-based network intrusion detection systems. In: Deze, Z., Huang, H., Hou, R., Rho, S., Chilamkurti, N. (eds.) Big Data Technologies and Applications. BDTA WiCON 2020. Lecture Notes of the Institute for Computer Sciences, Social Informatics and Telecommunications Engineering. vol. 371. Springer, Cham (2021). https://staff.itee.uq.edu.au/marius/NIDS_data sets/
4. Ahmed, S., et al.: Effective and efficient DDoS attack detection using deep learning algorithm, multi-layer perceptron. Future Internet **15**(2), 76 (2023)
5. Althamir, M.A., Boodai, J.Z., Hafizur Rahman, M.M.: A mini literature review on challenges and opportunities in threat intelligence. In: 2023 International Conference on Artificial Intelligence in Information and Communication (ICAIIC), Bali, pp. 558–563 (2023)
6. Sarhan, M., Layeghy, S., Portmann, M.: Towards a standard feature set for network intrusion detection system datasets. Mob. Netw. Appl. **103**, 108379 (2022)
7. Ring, M., Wunderlich, S., Scheuring, D., Landes, D., Hotho, A.: A survey of network-based intrusion detection data sets. Comput. Secur. **86**, 147–167 (2019)
8. Agarap, A.F.: Deep learning using rectified linear units (ReLU). arXiv preprint arXiv:1803.08375 (2018)

Harnessing Social Robotics and the Internet of Things to Reduce the Risk of Older Adults Developing Hypothermia and Dehydration

Hani Sindi[1,2(✉)] and Rachel McCrindle[2]

[1] Biomedical Engineering, University of Reading, Reading, UK
h.sindi@pgr.reading.ac.uk
[2] Information Technology Department, Faculty of Computing and Information Technology,
King Abdulaziz University, Jeddah, Saudi Arabia
r.j.mccrindle@reading.ac.uk

Abstract. Many older adults are at risk of developing hypothermia or becoming dehydrated, both of which can be dangerous conditions requiring hospitalization. This paper describes the development and evaluation of a novel support system, Hypothermia and Dehydration Advising Companion (HyDeAdCo), that integrates a social robot with off-the-shelf technologies within an IoT infrastructure, to help reduce the risk of older adults becoming hypothermic or dehydrated.

Keywords: dehydration · hypothermia · internet-of-things · social robots · older adults

1 Introduction

Hypothermia and dehydration are two conditions that pose significant risks to older adults which if left undetected may result in hospitalization [1]. For example, studies have shown that dehydration, which occurs when the body loses more fluid than it takes in, resulting in an upset to the balance of the minerals required for the body to carry out its normal functions [2], is prevalent in 20% of older adults living independently in the community [3] and in 40% of older adults admitted to hospital [4]. Hypothermia, which occurs when core body temperature drops below 35 ^{0}C (95 ^{0}F) [5–8] is common in the older population but whilst associated with substantial morbidity and frailty is to some extent preventable if caregivers can adopt preventative measures to lower its occurrence [9]. Preventative measures such as wearing warm clothing, maintaining indoor temperatures, staying active and ensuring adequate nutrition and hydration are important in reducing the risk of hypothermia in older adults. These conditions may be exasperated by physiological changes during the ageing process, the onset of long term conditions, limited mobility, as well as social issues such as loneliness, and financial hardship. For example some older adults may face 'heat or eat' dilemmas [10–13], some

This research was funded by King Abdulaziz University, Saudi Arabia.

will be housebound due to limited mobility, and others may lack regular visitors such that making a cup of tea 'just for themselves' becomes less of a priority [1, 14, 15]. By helping older adults to understand the severity of these conditions and the underlying causes of them, unobtrusively monitoring them in their homes using simple and affordable technology and advising them on actions to take based on the data obtained it may be possible to reduce the risk of them developing hypothermia or becoming dehydrated. Internet of Things technology incorporating sensors, real-time detection and alerts, and simple interactions with the user offer enormous potential to reduce the incidence of hypothermia and dehydration in older adults.

2 Background

Ambient Intelligent (AmI) systems enhance the way people interact with their environment through real-time information gathered from sensors and devices interconnected through a network and the accumulation of historic data [16]. When such systems are used to assist older adults to live independently this is frequently referred to as Ambient Assisted Living (AAL) [17, 18]. AAL systems should be user friendly, easy to use, user specific [19] and able to track in real-time an older person's environment as well as their particular behaviours and health related characteristics, with the system triggering alerts based on registered events. AAL is most effective when tailored to be user specific inside their house or environment [20].

A number of projects have been undertaken to monitor the hydration status or water intake of individuals including the use of smart bottles, throat microphones; kinetic movements; urine colour [21] and AR/QR codes with gamification to detect drinking events [22–26]. IoT systems that target body temperature monitoring, include the Vivago WristCare [27], Honeywell HomMed devices [28] and flexible sensors embedded in clothing that continuously monitor body temperature and environmental conditions [29]. A range of comprehensive smart home platforms that support Ambient Assisted Living (AAL) have also been developed including those of SPHERE [30], CAALYX [31], Casattenta [32] and TAFETA [33] which whilst they may monitor temperature and other vital signs are not developed specifically to address hypothermia and dehydration.

The aim of this paper is to describe an integrated yet simple and targeted AAL support system, HyDeAdCo (Hypothermia and Dehydration Advising Companion), that integrates current smart sensors and devices within an IoT infrastructure to specifically target the reduction of hypothermia and dehydration among older adults.

3 $H_Y D_E A_D C_O$ Framework

The HyDeAdCo IoT system uses a COTS (Components-off-the-shelf) based approach in order that readily available devices and sensors can be bought over the counter and integrated into the system through a plug-and-play interface, thereby enabling HyDeAdCo to have lower setup costs and higher personalization compared to many other AAL systems as different sensors and devices can be selected according to a person's medical, lifestyle and financial circumstances. As part of the COTS approach, HyDeAdCo uses, the commercially available Temi service robot as a natural language interface to the system and as a companion element of the system offering advice related to reducing the risk of developing hypothermia and dehydration. As such, the key features of the HyDeAdCo system are that it is:

- Targeted on reducing the risk of older people developing hypothermia or becoming dehydrated rather than on identifying the occurrence of falls or on monitoring long-term health conditions more generally.
- A monitoring system to detect any issues that might indicate a person is at risk of developing hypothermia or becoming dehydrated, as well as an advice system to help inform people about actions they can take to help prevent the onset of risk situations. The system also helps to alleviate loneliness by acting as a way of connecting the user with their friends and family through a video calling facility so that they might have a chat or enjoy a cup of tea together.
- Made as affordable, accessible, and personalized as possible though the use of COTS, rather than bespoke or single manufacturer components, in order that the number of devices integrated, and the cost of devices selected can reflect the users budget, needs and any devices they may already own.
- Able to be extended through the API (Application Programming Interface) as sensors develop and new devices come onto the market, or to accommodate changes in users financial, lifestyle or health needs.
- Easy to set up within a home or other care environment by a care giver or other family member with basic knowledge of smart devices centred on the current trend for home-based smart devices controlled by cloud-based voice services such as Alexa [34] and Google Home [35].
- Easy to use without requiring any technological experience or expertise via voice commands and responses with the human-system interaction being provided by the natural language interface of a social robot such as Temi [36].

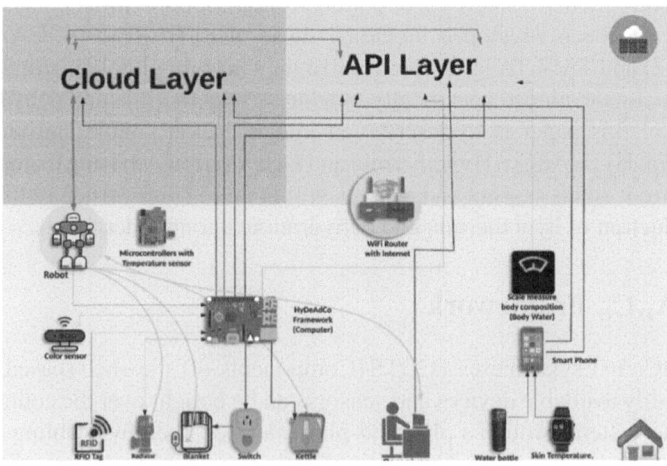

Fig. 1. Details of the HyDeAdCo Architecture and Components

- Able to visually show real-time data recorded from the sensors and devices on a single dashboard or with more detail on a computer screen, TV or smartphone app. The user may elect whether to see this data and it may if consented be viewed by or shared with a care giver, friends, or family.
- Offers reassurance that should the recorded data indicate that a person might be at increased risk of developing hypothermia or becoming dehydrated then increasing levels of alerts can be sent, firstly to the older person themselves so that they or the system can take some corrective action; then if there is continued cause for concern to a nominated care giver or family member; and finally, to the emergency services if a person become unresponsive for a prolonged and defined period of time.

These features are provided through a three-layered architecture – (A) the cloud-based layer, (B) the Application Programming Interface (API) layer, and (C) the local devices layer which includes a social robot as shown in Fig. 1.

3.1 Cloud Layer

The cloud layer is responsible for the storage, processing, analysis, and visualization of the data collected from the devices and sensors. As such it acts as the database for temperature, humidity, water consumption and other readings. Additionally, it is has been used to construct the conversational app installed in the companion robot, and to promote on/off action execution and notifications and alerts. Data stored in the cloud is utilized through a website to create the graphs and gauges of the monitoring feature.

3.2 API Layer

The API layer has a number of functions including collecting data from sensors and COTS devices such as those used to measure temperature, humidity, water consumption, body water percentage and pulse rate etc. which it then sends to the cloud-based layer where the data is stored, processed and aggregated so that decisions can be made and sent back to the local devices layer in the form of advice to the user or text notifications to care givers and family members. The API is also used to synchronize with the smart device apps for example those of smart bottle, smart plugs and HVAC (heating, ventilation and air conditioning) devices.

3.3 Local Device Layer

This layer includes the commercial off-the-shelf (COTS) devices that are used by the older adults either directly or via Temi, a social robot, that forms the natural language interface between the system and the user. The integrated devices have been selected based on being easy to use, affordable, personalized and having some part to play in reducing the risk of an older adult developing hypothermia or becoming dehydrated. The addition or removal of any device is based on users preferences, changing needs or new relevant smart devices coming onto the market. Aside from basic set-up many of the COTS components can be used in a turnkey manner, although a few are connected to the API and cloud layers via Raspberry Pi or Arduino microcontrollers. Sensors and devices within the HyDeAdCo system might include:

- Smartphone: keeps track of hydration and temperature conditions to predicts early stage of dehydration. Connects via Bluetooth to APIs of other devices such as smart bottle and health watch to sync and upload data and send messages to friends and family.
- Smart bottle: keeps track of water intake to improve frequency of drinking water or other fluids.
- Health sensor watch: takes skin temperature and pulse readings to help predict occurrence of hypothermia
- Temperature and humidity sensors: monitors temperature and humidity of bedrooms, bathroom, living room and under blankets.
- Smart scales: keeps track of percentage body water content and informs users/care givers if readings fall below a norm
- Smart plugs: turns on devices such as the kettle (increase fluid intake) and electronic blanket (increase warmth)
- Smart radiator and AC thermostats: maintains ideal indoor temperature of the home.
- Motion sensor (Kinect): tracks body movements to detect drinking motion, if a person has not moved for a long period of time, or if they are horizontal in an unexpected part of the home.
- Colour sensor: detects the early stages of dehydration based on urine colour
- Flush sensor: counts times the toilet is flushed as a potential risk indicator of dehydration.
- Thermal camera: checks body temperature and environment for example to identify home energy leakage.
- RFID positioning: used to map, track and time where a user spends most time indoors and detects abnormal patterns.
- Chatbot: sends alerts to the older adult suggesting actions to take, or to their care giver/family members should abnormal patterns or risk factors associated with dehydration or hypothermia be identified. Also enables family members/caregivers to ask the Bot rather than the elderly person about the amount they have drunk, their current location, the temperature of their home and their body temperature. In extreme circumstances can contact emergency services.
- Voice recognition (Alexa and Google Home): keeps track of status updates regarding hydration and temperature data and encourages users to improve their fluid intake. Informs the older adult and then caregivers if there is an oncoming risk related to dehydration or hypothermia. Accepts voice command to retrieve information or make voice in/out calls. Works in conjunction with the Temi robot.
- Raspberry Pi: Acts as the main 'brain' for the HyDeAdCo system connecting to all components and the API.
- Device APIs (Fitbit, Withings, Google Cloud etc.): enables exchange of data between layers of the system, the sensors and devices and the user.

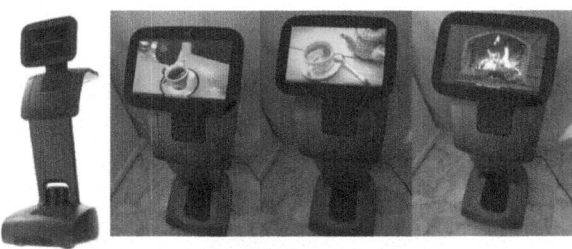

Fig. 2. Tēmi social robot

3.4   Social Robot Interface

A key component of the HyDeAdCo system is Temi (see Fig. 2), a 3-foot high commercially available off-the-shelf social robot supplied with a developer SDK [41]. Temi performs several very important functions (1) it acts as a friendly natural language interface between the person and the system using voice to speak with the user and to take their responses; (2) it helps to reinforce the importance of keeping warm and hydrated through daily advice messages and alerts as well as showing appropriate images, animations and videos via its screen; (3) it can entertain by showing videos or playing music or by calling a friend or family member so that a cup of tea can be shared virtually helping to both reduce loneliness and to encourage fluid consumption; and (4) if a person becomes unresponsive for a long period of time or abnormal sensor readings are detected Temi can instigate messages or calls at the appropriate level (personal, family, emergency services).

4   Example $H_Y D_E A_D C_O$ Scenario

The HyDeAdCo system can be set up in a person's home such that it is tailored to an individuals' needs and conditions. In this paper we consider two example scenarios Hannah and Michael. Hannah is 70 years old, has type one diabetes and thyroid issues and is regarded as being at high risk of developing hypothermia. Hannah lives independently but has a daughter living close by. Michael is 85 years old with a history of hospitalizations for kidney stones. Michael tends to become dehydrated as he does not consume enough water during the day, although he does enjoy drinking coffee in moderation and eating fruits high in water content such as strawberries, watermelons and cantaloup melons. He lives alone and is tech savvy and loves to interact with people including his friends and children.

In Hannah's case emphasis is placed on lowering the risk of her developing hypothermia with the key components in her HyDeAdCo system including as shown in Fig. 3:

- Social Robot (Tēmi)
- Smartphone (CAT S61 with Android OS)
- Smart watch (MAXREFDES101# health platform)
- E-Switch (Energenie)

- Electric kettle (Russell Hobbs 21600)
- Heated blanket (Pifco PE109)
- Electric heater via infrared (Broadlink RM Mini 3)
- Arduino with DHT11 sensor

Fig. 3. Social robot, smartphone, smart watch, E-Switch, E-Kettle, heated blanket, infrared device and Arduino with DHT11 sensor

These devices work together within the IoT framework to monitor and advise Hannah on how warm throughout the day. For example, the smartwatch (MAXREFDES101#) will monitor her body temperature every 5 min (Fig. 4). The resulting real-time data is sent to her smartphone (CAT S61-Android OS), and subsequently exported from the smartphone to Google Cloud where the data is stored in a Google Sheet (Fig. 5).

C	B	A	
Temperature (°C)	Sample Count	Time	1
35.56	0	19:09.5	2
35.56	1	19:10.0	3
35.55	2	19:10.5	4
35.57	3	19:11.0	5
35.56	4	19:11.5	6

Fig. 4. Data exported from Smart watch MAXREFDES101# health platform

If Hannah's temperature drops below 36°, the system notifies her via Alexa and/or her Temi robot (equipped with built-in Alexa) (Fig. 6). Communication with both Alexa device and Temi is achieved via a Raspberry Pi 3 utilizing the Alexa Skills Kit (ASK) via the internet.

HyDeAdCo will recommend to Hannah that she has something hot to drink such as tea or coffee (Fig. 7, 8). If Hannah agrees to this then the electric kettle (Russell Hobbs 21600) is turned on via an e-Switch (Energenie) and MiHome gateway connection between Alexa and the e-Switch. These actions can be programmed into HyDeAdCo via the Temi Centre which enables actions, interactions and dialogues to be programmed, including the option of using speech, images and video as a means of interaction.

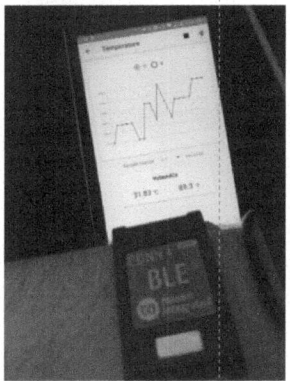

Fig. 5. Sending skin body temperature from smart watch to Anderiod app

```
1.  MAXREFDES101# measures body temperature
2.  MAXREFDES101# sends body temperature data
    to CAT S61(Android OS)
3.  CAT S61 sends body temperature data to
    Google Sheet (Google Cloud)
4.  Raspberry Pi (HyDeAdCo Processor) imports
    body temperature data from Google Sheet
    (Google Cloud)
5.  Raspberry Pi (HyDeAdCo Processor) checks
    body temperature data every 5 minutes
6.  If <36
7.  Raspberry Pi (HyDeAdCo Prcessor) activates
    specific pre-programmed functions (stored
    in semi center) via temi SDK
8.  Pre-programmed functions sequenced as per
    the following:
9.      1st TeaTime(),
10.     2nd Blanket(),
11.     3rd Clothes(),
12.     4th ShowerTime(),
13.     5th Heater()
```

Fig. 6. HyDeAdCo action plan once body temperature drop below 36°

If Hannah does not want to drink something hot, HyDeAdCo will ask her if she would prefer a heated blanket; if Hannah agrees, Alexa sends a signal via the ZigBee protocol

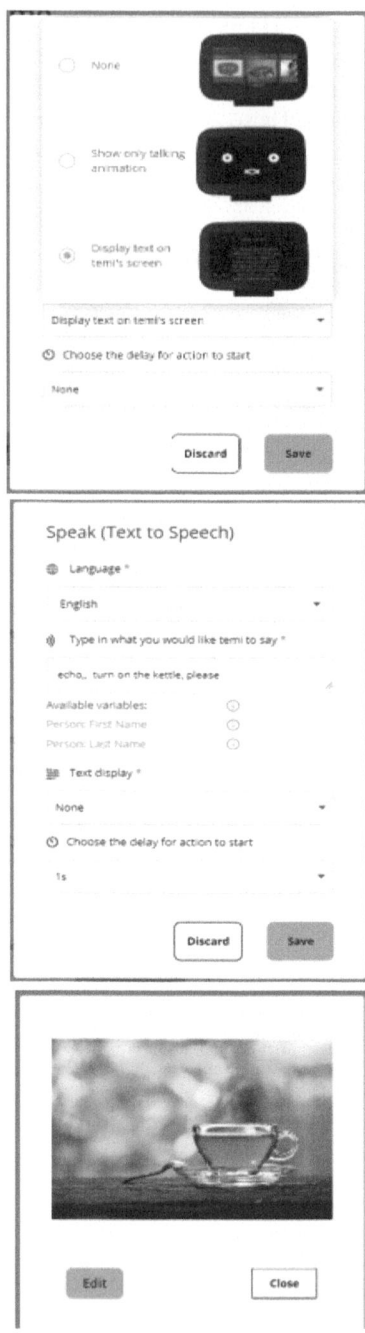

Fig. 7. TeaTime(). A, tēmi interface options. B, tēmi message for echo. C, Displayed image.

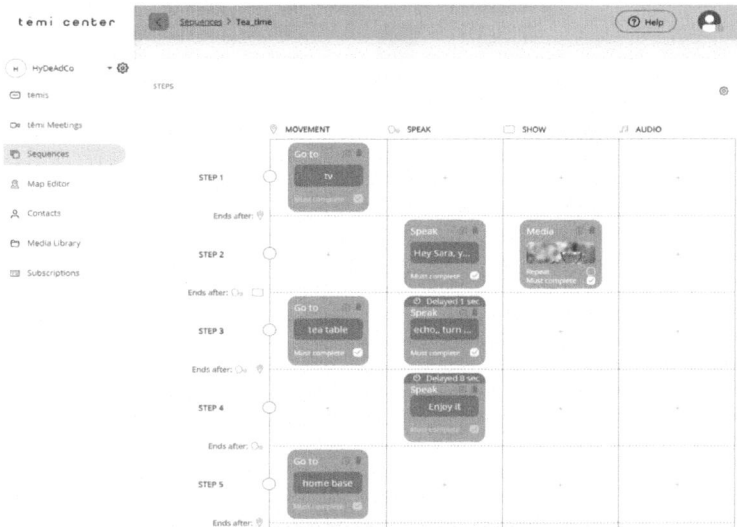

Fig. 8. TeaTime() sequence in tēmi center

to the MiHome gateway connection between Alexa and the e-Switch (Energenie) which is utilized to heat the blanket. If Hannah does not want to use the electrical blanket, other options include asking Hannah if she would like to put on a jumper or take a hot bath or shower. If her temperature remains low then HyDeAdCo can automatically turn on the heater using Alexa Skills Kit (ASK) via the internet. Should her monitored temperature drop below 35 degrees then the health service or family member can be contacted so that they can check on Hannah (Fig. 9).

There are also external sensors (DHT11) that can monitor the temperature of Hannah's home and which will alert her should it fall below a certain threshold (e.g. 25 °C). In a similar process to that described above data from the DHT11 is sent via an Arduino to the Google Sheet Spreadsheet API (Google Cloud). Communication with both the Alexa device and Temi is achieved via a Raspberry Pi 3 utilizing the Alexa Skills Kit (ASK) via the internet to wear warm clothes and drink hot fluids. Hannah's daughter will also receive constant notification via Telegram Bot.

In Michael's case the HyDeAdCo System technology utilises similar protocols but the personalized emphasis for Michael is on monitoring his hydration status and on encouraging him to drink more frequently throughout the day for example by:

- Tracking his fluid intake via a H2OPal smart-bottle, using Bluetooth to communicate with an App on his smartphone (Android and iOS), that uses a Fitbit API to uploads his fluid intake for storage and processing in the Google Cloud.
- HyDeAdCo periodically reminding Michael of his hydration status and encouraging him to drink more throughout the day or to eat high water content food.
- Sending notifications to members of his family should his fluid intake drop off so that they can remind him about the need of drinking water (Fig. 10).
- Encouraging him to contact his friend so that they can share a real or virtual coffee break together.

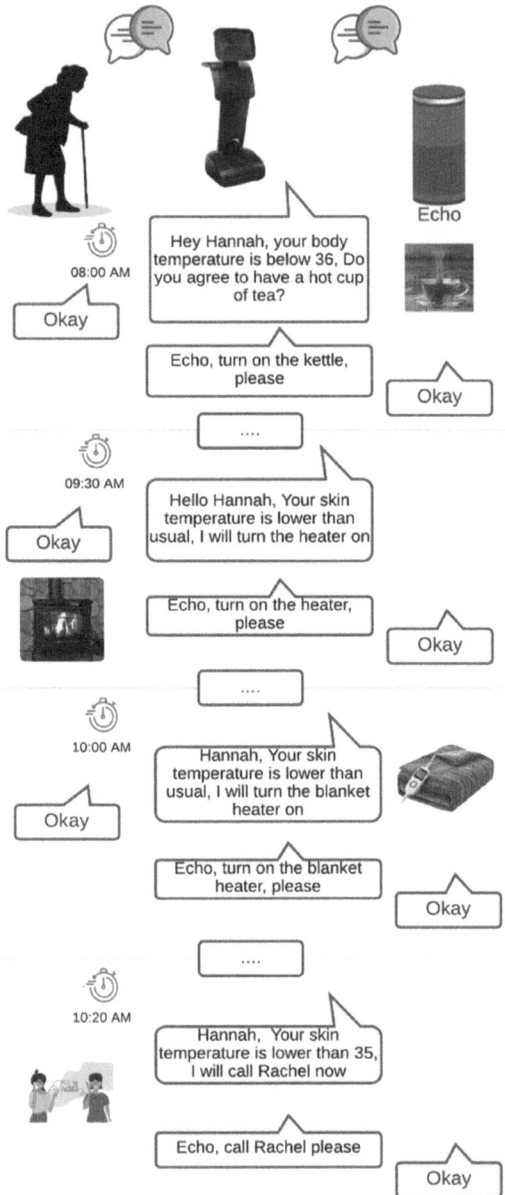

Fig. 9. Sample interaction between Temi and Hannah

- Contacting family and potentially emergency services should there be a prolonged lack of response to Temi's questions. An example dialogue is shown in Fig. 11.

In both scenarios data recorded for each of the sensors is processed, aggregated in the cloud with other data sets and compared to historic norms to influence the response and

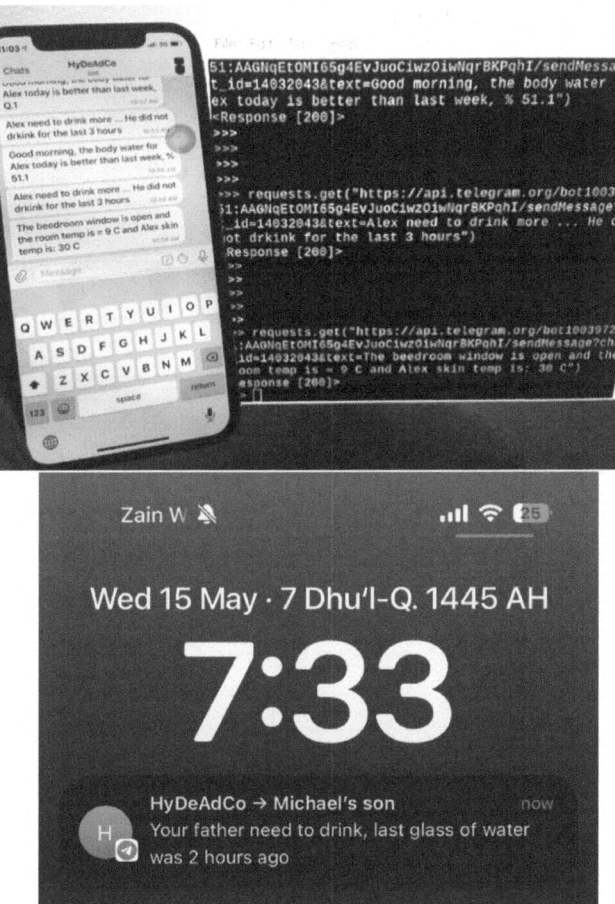

Fig. 10. Telegram Bot

prompts delivered by Temi. This data may be viewed on the overall system dashboard by the users themselves, or more likely viewed by a family member of caregiver (locally or remotely) on their computer, television, or phone. Figure 12 shows an example of the real-time data dashboard, whilst Figs. 13 and 14 show some of the more detailed historical data related to time spent in different rooms of the house, number of toilet flushes, when fluid intake occurred and body temperature.

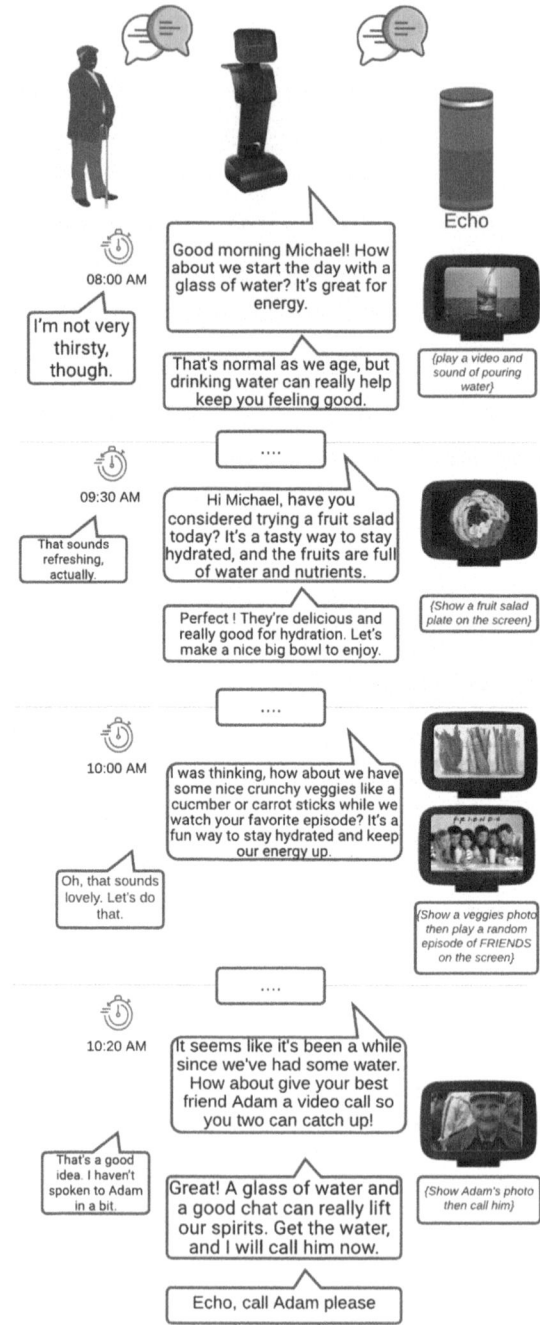

Fig. 11. Sample interaction between Temi and Micheal

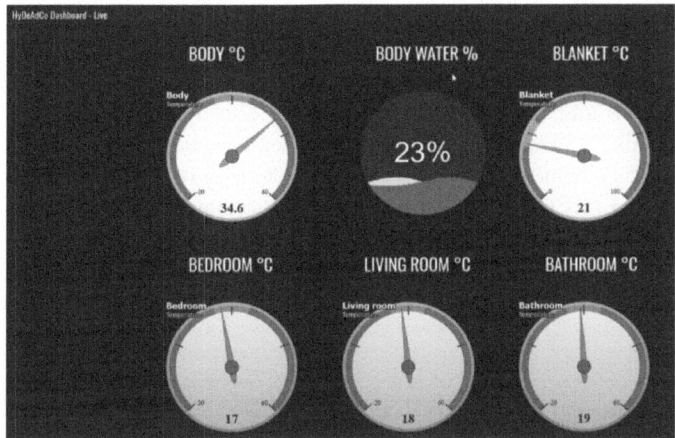

Fig. 12. Sample of HyDeAdCo main dashboard

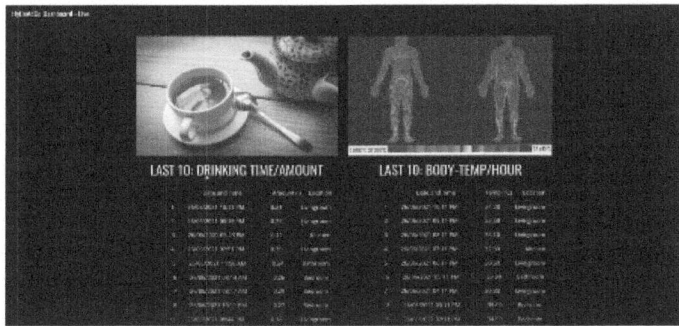

Fig. 13. Sample of room duration and toilet flush

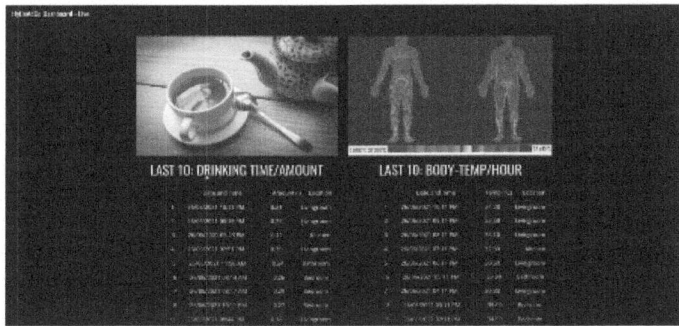

Fig. 14. Sample of drinking time and body temperature

5   Evaluation

HyDeAdCo (Hypothermia and Dehydration Advising Companion) is a prototype proof of concept system and as such has not yet been able to be installed and evaluated within individuals' homes. The concept and its features have however been evaluated through technology demonstrations, by showing videos of usage scenarios similar to those described in this paper, and through a questionnaire. Of the 21 respondents 15 (71.4%) were aged 65 and above and hence firmly in the target age demographic. There is not space in this paper to present the entire set of questionnaire results but those pertaining to the installation and features of HyDeAdCo are included and shown in Tables 1 and 2.

Table 1. Results from 21 respondents about their perceived importance of system installation

	Very useful No. (%)	Somewhat useful No. (%)	Not useful No. (%)	Not sure No. (%)
Use of readily available and low-cost components purchased online or in stores	15 (71.4)	5 (23.8)	1 (4.8)	0 (0.0)
Adapted to fit an individual's needs and lifestyle	14 (66.7)	4 (19.0)	2 (9.5)	1 (4.8)
Easily changed or extended with new applications and devices as a person's needs change	15 (71.4)	6 (28.6)	0 (0.0)	0 (0.0)
Use components from a range of manufacturers	15 (71.4)	5 (23.8)	1 (4.8)	0 (0.0)
Easily installed in a person's home without the need for any structural change or rewiring	15 (71.4)	5 (23.8)	1 (4.8)	0 (0.0)
Easy to use by people with little experience of using technology	18 (85.7)	2 (9.5)	1 (4.8)	0 (0.0)

With regards to the HyDeAdCo making use of a readily available and low cost components that can be purchased across a range of stores and updated as technology or an individual's needs change, responses were very positive being over 85% (18–20 respondents) in the 'very useful'/'somewhat useful' categories for all questions. The importance of HyDeAdCo being able to be used by people with little experience of using technology received the most 'very useful' scores with 18 out of 21 respondents selecting this.

With regards to the perceived usefulness of the features incorporated in HyDeAdCo if it were to be installed in their homes, again feedback was predominately very positive with responses being above 85% (at least 18 out of the 21 respondents) in the 'very useful'/'somewhat useful' categories and at least 14 selecting the 'very useful' category for each feature.

Some respondents voiced concerns about the risk of the Temi robot catching fire; about the robot being damaged during use; about being electrocuted by the electric blanket; the unfamiliarity of talking with a robot; high cost of purchasing the robot and

Table 2. Results from 21 respondents about how useful they thought features of the HyDeAdCo system are

	Very useful No. (%)	Somewhat useful No. (%)	Not useful No. (%)	Not sure No. (%)
Give daily tips on how to reduce risk of developing hypothermia or dehydration	15 (71.4)	5 (23.8)	1 (4.8)	0 (0.0)
Ask a person how they are feeling on a particular day and adapt its responses accordingly	14 (66.7)	4 (19.0)	2 (9.5)	1 (4.8)
Warn a person if their body temperature becomes too low and they need to act	15 (71.4)	6 (28.6)	0 (0.0)	0 (0.0)
Let a person know if they need to drink more water or take other action to avoid the risk of dehydration	15 (71.4)	5 (23.8)	1 (4.8)	0 (0.0)
Interact with a person through voice interface	15 (71.4)	5 (23.8)	1 (4.8)	0 (0.0)
Set up a video call with a friend/relative	18 (85.7)	2 (9.5)	1 (4.8)	0 (0.0)
Play a person's favourite music or TV programmes	18 (85.7)	2 (9.5)	1 (4.8)	0 (0.0)
Automatically call a friend/relative if a person appears to be at risk of dehydration or hypothermia	15 (71.4)	4 (19.0)	2 (9.5)	0 (0.0)
Automatically call emergency services if a person becomes unresponsive	20 (95.2)	1 (4.8)	0 (0.0)	0 (0.0)
Maintain a record of the sensor data	20 (95.2)	1 (4.8)	0 (0.0)	0 (0.0)
Visually display the sensor data if requested	16 (76.2)	5 (23.8)	0 (0.0)	0 (0.0)
Have a social robot chat with you and ask you questions about your needs and wants	15 (71.4)	4 (19.0)	2 (9.5)	0 (0.0)

its need for maintenance; loss of privacy; and of cyber security and camera footage data being leaked.

6 Summary

This paper has described the HyDeAdCo AAL support system, that integrates current smart sensors and devices within an IoT infrastructure to specifically target the reduction of hypothermia and dehydration among older adults. It should be noted that this is a technology driven project, with the focus being on developing a technology infrastructure and prototype demonstrator that can advise and support older adults to reduce their risk of becoming dehydrated or hypothermic, rather than a clinically focused project that aims to detect when a person is dehydrated or hypothermic. This paper describes the concept of the HyDeAdCo system and shows images taken from the prototype system which has undergone evaluation with an older adult user group.

Although this was a relatively small evaluation group it is encouraging to see the potential acceptance of a system such as HyDeAdCo to help reduce the risk of older adults developing hypothermia or becoming dehydrated. Based on their feedback the HyDeAdCo system will be updated to reflect their opinions.

Areas of future work also include translation of the voice recognition and responses to other languages including Arabic as well as further investigation into whether the system can in practice reduce hypothermia and dehydration from occurring, a study, that is outside the scope of this PhD project.

Acknowledgment. We would like to thank the King Abdulaziz University, Saudi Arabia who funded this work through a PhD scholarship to Hani Sindi.

References

1. NHS Digital, Hospital Episode Statistics (HES) (2012–2017)
2. NHS inform. Dehydration (2021). https://www.nhsinform.scot/illnesses-and-conditions/nutritional/dehydration. Accessed 12 July 2021
3. Hooper, L., Bunn, D.K., et al.: Water-loss (intracellular) dehydration assessed using urinary tests: how well do theu work? Diagnostic accuracy in older people. Am. J. Clin. Nutr. **104**(1), 121–131 (2016)
4. Fortes, M.B., Owen, J.A., et al.: Is this elderly patient dehydrated? Diagnostic accuracy of hydration assessment using physical signs, urine, and saliva markers. J. Am. Med. Dir. Assoc. **16**(3), 221–228 (2015)
5. Herity, B., Daly, L., Bourke, G.J., Horgan, J.M.: Hypothermia and mortality and morbidity. An epidemiological analysis. J. Epidemiol. Commun. Health **45**(1), 19–23 (1991)
6. Taylor, N., Griffiths, R., Cotter, J.: Epidemiology of hypothermia: fatalities and hospitalisations in New Zealand. Aust. N. Z. J. Med. **24**(6), 705–710 (1994)
7. Gross, C.R., Lindquist, R.D., Woolley, A.C., Granieri, R., Allard, K., Webster, B.: Clinical indicators of dehydration severity in elderly patients. J. Emerg. Med. **10**(3), 267–274 (1992)
8. MedlinePlus. Dehydration. 2021 (2016). https://medlineplus.gov/dehydration.html. Accessed 12 July 2021
9. Dharmarajan, T.S., Widjaja, D.: Hypothermia in the geriatric population. Aging Health **3**(6) (2007)
10. Beatty, T.K.M., Blow, L., Crossley, T.F.: Is there a 'heat-or-eat' trade-off in the UK? J. Roy. Stat. Soc. Ser. A (Stat. Soc.) **177**(1), 281–294 (2014). http://www.jstor.org/stable/43965682
11. Eurostat. People in the EU - statistics on an ageing society 2017. https://ec.europa.eu/eurostat/statistics-explained/index.php?oldid=408420. Accessed 04 Dec 2019
12. Office for National Statistics, Overview of the UK population (2017)
13. Age UK, Later Life in the United Kingdom (2018)
14. Amarya, S., Singh, K., Sabharwal, M.: Changes during aging and their association with malnutrition. J. Clin. Gerontol. Geriatr. **6**(3), 78–846 (2015)
15. Clegg, M.E., Williams, E.A.: Optimizing nutrition in older people. Maturitas **112**, 34–38 (2018)
16. Augusto, J.C., McCullagh, P.: Ambient Intelligence: concepts and applications. Comput. Sci. Inf. Syst. **4**, 1–27 (2007)
17. Memon, M., Wagner, S., Pedersen, C., Beevi, F., Hansen, F.: Ambient assisted living healthcare frameworks, platforms, standards, and quality attributes. Sensors **14**(3), 4312–4341 (2014)
18. Calvaresi, D., Cesarini, D., Sernani, P., Marinoni, M., Dragoni, A.F., Sturm, A.: Exploring the ambient assisted living domain: a systematic review. J. Ambient. Intell. Humaniz. Comput. **8**(2), 239–257 (2017)

19. Caballero-Gil, P., Georgieva, L., Brankovic, L., Burmester, M.: Ambient assisted living and ambient intelligence for health. Mob. Inf. Syst. **2018**, 7560465 (2018)
20. Gomez-Donoso, F., Escalona, F., Rivas, F.M., Cañas, J.M., Cazorla, M.: Enhancing the ambient assisted living capabilities with a mobile robot. Comput. Intell. Neurosci. **2019**, 9412384 (2019)
21. Gunawan, A.A.S., Brandon, D., Puspa, V.D., Wiweko, B.: Development of urine hydration system based on urine color and support vector machine. Procedia Comput. Sci. **135**, 481–489 (2018)
22. Jovanov, E., Nallathimmareddygari, V.R., Pryor, J.E.: SmartStuff: a case study of a smart water bottle. In: 2016 38th Annual International Conference of the IEEE Engineering in Medicine and Biology Society (EMBC). IEEE (2016)
23. Pankajavalli, P.B., Saikumar, R., Maheswaran, R.: Hydration reminding smart bottle: IoT experimentation. In: 2017 Innovations in Power and Advanced Computing Technologies (i-PACT) (2017)
24. Mengistu, Y., Pham, M., Do, H.M., Sheng, W.: AutoHydrate: a wearable hydration monitoring system. In: 2016 IEEE/RSJ International Conference on Intelligent Robots and Systems (IROS) (2016)
25. Cebanov, E., Dobre, C., Gradinaru, A., Ciobanu, R., Stanciu, V.: Activity recognition for ambient assisted living using off-the-shelf motion sensing input devices. In: 2019 Global IoT Summit (GIoTS) (2019)
26. Lehman, S., Graves, J., Mcaleer, C., Giovannetti, T., Tan, C.C.: A Mobile Augmented Reality Game to Encourage Hydration in the Elderly. Springer, Cham (2018)
27. Lötjönen, J., Korhonen, I., Hirvonen, K., Eskelinen, S., Myllymäki, M., Partinen, M.: Automatic sleep-wake and nap analysis with a new wrist worn online activity monitoring device vivago WristCare. Sleep **26**(1), 86–90 (2003)
28. Bal, M., Shen, W., Hao, Q., Xue, H.: Collaborative smart home technologies for senior independent living: a review. In: Proceedings of the 2011 15th International Conference on Computer Supported Cooperative Work in Design (CSCWD) (2011)
29. Khundaqji, H., Hing, W., Furness, J., Climstein, M.: Smart shirts for monitoring physiological parameters: scoping review. JMIR Mhealth Uhealth **8**(5), e18092 (2020)
30. Zhu, N., et al.: Bridging e-health and the internet of things: the SPHERE project. IEEE Intell. Syst. **30**(4), 39–46 (2015)
31. Rocha, A., Martins, A., Freire Junior, J.C., Kamel Boulos, M.N., Vicente, M.E., et al.: Innovations in health care services: the CAALYX system. Int. J. Med. Inform. **82**(11), e307-20 (2013)
32. Farella, E., Falavigna, M., Riccò, B.: Aware and smart environments: the Casattenta project. Microelectron. J. **41**, 697–702 (2010)
33. Arcelus, A., Jones, M.H., Goubran, R., Knoefel, F.: Integration of smart home technologies in a health monitoring system for the elderly. In: 21st International Conference on Advanced Information Networking and Applications Workshops (AINAW 2007) (2007)
34. Lit, Y., Kim, S., Sy, E.: A survey on Amazon Alexa attack surfaces. In: 2021 IEEE 18th Annual Consumer Communications & Networking Conference (CCNC) (2021)
35. Këpuska, V., Bohouta, G.: Next-generation of virtual personal assistants (Microsoft Cortana, Apple Siri, Amazon Alexa and Google Home). In: 2018 IEEE 8th Annual Computing and Communication Workshop and Conference (CCWC) (2018)
36. Temi Robot. Temi Robot Specs (2021). https://www.robotemi.com/specs/. Accessed 21 July 2021

Internet Computing and IoT (ICOMP) - Algorithms and Applications

Re/Imagining Smart Home Automation Framework in the Era of 6G-Enabled Smart Cities

Byungkwan Jung$^{(\boxtimes)}$ ⓘ, Suman Kumar ⓘ,
and Adityasinh Manthansinh Chauhan ⓘ

Troy University, Troy, AL 36082, USA
{bjung,skumar,achauhan200456}@troy.edu

Abstract. Smart home automation systems represent a seamless integration of Internet of Things technologies, facilitating the monitoring, management, and regulation of various aspects of our daily life. By leveraging advancements in communication, computing, sensing, and actuator technologies, they hold promises for enhancing the living experience. However, they face challenges such as the need for timely updates, efficient data management, real-time Big data processing, robust security measures, and advanced analytics. In this paper, we propose a novel framework that capitalizes on the capabilities of 6G networks and 6G-enabled cloud computing to address these challenges and improve the overall landscape of smart cities. This framework features enhanced security, data pre-processing, big data intelligence, and security service virtualization in the cloud. Through various application scenarios and a case study-focusing on safe routing during disasters, we demonstrate the utility of this framework and the critical role 6G networks and 6G-enabled cloud computing play in smart home automation.

Keywords: Machine Learning · Internet of Things (IoTs) · Cloud Computing · Network Security

1 Introduction and Motivation

Modern living has been rapidly evolving within our homes, where an array of electronic devices now seamlessly monitor, manage, and regulate various facets of our daily lives. Advancements in communication, sensing and actuator technologies are transforming these devices into Internet of Things (IoTs) collectively forming a home automation system [23], enriching the way we experience and interact with our living spaces. From controlling ambiance to ensuring security and efficiency in managing diverse home subsystems like refrigerators, trash cans, and even pet monitoring, these systems have evolved into intelligent, interconnected ecosystems, thanks to high-speed internet connectivity and cloud computing [2]. Continued advancements in smart home automation systems will undoubtedly unlock endless possibilities for enhancing our homes and ultimately

© The Author(s), under exclusive license to Springer Nature Switzerland AG 2025
H. R. Arabnia et al. (Eds.): CSCE 2024, CCIS 2260, pp. 137–150, 2025.
https://doi.org/10.1007/978-3-031-85923-6_11

improving our quality of life. However, limitations inherent in IoT devices with constrained storage and processing power, as well as the current state of network itself pose critical obstacles in the future evolution of Smart home automation systems.

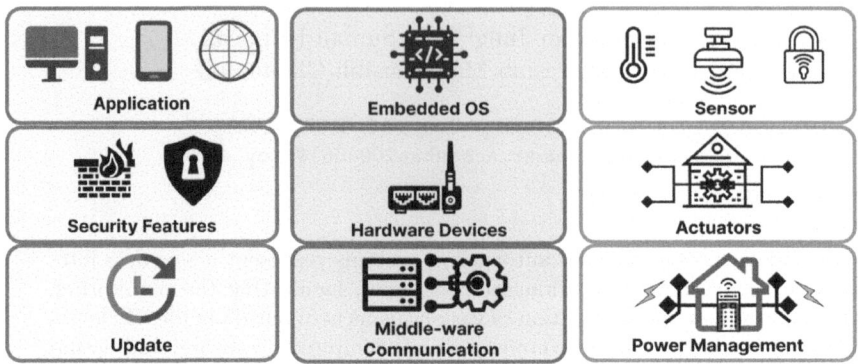

Fig. 1. State of Art HW/SW Architecture of IoT Devices.

The architecture of such devices (Fig. 1) typically includes IoT applications, security features, and update modules at the top layer. Beneath are embedded OS, hardware drivers, and middleware for communication. Sensors gather data, actuators respond to commands, communication modules enable data exchange, and power management regulates energy usage. However, because of resource limitations this framework struggle with handling big data efficiently, ensuring security against evolving threats, and managing updates effectively [13,14]. The dynamic landscape of security and privacy issues surrounding data sharing further complicates the challenge of harnessing collective data intelligence from smart homes, presenting a significant obstacle to realizing a truly responsive smart city ecosystem. These issues become more pronounced for real-time IoT devices which have stricter design constraints, with optimized operating systems, processors, and dedicated sensor interfaces. They often keep services on the device itself, as network latency becomes a critical bottleneck even with low-latency wireless protocols such as Zigbee and Z-wave. Furthermore, the outer network typically relies on legacy technologies like 4G and 5G, which suffer from latency and connection reliability issues.

There have been significant efforts to accommodate the growing number of IoT devices and their demanding applications [29]. The deployment of fifth-generation (5G) cellular technology has significantly enhanced network capacity and reduced latency compared to fourth-generation (4G) networks, leading to a surge in adoption of wireless devices. However, with the continuous influx of IoT devices into the network, the demand for capabilities such as massive data rates, ultra-low latency, enhanced computation power, scalability, and heightened security measures continues to escalate. The upcoming sixth-generation

(6G) technology aims to tackle these evolving demands through innovative concepts like swarm networks, self-sustained networks, and edge intelligence. With the integration of 6G-enabled cloud computing, the service burden will shift from application devices to virtualized infrastructure, offering greater flexibility and efficiency. Technologies such as big data intelligence, digital twins, and the ever expanding landscape of cloud-based services are reshaping the way we perceive, receive, and consume services. In this paper, we demonstrate how a 6G-enabled cloud coupled with 6G network effectively addresses the numerous challenges currently affecting smart home automation systems.

In this paper, a smart home framework that harnesses the capabilities of the 6G network and 6G-enabled cloud is presented. The framework enhances the spectrum of services offered to smart homes and smart city and also offloads as many tasks as possible to the cloud from IoT devices, thereby enabling the devices to perform minimal tasks. we demonstrate the framework through a case study: smart home automation systems computing real time safe routing in disaster situations. The proposed framework consisting of 5-layer service and infrastructure architecture for the cloud and a 4-layer IoT architecture for smart home side communicating over 6G networks includes the following features:

- Enhanced zero-day security and device auto-updates.
- Data pre-processing and advanced security services in the cloud utilizing the ultra low latency and high reliability features of 6G networks.
- Big data intelligence and analytics for secure and optimized operations.
- Dynamic management of security compliance landscape.
- IoT security services virtualizations in the cloud for efficient, flexible, and scalable secure smart home operations.

The paper is organized as follows: Sect. 2 presents background, challenges, opportunities and a brief past work. Our proposed novel smart home automation framework is presented in Sect. 3. Section 4 describes application scenarios and a case study illustrating safe routing in the even of disaster within our proposed framework. The paper concludes with possible future work in Sect. 5.

2   Background, Challenges, Opportunities, and Past Work

2.1   Smart Home Automation

Evolution. Figure 2 shows the evolution of Home automation system. In more recent decade, say 2000s, with the advent of wireless tech, basic control features like automated air conditioning and lighting emerged. However, not all devices in a home are managed by one interface yet. it is still isolated but connecting multiple home appliances [25]. As 4G and 5G technologies are introduced and IoTs are becomes a new trend, not only the home appliances but also other devices becomes a part of the devices managed by interfaces. With higher data rates and faster responses from low latency, more data throughput and diverse activities are in place. Home systems supporting voice over IP (VoIP), home security sensors, and smart lights and thermostats that can be managed by a individual remotely becomes common in many home system today. However, security and privacy concerns loom large, necessitating rigorous device interaction analysis for user safety [19]. Future smart homes, leveraging 6G, promise intelligent management and decision support via localized cloud services (edge intelligence), advancing towards all-in-one applications [4].

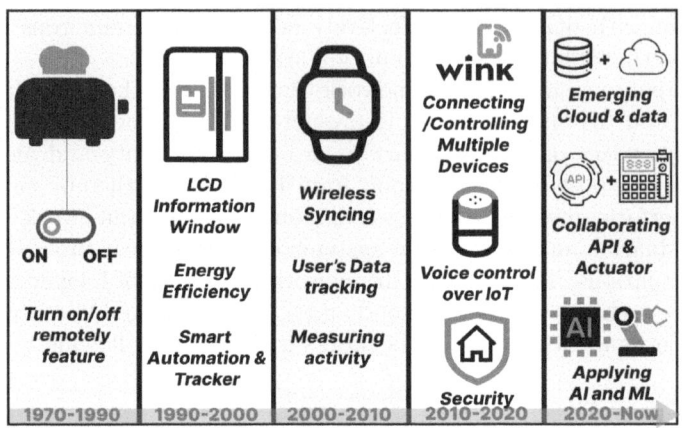

Fig. 2. Home Automation Evolution.

State of Art and Challenges

Update Mechanism: Smart home IoT devices often suffer from outdated software components, necessitating frequent and timely updates to mitigate vulnerabilities [21]. Many smart home IoT devices still rely on outdated and vulnerable software components, posing security risks.

Data Management: IoT systems in smart homes generate vast amounts of data crucial for improving customer experience and system monitoring [28]. The influx of data from IoT devices can overwhelm traditional data management systems, necessitating efficient data comparison, storage optimization, and processing techniques.

Real Time Data Processing and Decision Making: Authenticated data transfer methods facilitate real-time data processing between IoT devices and the cloud, enhancing smart home IoT capabilities [5]. However, large volumes of real-time data can lead to bottlenecks and delays, hindering timely decision-making and system responsiveness.

Security Measures: Securing cloud-based IoT involves implementing encryption, firewalls, secure communication protocols, multi-factor authentication, and secure data storage techniques [18]. These remain major concerns in smart home automation systems, with potential vulnerabilities in communication protocols, firmware updates, and network infrastructure. Ensuring the privacy and security of data transmitted and stored by IoT devices remains a significant challenge in smart home environments.

Big Data Analytics, Prediction and Modeling: IoT devices play a crucial role in leveraging machine learning (ML) and IoT technologies for various applications. Data driven security mechanisms such as Intrusion Detection Systems (IDS) analyze patterns of attacks and mitigate security threats in real-time [24]. Integrating diverse data sources, protocols, and formats requires interoperability standards and middleware solutions.

2.2   6G-Network

Increase in number of IoTs in the network and personal data usage throughout 5G deployment exposed its limitations. 6G holds the promise to achieve high bandwidth and ultra low latency of the order of fraction of a millisecond [30]. 6G aims to utilize higher frequency wave to significantly increase the data rates. With estimated bandwidth upto 1 Tbps, real-time decision making services, such as safe passage proposal and real-time incident detection and monitoring can benefit from the huge data rates. Real-time data analysis and distribution using machine learning and artificial intelligence are key services which can mutually benefit one another [27]. Techniques like evolutionary computing, neural computing and fuzzy systems can enhance the performance of 6G mobile networks by effectively managing massive data loads and diverse scenarios [9]. 6G-enabled IoT systems can leverage Federated learning(FL) among IoT devices and edge computing to ensure trust and low energy [1]. Data leakage from data training process increase concerns as not all IoTs are equipped with computing power to perform cryptographic algorithms [30]. IoT devices, having feeble computation power and limited functionality unlike desktops, are targeted as a point of attack in the connected network. Due to heterogeneous characteristic of IoTs, the 6G network aims to incorporate diverse security capabilities.

2.3   6G-Enabled Cloud

As the number of IoT devices increases, centralized cloud servers struggle to meet the demands of low latency high throughput applications [16], motivating the need for edge computing and a distributed cloud framework [7]. In a 6G network environment, end systems can deliver intelligence [8], by moving heavy computation services such as big data analysis close to data sources [1]. Big data services, such as cloud-based IoT healthcare networks, utilize data from body sensors and apply machine learning [17]. IoT devices can leverage machine learning and AI technologies for real-time monitoring, and can be deployed on cloud platforms enhancing efficiency and accuracy in smart home environments. Security measures in cloud-based IoT networks, such as fully homomorphic encryption aided by semi-trusted servers [22] and CP-ABE [12], employ encryption/decryption on attributes/data generated by IoT devices. Intrusion Detection Systems (IDS) analyze possible intrusions based on previous attack patterns for smart home systems [24]. Through the utilization of NFV and SDN, a myriad of IoT virtualization techniques have been proposed [3]. These techniques are limited in compatibility and security.

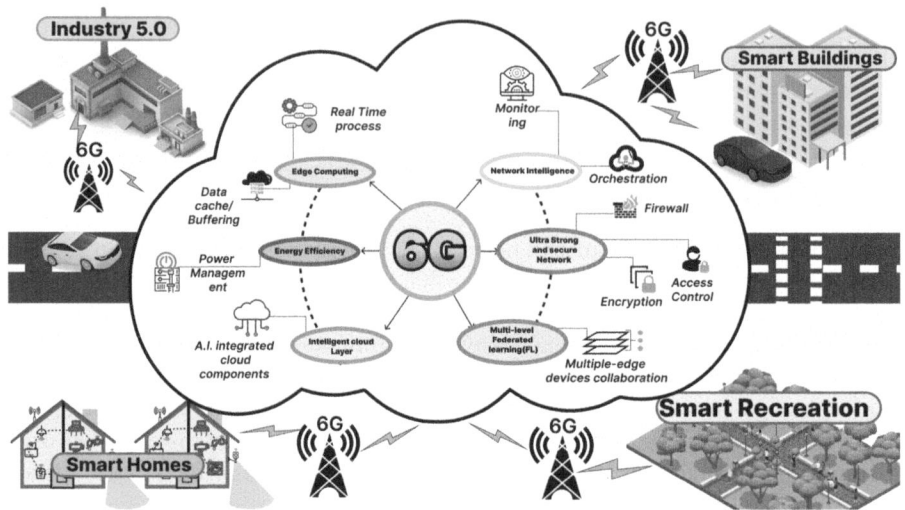

Fig. 3. 6G Enabled Smart City Eco System.

2.4 Past Work on Home Automation Systems

Various methods, such as analyzing user agent strings using IoT inspector's dataset and employing OTA smart updates, ensure uninterrupted service through smart patching [21,26]. Effective data management techniques, including data comparison, storage optimization, and utilization of big data services, optimize resource usage and ensure security with minimal delays [17]. Comparative analysis of IoT cloud providers aids in selecting the most suitable platform for industrial and home automation applications based on various factors like latency and user-friendliness [11]. Advanced encryption schemes, decentralized blockchain-based security solutions, and hardware-based isolation mechanisms are proposed to secure and protect IoT systems [12,22]. An authenticated search method for data transfers between IoT devices and the cloud is proposed for real-time data processing in IoT applications [5]. To assess Data sharing in Cloud-Assisted IoTs, five IoT cloud providers (Adafruit IO, Amazon Web Service, Blynk, Thingspeak, and Ubidots) are compared for industrial and home automation where latency, interval for update, user-friendliness, IFTTT compatibility [11].

3   Smart Home Automation Architecture

Figure 3 shows a 6G-enabled smart city infrastructure that serves as the underlying structure by integrating diverse network applications and their associated services, facilitating seamless data communication across the smart city's nodes. Leveraging its advanced features and enhanced network capabilities, 6G technology offers substantial operational flexibility for smart city infrastructures. Noteworthy attributes include an expanded spectrum, ultra-low latency, guaranteed Quality of Service (QoS), integrated intelligence, built-in optimization capabilities, broader integration capabilities, an improved air interface, and reduced operational costs all the while providing ultra-high reliable connectivity. These features are poised to transcend barriers such as time and space constraints, enabling efficient communication among various smart city devices and systems [30]. By co-designing communication and management protocols, smart cities can achieve cost reductions, enhance data transmission rates, and foster the proliferation of innovative applications, particularly in areas such as industry, transportation, recreation, and public safety. Ultimately, the integration of 6G technology promises to revolutionize the connectivity landscape of smart cities, driving efficiency, sustainability, and improved quality of life for residents.

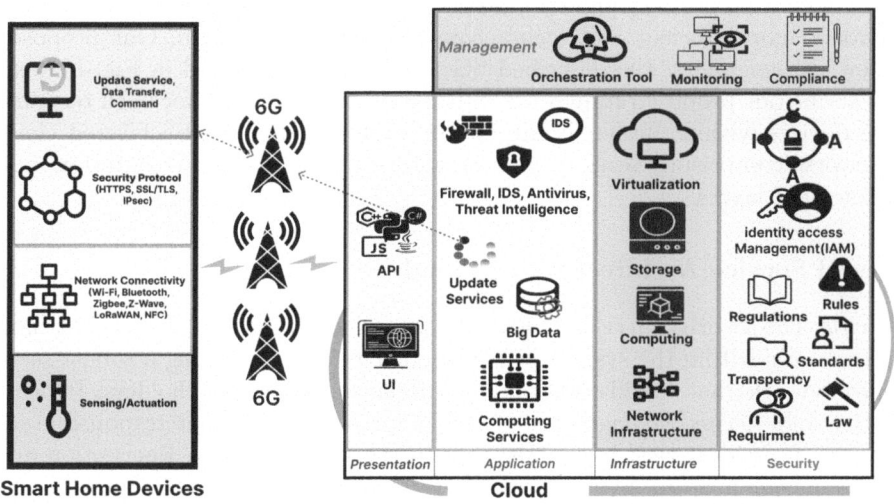

Fig. 4. Proposed Layered Smart Home Automation Framework.

Energy consumption is a significant concern when transmitting raw data from home units to the cloud [5]. However, recent advancements in energy technologies, ranging from renewable sources to wireless energy transfer mechanisms, offer promising solutions. With these advancements, it's assumed that home devices will consistently have access to power. Given their limited computational and storage capabilities, it is more efficient for these devices to process raw data in the cloud. The cloud possesses sophisticated techniques to address various data issues, including bad data, missing data, anomalies, and outliers, ensuring accurate and reliable data processing. Privacy and security issues can be addressed by using Federated learning [6] from each home. Using 6G-enabled edge intelligence, sophisticated machine learning algorithms and artificial intelligence models can be deployed. Raw sensor data can effectively processed for a diverse range of applications, from real-time monitoring to analytics.

In the context of a 6G-enabled cloud, end systems have the capability to provide intelligence by offloading heavy computational tasks, such as big data analysis, to the network's edge where the data is located. This approach enables edge intelligence to significantly reduce latency by handling data storage, processing, and analysis closer to the data source [1,8]. Moreover, edge intelligence plays a crucial role in enhancing privacy by shifting computational tasks to the network edge, sensitive data can be processed locally, minimizing the need for data transmission and storage in potentially vulnerable centralized locations. Furthermore, advancements in generative AI enable the automatic generation of updates based on the detection and identification of vulnerabilities. These updates can be rapidly tested and deployed to end devices, ensuring timely mitigation of security risks [10].

Overall, the integration of edge intelligence in 6G networks promises to revolutionize data processing, privacy protection, and security measures, paving the way for a more efficient and secure communication ecosystem. Our proposed framework, leveraging the described 6G features, is illustrated in Fig. 4. Next, we describe our proposed framework with layered architecture for both terminal home devices within the home automation system (SHA) and a layered cloud framework, comprising Security, Infrastructure, Application, Presentation, and Management layers.

Layered Service Architecture in Cloud

Security: The security layer includes critical tasks essential for safeguarding data and resources within the system. It is responsible for establishing a robust security framework that instills trust and confidence among stakeholders. It hosts Identity and Access Management (IAM), a pivotal component responsible for managing user identities, home IDs, facilitating access control. Encryption and Key Management form integral parts of this layer, playing crucial roles in protecting data both at rest and in transit. Key management module of this layer is responsible for generation, distribution, and rotation of encryption keys, ensuring the confidentiality and integrity of encrypted data [16]. The changing landscape of security rules and government regulations sit at this layer, serving as the repository of current security standards and protocols. Any additional security requirements related to data movement, whether internal or external to the cloud environment, are addressed within this layer.

Infrastructure: The infrastructure layer serves as the bedrock for both physical and virtual infrastructure within the system. Within this layer, the networking infrastructure plays a central role in facilitating communication among various physical and virtual network components, such as routers and switches. These components form the backbone of the system's connectivity, enabling seamless data exchange and resource utilization. Resource virtualization ensures scalability, flexibility, and efficiency in resource allocation and utilization [20]. The infrastructure layer relies on security features provided by the layer below to enforce access control and security measures. Conversely, the security layer depends on access to the infrastructure layer for key management and storage of security rules, establishing a symbiotic relationship.

Application: The application situated above the security layer contains application logic and services. Within this layer, security measures encompass firewalls, intrusion detection systems (IDS), antivirus software, and threat intelligence services, working harmoniously to ensure the security of both cloud infrastructure and IoT devices [24]. The application layer contains data preprocessing services tasked with cleaning and refining raw streaming data originating from SHA devices. These services deal with issues such as missing data, anomalies, and erroneous entries while performing tasks such as aggregation and filtering to optimize the data. Computational services are dedicated to executing intricate algorithms for analytics, machine learning, and automation. These services empower the system to derive actionable insights from the data, driving informed decision-making and facilitating automated processes. Update service is a critical component that interfaces with terminal SHA devices to identify and rectify any vulnerabilities promptly. By managing and implementing updates on demand, this service ensures that the devices remain current with the latest security patches and software updates. The application layer hosts big data services, facilitating comprehensive city-wide data analysis. This capability not only supports informed decision-making but also enables privacy-preserving federated learning, bolstering data security and privacy [28]. The application layer is positioned above the security layer to enforce adherence to the requisite security standards and protocols, fostering a secure and reliable computing environment.

Presentation: The presentation layer encompasses two vital components: user interfaces (UI) and Application Programming Interfaces (APIs). UIs serve an array of dashboards and handheld device interfaces. These interfaces empower users to seamlessly interact with their home devices, enabling them to observe, monitor, and issue commands with ease. From adjusting settings to monitoring activity, UIs provide intuitive pathways for users to engage with their smart home ecosystem. On the other hand, API play aims to extend the functionality of the system by providing programmable interfaces to third-party applications and developers [19]. These APIs offer controlled access to data and devices, enabling developers to build cloud-based services and applications tailored to specific needs. Additionally, APIs grant access to a variety of services located within the Application layer, fostering interoperability and enabling the integration of diverse applications into the smart home ecosystem.

Management: The Management Layer is and umbrella layer, responsible for over-seeing, orchestrating, and automating system operations. Its tasks are enforcing security policies to ensure compliance with regulations, standards, and policies [21]. Additionally, the Management Layer handles resource provisioning, auto-matic deployment, and system scaling through monitoring. By generating a range of metrics, it offers administrators visibility into various aspects of the system, including compliance status and system events, facilitating effective tracking and management of tasks.

Layered Framework for Terminal SHA Devices. The SHA devices are streamlined to bare minimum essential functionalities only, enabling them to perform key tasks such as data transmission, updates, command reception, and secure communications. These devices operate on a four-layer stack, prioritizing communication capabilities as outlined below.

Update, Data Transfer and Command: At this layer update services are respon-sible for tracking, scheduling, and performing updates. The update function is in communication with the update service at the cloud [21]. Cloud counterpart can also perform a rollback on the updates. In addition to these, this layer is responsible for raw data transfer using the massive data rate, ultra-low latency, and highly reliable feature of 6G. The raw data is preprocessed in the cloud as described in the last subsection. In addition, SHA devices can receive commands to perform suitable tasks.

Security Layer: The Security Layer is critical as it ensures the protection of data and communications within the framework. It encompasses encryption, authentication, and access control mechanisms, which are continually monitored and updated through the cloud's update feature.

Network: This layer serves as the backbone for network connectivity, offering a comprehensive suite of data communication protocols [7]. It includes various layer 2 protocols like Wi-Fi, Bluetooth, Zigbee, Z-Wave, alongside addressing and reliable transport protocols

Sensing and Actuation: This layer orchestrates the operation of sensors for data acquisition and actuators for executing desired and/or necessary actions [23].

4   Application Scenarios and a Case Study

As cities attract more residents seeking better opportunities and lifestyles, the demand for essential services rises, leading to increased living costs, crime rates, and strain on infrastructure. The proposed architecture utilizes the data col-lected from smart homes in providing critical information and insights to city government and residents. This section delves deeper into application scenarios and a case study within smart cities operating in a 6G network environment, where our proposed smart home automation architecture yields significant ben-efits as compared to existing ones.

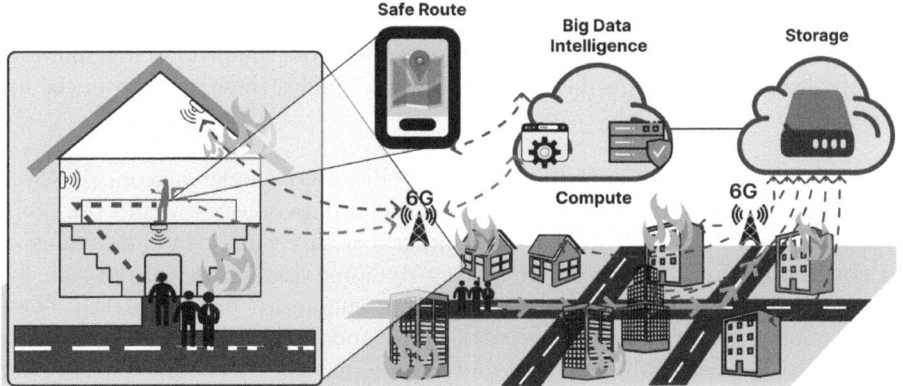

Fig. 5. Smart Home Automation Framework: Safe Route Computation and Dissemination in the Event of Local Disaster (Fire).

4.1 Application Scenarios

The proposed framework enhances public safety and aids in search and rescue efforts for missing individuals. Sensors in nearby buildings swiftly detect suspects, triggering immediate alerts to local authorities, thus preventing their escape. Continuous monitoring and seamless data sharing among buildings enable real-time suspect tracking. Surveillance cameras monitor civilian activities, promptly identifying and reporting suspicious behavior. Anomalies are quickly communicated to the smart city cloud, which collaborates with neighboring cities for regional monitoring and pursuit. Leveraging 6G network services, IoT devices access cloud resources for functionalities like facial recognition and object identification. Citywide home intelligence emerges as a prominent application of the proposed architecture, capable of performing citywide analyses and pattern recognition based on data collected from multiple IoT devices integrated into smart home automation systems. With a diverse array of sensors deployed both inside and outside buildings, civilians can receive personalized analysis reports detailing various aspects of home activities.

4.2 Real Time Safe Routing in the Event of Disasters

The proposed framework offers a comprehensive solution for enhancing safety and rescue operations in both home and city. We present a case study that illustrate how the proposed framework proves immensely beneficial in real-time applications, particularly in the event of natural disasters. Figure 5 illustrates a scenario in a city where multiple buildings are engulfed in fire. Until emergency services arrive on the scene, civilians must take immediate action to avoid potential danger zones. Without accurate situational details, choosing an improper evacuation route could result in casualties. In a smart city environment, 6G technology enables real-time dissemination of situation updates to all individuals through their personal devices. Real-time data analysis assesses nearby conditions, while sensors both inside and outside buildings continuously monitor the spread of the fire, guiding people to safety. This case study demonstrates how the proposed framework not only directs civilians inside buildings but also guides them away from the fire danger zone.

Smart Home Sensing and Data Collection: Fire and smoke sensors deployed both inside and outside buildings serve as crucial data sources within the home automation systems. The architecture integrates three main modules: sensing and communication, databases for storing dynamic and historical data on fire spread and rescue operations, and a compute engine for data analysis. These data are stored in two types of databases: static and dynamic. Static data include information such as building layouts and road maps, while dynamic data provide real-time updates on fire and environmental factors influencing its spread. Ultra-low latency and massive capacity of the 6G network swiftly transport real-time raw data to the abundant compute and storage resources of the cloud.

Edge Cloud Compute Engine: In the framework, the 6G-enabled cloud brings computing capabilities to the edge of the network. Here, the compute engine utilizes machine learning models like Bayesian networks (See [15]) to assess safety probabilities for various route segments. During a disaster, the cloud can prioritize this computation intelligently. By analyzing historical data alongside real-time inputs, the engine discerns the safest routes for fire rescue operations. Continuously updating with streaming real-time data from fire sensors, the Bayesian network ensures precise and adaptive decision-making in dynamic fire scenarios.

Safety Route Dissemination: The proposed home automation architecture facilitates coordination and decision-making in fire rescue operations by leveraging real-time data from smart homes and city infrastructure. Through integration with 6G networks and cloud computing, the architecture empowers civilians to make informed decisions about safe route options. This information is delivered directly to their mobile devices and on the map application.

End-to-End Communication Between Civilians in Distress and Fire Authorities: Information regarding trapped civilians, collected by a variety of home automation sensors (such as indoor localization and user behavior monitoring without privacy violations), is relayed to emergency services, ensuring they have timely and accurate information about those in need of rescue.

5   Conclusion and Future Work

An innovative approach to address the challenges of state-of-the-art smart home automation systems is proposed. By harnessing the capabilities of 6G networks and 6G-enabled cloud computing, the proposed architecture offers novel solutions to enhance security, data processing, and analytics in smart cities, improving the efficiency and functionality of smart cities. It features enhanced security measures, data preprocessing, big data intelligence, and IoT service virtualization in the cloud, contributing to the development of a robust and efficient smart home ecosystem and paving the way for the realization of true smart cities. Through explorations of various application scenarios and a case study, the impact of the proposed architecture is demonstrated. The future work could focus on further refining the architecture and exploring additional application domains. This could involve optimizing security measures, enhancing data processing algorithms, and expanding the scope of IoT services virtualization in the cloud. Additionally, exploring novel ways to integrate emerging technologies such as AI and edge computing could unlock new opportunities for advancing smart home automation systems in the era of 6G-enabled smart cities.

References

1. Adhikari, M., Hazra, A.: 6G-enabled ultra-reliable low-latency communication in edge networks. IEEE Commun. Stand. Mag. **6**(1), 67–74 (2022)
2. Alaa, M., Zaidan, A., Zaidan, B., Talal, M., Kiah, M.: A review of smart home applications based on internet of things. J. Netw. Comput. Appl. **97**, 48–65 (2017). https://doi.org/10.1016/j.jnca.2017.08.017
3. Alam, I., et al.: A survey of network virtualization techniques for internet of things using SDN and NFV. ACM Comput. Surv. (CSUR) **53**(2), 1–40 (2020)
4. Antzoulis, I., Chowdhury, M.M., Latiff, S.: IoT security for smart home: issues and solutions. In: 2022 IEEE International Conference on Electro Information Technology (eIT), pp. 1–7. IEEE (2022)
5. Condon, F., Martínez, J.M., Eltamaly, A.M., Kim, Y.C., Ahmed, M.A.: Design and implementation of a cloud-IoT-based home energy management system. Sensors **23**(1), 176 (2022)
6. Duan, Q., Huang, J., Hu, S., Deng, R., Lu, Z., Yu, S.: Combining federated learning and edge computing toward ubiquitous intelligence in 6G network: challenges, recent advances, and future directions. IEEE Commun. Surv. Tutor. **25**(4), 2892–2950 (2023). https://doi.org/10.1109/COMST.2023.3316615
7. Garcia Lopez, P., et al.: Edge-centric computing: vision and challenges (2015)
8. Giordani, M., Polese, M., Mezzavilla, M., Rangan, S., Zorzi, M.: Toward 6g networks: use cases and technologies. IEEE Commun. Mag. **58**(3), 55–61 (2020)
9. Guo, F., Yu, F.R., Zhang, H., Li, X., Ji, H., Leung, V.C.: Enabling massive IoT toward 6G: a comprehensive survey. IEEE Internet Things J. **8**(15), 11891–11915 (2021)
10. Gupta, M., Akiri, C., Aryal, K., Parker, E., Praharaj, L.: From chatGPT to threatGPT: Impact of generative AI in cybersecurity and privacy. IEEE Access **11**, 80218–80245 (2023)
11. Haghnegahdar, L., Joshi, S.S., Dahotre, N.B.: From IoT-based cloud manufacturing approach to intelligent additive manufacturing: industrial internet of things-an overview. Int. J. Adv. Manuf. Technol. **119**(3), 1461–1478 (2022)
12. Hahn, C., Kim, J., Kwon, H., Hur, J.: Efficient IoT management with resilience to unauthorized access to cloud storage. IEEE Trans. Cloud Comput. **10**(2), 1008–1020 (2020)
13. Hategekimana, F., Whitaker, T.J., Pantho, M., Bobda, C.: IoT device security through dynamic hardware isolation with cloud-based update. J. Syst. Architect. **109**, 101827 (2020)
14. Kolias, C., Kambourakis, G., Stavrou, A., Voas, J.: DDoS in the IoT: mirai and other botnets. Computer **50**(7), 80–84 (2017)

15. Liu, Q., Kumar, S., Mago, V.: SafeRNet: safe transportation routing in the era of internet of vehicles and mobile crowd sensing. In: 2017 14th IEEE Annual Consumer Communications & Networking Conference (CCNC), pp. 299–304. IEEE (2017)

16. Mao, B., Liu, J., Wu, Y., Kato, N.: Security and privacy on 6g network edge: a survey. IEEE Commun. Surv. Tutor. (2023)

17. Mehta, K., Gaur, S., Maheshwari, S., Chugh, H., Anibhushan Kumar, M.: Big data analytics cloud based smart IoT healthcare network. In: 7th International Conference on Trends in Electronics and Informatics (ICOEI), pp. 437–443 (2023)

18. Mishra, A.K., Wazid, M.: Design of a cloud-based security mechanism for industry 4.0 communication. In: 2023 Third International Conference on Secure Cyber Computing and Communication (ICSCCC), pp. 337–343. IEEE (2023)

19. Mladenova, T., Cankov, V.: Smart home based on IoT-architecture and practices. In: 2023 5th International Congress on Human-Computer Interaction, Optimization and Robotic Applications (HORA), pp. 1–5. IEEE (2023)

20. Ogawa, K., Kanai, K., Nakamura, K., Kanemitsu, H., Katto, J., Nakazato, H.: IoT device virtualization for efficient resource utilization in smart city IoT platform. In: 2019 IEEE International Conference on Pervasive Computing and Communications Workshops (PerCom Workshops), pp. 419–422. IEEE (2019)

21. Prakash, V., Xie, S., Huang, D.Y.: Software update practices on smart home IoT devices. arXiv preprint arXiv:2208.14367 (2022)

22. Rezaeibagha, F., Mu, Y., Huang, K., Chen, L., Zhang, L.: Toward secure data computation and outsource for multi-user cloud-based IoT. IEEE Trans. Cloud Comput. **11**(1), 217–228 (2021)

23. Sai, M.R., Teja, K.K., Sasank, V.P., Kavitha, M., Aravinth, S.: Smart home messenger notifications system using IoT. In: 2023 Third International Conference on Artificial Intelligence and Smart Energy (ICAIS), pp. 87–92. IEEE (2023)

24. Sasirekha, G., Bangari, A., Rao, M., Bapat, J., Das, D.: Synthesis of IoT sensor telemetry data for smart home edge-ids evaluation. In: 2023 International Conference on Computer Science, Information Technology and Engineering (ICCoSITE), pp. 562–567. IEEE (2023)

25. Sovacool, B.K., Del Rio, D.: Smart home technologies in Europe: a critical review of concepts, benefits, risks and policies. Renew. Sustain. Energy Rev. **120**, 109663 (2020)

26. Srinivas, A.K., Vikram, D., Sharma, S., et al.: Deployment automation for blockchain enabled IoMT. In: 2022 OITS International Conference on Information Technology (OCIT), pp. 1–4. IEEE (2022)

27. Sun, Y., Liu, J., Wang, J., Cao, Y., Kato, N.: When machine learning meets privacy in 6G: a survey. IEEE Comm. Surv. Tutor. **22**(4), 2694–2724 (2020)

28. Vajagic, N., Antic, M.: Smart home IoT network diagnostics using big data services. In: 2022 30th Telecommunications Forum (TELFOR), pp. 1–4. IEEE (2022)

29. Wang, C., Cai, Z., Li, Y.: Sustainable blockchain-based digital twin management architecture for IoT devices. IEEE Internet Things **10**(8), 6535–6548 (2022)

30. You, X., et al.: Towards 6G wireless communication networks: vision, enabling technologies, and new paradigm shifts. Sci. China Inf. Sci. **64**, 1–74 (2021)

Smart Roadway Monitoring: Pothole Detection and Mapping via Google Street View

Shazab Ali, Meng Xu, and Daehan Kwak

Department of Computer Science and Technology, Kean University, Union, USA
{alisha,mengxu,dkwak}@kean.edu

Abstract. Potholes pose significant financial and safety hazards to motorists worldwide, emphasizing the demand for innovative solutions for detection and repair. Conventional methods, reliant on manual inspection and patching, prove to be inefficient and unsustainable, prompting the need for automated detection systems. However, merely expediting the patching process does not address the underlying issues that cause the potholes in the first place. This paper introduces a pothole detection and mapping system over Google Street View, utilizing highly effective learning models and Google Map's APIs. Our system extracts images along specified routes from the Google Street View API, processes them using a detection model, and plots the results on an interactive map. Additionally, it compiles these findings into a video that simulates a drive along the route. By leveraging deep learning techniques, we provide users with valuable insights into road conditions, facilitating proactive maintenance strategies. The evaluation demonstrates high classification accuracy and sensitivity in pothole detection. Additionally, the system's capacity to analyze data over time enables municipalities to identify and pinpoint persistent pothole-prone areas, paving the way for targeted interventions to prevent future hazards. Future work includes expanding the dataset and developing a user-friendly interface to enhance the system's capabilities and usability. Our system offers a promising solution for long-term pothole repair and maintenance, contributing to safer and more sustainable transportation infrastructure for communities around the world.

Keywords: Deep learning · Google Street View · Pothole detection · Pothole mapping · Roadway monitoring system

1 Introduction

Potholes are holes in road surfaces that result from gradual damage caused by traffic and weather. Asphalt, commonly used in road surfaces for its durability, flexibility, and low cost, paradoxically becomes a breeding ground for potholes. Potholes arise in four main steps [6]. Moisture infiltrates the asphalt which allows

H. R. Arabnia et al. (Eds.): CSCE 2024, CCIS 2260, pp. 151–163, 2025.
https://doi.org/10.1007/978-3-031-85923-6_12

water to drain into it allowing for the moisture to become trapped underneath. During freezing and thawing, ice expands and causes cracks within the asphalt. Voids form as hollow spaces accumulate moisture and rapid freeze-thaw cycles. With the impact of traffic, the pavement begins to collapse, causing potholes to become larger and larger overtime.

The damage caused by potholes may seem trivial, but the extent of the damage they cause is significant, both financially and physically. A study investigating the impact of potholes on motorists across 11 distinct regions in the UK between 2019 and 2020 revealed that the cumulative damage inflicted on motorists annually exceeded 1.25 billion dollars [6]. Furthermore, the study [6] indicated that 32% of drivers who encountered potholes in the past year reported sustaining damage to their vehicles. These damages encompassed a range of issues, including but not limited to tire damage, wheel misalignment, and suspension repairs.

Potholes not only pose a financial burden, but also create significant safety hazards as well, with the potential for serious and fatal consequences. Road accidents attributed to potholes claimed 5,626 lives between 2018 and 2020 [21]. These accidents highlight the critical need for improved road maintenance and proactive measures. The intersection between financial burden and loss of life underscores the urgent need for effective pothole detection and mapping systems. By prioritizing these systems, we can enhance road safety, facilitate timely repairs, and reduce the economic and safety impact.

Traditional methods of pothole detection and repair rely on manual inspection and patching, both of which are inefficient. Patching, a common practice, involves filling potholes with temporary asphalt, however, this "quick fix" does not last long and constantly requires refilling especially in areas that receive bad weather or traffic frequently. Alternatively, methods such as reconstruction and overlays [9] provide long-term solutions by replacing entire sections of asphalt. However, the cost associated with these approaches limits their capability of widespread implementation.

In this paper, we introduce a pothole detection and mapping system leveraging well-established deep learning models and Google Maps APIs. Our system operates along a route of interest and extracts images from the Google Street View API, which are then analyzed using a pothole detection model. The detected potholes are plotted on a map before being converted into video. This facilitates both visual and statistical assessment of road conditions in a given area over time. This approach allows us to pinpoint the areas where there is recurring road damage and implement targeted reinforcement to prevent potholes from forming. By eliminating the need for constant road surveying and patching, our system aims to mitigate both injury and financial burdens caused by pothole-related incidents.

The paper is organized as follows. Section 2 introduces the related work to our approach and potential alternatives, and Sect. 3 discusses and explains the methodology of our proposed approach. Section 4 delves into the implementation and application, and Sect. 5 summarizes our results. Section 6 explains the challenges faced and the resulting output, and Sect. 7 summarizes our approach and discusses future work.

2   Related Work

Advancements in computer vision [20,22,23,27] and intelligent transportation systems [7,8,15] have led to more sophisticated methods for monitoring roadway conditions and supporting autonomous decision-making. Numerous studies have concentrated on refining models for enhanced pothole detection using image-based approaches [2,3,17,24,28]. At the same time, crowdsourcing has emerged as an invaluable approach for the real-time collection and dissemination of information across various domains [11–14,16]. Research has increasingly focused on combining these two methods to tackle real-world pothole detection. For example, several approaches leverage image-based machine learning algorithms alongside sensor technologies for pothole detection, while utilizing crowdsourcing mechanisms to disseminate pothole locations [10,19,26]. This dual approach not only aids in the precise detection of potholes but also allows real-time reporting and subsequent mitigation, therefore enhancing the practical implementation.

Studies in [10] and [19] have explored the option of using vehicle-mounted cameras in order to automate the process and improve detection accuracy. In [19], the You Only Look Once version 5 (YOLOv5) deep learning algorithm was used to detect potholes from dash camera images. These images served as input to CNN models within the YOLOv5 framework. During training, the CNN models were fine-tuned using transfer learning techniques. This involved leveraging pre-trained weights from models trained on larger datasets like COCO to expedite the learning process and improve performance. Next, three different architectures of YOLOv5 (small, medium, large) were evaluated during training of 500 epochs. The effectiveness of the YOLOv5 approach is demonstrated through its ability to detect potholes accurately and in real time. By analyzing the trade-offs between detection accuracy and speed across the different model sizes, the proposed solution offers flexibility in optimizing its performance based on the task presented.

YOLOv5 is not the only machine learning approach that has been used for this task. The study in [18] highlights a range of deep learning techniques suitable for pothole detection, composed of both object detection and semantic segmentation algorithms. The object detection methods range from single-shot multi-box detectors (SSD) to region-based convolutional neural networks (R-CNN) similar to what we employed in our experiment. In addition, semantic segmentation-based methods have also gained traction, utilizing networks such as U-Net and DeepLabv3+ to segment road images at the pixel level, providing us with a detailed understanding of road anomalies. These techniques leverage attention mechanisms and data fusion strategies to refine features and improve the accuracy of the segmentation.

Additionally, researchers have explored using crowd-sourcing for pothole detection and accelerometers to collect data on road conditions [18,26]. In [26], two groups of experiments were conducted utilizing smartphones in one group and high-precision devices in the other. In the smartphone group, three phones were positioned in different locations of the vehicle, with the high-precision device on the floor. Supervised learning models were then employed to identify the potholes, while the acceleration data was labeled using the ground truth from the windshield camera. The labeled data were used in the training of these models to recognize patterns in the acceleration data that indicated the appearance of road anomalies. The algorithms were fine-tuned using the collected data from both the experimental and verification groups to ensure their effectiveness in different driving conditions. This information would be uploaded by the users to further train the model around different road conditions.

It is important to note that although these approaches are good for detecting potholes, they lack any real-world application beyond monitoring and detecting. In addition, crowdsourcing from users is challenging to achieve and creates privacy and data authenticity concerns. To address these challenges, our system utilizes deep learning techniques and leverages Google Street View and Google Maps APIs to obtain real-world street-level road data. Additionally, we implement a mapping system to make use of the detections as a comprehensive data tool rather than a plain detection tool.

3 Methodology

3.1 Proposed System

Our proposed pothole detection system aims to provide users with a seamless and efficient way to not only detect potholes but monitor them as well. By combining powerful machine learning techniques and Google Street View imagery, the system offers users valuable insights into road conditions in their area and long-term data to prevent future hazards before they arise.

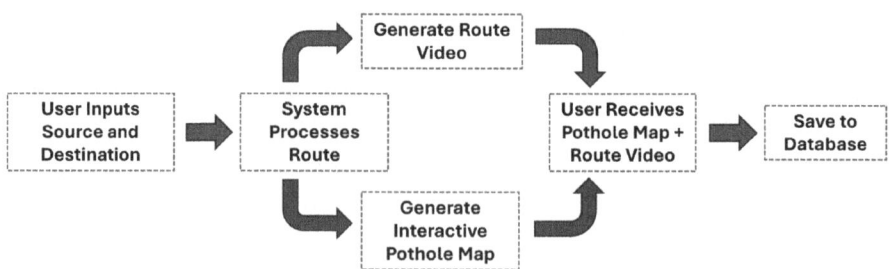

Fig. 1. Workflow of the pothole detection and mapping system.

3.2   System Implementation

The user flow of the proposed system is depicted in Fig. 1. The program starts with user input of the route of interest, where users can specify the source and destination. The system then takes this information and begins processing it using the Google Maps Directions and Street View APIs followed by a deep learning model, as seen in Fig. 1. Once the information is processed, an interactive map is generated that displays the location of the potholes at the exact coordinates where they were detected. In addition to the interactive map, the system compiles the detected potholes into a video simulation of the route for users to view. Lastly, the user receives the map and video and can store them in a database to monitor the road conditions over time in their town or area. Google Street View updates its imagery at varying frequencies, with urban areas typically updated once every year, while less populated areas may take three or more years [4]. This is beneficial for our system since we are not trying to simply gather road data or detect potholes for the current day but to gather data over time to prevent the potholes from forming in the first place. By leveraging these images and maps, within a few years, municipalities can discern patterns of road degradation and prioritize areas for appropriate intervention. For instance, areas exhibiting frequent and recurring pothole formation may warrant more extensive measures such as complete reconstruction and recurrence rather than just patching. As described earlier, reconstruction and reinforcement are expensive procedures and cannot be done everywhere, so utilizing our system, enables implementation in places where it is needed. Conversely, areas experiencing sporadic or isolated potholes will suffice with simpler solutions such as patching.

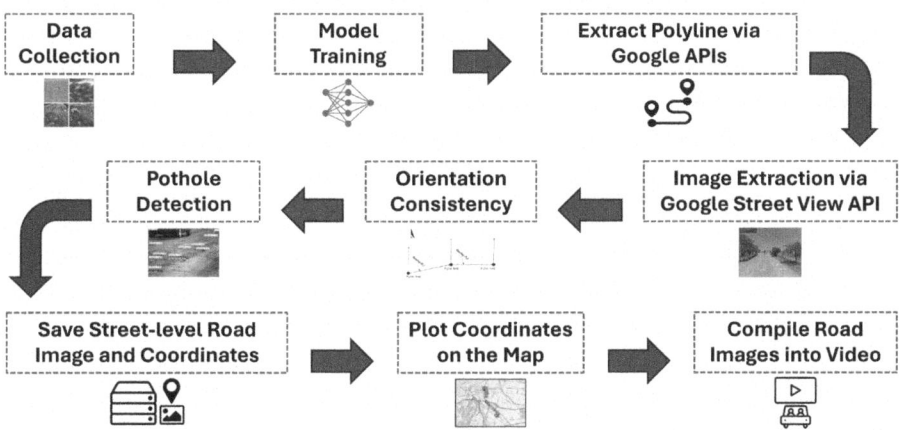

Fig. 2. System architecture of the pothole detection and mapping system.

3.3   System Architecture

Figure 2 illustrates the proposed systems architecture, while Fig. 1 depicts the user implementation. This highlights the various steps the data must go through to get the results. The first step in building the system's architecture was to collect a large dataset of potholes. A dataset used by a related paper that used deep learning to detect potholes which consisted of pothole images from various locations all around the world [5] was utilized. This dataset consisted of thousands of images; however, only the United States data was used as it was the closest to the type of images desired for detection. Additionally, the dataset was augmented with our images to enhance its size and diversity. The augmented images were from routes that were set from different parts of the region such as Wayne, New Jersey, to Newark, New Jersey, then the images were extracted and annotated manually using Roboflow [1].

Following data collection, we trained a Detectron2 model using the RCNN R50 FPN architecture from the model zoo [25]. This model was chosen due to its efficiency and relatively high accuracy compared to other available methods and models. The Feature Pyramid Network (FPN) incorporated into the architecture enables effective feature extraction allowing the model to capture both fine-grained details and broader contextual information in the training images. The ResNet-50 backbone provides a balance between the model efficiency and complexity making it suitable for this application where speed is an important factor. Overall, the choice of the RCNN R50 FPN architecture was because of our emphasis on achieving both high accuracy and efficiency in pothole detecting tasks.

Next, utilizing the Google Maps Directions API and the polyline library in Python, a polyline representation of the route of interest entered by the user was extracted. This ensured all the data points along the route were captured. We then employed the Google Maps Street View API to extract images at each data point along the route. Additionally, the bearing between each current and previous point was calculated to ensure the consistent orientation of the captured images. This step was crucial because without it, all the images would be facing different directions, making the last step of video compilation impossible but most importantly, preventing the detection of potholes if the orientation were not facing the direction of the road in progress. For example, without consistent bearings, the orientation of the street view image might face a home or the side of the road instead of the road itself, leading to inaccurate and unusable data.

With the images extracted, they were run through the model as they arrived. This process allowed for the detection of potholes as they were encountered and saved the coordinates in a CSV file. Running the images through the model in this order prevented duplicate images of detected and undetected potholes and eliminated the need to run the program twice to obtain the coordinates.

Upon saving of all the images and coordinates, the CSV file that stored the pothole coordinates was used to create the map. We used the folium library to create an interactive map, as seen in Fig. 6, to visualize the potholes along the route. Lastly, all the saved images were compiled into a video using OpenCV, with the addition of interpolation between the frames to give the illusion of a seamless driving experience as it progressed through the route.

4 Experiments

4.1 Dataset

The dataset used in our experiment comprises of street-level images obtained from the Google Street View Static API [5]. These images were captured under sunny conditions but at different times of the day and with varying sunlight intensities. The dataset consists of 1,977 images in the training set and 50 images in the test set, totaling 2,027 images. No separate validation set was used in this study, as it was not the scope of this research. Image annotations were provided in COCO format, allowing compatibility with our deep learning framework. Each image was annotated with bounding boxes delineating the location of the potholes. Prior to model training, images were preprocessed to ensure uniformity and compatibility with the model. Images were resized to a resolution of 640×640 pixels. A single class label, "pothole", was assigned to all annotated images, indicating the presence of a pothole within a bounding box region. In this study, data augmentations such as exposure and saturation adjustments were not applied to the dataset. We hope to test this in the future to enhance the model's performance.

4.2 Implementation Details

The training process was conducted using the Detectron2 library, leveraging the Faster R-CNN architecture with a ResNet-50 backbone pre-trained on the COCO dataset. The implementation details are as follows: The learning rate was set to 0.0025; the batch size was 256; the model was trained for 3,000 iterations; no preprocessing was done as this was completed while annotating the images; lastly, the optimizer that was used during training was stochastic gradient descent (SGD). The training was conducted in a GPU-enabled environment in Google Colab to accelerate computation. After training, the model's performance was evaluated on the test set using a detection threshold of 0.8.

5 Results

Figure 3 highlights the performance of the model in terms of classification accuracy, total loss, and false negatives, as expressed through the TensorBoard library. The classification accuracy peaked at 91% by the end of the training process. This demonstrates the model's high capability of predicting the classification of potholes correctly. In Fig. 3c, we can see the total loss of the model starting at 0.65 and bottoming out at around 0.15 by the end. This difference between the beginning and the end indicates that the model was learning throughout the training process and no errors occurred during training. Lastly, the false negative rate was initially high but neared zero at the end. This decrease reflects

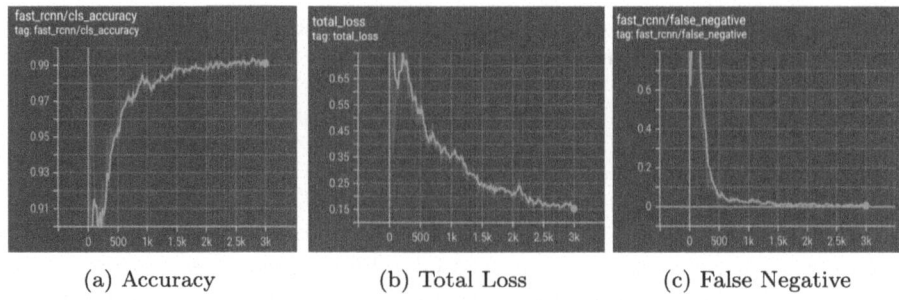

(a) Accuracy   (b) Total Loss   (c) False Negative

Fig. 3. Model performance in terms of accuracy, loss, and false negatives.

the model's enhanced sensitivity to detecting potholes, which is important for our task. Overall, these graphs collectively demonstrate the good health of the model and its effectiveness for the task.

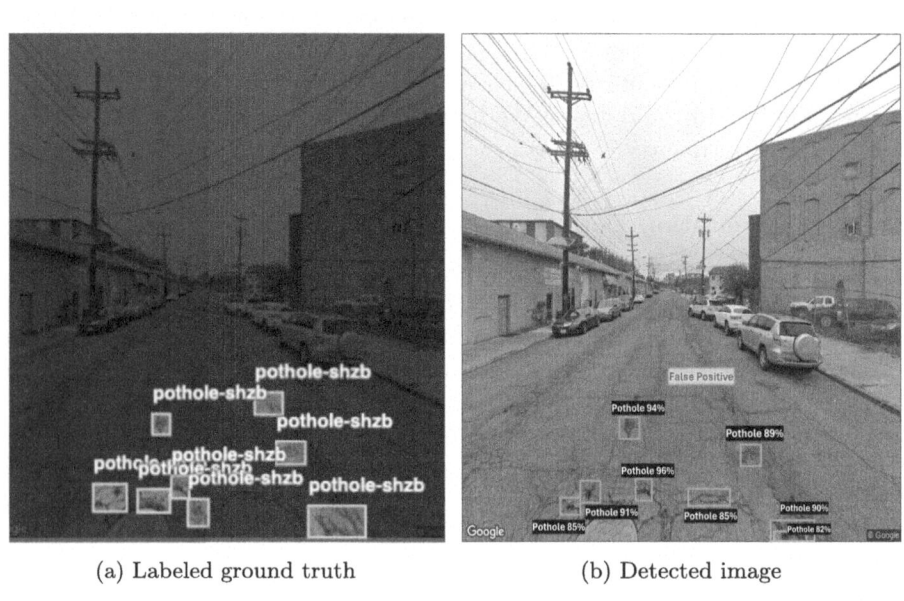

(a) Labeled ground truth   (b) Detected image

Fig. 4. Comparison of ground truth and system detection for pothole identification.

We selected a challenging route for a case study to test the effectiveness of the system. The chosen route was from 42 Maryland Ave, Paterson, New Jersey to 26 19th Ave, Paterson, New Jersey. This route was specifically selected because it is known to have a dense population of potholes, which is an ideal environment for evaluating the performance of the system. To establish the ground truth of this area, we extracted images from the polyline using the Google Maps Street

View API and Directions API and manually labeled the route. This was done to ensure the accuracy of our evaluation.

Figure 4 represents a side-by-side comparison between a snapshot from the ground truth video Fig. 4a and the snapshot obtained from our system's detection Fig. 4b. Despite the large population of potholes in the area, the system only missed two predictions and detected one false positive compared to the ground truth.

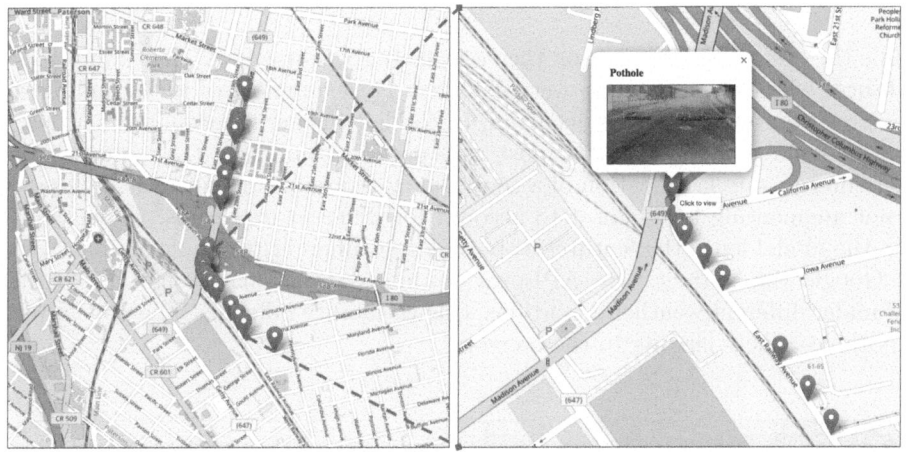

Fig. 5. Pothole detection mapping system. This figure provides a visual representation of pothole distribution along the route of interest, offering valuable insight into the road's condition.

Our proposed system's mapping layout is illustrated in Fig. 5, which provides a visual representation of pothole distribution along the route of interest, offering valuable insight into the road's condition. When a request is sent to the Directions API to create a polyline of the route, a JSON file containing the metadata of the latitude and longitude coordinates is generated. The Google Street View Static API reads these coordinates and returns street-level road images. When the image is run through the model to detect a pothole, if a pothole is detected, the coordinates are saved in a CSV file. However, if nothing is detected, the metadata is discarded even though the image is still saved. The coordinates in the CSV file indicate where the potholes are to be marked as pinpoints on the map, as seen in Fig. 5. Once this process is complete, the CSV file is saved and loaded into the Folium Python library, which marks the pothole positions on the map using the saved coordinates and creates an interactive map for the user to swipe through and analyze. The interactive map allows users to swipe through, zoom in and out, and click on any pinpoint location to view the actual potholes to conduct a more thorough investigation of the area of interest.

The map illustrates scattered pothole pinpoints at the beginning and end of the route, with a higher density concentration observed in the middle. This higher density indicates that the middle segment of the route receives a higher frequency of road deterioration, which could be due to several factors such as heavy traffic or bad weather. By identifying these segments, authorities can prepare these areas for additional measures such as reinforced construction or enhanced road surface materials. This addresses safety concerns for motorists and the financial burdens associated with frequent patching.

6   Challenges

While the overall accuracy along the case study route was high, there were a few instances where false positives were detected. For example, in Fig. 6a and 6b we see two instances where this occurred. In the left image, the system incorrectly identified the shadow of a light post as a pothole. Similarly, the image on the right shows a misclassification of a sewer lid as a pothole. This was likely due to us not augmenting the dataset to account for different exposures, which would help the model learn the features of potholes at different times of the day. Since the Google Maps Street View API provides images taken at various times of day and under different weather conditions, this variability influences the appearance of potholes, likely leading to these errors.

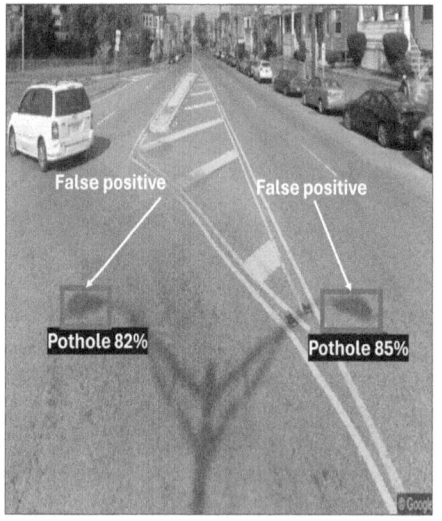 

(a) Lamp shadow detected as pothole   (b) Sewer detected as pothole

Fig. 6. Examples of false positives in pothole detection.

7   Conclusion and Future Work

In conclusion, our system presents a promising solution for pothole detection and mapping using deep learning techniques and real-world street-level road data from Google Street View API. The system's ability to analyze data over time will allow municipalities to identify persistent pothole-prone areas, enabling proactive intervention before the potholes even occur. This will not only reduce repair frequency and cost but will also increase safety. Through continued innovation, we hope to create a safer and more sustainable transportation infrastructure for all communities.

Moving forward, we aim to enhance the system's capabilities by expanding and augmenting the pothole dataset to include a wider range of road conditions and lighting scenarios. We plan to be able to adjust the images to account for the discrepancies caused by the different times of day when Google Street View car collected its images. Additionally, we plan to develop a user-friendly GUI to streamline route and input data retrieval so users of all technological backgrounds can use it. Furthermore, enabling users to upload their data to a cloud server will allow municipalities to efficiently input and track their data over time.

Acknowledgment. This work was supported in part by NSF grant DUE-2247157, CNS-2318696, and the Office of Research and Sponsored Programs, Kean University.

References

1. Roboflow: Computer vision tools for developers and enterprises. https://roboflow. com/. Accessed 16 May 2024
2. Akagic, A., Buza, E., Omanovic, S.: Pothole detection: an efficient vision based method using RGB color space image segmentation. In: 2017 40th International Convention on Information and Communication Technology, Electronics and Microelectronics (MIPRO). IEEE (2017). https://doi.org/10.23919/mipro.2017. 7973589
3. Ansari, S.: Building a realtime pothole detection system using machine learning and computer vision. https://towardsdatascience.com/building-a-realtime-pothole-detection-system-using-machine-learning-and-computer-vision-2e5fb2e5e746. Accessed 16 May 2024
4. Antonelli, W.: It can take years for google maps to update certain features - here's how they get the data to update street view, traffic, and more (2021). https://www.businessinsider.com/guides/tech/how-often-does-google-maps-update. Accessed 06 Sept 2024
5. Arya, D., Maeda, H., Ghosh, S.K., Toshniwal, D., Sekimoto, Y.: RDD2022: a multi-national image dataset for automatic road damage detection (2022). https://doi. org/10.48550/ARXIV.2209.08538
6. Bučko, B., Lieskovská, E., Zábovská, K., Zábovský, M.: Computer vision based pot-hole detection under challenging conditions. Sensors **22**(22), 8878 (2022). https:// doi.org/10.3390/s22228878

7. Dacayan, T., Ponte, E., Huang, K., Kwak, D.: Utilizing a spatial grid for automated parking space vacancy detection. In: 2023 International Conference on Computational Science and Computational Intelligence (CSCI). IEEE (2023). https://doi.org/10.1109/csci62032.2023.00169

8. Devarakonda, S., Chittaranjan, S., Kwak, D., Nath, B.: In: MobiQuitous 2020 - 17th EAI International Conference on Mobile and Ubiquitous Systems: Computing, Networking and Services, MobiQuitous 2020, pp. 206–214. ACM (2020)

9. Hafezzadeh, R., Autelitano, F., Giuliani, F.: Asphalt-based cold patches for repairing road potholes - an overview. Constr. Build. Mater. **306**, 124870 (2021). https://doi.org/10.1016/j.conbuildmat.2021.124870

10. Hoseini, M., Puliti, S., Hoffmann, S., Astrup, R.: Pothole detection in the woods: a deep learning approach for forest road surface monitoring with dashcams. Int. J. For. Eng. **35**(2), 303–312 (2023). https://doi.org/10.1080/14942119.2023.2290795

11. Kwak, D., Kim, D., Liu, R., Iftode, L., Nath, B.: Tweeting traffic image reports on the road. In: Proceedings of the 6th International Conference on Mobile Computing, Applications and Services. MobiCASE (2014). https://doi.org/10.4108/icst.mobicase.2014.257815

12. Kwak, D., Kim, D., Liu, R., Nath, B., Iftode, L.: DoppelDriver: counterfactual actual travel times for alternative routes. In: 2015 IEEE International Conference on Pervasive Computing and Communications (PerCom), pp. 178–185. IEEE (2015). https://doi.org/10.1109/PERCOM.2015.7146525

13. Kwak, D., Liu, R., Kim, D., Nath, B., Iftode, L.: Seeing is believing: sharing realtime visual traffic information via vehicular clouds. IEEE Access **4**, 3617–3631 (2016). https://doi.org/10.1109/ACCESS.2016.2569585

14. Liu, R., et al.: Themis: a participatory navigation system for balanced traffic routing. In: 2014 IEEE Vehicular Networking Conference (VNC), pp. 159–166. IEEE (2014). https://doi.org/10.1109/VNC.2014.7013335

15. Liu, R., et al.: Balanced traffic routing: design, implementation, and evaluation. Ad Hoc Netw. **37**, 14–28 (2016). https://doi.org/10.1016/j.adhoc.2015.09.001

16. Liu, R., Yang, Y., Kwak, D., Zhang, D., Iftode, L., Nath, B.: Your search path tells others where to park: towards fine-grained parking availability crowdsourcing using parking decision models. Proc. ACM Interact. Mob. Wearable Ubiquit. Technol. **1**(3), 1–27 (2017). https://doi.org/10.1145/3130942

17. Liu, Z., Gu, X., Chen, J., Wang, D., Chen, Y., Wang, L.: Automatic recognition of pavement cracks from combined GPR B-scan and C-scan images using multiscale feature fusion deep neural networks. Autom. Constr. **146**, 104698 (2023). https://doi.org/10.1016/j.autcon.2022.104698

18. Mednis, A., Strazdins, G., Zviedris, R., Kanonirs, G., Selavo, L.: Real time pothole detection using android smartphones with accelerometers. In: 2011 International Conference on Distributed Computing in Sensor Systems and Workshops (DCOSS), pp. 1–6 (2011). https://doi.org/10.1109/DCOSS.2011.5982206

19. Patel, R., Huang, L., Vejarano, G.: Pothole detection from dash camera images using yolov5. In: 26th International Conference on Image Processing, Computer Vision, & Pattern Recognition (IPCV 2022), Las Vegas, NV, USA (2022)

20. Ponte, E., Amparo, X., Huang, K., Kwak, D.: Automatic pill identification system based on deep learning and image preprocessing. In: 2023 Congress in Computer Science, Computer Engineering, & Applied Computing (CSCE). IEEE (2023). https://doi.org/10.1109/csce60160.2023.00324

21. PTI: Accidents caused by potholes killed 5626 people during 2018–2020. https://www.tribuneindia.com/news/nation/accidents-caused-by-potholes-killed-5626-people-during-2018-2020-424252. Accessed 15 May 2024

22. Serrano, G., Kwak, D.: Real-time sign language recognition using computer vision and AI. In: 2023 International Conference on Computational Science and Computational Intelligence (CSCI). IEEE (2023). https://doi.org/10.1109/csci62032.2023.00198

23. Shahzad, M., Ali, F., Shirazi, S.H., Rasheed, A., Ahmad, A., Shah, B., Kwak, D.: Blood cell image segmentation and classification: a systematic review. PeerJ Comput. Sci. **10**, e1813 (2024). https://doi.org/10.7717/peerj-cs.1813

24. Wang, D., Liu, Z., Gu, X., Wu, W., Chen, Y., Wang, L.: Automatic detection of pothole distress in asphalt pavement using improved convolutional neural networks. Remote Sens. **14**(16), 3892 (2022). https://doi.org/10.3390/rs14163892

25. Wu, Y., Kirillov, A., Massa, F., Lo, W.Y., Girshick, R.: Detectron2 (2019). https://github.com/facebookresearch/detectron2

26. Xin, H., et al.: Sustainable road pothole detection: a crowdsourcing based multi-sensors fusion approach. Sustainability **15**(8), 6610 (2023). https://doi.org/10.3390/su15086610

27. Xu, M., Huang, J., Huang, K., Liu, F.: Incorporating tumor edge information for fine-grained BI-RADS classification of breast ultrasound images. IEEE Access **12**, 38732–38744 (2024). https://doi.org/10.1109/access.2024.3374380

28. Zhang, Y., et al.: Road damage detection using UAV images based on multi-level attention mechanism. Autom. Constr. **144**, 104613 (2022). https://doi.org/10.1016/j.autcon.2022.104613

Energy-Efficiency Modeling for AI Applications on Edge Computing

Vamsi Krishna Bhagavathula, Xian Gao, Yi Zhou$^{(\boxtimes)}$, Rania Hodhod, and Lixin Wang

TSYS School of Computer Science, Columbus State University, Columbus, GA, USA
{bhagavathula_vam.s,gao_xian}@students.columbusstate.edu,
{zhou_yi,hodhod_rania,wang_lixin}@columbusstate.edu

Abstract. This research explores optimizing energy use in AI applications on edge devices like Raspberry Pi. We developed two models to predict resource usage and power consumption of AI algorithms, considering factors like CPU and memory use, algorithm speed, dataset size, and types. By using regression-based methods, we quantified the impact of these factors on energy consumption. The models provide developers with practical tools to evaluate and optimize the energy efficiency of AI deployments on edge servers without sacrificing performance.

Keywords: Edge computing · Energy efficiency · Predictive modeling · Machine learning regression · Resource utilization · AI algorithms

1 Introduction

Edge computing involves processing data close to its source, using sensors and IoT devices, rather than relying on distant data centers [1]. This approach enhances responsiveness and reduces bandwidth needs, especially relevant with the rise of IoT and AI [2].

AI algorithms, which include supervised, unsupervised, and deep learning type [3,4], aim to emulate human intelligence by processing data and making predictions. Deploying these algorithms on cost-effective edge devices like the Raspberry Pi is challenging due to their limited resources [5]. Understanding the energy impacts of AI tasks on such devices is crucial [6].

To address this, we create two machine-learning models for predicting power consumption and resource utilization. These models help optimize the performance of AI applications on edge devices by forecasting energy use and resource demands based on algorithm characteristics and dataset features [7,8]. The goal is to improve the efficiency and sustainability of AI in edge computing, supported by extensive statistical analysis.

H. R. Arabnia et al. (Eds.): CSCE 2024, CCIS 2260, pp. 164–177, 2025.
https://doi.org/10.1007/978-3-031-85923-6_13

1.1   Motivation

The motivations for this thesis are as follows:

Motivation 1: Edge computing, known for reduced latency and real-time processing, is widely used in industries like healthcare and transportation [9]. This project uses a Raspberry Pi as an edge server due to its cost-effectiveness, power efficiency, and support for various operating systems suitable for AI tasks [5].

Motivation 2: Running AI algorithms on edge servers rather than cloud servers allows real-time data analysis at the network edge, reducing latency and enhancing privacy and security [10, 11].

Motivation 3: The main challenge in edge computing is efficiently managing resources for AI tasks, especially on battery-operated servers [12]. While existing research often focuses on either speed or energy efficiency, this study addresses the gap by modeling the energy impacts of AI algorithms on edge devices, considering factors like dataset size, CPU and memory usage, and execution time [13].

1.2   Methodology

The overarching goal of this study is to construct energy and resource models for CPU- and memory-intensive AI algorithms on edge servers. We begin by rigorously profiling an edge server's power consumption and utilization (CPU, memory) while executing a suite of representative AI algorithms. This experimental phase considers algorithms with diverse computational complexities and varying dataset sizes, providing a comprehensive dataset for analysis. Then, we develop regression models that facilitate modeling the impacts of AI algorithms on their underlying Raspberry Pi server. By proposing a predictive energy model based on CPU and memory usage, dataset size, and AI algorithm type, this work aims to guide the development of sustainable AI schedulers for edge servers that strike a balance between energy efficiency and optimal performance.

The contributions of this study are summarized as follows:

* We profile the resource usage and power consumption of CPU-intensive and memory-intensive AI algorithms on a low-cost edge computing server.
* We develop models that predict resource utilization and power consumption using regression-based AI algorithms.

2   Literature Review

The rapid growth of the Internet of Things (IoT) has underscored the importance of edge computing, which processes data near its source to reduce latency and conserve bandwidth [2]. This is crucial as the proliferation of IoT devices generates massive amounts of data, necessitating efficient processing [5]. Edge computing has enabled real-time applications like autonomous vehicles, smart cities, and industrial automation [6].

However, the limited resources of edge devices pose challenges for AI applications, impacting their performance [7]. Despite this, AI-integrated edge computing offers transformative potential, enabling innovations such as predictive maintenance, personalized healthcare, and intelligent transportation [1,14,15].

Research highlights the significant impact of AI on edge device resources, emphasizing the need to optimize deployment for efficiency [3,5]. Advances like model compression have improved AI execution on constrained devices [4]. Yet, many energy-efficiency strategies lack comprehensiveness, failing to address the diverse needs of AI applications [10,11].

There is a clear need for detailed models that predict energy consumption by considering various factors like hardware usage and AI type [16]. Developing such models is crucial for optimizing AI deployment on edge devices, supporting their effective operation within resource limits [17], and driving innovation across industries [2].

3   Experimental Design and Implementation

3.1   System Design

This section presents a comprehensive study of the system designed to evaluate the energy efficiency and resource utilization of AI algorithms on Raspberry Pi. The system integrates both hardware and software components seamlessly, providing a robust platform for conducting controlled experiments with various algorithms and datasets.

System Overview. The core of this investigation involves a Raspberry Pi 3 Model B, which is used as a standalone edge computing platform to assess the efficiency of various machine learning models. This device is outfitted with 1 GB of RAM and a 32 GB microSD card, which accommodates the operating system and the data needed for testing. The goal is to analyze how different algorithms perform under varying workloads and to understand the resource dynamics of edge computing within real-world constraints.

Hardware Configuration. The chosen hardware, the Raspberry Pi 3, epitomizes typical edge devices-limited in power yet critical for on-site data processing tasks. It is connected to a power meter that meticulously records the energy usage during the execution of each algorithm. Automated scripts developed in Python track other essential metrics, including CPU and memory usage, along with the execution time of each task.

Software Environment. The system uses a Linux-based OS for its stability and lightweight footprint. Python, renowned for its robust library ecosystem and suitability for scientific computing, supports the implementation of all machine learning algorithms through the Scikit-learn library. This setup mirrors a typical edge computing software stack, providing a realistic experimental environment.

Algorithm Selection and Configuration. The study incorporates three distinct algorithms to address various machine learning challenges in edge computing, and these three algorithms are shown in Fig. 1.

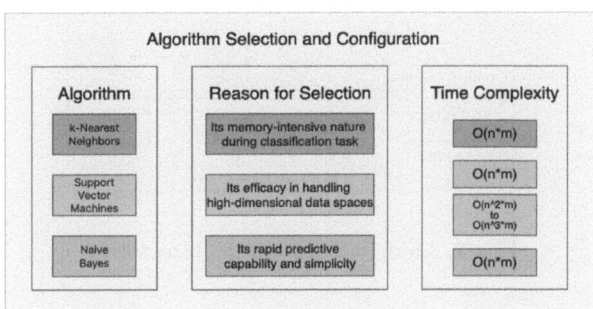

Fig. 1. Algorithm Selection and Configuration.

The k-Nearest Neighbors (KNN) algorithm was selected for its memory-intensive nature, as it classifies data based on proximity to k neighbors, with complexity scaling linearly with both training examples and dimensions ($O(n * m)$). The Support Vector Machines (SVM) algorithm was chosen for its ability to handle high-dimensional data, finding an optimal hyperplane for class separation, with complexity varying from $O(n * m)$ for linear kernels to $O(n^2 * m)$ or higher for non-linear kernels. Lastly, Naive Bayes was included for its simplicity and rapid predictions, with linear complexity ($O(n * m)$), making it suitable for resource-constrained edge environments.

Performance Metrics. Metrics such as CPU utilization, memory utilization, run time, and dataset size are systematically recorded to evaluate the performance of each algorithm. These metrics offer insights into the practical limitations and capabilities of deploying sophisticated machine learning models in edge computing scenarios. The modeling system orchestrates a set of AI algorithms running independently on an edge server. After collecting computing resource utilization and power consumption data from the underlying edge server, models are trained to predict future resource utilization and power consumption. This process is explained in Fig. 2.

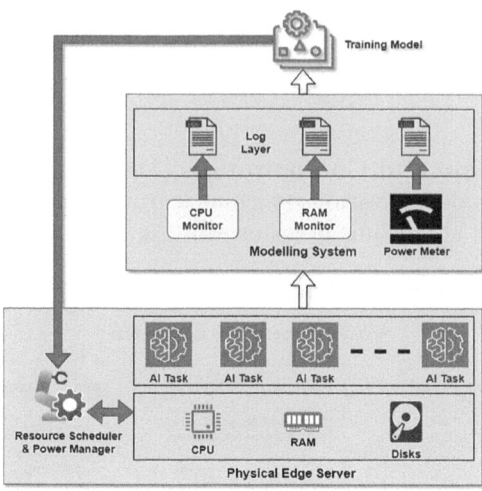

Fig. 2. Modeling System Architecture.

3.2 Methodology

Dataset. This study incorporates three distinct datasets, each presenting unique challenges and characteristics, to explore the performance and energy utilization of AI algorithms on Raspberry Pi devices: the Iris dataset, the Pima Indian Diabetes dataset, and the Breast Cancer dataset. These datasets were carefully chosen to examine a range of computational challenges and demonstrate how AI algorithms can be tailored for energy efficiency on constrained devices. The sizes of the datasets will vary each time the algorithms are run on the Pi.

Iris Dataset: Overview: The dataset comprises 150 observations, each with four attributes describing the dimensions of iris plant species.

Importance: This dataset is particularly useful for establishing a performance testing baseline due to its simplicity and minimal data volume, making it suitable for initial algorithm calibration on edge devices.

Pima Indian Diabetes Dataset: Overview: This database contains 768 instances, each with eight predictive attributes plus a target attribute indicating diabetes in Pima Indian women.

Importance: This medically oriented dataset presents a medium complexity challenge, enabling the assessment of how effectively edge computing devices handle health-related data with multiple input variables.

Breast Cancer Dataset: Overview: It includes 569 samples with 30 attributes derived from breast mass images used to classify tumors as malignant or benign.

Importance: Given its high-dimensional data, this dataset tests Raspberry Pi's capacity to manage and analyze detailed information, which is essential for critical health applications like tumor classification.

Performance metrics such as run time, CPU and memory usage, energy consumption, and dataset size will be recorded for each dataset processed by the AI algorithms, providing comparative insights and guiding the optimization of AI deployment on the Raspberry Pi.

The experiment involves altering the sizes of each dataset to test the algorithms under different data volumes. This variability helps to explore scalability and the impact of increased data complexity on resource consumption and operational efficiency.

Data Preprocessing. Following the execution of the selected AI algorithms using the Iris, Pima Indian Diabetes, and Breast Cancer datasets on the Raspberry Pi, we compiled comprehensive data for the following metrics:

Power Consumption: This measure quantifies the total energy consumed by the Raspberry Pi during the execution of each algorithm. It is essential for identifying energy-efficient algorithms suitable for edge devices.

CPU Utilization: This indicator represents the percentage of CPU resources engaged during the processing of each dataset. This data helps us understand how different algorithms leverage CPU capacity.

Memory Utilization: This metric tracks the amount of RAM the Raspberry Pi uses while running the algorithms. Memory demand can significantly affect the feasibility of deploying specific AI models on edge devices.

Run Time: This metric records the time taken to complete each task. It is critical for evaluating the operational efficiency of algorithms in real-time applications.

Dataset Size: Since the size of the datasets was deliberately varied, this metric provides insights into how changes in data volume impact the algorithms' performance and resource requirements.

Algorithm Category: This category classifies the algorithm used, providing a basis for comparative analysis across various types of AI methodologies.

Dataset Type: This metric identifies the specific dataset processed, aligning performance metrics with dataset characteristics to discern how different data types influence algorithm behavior.

Once the algorithms and datasets are ready, we can go ahead and collect the data.

One-Hot Encoding: In statistical modeling, particularly in regression analysis, all input data must be correctly formatted. Categorical variables, such as algorithm type (KNN, SVM, Naïve Bayes) or dataset type (Iris, Breast Cancer, Pima), inherently lack numerical properties and are not directly suitable for inclusion in regression models, which require numerical inputs for computation. To meet this requirement, one-hot encoding is utilized. This process converts categorical variables into a set of binary columns, with each column representing a single category. Such transformation is critical as it enables the inclusion of categorical data in regression analysis, preserving the statistical validity and functionality of the model.

One-Hot Encoding Implementation: In this study, one-hot encoding was implemented on the categorical variables concerning algorithm and dataset types. Each category within these variables was converted into a unique binary variable. For example, the "Algorithm Category" was separated into three binary variables: Algorithm_Category_KNN, Algorithm_Category_SVM, and Algorithm_Category_Naïve Bayes. The "Dataset Type" was similarly divided into Dataset_Type_Iris, Dataset_Type_Breast Cancer, and Dataset_Type_Pima. Within these binary variables, a category's presence in a data point is denoted by 1, and absence by 0. This technique avoids any potential ordinal interpretations by the regression model, ensuring that each category is treated as an independent feature, which enhances the accuracy of the model's assessments. And the data collected after applying this technique.

Data Cleaning: Data cleaning is crucial in this study as it ensures the accuracy and reliability of our results. By removing errors and inconsistencies, data cleaning ensures that the analysis of AI algorithms' performance on the Raspberry Pi is based on accurate data, which is essential for drawing valid conclusions about energy and resource usage. Furthermore, clean data significantly improves the performance of machine learning models, which are central to developing effective predictive models for energy consumption and resource utilization. It also facilitates the integration of various datasets, critical for a comprehensive analysis across different algorithms. Moreover, clear and clean data aids in straightforward interpretation and decision-making, essential for optimizing edge device AI applications. Proper data cleaning also enhances the reproducibility of our research, adding credibility and scientific value. Lastly, in the context of edge computing, where resources are at a premium, ensuring data is clean means computational resources are not wasted on processing irrelevant or erroneous information, optimizing the capabilities of the Raspberry Pi.

Figure 3 represents how often each algorithm and dataset type appears in my dataset after the one-hot encoding process. It shows Algorithm Category$_{KNN}$, Algorithm Category$_{Naïve Bayes}$, and Algorithm Category$_{SVM}$, where each graph counts how many data points the respective algorithm uses. This is important because it shows whether our data is balanced or if one algorithm is overrepresented, which might affect the reliability of our models. On the other hand, it shows Dataset Type$_{Breast Cancer}$, Dataset Type$_{Pima}$, and Dataset Type$_{Iris}$ graphs, which count how many data points are involved in each dataset. This information is crucial for understanding if some datasets are used more often.

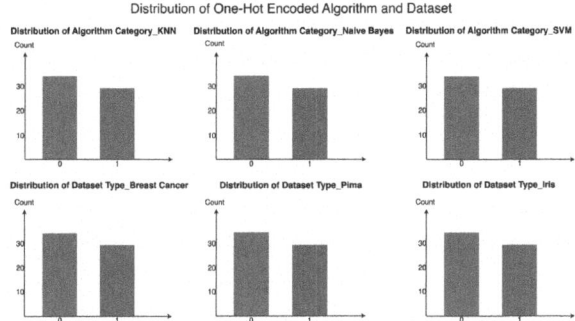

Fig. 3. Distribution of One-Hot Encoded Algorithm and Dataset.

3.3   Application of OLS Regression

With the dataset in the appropriate format, I applied Ordinary Least Squares (OLS) regression to model the relationships between various predictors and the performance metrics of interest: CPU Utilization, Memory Utilization, Run Time, and Power Consumption. OLS regression is advantageous due to its simplicity and effectiveness in estimating the parameters.

Model Specifications:

In the regression models:

* The dependent variables were the performance metrics I aimed to predict.
* The independent variables included one-hot encoded algorithm categories, dataset types, and other relevant predictors such as Dataset Size.
* The coefficients from these models provided critical insights, quantifying how changes in each predictor are expected to influence the dependent variables, assuming all other variables are held constant.

4   Discussion of Results and Conclusion

In this section, we will present our findings and discuss the developed predictive models after completing the data preprocessing steps, including one-hot encoding. We utilized Ordinary Least Squares (OLS) regression to explore the relationships within the data. Following the regression analysis, we meticulously developed models to predict the primary factors affecting hardware performance.

4.1   Results

In this section, we will provide a thorough explanation of these models. The insights we gathered from these models provide a good understanding of how many factors affect the energy efficiency and resource utilization of AI algorithms on edge devices.

CPU Utilization Model. To predict this model, we used CPU utilization as the dependent variable, and the independent variables are the algorithm category, dataset size, and dataset type.

Equation

$$
\begin{aligned}
\text{CPU Utilization} = {} & 0.0576 + (3.708 \times 10^{-5} \times \text{Dataset Size}) \\
& + 0.0184 \times \text{Algorithm Category}_{\text{KNN}} \\
& + 0.0198 \times \text{Algorithm Category}_{\text{Naive Bayes}} \\
& + 0.0194 \times \text{Algorithm Category}_{\text{SVM}} \\
& + 0.1814 \times \text{Dataset Type}_{\text{Breast Cancer}} \\
& - 0.0728 \times \text{Dataset Type}_{\text{Pima}} \\
& - 0.0510 \times \text{Dataset Type}_{\text{Iris}}
\end{aligned}
$$

Key Findings and Interpretation

* Dataset Size: Incremental increases in CPU utilization were observed with larger datasets, indicating increased computational demands.
* Algorithm Category: Both KNN and SVM algorithms exhibited higher CPU utilization, suggesting these algorithms are more computationally intensive, especially with increasing dataset sizes. The Naïve Bayes algorithm also showed heightened CPU usage, indicating significant computational requirements in handling large datasets or complex transformations.
* Dataset Type: The Breast Cancer dataset significantly increased CPU usage, reflecting its complexity, whereas the Pima and Iris datasets showed reduced CPU demands.

Figure 4 shows the CPU Utilization across different algorithms and datasets. It gives a clear overview of how each algorithm performs in terms of CPU usage when applied to several types of data.

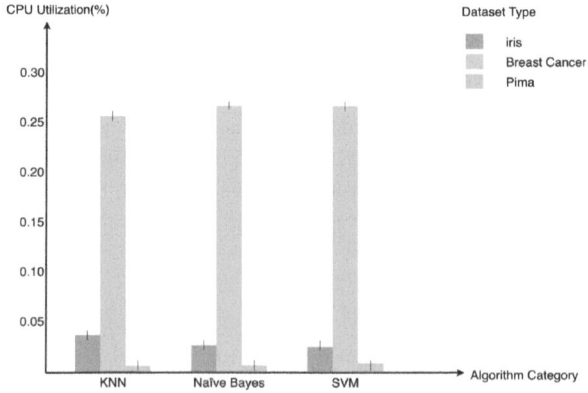

Fig. 4. CPU Utilization across algorithms and datasets.

Memory Utilization Model. To predict this model, we used the Dependent Variable memory utilization, and the independent variables are the algorithm category, dataset size, and dataset type.

Equation

$$\text{Memory Utilization} = 0.5421 + (0.0056 \times \text{Dataset Size})$$
$$- 0.4360 \times \text{Algorithm Category}_{\text{KNN}}$$
$$+ 1.4612 \times \text{Algorithm Category}_{\text{Naive Bayes}}$$
$$- 0.4831 \times \text{Algorithm Category}_{\text{SVM}}$$
$$- 0.5288 \times \text{Dataset Type}_{\text{Breast Cancer}}$$
$$+ 1.6857 \times \text{Dataset Type}_{\text{Pima}}$$
$$- 0.6148 \times \text{Dataset Type}_{\text{Iris}}$$

Key Findings and Interpretation

* Dataset Size: A slight increase in memory demands corresponds with larger dataset sizes.
* Algorithm Impact: The Naïve Bayes algorithm leads to a significant rise in memory use, demonstrating its substantial memory requirements for probability computations and data transformations. Conversely, both KNN and SVM algorithms show lower memory usage.
* Dataset Type: The Pima dataset type incurs higher memory utilization due to its complexity, while the Breast Cancer and Iris datasets are less demanding on memory.

Memory utilization, showing how memory usage varies with each algorithm when processing different datasets is displayed in Fig. 5. This visualization helps in comparing the memory demands of each algorithm across a range of conditions.

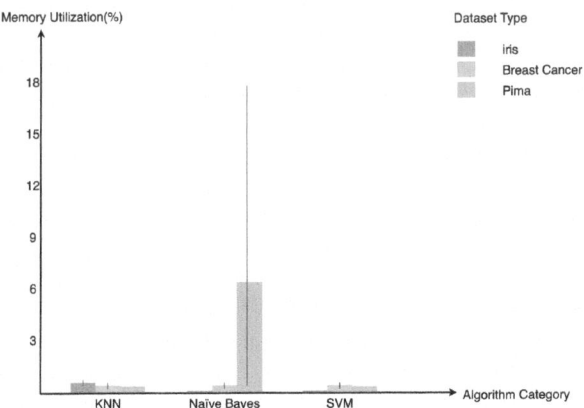

Fig. 5. Memory utilization across algorithms and datasets.

Run Time Model. To predict this model, we used the Dependent Variable run time, and the independent variables are the algorithm category, dataset size, and dataset type.

Equation

$$
\begin{aligned}
\text{Run Time} = {} & 1.5448 + 0.0149 \times \text{Dataset Size} \\
& - 2.9248 \times \text{Algorithm Category}_{\text{KNN}} \\
& - 2.2018 \times \text{Algorithm Category}_{\text{Naive Bayes}} \\
& + 6.6715 \times \text{Algorithm Category}_{\text{SVM}} \\
& - 1.4306 \times \text{Dataset Type}_{\text{Breast Cancer}} \\
& + 4.6358 \times \text{Dataset Type}_{\text{Pima}} \\
& - 1.6604 \times \text{Dataset Type}_{\text{Iris}}
\end{aligned}
$$

Key Findings

* The SVM algorithm significantly increases run time, indicating high computational complexity. In contrast, KNN is associated with faster execution times, reflecting efficiency in certain contexts.
* Dataset Type: Pima datasets increase run time, due to their inherent complexity.
* Dataset Size: Dataset size was not a significant factor, suggesting that other elements might mitigate its computational impact under certain conditions.

Power Consumption Model. To predict this model, we used the Dependent Variable power consumption, and the independent variables are the algorithm category, dataset size, dataset type, CPU utilization, run time, and memory utilization.

Equation

$$
\begin{aligned}
\text{Power Consumption} = {} & 2.9065 - 0.0005 \times \text{Dataset Size} \\
& + 1.0143 \times \text{Indicator for KNN} \\
& + 1.0004 \times \text{Indicator for Naive Bayes} \\
& + 0.8918 \times \text{Indicator for SVM} \\
& + 0.3461 \times \text{Indicator for Breast Cancer} \\
& + 1.6156 \times \text{Indicator for Pima} \\
& + 0.9447 \times \text{Indicator for Iris} \\
& + 5.5121 \times \text{CPU Utilization} \\
& + 0.0044 \times \text{Memory Utilization} \\
& + 0.0018 \times \text{Run Time}
\end{aligned}
$$

Key Findings and Interpretation

* Algorithm and Dataset Impact: The use of algorithms such as KNN, Naïve Bayes, and SVM leads to increased power consumption, emphasizing their energy demands. The Pima dataset notably elevates power usage due to its complex processing needs.
* CPU Utilization: A strong positive relationship with power consumption indicates that higher CPU activity escalates energy use.
* Dataset Size: The negligible and non-significant negative coefficient suggests a minor decrease in power consumption with larger datasets. This decrease may reflect the implementation of more efficient data processing techniques.

Figure 6 displays a consolidated bar chart illustrating Power Consumption across various algorithms and datasets. This visualization offers a straightforward comparison of power usage variations among different algorithms and datasets, effectively highlighting the energy efficiency or consumption linked to distinct computational tasks.

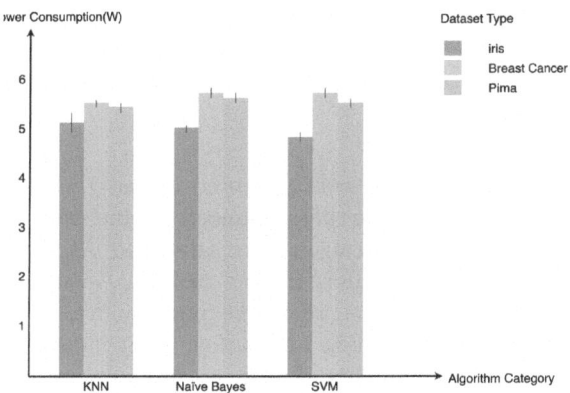

Fig. 6. Power Consumption across Algorithms and Datasets.

4.2   Conclusion

This thesis has successfully demonstrated the development and validation of predictive models for modeling energy consumption and resource utilization in AI applications on edge devices, particularly Raspberry Pi servers. Two main models were developed through rigorous experimental setup and data analysis: a power consumption model and a resource utilization model. These models employ regression techniques to predict how different AI algorithms affect energy usage and hardware resource demands based on various operational parameters such as algorithm type, dataset size, and execution times.

The findings from this study highlight several key insights:

* The choice of algorithm and the nature of the data being processed can significantly influence the power consumption and resource utilization of AI applications.
* The predictive models developed herein provide an empirical basis for making informed decisions about deploying AI applications on edge devices, helping to balance operational efficiency with energy conservation.
* The study contributes to the broader field of edge computing by offering a methodological framework that can be applied to other similar low-power edge computing scenarios, enhancing the sustainability and efficiency of AI technologies in resource-constrained environments.
* This research has significant implications for developers and system architects focusing on the edge computing paradigm, particularly in sectors where energy efficiency is paramount. It provides a foundation for further schedulers leveraging such models to dynamically adjust workloads and operational conditions.

This thesis not only addresses the practical challenges of AI deployments on low-power edge devices but also contributes to the theoretical understanding of energy dynamics in edge computing, thereby paving the way for more sustainable AI deployments across various industries.

4.3 Future Work

Building on the foundational research presented in this thesis, several exciting directions for future work could further enhance the efficiency and applicability of AI on edge devices. First, we can explore advanced AI methodologies that offer complex models considering more factors. Second, we can develop dynamic adjustment frameworks that utilize real-time performance and environmental data, to manage computational tasks and power settings adaptively, especially in variable operational environments. Third, we can explore the integration of renewable energy sources with edge devices, exploring how sustainable energy solutions can support autonomous edge operations. Last, we can extend optimization efforts to edge-cloud computing systems that could further reduce the energy footprint by intelligently offloading expensive AI tasks from edge servers to cloud servers.

Acknowledgments. Thank the authors of this paper for their contributions.

Disclosure of Interests. The authors have no competing interests to declare that are relevant to the content of this article.

References

1. Shi, W., Dustdar, S.: The promise of edge computing. Computer **49**(5), 78–81 (2016)

2. Zhu, S., Ota, K., Dong, M.: Energy-efficient artificial intelligence of things with intelligent edge. IEEE Internet Things J. **9**(10), 7525–7532 (2022)
3. Zhang, W., et al.: Lightweight fruit-detection algorithm for edge computing applications. Front. Plant Sci. **12**, 740936 (2021)
4. Schizas, N., Karras, A., Karras, C., Sioutas, S.: TinyML for ultra-low power AI and large scale IoT deployments: a systematic review. Future Internet **14**(12), 363 (2022)
5. Yu, W., et al.: A survey on the edge computing for the internet of things. IEEE Access **6**, 6900–6919 (2017)
6. Shi, W., Cao, J., Zhang, Q., Li, Y., Lanyu, X.: Edge computing: vision and challenges. IEEE Internet Things J. **3**(5), 637–646 (2016)
7. Satyanarayanan, M.: The emergence of edge computing. Computer **50**(1), 30–39 (2017)
8. Chang, Z., Liu, S., Xiong, X., Cai, Z., Guoqing, T.: A survey of recent advances in edge-computing-powered artificial intelligence of things. IEEE Internet Things J. **8**(18), 13849–13875 (2021)
9. Gamatie, A., Devic, G., Sassatelli, G., Bernabovi, S., Naudin, P., Chapman, M.: Towards energy-efficient heterogeneous multicore architectures for edge computing. IEEE Access **7**, 49474–49491 (2019)
10. Sodhro, A.H., Pirbhulal, S., De Albuquerque, V.: Artificial intelligence-driven mechanism for edge computing-based industrial applications. IEEE Trans. Ind. Inform. **15**(7), 4235–4243 (2019)
11. Cao, K., Liu, Y., Meng, G., Sun, Q.: An overview on edge computing research. IEEE Access **8**, 85714–85728 (2020)
12. Badhib, A., Alshehri, S., Cherif, A.: A robust device-to-device continuous authentication protocol for the internet of things. IEEE Access **9**, 124768–124792 (2021)
13. Bhattacharya, T., et al.: Performance modeling for I/O-intensive applications on virtual machines. Concurr. Comput. Pract. Exp. **34**(10), e6823 (2022)
14. Nguyen, H.H., Zhou, Y., Kushagra, K., Qin, X.: Computation offloading from edge to equipment for smart manufacturing. In: 2022 IEEE/ACM 15th International Conference on Utility and Cloud Computing (UCC), pp. 207–212. IEEE (2022)
15. Wang, C., Tian, Y., Shi, W., Zhou, Y., Zhou, Y.: Predicting drug response using two factors from cell lines-drug sensitivity and basal gene expression. In: 2023 Congress in Computer Science, Computer Engineering, & Applied Computing (CSCE), pp. 522–525. IEEE (2023)
16. Shi, Y., Yang, K., Jiang, T., Zhang, J., Letaief, K.B.: Communication-efficient edge AI: algorithms and systems. IEEE Commun. Surv. Tutor. **22**(4), 2167–2191 (2020)
17. Zhi Zhou, X., Chen, E.L., Zeng, L., Luo, K., Zhang, J.: Edge intelligence: Paving the last mile of artificial intelligence with edge computing. Proc. IEEE **107**(8), 1738–1762 (2019)

Optimizing Wireless Sensor Network Placement Using Bacterial Foraging Optimization

Rahul Priyadarshi[1]([✉]) [iD], Naga Raghuram Chinnapurapu[2] [iD], Piyush Rawat[3],
Tiansheng Yang[4], and Rajkumar Singh Rathore[5] [iD]

[1] Faculty of Engineering and Technology, ITER, Siksha 'O' Anusandhan (Deemed to be University), Bhubaneswar, India
rahul.glorious91@gmail.com
[2] Department of Electronics and Communication Engineering, Velagapudi Ramakrishna Siddhartha Engineering College, Vijayawada 520007, Andhra Pradesh, India
[3] School of Computer Science, UPES, Dehradun 248007, Uttarakhand, India
[4] University of South Wales, Llantwit Road, Pontypridd CF37, B1DL, UK
[5] Cardiff School of Technologies, Cardiff Metropolitan University, Llandaff Campus, Western, Avenue, Cardiff CF5 2QS, UK

Abstract. This paper investigates the application of Bacterial Foraging Optimization (BFO) for optimizing node placement in Wireless Sensor Networks (WSNs). Efficient node placement is crucial for enhancing network coverage, connectivity, and energy efficiency. BFO, inspired by bacterial foraging behavior, is particularly suited for this task due to its ability to adaptively explore and exploit search spaces. The study compares BFO against traditional optimization methods like Genetic Algorithms (GA) and Particle Swarm Optimization (PSO), highlighting its superior performance in achieving optimal node configurations. Experimental results demonstrate significant improvements in coverage, connectivity, and energy consumption metrics, validating BFO as an effective tool for optimizing WSN deployments. This research contributes insights into leveraging BFO for enhancing WSN performance and identifies avenues for further exploration in dynamic and large-scale deployment scenarios.

Keywords: Wireless Sensor Networks · Bacterial Foraging Optimization · Node Deployment · Coverage · Energy Efficiency

1 Introduction

Optimizing the placement of sensor nodes in Wireless Sensor Networks (WSNs) is crucial for ensuring efficient operation and maximizing the network's performance. The strategic placement of nodes directly impacts key aspects such as coverage, connectivity, energy consumption, and overall data reliability [1]. Inadequate node placement can lead to coverage gaps, poor connectivity, increased energy consumption, and reduced network lifespan. Therefore, the motivation to optimize node placement arises from the necessity to address these challenges comprehensively and to achieve optimal network performance in various application domains including environmental monitoring, industrial automation, healthcare, and smart cities [2].

Efficient node placement is pivotal for maximizing the coverage of the monitored area, ensuring that every point of interest is adequately covered by sensor nodes to detect events and collect data accurately. Moreover, optimal placement enhances network connectivity by establishing reliable communication links among nodes, which is essential for seamless data transmission and real-time decision-making. Energy efficiency is another critical factor as sensor nodes are typically battery-powered with limited energy resources. Strategic node placement aims to minimize energy consumption by balancing the workload among nodes, thereby prolonging the network's operational lifetime and reducing maintenance costs [3, 4].

Bacterial Foraging Optimization (BFO) emerges as a promising approach for optimizing node placement in WSNs due to its bio-inspired nature, which mimics the foraging behavior of bacterial colonies. BFO operates through iterative movements of virtual bacterial cells in a search space, guided by local environmental conditions (objective function landscape). This adaptive search strategy allows BFO to effectively explore diverse node placement configurations and exploit promising regions of the search space to find near-optimal solutions. Its ability to dynamically adjust node positions in response to environmental changes or network dynamics makes it suitable for handling the uncertainties and complexities inherent in WSN deployments [5, 6].

In summary, the integration of BFO holds significant promise for enhancing the performance of WSNs by optimizing node placement. This paper investigates the application of BFO in WSNs, compares its effectiveness against traditional optimization methods, and discusses practical implications for deploying BFO in real-world scenarios. The subsequent sections will provide a detailed exploration of BFO's methodologies, experimental findings, and implications for advancing the efficiency and reliability of WSN deployments.

2 Literature Review

The optimization of node placement in WSNs has been extensively studied in the literature, employing various optimization techniques to achieve optimal network performance [7, 8]. Traditional approaches often focus on maximizing coverage, improving connectivity, and minimizing energy consumption. One prevalent strategy involves grid-based placement, where nodes are uniformly distributed across the sensing area. However, grid-based methods may lead to suboptimal coverage and inefficiencies in dynamic environments [9, 10].

Furthermore, heuristic-based approaches have gained popularity for their ability to adapt to changing environmental conditions and network requirements [11, 12]. These approaches leverage optimization algorithms to strategically position nodes based on specific objectives such as maximizing coverage overlap, minimizing interference, or optimizing energy consumption [13, 14].

2.1 Comparison with Other Optimization Techniques

Several optimization techniques have been applied to WSN node placement, each offering unique advantages and trade-offs:

Genetic Algorithms (GA): GA is a popular evolutionary computing technique that mimics natural selection processes to iteratively evolve solutions. In node placement optimization, GA explores a population of candidate solutions through selection, crossover, and mutation operations to find optimal placements that maximize coverage and connectivity. However, GA may require significant computational resources and time to converge to a near-optimal solution, particularly in large-scale deployments [15, 16].

Particle Swarm Optimization (PSO): PSO is inspired by social behavior observed in bird flocking or fish schooling. It optimizes node placements by iteratively adjusting the positions of virtual particles in the search space. Each particle represents a potential solution, and its movement is influenced by its own best-known position and the global best position found by the swarm. PSO efficiently balances exploration and exploitation to find optimal node configurations, but its performance can be sensitive to parameter settings and may struggle with local optima in complex environments [17, 18].

Differential Evolution (DE): DE is a population-based stochastic optimization technique that iteratively improves candidate solutions by perturbing and recombining their parameter vectors. In node placement optimization, DE adjusts node positions based on the fitness function evaluation, aiming to enhance coverage and connectivity while minimizing energy consumption. DE is known for its robustness and effectiveness in handling multi-dimensional optimization problems, making it suitable for WSN deployments with diverse environmental conditions [19, 20].

These optimization techniques have been applied and compared in various WSN deployment scenarios, each offering distinct advantages in terms of solution quality, convergence speed, scalability, and robustness to uncertainties. The choice of optimization method often depends on specific application requirements, computational resources, and the desired trade-offs between performance metrics such as coverage, connectivity, and energy efficiency [21].

While grid-based and heuristic approaches provide foundational methods for node placement in WSNs, evolutionary and swarm intelligence techniques such as GA, PSO, and DE offer advanced capabilities to optimize node configurations effectively. The following sections will explore the application of BFO in comparison with these established methods, evaluating its performance and practical implications for optimizing WSN node placements in diverse real-world scenarios.

3 Proposed Methodology

BFO is a bio-inspired optimization algorithm that simulates the foraging behavior of bacterial colonies. The algorithm mimics how bacteria navigate through a chemical gradient to find optimal nutrient sources in their environment. BFO is characterized by its ability to balance exploration (searching for new solutions) and exploitation (improving known solutions) through iterative movement and interaction among virtual bacterial cells within a search space.

The main components of BFO include:

- **Chemotaxis:** This phase represents the movement of virtual bacteria towards regions of higher concentration of a chemical substance (nutrient). In the context of optimization, chemotaxis corresponds to exploring potential solutions (node placements) in the search space based on the objective function evaluation.
- **Swarming:** Swarming involves the interaction and communication among bacterial cells within the colony. In BFO, swarming enables sharing of information about promising solutions (optimal node configurations) discovered by individual bacteria, thereby guiding the search towards better solutions collectively.
- **Reproduction:** Reproduction in BFO involves creating new solutions (candidate solutions) based on the information gathered during chemotaxis and swarming phases. This phase ensures diversity in the solution space and promotes exploration of novel node placements.
- **Elimination-Dispersal:** This phase aims to eliminate less promising solutions (node configurations) and disperse bacteria to explore new regions of the search space. It helps in maintaining diversity and preventing premature convergence to suboptimal solutions.

3.1 Application of BFO to WSN Node Placement

BFO is particularly suited for optimizing node placement in WSNs due to its adaptive and decentralized nature. The application of BFO to WSN node placement involves translating the algorithm's principles into strategies for strategically positioning sensor nodes to maximize coverage, connectivity, and energy efficiency.

Steps Involved in the Optimization Process Using BFO:

Initialization:

- Define the search space: Represented as a set of potential node placement configurations within the monitored area.
- Initialize virtual bacterial cells (candidate solutions): Each bacterial cell corresponds to a potential node configuration.

Chemotaxis:

- Evaluate the fitness (objective function) of each bacterial cell based on coverage, connectivity, and energy efficiency metrics.
- Update the movement direction of each bacterial cell based on the gradient of the objective function (chemotactic movement).

The chemotactic movement of a bacterial cell i towards a new position x_i' is typically determined by the following equation:

$$x_i' = x_i + \delta_i \cdot \frac{\nabla f(x_i)}{||\nabla f(x_i)||}$$

where,

- x_i is the current position (node configuration) of bacterial cell i,
- δ_i is a step size,

- $\nabla f(x_i)$ is the gradient of the objective function at position x_i

Swarming:

- Share information among bacterial cells regarding their current positions and fitness values.
- Update each bacterial cell's best-known position (local best) and the global best position found by the swarm.

Reproduction:

- Generate new candidate solutions (node configurations) based on the information gathered during chemotaxis and swarming phases.
- Apply operators such as mutation or crossover to explore new solutions and maintain diversity in the population of bacterial cells.

Elimination-Dispersal:

- Evaluate the quality of candidate solutions.
- Remove less promising solutions (elimination).
- Introduce random perturbations or dispersal to explore new regions of the search space.

Termination:

- Repeat the chemotaxis, swarming, reproduction, and elimination-dispersal phases iteratively until a termination criterion is met (e.g., maximum number of iterations or convergence).

The iterative process of BFO continues until optimal or near-optimal node placements are found that maximize coverage, connectivity, and energy efficiency in the WSN deployment. The adaptive nature of BFO allows it to effectively handle dynamic environmental conditions and varying deployment requirements, making it a promising approach for optimizing WSN node placements in practical applications.

4   Simulation and Results

The simulation environment is configured to replicate a realistic WSN deployment scenario using the following parameters:

4.1   Network and Deployment Parameters

- Deployment area: 100 m × 100 m
- Number of sensor nodes (N): 50
- Sensing range: 10 m
- Communication range: 20 m

4.2 BFO Algorithm Parameters

- Population size (N): 50
- Swim Length (L): 100
- Step Size (δ): 0.1
- Chemotactic Step Size (α): 0.2

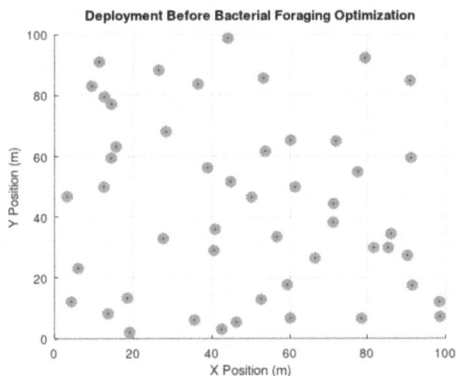

Fig. 1. Deployment Before Bacterial Foraging Optimization

Figure 1 illustrates the initial deployment of sensor nodes in a WSN within a 100 m × 100 m area, prior to the application of the BFO algorithm.

Coverage: Coverage is a critical metric for WSNs as it determines how well the sensor nodes can monitor the designated area.

BFO: Achieves the highest coverage at 94%. This indicates that BFO is highly effective in strategically placing sensor nodes to maximize the monitored area. The high coverage suggests that the algorithm can effectively reduce blind spots and ensure that most of the deployment area is under observation.

PSO: Attains a coverage of 92%, which is slightly lower than BFO but still very competitive. PSO's ability to maintain a relatively high coverage shows its effectiveness in distributing nodes evenly across the area.

GA: Results in 90% coverage. While lower than BFO and PSO, GA still provides a substantial coverage. However, the slightly reduced performance could be due to its tendency to converge prematurely or get trapped in local optima (Fig. 2).

Average Connectivity: Average connectivity measures the average number of direct neighbors each node has, which is crucial for maintaining robust communication networks.

BFO: Shows the highest average connectivity with 8 neighbors per node. High connectivity ensures that nodes can communicate efficiently, which is vital for data aggregation and transmission reliability.

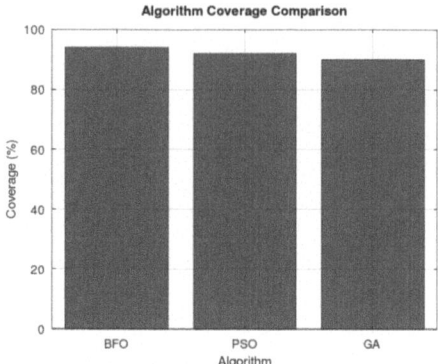

Fig. 2. Comparison of Algorithm Coverage

PSO: Achieves an average connectivity of 7.5 neighbors per node. This value indicates that PSO can also form a well-connected network, though slightly less interconnected than the network formed by BFO.

GA: Manages an average connectivity of 7 neighbors per node. While this indicates a decent level of network connectivity, it is the lowest among the three algorithms, which might lead to more isolated nodes or communication bottlenecks (Fig. 3).

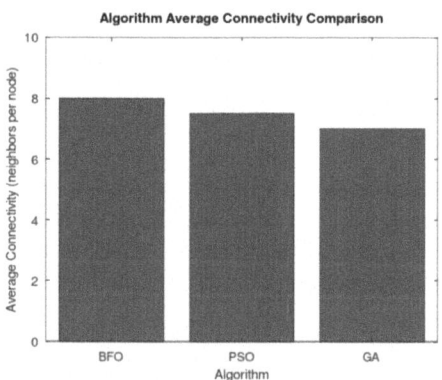

Fig. 3. Comparison of Algorithm Connectivity

Energy Consumption: Energy consumption is a crucial metric because WSN nodes are typically battery-powered, and efficient energy use can prolong the network's operational lifetime.

BFO: Consumes 205 J, the lowest among the three algorithms. This demonstrates BFO's efficiency in node placement, minimizing the energy required for communication and sensing operations.

PSO: Has an energy consumption of 220 J. Although higher than BFO, PSO still maintains a reasonable energy efficiency, balancing between achieving high coverage and maintaining good connectivity.

GA: Records the highest energy consumption at 230 J. This could be due to GA's less optimized node placement, leading to increased communication costs and more frequent retransmissions (Fig. 4).

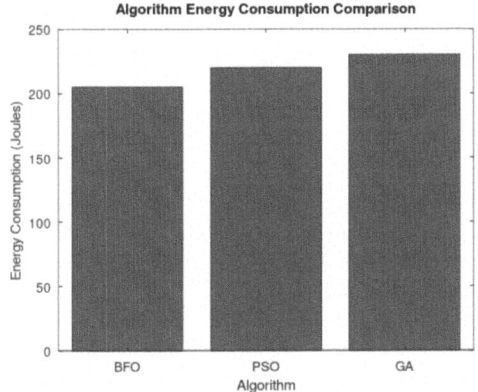

Fig. 4. Comparison of Algorithm Energy Consumption

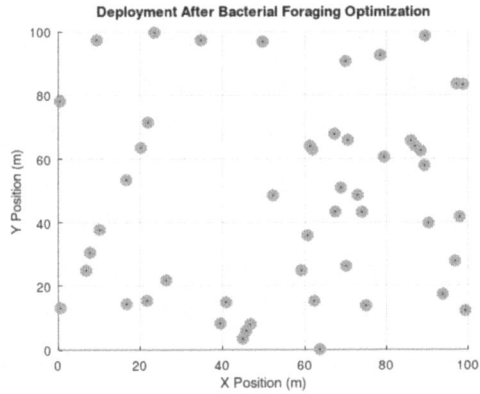

Fig. 5. Deployment After Bacterial Foraging Optimization

Figure 5 illustrates the deployment of sensor nodes in a WSN after applying the BFO algorithm.

5   Conclusion

In conclusion, this study has highlighted the efficacy of the BFO algorithm in optimizing node placement within WSNs. Through its application, BFO has demonstrated significant improvements over traditional methods like PSO and GA. Specifically, BFO achieved a notable coverage of 94%, ensuring comprehensive monitoring of the deployment area with minimal blind spots. The algorithm also enhanced connectivity by providing nodes with an average of 8 neighbors, thereby supporting robust data transmission and network reliability. Moreover, BFO exhibited superior energy efficiency, consuming only 205 J, which prolongs the operational lifespan of WSNs. These findings underscore BFO as a robust solution for optimizing WSN deployments, offering enhanced performance across coverage, connectivity, and energy consumption metrics, thus catering effectively to the demands of modern sensor network applications. Future research may further refine BFO's parameters and explore its application in diverse WSN environments to validate and extend its practical benefits.

References

1. Nagchoudhury, P., Maheshwari, S., Choudhary, K.: Optimal sensor nodes deployment method using bacteria foraging algorithm in wireless sensor networks. In: Emerging ICT for Bridging the Future-Proceedings of the 49th Annual Convention of the Computer Society of India CSI, vol. 2, pp. 221–228. Springer, Cham (2015)
2. Tabatabaei, S.: Provide energy-aware routing protocol in wireless sensor networks using bacterial foraging optimization algorithm and mobile sink. PLoS ONE **17**(3), e0265113 (2022)
3. Qiu, Y., Ma, L., Priyadarshi, R.: Deep learning challenges and prospects in wireless sensor network deployment. Arch. Comput. Methods Eng. (2024)
4. Deepa, S.R., Rekha, D.: Bacterial foraging optimization-based clustering in wireless sensor network by preventing left-out nodes. Intell. Comput. Paradigm Recent Trends 43–58 (2020)
5. Priyadarshi, R.: Energy-efficient routing in wireless sensor networks: a meta-heuristic and artificial intelligence-based approach: a comprehensive review. Arch. Comput. Methods Eng. (2024). https://doi.org/10.1007/s11831-023-10039-6
6. Bian, K., Priyadarshi, R.: Machine learning optimization techniques: a survey, classification, challenges, and future research issues. Arch. Comput. Methods Eng. (2024). https://doi.org/10.1007/s11831-024-10110-w
7. Ari, A.A.A., et al.: Bacterial foraging optimization scheme for mobile sensing in wireless sensor networks. Int. J. Wirel. Inf. Netw. **24**(3), 254–267 (2017)
8. Priyadarshi, R.: Exploring machine learning solutions for overcoming challenges in IoT-based wireless sensor network routing: a comprehensive review. Wirel. Netw. (2024). https://doi.org/10.1007/s11276-024-03697-2
9. Priyadarshi, R., Gupta, B.: Area coverage optimization in three-dimensional wireless sensor network. Wirel. Pers. Commun. **117**(2), 843–865 (2021). https://doi.org/10.1007/s11277-020-07899-7
10. Anurag, A., Priyadarshi, R., Goel, A., Gupta, B.: 2-D coverage optimization in WSN using a novel variant of particle swarm optimisation. In: 2020 7th International Conference on Signal Processing and Integrated Networks, SPIN 2020, pp. 663–668 (2020). https://doi.org/10.1109/SPIN48934.2020.9070978
11. Priyadarshi, R., Gupta, B., Anurag, A.: Deployment techniques in wireless sensor networks: a survey, classification, challenges, and future research issues. J. Supercomput. **76**(9), 7333–7373 (2020)
12. Abdulzahra, A.A., Khudor, I.B.A.Q., Alshawi, I.S.: Energy-efficient routing protocol in wireless sensor networks based on bacterial foraging optimization. Indonesian J. Electr. Eng. Comput. Sci. **29**(2), 911–920 (2023)

13. Priyadarshi, R., Gupta, B., Anurag, A.: Wireless sensor networks deployment: a result oriented analysis. Wirel. Pers. Commun. **113**(2), 843–866 (2020). https://doi.org/10.1007/s11277-020-07255-9

14. Lalwani, P., Das, S.: Bacterial foraging optimization algorithm for CH selection and routing in wireless sensor networks. In: 2016 3rd International Conference on Recent Advances in Information Technology (RAIT), pp. 95–100. IEEE (2016)

15. Priyadarshi, R., Gupta, B.: Coverage area enhancement in wireless sensor network. Microsyst. Technol. **26**(5), 1417–1426 (2020). https://doi.org/10.1007/s00542-019-04674-y

16. Hamidouche, R., Khentout, M., Aliouat, Z., Gueroui, A.M., Abba Ari, A.A.: Sink mobility based on bacterial foraging optimization algorithm. In: Computational Intelligence and Its Applications: 6th IFIP TC 5 International Conference, CIIA 2018, Oran, Algeria, May 8–10, Proceedings 6, pp. 352–363. Springer, Cham (2018)

17. Priyadarshi, R., Vikram, R., Huang, Z., Yang, T., Rathore, R.S.: Enhancing coverage in wireless sensor networks using machine learning techniques. In: 2024 4th Interdisciplinary Conference on Electrics and Computer (INTCEC), Chicago, IL, USA, pp. 1–6 (2024). https://doi.org/10.1109/INTCEC61833.2024.10603264

18. Hemavathi, P., Nandakumar, A.N.: Novel bacteria foraging optimization for energy-efficient communication in wireless sensor network. Int. J. Electr. Commun. Eng. **8**(6), 4755–4762 (2018)

19. Kaur, G., Bajwa, D.S.: Energy optimization in a wireless sensor network based on advanced Pegasis using bacterial foraging optimization in chain. Energy **10**(9), 27–32 (2014)

20. Priyadarshi, R., Vikram, R., Huang, Z., Yang, T., Rathore, R.S.: Multi-objective optimization for coverage and connectivity in wireless sensor networks. In: 2024 13th International Conference on Modern Circuits and Systems Technologies (MOCAST), Sofia, Bulgaria, pp. 1–7 (2024). https://doi.org/10.1109/MOCAST61810.2024.10615606

21. Moharamkhani, E., Zadmehr, B., Memarian, S., Saber, M.J., Shokouhifar, M.: Multiobjective fuzzy knowledge-based bacterial foraging optimization for congestion control in clustered wireless sensor networks. Int. J. Commun. Syst. Syst. **34**(16), e4949 (2021)

The Vital Role of Small and Marginal Farmer in Future of Our Climate: Democratization of Machine Learning, Artificial Intelligence, and Dairy Cow Necklace Sensors in Achieving the UN Climate Change Goals (COP21) and the Paris Agreement

Chandrasekar Vuppalapati[1]([⊠]), Anitha Ilapakurti[2], Sandhya Vissapragada[2], Vanaja Mamidi[2], Sriya Vuppalapati[2], Akshay Vuppalapati[2], Sharat Kedari[2], Santosh Kedari[3], Jaya Vuppalapati[3], Karthik Kallakur[3], Koduru Rajasri[3], and Narendra Lella[3]

[1] Computer Engineering (CMPE Department), San Jose State University, San Jose, USA
`chandrasekar.vuppalapati@sjsu.edu`
[2] Hanumayamma Innovations and Technologies, Inc., Fremont, USA
`{ailapakurti,svissapragada,sriya,sharath}@hanuinnotech.com`
[3] Hanumayamma Innovations and Technologiesa PVT Limited, Hyderbad, India

Abstract. Small and marginal dairy farmers are a crucial part of the global farming community, and there are approximately 570 million farms worldwide, with the majority being small farms, as per the Food and Agriculture Organization (FAO). The International Farm Comparison Network (IFCN) estimates that there are around 133 million dairy farms globally. Despite being a significant source of income for small dairy farmers, they often face challenges regarding cattle productivity and health issues. Interestingly, cattle rumination counts could be the solution to these issues, not only for small farmers but also for the world at large.

Cattle rumination count is a measure of how much time cows spend chewing cud, which is a mixture of partially digested food regurgitated from the cow's stomach to the mouth and further broken down by chewing before being swallowed again. Rumination count is a critical indicator of a cow's health and productivity since cows that chew more tend to have better digestion, absorb more nutrients from their feed, and produce more milk.

Cattle rumination count is also related to methane emissions, as cows release methane gas during the digestive process, especially during rumination. Methane is a potent greenhouse gas that contributes to climate change. By using Dairy IoT Cattle Cow Necklace sensors, small and marginal farmers worldwide can track rumination counts proactively. The Dairy Cow Necklace sensor records the time spent chewing cud, and this data can be used by small farmers and veterinarians to identify cows experiencing digestive issues or other health problems and adjust their feeding and management practices accordingly.

Reducing methane emissions from dairy cattle is a vital part of global efforts to mitigate climate change since livestock, including dairy cattle, contributes to around 14.5% of global greenhouse gas emissions. In a recent study, rumination counts were captured from three major dairy producing areas in India (Vishakhapatnam, Hyderabad, and Kashmir) between 2019 and 2024. The study demonstrated that improving dairy cattle health by reducing methane emissions is economically and sustainably advantageous to small farmers, rural economies, and the global climate overall.

Keywords: Methan emissions · Cow Necklace Sensor · Rumination · COP21

1 Introduction

Small farmers make a significant contribution to agriculture and dairy production worldwide. The Food and Agriculture Organization (FAO) highlights the importance of small farms in feeding the world's growing population [1]. Small farms account for 70% of the world's food production and are vital to the livelihoods of millions of people. Unlike their western counterparts, milk originates in highly decentralized villages, with small farmers owning three to five cattle and delivering milk twice daily to milk collection centers for payment. In essence, the livelihoods of around 2 billion people (26.7% of the world population) are dependent on agriculture, and climate change adversely impacts their survival.

Dairy Farming is the largest employer, with the majority of small-scale daily farmers relying on it for their livelihoods. Dairy farms are typically categorized into three groups based on size and output: marginal or small-scale, medium-scale, and large-scale. In Europe and Africa, small-scale farms are further divided into subsistence small-scale and small-scale farms. Subsistence dairy farming is performed to feed farmer families. Small-scale farmers worldwide operate as family-owned and highly fragmented businesses. Unfortunately, younger generations of these farms, typically youth, migrate to urban areas in search of industrial employment, leaving the burden of maintaining the farms to the women[1], elderly and seniors [2].

In addition, small farms face numerous challenges, including limited access to markets, credit, and technology, which can limit their productivity and profitability. The FAO calls for increased investment in small farms[2] and the development of policies that support their growth and resilience to ensure food security for all.

Small scale farmers tend to have lower productivity[3] than their medium and large scale counterparts. The quantity of milk produced per day varies greatly depending on the size of the dairy farm. Small-scale dairy farmers, who typically own a small number of cows (between three to five), usually produce between 5–20 L of milk per cow per day. As a result, their total daily milk production can range from 15–100 L per day.

---

[1] Chandrasekar Vuppalapati, Machine Learning and Artificial Intelligence for Agricultural Economics: Prognostic Data Analytics to Serve Small Scale Farmers, Publisher : Springer; 1st ed. 2021 edition (October 5, 2021), ISBN-13 : 978–3030774844.

[2] The Global Dairy Sector: Facts - https://openknowledge.fao.org/server/api/core/bitstreams/bee e9189-d92d-4a0d-86af-a1e3328c33d1/content.

[3] Lameness in Dairy Cow Herds: Disease Aetiology, Prevention and Management - https://www.mdpi.com/2624-862X/3/1/16.

On the other hand, medium-scale dairy farmers, who have between 10–50 cows, usually produce between 20–30 L of milk per cow per day, resulting in total daily milk production ranging from 200–1500 L per day.

One of the main reasons for productivity is lack of advanced insights into the health of the cattle. Rumination count, in addition to environmental and activity level key indicators, is a major parameter that can identify and forecast productivity of cattle. Dairy cattle rumination count is a measure of the time cows spend chewing cud. Cud is a mixture of partially digested food that is regurgitated from the cow's stomach to the mouth, where it is chewed before being swallowed again. This count is a significant indicator of a cow's health and productivity since cows that chew more tend to have better digestion, absorb more nutrients from their feed, and produce more milk. Integration of rumination count detection as part of small farmer information flow would be a game change to increase productivity.

Importantly, Methane emissions from livestock contribute to climate change, and cows release methane gas during rumination, making dairy cattle rumination count related to methane emissions. By using Dairy IoT Cattle Cow Necklace sensors, small and marginal farmers worldwide can track rumination counts proactively. These sensors record the time spent chewing cud, which small farmers and veterinarians can use to identify cows experiencing digestive issues and adjust their feeding and management practices accordingly [3].

The development of sensor technologies has provided us with an opportunity to tackle the problem of rumination in dairy cattle in a more thorough and data-driven manner. By utilizing activity data analysis and integrating AI and ML techniques, along with the possibility of including rumination scoring systems from veterinarians, we can create a system to identify early signs of lameness in dairy cattle that is highly efficient and successful.

This innovative approach has the potential to create a significant impact on animal welfare, farm management practices, and overall herd productivity. Early detection of higher rumination counts allows for timely treatment and care of affected animals, leading to improved welfare and health outcomes. Additionally, by proactively addressing rumination issues, we can minimize its impact on milk production, fertility, and methane emissions, ultimately leading to a greener world with less climate change potential. This not only benefits farmers and the agricultural sector, but also has positive economic implications.

The structure of this paper is presented as: Sect. 2 Data Capture by Sensor, Rumination Count, and Ensemble Machine Learning. Section 3 presents our dairy analytics service system by focusing on ML models. Section 4 discusses its related design and implementation decisions, and Sect. 5 shows a case study. The conclusion and future work are included in Sect. 6.

2 Understanding Computer Vision Models, Sensor Data and Machine Learning Models

2.1 Dairy Cow Necklace

Cow Necklace (please see Fig. 1) is a CLASS 10 Veterinarian Diagnostic sensor designed for improving the health and productivity of cows. The USPTO Trademark Class 10 encompasses an extensive range of medical and surgical instruments, apparatus, and devices utilized in the diagnosis, treatment, and prevention of diseases and medical conditions. This class includes surgical, medical, and dental instruments, orthopedic articles, suture materials, hearing aids, prosthetic limbs and eyes, as well as various types of medical and therapeutic equipment and devices. It also encompasses diagnostic apparatus and instruments, such as blood pressure monitors, thermometers, and medical imaging devices. By securing a trademark under Class 10, companies that produce and sell medical devices and equipment can protect their brand identity. More specifically, the Cow Necklace falls under Class 10 as a wearable veterinary sensor that captures a cow's vital signs, provides farmers with data to monitor milk productivity, and improves overall cow health [4].

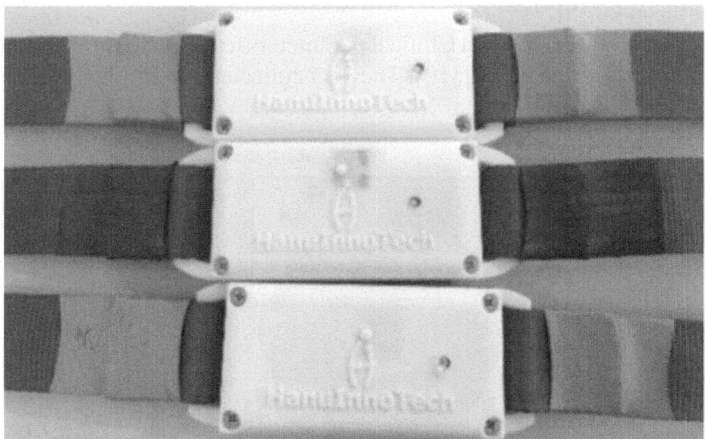

Fig. 1. Cow Necklace – Class 10 Sensor

2.2 Rumination Data Capture

Our team has gathered rumination count data from Dairy Cow necklace Sensors installed in Hyderabad, Vishakhapatnam, and Kashmir, India. The selection of these locations was purposefully diverse, allowing for both clinical and comprehensive data analysis. Our aim was to investigate the effects of fluctuating temperatures and humidity levels on rumination counts (please see Fig. 2 for Printed Circuit Board of the Sensor [5–9]). While we understand that numerous other factors can influence rumination counts, the

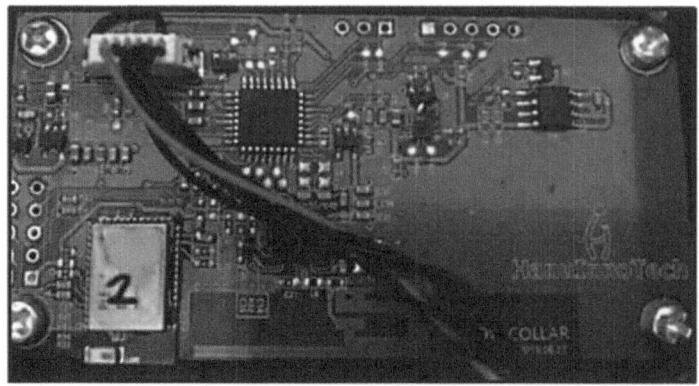

Fig. 2. Dairy Sensor Hardware

use of our innovative sensors provides an automated and non-invasive approach to data collection.

The use of AI and machine learning to monitor livestock health, including vital signs, daily activity levels, and food intake, is rapidly emerging as a prominent application in the agricultural sector [5].

The records are integrated with Clinical parameters to supplement Veterinarian decision processing (please see Fig. 8) [10]. The data collected has following details (please see Fig. 3):

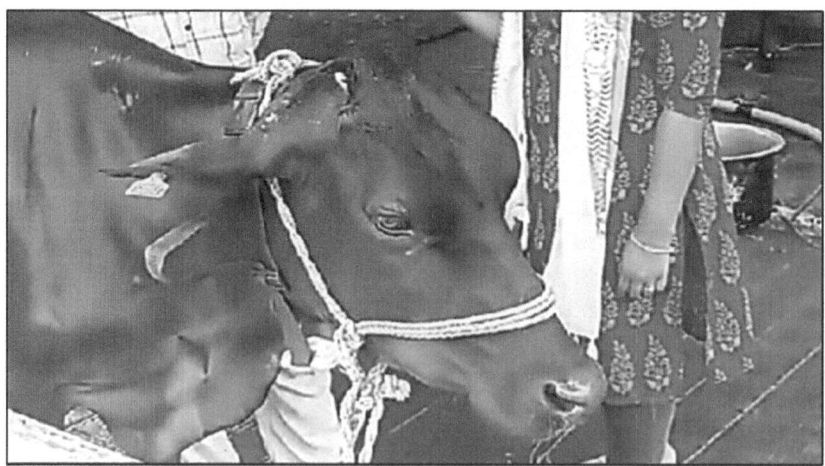

Fig. 3. Cow Necklace

2.3   Rumination and Supervisied Feed Management Data

Cow Necklace sensor utilizes a two-step data processing approach to optimize farm productivity. Firstly, we collect detailed feed management information from dairy farmers, which includes the feed given to the cows on a daily basis, as well as water consumption, grazing time, and milk parlor time. This in-depth analysis allows for a comprehensive understanding of the cows' nutritional intake and activity levels, enabling farmers to make informed decisions regarding their herd management.

The management of cattle is a complex task that shares many similarities with the feeding of 2-year-old children. Just as caring for a toddler requires a great deal of attention and effort, so too does the management of cattle (please see Table 1). However, unlike children who eventually outgrow this stage, cattle require a lifetime of care and attention. As a society, it is our ethical, moral, and emotional responsibility to take care of these gentle creatures that are an integral part of our lives as human beings. To achieve this, we must adopt advanced sensor technologies like cow necklace sensors to assist in their management. By doing so, we can define our true north as compassionate beings who value the well-being of all living creatures. A society that values animal husbandry is one that is mature and caring for all. Let us take up this responsibility with utmost sincerity and commitment.

Table 1. Cattle Feed and Rumination Timetable

Time of the day	Activity
6 am–7 am	Milk
7 am–8 am	Sweet Corn, Beans, Dhana
9:30 am–10:30 am	Green Fodder - More Green Fodder less Rumination
10:30 am–12:00	Rumination (Taking rest)
12:00–1:00 pm	Water
1:00 pm–2:00 pm	Rumination (Taking rest)
2:00 pm–4:00 pm	Green Fodder
4 pm–5:00 pm	Water or Rumination (Taking rest)
5:00 pm–6:00 pm	Green Fodder
6:00 pm–7:00 pm	Green Fodder
pm–5:30 am	Rumination (Taking rest)

The management of cattle feed varies considerably between South India and North India due to differences in climatic and weather conditions. Through our extensive work with farmers, we have observed that the daily input of green fodder typically averages around 40 kgs (88.1849 lb), while Sweet Corn, Beans, and Dhana are provided in quantities of 8 kgs (17.637 lbs). Additionally, 40 L (10 US liquid gallons) of water is a crucial component of daily feed management. Our exploratory data analysis has revealed a strong causative correlation between the amount of green fodder and the onset of effective rumination, resulting in reduced methane production. Conversely, excessive protein in the feed can lead to rumination complications, emphasizing the importance of a balanced diet. Furthermore, cattle in South India tend to perform 6 to 8 times more rumination than their counterparts in Kashmir and North India. By understanding these regional differences and utilizing advanced technologies like the Cow Necklace sensor, we can optimize cattle feed management and promote healthier, more sustainable practices for the benefit of our planet and all its inhabitants [11].

2.4 Rumination Algorithm

In rumination count calculation time scenarios, performing operations on the sensor rumination captures (Gyroscope and Accelerometer X, Y, and Z) contained in temporal windows is a common pattern. Fortunately, windowing functions enable calculating rumination count within a window (one minute or 30 s) of chewing cycle (please see Fig. 4). There are five types of temporal windows to choose from, including tumbling, hopping, sliding, session, and snapshot windows. These window functions can be used in the GROUP BY clause of the query within rumination data [12].

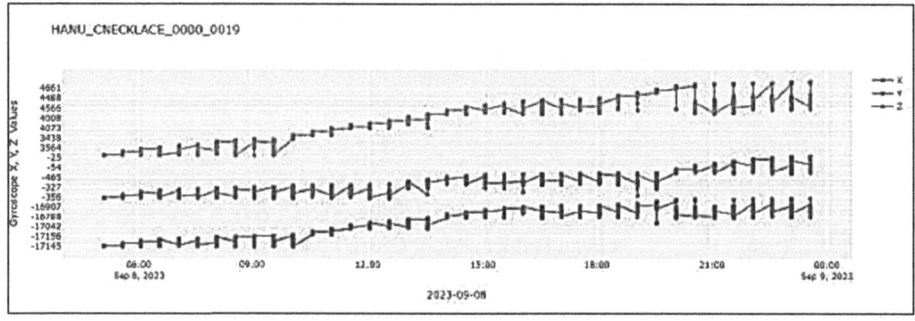

Fig. 4. Hanumayamma Vishkhapatnam Sensor

2.5 Democratization of Sensor

The performance of an algorithm can be measured by various metrics, such as accuracy, speed, memory, and scalability (please see Fig. 5). Accuracy refers to how well the algorithm can predict the correct output for a given input. Speed refers to how fast the algorithm can process the input and produce the output. Memory refers to how much space the algorithm requires to store the parameters and intermediate results. Scalability refers to how well the algorithm can handle large-scale data and complex tasks [13].

The following table summarizes the performance of the algorithms on the Rumination data (please see Table 2).

It's certain that the data calculates very close rumination count per sensor. The clinical value differs from cattle. The data collected for Jersey cattle [14].

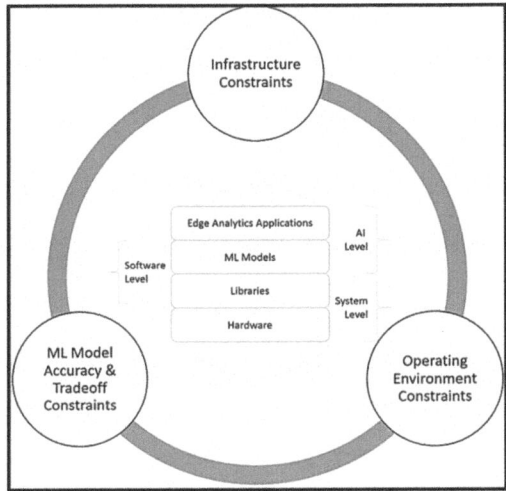

Fig. 5. ML Performance [5]

Table 2. Window Functions and Rumination

Algorithm	Location	Time Window	Rumination count
Sliding Window	Vishakhapatnam	30 s	14–16
Sliding Window	Hyderabad	30 s	12–14
Sliding Window	Kashmir	30 s	7–8
Tumbling Window	Vishakhapatnam	30 s	14–16
Tumbling Window	Hyderabad	30 s	12–14
Tumbling Window	Kashmir	30 s	7–8

2.6 Metane Gateway

The methane module deployed consists of methane gateway that collects data from dairy farms. This data overlapped with cattle data to detect changes in methane capture values (please see Fig. 6). Our goal is to fulfill COP21.

COP21[4], also known as the 2015 Paris Climate Conference, was a meeting of the United Nations Framework Convention on Climate Change (UNFCCC) held in Paris, France. The aim of COP21 was to negotiate and establish a legally binding international agreement on climate change, with the goal of limiting global warming to well below 2 degrees Celsius above pre-industrial levels and pursuing efforts to limit the increase to 1.5 degrees Celsius. The agreement was ultimately signed by 195 countries, making it a historic moment in the global fight against climate change [15].

---

[4] The Paris Agreement - https://unfccc.int/process-and-meetings/the-paris-agreement.

Fig. 6. Methane Gateway

3 System Overview

The system calculates the activity of the sensor using Gyroscope and accelerometer data. It will access the drop in movement of activity as the sensor data collection process. The consistent drop of sensor data triggers a process for proactive onset of Lameness, although not confirmed until proven via image analysis that is asked small farmer to upload.

Lambda architecture (please see Fig. 7) provides an effective solution for addressing the Rumination Count detection use case by creating two distinct paths for data flow. All data received through Bluetooth is processed through these two paths:

- The batch layer, or cold path, stores all incoming data in its raw form and processes it through batch processing, specifically for window functions. The result of this processing is stored as a batch view.
- The speed layer, or hot path, analyzes data in real-time, with a focus on low latency at the expense of accuracy. For rumination count, we can provide the farmer with daily counts, preferably at the beginning of the day, along with previous day's rumination count. This is because cows typically ruminate 7 to 8 times per day, with most rumination taking place at night.

The batch layer then feeds into a serving layer, which indexes the batch view for efficient window querying. In turn, the speed layer updates the serving layer with incremental updates based on the most recent data. By utilizing the lambda architecture, we can optimize data processing for rumination count detection, providing valuable insights into the health and wellbeing of cattle for farmers and industry professionals alike [5, 8, 9, 12].

3.1 Load Sensor Activity Data

The accelerometer data was used to detect Rumination count; The data window is from cattle feeding pattern table (please see Table 1).

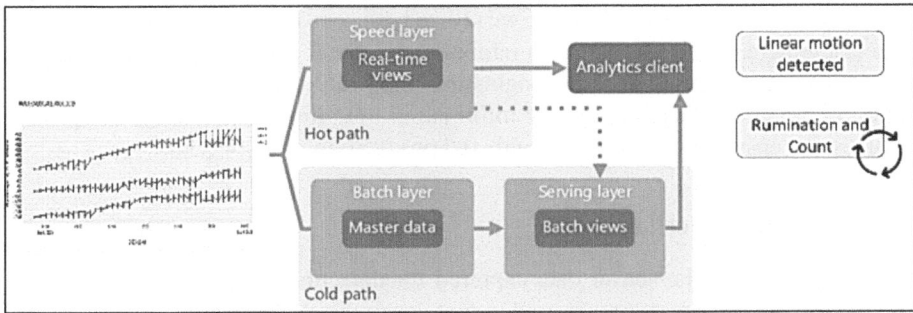

Fig. 7. Rumination Count Architecture

Step 1: load sensor data

```
df_G = pd.read_csv("sensor_19_G.csv", header = None) df_G
```

In the above code, we have loaded Hanumayamma Cow Necklace Sensor data that was installed in Kashmir.

Output: (please see Fig. 8).

The data capture process involves gathering Accelerometer and Gyroscope X, Y, and Z values. The Accelerometer measures the acceleration force in m/s2 that is applied to a device on all three physical axes (x, y, and z), with the exception of the force of gravity. Meanwhile, the Gyroscope measures the rate of rotation in rad/s around each of the three physical axes (x, y, and z) [12].

	0	1	2	3	4	5	6	7
0	Type	id	SensorDate	X	Y	Z	DateTime	Date
1	G	6694	230901002719	-1129	8042	-13914	2023-09-01T00:27:19.000Z	2023-09-01
2	G	6695	230901002721	-1148	8040	-13887	2023-09-01T00:27:21.000Z	2023-09-01
3	G	6696	230901002722	-1109	8022	-13878	2023-09-01T00:27:22.000Z	2023-09-01
4	G	6697	230901002724	-1161	8034	-13914	2023-09-01T00:27:24.000Z	2023-09-01
...	...	...	...	...	...	...	...	...
12022	G	6689	230831235754	-1143	8008	-13917	2023-08-31T23:57:54.000Z	2023-08-31
12023	G	6690	230831235756	-1149	8033	-13878	2023-08-31T23:57:56.000Z	2023-08-31
12024	G	6691	230831235757	-1147	8015	-13896	2023-08-31T23:57:57.000Z	2023-08-31
12025	G	6692	230831235758	-1125	8036	-13909	2023-08-31T23:57:58.000Z	2023-08-31
12026	G	6693	230831235800	-1152	8037	-13871	2023-08-31T23:58:00.000Z	2023-08-31

12027 rows × 8 columns

Fig. 8. Sensor Data

To calculate the rumination count, we utilize both sensor data, with the exception of the accelerometer, which serves as an inhibitor or initiator trigger. By combining these data points, we can gain valuable insights into the health and wellbeing of the cattle, providing farmers with the necessary information to optimize their feed management practices and ensure the continued health and productivity of their herds.

3.2   Rumination Detection

In the below Fig. 9, the sensor data captured for detection of rumination. As part of detection of rumination count, we need to first detect the cattle taking rest so as to filter out movement to gyroscope values.

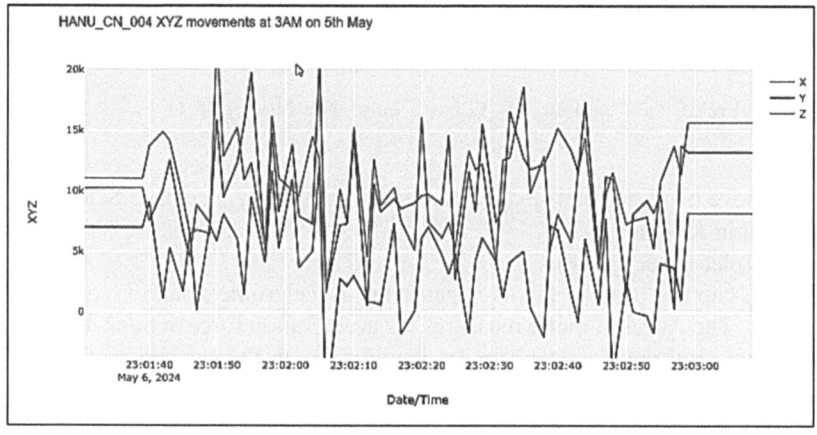

Fig. 9. Rumination Data

In the below (please see Fig. 10) linear movement detected by analyzing both accelerometer and gyroscope values.

4   System Design and Implementation

As part of the system design, the next step would be application of Window functions to detect rumination and then once detected calculated rumination count [10].

4.1   Tumbling Window to Calculate Rumination

Tumbling window functions provide an effective means of segmenting a cow necklace data stream into distinct time segments, allowing for efficient processing and analysis of data.

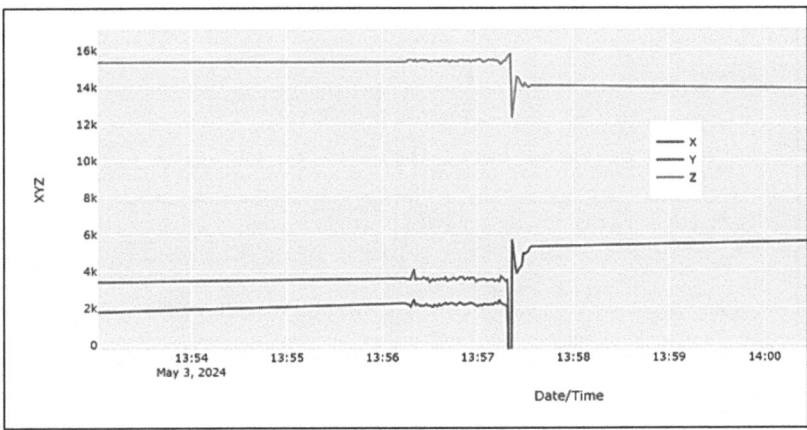

Fig. 10. Linear Motion

There are several key differentiators of a tumbling window, including the fact that they do not repeat or overlap with rumination initiating chewing. Additionally, an event can only belong to a single tumbling window, ensuring the accuracy and consistency of data processing.

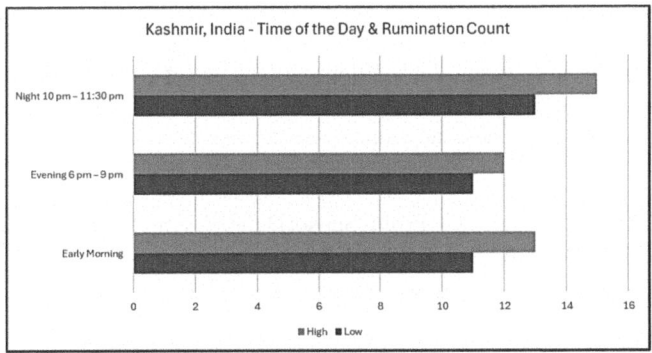

Fig. 11. Daily Rumination Count, Kashmir India

By utilizing tumbling window functions, we can streamline rumination count data analysis and gain valuable insights into the trends and patterns (please see Fig. 11).

```
Select TimeDetect, Count (*) From SensorDatatbl TimeStamp By CreatedAt
Group By TimeDetect, TumblingWindow(second, 30)
```

Output:

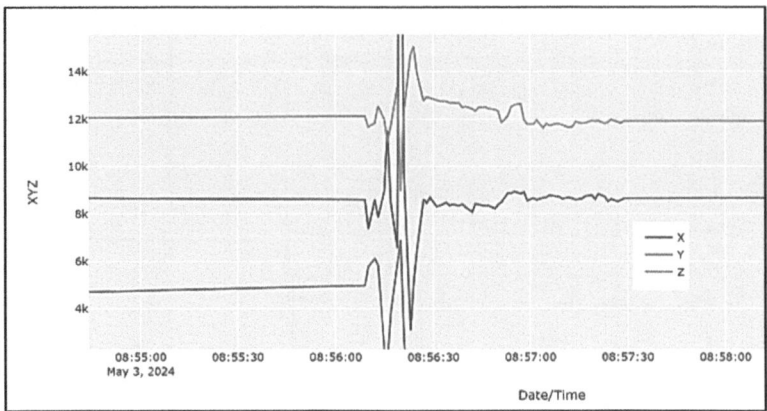

Fig. 12. Rumination Detection

4.2 Hopping Window to Calculate Rumination

Hopping window functions provide a flexible means of analyzing rumination count data by hopping forward in time by a fixed period. These functions can be viewed as similar to tumbling windows, but with the added ability to overlap and be emitted more frequently than the window size.

One key distinction of hopping windows is that events can belong to more than one result set, providing a more nuanced understanding of the data. Additionally, to ensure consistency with tumbling windows, the hop size can be set equal to the window size.

By utilizing hopping window functions, we can optimize data analysis and gain valuable insights into the trends and patterns within our datasets.

> Select TimeDetect, Count (*) From SensorDatatbl TimeStamp By CreatedAt Group By TimeDetect, HoppingWindow(second, 30, 30)

When utilizing window functions for rumination count, it is important to avoid double counting. One effective means of achieving this is by setting the hop size to be equal to the window size. This approach ensures that data is processed accurately and efficiently, without the risk of duplicate entries or inconsistencies in the rumination count (please see Fig. 12 and Fig. 13).

By carefully optimizing window functions for rumination count, we can gain valuable insights into the health and wellbeing of cattle, enabling farmers and industry professionals to make more informed decisions and optimize their feed management practices for optimal herd health and productivity.

The rumination count data for cattle in Kashmir, India varies based on the time of day. During early morning hours, the rumination count ranges from 11 to 13. In the evening from 6 pm to 9 pm, the rumination count ranges from 11 to 12. Finally, during the night from 10 pm to 11:30 pm, the rumination count ranges from 13 to 15 [6, 9, 13].

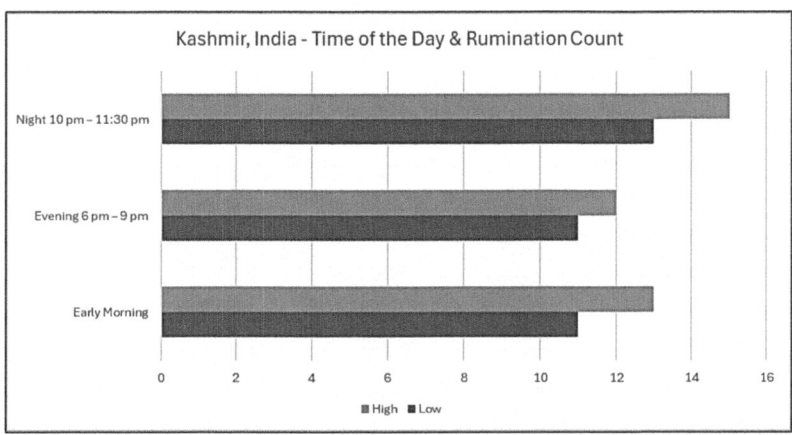

Fig. 13. Daily Rumination Count, Kashmir India

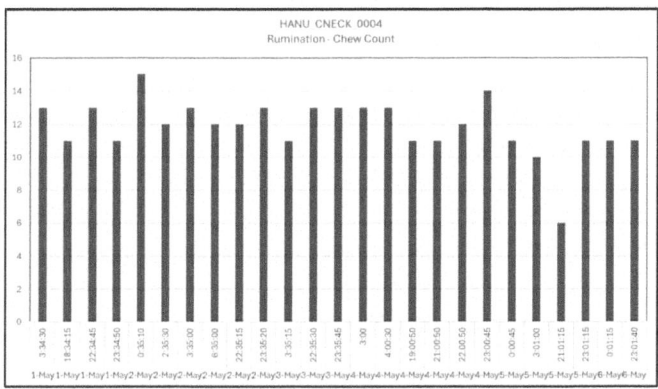

Fig. 14. Daily Rumination Count, Kashmir, India

4.3 Rumination Count and Methane Capture Data

Next step, signal change day to day rumination counts to the changes in thresholds of methane values at the dairy farm. The correlation model works by simply changes of thresholds of rumination count to the methane increase of decrease values.

What we observed was changes in feed and less glazing time of cattle due to weather and extreme climatic conditions could trigger increase in methane.

Ourt analysis clearly shows that better feed management, cattle activity, and water/milk time have direct correlation with methane emissions. By using our sensors and algorithms, major dairy milk producing countries (please see Fig. 14) could meet COP21 Paris agreement most economically (Fig. 15).

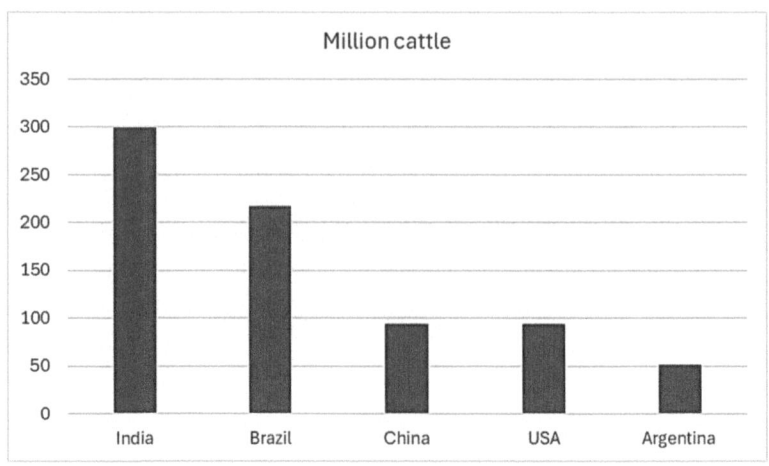

Fig. 15. Top five dairy milk producing countries

5   A Case Study

We have tested and deployed ML Model for predicting Rumination to serve small farmers around the world on our Hanumayamma[5] Data Analytics Platform. Credits at the company to provide access to sensors and field representatives in Vishakhapatnam (17.6868° N, 83.2185° E), Hyderabad (17.4065° N, 78.4772° E), India and Kashmir (34.0837° N, 74.7973° E), India.

6   Conclusion and Future Work

In the past, rumination count was calculated by manually observing the chewing time of cattle. However, due to the lack of human resources and the widespread distribution of cattle across small and medium-scale farms, electronic monitors are now more commonly used.

Given the influence of rumination on methane emissions, it is crucial for governmental agencies to regulate and monitor methane emissions to meet COP21 global climate emissions targets. Providing rumination count detection technology to small, subsistence, and marginal farmers is a mutually beneficial approach that promotes sustainable farming practices while reducing global emissions and creating a healthier planet for future generations.

---

[5] Hanumayamma Innovations and Technologies Inc. is a Delaware based Corporation founded in 2010. We are a U.S. based corporation with leading products in Agriculture Analytics, Dairy Analytics, Specialty Crops Sensors and Analytics, Wearable Veterinary Sensor (CLASS 10) for Animal Husbandry, and Data Analytics (DnA) platform made exclusively for Farmers worldwide. Our Analytics platform and Sensors help farmers around the world with practical suggestions on Yield Analytics, Sustainability, Extreme Weather, and Food Security.- https://www.hanuinnotech.com/.

We firmly believe that cutting-edge tools like rumination count detection, sensor data, machine learning, and artificial intelligence (AI) are essential for improving the livelihoods of small farmers worldwide. These technological advancements provide crucial data science advancements that empower small farmers with the knowledge and resources they need to make informed decisions about their farming practices and enhance their economic sustainability.

By embracing these advancements, we can work together with technology to secure the future of the agricultural industry and ensure that small farmers continue to thrive for generations to come.

References

1. FAO, Milk production. https://www.fao.org/dairy-production-products/production/en/. Accessed 18 May 2024
2. Vuppalapati, C.: Machine Learning and Artificial Intelligence for Agricultural Economics: Prognostic Data Analytics to Serve Small Scale Farmers, 1st edn. Springer, Cham (2021). ISBN-13: 978-3030774844
3. Garvey, M.: Lameness in dairy cow herds: disease aetiology, prevention and management. Dairy **3**, 199–210 (2022). https://doi.org/10.3390/dairy3010016
4. Vuppalapati, C.: Democratization of Artificial Intelligence for the Future of Humanity, 1st edn. CRC Press (2021). ISBN-1: 978-0367524098
5. Ranganathan, J., Waite, R., Searchinger, T., Hanson, C.: How to Sustainably Feed 10 Billion People by 2050, in 21 Charts (2018). https://www.wri.org/blog/2018/12/how-sustainably-feed-10-billion-people-2050-21-charts. Accessed 18 Sept 2019
6. Papastratis, I.: Comparison of Convolutional Neural Networks and Vision Transformers (ViTs) (2023). https://medium.com/@iliaspapastratis/comparison-of-convolutional-neural-networks-and-vision-transformers-vits-a8fc5486c5be. Accessed 10 Jan 2024
7. Columbus, L.: 10 Ways AI Has the Potential to Improve Agriculture in 2021 (2021). https://www.forbes.com/sites/louiscolumbus/2021/02/17/10-ways-ai-has-the-potential-to-improve-agriculture-in-2021/?sh=7f611e297f3b. Accessed 10 Mar 2021
8. Vuppalapati, C., Ilapakurti, A., Kedari, S., Vuppalapati, J., Kedari, S., Vuppalapati, R.: Democratization of AI, albeit constrained IoT devices & Tiny ML, for creating a sustainable food future. In: 2020 3rd International Conference on Information and Computer Technologies (ICICT), San Jose, CA, USA, pp. 525–530 (2020). https://doi.org/10.1109/ICICT50521.2020.00089
9. Vuppalapati, C., Ilapakurti, A., Kedari, S., Vuppalapati, R., Vuppalapati, J., Kedari, S.: The role of combinatorial mathematical optimization and heuristics to improve small farmers to veterinarian access and to create a sustainable food future for the world. In: 2020 Fourth World Conference on Smart Trends in Systems, Security and Sustainability (WorldS4), London, UK, pp. 214–221 (2020). https://doi.org/10.1109/WorldS450073.2020.9210339
10. Ilapakurti, A., Vuppalapati, C.: Building an IoT framework for connected dairy. In: 2015 IEEE First International Conference on Big Data Computing Service and Applications, Redwood City, CA, USA, pp. 275–285 (2015). https://doi.org/10.1109/BigDataService.2015.39
11. Ramalingam, A., Kedari, S., Vuppalapati, C.: IEEE FEMH voice data challenge 2018. In: 2018 IEEE International Conference on Big Data (Big Data), Seattle, WA, USA, pp. 5272–5276 (2018). https://doi.org/10.1109/BigData.2018.8622164
12. Vuppalapati, C.: Building Enterprise IoT Applications, 1st edn. CRC Press (2019). ISBN-13: 978-0367173852

13. Yang, X.-S., Sherratt, S., Dey, N., Joshi, A. (eds.) ICICT 2019, London, vol. 2, "Fourth International Congress on Information and Communication Technology", eBook ISBN 978-981-329-343-4 and Softcover ISBN 978-981-329-342-7

14. Luedeling, E., Zhang, M., Girvetz, E.H.: Climatic Changes Lead to Declining Winter Chill for Fruit and Nut Trees in California during 1950–2099 (2009). https://journals.plos.org/plosone/article?id=10.1371/journal.pone.0006166. Accessed 06 May 2023

15. Rothman, D.: Transformers for Natural Language Processing and Computer Vision - Third Edition: Explore Generative AI and Large Language Models with Hugging Face, ChatGPT, GPT-4V, and DALL-E 3. Packt Publishing (2024). ISBN-13: 978-1805128724

Autonomous Driving Prototype with Raspberry Pi by Using Image Processing Technology

Chris Zhang[1]([✉]), Jerry Yinran Huang[2], Eric Chen[3], Jinhui Shen[4], Mark Yining Liu[5], Yanxiao Wang[6], Haowei Ni[6], and Lang Qin[7]

[1] Cansight Technology Corporation, Vancouver, BC, Canada
head@roboca.org
[2] Nanjing Foreign Language School, Nanjing, Jiangsu, China
[3] R.C. Palmer Secondary School, Richmond, BC, Canada
[4] Communication University of China, Nanjing, Jiangsu, China
[5] University of Toronto, Toronto, ON, Canada
[6] Saint Patrick Regional Secondary School, Vancouver, BC, Canada
[7] High School Affiliated to Nanjing Normal University Jiangning Campus, Nanjing, Jiangsu, China

Abstract. With the development of the internet, the concept of self-driving cars is no longer unfamiliar with us. From military use to commercial use, autopilot technology is playing a bigger and bigger role in society nowadays. In order to make this kind of invention easier for us to use in daily life, a self-driving car prototype is designed. It comes with basic functions like detecting and moving ability which can help people do a few household necessities. This kind of robot may be connected to the household WIFI in the future to realize more complex functions.

Keywords: Raspberry Pi · self-driving · OpenCV

1 Introduction

Nowadays, the internet has become a significant part of our daily life [1] (Fig. 1). With the help of the internet, everything gets connected, and many things can be replaced by AI and robots. Driving, for example, is now gradually being replaced by self-driving with the technology of AI. The concept of self-driving cars first appeared more than decade ago. At first, this idea was more open to military affairs, since it can reduce the danger of human injuries. However, with the development of detecting technology, this concept is now more and more popular. In this project, a household self-driving car is designed in order to realize some of its functions like detecting roads and moving freely on the ground.

© The Author(s), under exclusive license to Springer Nature Switzerland AG 2025
H. R. Arabnia et al. (Eds.): CSCE 2024, CCIS 2260, pp. 205–212, 2025.
https://doi.org/10.1007/978-3-031-85923-6_16

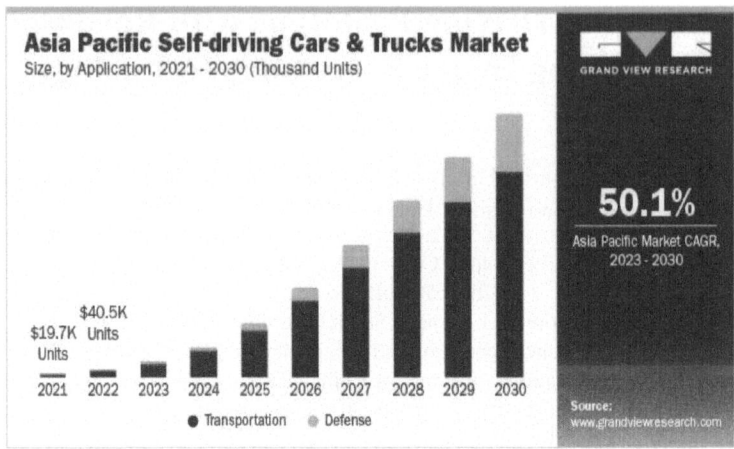

Fig. 1. Chart of Asia-Pacific Self-driving Cars & Trucks Market

2 Design and Methodology

2.1 3D Printing

All the materials are made by 3D printers, using environmentally friendly ingredients. These 3D printed boards are all designed on the computer. The designing part includes drawing lines, doing classifications, combining parts together, cutting off some extra parts, and eventually making it solid. (The principle of 3D printing [2]) (Figs. 2 and 3).

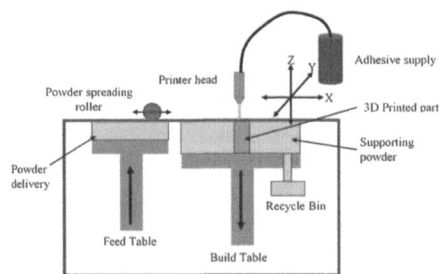

Fig. 2. Principles of 3D Printing: A Comprehensive Overview

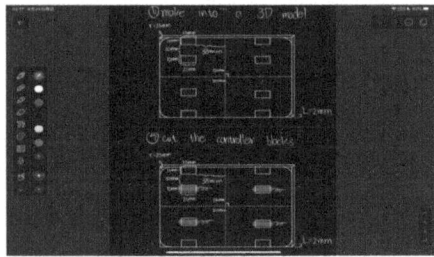

Fig. 3. Design Plan for Robot Chassis

2.2 Wheels

The regular wheels in the Raspberry Pi educational package are used in this project because these wheels have special patterns. These patterns will make the car more stable when running on the ground, and the friction level can be increased. In this way, the car sticks to the ground tightly without slipping (Figs. 4 and 5).

Fig. 4. A sample of the wheel used on the robot

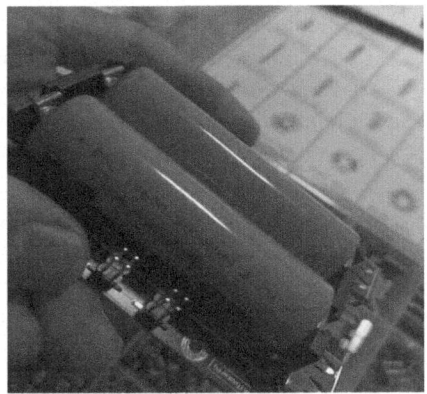

Fig. 5. 18650 LIPO batteries

2.3 Batteries

The 3.7 V batteries are used to power both the controllers and the motors. It is because the 3.7 V battery can last for longer hours while running. And another important reason is its special size since the chassis of the robot has a limit area for the powering section. So, the batteries should fit the limit position of a 15 cm*20 cm area [3].

2.4 3D Model Building

During the designing section, except for the basic 3D printing principles mentioned above, there are also many details have to be paid attention to. For example, some areas are shaded on the computers. It means that the two parts are overlapping. Under this circumstance, it cannot be printed. So, all sides have to be checked in order to ensure every part is separated from others [4]. Here are some key points of designing different parts of the robot (Figs. 6 and 7).

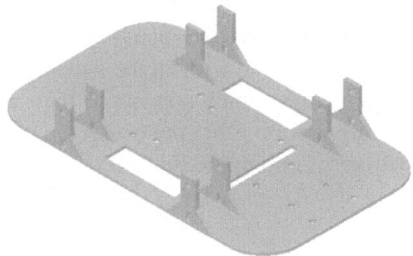

Fig. 6. Robot chassis design in Fusion 360

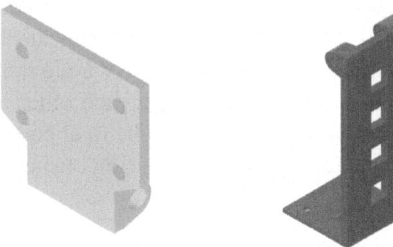

Fig. 7. Camera holder and Camera stand

- Camera stands

    When printing the camera stand, the triangle connection at the bottom of that part cannot be directly printed by the 3D printer. Therefore, both the vertical and horizontal lengths of the boards have to be increased.

- Chassis and motors

  Lots of holes are drilled at the bottom of the board in order the wires go through. Moreover, the distance between each motor stand needs to be measured so that the nails do not reach both sides of the stands.

- Camera holder

  Since the camera part is pretty small and fragile, both the camera, the holder, and the hole size need to be measured precisely. In that case, the camera is fixed in the holder very tightly and can also detect the environment freely.

3 Assembling All Parts Together

3.1 Assembling Plan

The first step to connect every part together is to put them together instead of directly connecting them together with tools. After considering the whole size, motor positions, wiring and the decoration all together, an assembling plan will be made to assemble them together (Figs. 8 and 9).

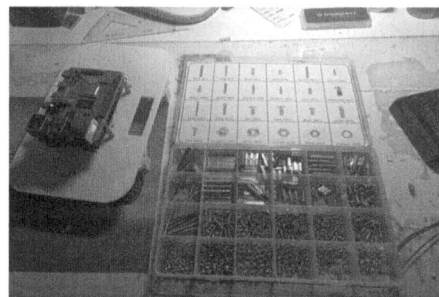

Fig. 8. Assembling parts

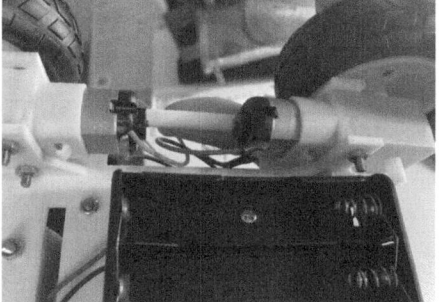

Fig. 9. Wiring

After putting all the materials together, check the space required in order to connect each hardware with wires. Electric soldering iron is used to connect the wires to the motors. During that process, some heat shrinking tubes are used to tighten the wires and the hot glue is used to stick the wire to the motors. After dealing with all the wires, make sure those wires match with each other because two wires which connect to the same motor are made into pairs. The final part of the wiring section is to connect all the wires to the motor controller. This time, using a screwdriver is enough to make it tight.

3.2 Assembling Camera

This is the most difficult part when assembling all the hardware together. Due to the small holes on the holder, no nuts can be used for assembling the camera (Figs. 10 and 11).

Fig. 10. Camera assembling

Fig. 11. Motors assembling and batteries

3.3 Motors Assembling and Batteries

After assembling the camera, it comes to the last part - motors and batteries. In order to make the whole robot smaller, the batteries should be set under the chassis. In this way, it can also make the whole robot heavier and more stable on the ground.

4 Programming and Testing

An HDM-to-HDMI wire is used to connect the robot to a computer screen. Therefore, it is easier to write code and do the editing. Virtual Network Computing (VNC) is used to looking for IP address and confirming some basic settings like the signing up and checking in process [5].

Import the basic code—making all the code suitable for Python form available for Thonny, the Python-based editor.

4.1 Motor Tests

Four motors will run independently. This is because when running on a rough lane, this method will make the car more stable and easier to control [6, 8] (Fig. 12):

- Going forward: All the four motors moving forward.
- Moving backward: All the four motors are moving backward.
- Turning left: Motors in the right will move forward, and motors at the left side will stop.
- Turning right: Motors in the left will move forward, and motors at the right side will stop.

The motors also have their own speed level: low speed, medium speed, and high speed. Different speed levels are used in different environments or different battery voltages.

Fig. 12. Finalized robot top and side view

4.2 Camera Tests

To ensure the camera will suit the Thonny version, camera driver code also need to be installed.

4.3 Color Picker

This is used to pick the color on the image. Therefore, the robot can recognize which the correct lane is, and where the correct destination is. In order to acquire the complete sight, color picker code should be set carefully to help the robot distinguish the roads from different background colors. Only under this circumstance, the robot is able to run properly without the disturbance of surroundings [8, 9]. While writing the code, different places are tested in order to obtain the parameters of different colors. Moreover, the shapes of the barrier objects should also be taken into consideration when recording the figures. A list of color parameters and shape parameters are matched to simulate different types of roads.

5   Conclusion

The autopilot car prototype is able to move smoothly on the ground by using of camera image processing detection. In the future, more approaches should be added, such as mechanic arm in order to improve the functionality.

Appendix

Code snippet 1:	def __init__(self, address, debug=False):	

```
PCA test :
#!/usr/bin/python
import time
import math
import smbus

# =============================
# Raspi PCA9685 16-Channel PWM Servo
Driver
# =============================

class PCA9685:
  # Registers/etc.
    __SUBADR1      = 0x02
    __SUBADR2      = 0x03
    __SUBADR3      = 0x04
    __MODE1        = 0x00
    __PRESCALE     = 0xFE
    __LED0_ON_L    = 0x06
    __LED0_ON_H    = 0x07
    __LED0_OFF_L   = 0x08
    __LED0_OFF_H   = 0x09
    __ALLLED_ON_L  = 0xFA
    __ALLLED_ON_H  = 0xFB
    __ALLLED_OFF_L = 0xFC
    __ALLLED_OFF_H = 0xFD
```

```
    self.bus = smbus.SMBus(1)
    self.address = address
    self.debug = debug
    if (self.debug):
      print("Reseting PCA9685")
    self.write(self.__MODE1, 0x00)


  def write(self, reg, value):
    "Writes an 8-bit value to the specified
register/address"
    self.bus.write_byte_data(self.address, reg,
value)
    if (self.debug):
      print("I2C: Write 0x%02X to register
0x%02X" % (value, reg))

  def read(self, reg):
    "Read an unsigned byte from the I2C device"
    result                                  =
self.bus.read_byte_data(self.address, reg)
    if (self.debug):
      print("I2C:  Device  0x%02X  returned
0x%02X from reg 0x%02X" % (self.address,
result & 0xFF, reg))
    return result
```

```
  def setPWMFreq(self, freq):
    "Sets the PWM frequency"
    prescaleval = 25000000.0   # 25MHz
    prescaleval = prescaleval / 4096.0    # 12-
bit
    prescaleval = prescaleval / float(freq)
    prescaleval = prescaleval - 1.0
    if (self.debug):
      print("Setting PWM frequency to %d Hz" %
freq)
      print("Estimated    pre-scale:    %d"    %
prescaleval)
    prescale = math.floor(prescaleval + 0.5)
    if (self.debug):
      print("Final pre-scale: %d" % prescale)

    oldmode = self.read(self.__MODE1);
    newmode = (oldmode & 0x7F) | 0x10    #
sleep
    self.write
```

Code Snippet 2: color picker		

```
import cv2
import numpy as np

frameWidth = 100
frameHeight = 200
cap = cv2.VideoCapture(1)
cap.set(3, frameWidth)
cap.set(4, frameHeight)
def empty(a):
  pass
cv2.namedWindow("HSV")
cv2.resizeWindow("HSV", 120, 240)
cv2.createTrackbar("HUE Min", "HSV", 0, 179,
empty)

cv2.createTrackbar("HUE Max", "HSV", 179,
179, empty)
cv2.createTrackbar("SAT Min", "HSV", 0, 255,
empty)
cv2.createTrackbar("SAT Max", "HSV", 255,
255, empty)
```

```
cv2.createTrackbar("VALUE Min", "HSV", 0,
255, empty)
cv2.createTrackbar("VALUE Max", "HSV", 255,
255, empty)

cap = cv2.VideoCapture(0)
# cap = cv2.VideoCapture('example.mp4')
frameCounter = 0

while True:
  frameCounter +=1
  if
cap.get(cv2.CAP_PROP_FRAME_COUNT)
==frameCounter:

cap.set(cv2.CAP_PROP_POS_FRAMES,0)
    frameCounter=0

  _, img = cap.read()
  imgHsv        =          cv2.cvtColor(img,
cv2.COLOR_BGR2HSV)

  h_min  =  cv2.getTrackbarPos("HUE  Min",
"HSV")
  h_max = cv2.getTrackbarPos("HUE Max",
"HSV")
```

```
  s_min  =  cv2.getTrackbarPos("SAT  Min",
"HSV")
  s_max  =  cv2.getTrackbarPos("SAT  Max",
"HSV")
  v_min = cv2.getTrackbarPos("VALUE Min",
"HSV")
  v_max = cv2.getTrackbarPos("VALUE Max",
"HSV")
  print(h_min)
  lower = np.array([h_min, s_min, v_min])
  upper = np.array([h_max, s_max, v_max])
  mask = cv2.inRange(imgHsv, lower, upper)
  result     =     cv2.bitwise_and(img,   img,
mask=mask)
  mask             =             cv2.cvtColor(mask,
cv2.COLOR_GRAY2BGR)
  hStack = np.hstack([img, mask, result])
  cv2.imshow('Horizontal Stacking', hStack)
  if cv2.waitKey(1) and 0xFF == ord('q'):
    break
cap.release()
cv2.destroyAllWindows()
```

```
Code snippet 3: camera test
import cv2
# Open the default camera (usually the built-in
webcam)
cap = cv2.VideoCapture(0)

# Check if the camera opened successfully
if not cap.isOpened():
    print("Error: Could not open camera.")
    exit()

# Set the width and height of the frame (you can
adjust these values)
width = 640
height = 480
cap.set(cv2.CAP_PROP_FRAME_WIDTH,
width)
cap.set(cv2.CAP_PROP_FRAME_HEIGHT,
height)

while True:
    # Read a frame from the camera

ret, frame = cap.read()
# Check if the frame was read successfully
if not ret:
    print("Error: Could not read frame.")
    break
# Display the frame
cv2.imshow('Live Video Stream', frame)
# Break the loop when the 'q' key is pressed
if cv2.waitKey(1) & 0xFF == ord('q'):
    break
# Release the camera and close the window
cap.release()
cv2.destroyAllWindows()
```

References

1. Self-driving Cars and Trucks Market Size | Statistics Report 2023 (2024). https://www.lin kedin.com/pulse/self-driving-cars-trucks-market-size-statistics-m93lf
2. Thakar, C.M.: 3D Printing: Basic principles and applications (2021). https://www.sciencedi rect.com/science/article/abs/pii/S2214785321046575
3. All You Need to Know About the 3.7V Lithium Ion Battery (2022). https://www.tycorun.com/ blogs/news/all-you-need-to-know-about-the-3-7v-lithium-ion-battery
4. Krishelle Hardson-Hurley, Thonny: The Beginner-Friendly Python Editor. https://realpython. com/python-thonny/
5. Seth Kenlon, How to connect to a remote computer using VNC in Linux (2022). https://www. redhat.com/sysadmin/vnc-screen-sharing-linux
6. Four-Wheel Drives - All You Need to Know About 4WDs (2023). https://www.directasia.com/ all-about-4WDs
7. Zhang, C., Wang, C., Dai, X., Liu, S.: Camera-based analysis of human pose for fall detection. In: The 24th International Conference on Internet Computing & IoT (ICOMP 2023), p. 116 (2023). ISBN # 1-60132-518-5
8. Zhang, K., Zhang, C.: Designing a low-cost microcontroller-based rover for microplastic detection using deep-learning image detection and near-infrared spectroscopy. In: The 21st International Conference on Embedded Systems, Cyber-physical Systems, & Applications (ESCS 2023), p. 36 (2023). ISBN # 1-60132-518-5
9. HTML color picker. https://htmlcolorcodes.com/color-picker/

Towards Implementation of Privacy-Preserving Federated Learning Aggregation Using Multi-key Homomorphic Encryption

Svetlana Boudko$^{(\boxtimes)}$ (ID)

Norwegian Computing Center, Oslo, Norway
`svetlana@nr.no`

Abstract. Federated Learning is a machine learning approach where a model is trained across multiple decentralized edge devices. Since the data are not uploaded to a server, this approach is particularly useful for data protection and efficient computation. Further, it can be combined with privacy-preserving technologies, e.g., homomorphic encryption for enhanced data protection. Considering all these elements, a practical solution will require an efficient multikey homomorphic encryption as well as an effective integration of federated model aggregation and multikey generation processes. The paper studies the related work for homomorphic encryption in the context of federated learning and outlines the rationale behind practical design of secure federated learning.

Keywords: Distributed Computing · Federated Learning · Federated Aggregation · Multi-key Homomorphic Encryption · Privacy-Preserving Technology

1 Introduction

To ensure data consistency and control, data centralization is a preferred solution for training machine learning models. However, data protection regulations. e.g. GDPR, as well as, industrial competition impose restrictions on information sharing among different organisations and individuals. Furthermore, this approach is technically challenging since the cost of collecting, storing and processing all data in one centralized location is too high and often not affordable.

Google introduced Federated Learning (FL) [24] in 2016 to facilitate collaborative training of machine learning models. The main intention was the reduction of data transfer costs and protection of privacy-sensitive information [3,19]. In contrast to traditional machine learning, FL does not require local data to be collected, stored, and processed on a central server. Instead, this method enables on-device model training using client-specific data with further aggregation of the obtained local model updates on a central server, as depicted in Fig. 1. This

© The Author(s), under exclusive license to Springer Nature Switzerland AG 2025
H. R. Arabnia et al. (Eds.): CSCE 2024, CCIS 2260, pp. 213–222, 2025.
https://doi.org/10.1007/978-3-031-85923-6_17

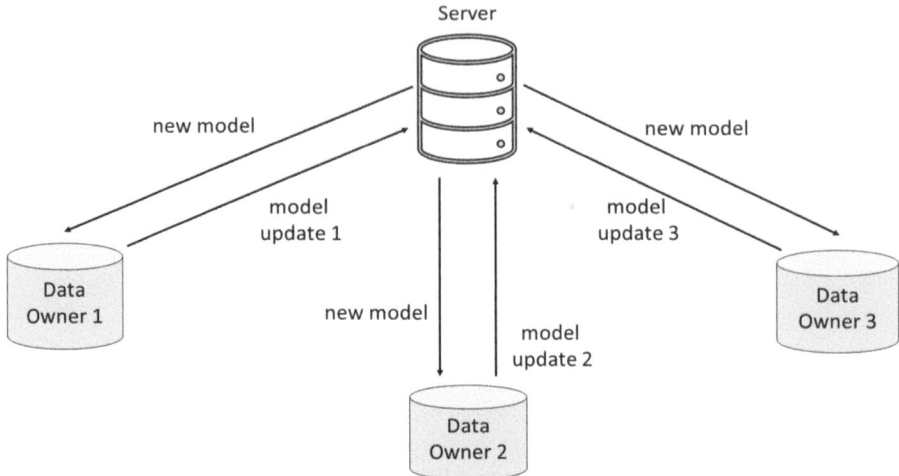

Fig. 1. Federated Aggregation process for three data owners and a central server. The data owners calculate their model updates and share these revisions with the server. The server then aggregates the received updates to generate a new model. This updated model is sent back to the data owners for further modifications.

approach can be particularly useful in scenarios where data privacy is a major concern, such as healthcare services or the financial sector.

FL can be further integrated with privacy-preserving technologies, e.g. homomorphic encryption (HE) for enhanced protection of personal data. In this case, an effective orchestration is required to ensure careful coordination between federated aggregation and key generation processes.

This work provides initial findings on practical implementation of secure federated aggregation of models in the context of federated learning including the following contributions: 1) analysis of HE within the context of federated learning and 2) design directions for privacy-preserving federated learning.

2   Theoretical Background

Federated learning, federated aggregation, and homomorphic encryption are all important concepts in the field of privacy-preserving machine learning and distributed data analysis. This section delves deeper into each of these concepts.

2.1   Federated Learning

FL relies on a distributed infrastructure comprised of a central server and multiple clients. The central server trains the initial model and sends it to all clients. The clients train their models using local data and send the obtained model updates back to the central server. After the updates are received from all clients, the server generates a new global model that is sent back to the clients to perform the next iteration step. The training process is an iteration process of several steps alternating between local updates and global aggregation.

The core of this method is the aggregation process. Different strategies have been proposed to facilitate the aggregation process, improve the convergence, and reduce communicational and computational expenses [1,20,22,23,31]. Federated Averaging is most commonly used due to its communication efficiency [23,32]. In this method, a subset of clients is selected to perform updates using stochastic gradient descent by processing several iterations. The process alternates between multiple local stochastic gradient updates and exchanging their averaged weights for updates of the global model.

Although the local data are not shared with external parties, there are still privacy concerns that must be addressed. Model updates can still reveal sensitive information and are prone to privacy attacks [17,26,30]. These attacks include inference attacks [25,28,29], data/gradient leakage attacks [2], and GAN-based attacks [18]. Launching GAN-based attacks, an attacker has a high chance to fully reconstruct users' private data. In these conditions, using privacy-preserving technologies can provide a secure way to aggregate the updates from different clients, and homomorphic encryption (HE) can be utilized to improve the protection of personal data.

2.2 Homomorphic Encryption

HE is an encryption technique that allows for computations on encrypted data without decrypting these data. This method can increase privacy preservation in federated learning. Each client encrypts its model updates using homomorphic encryption, and these encrypted updates can be securely sent to the central server. The server then performs aggregation operations on these encrypted updates. The result is received in encrypted form and is homomorphic to the result of the same computation on the unencrypted data. Different HE schemes have been proposed in the literature, each with their own benefits and drawbacks.

Partially Homomorphic Encryption (PHE). This is the simplest form of homomorphic encryption. PHE schemes can perform one type of operation, either addition or multiplication, an unlimited number of times. The most famous PHE scheme is the RSA algorithm, which is a multiplicative homomorphic encryption.

Somewhat Homomorphic Encryption (SHE). SHE schemes can perform both addition and multiplication operations, but only up to a certain degree. The limitation lies in the noise introduced into the cipher text after each operation, which grows exponentially with the number of operations. Therefore, the number of computations that can be performed is limited.

Fully Homomorphic Encryption (FHE). The first practical fully homomorphic encryption (FHE) scheme was proposed by Craig Gentry in 2009 [15]. FHE schemes overcome the limitations of SHE, allowing an unlimited number of both addition and multiplication operations. The major challenge with FHE is that it is computationally very intensive, which has limited its practical applications.

Following this, different homomorphic encryption schemes have been proposed in the literature [5,7,10,16] aiming to improve computational efficiency, The Dijk-Gentry-Halevi-Vaikuntanathan (DGHV) scheme [13] is a simpler FHE system proposed in 2010. It's based on the approximate greatest common divisor problem, a well-known problem in number theory. This scheme is simpler than Gentry's but also suffers from high computational costs.

The Brakerski-Gentry-Vaikuntanathan (BGV) scheme, proposed in 2011 [6], uses lattice-based cryptography with ring learning with errors (Ring-LWE) problem as its security basis. The BGV scheme is more efficient than earlier FHE schemes, making it more practical for real-world applications. This schemes supports computations over integer arithmetic circuits.

The Lopez-Alt-Tromer-Vaikuntanathan (LTV) scheme, proposed in 2012 [21], is an improvement on the BGV scheme. It simplifies some parts of the BGV construction, leading to further efficiency gains.

The Brakerski-Fan-Vercauteren (BFV) scheme, proposed in 2012 [5,14], is another variation on the BGV scheme. The BFV scheme simplifies the BGV scheme by removing the need for a relinearization step, leading to a more efficient algorithm.

In [9], the authors presented a homomorphic encryption scheme, known as the Cheon-Kim-Kim-Song (CKKS) scheme. This scheme features a plaintext space of approximations of real or complex numbers. and uses a rescaling operation for reducing noise growth from multiplications. It is designed to support real and complex numbers arithmetic operations, thus, particularly suitable for data analytics problems.

Though, these schemes when applying to the federated learning settings have a certain drawback. These are single key schemes implying that all clients use the same key and can decrypt updates from other participants. This problem is addressed in multi-key homomorphic encryption (MKHE), where each client holds its own secret key, and the server completes homomorphic calculations of data encrypted with different keys. The clients jointly decrypt the result using their secret keys.

The study [21] was the first to propose a multi-key homomorphic encryption scheme based on NTRU. It operates on inputs encrypted under multiple keys. The result is decrypted using the secret keys of all participants. In [11], the authors introduced a multi-identity IBFHE scheme that is selectively secure in the random oracle model under the hardness of Learning with Errors. The authors in [27] presented a fully dynamic multi-key FHE scheme that supports an unbounded number of homomorphic operations for an unbounded number of parties.

However, the MKHE schemes are computationally inefficient. The key generation is expensive. Additionally, computational runtime grows quadratically with the number of clients, and the generated ciphertext expands during homomorphic operations proportionally to the number of clients [8]. Further, the clients have to generate evaluation keys and send these keys to the server to perform homomorphic operations. Requiring expensive key generation and decryption, these schemes cannot be directly applied in real scenarios, and, to our knowledge, there is no practical solution that achieve this functionality.

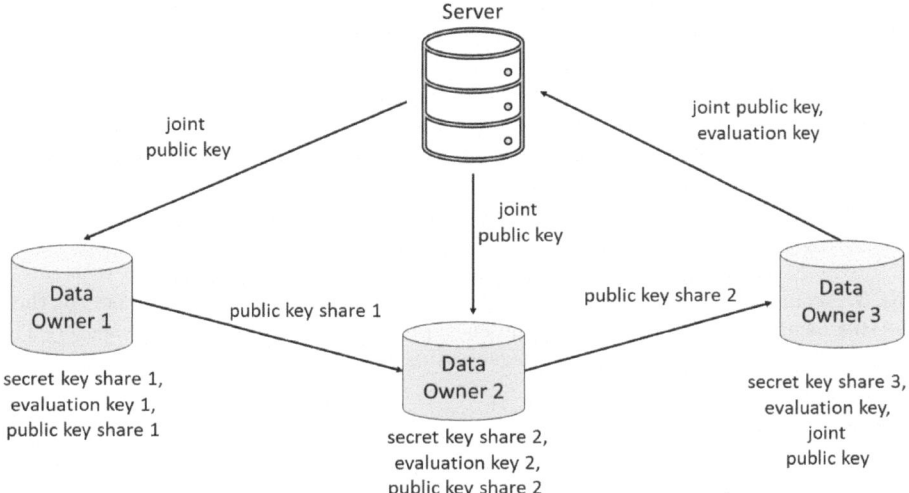

Fig. 2. Key generation process for three data owners and a central server. The data owners generate their secret keys, and interact to generate evaluation keys and a joint public key.

The threshold multi-key homomorphic encryption (TMKHE) is another method that can be applied for multiparty computation. It uses thresholdization [4,12] of fully homomorphic encryption schemes, e.g., BGV and CKKS. It relaxes the problem with ciphertext expansion and key generation making MKHE better suited for practical applications. This method involves three stages: (1) the generation of secret, evaluation, and public keys; (2) the process of encryption and homomorphic computation; and (3) decryption. The clients generate their own secret key shares and evaluation keys, and interact to generated a joint public key and a final evaluation key, as depicted in Fig. 2. The evaluation key is sent to the server, and the generated joint public key is shared among the participants. In contrast to the MKHE schemes, where clients utilize their own secret keys to encrypt data, in this scheme, each data owner encrypts their data using the jointly generated public key. The result is computed by the server in encrypted form using the evaluation key, Fig. 3. The encrypted result is decrypted collectively as in MKHE, and a new aggregated model is computed, Fig. 4.

Though the ciphertext length does not depend on the number of clients, it implies that the clients are predefined before generation of a common public key. These schemes also require phases that involves communication between

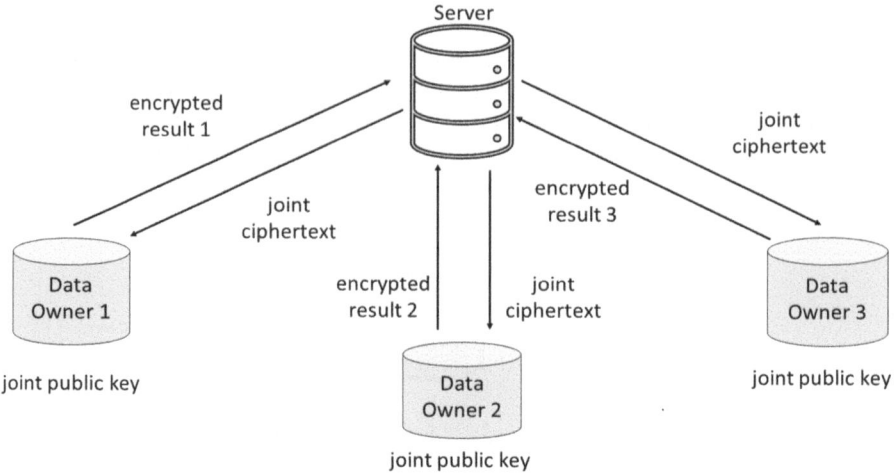

Fig. 3. Accumulation of encrypted results. The data owners compute and encrypt their updates using the joint public key. The encrypted updates are sent to the server. The joint ciphertext is generated by the server using the evaluation keys and sent back to the data owners.

all participants including a distributed key generation protocol, a homomorphic encryption algorithm, and a threshold decryption protocol.

3   Proposed Approach

This section outlines an approach designed to facilitate a multi-key homomorphic encryption process in the federated learning settings. Federated averaging is performed by a selected group of clients, with different groups for each round of model updating. Different groups of clients are selected in advance, and the key generation routine is run for all selected groups.

For the key generation routine, the server selects the leader of the process, defines the schedule of the joint public key computational process, and reports the schedule to the clients. The leading client starts the key generation process and sends its public key share to the next client. Upon receiving the public key share from its predecessor, each client performs its computation and sends the obtained public key share to the next client in sequence. The leading client sends the final result to the server. To facilitate this routine, the communication protocols and mechanisms must be in place.

All obtained public and evaluation keys are stored on both the server and the clients. The secret keys that are obtained are stored only on the clients. All keys are labeled according to the groups to which they belong. For each round of model updates, the server selects a group, and checks the availability of its members. If any member is unavailable, the next group is chosen. The model update is run if there is a group with all members available. The stored keys are

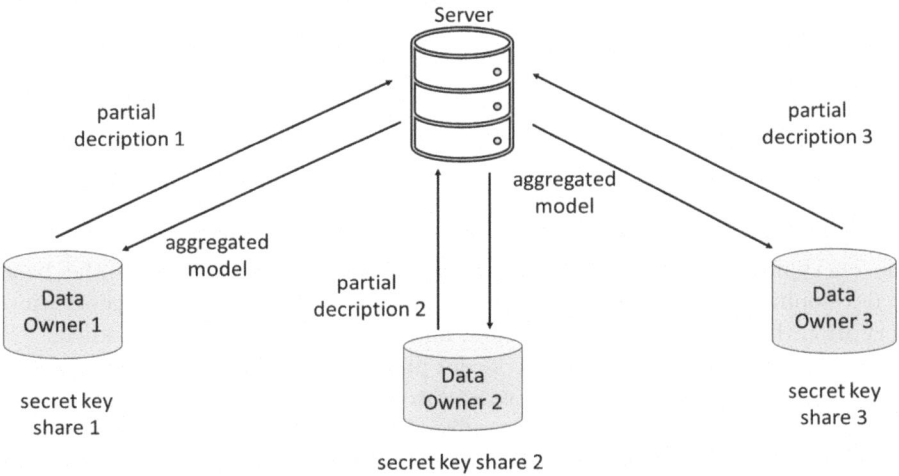

Fig. 4. Decryption process and model aggregation. The data owners decrypt the received ciphertext using their secret shares and send the results to the server. The server fuses the received results and generates a new model.

used for homomorphic encryption. If no group has all its members available, a new key generation routine is initiated.

4   Discussion

Despite considerable research conducted on multi-key homomorphic encryption, to the best of our knowledge, there are no practical solutions that implement necessary networking mechanisms and protocols, and are readily applicable in industrial distributed environments. Although TMKHE schemes are more efficient compared to MKHE, they present a problem when a new client joins the ongoing process. In federated learning aggregation, a new group of clients is selected in each iteration to perform mini-batch sampling of their local data. This implies that a new key generation process is required for each iteration.

The TMKHE workflow is complex as the key generation and decryption are interactive processes involving all the participating parties. In addition, TMKHE schemes operate in a peer-to-peer manner for key generation, while federated aggregation traditionally uses client-server communication. Thus, the interplay between these two paradigms should be considered to ensure effective integration. Furthermore, the key generation process is still a burden for clients with limited resources, as in industrial IoTs, requiring further adaptation to industrial settings and lightweight encryption schemes.

Several research challenges need to be addressed. If TMKHE schemes are used, it becomes necessary to define the routines for key generation in cooperation with the selection of client subsets for performing model updates. Appropriate protocols have to be implemented for the coordination of the key generation and model aggregation process. Modification of federated aggregation protocols may be required to comply with peer-to-peer communication.

5   Conclusion

This paper discusses the main components and directions for implementing privacy-preserving federated learning using the threshold multi-key homomorphic encryption. Multikey HE technologies have been analysed as the basis for developing data protection mechanisms. The workflows for key generation, encryption, homomorphic computation, and decryption have been studied.

At this stage, the work is in the concept phase, and additional research on how federated learning and TMKHE schemes can be integrated effectively is required. As of now, the proposed approach requires further design, implementation, and testing of communication protocols, mechanisms and key generation processes. Therefore, more detailed analyses and modeling will be conducted, in along with the integration of existing federated aggregation methods. Modifications to these methods will be made as necessary.

Acknowledgments. This work has been carried out in the context of the Center for Research-based Innovation NORCICS, funded by the Research Council of Norway, grant number 310105/F40.

Disclosure of Interests. The author has no competing interests to declare that are relevant to the content of this article.

References

1. Arivazhagan, M.G., Aggarwal, V., Singh, A.K., Choudhary, S.: Federated learning with personalization layers (2019). https://arxiv.org/abs/1912.00818. Accessed 01 Sept 2024
2. Bhowmick, A., Duchi, J., Freudiger, J., Kapoor, G., Rogers, R.: Protection against reconstruction and its applications in private federated learning (2019). https://arxiv.org/pdf/1812.00984. Accessed 01 Sept 2024
3. Bonawitz, K., et al.: Practical secure aggregation for federated learning on user-held data (2016). https://arxiv.org/abs/1611.04482. Accessed 01 Sept 2024
4. Boneh, D., et al.: Threshold cryptosystems from threshold fully homomorphic encryption. In: Shacham, H., Boldyreva, A. (eds.) Advances in Cryptology - CRYPTO 2018, pp. 565–596. Springer, Cham (2018)
5. Brakerski, Z.: Fully homomorphic encryption without modulus switching from classical GapSVP. In: Safavi-Naini, R., Canetti, R. (eds.) Advances in Cryptology - CRYPTO 2012, pp. 868–886. Springer, Heidelberg (2012)
6. Brakerski, Z., Gentry, C., Vaikuntanathan, V.: Fully homomorphic encryption without bootstrapping. Cryptology ePrint Archive, Paper 2011/277 (2011). https://eprint.iacr.org/2011/277.pdf. Accessed 01 Sept 2024

7. Brakerski, Z., Gentry, C., Vaikuntanathan, V.: (leveled) fully homomorphic encryption without bootstrapping. In: Proceedings of the 3rd Innovations in Theoretical Computer Science Conference, ITCS 2012, pp. 309–325. Association for Computing Machinery, New York (2012). https://doi.org/10.1145/2090236.2090262. Accessed 01 Sept 2024

8. Chen, H., Dai, W., Kim, M., Song, Y.: Efficient multi-key homomorphic encryption with packed ciphertexts with application to oblivious neural network inference. In: Proceedings of the 2019 ACM SIGSAC Conference on Computer and Communications Security, CCS 2019, pp. 395–412. Association for Computing Machinery, New York (2019). https://doi.org/10.1145/3319535.3363207

9. Cheon, J.H., Kim, A., Kim, M., Song, Y.: Homomorphic encryption for arithmetic of approximate numbers. In: Takagi, T., Peyrin, T. (eds.) Advances in Cryptology - ASIACRYPT 2017, pp. 409–437. Springer, Cham (2017)

10. Chillotti, I., Gama, N., Georgieva, M., Izabachène, M.: Faster fully homomorphic encryption: bootstrapping in less than 0.1 seconds. In: Cheon, J.H., Takagi, T. (eds.) Advances in Cryptology – ASIACRYPT 2016, pp. 3–33. Springer, Heidelberg (2016)

11. Clear, M., McGoldrick, C.: Multi-identity and multi-key leveled FHE from learning with errors. In: Gennaro, R., Robshaw, M. (eds.) Advances in Cryptology - CRYPTO 2015, pp. 630–656. Springer, Heidelberg (2015)

12. Desmedt, Y., Frankel, Y.: Threshold cryptosystems. In: Brassard, G. (ed.) Advances in Cryptology – CRYPTO' 89 Proceedings, pp. 307–315. Springer, New York (1990)

13. van Dijk, M., Gentry, C., Halevi, S., Vaikuntanathan, V.: Fully homomorphic encryption over the integers. In: Gilbert, H. (ed.) Advances in Cryptology - EUROCRYPT 2010, pp. 24–43. Springer, Heidelberg (2010)

14. Fan, J., Vercauteren, F.: Somewhat practical fully homomorphic encryption. Cryptology ePrint Archive, Paper 2012/144 (2012). https://eprint.iacr.org/2012/144. Accessed 01 Sept 2024

15. Gentry, C.: Fully homomorphic encryption using ideal lattices. In: Proceedings of the Forty-First Annual ACM Symposium on Theory of Computing, STOC 2009, pp. 169–178. Association for Computing Machinery, New York (2009). https://doi.org/10.1145/1536414.1536440. Accessed 01 Sept 2024

16. Gentry, C., Sahai, A., Waters, B.: Homomorphic encryption from learning with errors: conceptually-simpler, asymptotically-faster, attribute-based. In: Canetti, R., Garay, J.A. (eds.) Advances in Cryptology - CRYPTO 2013, pp. 75–92. Springer, Heidelberg (2013)

17. Gosselin, R., Vieu, L., Loukil, F., Benoit, A.: Privacy and security in federated learning: a survey. Appl. Sci. **12**(19) (2022). https://doi.org/10.3390/app12199901. https://www.mdpi.com/2076-3417/12/19/9901. Accessed 01 Sept 2024

18. Hitaj, B., Ateniese, G., Perez-Cruz, F.: Deep models under the GAN: information leakage from collaborative deep learning. In: Proceedings of the 2017 ACM SIGSAC Conference on Computer and Communications Security, CCS 2017, pp. 603–618. Association for Computing Machinery, New York (2017). https://doi.org/10.1145/3133956.3134012

19. Konečný, J., McMahan, H.B., Yu, F.X., Richtárik, P., Suresh, A.T., Bacon, D.: Federated learning: strategies for improving communication efficiency (2017). https://arxiv.org/abs/1610.05492. Accessed 01 Sept 2024

20. Li, T., Sahu, A.K., Zaheer, M., Sanjabi, M., Talwalkar, A., Smith, V.: Federated optimization in heterogeneous networks (2020). https://arxiv.org/abs/1812.06127. Accessed 01 Sept 2024

21. López-Alt, A., Tromer, E., Vaikuntanathan, V.: On-the-fly multiparty computation on the cloud via multikey fully homomorphic encryption. In: Proceedings of the Forty-Fourth Annual ACM Symposium on Theory of Computing, STOC 2012, pp. 1219–1234. Association for Computing Machinery, New York (2012). https://doi.org/10.1145/2213977.2214086. Accessed 01 Sept 2024

22. McMahan, B., Moore, E., Ramage, D., Hampson, S., Arcas, B.A.: Communication-efficient learning of deep networks from decentralized data. In: Singh, A., Zhu, J. (eds.) Proceedings of the 20th International Conference on Artificial Intelligence and Statistics. Proceedings of Machine Learning Research, vol. 54, pp. 1273–1282. PMLR (2017)

23. McMahan, H.B., Moore, E., Ramage, D., Arcas, B.A.: Federated learning of deep networks using model averaging (2016). http://arxiv.org/abs/1602.05629. Accessed 01 Sept 2024

24. McMahan, H.B., Moore, E., Ramage, D., Hampson, S., Arcas, B.A.: Communication-efficient learning of deep networks from decentralized data (2023). https://arxiv.org/abs/1602.05629. Accessed 01 Sept 2024

25. Melis, L., Song, C., Cristofaro, E.D., Shmatikov, V.: Exploiting unintended feature leakage in collaborative learning. In: 2019 IEEE Symposium on Security and Privacy (SP), pp. 691–706 (2018)

26. Mothukuri, V., Parizi, R.M., Pouriyeh, S., Huang, Y., Dehghantanha, A., Srivastava, G.: A survey on security and privacy of federated learning. Futur. Gener. Comput. Syst. **115**, 619–640 (2021). https://doi.org/10.1016/j.future.2020.10.007

27. Mukherjee, P., Wichs, D.: Two round multiparty computation via multi-key FHE. In: Fischlin, M., Coron, J.S. (eds.) Advances in Cryptology - EUROCRYPT 2016, pp. 735–763. Springer, Heidelberg (2016)

28. Nasr, M., Shokri, R., Houmansadr, A.: Comprehensive privacy analysis of deep learning: passive and active white-box inference attacks against centralized and federated learning. In: 2019 IEEE Symposium on Security and Privacy (SP), pp. 739–753 (2018)

29. Shokri, R., Stronati, M., Song, C., Shmatikov, V.: Membership inference attacks against machine learning models. In: 2017 IEEE Symposium on Security and Privacy (SP), pp. 3–18. IEEE Computer Society, Los Alamitos (2017). https://doi.org/10.1109/SP.2017.41

30. Truong, N., Sun, K., Wang, S., Guitton, F., Guo, Y.: Privacy preservation in federated learning: an insightful survey from the GDPR perspective. Comput. Secur. **110**, 102402 (2021). https://doi.org/10.1016/j.cose.2021.102402. https://www.sciencedirect.com/science/article/pii/S0167404821002261. Accessed 01 Sept 2024

31. Wang, H., Yurochkin, M., Sun, Y., Papailiopoulos, D., Khazaeni, Y.: Federated learning with matched averaging (2020). https://arxiv.org/abs/2002.06440. Accessed 01 Sept 2024

32. Wang, J., Das, R., Joshi, G., Kale, S., Xu, Z., Zhang, T.: On the unreasonable effectiveness of federated averaging with heterogeneous data. CoRR abs/2206.04723 (2022). https://doi.org/10.48550/ARXIV.2206.04723. Accessed 01 Sept 2024

Advancing Nursing Education Through Virtual Reality Training: A Revolutionary Approach to Ensuring Patient Safety

Sai Lokesh Reddy Gayam and Jiaofei Zhong$^{(\boxtimes)}$ (iD)

California State University East Bay, Hayward, CA 94542, USA
sgayam@horizon.csueastbay.edu, jiaofei.zhong@csueastbay.edu

Abstract. Ensuring patient safety is a primary concern in the healthcare industry, and nursing education plays a vital role in providing future professionals with the necessary skills to identify potential risks. Traditional training methods often lack the immersive and interactive experience that students need. In this paper, we proposed and implemented a Virtual Reality (VR) application as an educational tool to help students learn the best clinical practices they should follow in a hospital setting. This application created a 360-degree VR environment for the simulation lab, where the user needs to identify unsafe clinical practices in this virtual environment. By leveraging innovative VR technology, students can engage with virtual hospital scenes in a controlled and risk-free setting, allowing them to develop a deeper understanding of potential hazards and unsafe practices through the VR training application.

Keywords: Virtual Reality · VR · Nursing · Education · Safety · Simulation

1 Introduction

The recent COVID-19 pandemic has demonstrated the need for better healthcare professionals. One of our main goals is to train college students in the best possible way so that they become better healthcare professionals of tomorrow. With the rapid development of Virtual Reality (VR) technology, virtual scenes and objects look very realistic, making users feel like they are immersed in a computer-generated reality environment. Therefore, in this paper, we propose to build a VR-based application to facilitate education and training in the field of healthcare and nursing.

Ensuring patient safety is a primary concern in the healthcare industry, and nursing education plays a vital role in providing future professionals with the necessary skills to identify and mitigate potential risks. Traditional classroom-based and hospital-based training methods, while valuable, often lack the immersive and interactive experience students need to extensively practice identifying unsafe practices. This limitation may hinder the effective translation of theoretical knowledge into practical applications, potentially jeopardizing patient safety.

We propose to build an immersive VR simulation that addresses these limitations by providing students with a realistic and interactive training environment. A list of unsafe

H. R. Arabnia et al. (Eds.): CSCE 2024, CCIS 2260, pp. 223–231, 2025.
https://doi.org/10.1007/978-3-031-85923-6_18

practices was identified in a 360-degree scene of the simulation laboratory, which is a simulated ward in a hospital setting. These unsafe practices are flagged in this VR application, and users can point and click on these unsafe items using a VR headset and controllers. If the users select the correct items, they will receive points, and the application will display information about the unsafe item, along with updated total points the user has collected at that time.

By utilizing innovative virtual reality technology, students can participate in simulated hospital scenarios in a controlled and risk-free environment. This method of identifying unsafe clinical practices in a hospital setting from the comfort of home can give students a deeper understanding of potentially dangerous and unsafe practices and help them avoid making mistakes as they become healthcare professionals.

This study provides a revolutionary approach to nursing education by developing a game-based application to deliver VR simulation to our university's patient simulation laboratory. By combining realistic simulation, remote access and deliberate practice, the proposed solution aims to bridge the gap between theoretical knowledge and practical application, ultimately helping to improve patient safety and better prepare nursing professionals.

2 Related Work

Research and interest in the use of virtual reality (VR) simulations for training in healthcare education have grown recently. Many investigations were made into the possibilities of virtual reality technology in raising the learning standards in nursing education and other healthcare activities. The use of virtual reality is not limited to the nursing field, but to most of the fields related to engineering, healthcare, and communications.

A study by David Checa and Andres Bustillo of University of Burgos [1] claims that Immersive Virtual Reality Games have the potential to revolutionize the way we approach various learning and training tasks, if they have not already. As indicated by Pei Ning Woon et al. [2], computer-generated reality may be a viable training system for further development of information acquisition, while also being reasonable for augmenting common teaching strategies. Kyaw et al. [3] conducted a systematic review and meta-analysis of how virtual reality helps healthcare professionals. Their findings suggest that VR simulations in health professionals' education can have a majorly positive impact on their future. They found that VR simulations were helpful in better knowledge and skills acquisition when compared to traditional teaching methods.

Kiegaldie and Shaw [4] conducted a study and evaluated the effectiveness of Virtual Reality Simulations (VRS) compared to traditional Simulation-Based Education (SBE) for nursing students. This study involved 675 pre-registered students with the intervention group (n = 393) receiving four immersive VRS modules and the control group (n = 282) receiving standard SBE with simulated participants. The results showed that approximately 95% of students actively participated in the VRS scenarios compared to only 15% in the SBE group. Knowledge test scores were significantly higher for VRS compared to SBE. These students also reported higher preparedness for future practice. Also, Chen et al. [5] state that the effectiveness in areas of skills, confidence and performance is warranted with larger sampler size of students participating in the studies that use virtual reality. The results of a study by Grace Ryan [6] revealed that the knowledge gained using immersive technology is the same compared to traditional learning methods, however, the use of immersive technology such as virtual reality can improve the learning experience.

To ensure patients receive the best possible care, it is critical to incorporate safety skills into all training methods, whether for students or healthcare professionals. Despite the many obstacles presented by the COVID-19 pandemic, nursing educators are leveraging technology to share a wealth of information [7]. This, in turn, has helped many healthcare providers stay informed and adapt quickly during the pandemic. These technologies include virtual reality, augmented reality, and mixed reality. To achieve all these goals, it is essential for students to develop both technical proficiency and human-centered skills [8]. Although VR technology has recently been adopted in medical education, it is important to prioritize these skills in medical school. Supplementing didactic education with VR simulations will enable students to practice patient interactions effectively [9].

One unique feature of our proposed work compared to other existing works is that we use real photos of the physical laboratory and real objects in the photos to build the virtual environment of our VR application, while other works use animated scenes and animated objects within the scenes for their VR applications. Actual photos of patient rooms can provide users with a more immersive experience, allowing them to feel like they are standing in the room and be able to walk to various locations and observe every corner of the room.

3 Methods

The proposed immersive VR simulation for nursing education utilizes the Meta (Oculus) Quest 2 headset to enter the virtual simulation. The virtual simulation is achieved by integrating 360-degree photos of our patient simulation laboratory into a VR application developed with the help of the cross-platform game engine Unity. Students can take a comprehensive look at the patient simulation lab using their own VR headsets.

3.1 Design and Implementation

We decided to build the entire virtual scene of the simulation lab from scratch and provide more customization possibilities so that future changes of the VR application will be easy. Some existing studies [10] also suggest that creating our own applications or simulations can help students gain better understanding of the immersive technology. Figure 1 shows what the proposed VR application looks like, which displays the virtual patient room created from photos taken in the simulation laboratory on campus. The flowchart in Fig. 2 demonstrates the system workflow of the proposed VR application.

The first step in creating the proposed VR application is to obtain a series of 360-degree photos of a patient room in the simulation laboratory. After adding photos of the patient room to our VR project to create VR scenes, we identified a list of unsafe objects in these scenes with the help of our nursing professors, who provides us with 10 unsafe practices in photos and describes in detail what goes wrong in each situation. Detailed descriptions will be displayed to inform students when they identify each unsafe item

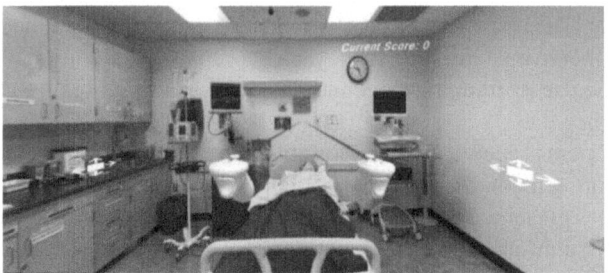

Fig. 1. A 360-degree Virtual Scene in the VR Application

in the virtual scene. While developing the application, we marked the locations of those 10 unsafe items in the virtual space and ensured that those markers are not visible to student users who would practice identifying those unsafe items in the virtual space.

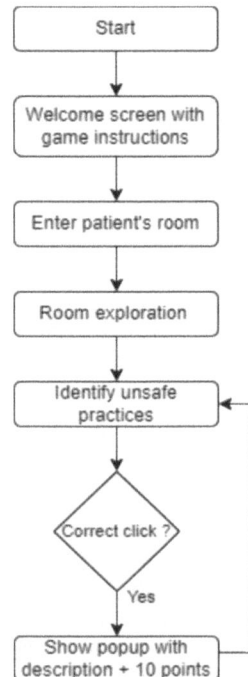

Fig. 2. System Workflow of the Proposed VR Application

3.2 Usage

In this gamified application, the primary task of the student users is to engage with the VR simulation to navigate the virtual space using the Meta (Oculus) Quest 2 VR headset and interact with different unsafe items in the scene. Users only need to wear the VR headset and turn their head to see the entire room of the simulation lab. Two VR controllers are also displayed in the scene, one for each hand. Users will be able to point to unsafe items and click on them using buttons on the controllers. For each unsafe item they identify in the scene, they are awarded 10 points, which are displayed in the upper right corner of the screen and updated after each correct click.

4   Application Overview

In this section, we will provide a complete overview of the application starting from what it looks like to how it works. Figure 3 shows the welcome screen when the VR application starts. Users can enter the VR scene by clicking on the button named "Enter into simulation" after reading the instructions.

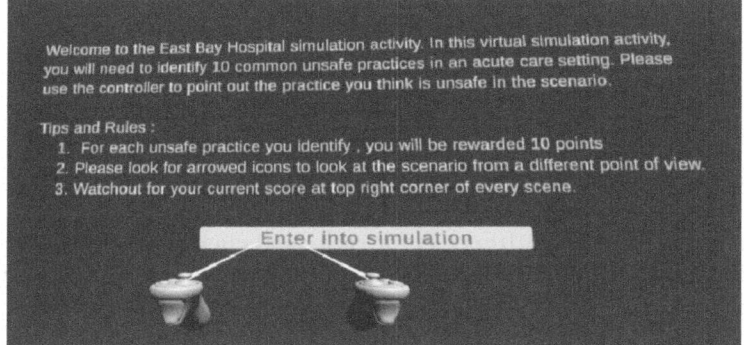

Fig. 3. Welcome Screen of the VR Application

4.1   User Interface: Patient Room Simulation

The VR application's complete user interface incorporates our university's simulation laboratory. Figure 4 shows a photo of the simulation laboratory in our university. Figure 5 shows the default front view of the VR scene through Meta (Oculus) Quest 2 VR headset, where users can see the controllers in the middle of the scene and the total score at the upper right corner.

4.2   Interactive Objects

We have marked 10 items in the virtual scene as unsafe and made these marks invisible to student users. The 10 locations are interactive, and students can click on them with the help of VR controllers to collect points.

Another interaction is that users can change their point of view by clicking on the icons on either side of the scene. In Fig. 5 of the default view, there are two white icons on both left and right sides. When users click on the left icon, their perspective changes to the left side, as shown in Fig. 6. Similarly, if they click on the right icon, their perspective changes to the right side, as shown in Fig. 7.

4.3 Controller Interactions and Scoring

In the given scenario, it is assumed that the oxygen nasal prong should be on the patient's nose, but this is not the case. This is an unsafe practice. If the users cannot see the patient's nose or the oxygen nasal prong from the default front view of the room, the viewing angle can be changed to the left side so that the patient's nose can be seen clearly and up close. Users can select the nose area using VR controllers. When they click on it, a pop-up window with a sound appears, notifying the users that they have discovered an unsafe condition.

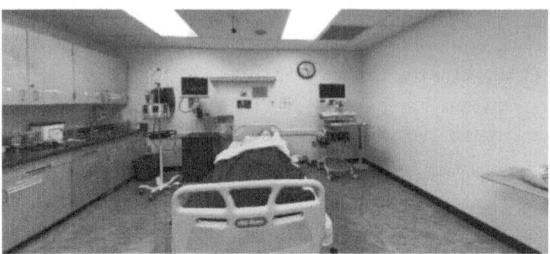

Fig. 4. A Photo of the Simulation Lab at the University

Student users will receive 10 points for each valid click on an unsafe item in the virtual scene, and a pop-up window will display a full description of what they found. The current score can be seen at the upper right corner of the screen and will be updated after each correct click. Figure 5, Fig. 6, and Fig. 7 show what the pop-up windows look like.

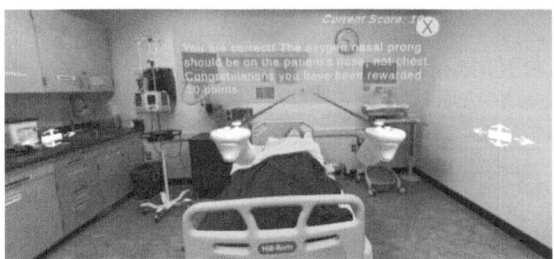

Fig. 5. Front View (Default Virtual Scene) of the Lab

We can see in Fig. 5 that the current score has been updated to 10 points immediately after the user identifies the first unsafe item. If the same user discovers another unsafe item, he or she will receive an additional 10 points, assuming that the newly discovered item has not been found before. See Fig. 6 and Fig. 7 for two new items identified in two different views and observe how the scores been updated to 20 points and then 30 points after two successful clicks on two more unsafe items in the scene.

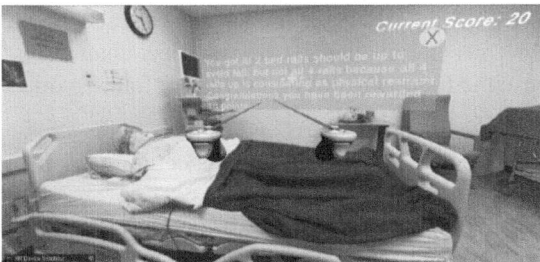

Fig. 6. Left Side View of the Lab

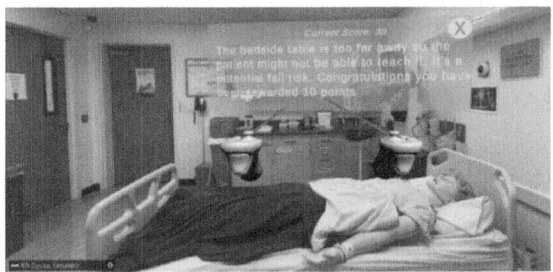

Fig. 7. Right Side View of the Lab

5   Discussion

Traditional methods of training nursing students at universities or hospitals can be very time-consuming and expensive, as time needs to be set aside to travel to the hospital each time practice is needed. The proposed VR simulations can greatly help nursing students continue to learn safe practices without having to travel directly to the hospitals. This is economical for universities because they don't need to purchase expensive patient simulators or hire real people to act as patients for students to practice. This also avoids any risk that the patient might face if the student behaves unsafely while practicing.

While this type of gamified VR simulation has many advantages, it also has its own limitations in terms of development and implementation. If students want to practice in a different virtual simulation room, the VR application must be updated by adding new 360-degree photos to build new scenes, and marking unsafe items in new scenes takes time and effort. This limitation also extends to the learning curve of students using VR applications. They need to know how to use a VR headset and controllers, and sometimes they need to connect the headsets to their laptops to run the VR simulations.

5.1   Future Directions

Integrating immersive VR training into nursing education not only solves the limitations of current traditional training methods, but also paves the way for future breakthroughs in medical training methods. By providing students with remotely accessible, realistic simulation experiences, this innovative approach aims to redefine the training environment and help students meet the challenges they will encounter throughout their careers. Therefore, we propose the following directions for our future work:

- Collaborate with subject matter experts and healthcare professionals to ensure simulation scenarios are accurate and relevant, reflecting current industry norms and practices.
- Conduct a long-term study to evaluate the impact of VR-based training on nursing students' performance, decision-making abilities, and patient outcomes in real-life clinical settings.
- Investigate the possibility of adding multi-user functionality, which would enable multiple students to participate in group training exercises and demonstrate collaboration and communication skills that are critical in a healthcare environment.

6   Conclusion

In this paper, we proposed and implemented a Virtual Reality (VR) application as an educational tool to help students learn the best clinical practices they should follow in a hospital setting. This application created a 360-degree virtual scene for the simulation lab, where the users can identify unsafe clinical practices in this virtual environment.

We found that adding immersive virtual reality training to nursing education has enormous potential to change the way healthcare professionals are trained. This innovative strategy overcomes the shortcomings of traditional training by providing students with realistic simulation experiences and remote access, better preparing nursing students for the challenges they may encounter in their future careers.

In addition to facilitating an immersive learning experience, gamified VR simulations improve patient safety by allowing students to practice in a virtual supervised environment. Future development and improvements in VR simulations are critical for nursing education, exploring new ways to tailor training to individual learners, and conducting long-term research to understand how VR-based simulations impact student learning outcomes in real clinical settings.

Acknowledgments. The authors would like to extend our gratitude to the Department of Computer Science at California State University East Bay (CSUEB) for the A2E2 grant, and the Collaborative Research Award from the College of Science. This work was also supported by CSUEB Center for Student Research (CSR) Scholar's Program.

References

1. Checa, D., Bustillo, A.: A review of immersive virtual reality serious games to enhance learning and training. Multimed. Tools Appl. **79**(9), 5501–5527 (2020)
2. Woon, A.P.N., et al.: Effectiveness of virtual reality training in improving knowledge among nursing students: a systematic review, meta-analysis and meta-regression. Nurse Educ. Today **98**, 104655 (2021)
3. Kyaw, B.M., et al.: Virtual reality for health professions education: systematic review and meta-analysis by the digital health education collaboration. J. Med. Internet Res. **21**(1), e12959 (2019)

4. Kiegaldie, D., Shaw, L.: Virtual reality simulation for nursing education: effectiveness and feasibility. BMC Nurs. **22**(1), 488 (2023)
5. Chen, F.Q., et al.: Effectiveness of virtual reality in nursing education: meta-analysis. J. Med. Internet Res. **22**(9), e18290 (2020)
6. Ryan, G.V., Callaghan, S., Rafferty, A., Higgins, M.F., Mangina, E., McAuliffe, F.: Learning outcomes of immersive technologies in health care student education: systematic review of the literature. J. Med. Internet Res. **24**(2), e30082 (2022)
7. Altmiller, G., Pepe, L.H.: Influence of technology in supporting quality and safety in nursing education. Nurs. Clin. North Am. **57**(4), 551 (2022)
8. Bradley, P.: The history of simulation in medical education and possible future directions. Med. Educ. **40**(3), 254–262 (2006)
9. Mistry, D., Brock, C.A., Lindsey, T.: The present and future of virtual reality in medical education: a narrative review. Cureus **15**(12) (2023)
10. Verkuyl, M., Atack, L., Mastrilli, P., Romaniuk, D.: Virtual gaming to develop students' pediatric nursing skills: a usability test. Nurse Educ. Today **46**, 81–85 (2016)

MultiDrone Simulator An Open Source Multi-plataform Tool to Use in Tests of Optimized Flight of Group of Drones

Robison Cris Brito[1]([✉]), Huilson José Lorenzi[1], Alfredo Weitzenfeld[2], and Eduardo Todt[3]

[1] Federal University of Technology, UTFPR, Akure, Brazil
robison@utfpr.edu.br
[2] University of South Florida, USF, Tampa, USA
aweitzenfeld@usf.edu
[3] Federal University of Paraná, UFPR, Curitiba, Brazil
todt@inf.ufpr.br

Abstract. This article presents an open source multiplatform tool for simulating flight of Drones group. From this tool, the user can perform an offline execution, loading the flight plan from a JSON file, or even allows a dynamic online execution, since the simulator accepts the connection via socket from other client, that can be developed in any language, and it only need to allow a connection via socket with the simulator to be able to sending/receiving JSON messages. This simulator displays the result of the flight execution, as well as presenting the task allocation in a Gantt chart. During the simulation, this tool allows execution step by step, thus changes in the environment data, such as wind speed/direction, inclusion and exclusion of Drones, request for immediate Drone return of the base, among other resources. The tool was tested for different scenarios, using different optimization algorithms, and for all tests, the simulator behaved well, presenting the expected results.

Keywords: Simulator · Optimization Flight · Drones Group · Dynamic Environment

1 Introduction

Unmanned Aerial Vehicles, also known as UAVs, were developed to facilitate monitoring, as well as information records, more quickly than terrestrial vehicles. With UAVs, data can be viewed from another perspective that until now, it was only possible by airplanes or helicopters, which significantly increased the cost of acquiring this data.

UAV flights can happen in two ways: remotely controlled or autonomous. In the second, there are the biggest advantages and, also, the biggest challenges. In autonomous flight, there is no limitation on the distance between the UAV and its controller. In controlled flight, this control often occurs using radio frequency,

H. R. Arabnia et al. (Eds.): CSCE 2024, CCIS 2260, pp. 232–241, 2025.
https://doi.org/10.1007/978-3-031-85923-6_19

which is limited to the power of the transmitter, not exceeding a few hundred meters. Thus, in autonomous flights, it is possible to cover a larger area, or even a higher flight altitude, which is better to capture information through sensors or cameras inside the UAV.

In the context of autonomous flight, several works were published, such as [1], which proposes a solution for the identification of vehicle traffic on the road. In this, the UAV is equipped with a camera and, during the flight, it captures and processes the images for the identification of vehicles on the roads. The images are processed using an image processing algorithm that identifies three types of vehicles: cars, trucks, and bicycles, computing how many of each is in the captured image. This information is subsequently transmitted to a device on land to feed a computer system.

Another autonomous UAVs example is presented in [2], which proposes the use of low-cost UAVs to assess and monitor mosquitoes that transmit diseases, such as malaria, dengue, chikungunya, and zika. The main idea is to use these autonomous vehicles to identify and spray in locations that have the focus of mosquitoes.

However, precision agriculture is where the use of autonomous UAVs stands out. According to [3], the concept of precision agriculture is usually associated with the use of high-tech equipment to assess, or monitor, conditions on a given space of land, then applying the various factors of production (seeds, fertilizers, water, etc.) accordingly with its necessity. Thus, based on specific data from geographically referenced areas, the agricultural automation process is implemented, dosing production inputs proportionally for each area, unlike traditional agriculture, in which the same amount of production inputs is used throughout all land.

Usually, in precision agriculture, UAVs called Fixed Wings, similar to small planes, are used, which the great advantage is their autonomy, that can exceed 60 min of flight, and since it can flight a high travel speed. It can easily fly a large amount of land in a short time.

However, a study developed by [4] presents all the advantages of using Rotating Wing UAV in relation to Fixed Wings UAV. The Rotary Wing UAV looks like a small helicopter, and it has pairs of propellers. It has limited autonomy, varying from 20 to 40 min. However, it has numerous other advantages in relation to the Fixed Wing, such as it can stop in the air to take a reading, it can fly at low speed. You can approach the ground for a detailed reading of the data, or going up in high speed for wider reading, but its main advantage is the cost. For example, with the price of a Fixed Wing Wingo, from UAVision Aeronautic (costs about $ 120,000 each), it is possible to buy a large swarm of Drones Phantom, from DJI company (costs around $ 400.00 each).

Given the limited autonomy of Rotative Wing UAV, from this moment just called as Drone, its application in precision agriculture only becomes viable if used in groups of UAVs flying over an area autonomously, thus, a swarm with 10 Drones, for example, autonomously, could fly over a large area without human intervention. A model proposal for the use of Drone groups applied to precision agriculture is presented by [5].

In this scenario, a research theme is still little explored: the optimization of the flight plan of this group of Drones, because as such optimization happens in a dynamic scenario, where can change in weather conditions, the algorithm has to provide good results to optimize the time of flight, and at the same time, be fast enough to adapt to the dynamics of the environment.

In this area, a big challenge is to test these kinds of optimization algorithms, since most of the existing simulators provide ways to test only the flight of a single Drone, and not of a group, where Drones are dynamically inserted/deleted in the scenario.

In this context, the present work aims to propose and evaluate a simulator to test flight optimization algorithms for a group of Drones, these applied to precision agriculture, being necessary to add to the simulator the dynamics of the environment, to identify how the algorithms behave with the changing the speed/direction of the wind, as well as the early termination of the battery of any Drone, or allocation/exclusion of Drones from a mission while it is happening.

2   Related Works

Regarding the tools and software commonly used for testing flight simulation of Drones, the tools that follow are the best known and have been tested by the author before the present work. In the following, there is a brief explanation of each tool, as well as its main characteristics:

- **Paparazzi UAV:** Available at http://wiki.paparazziuav.org, this is an open Software and Hardware project that covers autopilot systems and ground station software for UAVs of various types. This platform focuses on autonomous flights, although it can also be used on manual flights. One of its main features is the control of multiple UAVs. This system allows the definition of flight plans that happen as if they were missions, where way-points are treated dynamically;
- **JAUS - Joint Architecture for Unmanned Systems:** This architecture was designed by the United States Department of Defense in 1998. Available at http://openjaus.com, it has become an international standard for defining communication protocols for Unmanned Vehicle Systems. It employs an SOA-based approach (Service Oriented Architecture) to allow distributed command and control of these systems. This architecture is developed by the Society of Automotive Engineers under the Steering Committee of Unmanned Systems of Aerospace Standards. All documents that define JAUS can be purchased online directly from SAE. It is a heterogeneous architecture, which may involve land, water, and aerial vehicles; these can be autonomous or remotely controlled. JAUS is composed of the JAUS Service Interface Definition Language (JSIDL), which is the communication protocol and the JAUS Core Service Set (JSS Core), which is the set of tools;

- **AETOURNOS #: Airborne Embedded auTonomOUs Robust Network of Objects and Sensors:** This project is available at http:// aetournos.gforge.inria.fr. It aims to control multiple UAVs, as well as work with their flight training. The platform offers a complete environment for testing and simulation, allowing simulations in environments with land, air, and water vehicles. This project makes use of Parrot Drones, AR model. Drone 2.0;

- **TAEMS - Task Analysis, Environment Modeling and Simulation:** This framework allows to model environments to be used in complex computational tasks, in which agent-based approaches can be used. With it, it is possible to simulate a group of UAVs working cooperatively. It allows analyzing and simulating the behavior of a Multi-Agent System quantitatively about the relevant characteristics of the computational environment in which it is inserted. TAEMS is thus not only a language that allows specifying the characteristics of a multi-agent system, but also a simulation system that allows demonstrating the tasks graphically, actions of agents and statistical data;

- **Mission Planner - ArduPilot Fligth Controller:** This environment is presented at http://ardupilot.org/planner, and has the function of being a control and simulation model for UAVs. It is integrated with Google Maps and allows you to create missions, assigning way-points to a UAV. So, this environment is part of the ArduPilot project, and must be used with the UAV microcontrollers provided by it;

- **Simulink para Matlab:** Another way to perform UAV flight simulations on a computer is to use Simulink, a simulator available by Matlab that allows you to model software agents featuring as UAVs, which can communicate and perform tasks in a simulated environment. Therefore, the application must be coded using the Matlab programming language;

- **UAVSim:** It is a UAV open-source simulator, available at https://www. openhub.net/p/uavsim, most used for simulations where the UAV must search for a target and/or attack it. In this environment, UAVs are modeled as software agents and communicate to achieve a common goal;

- **The Network Simulator - ns-2:** Open Source project available at http:// www.isi.edu/nsnam/ns, it is a simple network simulator that allows simulating the communication between network elements. It is commonly used by projects that involve communication between UAVs for simulation and test environments.

With the study of the tools above, it was possible to identify the advantages and disadvantages of each environment, to propose a specific environment for the testing flight of Drone groups with the main objective of testing the optimization.

From the tools mentioned, some were proprietary without a free version for evaluation or providing a very limited version for testing. Others needed specific knowledge of some programming language to perform the tests and flight simulation, others were specific to a specific Drone model, or even, they had a focus more applied to the actual flight, not necessarily the simulation. Finally, many of them do not allow, at least without the use of a programming language, to treat the dynamics of the environment.

Thus, the present work proposes the MultiDrone Simulator, a software environment, developed in Java, that is, multiplatform, which allows the simulation of the flight of multiple Drones focusing on the dynamics of the environment, as well as on the ease of its use.

3   Proposed System

To simulate the environment, easier and quicker, without the need to program in a specific simulator, the Multidrone Simulator was developed. This is a free and open-source simulator. Developed on the Java platform, because of that, it can be run on multiple platforms, such as Windows, Linux, and Mac OS.

In the Multidrone Simulator, the user can upload a file containing the flight plan to be tested. This flight plan is a JSON file (JavaScript Object Notation), so this flight plan can be created in any language, making this simulator independent of the programming language.

Another feature supported by Multidrone Simulator is the possibility of dynamic testing. In static tests, the user loads the flight plan once, in JSON format, only at the beginning of the simulation, after the flight characteristics are placed, such as wind information, number of Drones, where they are found in the plane, and runs the simulation, from this moment on, it is not possible to interfere in the tests.

But the Multidrone Simulator has another mode of operation. It is named online mode. In this, the simulator opens a Socket server, allowing a client to connect and exchange information using its network. Thus, the client connects to the simulator's Socket server, sends the JSON of the initial flight plan, changes the characteristics of the environment directly in the simulator, and runs the tests. As the user changes some feature in the simulation environment, such as adding or removing Drone, or changing the information regarding wind speed or direction, the simulator, via Socket, sends such changes to the connected client, who has the opportunity to create new flight plans based on these changes and send it back to the simulator, which executes it.

Following are other features offered by Multidrone Simulator:

- **Definition of the size of the overflown area:** The simulator allows, graphically, to define the dimensions of the area to be overflown. This size is defined in a number of way-points, which are the points over which the Drone must fly;
- **Definition of Drones:** The environment allows add to the simulation one or more Drones, the user, when defining a Drone, must specify its name, which will be used for its visual presentation in the simulator. Also, it is possible to define its autonomy, which is defined in way-points, its initial position in the area to be flown, and still, a standard range for all Drones, if simulating with only one Drone model;

- **Import of the initial flight plan:** The environment allows to import an initial flight plan generated by other programs, this file must be in JSON format and will be executed by the simulator.

The following are some data visualization features offered by Multidrone Simulator.

- **Visual map of the routes:** The simulator graphically displays the flights performed by each Drone. Each flight is represented by a line, which is drawn on the way-points overflown by the flight. To differ the flight between different Drones, the lines have different colors;
- **Interactive Execution:** The user can opt for an interactive flight execution over time, in a step-by-step format, to check the behavior of each Drone, when they return to the charging base, how long they spend recharging the battery, among other information. The user, during this execution, can change characteristics in the environment, such as wind speed and direction, to see how his algorithm behaves, however, for that, he must use online execution, that is, his application must be connected to the simulator Socket server;
- **Complete Execution:** The user can click on the Play button on the simulator, to perform an execution without having to advance each step, however, at any time, the user can pause the complete execution and proceed with the execution step by step;
- **Gantt Chart:** Since the problem simulated by this environment is a resource allocation problem, where several Drones negotiate to fly over optimally several way-points, the environment also provides a Gantt Chart, in which the user can see the result of the execution from the allocation point of view, knowing at what time each Drone was overflight or was at the base reloading, as well as how many points it overflowed in each flight plan.

Finally, the environment also allows you to simulate the dynamics of an environment, which is the most important item in the Multidrone Simulator. In this simulator were implemented:

- **Adding/Removing Drones dynamically:** Allows you to simulate situations such as failure in Drones, or allocation of new Drones to the environment at the time of the mission's execution;
- **Early Drone Return to Base:** Even though the Drone's autonomy is known, at any time the user can request the Drone to return to base, simulating, for example, early termination of its battery and seeing how the system reacts to this adverse event;
- **Change in Weather data:** The cost of moving the Drone between one point and another change, basically, with the speed and direction of the wind. Thus, in the environment, the user can change this cost at any time in the four axes (North, South, East, and West), checking how the optimization algorithm behaves in these environmental changes.

4   Results

The results of the execution of two algorithms: Greedy flight allocation algorithm [6] and Algorithm based on recursive auctions [5], are tested in Multidrone Simulator.

Tests were carried out in various sizes of areas, aiming to know how the simulator behaved for different scenarios. The biggest scenario where the simulator was tested was the experimental area of the university where the study was carried out, which has a size of 340×340 m, with an area of 115,600 square meters, which is equivalent to 28 acres.

For all the examples tested here, each way-point was distance 10 m among them, so, to the real scenario was necessary 34×34 way-point, in total, 1,156 points - Fig. 1.

Fig. 1. Scenario 34×34 in a real area with resolution of 10 m.

For this scenario, the simulator could present the result in a graphic interface, but, due to the number of the point, the big images can not the showed with details in this paper, so, we reduce the area to 11×11 points, this way we can show all the information through the images.

A scenario of 11×11 crossing points was used, which gives a total of 121 crossing points. The computational complexity to find an optimal solution for this scenario is bigger, since this problem is similar to the Traveling Salesman Problem (TSP), with some more restrictions such as resource allocation. Still, it is as we had to go through 121 cities in the TSP.

As we can see, in Fig. 2, we have the result of executing the Greedy Optimization Algorithm (left) and the one result based on Recursive Auctions (right), for the 11 × 11 point scenario. The right result is the optimum global result. For these executions, it was considered only one Drone, with enough autonomy to overflown all the points.

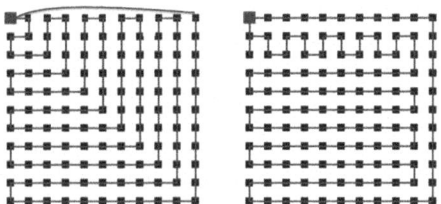

Fig. 2. Left. Flight plan generated for the Greedy Algorithm. Right. Optimal Flight plan for this scenario found using Recursive Auction Algorithm.

A second execution to test the simulator, where this same area (11 × 11) was overflight using 4 Drones, with 40 points of autonomy each. The result of the flight allocation is shown in Fig. 3.

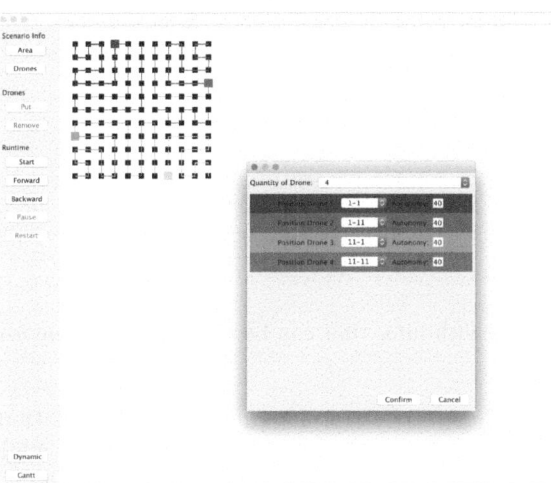

Fig. 3. Flight plan generated for the Greedy Algorithm using 4 Drones, with 40 points of autonomy each.

Another way to see the result of the flight and the allocation of resources is from a Gantt Chart, where on the y-axis we have the 4 Drones used in the simulation, and on the x-axis the time measured in time of flight between one point and another - Fig. 4.

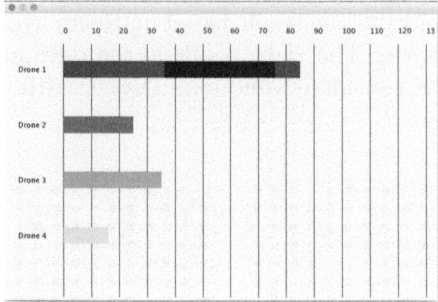

Fig. 4. Gantt Graph related to the allocation of four Drones in a Scenario with 121 points.

In this scenario, only Drone 1 had to make two flights. In the Graph, the waiting time at the base for recharging the battery is dark.

The dynamic screen of the environment is also presented, where resources can be allocated and removed at any time, as well as the direction and intensity of the wind, as shown in Fig. 5.

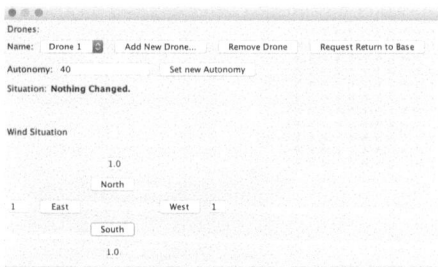

Fig. 5. Screen with infos that can be changed to the environment.

Other tests were done, for example, running the simulation using step-by-step, modifying values of the environment, deleting Drones while one execution is running. In all of these cases, the simulator works well and shows the results to the user.

5   Conclusion

The present study proposed and evaluated a simulator for optimization flights of a group of Drones, this applied to precision agriculture.

Before the development of this simulator, called Multidrone Simulator, eight simulators were studied: Paparazzi UAV, JAUS, AETORNOS, TAEMS, Mission Planner, Matlab Simulink, UAVSim and The Network Simulator. All have strengths, but also some weaknesses, which motivated the development of the simulator presented in this article.

Multidrone Simulator has characteristics such as the offline execution of one flight plan, as well as its online execution, in which it can exchange information with another application, through Socket, presenting the events and processing new flight plans.

The present simulator also has no limitations on the number of Drones and allows testing in dynamic environments, including simulating the inclusion/exclusion of Drones at runtime, changes in wind speed/direction, as well as the early termination of a Drone battery.

Step-by-step execution mechanisms for missions were also developed and tested, as well as visual presentation of data, using a Gantt Chart to verify the allocation of resources.

The Simulator worked well for different types of Drone group flight optimization algorithms, as well as in large scenarios, with more than a thousand crossing points, including overflight with several Drones.

As future work, now that the simulator has been tested and verified its functionality, it is to carry out its communication with the real Drones, making the simulator share the flight plan, which will be executed by the Drone itself, a resource that already exists in some tools studied before the development of this simulator.

References

1. Montanari, R., Tozadore, D.C., Fraccaroli, E.S., Romero, R.A.F.: Ground vehicle detection and classification by an unmanned aerial vehicle. In: 2015 12th Latin American Robotics Symposium and 2015 3rd Brazilian Symposium on Robotics (LARS-SBR). Institute of Electrical & Electronics Engineers (IEEE) (2015)
2. Amenyo, J.-T., et al.: MedizDroids project: ultra-low cost, low-altitude, affordable and sustainable UAV multicopter drones for mosquito vector control in malaria disease management. In: IEEE Global Humanitarian Technology Conference (GHTC 2014). Institute of Electrical & Electronics Engineers (IEEE) (2014)
3. Neto, M.C., Pinto, P.A., Coelho, J.P.P.: Tecnologias de informação e comunicação e a agricultura. Porto: Sociedade Portuguesa de Inovação (2005)
4. Lorencena, M.C., Brito, R.C., Loureiro, J.F., Favarim, F., Todt, E.: A comparative approach on the use of unmanned aerial vehicles kind of fixed-wing and rotative wing applied to the precision agriculture scenario. In: 2019 IEEE 43rd Annual Computer Software and Applications Conference (COMPSAC). IEEE (2019)
5. Brito, R.C., Loureiro, J.F., Guedes, A., Todt, E.: Optimization system for dynamic flight planning for groups of drones using cooperation with mobile recharge bases by means of multiagent system and recursive auctions. In: 2019 IEEE 43rd Annual Computer Software and Applications Conference (COMPSAC). IEEE (2019)
6. Thanh, P.D., Binh, H.T.T., Dac, D.D., Long, N.B., Phong, L.M.H.: A heuristic based on randomized greedy algorithms for the clustered shortest-path tree problem. In: 2019 IEEE Congress on Evolutionary Computation (CEC). IEEE (2019)

Revolutionizing Multiplayer Gaming: A Deep Dive into VisionXO, a 3D Multiplayer Tic-Tac-Toe Game

Mihir Kanjibhai Daka[1] ⓘ, Jiaofei Zhong[1]([✉]) ⓘ, and Deepak Shivrambhai Antiya[2] ⓘ

[1] California State University East Bay, Hayward, CA 94542, USA
mdaka@horizon.csueastbay.edu, jiaofei.zhong@csueastbay.edu
[2] Oracle Corporation, Pleasanton, CA 94588, USA

Abstract. This paper provides an in-depth exploration of VisionXO, a groundbreaking 3D multiplayer Tic-Tac-Toe game that we designed exclusively for Apple Vision Pro and iOS platforms. Leveraging a combination of SwiftUI for immersive user experience with RealityKit for seamless 3D model integration, VisionXO delivers remarkable gaming experience where multiple players can compete in real-time using unique room code. Through detailed analysis of technical complexity, challenges encountered, and future prospects, this paper highlights the far-reaching impact of VisionXO in the mobile gaming field.

Keywords: VisionXO · Apple Vision Pro · 3D · Multiplayer · SwiftUI · RealityKit

1 Introduction

With the recent release of Apple Vision Pro headsets, new opportunities for immersive gaming experiences have emerged. Recent studies [1–6] revealed that immersive mixed reality games have the potential to revolutionize the way we approach various learning and training tasks in different domains. This paper aims to dissect the technical complexities, obstacles overcome, and future prospects of VisionXO, an immersive real-time multiplayer 3D game that we developed for Apple Vision Pro headsets using software packages including SwiftUI and RealityKit. VisionXO represents a leap forward in multiplayer gaming, highlighting its importance in the mobile gaming field.

2 Methodology

The development methodology of VisionXO was meticulously designed to ensure seamless integration of emerging technologies and create engaging multiplayer gaming experiences. The following steps outline the methodology used during the design and development of VisionXO, which is a 3D multiplayer Tic-Tac-Toe game that we designed exclusively for Apple Vision Pro and iOS platforms.

© The Author(s), under exclusive license to Springer Nature Switzerland AG 2025
H. R. Arabnia et al. (Eds.): CSCE 2024, CCIS 2260, pp. 242–246, 2025.
https://doi.org/10.1007/978-3-031-85923-6_20

2.1 Requirement Analysis

The initial phase of development involved a thorough analysis of the project's requirements and objectives. This process requires a comprehensive understanding of the basic functionality of a multiplayer Tic-Tac-Toe game. Key considerations included the implementation of real-time gameplay mechanics, an intuitive user interface, and seamless player interaction. By defining the desired user experience early in the development cycle, the team could effectively guide subsequent decisions regarding technology selection and feature prioritization.

2.2 Selection of Technologies

The selection of technologies for VisionXO was driven by the project's specific requirements and the goal of delivering a high-quality gaming experience on Apple Vision Pro and iOS platforms. Swift and SwiftUI were chosen for front-end development due to their robustness, ease of use, and native integration with Apple's ecosystem. SwiftUI's declarative syntax enables the creation of responsive and visually appealing user interface, which is essential for engaging gameplay interactions. Meanwhile, RealityKit and RealityKitContent were identified as the optimal choices for 3D model integration. RealityKit provides a powerful framework for rendering realistic 3D graphics and handling complex scene interactions, while RealityKitContent provides a rich library of pre-existing 3D assets to simplify the development process. By leveraging these technologies, VisionXO can achieve a level of visual fidelity and immersion that sets it apart from traditional Tic-Tac-Toe games.

3 Technical Development

3.1 Front-End Development

Front-End development of VisionXO focuses on translating design concepts into functional user interfaces and gameplay mechanics. SwiftUI's declarative approach allows developers to express desired UI elements and behaviors neatly, resulting in clean and maintainable code. This facilitates the rapid iteration of UI designs and ensures consistency across different device form factors. Key aspects of front-end development include the implementation of responsive UI elements, intuitive gesture control for gameplay interaction, and dynamic scene management for 3D rendering. By leveraging SwiftUI's built-in support for animations and transitions, VisionXO delivers a smooth and immersive user experience that engages players from the moment they launch the game.

3.2 Back-End Infrastructure

The backbone of VisionXO's multiplayer functionality relies on a robust back-end infrastructure built using Dart web server and WebSockets technology. This architecture facilitates real-time communication between players, allowing them to seamlessly join and interact with shared gaming sessions. By leveraging WebSockets, VisionXO minimizes latency and ensures a responsive gaming experience, even over unreliable network connections. Key components of the back-end infrastructure include a matchmaking service for pairing players in multiplayer matches, session management to handle game state synchronization, and data persistence for storing player profiles and game progress. Carefully designed and optimized, VisionXO's back-end infrastructure provides a reliable foundation for multiplayer gaming, allowing players to easily connect and compete.

3.3 3D Model Integration

Integrating 3D models into VisionXO's gameplay environment requires a combination of technical expertise and creative vision. RealityKit and RealityKitContent play a vital role in this process, providing tools and resources for seamlessly importing, rendering, and animating 3D assets. The integration of 3D models, such as USDA files representing game components and environmental elements, enhances the visual fidelity and immersion of the VisionXO's gameplay experience. In addition to importing 3D assets, we also focused on configuring material properties, lighting conditions, and physical interactions to ensure a coherent and realistic 3D environment. By leveraging RealityKit's physics engine and collision detection capabilities, VisionXO can simulate dynamic interactions between game components and the surrounding environment, further enhancing gameplay immersion.

4 Testing and Optimization

Throughout the development cycle, VisionXO has been rigorously tested and optimized to ensure stability, performance, and user-friendliness. This encompasses a variety of testing methods, including unit testing to validate individual components, integration testing to verify system interactions, and user acceptance testing to evaluate the overall gaming experience.

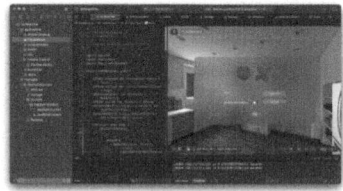

Fig. 1. Preview of VisionXO via Xcode

Performance optimization efforts focus on identifying and resolving bottlenecks related to rendering performance, network latency, and resource utilization. By analyzing and optimizing critical code paths, VisionXO's development team was able to achieve smooth and responsive gameplay across a variety of devices and network conditions. In Fig. 1, we can see a preview of VisionXO via XCode. Figure 2 shows the main screen of the VisionXO game board running on a virtual VisionOS simulator. In Fig. 3, the player is typing the room code using a virtual keyboard to enter the VisionXO game room. Figure 4 shows the VisionXO game settings where the player can choose to display immersive space. Finally, Fig. 5 is the VisionXO gaming screen main view.

Fig. 2. VisionXO Game Board View on Virtual VisionOS Simulator

Fig. 3. VisionXO Game Player Entered the Room Code

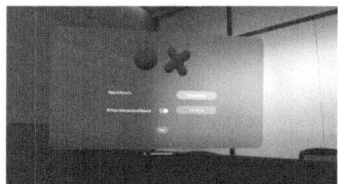

Fig. 4. Immersive View of the VisionXO Game Settings Screen

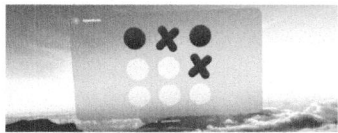

Fig. 5. Main View of the VisionXO Gaming Screen

We conclude from our testing results that VisionXO delivers an immersive and engaging multiplayer gaming experience that exceeds expectations. The combination of SwiftUI for front-end design and RealityKit for 3D model integration ensures a seamless gaming experience and stunning visual fidelity. Initial testing demonstrates the potential of RealityKitContent to enhance immersive gaming environment, raising the prospect of exciting future updates and expansions.

5 Conclusion and Future Work

VisionXO embodies the pinnacle of multiplayer gaming innovation, pushing the boundaries of immersive gameplay experiences on mobile platforms. Through meticulous technical development, seamless integration of cutting-edge technologies, and a commitment to continuous improvement, VisionXO sets a new standard for mobile gaming excellence. As development continues and future enhancements are implemented, VisionXO will continue to engage players and solidify its position as a trailblazer in the ever-evolving mobile gaming space.

Looking ahead, VisionXO has a roadmap of planned enhancements and expansions designed to further enrich the gaming experience. Key areas of focus include: (1). Integrate ARKit to enhance augmented reality compatibility, allowing players to immerse themselves in the game world through AR experience. (2). Implement better gesture interaction for intuitive control mechanics and enhance gameplay engagement. (3). Explore additional features and content updates to keep the game fresh and engaging for existing players while attracting new audiences.

By embracing innovative technology and listening to player feedback, VisionXO aims to grow into the premier destination for multiplayer gaming on Apple devices on the iOS platform, delivering an unparalleled combination of immersive gaming, social connection, and technological innovation.

Acknowledgments. The authors would like to extend their gratitude to the Department of Computer Science at California State University East Bay (CSUEB) for the A2E2 grant, and the College of Science for the Collaborative Research Award at CSUEB.

References

1. Araiza-Alba, P., Keane, T., Chen, W.S., Kaufman, J.: Immersive virtual reality as a tool to learn problem-solving skills. Comput. Educ. **164**, 104121 (2021)
2. Bian, S.: Research on the application of VR in games. Highlights Sci. Eng. Technol. **39**, 389–394 (2023)
3. Carvalho, B., Soares, M.M., Neves, A., Soares, G., Lins, A.: Virtual reality devices applied to digital games: a literature review. Ergonomics Des., 125–141 (2016)
4. Checa, D., Bustillo, A.: A review of immersive virtual reality serious games to enhance learning and training. Multimedia Tools Appl. **79**(9), 5501–5527 (2020)
5. Oyelere, S.S., Bouali, N., Kaliisa, R., Obaido, G., Yunusa, A.A., Jimoh, E.R.: Exploring the trends of educational virtual reality games: a systematic review of empirical studies. Smart Learn. Environ. **7**, 1–22 (2020)
6. Scher, S., Crabb, R., Davis, J.: Making real games virtual: tracking board game pieces. In: 2008 19th International Conference on Pattern Recognition, pp. 1–4. IEEE (2008)

DRIVE: A Mobile Application for Directed, Remote, Interactive Viewing and Exploring

Sonya Cates[✉], Rudolph Desanti, Roderick Ramirez, and Kyle Witham

Roger Williams University, Bristol, RI 02809, USA
scates@rwu.edu

Abstract. Technologies to support remote interaction hold great potential to expand opportunities for engagement and interaction. In this work, we present a mobile application to allow remote exploration of an environment by those who cannot be physically present due to geographic or mobility limitations. Our system is designed to place control of the experience with the audience or viewer to encourage greater engagement with the remote environment. After presenting the application, we discuss how the application will be used and tested in realistic contexts and present future extensions to create a more immersive experience.

Keywords: Mobile applications · Accessibility · Remote interaction · Remote environment · Cooperative applications

1 Introduction

The use of tools to support remote interactions has surged during the COVID-19 pandemic and even now shows little sign of disappearing [6, 12]. While these tools are not new, the pandemic has accelerated their adoption by more people and in more varied contexts. Widespread adoption of remote interaction was originally done out of necessity for many, and often with some reluctance, but the increased acceptance of remote interaction has expanded our ideas of what is possible and of what should be possible. Increased use and adoption of remote interaction has opened opportunities for more people to be engaged in ways they would not have been able to previously. While many found the shift to online restrictive and it has not been without drawbacks [7], others whose engagement was previously limited, for example due to mobility limitations, found more opportunity, for both work and socializing. Geographic limitations have also fallen as remote interaction has become not only more acceptable, but also the norm.

In this work, we are interested in exploring the benefits of remote technology and how those benefits can be applied to expand opportunities for engagement and interaction to overcome both mobility and geographic limitations. For example, consider remotely exploring a museum or park through a smart phone or tablet, but not through a prerecorded video or at the pace and discretion of a tour guide or docent, but rather choosing what to look at and for how long for yourself. In this paper, we present DRIVE, a mobile application for Directed, Remote, Interactive Viewing and Exploring, which

© The Author(s), under exclusive license to Springer Nature Switzerland AG 2025
H. R. Arabnia et al. (Eds.): CSCE 2024, CCIS 2260, pp. 247–253, 2025.
https://doi.org/10.1007/978-3-031-85923-6_21

supports this scenario. The DRIVE application creates a video connection between two participants; however, unlike existing video calling and conferencing applications, which support conversations and meetings, DRIVE is designed to support showing and remotely viewing a physical space or object. The two DRIVE participants have different rolls, which¬ we refer to as broadcaster and viewer. The broadcaster uses a mobile device to stream video of their surroundings to the viewer. The viewer is the audience. In the traditional presenter and audience model, the presenter controls the flow of information and the direction of attention. However, in the DRIVE application the viewer controls the experience by indicating where they would like to look and how they wish to remotely explore the environment in which the broadcaster is physically present. Giving the viewer control gives them a more active experience, mirroring that of a museum visitor exploring, rather than the passive experience of a lecture or recorded tour. A primary goal of DRIVE is to allow the viewer to indicate where they wish to look or explore in a way that is as nonintrusive as possible to provide an immersive experience. In addition, DRIVE is extremely lightweight, requiring only two off-the-shelf devices and no prior planning or setup to begin a remote interaction. After presenting the application, we describe several areas of in-progress and future work surrounding DRIVE, including user studies and the extension of the application to other hardware.

2 Related Work

A significant amount of prior work has explored tools for remote interaction, including applications for remote video conferencing, remote learning, telehealth, and others. While there exists a rich body of work conducted prior to the pandemic [1, 3, 10], the past two years have seen work in this area expand to reflect the societal shifts of the pandemic. A number of surveys [2, 11, 14, 15] summarize and explore the implications and open questions surrounding society's rapid adoption of tools for remote interaction.

Within this large body of work on remote interaction, DRIVE is particularly related to prior work on remote collaboration [4]. Gauglitz et al. describe a mobile system to support remote collaboration and apply it to the particular task of operating in an airplane cockpit [5]. Venerella et al. describe a system with a similar goal, but in addition make use of mixed reality [16]. These systems have similarities with DRIVE in that both look to support the remote user's ability to explore the environment; however, the systems differ in that DRIVE is not task focused or intended for peer-like collaboration. While the two DRIVE participants do collaborate in a sense, the goal of the collaboration is solely to support the remote participant's exploration of the environment, with the non-remote participant acting as a facilitator rather than equal participant in the interaction.

A second area of relevant prior work concerns remote exploration of an environment. Heshmat et al. describe the application of telepresence via a robot for physically participating in a remote environment, particularly applied to geocaching [8]. While others have considered the use of drones to allow for similar remote participation in outdoor activities [13]. While related in their goal of bring a remote participant into an environment these works differ from DRIVE in their use of significant hardware that may be expensive or not easily accessible. Kasahara et al. present a less hardware intensive method of providing immersion in a remote environment, but focus on prerecorded rather than live interaction [9]. DRIVE's aim is to support live, and potentially spontaneous, immersion in a remote environment with limited and accessible hardware.

3   The Drive Application

The two participants in a DRIVE interaction have asymmetric rolls and thus DRIVE has two different user interfaces to support these rolls.

3.1   Viewer Interface

The participant who accepts an incoming call becomes the viewer by default. The viewer may also request to swap rolls with the broadcaster at any time. In the application's settings, the viewer can select from three different mechanisms to indicate to the broadcaster where they would like to look. Three different control mechanisms are supported to allow for a variety of user preferences and abilities. Option one, shown in Fig. 1, displays buttons overlaying the video. There are eight directional controls and two zoom controls in the center. The viewer clicks a button to indicate where they would like the broadcaster to focus or move. The buttons may be easily hidden by tapping the hamburger menu on the bottom left corner to allow for an unobstructed view of the video. Option two does not use buttons at all, rather the user taps on the area of the screen where they would like to look, which is then mapped to one of the eight directions. Zoom functionality is controlled with a two fingered pinch motion. Option three, is visually similar to option two but the viewer indicates direction by moving the phone itself rather than tapping the screen. The phone's gyroscope is used to detect motion and translate the motion to a directional signal. The goal of the viewer interface is to be as non-intrusive as possible, allowing the viewer to focus on the remote environment. The viewer may also communicate with the broadcaster by speaking, as in a normal video call, if they wish.

3.2   Broadcaster Interface

The participant who initiates the call becomes the broadcaster by default. The broadcaster can also choose to swap rolls with the viewer at any time. The broadcaster interface screen indicates the direction the viewer would like to look using bars on the edges or corners of the screen. If the viewer wants a closer or wider view, the broadcaster sees a pop up indicating they should zoom in or out. Fig. 2 shows two views of the broadcaster screen. The broadcaster will see the left screen if the viewer indicates "left" and the right screen if the viewer indicates "zoom in." It is the broadcaster's responsibility to interpret the signals and move their device accordingly. The DRIVE application does not enforce that the viewer's directions are followed, rather its goal is to convey the viewers intent in an intuitive and easily interpretable way. The broadcaster may also communicate with the viewer by speaking, as in a normal video call, if they wish.

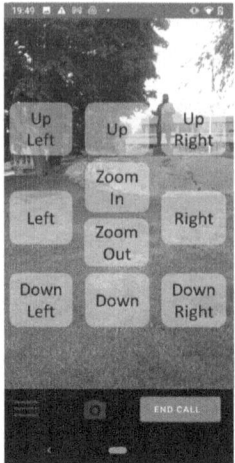

Fig. 1. The Viewer Interface. Users may choose a button based interface, touch based interface with multitouch gesture for zoom, or motion based interface for indicating where they wish to look.

Fig. 2. The Broadcaster Interface. Bars around the outer edge of the view screen indicate where the Broadcaster should move. A pop up in the center indicates if the Broadcaster should move closer or farther from the subject.

4 Ongoing and Future Work

Current and future work on DRIVE encompasses two topics: user studies to address research questions surrounding the application's utility and user experience as well as extensions to the current hardware and software systems to make the viewing experience more immersive.

4.1 User Studies

We identify two primary research questions. First, how does the viewer's experience using DRIVE compare to that of a prerecorded video or to a predetermined, guided tour? We are interested in both the subjective experience and preferences of participants as well as objective measures of engagement with the viewed environment, which may be measured by testing recall of the environment or objects that were viewed. Second, we ask to what extent the viewer chooses to indicate their preferences through the DRIVE interface versus verbally when both options are available. Do users prefer to talk to express where the broadcaster should aim their device rather than indicate direction through the DRIVE interface under certain circumstances, in particular to recover from misunderstandings? And a related question: does the extent to which users rely on the DRIVE interface versus oral communication depend on whether the participants previously knew each other or are communicating with a stranger?

4.2 Application Extensions

The primary focus of extensions to the DRIVE application is making the experience more immersive for the viewer. One option that we are investigating is the use of a virtual reality headset by the viewer. A second possibility for a more immersive experience uses a semi-circular, curved wall of monitors with gesture controls. This room sized viewing interface is depicted in Fig. 3. While both options would create a more immersive experience for the viewer, both also have the disadvantage of requiring expensive hardware, which may be uncomfortable for some or require significant, dedicated space. In its current form, DRIVE requires only two small devices, either smart phones or tablets. Increased immersion in the experience will need to be weighed against the downsides of other hardware approaches.

Fig. 3. Immersive room-sized viewing interface.

5 Conclusions

In this paper we have presented DRIVE: a mobile application to support remotely exploring a physical environment or object. Broad goals of this work are to explore the benefits of remote technology and how those benefits can be applied to expand opportunities for engagement and interaction to overcome both mobility and geographic limitations. This work is ongoing with work underway to explore research questions around how people explore remote environments and to explore alternative hardware for a more immersive experience.

References

1. Bailey, D.E., Kurland, N.B.: A review of telework research: findings, new directions, and lessons for the study of modern work. J. Organ. Behav. **23**, 383–400 (2002). https://doi.org/10.1002/job.144

2. Bond, M.: Schools and emergency remote education during the COVID-19 pandemic: a living rapid systematic review. Asian J. Dist. Educ. **15**(2), 191–247 (2021). https://doi.org/10.5281/zenodo.4425683

3. Dorsey, E., Topol, E.: State of telehealth. N. Engl. J. Med. **375**(2), 154–161 (2016). https://doi.org/10.1056/NEJMra1601705

4. Druta, R., Druta, C., Negirla, P., Silea, I.: A review on methods and systems for remote collaboration. Appl. Sci. **11**, 10035 (2021). https://doi.org/10.3390/app112110035

5. Gauglitz, S., Lee, C., Turk, M., Höllerer, T.: Integrating the physical environment into mobile remote collaboration. In: Proceedings of the 14th International Conference on Human-Computer Interaction with Mobile Devices and Services (MobileHCI '12) , pp. 241–250. Association for Computing Machinery, New York (2012). https://doi.org/10.1145/2371574.2371610

6. Goldberg, E.: A Two-Year, 50-Million-Person Experiment in Changing How We Work. https://www.nytimes.com/2022/03/10/business/remote-work-office-life.html. Accessed 19 May 2022

7. Hanno, E., Fritz, L., Jones, S., Lesaux, N.: School learning format and children's behavioral health during the COVID-19 pandemic. JAMA Pediatr. **176**(4), 410–411 (2022). https://doi.org/10.1001/jamapediatrics.2021.5698

8. Heshmat, Y., et al.: Geocaching with a beam: shared outdoor activities through a telepresence robot with 360 degree viewing. In: Proceedings of the 2018 Conference on Human Factors in Computing Systems (CHI '18), pp. 1–13. Association for Computing Machinery, New York (2018)

9. Kasahara, S., Nagai, S., Rekimoto, J.: First person omnidirectional video: system design and implications for immersive experience. In Proceedings of the ACM International Conference on Interactive Experiences for TV and Online Video (TVX '15), pp. 33–42. Association for Computing Machinery, New York (2015). https://doi.org/10.1145/2745197.2745202

10. Kolias, V., Anagnostopoulos, I., Kayafas, E.: Remote experiments in education: a survey over different platforms and application fields. In: 2008 11th International Conference on Optimization of Electrical and Electronic Equipment, pp. 181–188 (2008). https://doi.org/10.1109/OPTIM.2008.4602519

11. García, N.O., Velásquez, M.D., Romero, C.T., Monedero, J.O., Khalaf, O.: remote academic platforms in times of a pandemic. Int. J. Emerg. Technol. Learn. (iJET) **16**(21), 121–131 (2022). https://www.learntechlib.org/p/220531/. Accessed 19 May 2022

12. Popken, B.: Full return to office is 'dead,' experts say—and remote is only growing. https://www.nbcnews.com/business/economy/full-return-work-dead-experts-say-remote-only-growing-rcna11323. Accessed 19 May 2022

13. Shakeri, H., Neustaedter, C.: Teledrone: shared outdoor exploration using telepresence drones. In: Conference Companion Publication 2019 Computer Supported Cooperative Work and Social Computing, pp. 361–371 (2019)

14. Shanbehzadeh, M., Kazemi-Arpanahi, H., Kalkhajeh, S.G., Basati, G.: Systematic review on telemedicine platforms in lockdown periods: lessons learned from the COVID-19 pandemic. J. Educ. Health Promot. **10**, 211 (2021). https://doi.org/10.4103/jehp.jehp_1419_20

15. Vargo, D., Zhu, L., Benwell, B., Yan, Z.: Digital technology use during COVID-19 pandemic: a rapid review. Human Behav. Emerg. Technol. **3**(1), 13–24 (2020). https://doi.org/10.1002/hbe2.242

16. Venerella, J., Sherpa, L., Tang, H., Zhui, Z.: A lightweight mobile remote collaboration using mixed reality. In Proceedings of Computer Vision and Pattern Recognition, pp. 1–4 (2019)

Soft Actor Critic Based End-to-End QoS Path Selection in Multi-Domain SDN Environments

Gyumin Lee[1], Junghyun Lim[2], and Byeong-hee Roh[2(✉)] ⓘ

[1] Tactical Communication System Waveform R&D, LIG Nex1 Co., Ltd.,
Seongnam 13488, South Korea
gyumin.lee@lignex1.com
[2] Department of AI Convergence Network, Ajou University,
Suwon 16499, South Korea
{wjdguszoqt,bhroh}@ajou.ac.kr

Abstract. Software Defined Networking (SDN) uses an architecture that is vertically separated into a control plane, a data plane, and an application plane. Though research has been conducted to apply reinforcement learning methods for path selections in SDN environments, they have still problems with limited and unstable features in variable network conditions. In this paper, we propose a Soft Actor Critic (SAC)-based learning methods that can be applied to dynamic, to solve the problems in DDPG-based methods with the problem that do not converge quickly in continuously changed networking environments.

Keywords: Software Defined Networking (SDN) · Deep Deterministic Policy Gradient (DDPG) · Path Selection

1 Introduction

With the proliferation of multimedia applications such as video conferencing, Internet telephony, streaming, and online gaming, which have Quality of Service (QoS) requirements, robust and effective inter-domain control is essential to ensure end-to-end QoS guarantees in multi-domain networks [1].

Software Defined Networking (SDN) uses an architecture that is vertically separated into a control plane, a data plane, and an application plane. This architecture allows network operators to handle flows in greater detail than traditional networks through controllers [2].

Various studies have been conducted to optimize end-to-end routing performance to ensure QoS in SDN [3–6]. Also, Deep Deterministic Policy Gradient (DDPG)-based methods have also been proposed in which parameters affecting QoS are generally considered to be data with continuous regression that changes over time [7–10]. Though research has been conducted to apply reinforcement learning methods for path selections in SDN environments, they have still problems with limited and unstable features in variable network conditions.

H. R. Arabnia et al. (Eds.): CSCE 2024, CCIS 2260, pp. 254–262, 2025.
https://doi.org/10.1007/978-3-031-85923-6_22

In this paper, we propose a Soft Actor Critic (SAC)-based learning methods that can be applied to dynamic, to solve the problems in DDPG-based methods with the problem that do not converge quickly in continuously changed networking environments.

2 Soft Actor Critic Based for ETE QoS Path Selection

The SAC-based learning structure in our proposed method consists solely of Q and policy networks without a value network, as shonw in Fig. 1. In a discrete action space, the expected value can be calculated directly without the need for approximation through sampling. Instead, the data stored in the replay buffer can be utilized directly.

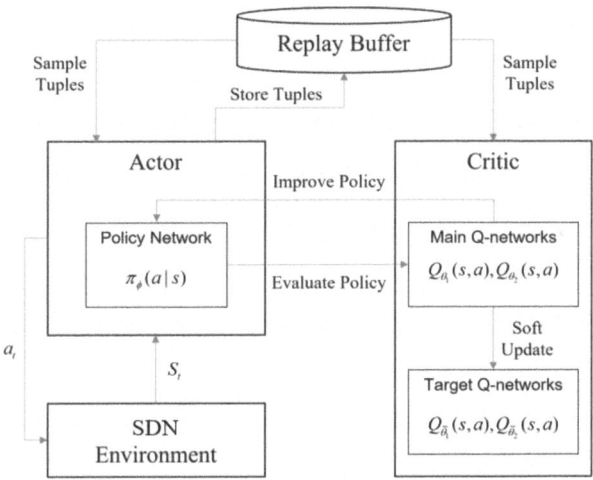

Fig. 1. SAC based QoS optimization structure

2.1 Problem Statement

The network environment considered in this paper considers a graph G with N nodes and E edges.

The network is partitioned into L local domains managed by respective local controllers. Each local controller exchanges the networking and control information with its local switches. There is a global controller, which exchange the global information with all local controllers for path selections of flows beyond local domain area. Because each local controller does not know in advance the emerging traffic flow, the local controller computes the end-to-end flow through the global controller overseeing the entire network across the domain (finding switches, training, collecting experience replay samples, updating agent policies). etc.) are requested.

Assume an environment in which K unique paths are pre-computed by the global controller for each pair of nodes. Decision agents located at the nodes can access message information received from both the local domain and neighboring domains to make more informed decisions. The primary information available for training includes flow propagation delay, packet drops, achieved throughput, link utilization, and jitter. The data is periodically collected to update the objective and compensation functions. We identified the optimal combination of network metrics required to design an efficient compensation function. Using these identified metrics, the traffic allocation ratio is determined, and the path selection process is executed whenever a new flow request is received. This repeated process accelerates the convergence of flows to the target ratio, enhancing overall network performance.

2.2 DDPG Based Learning Agent Design

The distinguishing characteristic of the DDPG is that it combines the Actor-Critic structure with the Q-network structure of DQN. This approach is advantageous in large and continuous workspaces. To adapt a structure that is typically limited to discrete environments, as is the case with DQN, for use in continuous environments, a deep neural network (DNN) is employed to determine actions based on the state.

As similarly in [11], the DPG of the proposed method has a network of actors (policy π) and critics (value function Q) with parameters θ^{μ} and θ^{Q}, and there are also two actors and critic copies, denoted by parameter $\theta^{\mu'}$ and $\theta^{Q'}$, respectively. The Q function is updated periodically with time differences in the same way as the DQN. By applying the policy gradient algorithm, the actor network is updated according to the evaluation result of the critical network. In this approach we consider $s_t = o_t$. The state space reward is meaning as the sum of the discounted future rewards and is calculated as follow Algorithm 1:

2.3 SAC Based Learning Agent Design

Soft Actor-Critic (SAC) is a learning method from the Experience Replay family that applies importance-sampling weights to eliminate bias towards frequently visited experiences. In this paper, we apply an algorithm that maximizes entropy given as

$$\pi^* = \arg \max_{\pi} E_{(s_t, a_t)} \sum_{i=t}^{\infty} \psi_{i-t}(\gamma_i + \sigma \mathcal{H}(\pi(\cdot | \chi_i))), \tag{1}$$

where σ represents a temperature parameter that can balance entropy with system compensation, and $\mathcal{H}(\pi(\cdot | \chi_i))$ represents the policy entropy. The algorithm collects local state information that the agent updates to each domain controller in each training episode. Thereafter, the global controller agent generates a traffic allocation task based on the local state. The assignment task and local state

---

Algorithm 1: DDPG optimization Algorithm

---

1   Initiailize: init $Q_{\theta_1}(s,a), Q_{\theta_2}(s,a), Q_{\theta_1'}(s,a), Q_{\theta_2'}(s,a)$ with weights θ_1 and θ_2

2   Initiailize: init target network $Q_{\theta_1'}, Q_{\theta_2'}$ with weights $\theta_1' \leftarrow \theta_1$ and $\theta_2' \leftarrow \theta_2$

3   Initiailize: replay buffer rb

4   $s_t = U_t = [u_{i,j}]_{n \times n}$

5   $A_t = W_t = [w_{t,1}, w_{t,2}, ..., w_{t,l}]$

6   **while** *convergence* **do**

7 | Randomly sample a mini-batch of transition

8 | Update critic loss function with

$$\underset{s_n \sim \rho^X, a_n \sim X, R_n \sim X}{E} \left[\left(Q(s_n, a_n | \theta^Q) - Y_n\right)^2 \right]$$

9 | $\theta_1' \leftarrow \delta\theta_1 + (1-\delta)\theta_1'$

10 | $\theta_1' \leftarrow \delta\theta_2 + (1-\delta)\theta_2'$

11 | **if** $c > 0$ **then**

12 | | update reward with $R_t = -c(f(U_t) - f(U_1))$

13 | **end**

14 **end**

---

information act as input values and are evaluated by the Critical Network. The Critical network is then updated on the primary network.

According to the SAC approach, in addition to maximizing entropy, the actor seeks to maximize the expected reward. In this method, an infinite horizontal MDP is defined as a continuous tuple (S, A, p, r) with a state space A and an operational space A, and the unknown state transition probability $p : S \times S \times A \to [0; 1)$ represents the probability of the next state s_{t+1} based on the current state s_t.

We assume a parameterized Q function $Q_\phi(s, a)$ and a policy π_θ. Also, the target Q network is defined as $Q_{\tilde{\phi}}$, where the parameter $\tilde{\phi}$ is computed as an exponential moving average of ϕ. By minimizing the soft Bellman residual, we can learn the Q function as

$$Q(\phi) = E\left[\left(Q(s_t, a_t) - r(s_t, a_t) - rE\left[V_{\tilde{\phi}}(s_{t1})\right]\right)^2 \right], \qquad (2)$$

where $V_{\tilde{\phi}}(s)$ is $V_{\tilde{\phi}}(s) = E_{\pi_\theta}\left[Q_{\tilde{\phi}}(s, a) - \varphi \log \pi_\theta(a|s)\right]$

The policy $\pi(\theta)$ is expressed by

$$\pi(\theta) = E_{s \sim B}\left[E_{a \sim \pi(\theta)}[\varphi \log \pi_\theta(a|s) - Q_\phi(s, a)]\right], \qquad (3)$$

where B represents a previously sampled state and workset or replay buffer. To reduce the problem of biased Q values, SAC uses two Q-networks (also two target

Q-networks). That is, $Q_\phi(s,a) = \min(Q_{\phi_1}(s,a), Q_{\phi_1}(s,a))$. There are many ways to optimize $\pi(\theta)$.

The target density of SAC is a Q function with a similar meaning to that used in neural networks, and since it is impossible to calculate the differential of the expected value for the loss function as a sampling average, a re-parameterization method for policy networks can be used to solve this problem. To this end, we parameterize the policy again using neural network transformations that use both state and noise vector ε as inputs as follows.

$$a = f_\theta(s, \varepsilon). \tag{4}$$

We can rewrite Eq. (3) as

$$\pi(\theta) = E_{s \sim B, \varepsilon \sim N} \left[\varphi \log \pi_\theta(f_\theta(s,\varepsilon)|s) - Q_\phi(s, f_\theta(s,\varepsilon)) \right]] \tag{5}$$

For each time period, the local controller learning agent of the domain manages the traffic information in the domain and updates it in the state space. In the local domain environment, the controller collects the following parameters and passes them to the global controller.

1) $\gamma_k(t)$: accumulated delay bound of the flow k at time t.
2) $F_{v^d}(t)$: The remaining bandwidth of the domain switch v^d at time t.
3) $\nu_k(t)$: The service availability of k flow at time t.
4) $D(t)$: Data size at time t.
5) $C(t)$: Computation size at time t.

Let S be the state space with state vectors at time t, s_t. Then, we have

$$s_t = [\gamma_1(t), \gamma_2(t), ..., \gamma_K(t), \tag{6}$$
$$F_{1^1}(t), F_{2^1}(t), ..., F_{v^d}(t), \eta_1(t), \eta_2(t), ..., \eta_K(t), \tag{7}$$
$$D(t), C(t)]. \tag{8}$$

The SAC learning process is described in Algorithm 2.

3   Evaluation

For the experiments, we implemented the proposed framework and set up the environment using OMNET++ simulator. The deep neural networks (i.e., actor and critic networks) were implemented using TensorFlow. Simulations were performed on a system equipped with an Intel i7-10700 K CPU, a GeForce 2080Ti GPU, and 32 GB RAM. The topology we considered is a well-known network topology, called GEANT. The number of flows were set varying between 50 and 250, and each flow has randomly selected source and destination nodes. The proposed method (SAC) are compared with the greedy-based route constrained optimization (RCO) [5] and actor-critic-based DDPG (DDPG) [11].

Algorithm 2: SAC based QoS optimize Algorithm

---

1 Hyperparameters : step size λ_π,λ_Q, λ_φ, target entropy e, exponentially moving average coefficient τ
2 Input: Initial Q value function parameters ϕ_1, ϕ_2
3 Output: Calculated policy parameters θ
4 $B = \varnothing$, $\tilde{\phi} = \phi$
5 **foreach** *iteration in function* $i \in \{1,2\}$ **do**
6   **foreach** *iteration in function* $i \in \{1,2\}$ **do**
7        $a_t \sim \pi_\theta(\cdot|s_t)$
8        $s_{t+1} \sim p(s_{t+1}|s_t, a_t)$
9        $B \leftarrow B \cup \{s_t, a_t, r(s_t, a_t), s_{t+1}\}$
10   **end**
11   **foreach** *each gradient step* **do**
12       $\theta \leftarrow \theta - \lambda_\pi \nabla_\theta J_\pi(\theta)$
13   **for** $i \in \{1,2\}$ **do**
14          $\phi_i \leftarrow \phi_i - \lambda_Q \nabla J_Q(\phi_i)$
15   **end**
16       $\varphi \leftarrow \varphi - \lambda_\varphi \nabla J(\varphi)$
17   **for** $i \in \{1,2\}$ **do**
18          $\tilde{\phi}_i \leftarrow \tau \tilde{\phi}_i + (1 - \tau)\phi_i$
19   **end**
20   **end**
21 **end**

Figure 2 shows the rewards for SAC, DDPG, and RCO. The reward remains unchanged for the greedy RCO approach because it operates by simply delivering traffic without feedback on the flows that have met QoS requirements. DDPG, a representative algorithm that simultaneously learns a deterministic policy and a Q-function, is strongly influenced by its initial parameters, as evident in the graph. The reward reflects the initial parameters up to the 200th episode, and although it increases slightly after the 600th episode, the reward tends to stabilize. Additionally, sections where parameter updates cause rapid changes in reward values are observable. The SAC method maximizes the sum of entropy along with the reward function, allowing the actor and critic networks to adapt to various environments. So, SAC has the advantage of stably performing learning in a continuous space compared to the DDPG method.

As traffic increases, link utilization rises, which cause some bottleneck links. So, traffic load distribution evenly over the network while guaranteeing QoS should be provided to alleviate the effect. Figure 3 shows the average link utilization varying the number of flows. For SAC and DDPG, since traffic allocation considering QoS is reflected in the reward function, the domain switch can smoothly deliver traffic in the 200–250 flow section. However, RCO, which transmits traffic using a greedy method, cannot distribute traffic considering

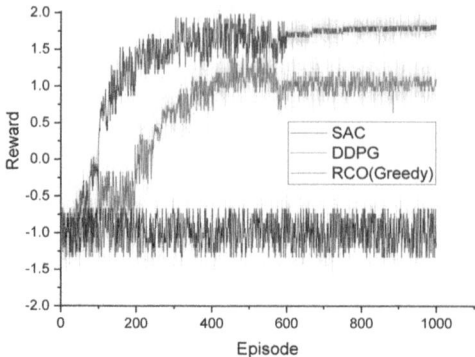

Fig. 2. Reward comparison between Reinforcement learning approach

the network conditions, resulting in a rapid increase in usage in the 200 and 250 flow sections. In the case of DDPG, it was confirmed that the link usage increased more than in other approaches due to the issue of initial parameter settings, particularly in the 50 flow section. This demonstrates the significant impact of initial parameters on performance. Since the SAC approach performs probability-based learning, it can effectively distribute traffic considering QoS in various environments.

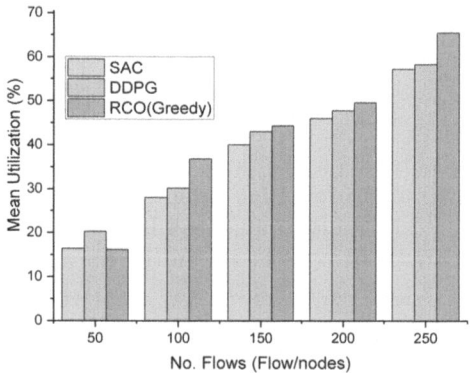

Fig. 3. Average Link Utilization

Figure 4 shows the average delay varying the number of flows. We can see that the delay increases as the number of flows increases. It is evident that delays are similar in the range of 50–100 flows where there is ample link capacity. However, with the greedy-based method, there is an overlap in traffic delivery, leading to increased delays compared to others. The delay of RCO for 250 flows rapidly increases exceeding 60% of the link capacity, due to the increase of bottleneck links. There is no significant difference between SAC and DDPG in general. However, a local optimal value of DDPG for 250 flows leads to higher delays compared to SAC.

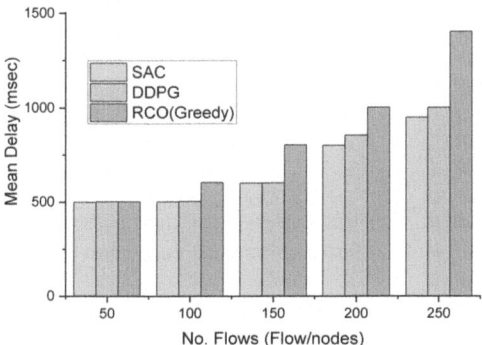

Fig. 4. Mean Delay

Figure 5 shows the degree of QoS satisfaction. In general, SAC and DDPG exhibit high QoS satisfaction. On the other hand, in the 200 and 250 flow sections, the greedy RCO method fails to satisfy QoS requirements. This is due to increased traffic delay in bottleneck sections, as traffic continues to be delivered through the same path.

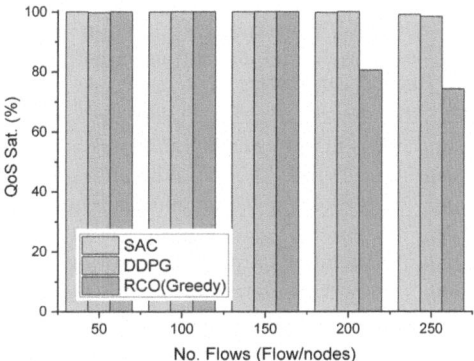

Fig. 5. Degree of QoS Satisfaction

4   Conclusion

This paper proposed the end-to-end path selection methods to guarantee QoSs in SDN environments, taking into account uncertainties in the QoS requirement of each traffic flow. We employed the Soft Actor-Critic (SAC) method as the primary approach and compared it with other methods under various conditions. The results demonstrated that the SAC method, with its capacity to efficiently learn in continuous and highly complex multi-domain environments, can be applied immediately in real-world scenarios despite being a model-free reinforcement learning algorithm. In addition, it was confirmed that the SAC method is more efficient than both the DDPG approach and the greedy-based RCO approach.

Acknowledgments. This work was partially supported by the Ajou University research fund, South Korea.

Disclosure of Interests. The authors declare that they have no known competing financial interests or personal relationships that could have appeared to influence the work reported in this paper.

References

1. Duan, Q.: Network-as-a-service in software-defined networks for end-to-end qos provisioning. In: 2014 23rd Wireless and Optical Communication Conference (WOCC), pp. 1–5. IEEE (2014)
2. Ali, J., Roh, B., Khan, S.: Performance evaluation methods for SDN controllers: a comparative analysis. In: Sahoo, K.S., Solanki, A., Mishra, S.K., Sahoo, B., Nayyar, A. (eds.) SDN-Supported Edge-Cloud Interplay for Next Generation Internet of Things. vol. 6, pp. 105–124. Chapman and Hall/CRC (2022)
3. Mondal, A., Misra, S.: Flowman: qos-aware dynamic data flow management in software-defined networks. IEEE J. Sel. Areas Commun. **38**(7), 1366–1373 (2020)
4. Bastam, M., RahimiZadeh, K., Yousefpour, R.: Design and performance evaluation of a new traffic engineering technique for software-defined network datacenters. J. Netw. Syst. Manag. **29**(4), 1–26 (2021)
5. Bera, S., Misra, S., Saha, N., Sharif, H.: Q-soft: qos-aware traffic forwarding in software-defined cyber-physical systems. IEEE Internet Things J. (2021)
6. Ghazizadeh, A., Akbari, B., Tajiki, M.M.: Joint reliability-aware and cost efficient path allocationfig and vnf placement using sharing scheme. J. Netw. Syst. Manag. **30**(1), 1–28 (2022)
7. Stampa, G., Arias, M., Sánchez-Charles, D., Muntés-Mulero, V., Cabellos, A.: A deep-reinforcement learning approach for software-defined networking routing optimization. arXiv preprint arXiv:1709.07080 (2017)
8. Yu, C., Lan, J., Guo, Z., Hu, Y.: Drom: optimizing the routing in software-defined networks with deep reinforcement learning. IEEE Access **6**, 64533–64539 (2018)
9. Huang, X., Yuan, T., Qiao, G., Ren, Y.: Deep reinforcement learning for multimedia traffic control in software defined networking. IEEE Netw. **32**(6), 35–41 (2018)
10. Jeong, Y., Lim, J., Choi, G., Roh, B.: Deep deterministic policy gradient-based Load balancing method in SDN environments. In: SmartNets 2024, Harrisonburg. IEEE (2024)
11. Lillicrap, T.P., et al.: Continuous control with deep reinforcement learning. arXiv preprint arXiv:1509.02971 (2015)

Embedded Systems, Cyber-Physical Systems, and Applications (ESCS)

Container Performance in Space Systems

Shariar M. Alamgir[1][✉], Dhruv L. Bohra[1], and Elisabeth A. Nguyen[2]

[1] Embedded and Specialized Computing Department, The Aerospace Corporation, El Segundo, CA, USA
{shar.m.alamgir,dhruv.l.bohra}@aero.org
[2] Software Architecture and Engineering Department, The Aerospace Corporation, El Segundo, CA, USA
enguyen@aero.org

Abstract. Critical embedded software, such as spacecraft flight software, requires high reliability, efficiency, and real-time performance while being capable enough to meet application needs. The increasing prevalence of Linux, and in particular Linux containers, presents opportunities for space systems but also poses potential risks since Linux was not designed to be a real-time operating system. In this study, we conducted a variety of experiments to look at both the overhead imposed by containers and the latency experienced in Linux using various combinations of patched OS and containers running on a Raspberry Pi 4. We found that containers have little impact on CPU utilization but do incur penalties in RAM, disk storage, and startup time. We also found the unpatched Linux kernel performs well for real time; and that, while the real-time kernel patch reduces both overall and maximum latency, it can negatively impact performance, particularly on single-core systems running non-real-time tasks.

Keywords: containers · embedded · performance · real-time systems

1 Introduction

High-criticality real-time embedded systems, such as those built for aerospace applications, rely on operating systems (OSs) to execute high-criticality tasks reliably and with low latency. Traditionally, designers have used real-time operating systems (RTOSs) designed specifically to support high reliability and small, well-defined latencies in the start of task execution. More recently though, they have begun using Linux due to its low cost, many features, and wide developer base. We have seen Linux successfully used on space systems but did not know in what circumstances it could be used safely, or what the risks of its use would be.

Furthermore, designers have started to take advantage of Linux's ability to run containers as a multi-tenancy solution presenting a lightweight alternative to virtual machines. Containers allow a developer to group all dependencies associated with an application into a single executable package of software, helping user applications to run consistently across different computing environments. Although Docker containers

H. R. Arabnia et al. (Eds.): CSCE 2024, CCIS 2260, pp. 265–281, 2025.
https://doi.org/10.1007/978-3-031-85923-6_23

have numerous benefits, they do still require synthesis of an abstraction layer between the application and the host operating system, which in turn introduces the potential for performance impacts. We also are working with upcoming space computing designs incorporating containers and wanted to understand their implications.

In this paper, we present results of nine different experiments we conducted to determine the performance implications of Linux and containers. These experiments are:

1. *File Operations*: tested performance impact of the container runtime's intercepting system calls
2. *Response time*: tested performance impact of the container runtime intercepting application communication into/out of a container
3. *CPU Utilization*: tested CPU utilization overhead of the container runtime
4. *Parallel Processing*: tested performance impact of the container runtime on multi-threaded workloads
5. *Base Layers*: tested how different base layers affect startup time, memory utilization, and size on disk
6. *Container Count*: tested how many containers the OS and runtime can support, given memory constraints
7. *Thread Wakeup Time*: tested latency of waking real-time scheduled threads
8. *Patched Kernel Runtime Overhead*: measured the runtime of non-real-time applications when executed on a real-time patched OS kernel.

The rest of this paper is organized as follows. Section 2 describes the setup of all our experiments. Section 3 details experiments 1–7, which emphasize questions about container overhead. Section 4 details experiments 8 and 9, which emphasize questions about latency for real-time systems. Section 5 draws overall conclusions.

2 Related Work

Our study's motivation came from existing research studies, including Ruan et al. and their study on containers with cloud environments [1], Bachiega et al. and their survey on existing container-based performance research [2], and Espe et al. and their research evaluating different container runtimes and the performance impact on a shared host [3].

3 Experiment Setup

3.1 Processor and Operating System

For our study we used an 8 GB RAM Raspberry Pi 4 running Ubuntu 22.04 as a primary platform for testing and evaluating flight-like embedded programs and their effect on hardware. Although far more powerful than the radiation-tolerant processors used on many of today's spacecraft, the Raspberry Pi 4 was a good choice to represent our use case for next-generation systems willing to use less traditional operating systems. It does have flight heritage [4], and its quad-core Cortex-A72 powered System on Chip (ARMv8) can run at 1.5 GHz, resembling newer processors such as AMD's Versal

Adaptive Compute Acceleration Platform (ACAP) [5, 6]. We note that newer processors may have increased memory capacity; We did not believe that this type of difference would fundamentally alter our experiment's results, however, since we did not use a memory-intensive application.

3.2   Container Setup

We used Docker version 23.0.2 as our container runtime since it has by far the widest support from both industry and community software organizations. Each containerized experiment contained the following three components:

- Its own Dockerfile and outlined base layer image
- Required dependencies
- The application to run inside the container

We measured timing results by leveraging the capabilities of Linux's built-in `time` command along with customized python and bash scripts to automate invoking the command at different checkpoints of each experiment.

For our containerized experiments, we ensured that the required container images were available locally, to avoid incurring the overhead of Docker having to pull images from a repository. The first step of each experiment was to set up the container using the `docker run` command. `docker run` performs the following steps:

- Create a new container from a specified image
- Allocate a filesystem and mount a read-write layer
- Allocate a network/bridge interface
- Set up an IP address
- Execute the main embedded program ("containerized application") within the container

Except where otherwise noted, our performance numbers include only execution of the containerized application.

3.3   Real-Time Kernal Patch

The standard version of the Linux kernel does not support hard real time, meaning, there is not a way to interrupt the operating system kernel if a user process needs to be switched in on a clock tick. However, a patch called PREEMPT_RT can be built into the kernel to enable OS preemption. PREEMPT_RT replaces Linux's default Completely Fair Scheduler, which attempts to allocate time fairly among user processes, with a real-time scheduler, which supports process priorities and schedules processes strictly based on priority. PREEMPT_RT also enables interrupt handlers to execute as separate kernel threads with assigned priorities, minimizing interrupt latencies. These features make scheduling deterministic and hence enables developers to prioritize and guarantee the execution of time-critical processes.

To apply the PREEMPT_RT patch onto a Linux kernel, we used kernel version 5.15.39-rt42-raspi, which allowed for our kernel to run on the Pi 4. We applied the patch command to the kernel image directory and updated the configuration file to enable the

High-Resolution Timer (HRT) as well the selecting "Fully Preemptible Kernel (RT)" as our preemption model from the menu configuration. This allowed for us to not only have a real-time patched kernel but leverage precise timing and lower latency for our timers and threads using the HRT.

4   Container Performance Experiments

We wrote all applications in Python and ran all Variations for all experiments 25 or more times. The data presented in all figures and tables represent data observed from the corresponding sample set of runs.

4.1   Experiment 1: File Operations

Our first experiment tests performance impact of the container runtime intercepting system calls for file operations. This experiment's containerized application opens a file that contains numbers on every line. After making a system call to the host OS to read each line of the file, the application increments the read number, and then makes another system call to write (append) that incremented value to a new file. We tested this base experiment through six variations:

- Variation A: The `docker run` command was executed 25 times in sequence.
- Variation B: The `docker run` command was executed 1 time, but the embedded program was modified to loop 25 times in sequence.
- Variation C: The embedded program was run on the host OS 25 times in sequence. This involved no containerization at all.
- Variation D: Same as Variation A, but with a longer embedded program runtime.
- Variation E: Same as Variation B, but with a longer embedded program runtime.
- Variation F: Same as Variation C, but with a longer embedded program runtime.

Table 1 shows the mean and standard deviation data taken from 25 runs of each variation specified. Variation A and D had a higher mean runtime and Variation A, specifically, had a higher standard deviation that its counterparts. However, the increase in runtime between both Variation A versus Variation B and Variation D versus variation E is below 2 s, indicating that the spin-up time for the docker container using this program's necessary base image and libraries takes about 2 s regardless of programs runtime. Our values do indicate that Variations B and E had similar runtimes to control Variations C and F, respectively. This suggests containerization did not have a negative impact on the execution time of the embedded program. In fact, the containerized Variations (B and E) ran faster than their non-containerized counterparts (C and F). We believe this is due to the isolation property of containers, providing dedicated resource allocation for the single-program containers, thus minimizing the multiprocessing conflicts or resource scarcity slowdowns our programs likely encountered when running on the host OS directly.

Table 1. Experiment 1: File Operations.

Variation	Runtime Mean (s)	Runtime Std. Dev. (s)
A: Inside Container 25x `docker run`; 1x short runtime	1.68	0.19
B: Inside Container 1x `docker run`; 25x short runtime	0.14	0.004
C: Outside Container 25x short runtime	0.19	0.02
D: Inside Container 25x `docker run`; 1x long runtime	20.51	0.54
E: Inside Container 1x `docker run`; 25x long runtime	18.66	0.60
F: Outside Container 25x long runtime	21.97	0.55

4.2 Experiment 2: Response Time

This experiment tested performance impact of the container runtime's intercepting application communication into/out of a container. We used Python's socket library to send a "command" (string of characters) between a server and a client. We conducted two variations of this experiment:

- Containerized client: The server existed outside the container on the host OS, while the client existed inside a container.
- No containers: Both the server and client existed on the host OS – no containerization was involved.

In order to independently investigate the time taken to send data from server to client and from client to server, for both variations we timed the following operations:

- One-way: server sends command to client, and client receives that command.
- Round-trip: server sends command to client; client receives that command; client echoes the same command back to the server; server receives that same command.

As shown in Table 2, the one-way and two-way latencies increased by about 22% when adding containerization. Though these latencies are significant as percentages, they represent maximum overall increases of about 0.002 s. We believe that a system designer would not plan to have any functionality this sensitive to timing execute on a container-capable general purpose embedded CPU; they would instead accelerate such algorithms with an ASIC or FPGA. Similarly, jitter increased with containerization, but was still well within the constraints of the spacecraft flight software we have seen executing in a CPU.

Table 2. Experiment 2: Response Time.

Variation	Response time Mean (μs)	Response time Std. Dev. (μs)
No containerization, one way	73	2
No containerization, round trip	199	11
Containerized app, one way	89	11
Containerized app, round trip	244	23

4.3   Experiment 3: CPU Utilization

This experiment tested CPU utilization overhead of the container runtime using a single application with high CPU demand. The application used a purposefully inefficient algorithm to test for prime numbers by performing divisions and checking for a zero remainder. This algorithm drove CPU utilization to over 98% during the entire runtime of the application (it was inefficient in a way that the Python interpreter did not optimize out).

Figure 1 shows our initial results. We saw some increase in runtime with containerization, and a substantial increase in standard deviation. We were concerned that much of what we were seeing was related to container startup time, however, and we wanted to understand runtime independent of startup time, so we added additional loops to our program to increase the runtime. Table 3 shows the results of the longer-runtime experiment.

Table 3. Experiment 3: CPU Utilization, Increased Program Runtime.

Variation	Runtime Mean (s)	Runtime Std. Dev. (s)
No containerization	31.6	0.8
Containerized application	32.4	1.2

The containerized version experienced only an approximately 2.5% increase in mean runtime but saw an approximately 50% increase in standard deviation. Though we are not certain why the standard deviation is so much higher, we believe it could be due to some network overhead, resource isolation issue, or Docker characteristic unrelated to the high CPU utilization of the embedded algorithm. More testing would be required to isolate and identify the cause.

4.4   Experiment 4 and 5: Parallel Processing

Modern flight software is often natively programmed, or optimized through compilation, to take advantage of the parallel computing resources available in embedded hardware. This experiment investigated whether Docker effectively allocates embedded CPU cores to multithreaded containerized applications.

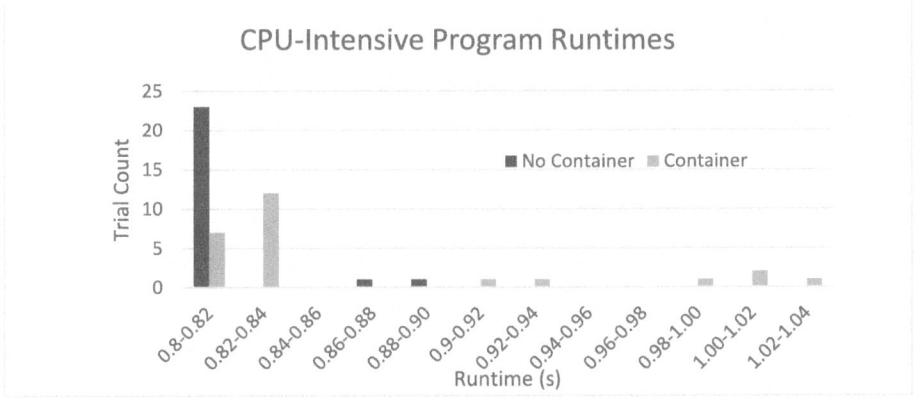

Fig. 1. Runtimes of CPU-Intensive program inside versus outside container

In this experiment, we first reused the CPU intensive application from Experiment 3, and varied the allowable number of CPU cores. Table 4 shows the results, with total CPU utilization in the multicore case added for all 4 cores.

Table 4. Experiment 4: Parallel Processing Part 1.

Variation	Runtim Mean (s)	Runtime Std. Dev. (s)	Utilization (%)	Utilization per Core (%)
Containerized 1 core	29.6	1.4	98–100	98–100
Containerized 4 cores	12.5	0.9	350–365	88–91
No Container 1 core	29.9	1.8	95–100	95–100
No Container 4 cores	12.1	0.2	360–385	90–96

Table 4 shows no correlation between containerization and the runtime of the algorithm, regardless of the number of cores allowed. It also shows that when executing the single-thread algorithm inside the container, the minimum CPU utilization was higher by 3% when compared to the same algorithm executed on the host OS outside a container. This may explain the very slight difference in runtimes.

The 3–5% decrease in maximum utilization seen when containerizing the 4-core experiment suggests that Docker may have some difficulty efficiently allocating multiple simultaneous CPU resources to a containerized algorithm. This had little impact on the total runtime of the algorithm, as the difference in average runtime between those two variants was only about 3%.

We also wanted to understand how varying numbers of containers might impact the scheduler's ability to fairly allocate time across applications. To investigate this, we again used the CPU intensive application from Experiment 3 but adjusted its runtime to take around 2 min. We then ran 20 concurrent processes with a mix of core counts and container counts. Table 5 shows the results from these runs:

Table 5. Experiment 5: Parallel Processing Part 2.

Variation	Runtim Mean (s)	Runtime Std. Dev. (s)
No Container 4 cores	119	5.0
1 Container 4 cores	122	3.8
4 Containers 4 cores	124	4.1
4 Containers 1 core each	123	4.1
5 Containers 4 cores	122	3.9
20 Containers 4 cores	118	6.1

Table 5 shows that the average runtime is within 6 s for all variations, with standard deviations of all variations within 6 s as well–that's a 5.24% difference in average runtimes, regardless of the number of cores or containers the algorithm was split across. The containerized experiments show that putting more processes within fewer containers reduces the standard deviations and narrows the confidence interval, suggesting that containers fairly allocate resources across the processes within.

4.5 Experiment 6: Base Layers

Container images require not just the application to be run, but also OS and other dependencies to support it. A developer's choice of both the base layer (set of OS dependencies) and additional dependencies will impact image size on disk, runtime memory footprint, and container startup time.

While all previous experiments in this paper used Ubuntu as the base image, realistic embedded deployments of Linux systems often don't need many of the userspace features of Ubuntu. Scratch is a very minimal base image, taking 194 Bytes of space on disk and inflating to < 5 MB on disk when adding sufficient dependencies to run C programs. Both of these numbers are dramatically smaller than the nearly 100 MB+ of space required to house an Ubuntu image or other image based on a "full size" base layer.

We wanted to understand the impact that different base layers would have on startup time, memory utilization, and disk utilization. Because we wanted fewer dependencies, we switched from using Python scripts (which require a Python interpreter) to a statically-linked C program. Since we wanted to analyze startup time rather than overall utilization, we designed our C program to simply allocate 256 KB of memory and then sleep.

As shown in Table 6, the average runtime difference between the Scratch and Ubuntu bases was about 1%. Although their standard deviations differed by over 50%, Fig. 2 shows that this is because the standard deviation was very small to begin with. This data

Table 6. Experiment 6: Base Layers - Runtime.

Variation	Runtime Mean (s)	Runtime Std. Dev. (s)
No Container	0.007	0.001
Scratch Base	0.98	0.036
Ubuntu Base	0.99	0.055

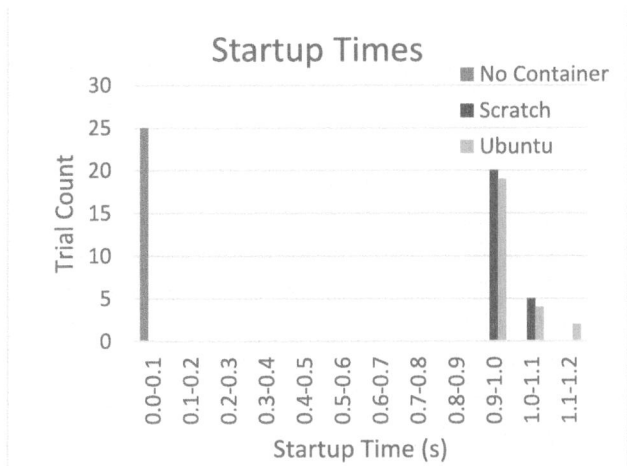

Fig. 2. Startup time comparison between no container, scratch, and ubuntu base layer images

indicates that the base layer of a container does not significantly affect its startup time, which may be in part due to Docker's ability to analyze an image's construction, before executing it as a container, and pull from cache or ignore any instructions unused by the executed program.

In terms of memory usage, each container requires (1) the amount of memory needed by the application; (2) memory to support its isolated runtime environment; and (3) memory to support a utility function called containerd-shim, which bridges the Docker daemon to the container and manages low-level details of the container such as the optimization function detailed previously. Table 7 shows the memory usage for each component of each base layer experiment.

Physical Memory is the "Resident Size" memory actually taken up on RAM by a process, and allocated for ownership by that process specifically. Shared memory physical memory optimized by the OS and designated for re-use by multiple processes; a high level of shared memory can indicate substantial memory optimization.

Virtual memory is different: the OS uses virtual memory to "virtually" expand the total pool of available memory by writing out the contents of memory to disk. Linux refers to virtual memory space as "swap space," because the OS will swap memory contents in active use into RAM, while swapping inactive contents out to disk. Virtual memory is typically allocated by whoever will use it; in this case, Docker is allocating the virtual memory–meaning, setting aside a certain amount of disk space–at container startup. This does not mean that Docker will use all (or any) of the virtual memory it allocates, and it is possible to tune this parameter to meet the user's needs. Hence, we think the virtual memory values are something of a red herring, but we include them here for the reader's awareness.

Table 7. Experiment 6: Base Layers – Memory Usage Breakdown.

Variation	Virtual Memory (MB)	Physical Memory (MB)	Shared Memory (MB)
Program Only	1.20	0.80	0.59
Scratch containerd-shim	711	9.0	6.9
Ubuntu containerd-shim	712	9.2	6.9
Scratch Container	1.20	0.56	0.59
Ubuntu Container	1.20	0.76	0.59
Scratch Docker environment	1270–1450	32–35	24–26
Ubuntu Docker environment	1270–1450	32–35	24–26

While the application itself was programmed to request only 256 KB of RAM, when run on the host OS it used over 3.1x that much physical memory and was given over 4.6x that much virtual memory to use. This is likely due to all the statically linked C libraries and dependency calls and processes invoked when running the program. When executing in a container with the Scratch base layer, the whole container actually used less physical memory than just the program did on the host OS. This is likely due to containerd-shim optimizations. The Ubuntu-based container occupied more physical memory than the Scratch container, though still below the memory usage of the program when executing on the host OS. Both containers used the same amount of virtual and shared memory as the original program.

Although the memory usage of the containers was highly optimized by the Docker runtime and containerd-shim, the shim itself occupied over 9 MB of physical memory, and the runtime environments each used 32–35 MB of physical memory. Our memory readout program reported that around 33 MB of this memory was shared–likely with each other–for the Scratch and Ubuntu versions. Interestingly, the Docker runtime allocated over 711 MB of virtual memory to its container shims, and 1.27–1.45 GB of virtual memory to its runtime environments. While these are relatively large values, the following points must be taken into consideration:

- The memory values of both the containerd-shim and the Docker environments did not change as the internal program's memory allocation changed, indicating these are configurable container runtime parameters.

- We observed a large discrepancy between physical memory used and virtual memory allocated, suggesting that the amount of virtual memory Docker allocates to its containers can be configured to be lower, with little to no effect on the containerized algorithm.

During our trials, the utilization of virtual memory by all processes in the system reached 26 GB+. It is important to note that virtual memory overallocation generally does not lead to the same types of catastrophic functional errors experienced by real memory overutilization, as seen in Experiment 7. Virtual memory is also shared, reducing the net utilization in the system.

4.6 Experiment 7: Container Count

While Docker optimizes resource usage across containers, we still wanted to know how many containers the runtime can manage before causing host OS performance degradation. Given the results of earlier experiments, which suggested containers introduce little performance overhead but substantial memory overhead, this experiment launched enough containers to drive physical memory utilization to near 100% (8 GB on our Raspberry Pi 4s). Experiment 7 tested three variations:

- Up to 32 containers launched in series, each using 256 MB of memory.
- Up to 16 containers, each using 512 MB of memory.
- Up to 8 containers, each using 1 GB of memory.

For each variation, we:

- Monitored the host OS for a slowdown between container launches.
- Recorded average and maximum container startup times for each container launch.
- Timed execution of our application for each container launch.

Table 8. Experiment 7: Host OS Slowdown Points.

Variation	Actual Container Memory Usage	Slowdown Point (# of Concurrent Containers)
32 containers, 256 MB each	221–257 MB	30
16 containers, 512 MB each	495–528 MB	15
8 containers, 1 GB each	1.0–1.06 GB	7

Table 8 shows that our system under test experienced a slowdown whenever the total memory usage approached 90%, regardless of the memory usage size of each individual container. This means that the number of containers it takes to degrade the performance of the host OS is roughly linear with the memory usage of each container. The peaks in Fig. 3 depict the effect this slowdown has on container startup times.

For the 256 MB containers, Tables 9 and 10 show that both startup and runtime performance degrades very substantially after the point of physical memory saturation. For

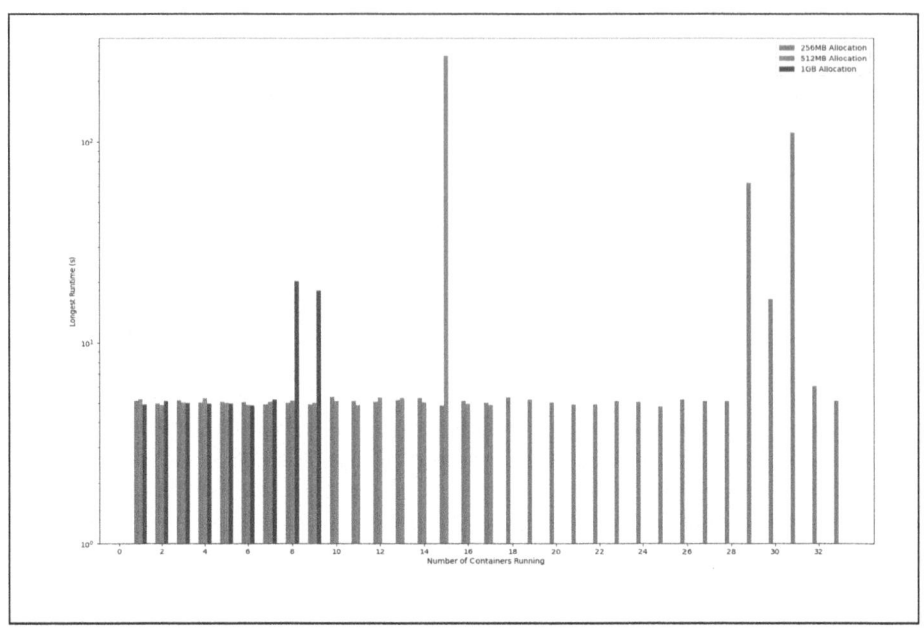

Fig. 3. Longest container application runtime as container count changes for varying memory utilization per container.

Table 9. Experiment 7: Container Startup Times Before & After Physical Memory Saturation.

Variation	Max Startup Time Before Saturation (s)	Mean Startup Time After Saturation (s)	Max Startup Time After Saturation (s)
32/256 MB	2.26	48	143
16/512 MB	1.17	1.9	Startup failure
8/1 GB	2.23	1.2	Startup failure

Table 10. Experiment 7: Application Runtimes Before & After Physical Memory Saturation.

Variation	Max Runtime Before Saturation (s)	Mean Runtime After Saturation (s)	Max Runtime After Saturation (s)
32/256 MB	5.34	40	111
16/512 MB	5.32	70	267
8/1 GB	5.21	5	20

the larger containers, although in some cases startup time was reasonable, in other cases startup failed completely; the lack of data for these cases makes the mean misleadingly low.

Analysis of the external program runtime is slightly more complicated. As shown in Table 10, all three variations had consistent runtimes when sufficient memory was available. Likewise, when the slowdown occurred, the worst-case runtime for all three variations spiked significantly. However, Fig. 4 shows that the external program runtimes return to normal after the spike occurs. This is likely due to termination of containers executed earlier in the experiment; container termination means that memory is no longer saturated. Using virtual memory (i.e., reading from disk, as discussed above) when memory is oversubscribed may also contribute to the delays.

Traditional embedded system design requires strict memory management; recursive functions, which can produce an unbounded number of function calls, are discouraged, for example, and in critical systems even dynamically allocated memory may be disallowed. Maximum memory usage is often reported as a Technical Performance Measure. Hence, our takeaway from our experimental results is that containerized applications have the same limitations as their heritage counterparts, but containerization does not by itself pose a significant new concern.

5   Real-Time Patch Experiments

To understand the implications of Linux and containers for processes with real-time deadlines, we conducted two experiments to examine the timing overhead of both real-time and non-real-time programs, when executed on a Linux kernel patched to support real time. We assessed outcomes using a combination of 3 different configuration options:

- Kernel: Unpatched Ubuntu 22 kernel (control) or PREEMPT_RT patched Ubuntu 22 kernel (experimental).
- No containerization (control) or experimental application placed inside a Docker container (experiment).
- Single core or multi core (both common options in our systems of interest).

The experiments gathered metrics on response time latencies for scheduled threads as well as runtime for multi-threaded programs running with non-real-time priorities. These metrics helped us understand the prioritization advantages and disadvantages of using a real-time patched Linux kernel and indicate which kernel to use for certain capabilities, along with the impact of containerization on different Linux builds.

5.1   Experiment 8: Real-Time Priority Scheduled Threads

Experiment 8 tested latency of switching to a high-priority task, both using a standard Linux kernel build and a build patched with PREEMPT_RT. This task switching latency translates into task activation time jitter in the system, and could potentially cause problems for timing-sensitive functionality such as attitude control loops. For this experiment, we only used one processor core; single-core processing relates most closely to heritage space systems, and further, we had no reason to expect that using multiple cores would change the overall results.

To automate task switching, we used The Linux Foundation's rt-tests suite containing the Cyclictest program. Cyclictest runs a master thread which starts a determined number of real-time priority threads and wakes them up repeatedly using a cyclic alarm expiring timer. The difference between the intended wake-up time and the actual wake-up time is measured as the latency. Cyclictest provides the average, minimum, and maximum latencies, where the maximum latencies indicate potential worst case response time for a scheduled thread.

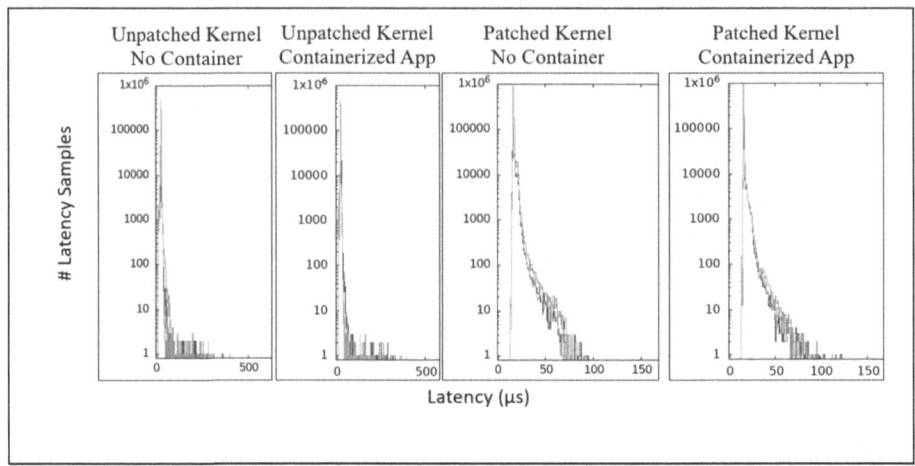

Fig. 4. Latency comparison for real-time scheduled threads between unpatched and patched kernel and containerized or non-containerized application.

Our Cyclictest script ran 1,000,000 samples of the test. The maximum latencies were gathered into a plot for all four CPU cores on the system. The plot also captured the absolute maximum latency from the samples, giving us an idea of the worst case wake-up time delay for the threads.

Figure 4 shows the results of our tests. Different CPUs are shown in different colors, but the tests did not distinguish between CPUs. The figures indicate that the real-time patched Linux kernels have lower maximum latency than a regular Linux kernel. The figures also indicate that on the real-time patched Linux kernel, the containerized test had higher latency than directly on the OS, but the containerized test on the regular Linux kernel had lower latency than directly on the OS. This difference in latency time could be attributed to Docker's kernel configuration and the scheduling and resource management differences within Docker containers.

5.2 Experiment 9: Real-Time Patch Performance Overhead

PREEMPT_RT modifies the context switching behavior in Linux. By default, the Linux kernel uses voluntary kernel preemption. With the PREEMPT-RT patch, the kernel can be preempted even while executing in kernel mode, allowing for more deterministic and responsive behavior. The patch modifies the kernel's context switching mechanism to handle preemption within the kernel more efficiently. While it improves real-time capabilities, it introduces additional overhead due to more frequent context switches, which can affect the overall system performance for non-real-time tasks.

This experiment investigates Docker's effectiveness in isolating and dedicating embedded CPU cores to individual containers, which holds significant value for flight software optimization. Efficient containerization and parallel computing utilization can enhance flight software performance and resource management, crucial in aerospace applications with stringent demands on computing resources.

To drive our performance experiment, we used the application from Experiment 3 that runs an algorithm using a purposefully inefficient way to test if many numbers are prime, which fully loaded multiple cores even after being optimized by Python's multiprocessing library. We calculated averages from 25 runs of the application, each run looping the application 25 times. Table 11 reports runtime and CPU utilization over our 25 application runs, where a single core system has a maximum 100% utilization and a 4-core system has a maximum 400% utilization:

Table 11. Experiment 9: Runtime Data for Unpatched and Patched Kernels.

Variation	Runtime Mean (s)	Runtime Std. Dev. (s)	Total Utilization (%)	Utilization per Core (%)
Unpatched kernel Inside container 1 core	27.7	1.4	98–100	98–100
Unpatched kernel Inside container 4 cores	13.6	0.9	350–365	88–91
Unpatched kernel No container 1 core	28.0	1.5	95–100	95–100
Unpatched kernel No container 4 cores	14.8	1.0	360–385	90–96
Patched kernel Inside container 1 core	35.2	1.7	96–99	96–99
Patched kernel Inside container 4 cores	10.9	1.0	350–365	88–91
Patched kernel No container 1 core	34.9	1.4	98–100	98–100
Patched kernel No container 4 cores	10.6	1.0	372–385	93–96

Table 1 indicates that for single CPU restricted variations, the average runtime is greater on the patched kernel than an unpatched kernel. However, the 4 CPU variations had opposite results. The data also showed that in the unpatched kernel, the containerized versions performed slightly faster than their non-containerized counterparts, but the opposite was observed for the patched kernel. The real-time patch and containerization introduce different optimization mechanisms but also different overhead additions. It may be the case that the real-time optimizations work best directly on the OS rather than through the container, whereas the containerization isolation provides better performance on the unpatched kernel. This coincides with Table 2's data, indicating that the observed CPU utilization for 4 CPU variations were higher on the patched kernel than the unpatched kernel.

6 Conclusion

Industry adoption clearly shows that Docker containers provide significant advantages in terms of deployment, scalability, and isolation. While these benefits make them a potentially attractive option for deploying applications in tactical resource-constrained environments, this study focused on evaluating concerns of using Docker containers for deploying applications on embedded systems.

We found that Docker containers do not significantly impact the performance of an application's runtime or CPU utilization, even on embedded hardware. Although our results did suggest that the latency introduced by containerization may make this approach unsuitable for algorithms that require sub-millisecond timings, such algorithms would generally not be run on a non-real-time version of Linux on COTS CPUs.

However, our results present significant concerns related to memory usage of the application within the container, and the containerd-shim utility. We believe this concern could be mitigated by carefully monitoring memory usage, limiting the application's internal memory usage, and limiting the number of containers per system. Though memory usage is an important metric for all system designers to consider, it is particularly critical in embedded space software.

Regardless of containerization, the patched kernel consistently exhibited reduced latency and jitter for real-time tasks; we believe that Linux can be reasonably used in spacecraft software without patching. Containerization led to a small increase in latency in the patched kernel, but a small decrease in latency in the unpatched kernel.

For non-real-time tasks, the unpatched kernel demonstrated faster performance for programs constrained to a single CPU, whereas the real-time patched kernel outperformed for 4-CPU programs. This discrepancy suggests that the real-time system optimizations might have certain disadvantages for non-real-time tasks, particularly when running on a single CPU core.

In conclusion, the evaluation of real-time Linux and containerization for spacecraft technology reveals valuable trade-offs and considerations. Containerization has little impact on performance if sufficient memory is available. The PREEMPT_RT patch controls latency for real-time tasks but may add CPU overhead. These insights provide critical guidance for developers seeking to use Linux and containers in space systems. With knowledge of the performance impact, designers wishing to use containerization in different applications can proceed with little worry. Containerization can greatly improve the deployment, isolation, and scalability of many different environments, such as reconfigurable modules for the International Space Station, deploying applications for autonomous reconfigurable lunar rovers, adding secure, low-overhead support for applications in government technology such as the Department of Transportation's traffic regulators, and providing support of DevSecOps for Internet-of-Things (IoT) ecosystems.

Disclosure of Interests. The authors have no competing interests to declare that are relevant to the content of this article.

References

1. Ruan, B., Huang, H., Wu, S., Jin, H.: A performance study of containers in cloud environment. In: Advances in Services Computing (2016)
2. Bachiega, N.G., Souza, P.S.L., Bruschi, S.M., de Souza, S.d.R.S.: Container-based performance evaluation: a survey and challenges. In: IEEE International Conference on Cloud Engineering, Orlando (2018)
3. Espe, L., Jindal, A., Podolskiy, V., Gerndt, M.: Performance evaluation of container runtimes (2020)
4. Guertin, S.: Raspberry pis for space guideline. Nat. Aeronaut. Space Adm. (2001)
5. Versal architecture and product data sheet: overview (DS950) 2023. https://docs.xilinx.com/v/u/en-US/ds950-versal-overview. Accessed 16 Nov 2023
6. Versal Adaptive SoC Technical Reference Manual (AM011) 2023. https://docs.xilinx.com/r/en-US/am011-versal-acap-trm/Introduction. Accessed 16 Nov 2023

Using Heuristics and Byte Histograms to Detect Anomalies in OT Network Traffic

Philip Rahal$^{(\boxtimes)}$ ⓘ, Jack Nunnelee ⓘ, Alex Howe ⓘ, and Mauricio Papa ⓘ

The University of Tulsa, Tulsa, OK 74104, USA
{pjr4516,jen2603,alex-howe,mauricio-papa}@utulsa.edu
http://www.utulsa.edu

Abstract. Anomaly detection is a significant problem in Operational Technology (OT) networks. Given a collection of network traffic, detecting anomalies is paramount due to safety and functionality concerns. This paper seeks to prove the effectiveness of anomaly-based Intrusion Detection Systems (IDS) to protect Industrial Control Systems (ICS) from cyberattacks. Our two-stage anomaly detection strategy employs heuristics and the byte histogram data structure to detect malicious activity as packets enter the network. The novelty of our byte histogram data structure is the ability to detect anomalies in packets where the details of every protocol in the packet are unknown. This paper discusses the heuristics used in Stage One, the usage and effectiveness of byte histograms used in Stage Two, and the algorithms used to process packet information. Using an OT network traffic dataset, we evaluate our approach using multiple attack examples, achieving an average F2 Score of 99.81%.

Keywords: Cyber-Physical Systems · Cybersecurity · Intrusion Detection Systems · Anomaly Detection · OT Environment · SCADA Systems

1 Introduction

Operational Technology (OT) networks are vital components of critical infrastructure operations. However, many of these networks heavily rely on legacy hardware and proprietary communication protocols, which provide broad attack surfaces to malicious actors.

Introducing modern technology into these systems provides the benefit of constant monitoring and maintenance capabilities. However, traditional cybersecurity measures need improvement in combating cyber attacks on these networks for two primary reasons: The sophisticated and evolving nature of cyber attacks and the reliance on legacy hardware and proprietary communication protocols. Malicious actors can spy on, manipulate, or control machines in an OT network without proper security measures.

Recent research efforts have focused on implementing flexible tools to bolster the security posture of these networks. Anomalous Intrusion Detection Systems (IDSs) are one example of a model of normal network behavior that is

H. R. Arabnia et al. (Eds.): CSCE 2024, CCIS 2260, pp. 282–298, 2025.
https://doi.org/10.1007/978-3-031-85923-6_24

constructed and used to identify anomalous network traffic. Properly trained anomalous IDSs can detect a wide range of attacks (including zero-day or never-before-seen attacks) with minimal impact on network performance. Machine learning has become a promising solution for creating these normal models due to its capability of generalizing from a large amount of data. However, machine learning algorithms require extensive domain knowledge to transform raw network traffic into features processable by the models [1].

Transforming network traffic into quality features capable of fully defining network behavior requires detailed information about network specifications. Relying on domain-focused features (e.g., variables describing Modbus/TCP transaction statistics or MQTT communication flows) reduces the tool's generalizability and restricts it to one domain. Due to the prevalent usage and creation of different proprietary protocols in OT networks, it is infeasible to design an anomaly-based IDS that caters to each protocol.

This work proposes an application-agnostic IDS to model/profile normal network behavior using a set of heuristic rules and raw byte analysis. Specifically, our byte analysis includes creating a set of byte histograms that record the observed frequency of byte data and can be used to determine anomalous byte information in incoming network traffic. Due to the precise nature of the proposed byte analysis, the IDS can generate highly detailed reports that contain specific information regarding which aspects of the packet triggered the alert. These detailed reports can significantly reduce the strain on security operators, improving overall security posture.

Developing new security systems for OT networks has proved challenging due to the cost of creating new OT environments for research and the critical nature of their operations. In the interest of publicly available data for research in ICS network security, [3] has generated 19 datasets (consisting of raw network traffic files)in a Supervisory Control And Data Acquisition (SCADA) sandbox. This work considers six of these datasets, aiming to expose the shortcomings of current anomaly-based detection methods and demonstrate how heuristics, byte histograms, and frequency of byte data can be used to provide a more accurate and precise way of detecting anomalies in OT environments.

In Sect. 2, we evaluate existing works that aim to build heuristic approaches to anomaly-based IDS. Sections 3 and 4 introduce the training profile and define the byte histogram. We discuss using the trained profile to detect anomalies in Sects. 5 and 6. Finally, in Sects. 7 and 8, we propose possible future work and offer our conclusions.

2   Related Work

This work proposes an explainable anomaly-based intrusion detection system designed to identify anomalous network packet behavior using a byte histogram. Performing a context-free analysis of the byte values results in a general IDS that can be adopted into multiple environments regardless of network specifications or protocols. Several other works have approached constructing statistics-based normal network behavioral profiles. However, existing works are often applied at the application level, restricting the adaptability of the resulting detection system. Additionally, previous byte-based approaches fail to take advantage of the context-free analysis of byte-level intrusion detection.

In their work, Sekar et al. take a specification-based anomalous IDS augmented with statistical information regarding the network [4]. Specifically, the work constructs a series of specifications, or rules, using extended finite state automata based on network traces to define normal network behavior. Additionally, machine learning is used to capture the statistical properties of the network traces and detect anomalous behavior within them. While effective, this method is highly dependent on the state specifications, which are based on network protocols, which can limit the system's use cases.

Krügel et al. developed a service-specific anomaly detection system based on application knowledge to detect malicious payloads [2]. In addition to service-specific information, the detection system attempts to model normal payload distributions by recording the frequencies of the observed ASCII characters. Statistical tests then calculate the likelihood that a particular payload is derived from the modeled "normal" payload. While practical, this approach focuses on ASCII characters in the payload, limiting the statistical model's scope.

In [6], the authors develop a low-cost approach to detecting anomalous network traffic events. The approach focuses on collecting packet header information and statistical methods such as cluster analysis and PCA to model normal network behavior and identify anomalies. Focusing on only header information is computationally efficient but can result in a shallow model.

In their work, Valdes and Cheung proposed an anomaly detection technique to statistically learn standard communication patterns to identify anomalous network traffic instances [7]. Specifically, they take advantage of the request/reply scheme found in most process control systems (their work focuses on the Modbus/TCP protocol) and attempt to model communication flows between devices on the network. The proposed approach is computationally efficient and effective, but it does not attempt to model the payload of network packets, which can lead to inaccuracy in detecting discrete attacks.

Smolarczyk et al. propose a deterministic finite automaton-based approach that detects anomalies in Modbus TCP networks [5]. The proposed approach leverages the repetitive nature of OT communication protocols to construct cycles that describe the network's traffic flow. Anomaly detection is performed in real-time on the created cycles and can be extended into the time domain to detect irregular message intervals. However, this approach is highly domain-specific and requires extensive domain knowledge to adapt to a new environment.

3   Normal Network Traffic Profile

This section introduces the training, or "normal", profile and its creation. Table 1 lists symbols and abbreviations used throughout this paper and their descriptions. A normal network traffic profile consists of a structured set of histograms and heuristic rules. Byte histograms are built over a set of packets X. A byte histogram is a collection of dictionaries D_i where i is the byte index; for example, the third byte in a packet is represented by D_3. The *key set* for dictionary D_i is the set of all values observed in X at byte position i. In other words, if $D_i[j] = k$, we have observed the byte value j in byte position i a total of k times. The process for creating and updating the byte histograms is shown in Algorithm 1.

Table 1. Frequently Used Symbols and their Descriptions

Symbol	Description
X	Set of all packets
C	Set of all Clients in Training Data
S	Set of all Servers in Training Data
P_s	Set of all open Ports in Training Data
i	Byte index
j	Numerical value of the byte
k	Number of times j has been seen at i
p	An arbitrary packet $\in X$
c_x	An arbitrary client $\in C$
s_x	An arbitrary server $\in S$
pt_x	An arbitrary open port $\in P_s$
eth_src	Source MAC Address
eth_dst	Destination MAC Address
eth_type	Ethertype
ip_src	Source IP Address
ip_dst	Destination IP Address
$ip\_protocol$	IP Protocol
src_port	Source Port of a TCP packet
dst_port	Destination Port of a TCP packet
th	Threshold: maximum size of a dictionary

While the number and hierarchy of histograms and heuristic rules could be arbitrary, this work considers seven types of histograms and three types of heuristic rules.

The following histogram hierarchy is defined:

1. **Global:** one histogram over the entire set of packets used to describe and generate "normal" traffic,
2. **Ethernet source:** one histogram for each eth_src,
3. **Ethernet source-destination:** one histogram for each (eth_src, eth_dst) tuple,
4. **Ethernet source-destination-type:** one histogram for each $(eth\_src, eth\_dst, eth\_type)$ tuple,
5. **IP source:** one histogram for each ip_src. Note that the IP address could be version 4 or version 6,

6. **IP source-destination:** one histogram for each (*ip_src*, *ip_dst*) tuple,
7. **IP source-destination-protocol:** one histogram for each (*ip_src*, *ip_dst*, *ip_protocol*) tuple.

Histogram types 5–7 only apply to IP packets. Furthermore, the histogram hierarchy closely and intentionally follows the TCP/IP layers.

Three heuristic rules are used and supported by three tables:

1. **IP→MAC:** a table of mappings from IP addresses to ethernet addresses (similar to an ARP table). They are used to check that IP hosts are using valid MAC addresses.
2. **Server→Port→Client:** a table of TCP *clients* that have communicated to *server* on open *port*. Used to check TCP communications.
3. **(ip_src, src_port)→(ip_dst, dst_port):** a table of UDP hosts that have communicated on the indicated ports, i.e., host *A* has used the source port to communicate with host *B* on the destination port, used to check UDP communications.

As defined, heuristic rules only apply to IP packets.

3.1 Constructing the Normal Profile

The normal network traffic profile is constructed by inspecting each packet and then extracting (i) packet contents (as a byte array) to update histograms and (ii) packet header info needed for each type of histogram and heuristic rule. Histograms, for a given set of packets X, are updated using Algorithm 1.

For each $p \in X$, one histogram will be updated (or created, if necessary) for each type of histogram. If p happens to be an IP packet, then seven histograms would be involved. However, if p is not an IP packet, only the first four histogram types would take part in the update process. For example, if p has *eth_src* and *eth_dst* A and B, the Ethernet source-destination histogram associated with a tuple (*A,B*) would be updated (or created if this is the first packet we see from A to B). In other words, one histogram from each applicable type is updated or created.

The next step involves using packet header data to update the tables and evaluate the heuristic rules. The first table stores valid IP to ethernet address mappings for all IP packets in normal network traffic.

Building the **Server→Port→Client** table relies on identifying $SYN+ACK$ TCP packets. For a given $SYN+ACK$ packet, the source IP address identifies the server, the source port identifies the server's port to listen for incoming connection requests, and the destination IP is recognized as the client. The port used by the client on an inbound connection to the server is assumed to be an ephemeral port and is not stored or considered.

Finally, for the third table **(Src IP, Src Port)→(Dst IP, Dst Port)**, information associated with UDP traffic is stored. The approach assumes hosts communicating over UDP will use a predefined set of ports under normal circumstances. Figure 1 shows the general process for constructing the profile.

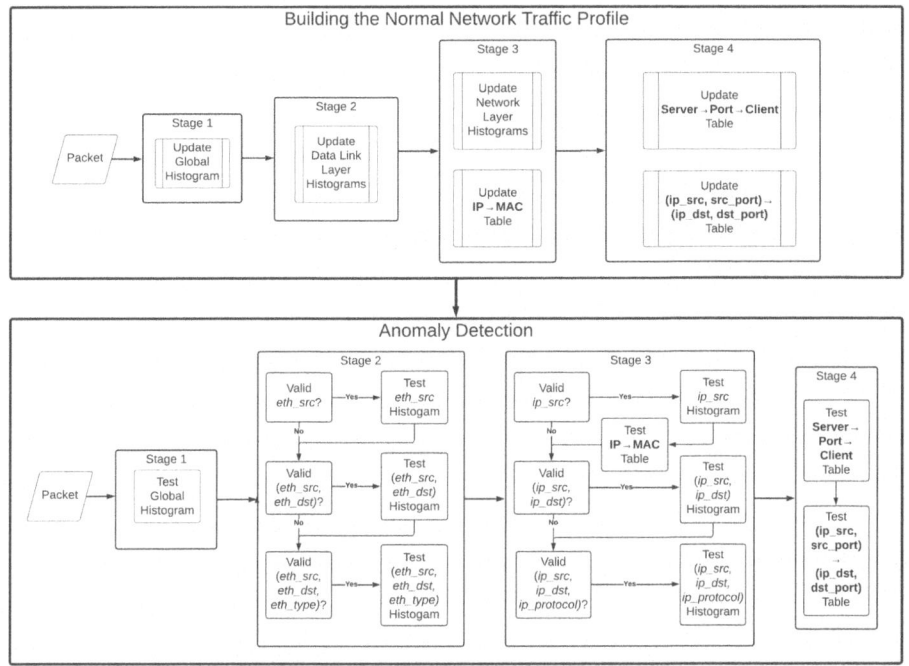

Fig. 1. Two-Stage IDS Algorithm Overview

4   Byte Histograms

The use of histograms is key for the framework. Packets are, in many instances, tested against histograms to evaluate or detect anomalies. The following subsections describe a technique for reducing the number of dictionaries used and how histogram testing is conducted.

4.1   Histogram Reduction

It is possible to decrease histogram evaluation time by reducing the number of dictionaries in a histogram as prescribed by some predefined rationale. One possible histogram reduction technique analyzes the variance of the recorded byte values and removes byte positions with high variance in their corresponding recorded values. This technique reduces the algorithm's overall spatial complexity and removes byte positions irrelevant to identifying anomalous network behavior.

For instance, a D_i for which $size(D_i) = 256$ is irrelevant as it contains all possible byte values and therefore does not provide a meaningful test. This can be done by setting a threshold, (th), for the maximum size of a particular dictionary. Any dictionaries that exceed this size threshold are removed from the corresponding histogram. For example, if we set $th = 7$ for the maximum number

---

Algorithm 1. Histogram Update Process

Require: *Packet, Byte_Histogram*
1: $i \leftarrow$ *Packet Byte Index*
2: $j \leftarrow$ *Byte Value*
3: **while** *Packet* has next i **do**
4:     **if** i in *Byte_Histogram* **then**
5:         **if** j in *Byte_Histogram*$[i]$ **then**
6:             *Byte_Histogram*$[i][j] \leftarrow Count + 1$
7:         **else**
8:             *Byte_Histogram*$[i]$ append $\{j : Count = 1\}$
9:         **end if**
10:     **else**
11:         *Byte_Histogram*$[i] \leftarrow \{j : Count = 1\}$
12:     **end if**
13: **end while**

---

of distinct values in the same *run1_6rtu.pcap* file, the number of dictionaries is reduced to 15 for the global histogram. In this case, the remaining dictionaries are 0–2, 6–8, 12–16, 20–23, 30, and 46 (Fig. 2).

In our research with the *run1_6rtu.pcap* data set, important positions tend to have four to twenty different byte values, whereas procedurally generated fields (i.e., TCP sequence numbers and checksums) are flooded with anywhere from 20 to 255. Due to the nature of machines in an OT network, the variability of payloads and protocols should be low. Thus, this work considers $th = 20$ byte values, eliminating byte positions with more than twenty observed values. This value was attained by analyzing dictionary lengths for procedurally generated byte positions. Some fields, such as the transaction ID field in MODBUS packets, contained values different from the training data, even for entirely normal packets. Therefore, we additionally applied a post-processing mask technique. This process involves evaluating the anomaly report after all testing has concluded, if the number of anomalies is contained to one byte position and that position is 54, then we ignore the report and allow the packet through. In practice, on-site operators could view and evaluate the anomaly reports for actual abnormality.

4.2   Histogram Testing

Histograms generated when building the normal profile contain summary information related to byte values for every packet in a set. A packet containing n bytes is an array of bytes $B[i]$ where $0 \leq i \leq n - 1$. A packet passes the *histogram test* if every byte value $B[i] = j$ in the packet passes the *dictionary test* for every D_i in the histogram. A packet passes the *dictionary test* associated with D_i if and only if j is in D_i's key set. For example, consider the dictionary $D_0 = \{0 \rightarrow 13444, 1 \rightarrow 2, 51 \rightarrow 57, 255 \rightarrow 187\}$ showing how many times a byte value has been observed at index 0 in a set of packets. An incoming packet with value 255 at byte position 0 will pass the "dictionary test" for D_0, i.e. 255 is a key in D_0, while a packet with value 32 at byte index 0 will not, i.e., 32 is not a key in D_0. This particular example for D_0 corresponds to the file *run1_6rtu.pcap* containing 134,690 packets in the Fernandez data set [3] (Fig. 2).

A histogram for a network with an MTU=N will have a maximum of around N dictionaries D_i where $0 \leq i \leq N$ and $size(D_i) \leq 256$ (since each byte value is in the range 0–255). For an Ethernet network, N is expected to be 1514 since an Ethernet header is 14 bytes long and the maximum payload is 1500 bytes (unless jumbo packets are used). This is precisely the number of dictionaries produced for the same file when generating a histogram for the set of all packets.

i	Dictionary
0	0→134444, 1→2, 51→57, 255→187
1	0→2, 12→133113, 51→57, 80→1331, 255→187
2	0→57, 41→133113, 86→1331, 94→2, 255→187
6	0→134690
7	12→130589, 80→4101
8	41→130589 ,86→4101
12	8→134633, 134→57
13	0→134338, 6→295, 221→57
14	0→295, 69→134338, 96→57
15	0→134176, 1→295, 16→4, 192→215
16	0→128390, 1→1744, 2→254, 3→12, 4→1145, 5→2850, 8→295
20	0→4365, 17→57, 64→130268
21	0→134338, 1→214, 2→138
22	0→295, 1→1, 16→4, 64→8471, 128→125861, 254→57, 255→1
23	6→133853, 12→231, 17→485, 80→64, 128→57

Fig. 2. Global histogram using dictionaries with a size threshold of 7 for file *run1_6rtu.pcap* (134,690 packets)

5   Anomaly Detection

Detecting anomalous network packets relies on the histograms and tables generated from normal traffic, as described in the previous sections. Similar to the hierarchy of histograms, testing incoming network traffic follows the TCP/IP model and is organized into four stages. Specifically, when a new packet is received, it is tested against the first stage (physical layer) and then against the second stage (data link layer). The packet is then tested against the third and fourth layers, corresponding to the internet and transport layers. Each stage comprises a set of histograms or heuristic rules the packet must adhere to. If a packet successfully passes all stages, it is considered normal.

Information extracted from the packet header determines which stages the packet needs to be tested against. The approach is agnostic regarding the application layer; i.e., no histogram is generated based on packet headers beyond the transport layer. Currently, the approach relies only on histograms to identify anomalies beyond the transport layer, i.e., for application layer protocols that are unknown or not presently considered.

Since packets are evaluated on a layered basis, if one packet is classified as abnormal at one point, it will also fail all subsequent tests. For example, a packet that fails the "ethernet source-destination" test, i.e., the ethernet source host was never observed communicating with the destination ethernet host, will also fail the "ethernet source-destination-type" test. This makes the approach amenable to "short circuit evaluation", which minimizes the time needed to classify the packet. Alternatively, strict rule evaluation across the histogram hierarchy may also be used to obtain a more detailed report explaining the resulting classification. This work considers the strict evaluation approach, which provides the most information and reduces the overall strain on security analysts.

5.1   Stage 1: Physical Layer

The first test in the evaluation chain involves the singular global histogram. This histogram is evaluated over all the normal packets without any assumptions being made about packet structure. This test is related to the physical layer since it only involves transmitted raw bytes. For example, Fig. 2 shows the dictionaries (with a maximum size of 10) that make up a reduced global histogram for file *run1_6rtu.pcap*. This file contains a total of 134,690 packets.

Test 1. *Evaluate packet against global histogram. Test passes if the packet passes the histogram test.*

5.2   Stage 2: Data Link Layer

The second stage includes three Ethernet-based histogram collections: source, source-destination, and source-destination-type. The source collection contains one histogram for each ethernet source address observed in normal traffic. Each one of these histograms is constructed using only ethernet packets from the associated source address.

Similarly, the source-destination collection contains one histogram for each ethernet source-destination tuple. For instance, the histogram for source-destination tuple (A, B) comprises all ethernet packets sent from host A to host B. It is important to note that the histogram for the source-destination tuple (A, B) differs from that for the tuple (B, A).

Finally, the source-destination-type collection contains one histogram for each ethernet source-destination-type triple. Specifically, given some source-destination tuple (A, B), we construct a separate histogram for each ether type of packet sent from A to B. For example, consider A and B communicating IPv4 (ethertype texttt 0x0800) and IPv6 (ethertype texttt 0x86DD). By constructing histograms that consider the ether type, it is possible to construct separate histograms for each ether type protocol they use.

Six tests are defined for Stage 2. An implicit pre-condition for histogram tests is that the associated histogram must exist.

Test 2. *Ethernet source. Test passes if the source address has a corresponding source histogram.*

Test 3. *Ethernet source histogram. Test passes if a packet from the ethernet source passes the histogram test.*

Test 4. *Ethernet source–destination. Test passes if the source-destination tuple has a corresponding source-destination histogram.*

Test 5. *Ethernet source–destination histogram. Test passes if a packet from the ethernet source to the ethernet destination passes the histogram test.*

Test 6. *Ethernet source–destination–type. Test passes if source–destination–type triple has a corresponding source–destination–type histogram.*

Test 7. *Ethernet source–destination–type histogram. Test passes if the packet from the ethernet source to the ethernet destination using the ether type passes the histogram test.*

For example, for the *run1_6rtu.pcap* file:

- The source collection contains 13 histograms. The histogram for host `00:0C:29:EE:B7:84` was computed over 35,329 packets.
- The source-destination collection contains 46 histograms. The histogram for packets sent from `00:0C:29:EE:B7:84` to `00:0C:29:DC:42:E5` was computed over 5,410 packets while the histogram from `00:0C:29:DC:42:E5` to `00:0C:29:EE:B7:84` was computed over 4,333 packets.
- The source-destination-type collection contains 67 histograms. The histogram for packets sent from `00:0C:29:EE:B7:84` to `00:0C:29:DC:42:E5` for ether type 0x0800 (IPv4) was computed over 5,410 packets while the histogram from `00:0C:29:EE:B7:84` to `FF:FF:FF:FF:FF:FF` for ether type 0x0806 (ARP) was computed over 41 packets.

5.3   Stage 3: Network Layer

Network layer tests focus on IP packets (version 4 or 6). Similar to the strategy followed before, the histogram hierarchy has a similar structure to the one used in Stage 2: a source collection, a source-destination collection, and a source-destination-protocol collection. The source collection is a set of histograms for each unique IP host in the observed network packets. The source-destination collection contains histograms constructed for each unique (ip_src, ip_dst) tuple or unidirectional flow. Finally, the source-destination-protocol collection contains one histogram for each unique application-level protocol for each (ip_src, ip_dst) flow.

Seven tests are defined for Stage 3. The following pre-condition applies to these seven tests: packet has ether type 0x0800 (IPv4) or 0x86DD (IPv6). As in Stage 2 testing, there is an implicit pre-condition for histogram tests that the associated histogram must exist.

Test 8. $IP \rightarrow MAC$: *Test passes if source IP maps to hardware address in the table.*

Test 9. *IP source: The test passes if the packet from the IP source address has a corresponding histogram.*

Test 10. *IP source histogram: The test passes if the packet from the IP source passes the histogram test.*

Test 11. *IP source-destination: The test passes if the packet (ip_src, ip_dst) tuple has a corresponding histogram.*

Test 12. *IP source-destination histogram: The test passes if the packet for the (ip_src, ip_dst) tuple passes the histogram test.*

Test 13. *IP source-destination-protocol: Test passes if the packet for the (ip_src, ip_dst, ip_protocol) triple has an existing histogram.*

Test 14. *IP source-destination-protocol histogram: Test passes if the packet for the (ip_src, ip_dst, ip_protocol) triple passes the histogram test.*

Using the same *run1_6rtu.pcap* file we observed:

- the IP→MAC table has 23 entries (with the exception of one IPv6 entry, all others are IPv4 addresses). IPv4 address 192.168.1.100 maps to ethernet address 00:0C:29:EE:B7:84
- The IP source collection, as expected, contains 23 histograms. The histogram for packets sent from IPv4 address 192.168.1.100 was computed over 35,287 packets.
- The IP source-destination collection contains 58 histograms. The histogram for packets sent from IPv4 address 192.168.1.100 to IPv4 address 192.168.1.103 was computed over 5,410 packets while the histogram for IPv4 packets sent from 192.168.1.103 to IPv4 address 192.168.1.100 was computed over 4,328 packets.
- The IP source-destination-protocol collection contains 61 histograms. The histogram for packets sent from IPv4 address 192.168.1.100 to IPv4 address 192.168.1.103 using protocol 6 (TCP) was computed over 5,410 packets (all the IPv4 packets exchanged between these two hosts were TCP packets).

5.4   Stage 4: Transport Layer

The final stage focuses on the two primary transport-level protocols used with IP: TCP and UDP. The first rule applies to the connection-oriented TCP protocol. More specifically, the rule seeks to validate server-client communication behavior. The three parameters used to evaluate server-client communications are the server's IP address, ports the server has open for inbound connections, and the IP address of clients with established connections to the open ports. The port used by the TCP client is assumed to be ephemeral and is not considered, i.e., this is a field in the packet that could have any value and still be regarded as a normal packet.

The three relevant parameters are collected from $SYN + ACK$ packets: the server's IP address is the source address, the server's open port is the source port, and the client's IP address is the destination address. This information is stored in a corresponding data structure. The following two tests can be conducted using the $Server \rightarrow Port \rightarrow Client$ data structure.

Test 15. Any TCP packet *Extract source address ip_src, source port src_port, destination address ip_dst, and destination port dst_port. The test has four possible outcomes:*

1. *If: ip_src $\notin S \cap$ ip_dst $\notin S$, the test fails, i.e., neither host is a recorded server. Otherwise, identify potential s_x, pt_x and c_x. Note that there could be two of each, one for each IP address involved.*
2. *Else If: $pt_x \notin P_s$, the test fails, i.e., s_x is a server but pt_x is not a recorded open port.*
3. *Else If: $c_x \notin C$, the test fails, i.e., s_x is a server with open port pt_x but c_x is not a recorded client.*
4. *Else: the test passes, i.e., this packet is related to a s_x that has been observed communicating with c_x on this server pt_x.*

Test 16. Connection Establishment *For any SYN–only packet, the source address is designated as c, the destination address is defined as s, and the destination port is designated as p. For any $SYN + ACK$ packet, the source address is designated as s, the destination address is designated as c, and the source port is designated as pt.*

1. *If: $s_x \notin S$, the test fails, i.e., c_x is attempting to establish a connection to host s_x which is not a recorded server.*
2. *Else If: $pt_x \notin P_s$, test fails, i.e., s_x is a server but pt_x is not a recorded open port.*
3. *Else If: $c_x \notin C$, test fails, i.e., s_x is a server with open port pt_x but c_x is not a recorded client.*
4. *Else: test passes, i.e., this packet is related to a s_x that has been observed accepting inbound connections from c_x on port pt_x.*

For the *run1_6rtu.pcap* file:

– a total of 12 servers were identified
– host 192.168.1.102 was found to have ports 502 and 139 open for inbound connections. Furthermore, 1078 connections were established from 192.168.1.99 on port 502, 1078 connections from 192.168.100 on port 502 and 10 connections from 192.168.1.100 on port 139

The second rule applies to the UDP protocol. Unlike TCP, UDP is a connection-less protocol, meaning it does not support the concept of an established connection. If IP two hosts are going to communicate over UDP, the port numbers used are not likely to be ephemeral. For that reason, four parameters are used to evaluate UDP communications between two hosts: the IP address of the sender, the source port, the IP address of the destination, and the destination port. These numbers are also stored in an appropriate data structure.

One simple test is conducted on UDP traffic using the **(Src IP, Src Port)→(Dst IP, Dst Port)** data structure.

Test 17. *For all UDP traffic, the test passes if the source address, source port, destination address, and destination port are an entry in the data structure.*

For the *run1_6rtu.pcap* file:

- A total of 37 UDP flows were identified, i.e., the set of unique (Src IP, Src Port)→(Dst IP, Dst Port) values; for example:
- host `192.168.37.129` sent a packet from port `123` to host `91.189.94.4` on port `123` a total of 42 times

6   Experimental Results

The proposed approach using heuristic rules and histograms to detect abnormal traffic was tested against the Lemay-Fernandez dataset [3]. The dataset provides several files with normal traffic and attacks. The approach was tested using one file for normal traffic and five attacks (Table 3). Attack files in the dataset are accompanied by spreadsheets that label each packet in the attack files as normal or abnormal.

The following three standard metrics evaluate results: precision, recall, and F-Beta score (Table 2). In industrial control systems security, misclassifying an anomalous packet (false negatives) can have a much more significant impact than a false alarm (false positives). Therefore, we use a beta value of two to emphasize recall.

Table 2. Testing Results

File	Precision	Recall	F-Beta Score ($\beta = 2$)
characterization	99.64%	100%	99.93%
CnC_uploading_exe	100%	99.17%	99.34%
exploit_ms08_netapi	99.50%	100%	99.90%
moving_two_files	100%	100%	100%
send_a_fake_command	18.87%	100%	53.76%
Total	**99.11%**	**99.99%**	**99.81%**

Precision measures the proportion of correctly identified anomalies among all instances classified as anomalies. A precision of 99.11% indicates that the algorithm has a low false positive rate, meaning it accurately identifies anomalies without misclassifying normal instances as anomalies. In practical terms, this suggests that when the algorithm flags an event as anomalous, it is highly likely to be a genuine anomaly, reducing unnecessary alerts and improving the efficiency of response measures.

Recall measures the proportion of actual anomalies that the algorithm correctly identifies. A recall of 99.99% indicates that the algorithm captures almost all anomalies in the data, minimizing the risk of false negatives where actual anomalies are missed. High recall ensures comprehensive coverage of anomalous events in OT environments, reducing the likelihood of undetected security breaches or operational failures.

The F-beta score is a harmonic mean of precision and recall, weighted by the parameter beta. An F-beta score of 99.81% indicates a balance between precision and recall, emphasizing the importance of recall in this context. In anomaly detection, where identifying all anomalies is crucial, a high F-beta score reflects both the low false positive rate and high anomaly detection rate, demonstrating the algorithm's effectiveness in accurately identifying anomalies while minimizing false alarms.

Table 3. Modbus/TCP Datasets

PCAP File	Total Packets	Attack Packets	Description
run1_6rtu	134690	0	Strictly normal traffic used for training
characterization	12296	6719	Compromised RTU sends read commands to enumerate registers on other RTUs
CnC_uploading_exe	1426	121	Compromised RTU Uploads an executable file to another RTU
exploit_ms08_netapi	1857	1199	exploit_ms08_netapi used to compromise a PLC
moving_two_files	3319	75	Compromised RTU uploads files to two other RTUs on the network
send_a_fake_command	11167	10	Compromised RTU sends a forged Modbus TCP write command to RTU

6.1   Mislabeled Packets

Our analysis identified 73 mislabeled packets. We define mislabeled packets as those with a "normal" label but whose contents are anomalous. Specifically, an anomaly is any concept that was not represented in the original training data. Thus, mislabeled packets signify that the training data fails to characterize normal network behavior fully.

The misclassification of one such packet indicates a need to redefine the training data rather than the detection algorithm.

Our analysis indicates that these mislabeled packets were overlooked, as identical packets were found in other attack datasets and correctly labeled anomalous. Another consideration is that some packets are residuals of the injected attacks, so the packets should still be labeled anomalous.

6.2   Characterization

The proposed approach achieved excellent performance on this attack, achieving an F-Beta score of 99.93% Our dataset analysis indicates that the precision score loss is due to mislabeled packets. Specifically, packets 1–2 display an abnormal ARP request where host A attempts to discover the hardware address of host B. This sequence of packets aligns with our definition of anomalous and should have been labeled as such. Further analysis indicates that packet 1739 was also mislabeled due to the 263 anomalies. A long sequence of packets 10078–10095 was also mislabeled due to the frequency of byte value anomalies and the absence of such sequence in the training data. Further, we cross-referenced some packets in this sequence, such as LANMAN packets 10090 and 10091, and found them identical to correctly labeled packets 825 and 826 in CnC_uploading_exe.

6.3   CnC_uploading_exe

The proposed approach performed nearly perfectly for this attack, producing an F-beta score of 99.34%. This dataset proved to be an outlier, as it was the only dataset to produce a recall score of less than 100%. Our result was due to a packet labeled as anomalous but containing completely normal information. Further analysis indicates this packet was labeled anomalous as a residual of the injected attack since the packet lies in a long sequence of correctly labeled anomalous packets, starting from packet 208 and ending with 1090. Due to the consequences of an attack on OT networks, it would be preferred to label this packet anomalous like other residual packets.

6.4   exploit_ms08_netapi

The proposed approach was largely successful for this attack, achieving an F-Beta score of 99.90%. Our IDS flagged abnormal ARP requests found in 2–4, 550, 1038, and 1427 as false alarms during this attack, causing a loss in precision. An abnormal ARP request is defined as host A attempting to discover the hardware address of host B when this behavior was not observed in the training set. With this in mind, we believe the original researchers also overlooked these packets. Additionally, since the ARP requests are anomalous, it should follow that we flag the response as well.

6.5   moving_two_files

The proposed approach could correctly identify all packets related to this transfer attack. Additionally, no false alarms were generated, resulting in a perfect F-Beta score of 100%.

6.6   send_a_fake_command

The *send_a_fake_command* (SFC) dataset produced an abnormal number of false alarms compared to the other data sets, achieving an F-Beta score of only 53.76%. The sequence of packets 1817–1848 specifically showed frequent anomalies during histogram testing, such as packet 1839, which contained over 335 anomalies. Due to the number of anomalies, further analysis was conducted to determine whether our IDS was error-prone or if the mislabeled packets should have been labeled anomalous. Coincidentally, the *moving_two_files_modbus_6RTU* dataset contains an almost identical sequence of packets from 331 to 362, but this sequence is correctly marked anomalous. Furthermore, the remaining mislabeled packets from SFC were cross-referenced with other datasets where identical packets were correctly labeled anomalous. Considering these facts and the abnormal number of anomalies produced by these packets, the Fernandez-Lemay researchers likely overlooked certain exchanges between machines that should have been labeled anomalous.

7   Future Work

Future research involves developing heuristic rules based on FIN packets to bolster intrusion detection capabilities. Specifically, establishing criteria for identifying anomalous behavior in TCP connections, such as the timing and sequence of FIN and ACK packets, could contribute to more robust detection mechanisms. However, potential challenges must be acknowledged, including the adaptability of these rules across diverse network environments and the scalability of the approach in handling large-scale data.

Additionally, real-time anomaly detection using metrics such as packet lengths and inter-packet timings could improve the effectiveness of the proposed approach. By continuously monitoring network traffic and comparing observed patterns against expected norms, anomalies indicative of potential intrusions can be promptly identified.

8   Conclusion

Network security has been challenging in OT environments due to reliance on legacy hardware and proprietary communication protocols. This paper presents a two-part method for detecting anomalies in network traffic. First, we demonstrate how to create a testing profile from normal network traffic and then describe the testing process.

Heuristics and byte histograms have proven highly effective in creating an intrusion detection system for OT Environments. Our approach is applicable across all OT environments because it does not utilize information about proprietary protocols. Our IDS also provides detailed information regarding the part or parts of a packet that make it anomalous. The SFC dataset proved to be an outlier; however, we believe that our IDS flagged false alarms were anomalous packets that were overlooked during the dataset's creation.

Acknowledgement. This material is based upon work supported by the ERDC under Contract No. W912HZ23C0011.

References

1. Howe, A., Papa, M.: Feature engineering in machine learning-based intrusion detection systems for OT networks. In: 2023 IEEE International Conference on Smart Computing (SMARTCOMP), pp. 361–366. IEEE (2023)
2. Krügel, C., Toth, T., Kirda, E.: Service specific anomaly detection for network intrusion detection. In: Proceedings of the 2002 ACM Symposium on Applied Computing, pp. 201–208 (2002)
3. Lemay, A., Fernandez, J.M.: Providing SCADA network data sets for intrusion detection research. In: 9th Workshop on Cyber Security Experimentation and Test (CSET 16) (2016)
4. Sekar, R., et al.: Specification-based anomaly detection: a new approach for detecting network intrusions. In: Proceedings of the 9th ACM Conference on Computer and Communications Security, pp. 265–274 (2002)
5. Smolarczyk, M., Plamowski, S., Pawluk, J., Szczypiorski, K.: Anomaly detection in cyclic communication in OT protocols. Energies **15**(4), 1517 (2022)
6. Taylor, C., Alves-Foss, J.: NATE: network analysis of a nomalous traffic events, a low-cost approach. In: Proceedings of the 2001 Workshop on New Security Paradigms, pp. 89–96 (2001)
7. Valdes, A., Cheung, S.: Communication pattern anomaly detection in process control systems. In: 2009 IEEE Conference on Technologies for Homeland Security, pp. 22–29 (2009)

Reliable I/F Circuit for Embedded Self-Timed Data-Driven Processors

Riku Uemoto[1] and Makoto Iwata[2(✉)]

[1] Graduate School of Engineering, Kochi University of Technology,
Kami, Kochi 782-8502, Japan
275097y@gs.kochi-tech.ac.jp
[2] School of Informatics, Kochi University of Technology,
Kami, Kochi 782–8502, Japan
iwata.makoto@kochi-tech.ac.jp

Abstract. A self-timed data-driven processor (DDP) is one of the promising embedded processor architectures realizing high-performance and low-power operations. The DDP is implemented by a self-timed pipeline (STP) circuit, i.e., asynchronous circuits. In order to realize a practical embedded system employing the DDP, the DDP could play a powerful accelerator with a commodity application processor. In such a case, an I/F circuit with buffers is required to synchronize operation timing, convert data transfer control protocols, and perform data input/output according to the DDP's pipeline processing capability. This paper proposes a reliable I/F circuit using asynchronous FIFOs that guarantee a required MTBF with minimized synchronization circuits. The prototype circuit operating at 50 MHz clock frequency is implemented and evaluated on an FPGA chip. Results demonstrate that it achieves over 3.8 times higher input/output throughput while maintaining comparable reliability to a synchronous FIFO-based I/F circuit. Furthermore, it has been shown that the proposed I/F circuit outperforms the synchronous FIFO-based I/F circuit in terms of throughput per resource.

Keywords: I/F circuit · reliability · asynchronous FIFO · data-driven processor · self-timed pipeline

1 Introduction

With the widespread adoption of modern embedded devices, such as those in the Internet of Things (IoT), there is an increasing demand for greater flexibility, enhanced performance, and reduced power consumption. These devices often need to gather data from multiple sensors, analyze the data to control actuators, and communicate with other edge devices and cloud servers, requiring them to efficiently handle multiplexed processing of diverse data types.

A self-timed data-driven processor (DDP), such as the DDMP [1], is a promising architecture due to its parallel processing capabilities. The DDP can achieve

© The Author(s), under exclusive license to Springer Nature Switzerland AG 2025
H. R. Arabnia et al. (Eds.): CSCE 2024, CCIS 2260, pp. 299–312, 2025.
https://doi.org/10.1007/978-3-031-85923-6_25

low-power operation because it operates only when data arrives, as it is implemented using a self-timed pipeline (STP), a type of asynchronous circuit. In our research project, we aim to realize the DDP on a field-programmable gate array (FPGA) chip, allowing for more flexible functionality in various embedded applications.

When using the DDP as an accelerator in coordination with a commodity application processor (AP), it is essential to interface between self-timed asynchronous circuits and clocked synchronous circuits. This requires an interface (I/F) circuit with buffers to synchronize operation timing, convert data transfer control protocols, and manage data input/output according to the DDP's processing. In asynchronous-synchronous interface circuits, timing violations related to the setup/hold time constraints can occur in the timing paths to the D flip-flop (DFF) within the synchronous circuit. This can lead to metastability events that impair reliability, as the synchronous circuit relies on a clock signal, whereas the DDP operates using a 4-phase self-timed handshake protocol without a global clock. Due to the producer-consumer problem and potential mismatches between the data transfer rate of the application processor and the data processing rate of the DDP, a buffer for temporary data storage is necessary to manage these fluctuations. Therefore, the I/F circuit must be reliable in synchronizing operation timing, converting protocols, and buffering data.

Although interface circuits between synchronous and asynchronous circuits have been studied extensively—such as cascaded flip-flop synchronizers [2,3], asynchronous FIFOs [4], pausible clocks [5], and click-elements [6]—there has been no study addressing all of the requirements outlined above. To fill this gap, this paper proposes a self-timed DDP-oriented I/F circuit designed to synchronize operation timing, convert protocols, and buffer data for efficient input/output transfer between the self-timed DDP and the clock-synchronous application processor. We then discuss the implementation of the proposed I/F circuit on an FPGA chip to achieve more reliable and faster data transfer. Finally, the proposed I/F circuit, implemented on AMD's Zynq-7010 FPGA chip, is evaluated in terms of reliability, performance, and resource usage.

2   Functionality and Reliability

The 4-phase handshaking protocol of the STP circuit realizing the DDP is briefly introduced. Then, how to coordinate the clock-synchronous application processor with the self-timed DDP is discussed. Finally, reliable timing synchronization between their interface is detailed.

2.1   Self-Timed Pipeline

A basic structure of STP [1] realizing the DDP is shown in Fig. 1. The data transfer in each pipeline stage of the STP is controlled by a data transfer control circuit called a coincidence flip-flop (C-element), i.e., each pipeline register (data

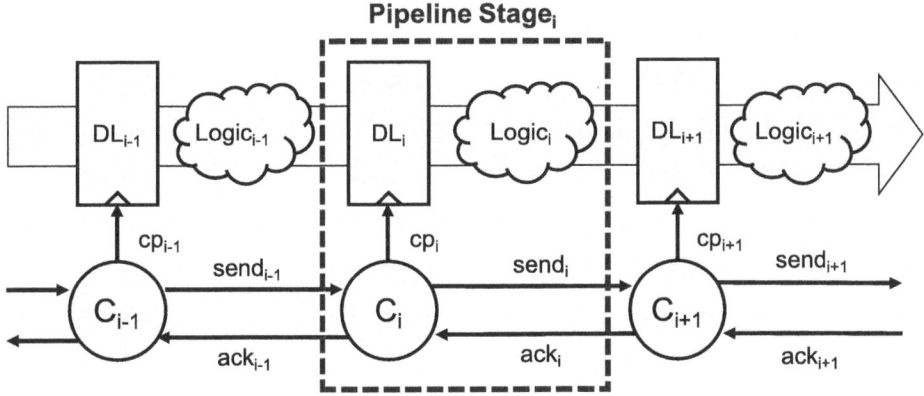

Fig. 1. Basic structure of STP.

latch) is opened through handshaking between adjacent C-elements based on the following 4-phase protocol.

Before data is transferred to the pipeline stage i, the data transfer request signal, $send_{i-1}$, falls, and the data transfer acknowledgment signal, ack_{i-1}, then falls at the C-element, C_i. After that, $send_{i-1}$ rises, and the data-latch open signal cp_i rises as a localized clock of the data latch, DL_i, i.e., the data is transferred from the stage i–1 to the stage i. At the same time, ack_{i-1} rises, allowing stage i to accept the next data again. While processing data at the stage logic $Logic_i$, $send_i$ falls, starting a handshake between C_i and C_{i+1}.

As long as the authors have surveyed, there has been no reliable asynchronous-synchronous interface circuit supporting the 4-phase handshaking protocol.

2.2   AP-DDP Coordinated System

The practical application of this research involves constructing an IoT system that coordinates an application processor (AP) with the DDP. This necessitates an interface with buffering capabilities to effectively manage the interaction between synchronous and asynchronous circuits.

As shown in Fig. 2, this IoT system assumes that sensor data acquisition, actuator operation, and communication with other IoT devices and cloud servers are performed on the clock-synchronous AP, and data processing is accelerated on the self-timed DDP.

To prevent data overflow, the average input/output rates between the synchronous circuit and the I/F circuit, as well as between the I/F circuit and the

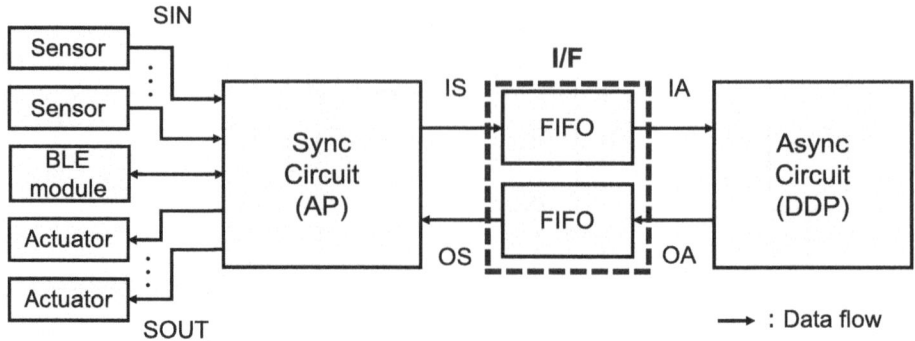

Fig. 2. A structure of AP-DDP coordinated system.

DDP, should be as equal as possible, $R_{IS} = R_{IA}$, and $R_{OS} = R_{OA}$, where R_{IS} and R_{OS} denote the average input/output rates between the synchronous circuit and the I/F circuit, respectively, as well as R_{IA} and R_{OA} denote the average input/output rates between the I/F circuit and the DDP, respectively.

It is necessary to consider that multiple data are processed together using direct memory access (DMA) or interrupt processing for data transfer between the synchronous circuit and the DDP. In such cases, the I/F circuit needs a buffer to temporarily store data since the input/output data rate fluctuates instantaneously. Thus, we cope with this issue by incorporating a FIFO inside the I/F circuit.

2.3   Timing Synchronization

The AP-DDP coordinated system involves nondeterministic signal timing between synchronous and asynchronous circuits. Generally, if an asynchronous control signal is input to the DFF of the synchronous circuit leading to circuit malfunction since the setup/hold time constraints violation may occur, resulting in a metastable state. Therefore, the I/F circuit in the system must also synchronize the asynchronous signals produced from the DDP and utilize them for the reliable operations of the synchronous circuit.

The cascaded flip-flop synchronizer [2,3] is a useful circuit for synchronizing asynchronous signals. This circuit suppresses the possibility of the final output signal being metastable by cascading n stages of DFFs, which is called n-flop synchronizer. The probability of circuit malfunction can be further reduced by increasing the number of DFF stages since the duration of the metastable state is determined probabilistically, and the longer the duration, the lower the probability of metastable states. However, since the delay time depends on the number of DFF stages, it is necessary to determine the number of DFF stages as needed to minimize the amount of delay while guaranteeing the reliability of the circuit.

The n-flop synchronizer can be embedded in other circuits, e.g., the asynchronous FIFO [4] and I/F circuit using click-element [6]. Since n might be

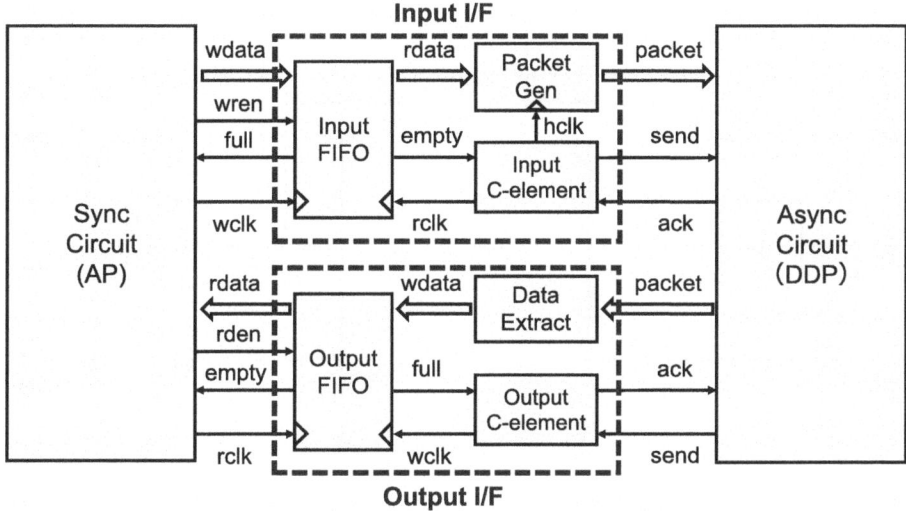

Fig. 3. Basic structure of DDP I/F circuit.

enough for two or three, the amount of circuits could be smaller than that of the pausible clock [5] pausing the clock without using the synchronizer. Therefore, we adopted the n-flop synchronizer for our AP-DDP coordinated system.

As for the buffering function discussed in the previous subsection, there are two types of FIFOs embedded in the proposed I/F circuit. One is a synchronous FIFO, in which data is read/written simultaneously. The other is an asynchronous FIFO, in which data is read/written at different times. The I/F circuit equipped with the synchronous FIFO requires synchronizing signals outside the FIFO, while that equipped with the asynchronous FIFO can deal with asynchronous signals because the signals are synchronized during the generation of empty/full flags inside the asynchronous FIFO. Therefore, the I/F circuit equipped with the asynchronous FIFO has no delay caused by the n-flop synchronizer when reading and writing data into the asynchronous FIFO. Both I/F circuits use the n-flop synchronizer, so the reliability of the circuits could be comparable, but the I/F circuit equipped with the asynchronous FIFO has a higher throughput, so it is adopted in this paper.

3   DDP I/F Circuit

Based on the discussion in the previous section, we propose a DDP I/F circuit shown in Fig. 3. The data input part (Input I/F) from the AP to the DDP consists of three modules: Input FIFO, Input C-element, and Packet Gen. The data output part (Output I/F) from the DDP to the AP consists of three modules: Output FIFO, Output C-element, and Data Extract. The Input FIFO and Output FIFO temporarily store input and output data and synchronize the operation timing between the clock-synchronous AP and the self-timed DDP. The

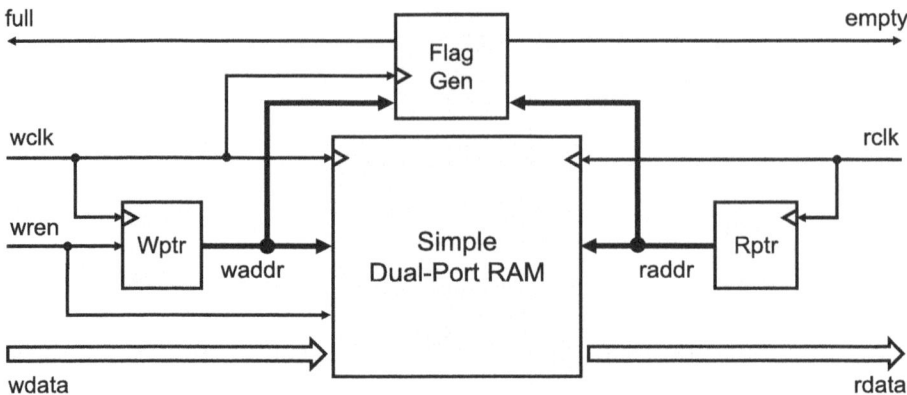

Fig. 4. Block diagram of Input FIFO.

Input C-element and Output C-element perform protocol conversion for data transfer between an asynchronous FIFO and the self-timed DDP. The Packet Gen module performs to generate a packet from data accessing an inside header memory. This is because the DDP requires input/output in the form of packets with the necessary header fields for data processing. The Data Extract module performs to extract data from the output packet from the DDP. In this section, we describe the details of Input FIFO, Output FIFO, Input C-element, and Output C-element. Furthermore, we discuss implementing the proposed I/F circuit on an FPGA chip for more reliable and faster data transfer.

3.1 Input FIFO and Output FIFO

As discussed in Sect. 2.2, the DDP-oriented I/F circuit is equipped with an asynchronous FIFO. Figure 4 shows a structure of Input FIFO which can synchronize timing while functioning as a buffer to store data. This asynchronous FIFO consists of a write address management module (Wptr), a read address management module (Rptr), a ready flags (full/empty) generation module (Flag Gen), and Simple Dual-Port RAM, just like a general one. In the Input FIFO, there is no read enable signal, and data is read at the rising timing of the read clock signal (rclk). In the Output FIFO, there is no write enable signal, and data is written at the rising timing of the write clock signal (wclk). The asynchronous FIFO generates the ready flag (full/empty) in the Flag Gen module by comparing the write address (waddr) with the read address (raddr). It is necessary to synchronize timing since waddr and raddr are operated at different timings. In particular, we use an n-flop synchronizer (Sync) for the Input FIFO as shown in Fig. 5, to synchronize the asynchronous signal raddr when generating the full flag. The Flag Gen module temporarily encodes raddr to a gray code before it is input to Sync. As a result, we can suppress the occurrence of metastable conditions since, at most, only one bit within the gray code could change at the synchronization timing.

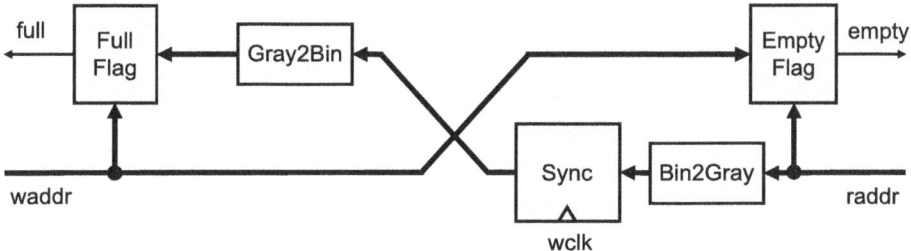

Fig. 5. Block diagram of Flag Gen in Input FIFO.

On the other hand, the Sync module and gray code converters (Bin2Gray and Gray2Bin) for synchronization of waddr is not needed in the Input FIFO since the waddr comes from the synchronous part and goes to the asynchronous part. However, since the empty flag is generated by comparing the multi-bit signals waddr and raddr, glitches can occur when their values change. Since the empty flag is set to 1 only when the values of waddr and raddr match, each address change during the empty state always results in a non-empty state. In other words, a glitch that becomes 0 when the value of the empty flag is 1 (empty $1 \rightarrow 0 \rightarrow 1$) does not occur, and only a glitch that becomes 1 when the value of the empty flag is 0 (empty $0 \rightarrow 1 \rightarrow 0$) can occur. Therefore, it is necessary to deal with this glitch in the Input C-element. As for the Output FIFO, we synchronize waddr using the Sync module when generating the empty flag. It is also necessary to deal with the glitch (full $0 \rightarrow 1 \rightarrow 0$) in the Output C-element since it can occur when the generation of the full flag.

3.2   Input C-Element

Figure 6 shows the Input C-element circuit where send and ack signals are the transfer request and acknowledgment signals of the C-elements of the DDP, respectively, empty signal represents that the Input FIFO is empty, rclk denotes the read clock signal of the Input FIFO, hclk is the read clock signal for the header memory, mr is the master reset signal of the system. Based on this circuit, data transfer is controlled by handshaking with the C-elements of the DDP only when data exists inside the Input FIFO. Dealing with an empty glitch (empty $0 \rightarrow 1 \rightarrow 0$) as described in Sect. 3.1 is also necessary. The set-reset latch (SR latch) within the Input C-element can absorb the glitch to prevent circuit malfunctions.

The proposed DDP I/F circuit must satisfy the setup/hold time constraints for the registers, RAM used within the Input I/F, and the DDP internal data latch connected to the Input I/F to ensure correct operation. Since those are driven by the local clock signals, i.e., rclk and hclk, the proper clock timings must be guaranteed by adjusting the delay element D_{sh} shown in Fig. 6. The D_g is also a delay element to prevent the hatched NAND gate from generating the glitch signals.

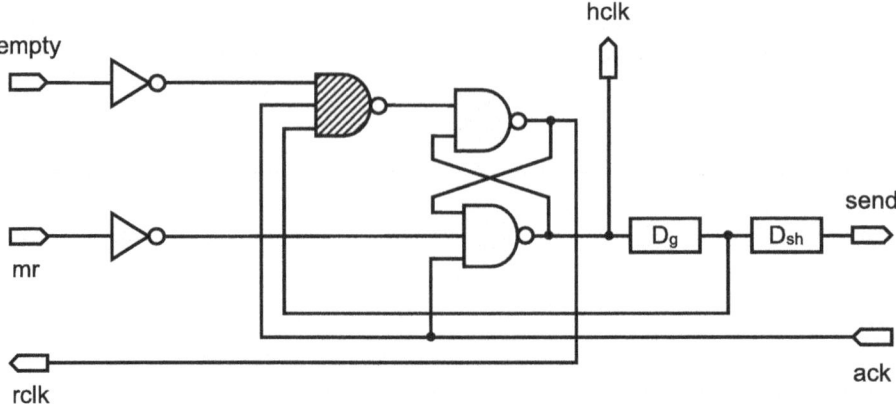

Fig. 6. Input C-element.

3.3   Output C-Element

Figure 7 shows the Output C-element circuit where full indicates that the Output FIFO is full, and wclk is a data write clock signal for the Output FIFO. The other signals, send, ack, and mr, have the same meaning as those in the Input C-element. The Output C-element also must convert the data transfer protocol between the asynchronous FIFO and the DDP. In this circuit, data is output by handshaking with the C-elements when there is a room in the Output FIFO. As in the Input C-element, the inside SR latch absorbs the glitch (full $0 \rightarrow 1 \rightarrow 0$) to prevent circuit malfunctions from occurring.

The proposed DDP I/F circuit must satisfy the setup/hold time constraints for the registers, RAM used within the Output I/F, and the DDP internal data latch connected to the Output I/F to ensure correct operation. Since those are driven by the local clock signal, i.e., wclk, the proper clock timing must be guaranteed by adjusting the delay element D_{sh} shown in Fig. 7. The D_g is a delay element to prevent the hatched NAND gate from generating the glitch signals.

3.4   FPGA Implementation

The synchronizer must prevent metastable signals from propagating for an extended period to avoid causing a metastable condition in subsequent D flip-flops (DFFs), even if a metastable condition occurs in the first-stage DFF. Therefore, the DFFs within the synchronizer should be placed as close together as possible, and the wiring between them should be minimized. The AMD FPGA chip used in this paper supports the async_reg attribute in the EDA tool Vivado. We use this attribute to reduce wiring latency between DFFs by assigning it to each DFF.

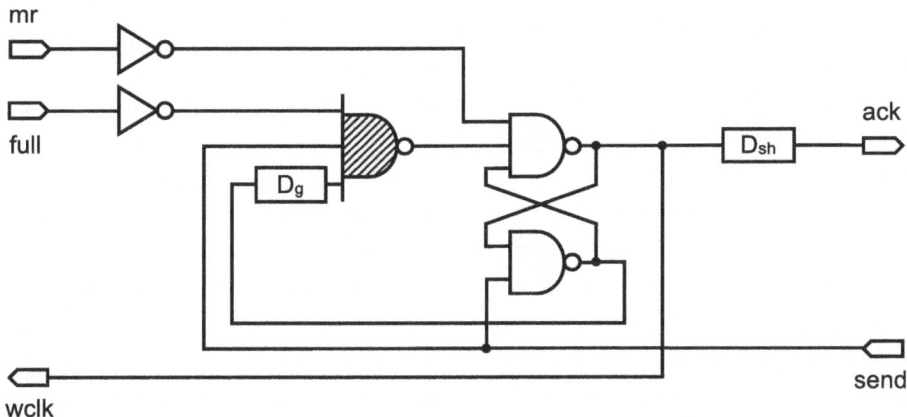

Fig. 7. Output C-element.

The Simple Dual-Port RAM that constitutes the Input FIFO and Output FIFO uses the Intellectual Property (IP) provided by AMD and uses Block RAM, a circuit resource on the FPGA. The Single Port RAM that constitutes the header memory is also implemented using Block RAM. The delay elements in the Input C-element and Output C-element are implemented by cascading lookup tables (LUTs).

4 Evaluation

We implemented the proposed I/F circuit equipped with asynchronous FIFOs (Async-FIFO I/F) on a Zynq-7010 FPGA chip using AMD's Vivado EDA tool and evaluated its reliability, throughput, and FPGA resource usage. For the comparative evaluation, we implemented the I/F circuit equipped with synchronous FIFOs (Sync-FIFO I/F) on the same FPGA chip. Its circuit configuration is described in Appendix.

Both of the implemented I/F circuits employ the specifications shown in Table 1. Since we assumed that the data processed by DDP is 16 bits, the DDP input/output packet consists of 16-bit data and a 22-bit header. The data stored in the Input FIFO consists of 16-bit data and a 7-bit address to the header memory, and the data stored in the Output FIFO consists of 16-bit data and a 7-bit destination address. The destination address is included in the packet header and is the address to the program storage used inside DDP, i.e., it indicates the destination of the data. The Input/Output FIFO and header memory size were set as shown in Table 1 to be able to run a simple program on the DDP. Every

Table 1. Specification of both I/F circuits

DDP input/output packet	38 bit
Header memory	22 bit × 128 words
Input/Output FIFO	23 bit × 32 words
Every delay element	approx. 4 ns (8 LUTs)
Clock freq. on synchronous circuit	50 MHz

delay element inserted in the C-elements used in the DDP and the I/F circuits was set to approximately 4 ns as a sufficient delay to allow the implemented circuit to operate with all timing constraints satisfied. This delay element is configured by cascading 8 LUTs.

4.1 Reliability

Before Implementing the Async-FIFO I/F and Sync-FIFO I/F on the FPGA, we evaluate the reliability of the n-flop synchronizer and predetermine the appropriate number of DFF stages.

Mean time between failures (MTBF) is used as an indicator of reliability regarding circuit malfunction due to metastability event occurrences and is obtained by (1) [7].

$$MTBF = \frac{e^{S/\tau}}{T_W \times F_C \times F_D} \tag{1}$$

where F_C is the clock frequency, F_D is the data rate, S is the time reserved for metastable resolution, T_W is the setup/hold time window, and τ is the time associated with metastable resolution. T_W and τ are device-specific constants.

First, we implemented the test circuit described in [8] on the FPGA, measured the number of metastability events in 30 s, and calculated MTBF. The averaged τ, an unknown device-specific constant, is calculated through five times measurements. That is $\tau = 43.4$ ps at DFF where $T_W = 322.0$ ps when $F_C = 50$ MHz, $F_D = 30$ MHz, $S = 681.7$ ps.

Based on the averaged τ and (1), the MTBF can be obtained in the cases of 2- or 3-flop synchronizers implemented on the FPGA. Precise F_D of the DDP could not be estimated because the DDP is an asynchronous circuit and does not input/output data in a constant cycle. However, we can estimate that the maximum F_D of the DDP would be approximately 30 MHz, based on the timing report of its FPGA implementation of the DDP. Consequently, S at 2-flop and 3-flop synchronizers were 18107.4 ps and 37340.6 ps, respectively. The average T_W of them were 278.5 ps and 276.0 ps, respectively.

As a result, the malfunction probability of the circuit was 5.3×10^{-178} ppm in the 2-flop synchronizer and 1.8×10^{-370} ppm in the 3-flop one. This indicates that 2 DFF stages are sufficient for the synchronizer because they are far less than the reliability requirement of commercial embedded hardware, 10 ppm.

On the other hand, even when operating at 250 MHz, the maximum operating frequency of the FPGA part on the Zynq-7010, a malfunction probability of the 2-flop synchronizer will be 6.8×10^{-18} ppm.

Although the synchronizer built in the Async-FIFO I/F is slightly different from that built in the Sync-FIFO I/F, these I/F circuits have the same probability of malfunctioning the circuit in synchronizing the asynchronous signal. This is because an asynchronous signal input to the synchronizer is limited to only one bit per data in both I/F circuits.

4.2   Throughput and Resource Usage

The input/output throughput [packets/s] of the Async-FIFO I/F and the Sync-FIFO I/F with the 2-flop synchronizer is evaluated by post-implementation timing simulation. Furthermore, the FPGA resource usage of both I/F circuits implemented on the Zynq-7010 are compared, i.e., the usage of Slice LUTs (LUTs), Slice Registers (Registers), Slice, and Block RAM. Those are summarized in Table 2.

The Input I/F and Output I/F of the Async-FIFO I/F utilize about twice as many resources as those of the Sync-FIFO I/F, and the throughput is 3.8 times higher for the Input I/F and 4.7 times higher for the Output I/F. In terms of the throughput per resource [packets/s/slice], the Async-FIFO I/F is higher and superior to the Sync-FIFO I/F in both Input I/F and Output I/F.

In particular, the throughput of the Sync-FIFO I/F is basically determined by the clock frequency, and when the number of synchronizer stages is n, it takes at least $2(1 + n)$ clock cycles to transfer a single data. A clock frequency of 50 MHz or higher can achieve even higher speeds but increases power consumption.

As for resource usage, Bin2Gray and Gray2Bin used in the Flag Gen in the Async-FIFO I/F affect the increase in LUT usage. The input signals to these modules are the read/write address of the Input/Output FIFO, and the address width increases by 1 bit each time the FIFO size doubles. Without considering circuit optimization, a rise of 1 bit in address width increases the LUT usage by one since Bin2Gray and Gray2Bin require one additional XOR gate, respectively. The n-flop synchronizer in the Sync-FIFO I/F requires n DFFs, whereas the n-flop synchronizer in the Async-FIFO I/F requires mn DFFs. Since one bit more FIFO address width is needed to generate ready flags, w can be expressed as $m = w + 1$ if the address width of the FIFO is w. This indicates that the Async-FIFO I/F additionally requires wn DFFs compared to the Sync-FIFO I/F.

4.3   Discussion

The above evaluation results show that the proposed Async-FIFO I/F and Sync-FIFO I/F circuits are comparable in terms of circuit reliability when synchronizing asynchronous signals.

Table 2. Comparison of throughput and FPGA resource usage

	Input I/F		Output I/F	
Type of FIFO	Async	Sync	Async	Sync
Throughput [*packets/s*]	31.9 M	8.3 M	38.8 M	8.3 M
LUT	34	15	35	13
Register	24	17	24	15
Slice	18	7	16	6
Block RAM	1	1	0.5	0.5
Throughput/resource [*packets/s/slice*]	1.8 M	1.2 M	2.4 M	1.4 M

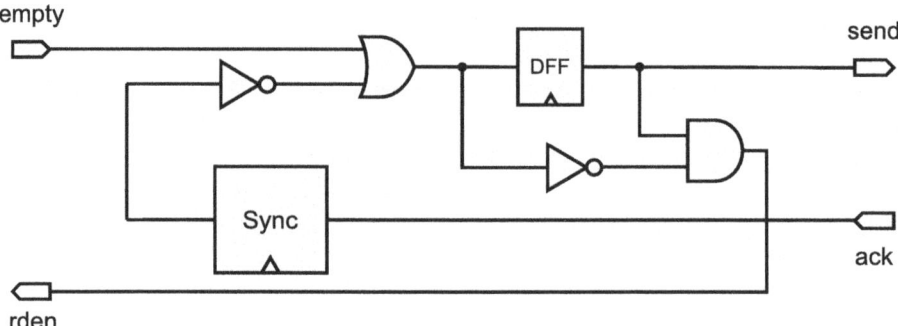

Fig. 8. Input C-element in Sync-FIFO I/F.

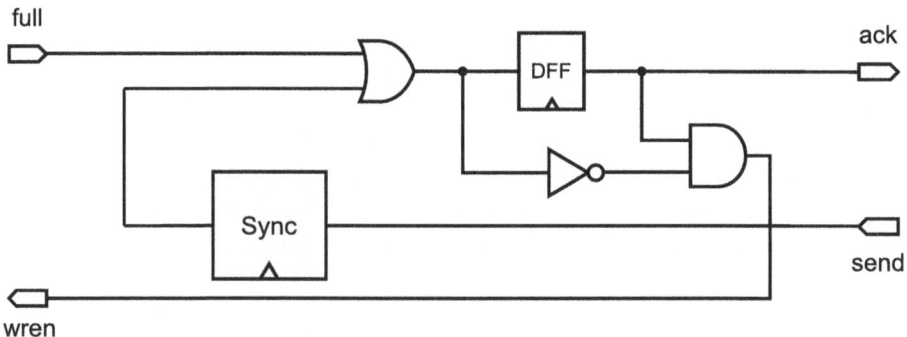

Fig. 9. Output C-element in Sync-FIFO I/F.

Considering the use in IoT devices that require low power operation, the Async-FIFO I/F is more useful because it can transfer data with the same reliability and without being affected by clock frequency, although the resource usage increases by about 20 units shown in Table 2. When a 2-flop synchronizer is used at a clock frequency of 50 MHz as in this experiment, the Async-FIFO

I/F uses 4 more LUTs and 2 more registers than the Sync-FIFO I/F for each time the FIFO size doubles. However, as the FIFO size and the DDP packet size increase, the resource usage of other common circuits also increases. Therefore, the throughput per resource of the Async-FIFO I/F could be improved further. In addition, 16 LUTs are used for each delay element in the Input I/F and the Output I/F of the Async-FIFO I/F, respectively. Since the number of LUTs used in the delay elements is not affected by the FIFO size and the DDP packet size, the throughput per resource could be improved similarly.

5   Conclusion

In this paper, we proposed a self-timed DDP-oriented I/F circuit that synchronizes operation timing, converts protocols, and buffers data to transfer input/output data between the self-timed DDP and the clock-synchronous application processor. We implemented the proposed I/F circuit on AMD's Zynq-7010 FPGA chip and evaluated its reliability, performance, and resource usage.

By employing an asynchronous FIFO instead of a synchronous FIFO for the I/F circuit, we have improved the throughput by 3.8 times for the input I/F circuit and 4.7 times for the output I/F circuit when the clock frequency of the synchronous circuit is 50 MHz, while the same reliability of both input and output I/F circuits can be guaranteed. However, the FPGA circuit resource of the proposed circuit becomes almost double that of the synchronous FIFO I/F circuit. Therefore, we must study smaller I/F circuits with similar reliability and throughput for future embedded systems.

Acknowledgments. Although it is impossible to give credit individually to all those who organized and supported our project, the authors would like to express their sincere appreciation to all the colleagues in the project.

Disclosure of Interests. The authors have no competing interests to declare that are relevant to the content of this article.

Appendix

The Sync-FIFO I/F is structured with similar modules shown in Fig. 3. The Input C-element and the Output C-element must be equipped with the n-flop synchronizer since the synchronous FIFO could not internally synchronize the asynchronous signals with the n-flop synchronizer. The Input FIFO is a synchronous FIFO, using the same clock signal for data read/write. Therefore, the rclk signal is not required to input data from the Input C-element into the Input FIFO, but instead, a read enable signal (rden) is required additionally. Similarly, the Output FIFO requires a write enable signal (wren) instead of wclk. Figure 8 shows the Input C-element circuit in the Sync-FIFO I/F. The handshake with the DDP is controlled using the ack signal synchronized by the n-flop synchronizer and the empty signal. The send signal is held in DFF before outputting, and the rden is asserted when the falling edge of the send signal is detected. Figure 9 shows the Output C-element circuit in the Sync-FIFO I/F. Similar to the Input C-element, the handshake with the DDP is controlled using the send signal synchronized by the n-flop synchronizer and full signal, and the wren is asserted when the falling edge of the ack signal is detected. Since the Input C-element contains DFF, at least 2 clock cycles are required for a 4-phase handshake to input one packet to the DDP. Therefore, the Sync-FIFO I/F does not require the hclk. Although it is possible to configure the Sync-FIFO I/F by simply connecting the n-flop synchronizer to the Input C-element and Output C-element of the proposed Async-FIFO I/F, additional DFF is required to generate the rden and the wren. To reduce the circuit resource, we adopted the unified circuit of the n-flop synchronizer and the Input/Output C-element for Sync-FIFO I/F as shown in Fig. 8 and 9.

References

1. Terada, H., Miyata, S., Iwata, M.: DDMP's: self-timed super-pipelined data-driven multimedia processors. Proc. IEEE **87**(2), 282–296 (1999). https://doi.org/10.1109/5.740021
2. Ginosar, R.: Fourteen ways to fool your synchronizer. In: Ninth International Symposium on Asynchronous Circuits and Systems, pp. 89–96 (2003). https://doi.org/10.1109/ASYNC.2003.1199169
3. Beer, S., Ginosar, R.: Eleven ways to boost your synchronizer. IEEE Trans. Very Large Scale Integrat. (VLSI) Syst. **23**(6), 1040–1049 (2015). https://doi.org/10.1109/TVLSI.2014.2331331
4. Hao, Z., Liu, L., Tian, B.: The principle and applications of asynchronous FIFO. In: IEEE 2nd International Conference on Electrical Engineering, Big Data and Algorithms (EEBDA), pp. 277–279 (2023). https://doi.org/10.1109/EEBDA56825.2023.10090696
5. Oliveira, D.L., Curtinhas, T., Faria, L.A., Romano, L.: A novel asynchronous interface with pausible clock for partitioned synchronous modules. In: IEEE 6th Latin American Symposium on Circuits & Systems (LASCAS), pp. 1–4 (2015). https://doi.org/10.1109/LASCAS.2015.7250441
6. Semba, S., Saito, H.: A study on the design of interface circuits between synchronous-asynchronous modules using click elements. In: SASIMI, pp. 139–144 (2022)
7. Dike, C., Burton, E.: Miller and noise effects in a synchronizing flip-flop. IEEE J. Solid-State Circ. **346**, 849–855 (1999). https://doi.org/10.1109/4.766819
8. Beer, S., Ginosar, R., Priel, M., Dobkin, R., Kolodny, A.: The devolution of synchronizers. In: IEEE Symposium on Asynchronous Circuits and Systems, pp. 94–103 (2010). https://doi.org/10.1109/ASYNC.2010.22

Analytical Study of Attacks and Defenses for IoT in Critical Infrastructure

Ali Al-Sinayyid(✉) ⓘ, Timothy Sanford, Alexander Sanchez, Rohith Reddy Battula, Sasidhar Kadiyala , and Venkatesh Mannuru

Department of Mathematics and Computer Science, West Virginia State University, Institute, USA

{ali.alsinayyid,tsanford,asanchez4,rbattula,skadiyala1, vmannuru}@wvstateu.edu

Abstract. Technological advancements in critical infrastructures have led to an increase in cyber-attacks. This paper studies a vulnerable aspect of these infrastructures - Internet of Things (IoT) which comprise Supervisory Control and Data Acquisition (SCADA) systems. Evaluating cyber-attacks and defenses in regard to: attack deployment, type, and impact scope; defensive algorithms, response, and efficiency. These attacks and defenses are then analyzed to provide insights on the most common and effective methods to deploy and combat IoT threats. Concluding that Denial of Service (DoS) attacks are the most common, and machine learning algorithms are currently the most effective defense.

Keywords: critical infrastructure · Internet of Things (IoT) · Supervisory Control and Data Acquisition (SCADA) · automation · cyber-attacks · systematic analysis · counter defenses · machine learning · cyber security

1 Introduction

Critical infrastructures are systems and networks that are necessary for life which include vital sectors such as water plants, transportation/traffic, public health, and energy plants [26]. Serving as the backbone of society, critical infrastructure has evolved with the growth of technology [27]. Many technologies have been incorporated into these sectors with one of the main technologies being Supervisory Control and Data Acquisition (SCADA) systems [8]. SCADA systems are comprised of Internet of Things (IoT) devices and systems [8].

IoT devices allow for major advancements such as providing automation, increased efficiency, the availability of artificial intelligence, and the interconnection of devices/networks [1]. While there are many advantages of using IoT, the use of IoT makes these areas targets for cyber-attacks, thus creating security concerns [12, 18].

In this paper, a comprehensive literature review focusing on cyber-threats targeting IoT and the corresponding defense mechanisms proposed against them are explored in Sect. 2. The literature review includes a wide range of research articles, each looking at various aspects of IoT security, from detection to prevention strategies. Following

H. R. Arabnia et al. (Eds.): CSCE 2024, CCIS 2260, pp. 313–322, 2025.
https://doi.org/10.1007/978-3-031-85923-6_26

the review, tables regarding common attacks and defenses from the literature review are organized. These tables arrange these attacks and defenses in a manner that can aid future researchers by showing commonality in attacks, what those attacks do, typical defenses against those attacks, and how accurate they are. Further analysis of these tables is given in Sect. 3 of this paper and final conclusions are drawn with suggestions for future studies in Sect. 4.

2 Literature Review

Alanazi et al. [1] investigates anomaly detection based on machine learning as a solution to multiple IoT cyber security attacks. This paper proposes a model that has a collaborative feature selection method that chooses the most optimal distinctive features and eliminates unnecessary features to create the most optimal model for IoT cyber-attack detection. Numerous learning techniques to improve classification for predicting diverse types of IoT attacks are also proposed in the detection phase of this paper. "The experimental results show that our proposed method can effectively and efficiently predict several IoT attacks with a higher accuracy rate of 99.984%, a precision rate of 99.982%, a recall rate of 99.984%, and an F1-score of 99.983%" [1].

With deep learning and machine learning showing promise in finding and addressing security threats in IoT, Alkhudaydi et al. [2] focused on using AI to precisely extract essential features from a "realistic-network-traffic BoT-IoT dataset. Then, this paper used ten distinct machine learning models to assess efficiency in finding malware. This paper also evaluated the "performance enhancement of these models when integrated with the SMOTE (Synthetic Minority Over-sampling Technique) algorithm to counteract imbalanced data" [2]. The research concluded by showing the potential of the AI techniques, along with balancing algorithms like SMOTE, to efficiently find IoT network attacks. "Notably, the CatBoost and XGBoost classifiers achieved remarkable accuracy rates of 98.19% and 98.50%, respectively. Our findings offer insights into the potential of the ML and DL techniques, in conjunction with balancing algorithms such as SMOTE, to effectively identify IoT network intrusions" [2].

Alanazi et al. [3] focuses on vulnerabilities of the Industrial Internet of Things (IIoT) to cyberattacks and proposes anomaly-based Intrusion Detection System as a solution. The Intrusion Detection System has three phases: pre-processing, feature selection, and classification. Techniques such as minimum redundancy, maximum relevance, and neighborhood components analysis were used. Classifiers such as support vector machine, decision tree, k-nearest neighbors, and linear discriminant analysis are used in the modeling phase. The experimental evaluation, conducted on the X-IIoTID dataset, showed the effectiveness of the proposed model with a high accuracy rate of 99.58%.

Alterazi et al. [4] focuses on providing high security for physical items via IoT by assigning distinct online addresses (Internet Protocol) for communication. An increase in hacker attacks during Internet data exchange has led to IoT devices facing security risks creating a need for attack detection. This study touches on performance-based AI models for predicting attacks and issues with IoT devices, using Particle Swarm Optimization (PSO), genetic algorithms, and ant colony optimization. The proposed method showed significant effectiveness with an accuracy of 99%.

To address the increase in cyber threats and data integrity in IoT, various Intrusion Detection Systems (IDS) have been proposed to identify malicious activities based on predefined attack patterns as seen in Abbas et al. [5]. This study introduces an ensemble-based IDS model that utilizes logistic regression, naïve Bayes, and decision tree with a voting classifier. When using the CICIDS2017 dataset, this paper's model outperformed existing techniques in terms of accuracy for both binary and multi-class classification scenarios while having an average classification accuracy of 99.67%.

Since there is not a default security in IoT devices there are a lot of risks that exist. To help mitigate these risks, Echeverría et al. [6] proposes a seven-step sequence for minimizing the attack surface via hardening processes. The methodology involves a systematic literature review using PRISMA techniques, leading to the development of a checklist for evaluating security level of an IoT solution across its three layers. Lastly, a risk matrix is established which facilitates the assessment of the attack surface of an IoT layer.

SCADA's integration with electronic devices enhances systemic efficiency and monitoring capabilities. However, the integration with public networks raises concerns about cyber-attacks and information security breaches. Yang et al. [7] suggests a token authentication module to deter Distributed Denial-of-Service (DDoS) attacks and experimental results in an energy management system show that this proposed security architecture effectively enhances system security in real-world applications.

IIoT is advancing industrial automation, transforming the SCADA network into an open and interconnected system. Integration with industrial electronic devices via Modbus protocol enhances control and monitoring, boosting operational efficiency. However, the increased connectivity exposes the SCADA system to security threats. To address this, Yang et al. [8] proposes a trusted token authentication service and Transport Layer Security (TLS) protocol for encryption and verification, aiming to prevent physical attacks. Experimental deployment in an energy management system field validates the effectiveness and compatibility of the proposed security defense architecture.

IoT systems face multiple attacks, but Denial of Service (DoS) and DDoS attacks have been among the most reported. Alaeddine et al. [9] focuses on detecting and mitigating DoS and DDoS attacks in IoT via machine learning. An architecture to combat these attacks would be composed of a detection component that offers fine-grained identification of attack/packet types and a mitigation component to deal with issues after they have been identified. To conclude, a multi-class classifier showed promising results with a Looking-Back-enabled Random Forest classifier reaching accuracy of 99.81% when tested on a Bot-IoT dataset.

Abdullahi et al. [10] offers a systematic literature review (SLR) to classify, map, and survey existing literature on AI methods used for detecting IoT cybersecurity attacks. Multiple databases were explored as well as deep learning and machine learning techniques regarding IoT security. Some studies proposed smart intrusion detection systems with intelligent architectural frameworks using AI to provide security while others showed how support vector machines and random forest are some of the most employed methods. Extreme gradient boosting, neural networks, and recurrent neural networks all also were methods seen implemented via this review.

Jhanjhi et al. [11] identifies possible cybersecurity threats and privacy issues and aims to provide solutions for them. Mainly, possible cyber-attacks on the four layers of IIoT are investigated. The research includes identifying threats, consequences, and countermeasures in a detailed literature review. A comprehensive framework to grasp the current state of cybersecurity is given in this paper with the intent to guide future research and applications.

A comprehensive survey on detecting and preventing various IoT-based security attacks is given in this paper. Muhammad et al. [12] outlines a framework focusing on representative attacks, potential solutions, threat analysis, and ranking the threats mentioned. Five main defense mechanism categories are identified: default password protection, distributed denial of service detection/prevention, intrusion detection/prevention, encryption mechanisms, and anomaly detection. There is also an emphasis on a need for threat modeling that considers resource consumption and implementation effort. Lastly, the paper highlights a lack of systematic studies evaluating frameworks/methodologies and proposed mechanisms in the current state of technology.

N. et al. [13] discusses the integration of IoT technology while also touching on the topics of the challenges it brings such as heterogeneity, scalability, quality of service, and security requirements. Security measurements often are not a priority because of things like cost, size/power, and causing potential risks. This paper has a comprehensive survey of security issues across the different IoT layers with extra focus on DDoS attacks. The paper also compares multiple Intrusion Detection and Prevention models while exploring anomaly detection techniques, machine learning, and deep learning for malware detection. The paper addresses research challenges, proposes solutions, and gives future visions of IoT security.

Malhotra et al. [14] discusses how crucial timely detection and prevention are to avoid cyber-attacks for the IoT in our lives. The survey focusses on attacks and anomalies in IoT with an emphasis on intelligent intrusion detection systems. An in-depth analysis of machine and deep learning-based network intrusion detection systems are given, including a healthcare IoT case study over architecture, security, privacy issues, and learning paradigms.

Various IoT intrusion detection systems (IDS) have been proposed. These IDS are classified based on detection, validation, and deployment strategies. Khraisat et al. [15] serves as a comprehensive review of current IoT IDS and covers techniques, deployment, and validation strategies along with using common datasets. How existing IoT IDS detects attacks, secures communications, and classifies IoT attacks is discussed in this paper. Future research challenges regarding enhancing IoT security are also discussed.

Podder et al. [16] systematically reviews IoT security by discussing its application in industrial and medical services, covering security threats over different layers of IoT healthcare architecture, and discussing multiple types of malwares. The main malware discussed in this paper are Mirai, Echobot, and Reaper. Machine learning algorithms' effectiveness and tools for ransomware detection are also discussed in this paper. The paper finishes with reviewing existing security issues, discussing open challenges, and examining the future possibilities of IoT security.

Abosata et al. [17] focuses on the integrity of IIoT systems. Security approaches are analyzed for IoT in industrial applications and security attacks are categorized based on

IoT layers architecture. The paper then goes to analyze existing security solutions such as communication protocols, networking, cryptography, and intrusion detection systems. Finally, this paper looks at tools and simulations for testing security mechanisms in IoT applications and outlines issues in IIoT and IoT security.

Existing Internet technologies were not designed for IoT which creates security concerns. Reddy et al. [18] focuses on giving a comprehensive overview of edge-side security threats and countermeasures for IoT. Three IoT reference models and their security are discussed in this paper along with applications of IoT, hacker motivations, outlines of serious threats, and potential countermeasures. The intent of this paper is to improve understanding of IoT security.

Cyber attackers use multiple tools of infiltration such as Phishing, Malware, SQL Injection, Ransomware, Cross-Site Scripting, Denial of Service, Session Hijacking, and Credential Reuse. Phishing is the most common of these attacks. Sadiq et al. [19] focuses on fighting phishing, categorizing the most up-to-date phishing detection techniques into Sata Mining, Deep Learning and Machine Learning-Based Approach, Search Engine-Based Approach, URL Scan-Based Approach, Blacklisting-Whitelisting Approach, and Visual Similarity-Based Approach. The paper then has a comparative analysis in each category.

As mentioned in Nagajayanthi et al. [20], IoT utilization examples include but are not limited to intelligent device control via cloud vendors like Amazon and Google and using AI for data analytics and digital assistants like Alexa and Siri. Security vulnerabilities in IoT architecture can be addressed with blockchain, ensuring transparency and data security according to this paper. This research also discusses the technical aspects of IoT such as interoperability, flexibility, scalability, mobility, security, transparency, standardization, and low energy.

José et al. [21] reviews vulnerabilities in wireless technologies giving connectivity to IoT and looks at the experiences using Software Defines Radio (SDR) for wireless attacks. This systematic literature review compares vulnerabilities and attacks that affect the IoT ecosystem and SDR platforms. From this study, the perception layer in the IoT reference model is seen as the most vulnerable. Attacks at the perception level tend to occur due to hardware limitations, physical device exposure, and technological heterogeneity. This paper concludes by suggesting future security measures of security systems use SDR technology and merge the SDR hardware with cognitive and intelligent techniques.

Mamoona et al. [22] focuses on ransomware attacks which have emerged as a major threat. Ransomware restricts access to information in IoT, demanding payment for the return of that access. This paper serves as a comprehensive survey on the evolution, prevention, and mitigation of ransomware in the context of IoT.

Integrating Cyber-Physical Systems (CPS) with IoT through cloud computing creates smart industrial systems for applications like smart transportation, grids, and healthcare. These systems often are reliant on SCADA for critical infrastructure monitoring. A. et al. [23] focuses on security challenges that industrial SCADA systems face in an IoT cloud environment. These vulnerabilities are worsened by complex architectures integrating IoT, cloud computing, and mobile wireless sensor networks. The paper provides best practices, recommendations, and outlines future research directions to secure critical CPSs.

Mesbah et al. [24] discusses how Operational Technology (OT) has transformed and how SCADA attacks on industrial control systems have risen. To combat cybersecurity concerns, OT operators should adopt the defense-in-depth concept, using layers of security like firewalls, endpoint solutions, and honeypots. Honeypots are the focus of this paper. Honeypots are a security layer for IT and OP in SCADA environments that are used to detect potential malicious tampering, understand attackers' techniques, and find network vulnerabilities. This paper employs the SCADA honeypot "Conpot" for early detection, analysis, and insights into attackers' goals.

SCADA systems have allowed for the rise of interconnected networks but also an increase in cyber-attack vulnerabilities. Manar et al. [25] explores SCADA system security vulnerabilities, categorizing threats based on architecture, vulnerabilities, attacks, intrusion detection techniques (IDS), and testbeds. Research challenges and open issues for future research in the field of SCADA security are discussed at the end of the paper.

3 Analysis

In Table 1: Attacks and Table 2: Defenses, cyber-attack types, their corresponding defenses, and their efficiency are shown. Table 1 highlights recent attack types from the literature review. Table 2 gives common defense strategies that correspond to the attacks given in Table 1.

There are different attack types as seen in Table 1. The most common type of attack is the DoS attack. The DoS attack is an attack that aims to make a targeted system unavailable to a user by flooding it with an abundance of traffic. The data from Table 1 also shows that most of the attacks employed on IoT systems are typically automated. Regardless of the attack type, there are negative repercussions for all, the most frequent repercussions are data loss, interception, and corruption.

Table 2 complements Table 1 by giving multiple defenses to counter the attacks in Table 1. Recent defenses use machine learning algorithms such as Decision Trees, Bagging, CatBoost, Extra Trees, Random Forrest, and XGBoost to accomplish high accuracy rates in identifying and mitigating attacks in IoT systems. As mentioned, the machine learning algorithms do well against their counterpart attacks as many of them exceed a 99% accuracy rate in identifying the attacks. Along with having a high accuracy

Table 1. Legend

Symbol	Refers to
T1	Man-In-The-Middle Attack
O1	Data Loss and Denial of Resources
G1	Extra Trees (ET), Random Forest (RF), XGBoost (XGB)
G2	Token Authentication Service
A1	No standard percentage of improvement rather general increase of security

rate, these machine learning algorithm defenses are automated which pairs well with the fact that many of the attacks are automated, leading to the defenses being able to combat the attacks in a timely manner.

While there are effective defenses, there are still areas that require further research such as how there are further studies needed for mathematical analysis for several defenses, especially the defenses regarding token authentication services. The way in which a defense is measured is also an area that can be further explored as there are different metrics used for different defenses. Overall, these tables give insights into cyber threats on IoT systems in Table 2, and corresponding defenses to combat them Table 3.

Table 2. Attacks

Paper/Year	Manual	Attack Type	Operational Disruption
[1] 2021	No	T1, Mirai botnet attack, Dark Nexus Attack, and Hide and Seek (HNS)	Data Loss, Data Interception, and Data Corruption
[2] 2023	No	DoS and DDoS attacks	O1
[3] 2022	No	T1, Dictionary Attack, and DoS	O1
[4] 2022	No	User-To-Root (U2R), DoS, and Data-Type Probing	Denial of Resources, Data Interception
[5] 2022	No	Benign Attacks: DoS, Brute force BOT: PortScan and Sql Injection DDos: Heartbleed, SSH-Patator, and XSS	O1
[6] 2021	No	DoS	Denial of Resources
[7] 2022	No	DDoS	Widespread Denial of Resources
[8] 2021	Yes	Physical Layer Attacks	Power Outages, Infrastructure Damage, and Communication Disruptions

Table 3. Defenses

Paper/Year	System	Algorithm(s)	Response Type	Accuracy
[1] 2021	IoT	Decision Trees (DT) and G1	Automatic	Accuracy: 99.984% Precision: 99.982% Recall: 99.984% F1-score: 99.983%"

(*continued*)

Table 3. (*continued*)

Paper/Year	System	Algorithm(s)	Response Type	Accuracy
[2] 2023	IoT	ML: Bagging, CatBoost, LGBM, AdaBoost, HistGBoost, SVM, KNN, <u>G1</u> DL: RNN, GRU, LSTM, ANN, MLP	Automatic	*Two Highest accuracies CatBoost Accuracy: 98.19% XGBoost Accuracy: 98.50%
[3] 2022	IIoT	Anomaly-based IDS to overcome IIoT Attacks	Automatic	Accuracy: 99.58% Sensitivity: 99.59% Specificity: 99.58% Low false positive: 0.4%
[4] 2022	IoT	Particle Swarm Optimization (PSO), Ant Optimization, and Genetic Optimization	Automatic	Outperformed existing systems by roughly 73% Accuracy: 99%
[5] 2022	IoT	Logistic Regression, Naive Bayes, and Decision Trees	Automatic	Average Classification Accuracy: 99.67%
[6] 2021	IoT	Threat Modeling, Vulnerability Analysis, and Hardening Process	Manual	Furter study is required to provide a mathematical analysis
[7] 2022	SCADA	<u>G2</u>	Manual	<u>A1</u>
[8] 2021	SCADA	<u>G2</u>	Manual	<u>A1</u>

4   Conclusion

This paper provides findings regarding the nature of IoT security in critical infrastructure via an analytical study and expands on the ongoing efforts to protect IoT systems from growing cyber threats. A comparative analysis of recent attacks and defenses shows that DoS attacks are the main IoT attacks and machine learning algorithms are the current effective solution. Though there are promising advancements in defenses, there are areas and challenges that remain which could be used for further research. The mathematical analysis of defense mechanisms and the standardization of defensive measurements are the main areas that could gain value from further research. This paper acts as a resource to understand the current state of IoT security and offers valuable perspectives on current effective defense strategies to aid in securing IoT systems against cyber threats.

Acknowledgments. The authors would like to acknowledge the support of the US Department of Education under subaward grant number R2301364. The DoE support made it possible to conduct this research and other research works like [28, 29] and [30] and to disseminate the findings. The authors are grateful for the DoE commitment to supporting cutting-edge research.

References

1. Alanazi, M., Aljuhani, A.: Anomaly Detection for Internet of Things Cyberattacks (2021)
2. Alkhudaydi, O.A., Krichen, M., Alghamdi, A.D.: A deep learning methodology for predicting cybersecurity attacks on the internet of things. Information **14**(10), 550 (2023). https://doi. org/10.3390/info14100550
3. Alanazi, R., Aljuhani. A.: Anomaly Detection for Industrial Internet of Things Cyberattacks (2022)
4. Alterazi, A.H., et al.: Prevention of cyber security with the internet of things using particle swarm optimization. Sensors **22**(16), 6117 (2022). https://doi.org/10.3390/s22166117
5. Abbas, A., Khan, M.A., Latif, S., et al.: A new ensemble-based intrusion detection system for internet of things. Arab. J. Sci. Eng. **47**, 1805–1819 (2022). https://doi.org/10.1007/s13 369-021-06086-5
6. Echeverría, A., Cevallos, C., Ortiz-Garces, I., Andrade, R.O.: Cybersecurity model based on hardening for secure internet of things implementation. Appl. Sci. **11**(7), 3260 (2021). https:// doi.org/10.3390/app11073260
7. Yang, Y.S., Lee, S.H., Chen, W.C., Yang, C.S., Huang, Y.M., Hou, T.W.: Securing SCADA energy management system under DDos attacks using token verification approach. Appl. Sci. **12**(1), 530 (2022). https://doi.org/10.3390/app12010530
8. Yang, Y.S., Lee, S.H., Chen, W.C., Yang, C.S., Huang, Y.M., Hou, T.W.: TTAS: trusted token authentication service of securing SCADA network in energy management system for industrial internet of things. Sensors **21**(8), 2685 (2021). https://doi.org/10.3390/s21082685
9. Mihoub, A., Fredj, O.B., Cheikhrouhou, O., Derhab, A., Krichen, M.: Denial of service attack detection and mitigation for internet of things using looking-back-enabled machine learning techniques. Comput. Electr. Eng. **98**, 107716 (2022)
10. Abdullahi, M., et al.: Detecting cybersecurity attacks in internet of things using artificial intelligence methods: a systematic literature review. Electronics **11**(2), 198 (2022). https:// doi.org/10.3390/electronics11020198
11. Jhanjhi, N.Z., Humayun, M., Almuayqil, S.N.: Cyber Security and Privacy Issues in Industrial Internet of Things (2020)
12. Shafiq, M., Zhaoquan, G., O., Cheikhrouhou, Alhakami, W., Hamam, H.: The rise of "internet of things": review and open research issues related to detection and prevention of IoT-based security attacks. Wireless Commun. Mob. Comput. **2022**(1), 8669348 (2022). https://doi.org/ 10.1155/2022/8669348
13. Mishra, N., Pandya, S.: Internet of things applications, security challenges, attacks, intrusion detection, and future visions: a systematic review. IEEE Access **9**, 59353–59377 (2021). https://doi.org/10.1109/ACCESS.2021.3073408
14. Malhotra, P., Singh, Y., Anand, P., Bangotra, D.K., Singh, P.K., Hong, W.C.: Internet of things: evolution, concerns and security challenges. Sensors **21**(5), 1809 (2021). https://doi.org/10. 3390/s21051809
15. Khraisat, A., Alazab, A.: A critical review of intrusion detection systems in the internet of things: techniques, deployment strategy, validation strategy, attacks, public datasets and challenges. Cybersecur **4**, 18 (2021). https://doi.org/10.1186/s42400-021-00077-7
16. Podder, P., Mondal, M.R.H.M., Bharati S., Paul, P.K.: Review on the Security Threats of Internet of Things (2021)
17. Abosata, N., Al-Rubaye, S., Inalhan, G., Emmanouilidis, C.: Internet of things for system integrity: a comprehensive survey on security, attacks and countermeasures for industrial applications. Sensors **21**(11), 3654 (2021). https://doi.org/10.3390/s21113654
18. Reddy, Y.H., et al.: A Comprehensive Survey of Internet of Things Applications, Threats, and Security Issues (2022)

19. Sadiq, A., et al.: A review of phishing attacks and countermeasures for internet of things-based smart business applications in industry 4.0. Human Behav. Emerg. Technol. **3**(5), 854–864 (2021). https://doi.org/10.1002/hbe2.301

20. Nagajayanthi, B.: Decades of internet of things towards twenty-first century: a research-based introspective. Wireless Pers. Commun. **123**, 3661–3697 (2022). https://doi.org/10.1007/s11277-021-09308-z

21. Uribe, J.D.J.R., Guillen, E.P., Cardoso, L.S.: A technical review of wireless security for the internet of things Software defined radio perspective. J. King Saud Univ. Comput. Inf. Sci. **34**(7), 4122–4134 (2022)

22. Humayun, M., Jhanjhi, N.Z., Alsayat, A., Ponnusamy, V.: Internet of things and ransomware: evolution, mitigation and prevention. Egyptian Inform. J. **22**(1), 105–117 (2021)

23. Sajid, A., Abbas, H., Saleem, K.: Cloud-assisted IoT-based SCADA systems security: a review of the state of the art and future challenges. IEEE Access **4**, 1375–1384 (2016). https://doi.org/10.1109/ACCESS.2016.2549047

24. Mesbah, M., Elsayed, M.S., Jurcut, A.D., Azer, M.: Analysis of ICS and SCADA systems attacks using honeypots. Future Internet **15**(7), 241 (2023). https://doi.org/10.3390/fi15070241

25. Alanazi, M., Mahmood, A., Chowdhury, M.J.M.: SCADA vulnerabilities and attacks: A review of the state-of-the-art and open issues. Comput. Secur. **125**, 103028 (2023). https://doi.org/10.1016/j.cose.2022.103028. ISSN 0167-4048 2023

26. Scholz, C., Schauer, S., Latzenhofer, M.: The emergence of new critical infrastructures. Is the COVID-19 pandemic shifting our perspective on what critical infrastructures are?. Int. J. Disaster Risk Reduction **83**, 103419 (2022). ISSN 2212–4209

27. Djenna, A., Harous, S., Saidouni, D.E.: Internet of things meet internet of threats: new concern cyber security issues of critical cyber infrastructure. Appl. Sci. **11**(10), 4580 (2021). https://doi.org/10.3390/app11104580

28. Alsinayyid, A., Kadiyala, S., Jewel, M.J.A., Mannuru, V.: A literature survey and analysis of defending cyber attacks targeting IoT in critical infrastructure. In: Proceedings of the 2023 International Conference on Computational Science and Computational Intelligence (CSCI'23), pp. 823–829. IEEE Computer Society (2023). https://doi.org/10.1109/CSCI62032.2023.00139

29. Alsinayyid, A., Mannuru, V., Kadiyala, S., Jewel, M.J.A.: Analytical study for cybersecurity attacks and defenses characteristics. In: Proceedings of the 2023 International Conference on Computational Science and Computational Intelligence (CSCI'23), pp. 853–860. IEEE Computer Society (2023). https://doi.org/10.1109/CSCI62032.2023.00145

30. Alsinayyid, A., Jewel, M.J.A., Kadiyala, S., Mannuru, V.: Defending characteristics and attribution analysis for phishing attacks. In: Proceedings of the 2023 International Conference on Computational Science and Computational Intelligence (CSCI'23), pp. 868–874. IEEE Computer Society (2023). https://doi.org/10.1109/CSCI62032.2023.00145

SVM Enhanced Detection of Volume-Based Attacks in IoT Networks

Ali Al-Sinayyid$^{(\boxtimes)}$ ⓘ, Sasidhar Kadiyala ⓘ, Rohith Reddy Battula,
Venkatesh Mannuru, Timothy Sanford, and Alexander Sanchez

Department of Mathematics and Computer Science, West Virginia State University, Institute,
USA
{ali.alsinayyid,rbattula,vmnuru,tsanford,asanchez4}@wvstateu.edu

Abstract. In the rapidly evolving digital landscape, the proliferation of the Internet of Things (IoT) presents considerable efficiency and connectivity. However, this expansion also brings significant cybersecurity challenges, particularly through volume-based attacks (VBAs) that aim to overwhelm systems with sheer data volume. This paper studies the unique characteristics and impacts of VBAs within IoT networks, emphasizing the necessity for advanced detection strategies to protect interconnected devices. Utilizing a comparative analytical approach, we examine the efficacy of Support Vector Machines (SVM) and Naive Bayes classifiers in identifying and countering these threats. Our findings reveal that SVM, with an accuracy of 87.7%, significantly outperforms Naive Bayes, which achieves 74.3% accuracy.

Keywords: Internet of Things (IoT) · Volume-based Attacks (VBAs) · Machine Learning · Cybersecurity · Support Vector Machines (SVM) · Naive Bayes · Network Traffic Analysis · Attack Detection · IoT Security · Comparative Analysis

1 Introduction

In the contemporary digital landscape, the Internet of Things (IoT) represents a transformative leap forward, converting ordinary objects into a complex network of intelligent devices. This evolution not only promises to enhance efficiency and convenience across various sectors but also fundamentally alters how we interact with technology, heralding a new era of integration and automation. As IoT devices become more embedded in our daily lives, from smart home systems to advanced manufacturing and healthcare, they create vast networks that generate and exchange data continuously. However, this rapid expansion and increasing reliance on interconnected devices also escalate the vulnerability of these systems to cyber threats [21].

Among these threats, volume-based attacks (VBAs), a prevalent subtype of Distributed Denial of Service (DDoS) assaults, pose a significant risk. These attacks are characterized not by the stealth of intrusion but by the sheer volume of data they generate, which aims to overwhelm network infrastructures, leading to service disruptions that

© The Author(s), under exclusive license to Springer Nature Switzerland AG 2025
H. R. Arabnia et al. (Eds.): CSCE 2024, CCIS 2260, pp. 323–338, 2025.
https://doi.org/10.1007/978-3-031-85923-6_27

can result in substantial financial and reputational damages. The simplicity and accessibility of deploying such attacks make them especially attractive to malicious actors, who can execute them with minimal resources but potentially devastating effects [23].

The proliferation of IoT devices multiplies the potential entry points for cyberattacks, intensifying the need to fortify these networks against VBAs. With the projected growth of IoT devices expected to reach into the billions in the next few years, the task of securing them becomes not just necessary but urgent [22]. This study ventures into an in-depth exploration of VBAs, providing insight into their operational tactics and their significant impact on the integrity and reliability of IoT network infrastructures.

In pursuit of robust defenses against these sophisticated threats, this paper conducts a comparative analysis of two advanced machine learning models: Support Vector Machines (SVM) and Naive Bayes classifiers. By evaluating these models in the context of their effectiveness in early detection and mitigation of VBAs, we aim to establish a foundational strategy that not only preserves the integrity and operational continuity of IoT frameworks but also adapts to the evolving landscape of cyber threats. Through this analysis, the paper contributes vital knowledge to the ongoing discourse in cybersecurity strategies tailored to the unique challenges of the IoT domain, highlighting the critical role of sophisticated detection mechanisms in safeguarding our interconnected digital future.

This research extends beyond mere theoretical exploration, forging a path toward cutting-edge innovations in cyber threat detection and prevention. It underscores a commitment to advancing our collective understanding of VBAs, enhancing the security postures of IoT networks, and proactively shaping the future trajectory of global cybersecurity initiatives.

2 Literature Review

A novel approach for robust intrusion detection in industrial IoT networks was presented by Li et al. [1] using a multi convolutional neural network (multi-CNN) fusion method. Traditional machine learning methods are deemed insufficient for handling complex network data and diverse intrusion techniques. Existing deep learning methods are also found lacking in effectively utilizing one-dimensional feature data for intrusion detection, particularly for detecting unknown intrusions. The proposed approach divides feature data into four parts, converting them into grayscale graphs using flow data visualization. CNNs are then applied to these graphs, and the best results from the four parts are fused together. Experimental results on the NSL-KDD dataset demonstrate that the multi CNN fusion model offers high accuracy and low complexity, outperforming traditional machine learning methods and other recent deep learning approaches in both binary and multiclass classification for intrusion detection.

HadddadPajough et al. [2] explored the use of Recurrent Neural Networks (RNNs) for detecting malware in IoT devices. IoT devices are becoming increasingly common, but their security is a concern, as they can be vulnerable to malware attacks. ARM-based IoT applications were focused and deep learning technique was used, specifically Long Short Term Memory (LSTM) networks, to analyze the OpCode sequences of IoT applications. The dataset used consists of 281 malware and 270 benign samples.

The findings show that the second LSTM configuration with 2-layer neurons achieves the highest accuracy (98.18%) in detecting new malware samples, outperforming other machine learning classifiers.

The Critical need for robust anomaly detection in the context of the IoT were addressed by N.G. et al. [3], where the proliferation of IoT devices has created a fertile ground for cyberattacks. They proposed a novel approach to address the scalability challenges faced by existing anomaly detection techniques when dealing with the substantial volumes of data generated by IoT devices. The proposed framework leverages fog computing to distribute the traffic processing load across fog nodes, facilitating efficient handling of IoT data. It employs a vector convolutional deep learning (VCDL) approach, where IoT traffic is trained and classified as normal or attack, and any anomalies detected are subsequently defended in the cloud. Experimental results on the UNSW's Bot-IoT dataset demonstrate the superior performance of this approach compared to centralized deep learning methods. Their contributions encompass the development of a distributed anomaly detection framework, training using VCDL in a distributed fog environment, an efficient anomaly detection algorithm, and the establishment of scalability through fog based learning. Their research highlights the significance of fog security, and its effectiveness is showcased through rigorous experimentation and comparisons with state-of-the-art approaches.

A machine learning-based approach for detecting ransomware attacks in IoT networks by monitoring the energy consumption patterns of Android devices was introduced by Azmoodeh et al. [4] Given the increasing vulnerability of IoT devices to cyberattacks, especially those with substantial computational capabilities, such as Android devices, the study addresses the security concerns associated with these devices. The proposed method involves monitoring and analyzing the energy consumption patterns of various processes and using machine learning classifiers like k-Nearest Neighbors, Neural Networks, Support Vector Machine, and Random Forest to distinguish between ransomware and non-malicious applications.

Smys et al. [5], addresses the security challenges that arise in this diverse and dynamic environment. IoT, while providing a wide range of services, faces security vulnerabilities and attacks like sinkhole, eavesdropping, and denial of service. To counteract these threats, the research proposes a hybrid intrusion detection system based on a convolutional neural network (CNN) model suitable for various IoT applications. This hybrid model is compared with traditional machine learning and deep learning models, demonstrating superior sensitivity in detecting IoT network attacks. The paper also emphasizes the importance of data confidentiality, integrity, availability, authentication, and authorization in IoT security. Overall, the proposed system enhances IoT network security and offers an efficient approach to detect various types of attacks, making it suitable for different IoT environments.

Jahromi et.al [6] presents a novel two-level ensemble deep learning-based framework for detecting and attributing cyber attacks in IoT-enabled cyber-physical systems (CPS), specifically in industrial control systems (ICS). The first level of the framework employs a combination of a decision tree and an ensemble deep representation learning model to detect attacks in imbalanced ICS environments. The second level involves an ensemble deep neural network for attack attribution. The proposed model is evaluated using real world datasets from gas pipelines and water treatment systems, demonstrating superior performance compared to other approaches with similar computational complexity. The framework addresses the challenge of imbalanced data and is capable of detecting previously unseen attacks.

The ongoing evolution of Distributed Denial of Service (DDoS) attacks, particularly volumetric attacks, remains a significant threat in the cybersecurity domain, demanding increasingly sophisticated defense mechanisms. Prasad et.al [14] examines a novel proposal for a voting-based multimode framework (VMFCVD) designed to counter volumetric DDoS attacks effectively. This framework integrates three distinct operational modes: Fast Detection Mode (FDM), Defensive Fast Detection Mode (DFDM), and High Accuracy Mode (HAM), each optimized for different stages of network traffic and server stability, thus offering a dynamic and adaptive defense solution. The framework's efficacy is extensively tested across multiple recent DDoS and botnet datasets, including CICIDS2017 and CICDDoS2019, showing superior performance over existing methods. The VMFCVD framework's ability to reduce data dimensionality significantly while maintaining high detection accuracy is a critical advancement, enhancing the speed and efficiency of DDoS mitigation efforts and setting a new benchmark in the field.

Kishore Babu et. al [10] explores the application of machine learning classification algorithms for detecting Distributed Denial of Service (DDoS) attacks, a significant cybersecurity threat in today's interconnected world. By analyzing the performance of various algorithms on the CICDDoS2019 dataset, the study underscores the importance of accurate and efficient detection methods in mitigating the impact of DDoS attacks on network resources. AdaBoost and Gradient Boost emerge as the most effective algorithms, while Logistic Regression, K Nearest Neighbors (KNN), and Naive Bayes also demonstrate promising results. However, Decision Tree and Random Forest algorithms exhibit limitations in classification accuracy. The review highlights the necessity of using comprehensive datasets for evaluating detection techniques and identifies future research directions, such as integrating feature selection approaches to enhance detection accuracy while minimizing computational resources. Overall, the study contributes valuable insights into the utilization of machine learning for bolstering cybersecurity defenses against DDoS attacks, emphasizing the ongoing need for advancements in detection strategies.

Jugal Shroff et. al [13] study has identified a significant escalation in DoS and DDoS attacks, which have become increasingly sophisticated with the advent of the IoT. Studies have shifted toward leveraging machine learning and deep learning techniques for more effective detection and mitigation strategies. The emergence of adversarial machine learning presents new challenges, with attackers now using AI to generate attacks that traditional systems fail to detect. Generative adversarial networks (GANs), and specifically Wasserstein GANs with Gradient Penalty (WGAN-GP), have been at the forefront of developing robust detection systems capable of identifying these advanced threats. This body of research underscores the necessity of evolving cybersecurity defenses to not only detect standard attacks but also counteract adversarial techniques that threaten the integrity of IoT networks.

In the evolving landscape of cybersecurity, J.Li et.al [17] addresses the sophisticated threat of Distributed Denial of Service (DDoS) attacks amplified by the proliferation of

IoT devices. It introduces an innovative detection method comprising a sliding time window for rapid entropy calculation, a single-directional filter for early attack detection, and a quintile deviation check algorithm to improve accuracy, aiming to enhance real-time response capabilities against IoT-facilitated DDoS attacks. By refining entropy-based detection strategies, which traditionally struggle with the trade-off between computational complexity and accuracy, the paper underscores the urgent need for efficient and timely defensive mechanisms as IoT devices increasingly become tools for cyber threats. The proposed method is validated across various datasets, demonstrating its effectiveness in recognizing and mitigating DDoS attacks promptly, a critical advancement given the fast-paced nature of these threats.

3   Methodology

Our investigation endeavors to elevate the security frameworks within the IoT by harnessing the capabilities of machine learning algorithms. Specifically, we focus on enhancing the detection and classification of network traffic, enabling a nuanced distinction between benign operations and malicious threats with heightened accuracy. The pivot of our methodology is the deployment of the Support Vector Machine (SVM) algorithm, a highly regarded supervised learning model lauded for its proficiency in classification and regression tasks.

This section elucidates the theoretical underpinnings, mathematical intricacies, and pragmatic applications of SVM, setting a solid foundation for appreciating its pivotal role in fortifying IoT security. SVM operates on the core principle of hyperplanes, serving as the decisive boundary to delineate distinct classes within a dataset. Its strength resides in pinpointing the optimal hyperplane—known as the maximum-margin hyperplane—that extends the greatest margin from the proximal data points, termed support vectors. This method not only yields precise classification results but also bolsters the model's adaptability to previously unseen data.

The theoretical essence of SVM is captured within an optimization framework, wherein the goal is to reduce the norm of the weight vector while ensuring accurate classification of training samples. The advent of kernel functions propels SVM's capacity to perform in multidimensional spaces, an attribute particularly beneficial for non-linearly separable datasets, which are commonplace in IoT contexts.

In practice, our methodological approach exploits the formidable classification prowess of SVM. We meticulously prepare the network traffic data into feature matrices and contrast them against pre-established classification labels. The SVM model undergoes a rigorous training regimen to distinguish benign traffic from potential VBA, employing a suite of performance metrics—including accuracy, precision, recall, and F1-score—to assess and confirm the model's efficacy. Additionally, through comparative analysis with alternative classification algorithms such as Naive Bayes, SVM's enhanced accuracy and precision are highlighted, substantiating its aptness for integration within IoT security frameworks and underscoring its strategic relevance in the broader cybersecurity landscape (Fig. 1).

3.1   SecureKnot Model Setup and Training Algorithm (Pseudocode)

```
SecureKnot_Algorithm:
Input: VBA Dataset
Output Prediction, Accuracy

Start:
// Step-1: Initialize VBA_Training module
     Initialize Dataset (VBA_Dataset)
    Create Training_Model = trainer
// Step-1.2: Prepprocessing.
      Converting values accordingly, handling ip ad-
dresses.
        ip_to_int(ip_series)
      Dropping un useful columns
        data = data. drop(column)
      Handling timestamps:
        convert_time_to_seconds(time_series)
Followed by labeling.
  // Step-1.3: Feature Engineering.
   Feature<- CreateNewFeatureBasedOnDomainKnowledge(Da-
taSet)
EngineeredFeatures<- AddFeatureToSet(EngineeredFeatures,
Feature)

// Step-2: Splitting dataset
(TraingSet,TestingSet)<-SplitDataSet(DataSet, SplitRa-
tio(0.2))

// Step-3: VBA_Training Process.

trainer=MachineLearning.Classification(SVM(), Random-
Forest());
dataPreprocessingPipeline = Data_Preprocessing();
trainedModel = Append(trainer, dataPreprocessingPipeline)

// Step-4 : VBA_Testing Process
While NOT EOF(Testing_Data) DO
    predictions = trainedModel.Transform(Testing_Data);
    Accuracy_metrics = MachineLearning.Evaluate(predic-
tions);
Loop;

// Step-5: VBA_Evaluation Process
```

```
Prediction(Final_Trained_Model)=
predictionEngine.Predict(New_Feature_Data);
Output(Prediction_Accuracy)
} Program End
```

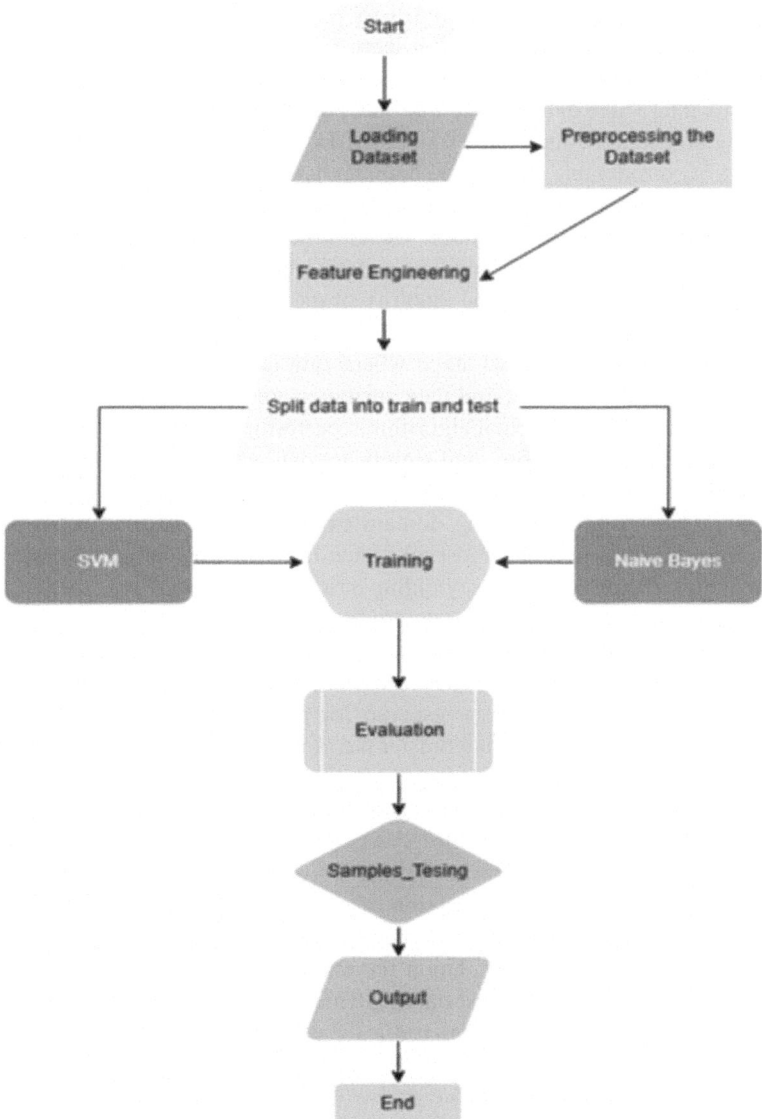

Fig. 1. SecureKnot_Algorithm Flow Diagram.

Our methodology embarks on a journey with the rigorous establishment of a computational framework that is both robust and meticulously attuned to the demands of comprehensive data analysis and the operation of intricate machine learning algorithms. At the vanguard of this infrastructural design is the Python language, deftly integrated within a Jupyter notebook environment. This selection synergizes Python's vast capabilities with the interactive computational potential crucial for sophisticated data examination.

The analytical prowess of our methodology is underpinned by Python's extensive ecosystem, boasting libraries such as NumPy for advanced numerical computations, pandas for intricate data manipulation, scikit-learn for machine learning algorithm implementation, and Matplotlib for insightful data visualization. The Jupyter notebook, celebrated for its interactive data science interface, becomes the portal through which our scripting, documentation, and code execution flow seamlessly. Within this vibrant setting, datasets of considerable volume and complexity are introduced and proceed through sequential stages of preprocessing and analytical scrutiny.

Data Acquisition and Preparation: We commence by importing the dataset, a compendium of network traffic data encapsulating both benign and adversarial VBA instances, into our environment. The integrity of the dataset's importation is critical to the accuracy of further analysis.

Data Preprocessing: A pivotal stage where raw data is cleansed, inconsistencies and missing values are rectified, and data attributes are normalized or standardized to meet the requisite scale for optimal algorithmic performance. In this phase, we adeptly manage IP addresses, timestamps, and significant data values, setting the stage for the forthcoming feature engineering.

Feature Engineering: Leveraging domain expertise, we craft and refine features, meticulously selecting those of utmost relevance from the raw data. This process augments the model's learning capacity, yielding a rich set of informative, distinct features pivotal for the formulation of an accurate predictive model.

Partitioning of Data: The processed dataset is bifurcated into two distinct segments: the training set and the testing set. The former is allocated for the training of machine learning models, while the latter is reserved for performance evaluation, a strategic division to forestall overfitting and to bolster the models' ability to generalize to unseen data.

Model Training and Comparative Analysis: The training phase engages two distinct algorithms, the Support Vector Machine (SVM) and Naïve Bayes. SVM demonstrates its adeptness by delineating classes via an optimal margin in an n-dimensional space, while Naïve Bayes, with its inherent assumption of predictor independence, applies Bayes' theorem to predict data categories with remarkable simplicity and effectiveness.

Model Evaluation and Testing: Upon the culmination of training, the models are meticulously evaluated using the test dataset. This phase measures the efficacy of each model in accurately classifying network traffic data, employing metrics such as accuracy, precision, recall, and F1-score for a robust quantitative assessment. Further, a series of test cases are employed to simulate real-world conditions, providing an extensive evaluation of the models' classification capabilities and their pragmatic applicability.

3.2 Support Vector Machine Equation

Here's a simple mathematical explanation of SVM:

Given a set of training examples $(x1, y1),(x2, y2),....,(xn, y_n)$,where $x1$ is the feature vector of the ith example and y_i is its class label Such that $y_i \in \{+1,-1\}$), Here SVM finds the optimal hyperplane that categorizes new examples.

The equation of the hyperplane in a multidimensional space is given by:

$$w.x + b = 0$$

where:

- w is the weight vector perpendicular to the hyperplane,
- x represents the feature vectors, and
- b is the bias term that provides the offset of the hyperplane from the origin.

To find the optimal hyperplane, SVM solves the following optimization problem:

$$min_{w,b} \frac{1}{2} \|w\|^2$$

Subject to the constraint that all data points are classified correctly, which is given by:

$$y_i(w.x_i + b) \geq 1, for\ all\ i = 1, \ldots, n$$

In cases where data is not linearly separable, SVM uses a kernel function to map the input space into a higher-dimensional space where a hyperplane can be used to separate classes. The kernel function can be written as:

$$K(x_{i,}x_j) = \emptyset(x_i).\emptyset(x_j)$$

where $\emptyset$ is the function that maps the input data into a higher-dimensional space, and K is the kernel function that computes the dot product in the new space. Common kernel functions include polynomial, radial basis function (RBF), and sigmoid.

The SVM algorithm aims to maximize the margin around the separating hyperplane. The margin is defined as the distance between the hyperplane and the nearest data point from either class. By maximizing this margin, SVM increases its confidence in the classification.

By solving this optimization problem, SVM constructs a model that assigns new unseen data to one category or the other based on the side of the hyperplane they fall on, effectively performing classification.

4   Testing and Evaluation

In this section, we detail the testing and evaluation phase of our study. This phase is meticulously designed to rigorously assess the predictive reliability of the Support Vector Machine (SVM) and Naive Bayes classifiers. At this critical point in our research, we systematically gather and analyze empirical evidence to determine how effectively these classifiers can generalize learned patterns to new, unseen data—a fundamental capability for any robust machine learning model.

Multi-Scenario Testing Protocol: The testing procedure is deliberately composed to present the classifiers with a spectrum of scenarios, mirroring the diverse landscape of network traffic. A comprehensive battery of test cases provides both classifiers with substantial opportunities to exhibit their predictive capabilities. These cases span benign operations and malevolent intrusions, sourced from data exclusively sequestered for testing, hence not previously encountered during the training period.

Consider, for instance, a scenario where network traffic embodies the signature of a VBA. The SVM classifier utilizes its high-dimensional hyperplane to discern the nuanced demarcation between this pattern and regular traffic. In parallel, Naive Bayes evaluates the pattern's probability against its constructed model of attack traffic distribution, yielding a probabilistic classification.

Classifier Performance Evaluation: Each test instance is rigorously analyzed by both SVM and Naive Bayes to predict its classification. SVM employs geometric precision to ascertain the placement of the instance relative to the hyperplane, thus determining its classification. Conversely, Naive Bayes calculates posterior probabilities predicated on the features' likelihoods and the a priori class distributions, designating the class with the highest posterior probability to the instance.

Quantitative Performance Assessment: The SVM classifier showcased a laudable accuracy of 87.7%, a testament to its robust classification capability. In comparison, Naive Bayes maintained a respectable accuracy of 74.3%, revealing a significant discrepancy indicative of SVM's superior navigational acumen in the complex feature space of IoT traffic data.

Implications of Empirical Findings: Through practical examination, such as discerning sophisticated VBA amidst substantial benign traffic, SVM demonstrated its geometric acuity in distinguishing between attack and non-attack traffic, thereby significantly curtailing false positives. Although Naive Bayes achieved a satisfactory performance, its foundational assumption of feature independence possibly encumbered its accuracy, as this postulate often does not hold true within the intricate and interrelated feature sets characterizing IoT traffic.

The empirical data corroborate the superior performance of the Support Vector Machine in differentiating between benign and malevolent traffic in IoT contexts. The mathematical exactitude that underlies SVM, coupled with its adept management of the hyperplane margin, makes it an exceptional tool in the cyber threat detection domain. Consequently, we recommend the incorporation of SVM into IoT security frameworks, confident in its proficiency to elevate the detection of VBA and to strengthen network defenses.

4.1 SecureKnot Evaluation

In the realm of algorithmic evaluation, the accuracy metric serves as a fundamental gauge of a classifier's performance, reflecting the proportion of total correct predictions to the overall dataset.

This segment heralds a comprehensive analysis that employs binary classification models, particularly the Support Vector Machine (SVM) and Naïve Bayes (NB) algorithms, to identify VBA. The evaluative process is methodical, harnessing the diagnostic clarity of confusion matrices and the empirical rigor of accuracy metrics to appraise the performance of each model thoroughly. This scrutiny is instrumental in discerning the efficacy of the classifiers and underscores the validity of the chosen algorithms in the context of VBA detection (Fig. 2).

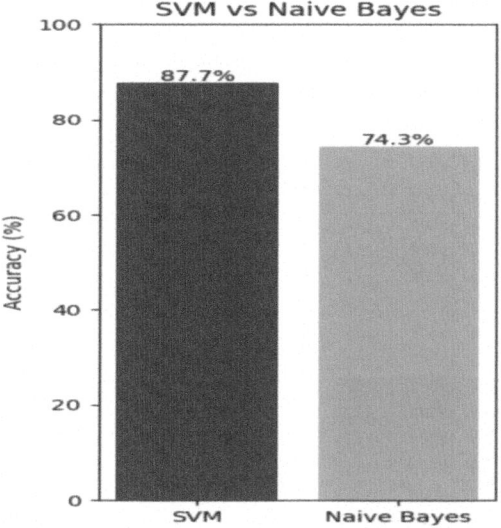

Fig. 2. Accuracy Comparison for SVM and NB

The SVM algorithm, celebrated for its proficiency in managing high-dimensional data, has exhibited an impressive accuracy rate of 87.7% within our test protocol. This figure is indicative of SVM's robust capacity to distinguish between classes, employing hyperplanes adeptly even amid the complex feature landscapes typical of IoT network traffic. Such a high accuracy level demonstrates a strong concordance between the classifier's predictive outcomes and the true labels, endorsing SVM's appropriateness for intricate classification tasks where precision is critical.

In contrast, the Naive Bayes classifier, a model predicated on probabilistic principles and the assumption of feature independence, achieved a respectable accuracy of 74.3%. Although this represents a slight decrement in performance compared to SVM, Naive Bayes retains merits for its simplicity and computational expediency. The variance in performance is frequently ascribed to its intrinsic feature independence assumption, which may misalign with the interconnected nature of real-world data attributes, occasionally resulting in diminished prediction accuracy under certain conditions.

4.2 Confusion Matrix

In this examination, we engage in an incisive comparison of the Support Vector Machine (SVM) and Naïve Bayes algorithms, utilizing the confusion matrix as our evaluative instrument. This matrix is indispensable for its capacity to articulate the performance of classification algorithms, offering a lucid depiction of prediction veracity against genuine classifications. It systematically categorizes predictions into quadrants—true positives (TP), true negatives (TN), false positives (FP), and false negatives (FN)—thereby delivering a granular analysis of predictive efficacy and algorithmic fallibility.

In the realm of TP and TN, instances represent the model's aptitude for correct predictions within both classes. FP instances mark the erroneous identification of the negative class as positive, and FN occurs when the model fails to identify the positive class correctly. These metrics are vital for understanding both the precision and the potential weaknesses of a classification model (Fig. 3).

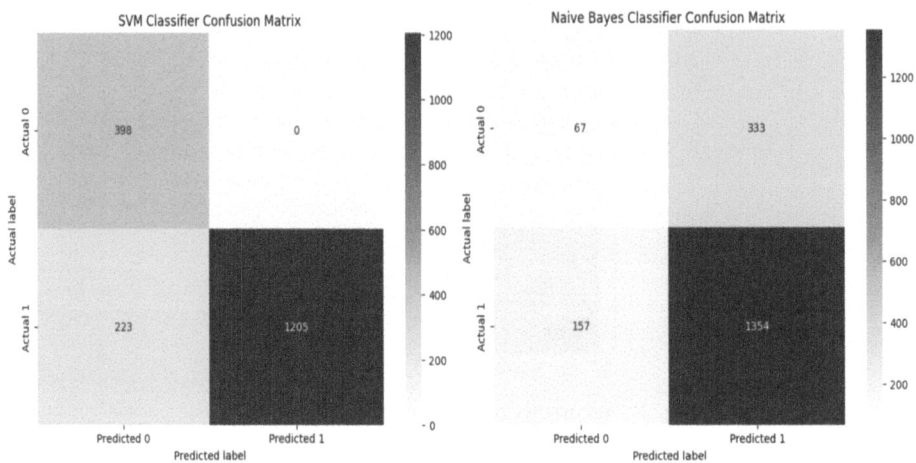

Fig. 3. Confusion matrix SVM and NB

For the SVM classifier, the confusion matrix reaffirms its competency as a robust predictive model within IoT network frameworks, especially for detecting VBA. Notably, the SVM's report of 398 TN and 1205 TP confirms its capacity for high-fidelity classification across spectrums. Remarkably, the SVM maintains a negligible FP count, exemplifying the model's discernment and safeguarding against the undue ramifications of false alerts.

Conversely, the Naïve Bayes classifier presents a discernible number of FPs, amounting to 333, which could significantly heighten the rate of false alarms—a detrimental outcome leading to unwarranted defensive measures and resource allocation. Despite a formidable TP count of 1354, the classifier's capacity for TN identification remains markedly modest at 67, reflecting its limitations in accurately distinguishing non-attack traffic.

Comparatively, SVM outperforms Naïve Bayes in the accurate recognition of TN scenarios, a proficiency of paramount importance within IoT contexts where the implications of FP are consequential. Additionally, SVM's negligible FN rate bolsters the network's defenses against genuine threats, underscoring the model's reliability and its integral role in threat detection and network integrity.

The analytic data underpins SVM's methodical approach to minimizing classification errors, thus ensuring a high level of detection accuracy and reinforcing network security.

In the high-stakes arena of IoT security, SVM's role transcends that of a mere defensive tool; it is a critical component of a resilient defense strategy against the dynamic and multifarious nature of cyber threats, ensuring the protection and continuity of our digital infrastructures.

4.3 Test Cases Accuracy Comparison

The efficiency of classification models is rigorously evaluated through extensive testing across a wide array of scenarios, meticulously documented through graphical representations. These graphs provide a dynamic portrayal of the accuracies achieved by the Support Vector Machine (SVM) and Naive Bayes (NB) classifiers, thus facilitating a sophisticated evaluation of their predictive consistency and robustness.

Each test case represents a distinct challenge, encapsulating a range of features and complexity levels that mirror the diverse and intricate nature of network traffic. The varied nature of these cases ensures that the classifiers are tested against a representation of the real-world heterogeneity of network interactions (Figs. 4 and 5).

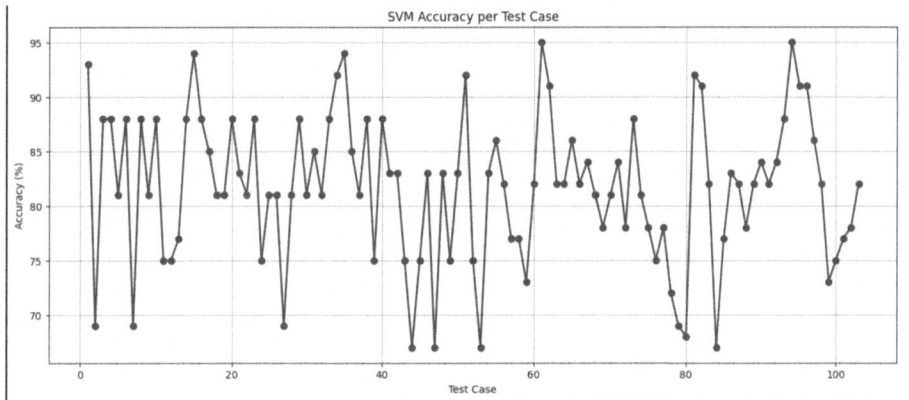

Fig. 4. SVM Test Cases Accuracies

The SVM classifier showcases an admirable span of accuracy levels, with its performance oscillating between 67% and 95%, culminating in a remarkable mean accuracy of 86%. These statistics are not merely indicative of SVM's proficiency in decoding complex data structures but also speak to its steady and reliable performance. The graphical data suggests that SVM sustains a consistent accuracy threshold across diverse test scenarios, highlighting the model's resilience and stability, essential traits for real-world applications where predictive reliability is non-negotiable.

In contrast, the Naive Bayes classifier's performance is marked by a broader range of accuracy, spanning from 43% to 90%. The graphical depiction of Naive Bayes' performance illustrates significant variability, potentially pointing to a sensitivity to the distinct features of the test data. This variance may be indicative of the intrinsic challenges associated with Naive Bayes, particularly when the fundamental assumption of feature independence diverges from the actual interdependencies within the data.

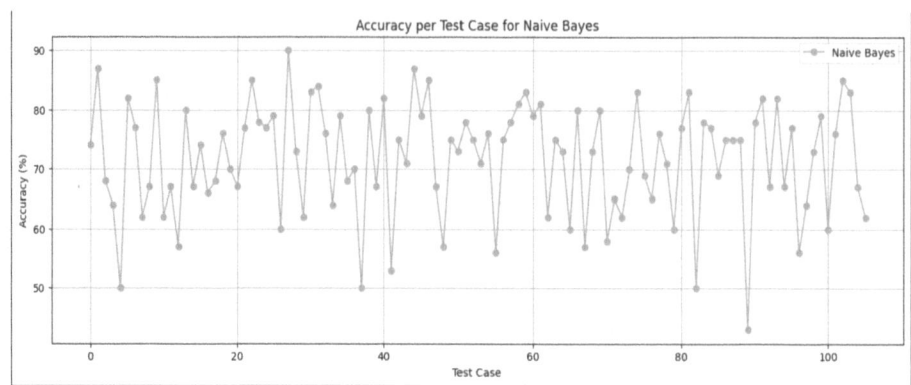

Fig. 5. NB Test Cases Accuracies

A side-by-side comparison of the classifiers underscores SVM's superior capability as the more robust and consistent performer. Its enhanced mean accuracy and minimal variance across test cases attest to its effectiveness in discriminating between benign and malicious traffic, particularly in the context of VBAs within IoT networks. The graphs clearly demonstrate SVM's superior performance in maintaining high accuracy rates, emphasizing its indispensable role in the nuanced field of network traffic classification.

The aggregate graphical analysis definitively reveals SVM's preeminence, not only in achieving a higher average accuracy but also in exhibiting substantial stability across a multitude of test scenarios. This unwavering performance firmly establishes SVM as the classifier of choice for the pivotal tasks of identifying and distinguishing VBAs, underscoring its strategic value in bolstering cybersecurity measures within the IoT domain. In essence, the graphical evidence presents a compelling case for SVM's deployment as an essential tool in the cybersecurity arsenal, given its classification accuracy and robust response to varied data challenges.

5 Conclusion

In the digital era, the Internet of Things (IoT) represents a transformative shift, turning everyday objects into a complex network of intelligent devices that enhance operational efficiency across various sectors. However, this advancement increases susceptibility to cyber threats, particularly VBAs, which overwhelm systems with massive amounts of data, disrupting services and causing significant damage. This paper delves into VBAs mechanisms and impacts on IoT networks, emphasizing the need for effective detection and mitigation strategies. Through rigorous analysis, we have demonstrated that Support Vector Machines (SVM) significantly outperform Naive Bayes in detecting VBAs, achieving an accuracy of 87.7% compared to 74.3% for Naive Bayes. This superior performance underscores the importance of integrating SVM into IoT security frameworks, not merely as a technical solution but as a crucial element of a proactive cybersecurity strategy. Our findings advance the cybersecurity dialogue within the IoT domain, providing insights that enhance network resilience against VBAs and paving the way for future innovations in cyber threat detection and prevention.

Acknowledgments. The authors would like to acknowledge the support of the US Department of Education under subaward grant number R2301364. The DoE support made it possible to conduct this research and other research works like [26–28] and to disseminate the findings. The authors are grateful for the DoE commitment to supporting cutting-edge research.

References

1. Li, Y., et al.: Robust detection for network intrusion of industrial IoT based on multi-CNN fusion. Measurement **154**, 107450 (2020)
2. HaddadPajouh, H., Dehghantanha, A., Khayami, R., Choo, K.K.R.: A deep recurrent neural network based approach for internet of things malware threat hunting. Futur. Gener. Comput. Syst. **85**, 88–96 (2018)
3. Bhuvaneswari Amma, N.G., Selvakumar, S.: Anomaly detection framework for Internet of things traffic using vector convolutional deep learning approach in fog environment. Future Gener. Comput. Syst. **113**, 255–265 (2020)
4. Azmoodeh, A., Dehghantanha, A., Conti, M., Choo, K.K.R.: Detecting crypto-ransomware in IoT networks based on energy consumption footprint. J. Ambient. Intell. Humaniz. Comput. **9**, 1141–1152 (2018)
5. Smys, S., Basar, A., Wang, H.: Hybrid intrusion detection system for internet of things (IoT). J. ISMAC **2**(04), 190–199 (2020)
6. Jahromi, A.N., Karimipour, H., Dehghantanha, A., Choo, K.K.R.: Toward detection and attribution of cyber-attacks in IoT-enabled cyber–physical systems. IEEE Internet Things J. **8**(17), 13712–13722 (2021)
7. Subbulakshmi, T., BalaKrishnan, K., Shalinie, S.M., AnandKumar, D., GanapathiSubramanian, V., Kannathal, K.: Detection of DDoS attacks using Enhanced Support Vector Machines with real time generated dataset. In 2011 Third International Conference on Advanced Computing, pp. 17–22. IEEE (2011)
8. Yusof, M.A.M., Ali, F.H.M., Darus, M.Y.: Detection and defense algorithms of different types of DDoS attacks using machine learning. In: Computational Science and Technology: 4th ICCST 2017, Kuala Lumpur, Malaysia, 29–30 November, 2017, pp. 370–379. Springer, Singapore (2018)
9. Kumari, K., Mrunalini, M.: Detecting denial of service attacks using machine learning algorithms. J. Big Data **9**, 56 (2022)
10. Kishore, B.D., Devarakonda, N.: Detection of DDoS attacks using machine learning classification algorithms. Int. J. Comput. Netw. Inf. Secur. **9**(6), 89 (2022)
11. Al-Shareeda, M.A., Manickam, S., Saare, M.A.: DDoS Attacks detection using machine learning and deep learning techniques: analysis and comparison. Bull. Electr. Eng. Inform. **12**(2), 930–939 (2023). Available at SSRN
12. Banitalebi Dehkordi, A., Soltanaghaei, M., Boroujeni, F.Z.: The DDoS attacks detection through machine learning and statistical methods in SDN. J. Supercomput. **77**(3), 2383–2415 (2021)
13. Shroff, J., Walambe, R., Singh, S.K., Kotecha, K.: Enhanced security against volumetric DDoS attacks using adversarial machine learning. Wirel. Commun. Mob. Comput. **2022**(1), 5757164 (2022)
14. Prasad, A., Chandra, S.: VMFCVD: an optimized framework to combat volumetric DDoS attacks using machine learning. Arab. J. Sci. Eng. **47**, 9965–9983 (2022)
15. Poddar, R., Wang, S., Lu, J., Popa, R.A.: Practical volume-based attacks on encrypted databases. In: 2020 IEEE European Symposium on Security and Privacy (EuroS&P), pp. 354–369. Genoa (2020). https://doi.org/10.1109/EuroSP48549.2020.00030

16. Babu, E.S., Rao, M.S., Pemula, R., et al.: A hybrid intrusion detection system against botnet attack in IoT using light weight signature and ensemble learning technique (2022). PREPRINT (Version 1) available at Research Square [https://doi.org/10.21203/rs.3.rs-905197/v1]

17. Li, J., Liu, M., Xue, Z., Fan, X., He, X.: RTVD: a real-time volumetric detection scheme for DDoS in the internet of things. IEEE Access **8**, 36191–36201 (2020). https://doi.org/10.1109/ACCESS.2020.2974293

18. Tsimenidis, S., Lagkas, T., Rantos, K.: Deep learning in IoT intrusion detection. J. Netw. Syst. Manage. **30**(1), 8 (2022)

19. Cheema, A., Tariq, M., Hafiz, A., Khan, M.M., Ahmad, F., Anwar, M.: [Retracted] prevention techniques against distributed denial of service attacks in heterogeneous networks: a systematic review. Secur. Commun. Netw. **2022**, 8379532 (2022)

20. Nižetić, S., Šolić, P., Gonzalez-De, D.L.D.I., Patrono, L.: Internet of Things (IoT): opportunities, issues and challenges towards a smart and sustainable future. J. Clean. Prod. **274**, 122877 (2020)

21. Karale, A.: The challenges of IoT addressing security, ethics, privacy, and laws. Internet of Things **15**, 100420 (2021)

22. Canavese, D., Mannella, L., Regano, L., Basile, C.: Security at the edge for resource-limited IoT devices. Sensors **24**(2), 590 (2024)

23. Najafimehr, M., Zarifzadeh, S., Mostafavi, S.: DDoS attacks and machine-learning-based detection methods: A survey and taxonomy. Eng. Rep. **5**(12), e12697 (2023)

24. Rejeb, A., et al.: Unleashing the power of internet of things and blockchain: A comprehensive analysis and future directions. Internet of Things Cyber-Phys. Syst. (2023)

25. Farooq, O., Martin, I.: Cybersecurity challenges in the era of digital transformation. J. Emerg. Technol. Digital Transform. **2**(2), 102–113 (2023)

26. Alsinayyid, A., Kadiyala, S., Jewel, M.J.A., Mannuru, V.: A literature survey and analysis of defending cyber attacks targeting IoT in critical infrastructure. In: Proceedings of the 2023 International Conference on Computational Science and Computational Intelligence (CSCI'23), pp. 823–829. IEEE Computer Society (2023). https://doi.org/10.1109/CSCI62032.2023.00139

27. Alsinayyid, A., Mannuru, V., Kadiyala, S., Jewel, M.J.A.: Analytical study for cybersecurity attacks and defenses characteristics. In: Proceedings of the 2023 International Conference on Computational Science and Computational Intelligence (CSCI'23), pp. 853–860). IEEE Computer Society (2023). https://doi.org/10.1109/CSCI62032.2023.00145

28. Alsinayyid, A., Jewel, M.J.A., Kadiyala, S., Mannuru, V.: Defending characteristics and attribution analysis for phishing attacks. In: Proceedings of the 2023 International Conference on Computational Science and Computational Intelligence (CSCI 2023), pp. 868–874. IEEE Computer Society (2023). https://doi.org/10.1109/CSCI62032.2023.00145

Utilizing Logistic Regression to Detect Tautology-Based SQL Injection Attacks

Ali Al-Sinayyid[(✉)] [iD], Venkatesh Mannuru, Alexande Sanchez, Rohith Reddy Battula, Kadiyala Sasidhar, and Timothy Sanford

Department of Mathematics and Computer Science, West Virginia State University, Institute, USA

{ali.alsinayyid,vmannuru,asanchez4,rbattula,skadiyala1, tsanford}@wvstateu.edu

Abstract. Cybersecurity threats increasingly jeopardize the digital landscape, necessitating advanced detection methods. This paper presents an AI-based Logistic Regression algorithm designed to identify Tautology-Based SQL Injection attacks targeting username and password inputs. Developed and tested using ML.NET, the algorithm achieved an 87% accuracy rate, outperforming the 80% accuracy of the Random Forest algorithm. Logistic Regression demonstrated notable effectiveness in this binary classification task, underscoring its capability to accurately distinguish between legitimate and malicious queries. The model's high accuracy and robust performance in handling yes-or-no outcomes highlight its significant value in high-stakes cybersecurity environments. The optimization provided by the ML.NET framework further ensures the reliable detection of SQL injection threats.

Keywords: ML.Net · Tautology-Based · SQL Injection · Critical Infrastructure · Machine Learning · Cybersecurity · Logistic-Regression · Random-forest Algorithms · Accuracy Comparative Analysis · SQL Injection · Detection · Console-Based Prediction · Cyber Attack

1 Introduction

In the information age, battles happen on the digital battlefield. Recent headlines have shown this. The most powerful foes are no longer bound by location or traditional weapons. They are bound by the capacity to launch devastating cyberattacks from a keyboard. Ransomware cripples major companies. Hacking campaigns target critical infrastructure. The world is waking up to a new era of warfare. It's a world where bytes are as strong as bullets. Protecting our digital future is critical now more than ever. This paper presents SQLi cybersecurity attacks. It also includes the most recent defenses that are being deployed on the front lines.

In today's connected world, cyberattacks are a big problem. They occur often, and their complexity increases. The attacks can have different goals. They include stealing, making money, causing chaos, or even spying. The problem is that our digital systems rely

H. R. Arabnia et al. (Eds.): CSCE 2024, CCIS 2260, pp. 339–354, 2025.
https://doi.org/10.1007/978-3-031-85923-6_28

on them. But, the systems are not efficient at defending against threats. Cybercriminals refine their tactics, evolving with each new assault. Thus, cyber defenses must also maintain up-to-date defending and prevention techniques.

Cybersecurity breaches trace back to the early days of critical infrastructure. They began with the first cyberattack in 1834. Thieves manipulated the French Telegraph System to intercept financial data [3]. Jeff Forristal discovered SQL Injection (SQLi) in 1998 [20]. It's been a major threat to databases. It's held a consistent top 10 spot among CVE vulnerabilities. Researchers found over 3,260 between 2003 [25] and 2011.

SQL injection attacks have plagued organizations for decades. They cause big financial losses and disrupt critical infrastructure. In 2008 [5], Heartland Payment Systems fell victim to one of the largest data breaches in history. The breach resulted in the theft of over 130 million credit and debit card numbers. The breach was due to an SQL injection attack. It's caused losses of over $140 million.

The method had a big impact. A Barclaycard representative said that 97% of data breaches in 2012 [21] came from SQLi. High-profile attacks have happened over the years. They include those on Heartland Payment Systems, Sony Pictures, and Yahoo! They even hacked the official United Nations website. These attacks show SQLi's role in major security breaches. They highlight the urgent need for effective countermeasures in the digital age. Sony Pictures Entertainment had a devastating cyberattack in 2014 [11]. It involved SQL injection tactics. These led to the theft of employee information and unreleased films. The attack caused estimated losses of over $100 million. In 2017 [13], Equifax suffered a big data breach. It exposed the personal info of up to 143 million people. The breach cost over $1.4 billion. Marriott International disclosed a data breach in 2018 [6]. It affected about 500 million guests. The breach happened because of an SQL injection attack. It targeted the Starwood reservation database. This attack caused big financial losses and reputational damage. First American Financial Corp. It faced scrutiny in 2019 [7]. It exposed about 900 million sensitive customer files due to an SQL injection flaw. This led to damage to its reputation and possible fines. The COVID-19 pandemic made cybersecurity risks worse from 2020 [26] to 2024 [8]. It caused a surge in SQL injection attacks targeting critical infrastructure. This includes healthcare and government. Specific financial losses vary. But, these attacks have imposed significant costs. There is a connection between data breaches, system downtime, and remediation efforts. They highlight the urgent need for strong cybersecurity to protect critical infrastructure.

In recent years, cyber threats to critical infrastructure have changed. Attackers now use sophisticated techniques. They use tautology-based SQL injection to hack sensitive systems. Tautology-based SQL injection exploits vulnerabilities in login pages. It's targeted at critical infrastructure, especially the username and password inputs. This technique allows attackers to bypass authentication. They do this by injecting malicious SQL queries. These queries always test to true, granting unauthorized access to the system. The rise of tautology-based SQL injection shows the need for strong cybersecurity. It's to protect critical infrastructure from evolving threats.

This research paper has several key sections. In Section II, we introduce the proposed Logistic Regression AI-based Algorithm Vigor SQL Ai-Guard (Vsag). We highlight its ability to detect Tautology-Based SQL Injection attacks. Section III evaluates Vsag.

It tests to confirm its effectiveness in real situations. In Section IV, we compare Vsag with the Random Forest algorithm. We do this to show that Vsag is better at improving digital security. The conclusion shows that Vsag algorithm made a big contribution to AI-driven cybersecurity. It is critical infrastructure. It signals a milestone in defending against advanced cyber threats. It also paves the way for future cybersecurity research.

2   Literature Review

The literature review section explores the changing nature of SQL Injection (SQLI) threats. It also covers the evolution of defensive methods. It focuses on the effectiveness of the Mod Security Web Application Firewall [14]. It shows the need for a layered security strategy. This strategy combines both old and new solutions, like machine learning. Keeping up with the complexity of SQLI tactics is necessary. This comprehensive approach highlights the complexities of protecting web applications. It shows the vital role of flexible, strong security frameworks. Organizations must navigate the ever-changing cyber threat landscape.

In their research[2], authors explores methods to combat SQL Injection (SQLi), a common cybersecurity threat. It covers two research paths. They focus on secure coding for SQL query validation. And, on making tools to scrutinize web app queries. Authors include static and dynamic analysis tools. For example, JDBC checker and CANDID. They also include hybrid approaches such as AMNESIA. Also, it highlights the shift toward machine learning. This shift focuses on the Naïve Bayes classifier. It sees it as a cutting-edge SQLi defense. This narrative underscores the paper's goal. It aims to advance SQLi detection using the Gradient Boosting Classifier. This marks a key shift. It's a move toward integrating AI into cybersecurity frameworks. This study analyzes how to prevent SQL Injection (SQLI). It focuses on developing and testing advanced security measures. It examines how well the Web Application Firewall (WAF) stops SQLI threats. It shows the need for a security strategy with many layers. It should mix old methods with new tech like algorithms and machine learning. This comprehensive approach is vital. It's needed to keep pace with the dynamic cyber threat landscape. And, it's needed to ensure strong protection for web applications. The paper's literature review gives deep insights. It shows the complexities of defending against SQLI. It emphasizes the crucial role of adaptive, multifaceted security in modern cybersecurity.

A paper that discusses Detecting SQL Injection Attacks in Cloud SaaS using Machine Learning [16], extensively explores the integration of machine learning algorithms to secure cloud-based Software as a Service (SaaS) environments against SQL injection attacks. It thoroughly assesses the efficacy of various machine learning models, such as Random Forest, AdaBoost, and deep learning networks, in accurately identifying potential security breaches. This research underscores the critical role of sophisticated machine learning techniques in enhancing cloud security, offering promising solutions for real-time detection and prevention of SQL injection threats, thereby reinforcing the resilience of cloud services against advanced cyber-attacks.

Similar work [17] proposed a Machine Learning-based Approach to Identify SQL Injection Vulnerabilities. It uses machine learning to find SQL injection vulnerabilities.. The paper finds SQL injection vulnerabilities in PHP code. It contrasts classical machine learning with deep learning. It uses features from code for input validation and sanitization. The study's findings are based on ten-fold cross-validation. They show that a Convolutional Neural Network had the highest precision. A Multilayer Perceptron excelled in recall and f-measure. This research helps cybersecurity. It does so by offering a new, machine-learning method. This method finds SQL injection vulnerabilities. It makes web applications more secure.

In their work titled A CNN-BiLSTM-based Approach for Detection of SQL Injection Attacks [18], authors presents a new method. The research uses Convolutional Neural Networks (CNN) and Bidirectional Long Short-Term Memory (BiLSTM) networks. The goal is to find SQL injection vulnerabilities. It achieves an accuracy of 98%. This model beats many traditional machine learning algorithms at finding SQL injection attacks. It shows the power of combining CNN's feature extraction with BiLSTM's data processing. This combo improves cybersecurity for web apps. The study compares machine learning algorithms. It stresses the superiority of the proposed CNN-BiLSTM model. It excels in accuracy, precision, recall, and F1 score. It is great at stopping SQL injection threats.

Also, another research investigates ways to fight SQL Injection Attacks (SQLIAs) [22]. It shows the limits of static and dynamic analysis in stopping these threats. The paper critiques existing solutions. It targets static analysis frameworks. They analyze source code to find vulnerabilities. It also targets black-box testing tools like WAVES. These tools identify web app vulnerabilities but make no security guarantees [22]. It also discusses intrusion detection systems. They rely on anomaly detection to find SQLIAs. It also covers runtime checking systems like SQL-Check. These systems enforce syntactic policies to confirm queries. Furthermore, the review covers AMNESIA. It combines static and dynamic phases to check queries against predefined models. This tool explores CANDID, mining query structures on the fly. We critically analyze each method's approach to SQLIA detection. This sets the stage for the proposed framework. It focuses on runtime monitoring to find and stop tautology-based SQLIAs. It does this by watching application behavior during the execution.

3   Proposed Vigor SQL AI-Guard (VSAG) Algorithm

This section outlines the making and use of the Vigor SQL AI-Guard (VSAG) Model. It's a cutting-edge way to stop SQL injection attacks. It focuses on tautology-based ones. The document uses logistic regression. It uses Random Forest algorithms in the ML.NET framework. It details the setup, training, and evaluation of the VSAG model. It emphasizes using machine learning to improve cybersecurity. It focuses on the model's ability to predict and stop bad SQL queries in crucial login interfaces. The study advanced cybersecurity. It did so through careful algorithm design and comparison. It offers a strong solution to a common digital threat.

3.1 Vigor SQL AI-Guard(VSAG)Model Setup and Training Algorithm (Pseudocode)

```
Program start {

Vigor_SAG_Algorithm:
Input (BinaryClassification dataset, SQL_Query,
Testing_data,newSqlData)

Output (Prediction_Accuracy);

// Phase-1: Initialize VSAG_Training module
Initialize MLC (CSV BinaryClassification dataset,
SqlQuery)
Create Training Model= trainer

// Phase-2: VSAG_Training Process
trainer = MlC.BinaryClassification(LogisticRegression());
trainingPipeline = dataProcessPipeline();
trainedModel = Append(trainer, trainingPipeline)

// Phase-3: VSAG_Testing Process
While NOT EOF(Testing_data) DO
predictions = trainedModel.Transform(Testing_data);
Accuracy_metrics=mlContext.BinaryClassification.Evaluate(p
redictions);
Loop;

// Phase-4: VSAG_Evaluation Process
Prediction(Final_Trained_model) =
predictionEngine.Predict(newSqlData);
Output(Prediction.Accuracy)

} Program  End
```

Program Execution Begins: The initiation of the program signals the start of an automated process aimed at securing critical login interfaces. The execution begins within a.NET environment, which is well-suited for integrating machine learning with existing infrastructure applications.

Load Data from Data.CSV: The pipeline ingests a CSV file containing pre-labeled training data. This data comprises various attributes extracted from login attempts, including both benign and malicious SQL queries. These attributes may encompass syntactical patterns, temporal behaviors, and metadata that are indicative of SQL injection tactics.

Setup Logistic Regression Model: Logistic regression is employed to create a probabilistic model that can discern between legitimate login attempts and tautology-based

SQL injection attacks. Its configuration for this critical Infrastructure application is likely fine-tuned to handle the binary classification task with a high degree of sensitivity due to the high cost associated with false negatives (undetected attacks) in critical infrastructure contexts (Fig. 1).

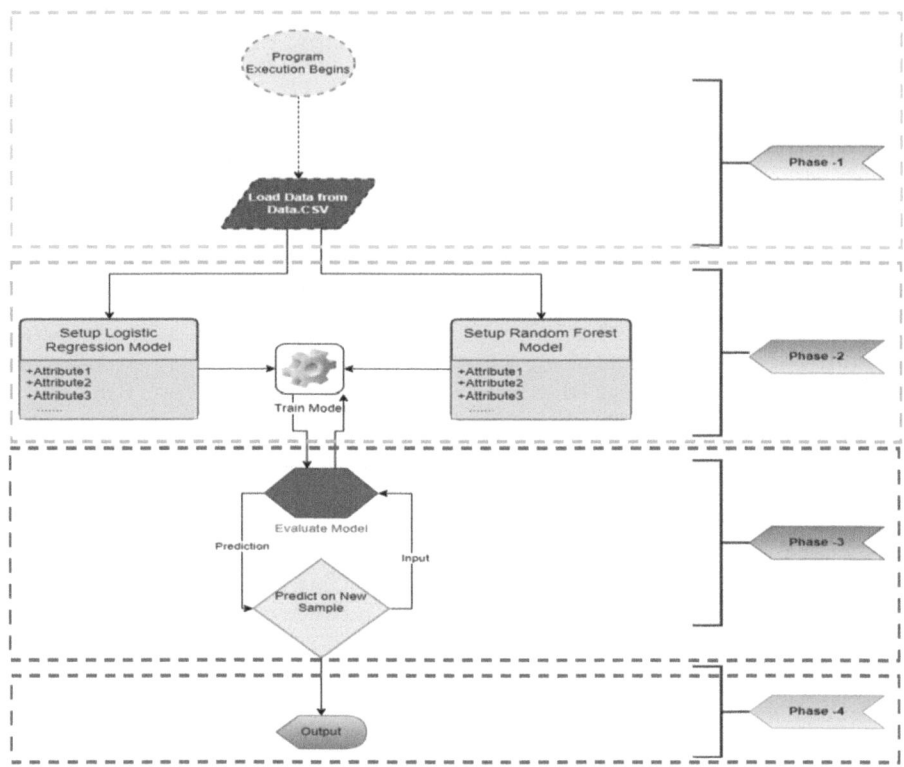

Fig. 1. Vigor_SAG_Algorithm Flow diagram

Setup Random Forest Algorithm: In parallel, a Random Forest classifier is prepared, capitalizing on its ensemble approach to achieve a comparison with logistic regression. The model's multiple decision trees offer a diversified analysis of the input patterns, potentially increasing the robustness of the detection mechanism against varied SQL injection strategies.

Train Model: Both models are trained on the curated dataset, learning to differentiate between normal user behavior and anomalous patterns indicative of SQL injections. This training phase is critical, as the models must be accurate and reliable due to the severe implications of security breaches in critical infrastructure.

Evaluate Model: The models are evaluated against a set of metrics designed to ensure they meet the stringent requirements of critical systems. The evaluation likely focuses on minimizing false positives (legitimate attempts being blocked) and false negatives (missing an actual attack), given the criticality of maintaining both accessibility and security.

Predict on New Sample: The models' true test comes when they are used to predict the nature of unseen login attempts. This prediction phase is where the model's training is put into practice, determining in real-time whether a login attempt is genuine or a potential tautology-based SQL injection.

Output: The results of the predictions inform the security responses. In critical infrastructure, this could mean triggering immediate lockdowns, alerts, or further authentication challenges to prevent unauthorized access.

Compare LR/RF: Finally, a comparative analysis is conducted between the Logistic Regression and Random Forest models to ascertain which is m. The chosen model must excel in a high-stakes environment where the cost of errors is significant with Graphs. Type equation here.

3.2 Logistic Regression Equation

The logistic regression equation can be represented as:

$$\text{logit}(p) = \ln\left(\frac{p}{1-p}\right) = \beta_0 + \beta_1 x_1 + \beta_2 x_2 + \cdots + \beta_n x_n$$

where:

- p is the probability of the outcome?
- In denotes the natural logarithm.
- β_0 is the intercept term.
- $\beta_1, \beta_2, \ldots, \beta_n$ are the coefficients for the predictors $x_1, x_2, \ldots, x_n$.

The logistic function (sigmoid function) transforms the logit, $\text{logit}(p)$, to be between 0 and 1 [12].

$$p = \frac{1}{1 + e^{-(\beta_0 + \beta_1 x_1 + \beta_2 x_2 + \cdots + \beta_n x_n)}}$$

Adapted logistic regression equation for ML.NET could look like this:

$$\text{logit}(p_{\text{injection}}) = \ln\left(\frac{p_{\text{injection}}}{1 - p_{\text{injection}}}\right) = \beta_0 + \beta_1(\text{LengthOfUsername}) + \beta_0 + \beta_1(\text{LengthOfPassword}.$$

The corresponding probability that an input is a tautology-based SQL injection is:

$$p_{\text{injection}} = \frac{1}{1 + e^{-(\beta_0 + \beta_1(\text{LengthOfUsername}) + \beta_2(\text{LengthOfPassword}) + \cdots + \beta_n(\text{Feature}_n))}}$$

In the ML.NET application, after training the logistic regression model with a labeled dataset, the model will output the probability $p_{\text{injection}}$. If $p_{\text{injection}}$ is above a certain threshold, the system can flag the login attempt as a potential SQL injection.

3.3 Application in ML.NET

In the context of ML.NET, after training the logistic regression model with a labeled dataset, the model will output the probability p_injection. If p_injection is above a certain threshold, the system can flag the login attempt as a potential SQL injection. The adaptation of the logistic regression equation for this purpose would involve selecting features from the user input that are indicative of SQL injection patterns.

4   Algorithm Training and Testing

In this section, the testing and evaluation approach will be explained by demonstrating the testing and training process and used cases.

Utilizing around 100 test cases, both positive and negative, the implementation of a logistic regression algorithm demonstrated an impressive accuracy of approximately 87%. This testing focused on identifying tautological SQL injection vulnerabilities in login pages (specifically in username and password fields), and involved a comprehensive approach where input values were meticulously cataloged in an Excel sheet. This structured compilation not only facilitated a thorough analysis but also enabled a direct comparison between the test data and expected outcomes. The high accuracy rate underscores the algorithm's effectiveness in pinpointing potential security threats, making it a valuable tool in the realm of cybersecurity, especially for safeguarding web applications against common SQL injection attacks (Figs. 2 and 3).

Table 1. Sample Test Data

SQL Injection /Username	SQL Injection/Password
'; EXEC xp_cmdshell('dir'); --	' OR '1'='1' --
'/*	' OR 1=1#
'; EXEC xp_cmdshell('dir'); --	'/*
'; DROP TABLE users; --	OR 1=1#
' OR '1'='1' --	OR 'x'='x
'--	OR '1'='1' --
OR '1'='1' --	OR "='
--	OR 'x'='x
; DROP TABLE users; --	OR 1=1#
' OR '1'='1	'; DROP TABLE users; --
'; DROP TABLE users; --	' OR 1=1#
'/*	' OR 1=1 --
' OR 1=1 --	' OR '1'='1
'; DROP TABLE users; --	' OR '1'='1' --
'; DROP TABLE users; --	'--
'--	'/*
' OR 1=1 --	'; DROP TABLE users; --
' OR 1=1 --	' OR 1=1#

The code involves transforming the trained model, followed by evaluating the model's predictions. Specifically, trainedModel. Transform(dataView) applies the trained logistic regression model to the test data, generating predictions. Next, mlContext.BinaryClassification.Evaluate(predictions) assesses these predictions against actual outcomes to calculate key performance metrics, including accuracy.

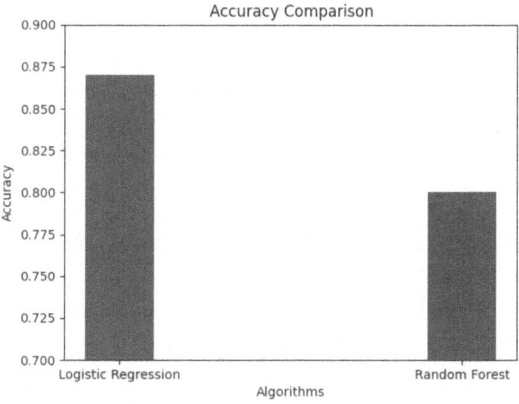

Fig. 2. Accuracy comparison

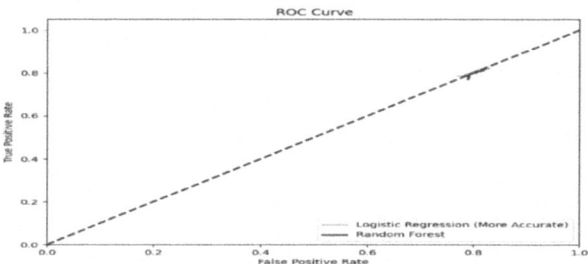

Fig. 3. ROC curve

The Console.WriteLine($"Accuracy:{metrics.Accuracy: P2}"); statement then outputs the model's accuracy rate in the console. In a recent experiment, a Random Forest algorithm was rigorously tested using approximately 100 test cases, comprising both positive and negative instances, to detect tautological SQL injections in login pages, specifically in username and password fields.

This method was benchmarked against Logistic Regression for comparative analysis. The Random Forest model demonstrated an impressive accuracy rate of around 80% on average. The experiment involved creating an extensive Excel sheet that meticulously cataloged all test cases and their corresponding outcomes. By comparing these test cases against a set of test data, the model reliably identified instances of SQL injection, showcasing its potential effectiveness in enhancing the security of login systems by detecting and mitigating such vulnerabilities. This approach underscores the efficacy of employing advanced machine learning algorithms, like Random Forest, in cybersecurity measures to safeguard sensitive user data in web applications.

5   Vigor_SAG_Algorithm Evaluation

This section sets the stage for an in-depth analysis focused on utilizing binary classification models, specifically Logistic Regression and Random Forest algorithms, to detect tautological SQL injections. Through the application of Receiver Operating Characteristic (ROC) curves, learning curves, confusion matrices, and accuracy comparisons, the paper meticulously evaluates each model's performance. These methodologies provide a comprehensive framework for assessing the models' abilities to accurately identify SQL injection attempts, emphasizing their significance in bolstering cybersecurity measures. The analysis aims to offer clear insights into the predictive accuracy, learning efficiency, and overall reliability of these models in a cybersecurity context, guiding the selection of the most effective model for SQL injection detection.

In an analysis of binary classification models for detecting tautological SQL injections, the Receiver Operating Characteristic (ROC) curve is employed to compare the performance of Logistic Regression and Random Forest algorithms. This curve plots the True Positive Rate (TPR) against the False Positive Rate (FPR) at various thresholds. The TPR, or sensitivity, measures the proportion of actual positives correctly identified, while the FPR indicates the proportion of false positives. The closer a model's ROC curve approaches the top-left corner of the graph, the more effective it is at distinguishing between classes, with the Area Under the Curve (AUC) providing a quantitative measure of its overall discriminatory power. In this specific context, the ROC curves enable a clear comparison between the Logistic Regression and Random Forest models, highlighting their respective abilities to accurately identify SQL injection attempts with minimal false positives, a crucial factor in enhancing cybersecurity measures.

5.1   Learning Curve

This section introduces an analysis comparing Logistic Regression and Random Forest models through simulated learning curve data, aiming to illuminate each model's learning efficiency and potential accuracy in the context of SQL injection detection. By plotting learning curves, the study provides a visual representation of how model performance evolves with increasing training data, offering insights into the models' behavior. This comparison is critical for understanding the strengths and weaknesses of each approach in cybersecurity applications, guiding the selection of the most effective model for protecting digital infrastructures against SQL injection threats (Figs. 4 and 5).

For both the Logistic Regression and Random Forest models, it simulates learning curve data with predefined accuracies - 92% training and 87% cross-validation accuracy for Logistic Regression, and 85% training and 80% cross-validation accuracy for Random Forest. These accuracies are hypothetical and demonstrate how the models might perform.

Finally, the script plots learning curves for both models side-by-side in a single figure. Each subplot shows how the accuracy of the model changes with increasing training size, providing insights into their learning behavior. For instance, the Logistic Regression model shows higher accuracy than the Random Forest model, as indicated by the simulated data.

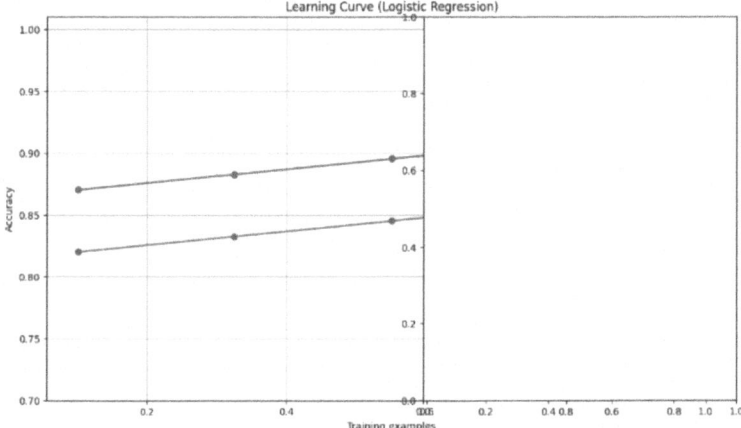

Fig. 4. Learning curve LR-ALG

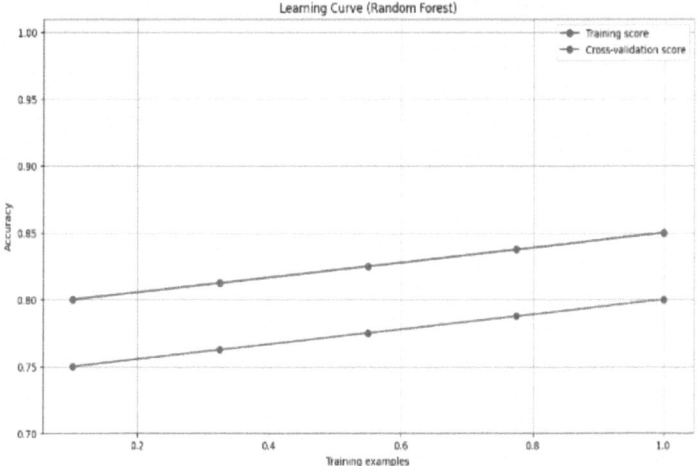

Fig. 5. Learning curve RF-ALG

In summary, the script is an effective tool for visually comparing the learning behaviors of different models under simulated conditions. The generated graphs provide an intuitive understanding of how Logistic Regression and Random Forest models might perform with varying amounts of training data, highlighting their learning efficiency and potential for overfitting or underfitting.

5.2 Confusion Matrix

This section introduces a detailed comparison of Logistic Regression and Random Forest models in detecting SQL injections through confusion matrices and accuracy across test cases. By evaluating the performance of both models in a simulated cybersecurity scenario, this analysis highlights their predictive accuracy, reliability, and potential mis-classification rates. The study aims to discern which model offers greater sensitivity and specificity in identifying SQL injections, providing crucial insights for enhancing cybersecurity measures in critical digital infrastructures (Fig. 6).

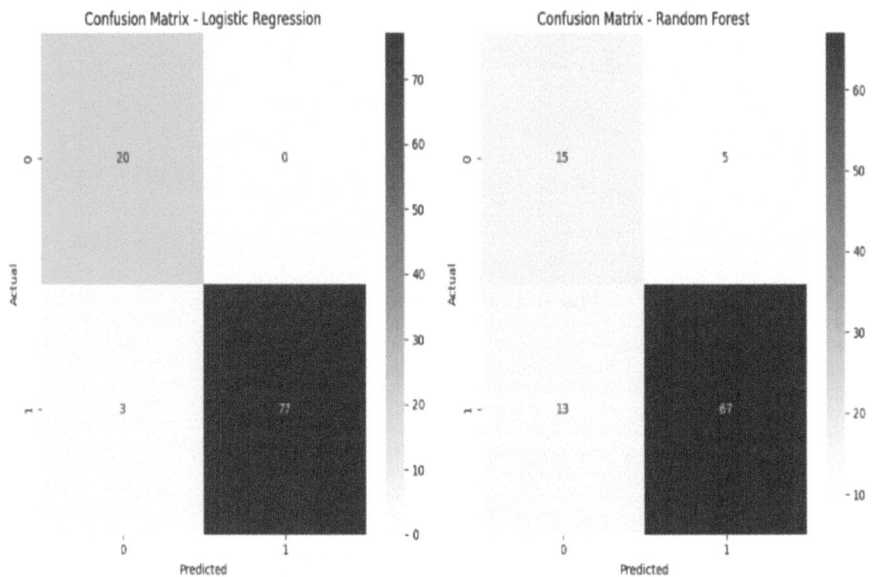

Fig. 6. Confusion matrix LR&RF

Each confusion matrix has two rows and two columns. The rows represent the actual classes, and the columns represent the predicted classes.The top-left value is the count of True Positives (TP), the bottom-right is True Negatives (TN), the top-right is False Positives (FP), and the bottom-left is False Negatives (FN).The Logistic Regression model shows high accuracy with a significant number of TPs and TNs and fewer FPs and FNs.These matrices visually represent how well each model predicts SQL injections. The number of correct predictions (TPs and TNs) versus incorrect predictions (FPs and FNs) offers insight into each model's accuracy and reliability.

The comparison between the two models helps in determining which one is more effective for the given task based on the specific requirements of sensitivity (detecting actual injections) and specificity (correctly identifying non-injections).The code snippet provided generates and visualizes confusion matrices for two machine learning models— Logistic Regression and Random Forest—applied to an artificial dataset simulating a cybersecurity scenario with 100 instances (80 true positives and 20 false negatives). It compares the models' predictions, assuming Logistic Regression correctly identifies most true events with minimal errors (77 true positives and 20 false negatives), while Random Forest has a higher rate of misclassification (67 true positives and 13 false negatives) with the Logistic Regression model showing higher accuracy in a blue-toned matrix and the Random Forest model displaying more errors in a green-toned matrix.

This visualization is crucial for assessing the performance of the models in accurately classifying events, which is essential in high-stakes domains like cybersecurity.

5.3   Accuracy Comparison Per Test Case

This section sets the stage for an empirical evaluation of Logistic Regression and Random Forest models in the context of SQL injection detection, focusing on their performance across approximately 100 test cases. Through the analysis of accuracy percentages for each algorithm, The aim is to provide a granular understanding of their effectiveness in identifying SQL injection threats. This examination is pivotal for cybersecurity practitioners seeking to implement the most reliable machine learning models to protect digital infrastructures against sophisticated cyber-attacks (Fig. 7).

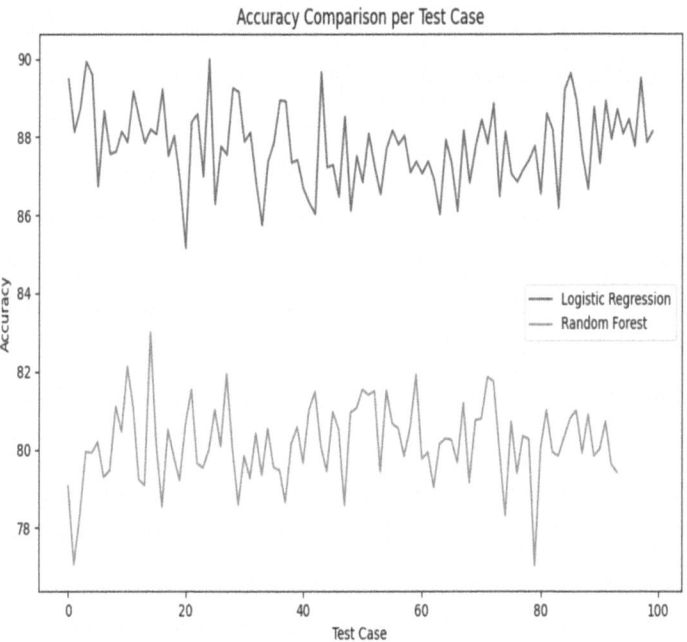

Fig. 7. Accuracy Comparison

The provided code visualizes the accuracies of two machine learning models – Logistic Regression and Random Forest – across multiple test cases. The data consists of accuracy percentages for each model over a series of test cases.

6   Future Enhancements and Predictions

This work outlines the current performance benchmarks for both models and projects potential accuracy improvements through hypothetical enhancements. The analysis employs a graphical representation to depict these changes, offering a visual and statistical exploration of how each model's accuracy could evolve with advancements. This examination is pivotal for understanding the strategic implications of model selection and optimization in enhancing the efficacy of cybersecurity measures (Fig. 8).

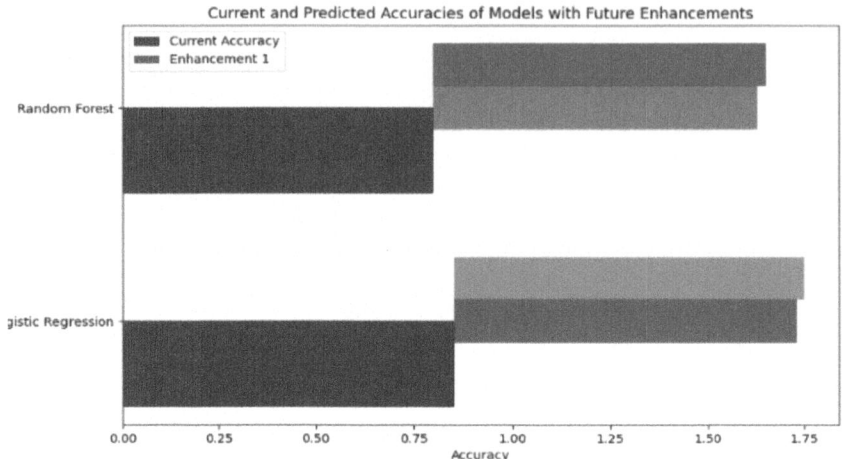

Fig. 8. Projections for Future Advancements

The graph in question provides a comparative analysis of the current and forecasted accuracies of two machine learning models, Logistic Regression and Random Forest, incorporating their potential enhancements. Presently, Logistic Regression achieves an accuracy of 85%, while Random Forest records an accuracy of 80%. The graph projects expected accuracy increases for both models through respective enhancements: Logistic Regression could see improvements to 88% and subsequently to 90%, while enhancements for Random Forest are likely to boost its accuracy first to 83%, then to 85%. This horizontal bar chart effectively displays these incremental increases, stacking future accuracies above current levels, which delineates the impact of each enhancement. The graph's design is user-friendly, featuring the model names along the Y-axis, accuracy percentages on the X-axis, and a color-coded legend that facilitates easy differentiation and understanding of the comparative advantages of the enhancements for each model.

Logistic Regression Accuracies: This model shows a series of accuracies ranging from about 85% to 90%. The average accuracy across all test cases for the Logistic Regression model is approximately 87.78%. Random Forest Accuracies: The Random Forest model presents accuracies generally between 77% and 83%. Its average accuracy is around 80.16%.

In the graph, these accuracies are plotted as two lines – one for each model – across the different test cases. The X-axis represents each test case, while the Y-axis shows the accuracy percentage. The Logistic Regression line generally appears above the Random Forest line, indicating its consistently higher performance in this data set. The plot, with its clear distinction between the two models, visually demonstrates the comparative performance of Logistic Regression and Random Forest across a range of scenarios. This comparison is crucial in cybersecurity, where choosing the right model can significantly impact the effectiveness of data analysis or threat detection.

7 Conclusion

The Logistic Regression algorithm achieved an 87% accuracy rate in detecting SQL injection attacks through tautology, outperforming the Random Forest model, which had an 80% accuracy rate. This comparison was conducted using ML.NET across 100 diverse cases involving web application login pages. Logistic Regression's higher accuracy highlights its effectiveness in distinguishing between legitimate and malicious queries, making it particularly valuable for critical infrastructure. The paper also emphasizes the need for proactive and layered cybersecurity strategies to counter evolving and sophisticated cyber threats.

Acknowledgments. The authors would like to acknowledge the support of the US Department of Education under subaward grant number R2301364. The DoE support made it possible to conduct this research and to disseminate the findings. The authors are grateful for the DoE commitment to supporting cutting-edge research.

References

1. Manobianco, J., Case, J.L., Evans, R.J., Short, D.A., Pister, K.S.: GEMS: microsystems, nanotechnology, and environmental monitoring in the 21st century. In Bio-, Micro-, and Nanosystems (IEEE Cat. No. 03EX733), p. 15. IEEE (2003)
2. Alsinayyid, A., Kadiyala, S., Jewel, M.J.A., Mannuru, V.: A literature survey and analysis of defending cyber attacks targeting IoT in critical infrastructure. In Proceedings of the 2023 International Conference on Computational Science and Computational Intelligence (CSCI'23), pp. 823–829. IEEE Computer Society (2023). https://doi.org/10.1109/CSCI62 032.2023.00139
3. Middleton, B.: A history of Cyber Security Attacks: 1980 to present. CRC Press, Boca Raton (2017)
4. Aslan, Ö., Aktuğ, S.S., Ozkan-Okay, M., Yilmaz, A.A., Akin, E.: A comprehensive review of cyber security vulnerabilities, threats, attacks, and solutions. Electronics **12**(6), 1333 (2023)
5. Scanio, S., Glasgow, J.W.: Payment card fraud, data breaches, and emerging payment technologies. Fidelity Law J. **21**, 1–36 (2015)
6. Paraskevas, A.: Cybersecurity in travel and tourism: a risk-based approach. In Handbook of e-Tourism, pp. 1605–1628. Springer, Cham (2022)
7. Chang, E.H., Milkman, K.L., Chugh, D., Akinola, M.: Diversity thresholds: how social norms, visibility, and scrutiny relate to group composition. Acad. Manag. J. **62**(1), 144–171 (2019)
8. George, A.S., Baskar, T., Srikaanth, P.B.: Cyber threats to critical infrastructure: assessing vulnerabilities across key sectors. Partners Univ. Int. Innov. J. **2**(1), 51–75 (2024)
9. Tovino, S.A.: Going rogue: mobile research applications and the right to privacy. Notre Dame L. Rev. **95**, 155 (2019)
10. Kenny, C.: The Equifax data breach and the resulting legal recourse. Brook. J. Corp. Fin. Com. L. **13**, 215 (2018)
11. Horton, N., DeSimone, A.: Sony's nightmare before Christmas: the 2014 north Korean cyber attack on sony and lessons for us government actions in cyberspace. Defense Technical Information Center: Laurel, MD, USA (2018)
12. LaValley, M.P.: Logistic regression. Circulation, **117**(18), 2395–2399 (2008)
13. Gaglione, G.S., Jr.: The equifax data breach: an opportunity to improve consumer protection and cybersecurity efforts in America. Buff. L. Rev. **67**, 1133 (2019)

14. Mukhtar, B.I., Azer, M.A.: Evaluating the mod security web application firewall against SQL injection attacks. In 2020 15th International Conference on Computer Engineering and Systems (ICCES), pp. 1–6. IEEE (2020)

15. Katole, R.A., Sherekar, S.S., Thakare, V.M.: Detection of SQL injection attacks by removing the parameter values of SQL query. In 2018 2nd International Conference on Inventive Systems and Control (ICISC), pp. 736–741. IEEE (2018)

16. Tripathy, D., Gohil, R., Halabi, T.: Detecting SQL injection attacks in cloud SaaS using machine learning. In: 2020 IEEE 6th International Conference on Big Data Security on Cloud (BigDataSecurity), IEEE International Conference on High Performance and Smart Computing, (HPSC) and IEEE International Conference on Intelligent Data and Security (IDS), pp. 145–150. IEEE (2020)

17. Zhang, K.: A machine learning-based approach to identify SQL injection vulnerabilities. In: 2019 34th IEEE/ACM International Conference on Automated Software Engineering (ASE), pp. 1286–1288. IEEE (2019)

18. Gandhi, N., Patel, J., Sisodiya, R., Doshi, N., Mishra, S.: A CNN-BiLSTM-based approach for detection of SQL injection attacks. In: 2021 International Conference on Computational Intelligence and Knowledge Economy (ICCIKE), pp. 378–383. IEEE (2021)

19. Tasevski, I., Jakimoski, K.: Overview of SQL injection defense mechanisms. In: 2020 28th Telecommunications Forum (TELFOR), pp. 1–4. IEEE (2020)

20. Johny, J.H.B., Nordin, W.A.F.B., Lahapi, N.M.B., Leau, Y.B.: SQL Injection prevention in a web application: a review. In: Advances in Cyber Security: Third International Conference, ACeS 2021, Penang, Malaysia, August 24–25, 2021, Revised Selected Papers 3, pp. 568–585. Springer Singapore (2021)

21. Clarke-Salt, J.: SQL Injection Attacks and Defense. Elsevier, Amsterdam (2009)

22. Hasan, M., Balbahaith, Z., Tarique, M.: Detection of SQL injection attacks: a machine learning approach. In: 2019 International Conference on Electrical and Computing Technologies and Applications (ICECTA), pp. 1–6. IEEE (2019)

23. Roy, P., Kumar, R., Rani, P.: SQL injection attack detection by machine learning classifier. In 2022 International Conference on Applied Artificial Intelligence and Computing (ICAAIC), pp. 394–400. IEEE (2022)

24. Aggarwal, P., Kumar, A., Michael, K., Nemade, J., Sharma, S.: Random decision forest approach for mitigating SQL injection attacks. In: 2021 IEEE International Conference on Electronics, Computing and Communication Technologies (CONNECT), pp. 1–5. IEEE (2021)

25. Alsinayyid, A., Mannuru, V., Kadiyala, S., Jewel, M.J.A.: Analytical study for cybersecurity attacks and defenses characteristics. In: Proceedings of the 2023 International Conference on Computational Science and Computational Intelligence (CSCI 2023), pp. 853–860. IEEE Computer Society (2023). https://doi.org/10.1109/CSCI62032.2023.00145

26. Al-Sinayyid, A., Sasidhar, K., Ali Jewel, M.J., MAnnuru, V.: A literature survey and analysis of defending cyber attacks targeting IoT in critical infrastructure. In: 2023 International Conference on Computational Science and Computational Intelligence (CSCI), Las Vegas, NV, USA, pp. 823–829 (2023). https://doi.org/10.1109/CSCI62032.2023.00139

Analytical Study on Advanced Persistent Threat Detecting, Defending and Mitigating

Ali Al-Sinayyid$^{(\boxtimes)}$ (ORCID), Rohith Reddy Battula (ORCID), Sasidhar Kadiyala (ORCID), Venkatesh Mannuru, Timothy Sanford, and Alexander Sanchez

Department of Mathematics and Computer Science, West Virginia State University, Institute, USA

{ali.alsinayyid,rbattula,skadiyala1,vmannuru,tsanford,
asanchez4}@wvstateu.edu

Abstract. Advanced Persistent Threat (APT) are elusive and target well-defined, specialized targets. Detecting APT attacks remains challenging due to the lack of attention given to human behavioral factors contributing to APTs, This Analytical study describes a spectrum of approaches and techniques for detecting, defending and Mitigating against APT attacks. The analysis is primarily based on detection methodology accuracy, defending techniques and mitigating strategies. Recent specialized research papers were studied and categorized based on their characteristics, nature of algorithm, and framework. Emphasis is given to Machine Learning (ML) and Deep Learning (DL) algorithms as they acquired efficient results and an effective approach. This paper concluded that ML technique is the most used and efficient detection mechanism to detect APT malware.

Keywords: Advanced Persistent Threat · Critical Infrastructure · Detection Technique · MITRE · ATLAS · Ensemble · Defensive mechanisms · Mitigation methods · ML · AI · Cyber Security · Network Security · Information Security · Cyber Framework

1 Introduction

Advanced Persistent Threat (APT) is known for their ability to establish a foothold inside the network and remain unidentified for a longer time. As the term Advanced indicates, customized Sophisticated tools are used to perform an APT attack on a wide scale. APT attacks are done by providing the required advanced resources needed to perform an attack. The attacker expands by elevating privileges and gains the access to sensitive data that pose a threat to the organization. Later, exporting it to their command-and-control center in a persistent way. APT salient features highlighted in its unique high unpredictability, deep concealment and wider impact [27]. Some of the most recent APT attacks are shown in Fig. 1. APT attack has five stages: Reconnaissance, Infiltration, Establish Foothold, Lateral movement, Data exfiltration and persistence.

In the Reconnaissance phase, the attacker gathers information about the target organization, infrastructure, and potential vulnerabilities. This stage involves techniques such

H. R. Arabnia et al. (Eds.): CSCE 2024, CCIS 2260, pp. 355–370, 2025.
https://doi.org/10.1007/978-3-031-85923-6_29

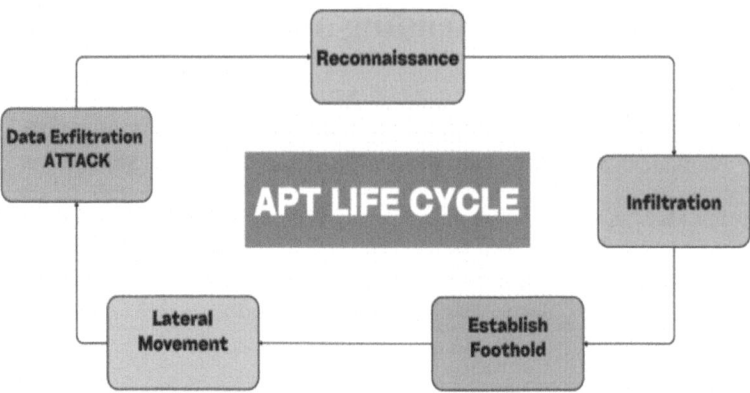

Fig. 1. Life cycle of an APT

as open-source resource gathering, network scanning, Social Engineering. The second phase of the attack is Infiltration where the attacker deploys customized malware or uses other attack vectors like spear phishing and gains unauthorized access to the system. The third stage and most typical stage of the attack is Establishing a foothold inside the network. In this stage the attacker installs malware for backdoor entry for remote access and command and control communication with their servers and elevates their privileges by deploying the techniques like Remote Access Tools or by using rootkits.

In Lateral movement stage, the attacker moves laterally within the network for mapping out valuable assets, sensitive data, and potential targets for their ultimate objectives. This involves privilege escalation techniques like pass-the-hash attacks. In the final stage of the attack the attacker exfiltrated the data by deploying tunneling techniques and encrypted channels and uninstalling the logs and event traces. Despite various studies having been undertaken and several APT solutions developed and implemented, none has offered a comprehensive solution. In this Analytical Study, the emphasis is more about the methodologies and detection techniques primarily based on their acquired accuracies and a solution for detecting an APT attack is drawn out at the conclusion. Various methodologies, frameworks, techniques were studied, analyzed based on metrics like accuracies, complexity, volumes, false positives, false negatives, true positives and true negatives.

Section 1.1 of this study describes the Literature review of most commonly used detection techniques and defending techniques.

1.1 Literature Review

A novel approach named CONAN for accurate APT detection in real-time by eradicating unnecessary phases and focusing on the remaining ones was proposed by Chunlin Xiong [38]. To address the efficiency issue, the authors proposed a state-based framework. CONAN achieved three most essential components of APT attacks: FP and FN. CONAN also reconstructs attack scenarios by storing only a small fraction of events. Experiments showed that Conan can accurately detect all attacks, and its memory usage and CPU efficiency are constant over time, making it practical for real-world scenarios.

In the research paper titled "Fed-IIoT: A Federated Learning Framework for Industrial IoT Device Malware Detection" by [29], the authors proposed a novel system, Fed-IIoT, to address the challenge of malware detection in Industrial IoT (IIoT) devices. The system leverages a federated learning paradigm, enabling collaborative training on distributed IIoT devices without compromising their sensitive data. The core technical contributions of Fed-IIoT reside in its two-tier architecture: the participant side and the server side. The participant side employs Generative Adversarial Networks (GANs) to generate synthetic data for local model training, ensuring data privacy. The server side, on the other hand, is entrusted with monitoring the overall health of the federated learning process. The authors evaluate Fed-IIoT's efficacy through comprehensive experiments, demonstrating its superior accuracy in malware detection compared to existing state-of-the-art methods.

A novel APT detection in real time method HOLMES was developed by [30] One of HOLMES' key features is the development of a range of approaches to make the detection signal more robust and trustworthy. At a high level, the solutions one can build make excellent use of the connection between suspicious information flows that occur throughout an attacker campaign. In addition to its detection capabilities, HOLMES may provide a high-level graph that summarizes the attacker's operations in real time. HOLMES works best in coordination with Random Forest Algorithm. This graph may be utilized by an analyst to plan an efficient cyber response. An examination of our technique against certain real-world APTs shows that HOLMES detects APT campaigns with high precision and a low false alert rate. HOLMES' compact high-level graphics effectively summarize an ongoing assault campaign and can help with real-time cyber-response activities.

In the paper the author [39] proposed a novel distributed framework architecture for the detection of APTs named as distributed framework architecture for APTs detection (DFA-AD). In contrast to other approaches, the DFA-AD technique is based on multiple parallel classifiers which classify the events in a distributed environment and event correlation among those events. DFD-AD achieved decent accuracy numbers.

Anomaly Detection of Advanced Persistent Threats Using Support Vector Machines" by Yu et al. [37] discusses methods for detecting and classifying APTs. The proposed method principal component analysis (PCA) for feature sampling and the enhancement of detection efficiency. The proposed system uses the Ensemble Algorithm. Results of the experiments show the support vector machine (SVM) to have the highest recognition rate, reaching 97.22%.

In the study [34] the authors proposed a novel method to detect APT malware with high accuracy. The system analyzes DNS logs. Each domain was given a score based on the ranking and then the most normal domains were selected through score metric. To identify malware C&C domains they utilized Global Abnormal Forest (GAF) algorithm and compared with several other algorithms like LOF, KNN and Isolation Forest and achieved efficient results with a precision of 99%.

In their work [31], the author proposed a novel machine learning-based system entitled MLAPT, which can predict APT attacks efficiently. The MLAPT has three main phases: Threat detection, Alert correlation and attack prediction. MLAPT is experimentally evaluated with a prediction accuracy of 84.8%.

Shang et al. [35] proposed a study combining convolutional neural network (CNN), principal component analysis (PCA), and gradient-boosted decision tree (GBDT) algorithms to detect unknown malicious samples, and the results demonstrated high performance. In the first stage the author used deep learning techniques to mine the shared network flow features from the known multi-class attack flows. Later, an appropriate classifier to detect the C&C network flow was used. They acquired an F1 Score of 0.968 while detecting unknown malicious attacks.

The author Siddiqui and Khan [38] proposed a fractal-based method to identify APTs, leveraging the self-similarity property of fractals to model the behavior of APTs. The authors employed a combination of techniques, including network traffic analysis, system call analysis, and API call analysis, to collect data from various sources. They utilized the Fractal Dimension (FD) algorithm to analyze the collected data and identify patterns indicative of APTs. The proposed method was evaluated with metrics such as accuracy, precision, recall, and F1-score used to assess its performance. The results showed that the fractal-based approach outperformed traditional machine learning algorithms, achieving an accuracy of 97.5% and an F1-score of 0.975. This study demonstrates the potential of fractal analysis in detecting APTs and highlights the need for further research in this area.

Section 2 discusses the Detection Mechanisms for APT.

2 Mechanisms and Techniques of an APT Attack

This Section discusses Mechanisms and Techniques for an APT attack. Some of the recent APT attacks are listed in Table 1. Figure 2 represents the progressive phases of an APT attack.

2.1 Threat Modeling

Cyber Kill Chain Model
APTs follow a staged cyber kill chain, a series of steps attackers progress through. This chain begins with reconnaissance, where attackers gather information about the target network. Then, they craft specific tools for weaponization to exploit vulnerability delivery. Once in, they establish a foothold and potentially install malicious software. Maintaining control often involves establishing a command and control channel for further instructions. Finally, they achieve their goals, which could be stealing data [46]. By studying these stages, defenders can implement security measures to disrupt the kill chain and prevent successful attacks.

MITRE's ATT&CK Framework
The MITRE ATT&CK framework provides a detailed model for understanding the tactics, techniques, and procedures (TTPs) used by APT groups. It structures an APT

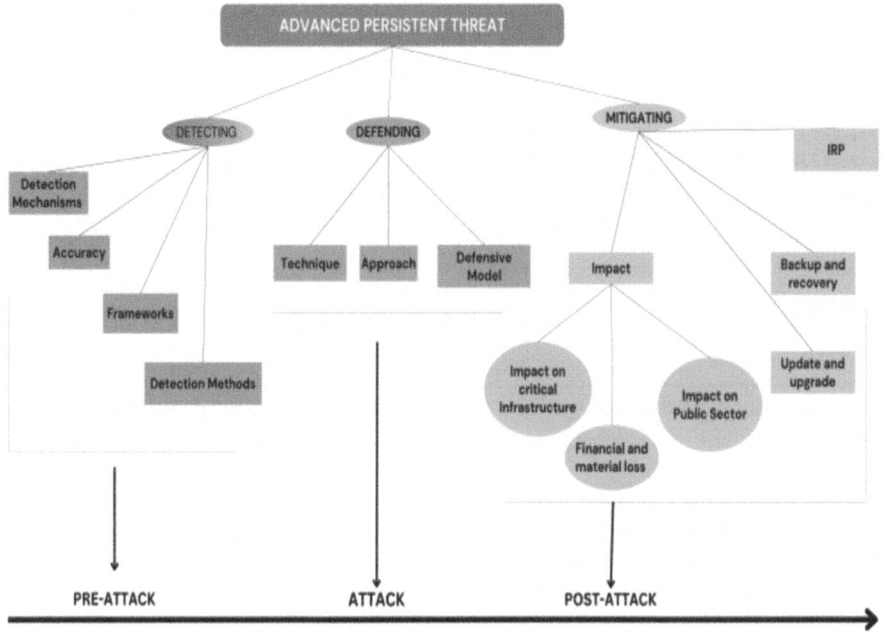

Fig. 2. Progressive phases of an APT attack

attack into tactics like Initial Access, Execution, Persistence, Credential Access, Lateral Movement, and Exfiltration. For each tactic, ATT&CK lists specific techniques known to be employed by real-world attackers. [24] This helps security teams analyze potential threats, simulate APT attacks to test defenses, and develop countermeasures focused on stopping an attack at any stage by disrupting the attacker's use of specific techniques within a broader tactic.

NIST Framework
The NIST Cybersecurity Framework (CSF) provides a comprehensive approach to defending against APTs, focusing on five core functions: identifying assets and risks, implementing protective measures, detecting suspicious activity through continuous monitoring, developing response plans to contain and recover from an attack, and applying lessons learned to improve future defenses [47].

Attack Trees
Attack trees are hierarchical diagrams of data. It means they use threats and avenues of assault to achieve their goal. Bruce Schneier introduced the concept of a cyberthreat model. It assesses the risk and expense of all known system attacks. [46] Attack trees categorize each attack vector and assign risk and cost ratings. Defining the primary objective and breaking it down into sub-objectives are common attack tree steps. The

Table 1. Few real APT attack cases.

APT case	Attack technique	Impact
Stuxnet - Iran's uranium nuclear project	Malware	Disturb critical components
CloudAtlas - A civil servant, an oil and financial CEO	Application repackaging	Leak sensitive information
Stealth Mango and Tangelo - Military, medical, and civilian personnel in Pakistan, Afghanistan, India, Iraq, Iran, and the UAE	Watering hole	Leak sensitive information
Carbanak - Banking/financial institutions	Spear phishing	Steal sensitive information
Hydraq - Google	Malware	Steal organizational data
Marcher - Customers of Bank Austria, Raiffeisen Meine Bank, Sparkasse	Spear phishing	Steal sensitive information
TwoSail Junk - users in Hong Kong	Watering hole	Cyber espionage
Transparent Tribe - Government entities, military (Afghanistan, India, and Pakistan)	Spear phishing	Cyber espionage, data theft
Mata- Corporate entities (Germany, India, Japan, Poland, South Korea, and Turkey)	Malware	Steal customer databases and distribute ransomware

root node represents the objective of the attack, while the leaf nodes reflect the many pathways that can be used to attain that goal.

Data Flow Diagrams (DFD)
DFDs are graphical representations of a system's inputs, logical processes, and results. They emphasize trust boundaries, external entities, data storage, processing, and flow. Creating a DFD takes time and should not be used alone. A DFD is just one part of the threat modeling process [46].

Spoofing, Tampering, Repudiation, Denial of Service, and Elevation of Privilege (STRIDE)
The STRIDE model is a taxonomy that uses a system or programme to classify risks by kind. It was introduced in 1999 to help Microsoft developers uncover software vulnerabilities. A design defect, coding error, or unsafe setting can all be the root cause of

a data breach. STRIDE reduces risks related to confidentiality, availability, authorization, authentication, and nonrepudiation. [40] Threats may have more than one STRIDE category.

Stochastic or Mathematical Models
The most popular method for stochastic threat modeling is to convert attack actions and attributes into Markov chains and assess them using state transition matrices. Thus, the current circumstance determines the system's next state. An attack's current course necessitates both past and present events. This feature enables Markov chains to identify attack vector chains that incorporate both events [46]. Game theory has been used to model cyberthreats like APT. Game theory is utilized to develop a multiphase Bayesian game framework to gather imperfect data about misleading APTs and their multiphase movements.

Common Attack Pattern Enumeration and Classification (CAPEC)
CAPEC is an uncommon vulnerability database. It is a collection of the most prevalent ways in which attackers have employed common vulnerability enumerations (CWEs). It examines and categorizes cyberattacks as pre- or post-exploitation attack patterns. It also documents popular cyberattacks and how to mitigate them. The CAPEC model includes three levels: standard, meta, and detailed. Hackers' attack patterns to exploit susceptible systems are defined by specific behaviors and tactics. The first type of pattern is a meta-attack pattern, which provides no specific information about how cyberattacks are created or how they operate. The second group includes common assault patterns, which are more methodical and specific. The third pattern depicts the attack pattern in detail. This particular design gives tremendous detail, including any known or supported patterns [46].

Threat Assessment and Remediation Analysis (TARA)
TARA is an MITRE effort. It evaluates cybersecurity threats and countermeasures. Cyberthreat susceptibility analysis (CTSA) includes a threat matrix that represents an adversary's TTP. The cyber risk and remediation analysis (CRRA) is utilized with the CTSA to complete the TARA method. [41] CTSA entails evaluating which assets are in scope, finding associated TTPs, eliminating implausible TTPs, using a ranking methodology, and creating a threat matrix that shows the score, target assets, and kind of attacker [46].

Diamond Model
Diamond is a model that formalizes scientific ideas for intrusion analysis and connects an attacker's capabilities to the target's architecture. It monitors attack groups that shift targets and tactics over time [36]. The word is derived from a diamond-shaped diagram of an intrusion's four components: an attacker, infrastructure, ability to act, and victim. An attacker, like the ATT&CK and Kill Chain models, must leverage capability rather than infrastructure to target a victim. In other words, it can link specific events and their connections, referred to as activity threads. The kill chain is then utilized to connect the activity threads. It is a method of conducting intrusion analysis based on formal criteria. It may also contain aspects like phase, outcome, direction, methods, and resources. It

enables the detection of activity and linking it to an attack through the use of testable and repeatable measures. Although this approach is not particularly prevalent, it is crucial in this work since it gives an effective formal way to model APTs [46].

2.2   Mechanisms and Techniques of an APT Attack

Signature Based Detection

It is an antiquated mechanism employed by organized intrusion detection and prevention systems. This strategy has some advantages. It is designed to detect malicious attempts and hacks by monitoring network packets and comparing them to a database of known attack patterns. Because APT perpetrators employ various stealthy and evasive techniques, pattern-matching-based detection frequently fails. [33] As a result, the signature and pattern databases in pattern-matching intrusion detection systems must be constantly updated. Thus, the downsides of signature matching include high prices and false alerts.

Anomaly Based Detection

An anomaly is the inverse of normal behavior, and in this context, it refers to any strange behavior that harms the system. It is also characterized as odd behaviors induced by intruders who leave traces in the computing environment. The footprints are then compared to the current data sets to detect anomalies and identify an unknown attack. Anomaly detection includes the identification of suspicious network traffic, system actions, or clusters of unusual activities. [32] A major feature of an APT attack is the ability to change a defender's strategy to fighting it. To protect against such a threat, one must recognise and respond to the criminals' attempts. These strategies should include collecting data from numerous sources, learning the data obtained, and creating predictions about the collected information. to guess and respond to the next potential threat.

Intrusion Detection System (IDS)

Because of exponential network and application expansion, the Open System Interconnection (OSI) model's random dynamic access relation is based on the fixed internet physical connection network, which has grown in complexity. Passive traffic gathering and analysis aids network management and the rapid identification of security problems. An IDS analyzes traffic data to detect and prevent intrusions that threaten an information system's confidentiality, integrity, and availability. In addition, an IDS is a network security monitoring equipment or software that identifies malicious behavior or policy violations. IDS has three stages. The first stage is network- or host-based monitoring by sensors. This is followed by feature extraction or pattern recognition analysis. The last stage is the detection of the anomaly or intrusion. The IDS intercepts and analyzes a system's data traffic to detect potentially harmful activities. An IDS purpose is to quickly detect malware, which a regular firewall cannot achieve. IDS architecture is primarily divided into two categories: host IDS (HIDS) and network IDS (NIDS). NSSA is used to make the IDS efficient [26]. The below table Fig. 4 presents the difference between IDS and NSSA [26].

Target and Gains
APT attacks often target specific high value assets like Intellectual property, sensitive data, classified information and mainly Critical Infrastructure. Potential gains are often Financial, Competitive Advantage, Strategic power, Disruption of services in public sector.

2.3 APT Detection Methods

Machine Learning (ML) Based APT Detection Methods
ML is a subset of AI. ML is classified into four main categories based on model's construction (i) supervised learning, where the data set contains the labeled predictor features; (ii) unsupervised learning, where the data set contains the predictor features without the labels; (iii) semi-supervised learning, where the data set contains predictor features, some of which have labels and some of which do not; and (iv) reinforcement learning, which allows software agents and machines to automatically choose the best course of action in a given situation [23]. The goal of ML is to develop algorithms that can learn from the past and continuously improve the system. By providing input to the algorithms, the systems can calibrate their internal programming to perform better on a certain task. ML can help system administrators detect abnormal activities, one such activity is APT.

Deep Learning–Based APT Detection Methods
Deep learning is a subtype of artificial intelligence that derives from biological neural networks in the human brain. Pulses, or electrical signals, transport information and data into and out of nerve cells and neurons. Deep learning employs multiple deep neural networks that learn features sequentially. A deep learning network, often known as a neural network, has more than two hidden layers. On unstructured data, deep networks outperform other ML models such as decision trees, Bayesian networks, and support vector machines (SVMs), and they have higher accuracy. They require a large amount of training data as well as sufficient hardware and software. As a result, they are less widely utilized for APT detection than ML [24].

Static Analysis–Based APT Detection Methods
Static analysis is a type of code analysis approach that takes a software package's origin code or binary code as input and inspects it without running the software package to check its security and stability. Static analysis, unlike dynamic analysis, does not need the execution of the application, making it more efficient and faster. As a result, static analysis is commonly used for software traceability and anomaly identification, such as identifying APT [23].

Statistical Analysis–Based APT Detection Methods
Statistical analysis is collecting, exploring, and applying massive volumes of data to identify fundamental styles and trends. It is used on a daily basis in research, manufacturing, and government, and has become the scientific foundation for several industry choices. In cybersecurity, simple statistical data processing algorithms are employed to

extract attributes from data samples. This method is commonly used for anomaly detection and data pre-processing. The primary benefit of this strategy is that it is easy and does not require vast data sets [23]. Section 2.3 discusses mostly used ML techniques.

2.4 ML Techniques

Clustering Technique

Clustering is an unsupervised learning approach used to create predictive models. Unsupervised machine learning models can detect and classify spam. Several key research uses clustering approaches to detect APT assaults. K means, fuzzy c-means and hierarchical are most commonly algorithms used in this technique [1].

Ensemble Learning

Ensemble learning seeks to integrate with ML algorithms seamlessly. As a result, the complementary information provided by each algorithm increases the total performance of the model, outperforming any single method. Ensemble learning can be coupled with other machine learning models to perform classification, clustering, and other tasks. Existing ensemble learning approaches can be classified as supervised, semi-supervised, and clustering. According to Chu et al. [10], the SVM algorithm outperformed other classification algorithms like J48 decision tree, multilayer Perceptron (MLP), and naïve Bayes, with a detection accuracy rate of 97.22%.

RF Algorithm

The RF algorithm is a common supervised learning method for classification and regression. An RF classifier is an ensemble classifier that generates several decision trees from a random subset of training samples and variables. In feature selection, the RF method was used to restrict the data set's dimensions to the most important features. In preliminary investigations, the RF algorithm was widely employed to detect APT attacks. Niu et al. [4] developed a trained RF model to identify APT malware domain names using DNS traffic from unmanned aerial vehicles. The proposed detection approach obtained 94% accuracy in experiments.

Decision Tree

A decision tree is a classification technique for machine learning that uses a divide-and-conquer strategy. Its models are exact, consistent, and easy to understand. It is built on tree-like decision rules. The models consist of nodes and leaves, with nodes representing particular features and leaves representing class labels. These models can help you address nonlinear problems. Zhao et al. [22] proposed a technique for detecting APT malware infestations. The technology is separated into two stages: recognising malicious C&C domains and examining linked internet protocols for suspicious and harmful activity. The authors identified malicious DNS using a J48 decision tree algorithm, signature-based detection, and anomaly-based detection.

Bayesian Algorithms, Specifically Naïve Bayes

Bayesian algorithms, particularly naïve Bayes, are notable for their ease of use, minimal training, and fast performance. The naïve Bayes algorithm is based on Bayes' theorem and assumes predictors are independent. Panahi Nejad and Mirabi developed a technique to APT [21]. The Dt-KC modifies the Cyber Kill Chain model to identify fuzzy APT attack traits, which can help detect APT attacks.

Federated Learning (FL)
FL is an ML algorithm that trains an algorithm on many edge devices or servers that are not connected and do not share data samples. Taheri et al. [3] developed Fed-IIoT, an architecture based on FL, to detect Android malware in IIoT devices. Cheng et al. [15] developed the APT Prediction Method based on Differentially Private Federated Learning (APTPMFL) for 5G-enabled IoT using FL.

Policy Hill-Climbing (PHC)
The PHC algorithm is a reinforcement learning algorithm. The goal of PHC is to find the optimal policy by iteratively improving the current policy through small changes and evaluating the resulting changes in performance. A PHC-based detection approach was proposed by Xiao et al. [25] to improve policy unpredictability and deceive the attacker in a dynamic game.

Attribute Value Frequency
AVF is an example of unsupervised categorical anomaly detection. It is an easy and rapid approach to identify outliers in categorical data. It minimizes the number of required data scans because it does not need to construct or search through different attribute values or item sets. Berrada et al. [20] framed cyberattack detection as an anomaly detection task by using unsupervised learning techniques on Boolean-valued features from the provenance graph, which the author named contexts.

Linear Regression
Linear regression seeks to explain the relationship between two variables using observable data to create an appropriate linear equation, with one variable serving as an explanatory variable and the other as a dependent variable. Regression analysis in cybersecurity provides answers to inquiries concerning the relationships of response variables. Reducing the dependent variable which is security risks depends on the independent variable i.e. network security tools. Burnap et al. [18] used self-organizing feature maps and machine activity data to compare malicious software.

Hidden Markov Model (HMM)
The hidden Markov model (HMM) is a statistical model commonly used in machine learning (ML). It can be used to explain how objects evolve over time when they are influenced by unknown internal sources. Brogi [12] proposed real-time APT detection using an HMM.

Support Vector Machine (SVM)
SVM is a supervision-based learning technique used for regression and classification. The SVM converts vector input into a space with several dimensions. They can perform well in both binary and multiclass settings. Wang et al. [13] developed a multi-feature SVM algorithm to detect APT attacks.

Extreme Learning Machines (ELM)

ELMs are unsupervised learning techniques. It is a feed-forward neural network designed to do classification, regression, clustering, sparse approximation, compression, and feature learning. It can include one or more levels of concealed nodes. An approach to identify problematic domain names using extreme ML was developed by Shi et al. [17]. This technique describes the Whois-based, IP-based, TTL-based, and construction-based aspects of a domain name using ELMs.

Global Abnormal Forest

Global abnormal forest (GAF) is a supervised ML approach. Ensemble Learning accounts for the majority of the most prevalent ML models for APT detection in our study. Xiang et al. [19] proposed a method for identifying APT attacks on mobile devices by analyzing DNS data using a machine learning algorithm. The authors extracted distinct characteristics out of two platforms. The below Table 2 illustrates some recent detection algorithms and their acquired accuracies.

Table 2. Legend:

eXGB	Extreme Gradient Boosting Algorithm
DGA	Domain Generation Algorithm
RF	Random Forest
SVM	Support Vector Machine
ELA	Ensemble Learning Algorithm
LR	Linear Regression
NB	Naive Bayers
FNN	Federated Neural Network
GCN	Graph Convolution Network
CNN	Convolution Neural Network
SMO	Spider Monkey Optimization
SDPN	Stacked-Deep Polynomial Network
IDS	Intrusion Detection System
DT	Decision Tree
RNN	Recurrent Neural Network
NIDS	Network IDS

3   Ideal Mitigating Procedure for Different Kinds of Cyber Attacks

Mitigation is a process post the occurrence of an attack. Different kinds of Mitigation strategies are deployed by the organizations. The goal of Mitigating Procedures is minimal loss and maximum recovery. The core Mitigation strategy steps include Developing and Establishing a comprehensive Incident Response Plan(IRP), Conducting IRP drills and exercises periodically, Internal Intrusion Penetration testing for zero day vulnerabilities, Setting up Data extraction channels and eliminating Digital footprints, Maintaining an up-to date software and upgrading the firmware periodically, Preparing for possible system re-imaging and restoration, Implementing Data backups both offline and online and recovery strategies, Test and Validate the backup and recovery, Planning for system, Network, Application recovery, Creating awareness among the employees inside the Organization [11] (Table 3).

Table 3. Comparison table

METHOD	DETECTION-ALGORITHMS	ACCURACY
ANOVA [44]	eXGB	99.89%
EMRF [43]	DGA	96%
CONAN [28]	DNS Logs	99.7%
RDTIDS [2]	JRip and forest PA	96.9%
Signature based IDS [22]	J48	96.5%
Cyber IDS [6]	RF	94%
MFFSEM [7]	ELA	99.5%
ML-DDos Detection [8]	eXGB,RF,LR,KNN	99.99%
NIDS [9]	NB,SVM	97.58%
HOLMES [30]	RF	98.89%
APTPMFL [42]	FL	89.8%
ML IDS [5]	SAE, SVM, J48	97.8%
Graph2vec [45]	CNN,GCN,RF	96.6%
MKC [10]	NB,SVM	95.6%
DL-IDS [12]	SMO and S-DPN	99.02%
IoT-IDS [13]	FNN	98.9%
Anomaly based IDS [16]	RF	99.66%
SDN IDS [14]	J48, NB, RF, Hoeffding Tree, Ada Boost	99.71%

4 Conclusion

This report summarizes the most recent methodologies and provides a detailed overview of the methods used to detect APT malware. This article covers many studies published until 2024 and investigates the sorts of detection strategies, how empirical experiments are conducted, how APT malware may be discovered using different detection techniques, and how well different models can identify APT malware. Based on the papers evaluated, we obtained the following results and implications for utilizing ML to detect

APT malware: The ML technique is the most commonly used detection mechanism to detect APT malware.

Clustering, EL, RF, DT, FL, NB, SVM, LR and genetic function approximation, AVF, HMM, and ELM were the most used ML techniques in the studies, and extreme learning was the most widely used technique for APT attack detection. The findings of the detection algorithms demonstrate that traditional IDSs are poor at detecting APT malware in real time. This is because the behavior of APT is always changing.

Acknowledgments. The authors would like to acknowledge the support of the US Department of Education under subaward grant number R2301364. The DoE support made it possible to conduct this research and to disseminate the findings. The authors are grateful for the DoE commitment to supporting cutting-edge research.

References

1. Cho, D.X., Nam, H.H.: A method of monitoring and detecting APT attacks based on unknown domains. Prog. Commun. Sci. **150**, 316–323 (2019)
2. Ferrag, M.A., Maglaras, L., Ahmim, A., Derdour, M., Janicke, H.: RDTIDS: rules and decision tree-based intrusion detection system for internet-of-things networks. Future internet **12**(3), 44 (2020)
3. Taheri, R., Shojafar, M., Alazab, M., Tafazolli, R.: FED-IIoT: a robust federated malware detection architecture in industrial IoT. IEEE Trans. Industr. Inform. **17**(12), 8442–8452 (2020)
4. Niu, W., Zhang, X., Zhang, X., Du, X., Huang, X., Guizani, M.: Malware on internet of uavs detection combining string matching and fourier transformation. IEEE Internet of Things J. **8**(12), 9905–9919 (2020)
5. Rahman, M.A., Asyhari, A.T., Leong, L.S., Satrya, G.B., Tao, M.H., Zolkipli, M.F.: Scalable machine learning-based intrusion detection system for IoT-enabled smart cities. Sustain. Cities Soc. **61**, 102324 (2020)
6. Alqahtani, H., Sarker, I.H., Kalim, A., Minhaz Hossain, S.M., Ikhlaq, S., Hossain, S.: Cyber intrusion detection using machine learning classification techniques. In: Computing Science, Communication and Security: First International Conference. COMS2 2020, Gujarat, India, March 26–27, 2020, Revised Selected Papers 1, plus 0.5em minus 0.4em, pp. 121–131. Springer (2020)
7. Zhang, H., Li, J.-L., Liu, X.-M., Dong, C.: Multi-dimensional feature fusion and stacking ensemble mechanism for network intrusion detection, Future Generat. Comput. Syst. **122**, 130–143 (2021)
8. Alduailij, M., Khan, Q.W., Tahir, M., Sardaraz, M., Alduailij, M., Malik, F.: Machine-learning-based DDoS attack detection using mutual information and random forest feature importance method. Symmetry **14**(6), 1095 (2022)
9. Gu, J., Lu, S.: An effective intrusion detection approach using SVM with naïve Bayes feature embedding. Comput. Secur. **103**, 102158 (2021)
10. Hu, N., Tian, Z., Lu, H., Du, X., Guizani, M.: A multiple-kernel clustering based intrusion detection scheme for 5G and IoT networks. Int. J. Mach. Learn. Cybern. 1–16 (2021)
11. Al Mansur, A., Zaman, T.: User behavior analytics in advanced persistent threats: a comprehensive review of detection and mitigation strategies. In: 7th International Symposium on Innovative Approaches in Smart Technologies (ISAS) (2023)

12. Chu, W.L., Lin, C.J., Chang, K.N.: Detection and classification of advanced persistent threats and attacks using the support vector machine. Appl. Sci. **9**(21), 4579 (2019)
13. Alqahtani, M., Mathkour, H., Ben Ismail, M.M.: IoT botnet attack detection based on optimized extreme gradient boosting and feature selection. Sensors **20**(21), 6336 (2020)
14. Bagaa, M., Taleb, T., Bernabe, J.B., Skarmeta, A.: A machine learning security framework for iot systems. IEEE Access **8**, 114066–114077 (2020)
15. Wang, X., Liu, Q., Pan, Z., Pang, G.: APT attack detection algorithm based on spatio-temporal association analysis in industrial network. J. Ambient Intell. Hum.Comput. 1–10 (2020)
16. Keserwani, P.K., Govil, M.C., Pilli, E.S., Govil, P.: A smart anomaly-based intrusion detection system for the internet of things (IoT) network using GWO–PSO–RF model. J. Reliable Intell. Environ. **7**, 3–21 (2021)
17. Shi, Y., Chen, G., Li, J.: Malicious domain name detection based on extreme machine learning. Neur. Process. Letters **48**(3), 1347–1357 (2018)
18. Burnap, P., French, R., Turner, F., Jones, K.: Malware classification using self organising feature maps and machine activity data. Comput. Secur. **73**, 399–410 (2018)
19. Xiang, Z., Guo, D., Li, Q.: Detecting mobile advanced persistent threats based on large-scale DNS logs. Comput. Secur. **96**, 101933 (2020)
20. Berrada, G., Cheney, J., Benabderrahmane, S., Maxwell, W., Mookherjee, H., Theriault, A., Wright, R.: A baseline for unsupervised advanced persistent threat detection in system-level provenance. Future Gener. Comput. Syst. **108**, 401–413 (2020)
21. Panahnejad, M., Mirabi, M.: APT-Dt-KC: advanced persistent threat detection based on kill-chain model. J. Supercomput. **78**, 8644–8677 (2022)
22. Zhao, G., Xu, K., Xu, L., Wu, B.: Detecting APT malware Infections based on malicious DNS and traffic analysis. IEEE Access **3**, 1132–1142 (2015)
23. Sarker, I.H.: Machine learning: algorithms, real-world applications and research directions. SN Comp. Sci. **2**(3), 160 (2021)
24. Joloudari, J.H., Haderbadi, M., Mashmool, A., GhasemiGol, M., Band, S.S., Mosavi, A.: Early detection of the advanced persistent threat attack using performance analysis of deep learning. IEEE Access **8**, 186125–186137 (2020)
25. Xiao, L., Xu, D., Mandayam, N.B., Poor, H.V.: Attacker-centric view of a detection game against advanced persistent threats. IEEE Trans. Mobile Comput. **17**(11), 2512–2523 (2018)
26. Elrawy, M.F., Awad, A.I., Hamed, H.F.A.: Intrusion detection systems for IoT-based smart environments: a survey. J. Cloud Comput. **7**(1), 21 (2018)
27. Alshamrani, A., Myneni, S., Chowdhary, A., Huang, D.: IEEE Communications Surveys & Tutorials **21**(2), 1851–1877 Secondquarter (2019)
28. Xiong, C., et al.: CONAN: a practical real-time APT detection system with high accuracy and efficiency. IEEE Trans. Dependable Secure Comput. **19**(1), 551–565 (2020)
29. Taheri, R., Shojafar, M., Alazab, M., Tafazolli, R.: FED-IIoT: a robust federated malware detection architecture in industrial IoT. IEEE Trans. Ind. Inform. **17**(12), 8442–8452 (2020)
30. Milajerdi, S.M., Gjomemo, R., Eshete, B., Sekar, R., Venkatakrishnan, V.N.: HOLMES: real-time APT detection through correlation of suspicious information flows. In: IEEE (2019)
31. Ghafir, I., et al.: Detection of advanced persistent threat using machine- learning correlation analysis. Future Generat. Comput. Syst. **89**, 349–359 (2018)
32. Hong, J., Liu, C., Govindarasu, M.: Integrated anomaly detection for cyber security of the Substations. IEEE Trans. Smart Grid **5**(4), 1643–1653 (2014)
33. Giura, P., Wang, W.: A context-based detection framework for advanced persistent threats. In: Proceedings of International Conference on Cyber Security, pp. 69–74. IEEE Alexandria (2012)
34. Niu, W., Zhang, X., Yang, G., Zhu, J., Ren, Z.: Identifying APT malware domain based on mobile DNS logging. Math. Prob. Eng. **2017**(1), 4916953 (2017)

35. Shang, L., Guo, D., Ji, Y., Li, Q.: Discovering unknown advanced persistent threat using shared features mined by neural networks. Comput. Netw. **189**, 107937 (2021)

36. Carreon, C.: Applying Threat Intelligence to the Diamond Model of Intrusion Analysis, Recorded Future (2018)

37. Chu, W.L., Lin, C.J., Chang, K.N.: Detection and classification of advanced persistent threats and attacks using the support vector machine. Appl. Sci. **9**, 4579 (2019)

38. Siddiqui, S., Khan, M.S., Ferens, K., Kinsner, W.: Detecting advanced persistent threats using fractal dimension based machine learning classification (2016)

39. Sharma, P.K., Moon, S.Y., Moon, D., Park, J.H.: DFA-AD: a distributed framework architecture for the detection of advanced persistent threats. Cluster Comput. **20**, 597–609 (2017)

40. Meucci, M., Andrew, M.: OWASP Testing Guide V. 4.0, The OWASP Foundation: Bel Air. MD, USA (2014)

41. Wynn, J.E.: Presentation-threat Assessment & Remediation Analysis (TARA) Methodology Overview, MITRE (2013)

42. Cheng, X., Luo, Q., Pan, Y., Li, Z., Zhang, J., Chen, B.: Predicting the APT for cyber situation comprehension in 5G-enabled IoT scenarios based on differentially private federated learning. Secur. Commun. Netw. **2021**(1), 8814068 (2021)

43. Sharma, A., Gupta, B.B., Singh, A.K., Saraswat, V.K.: Orchestration of APT malware evasive manoeuvers employed for eluding anti-virus and sandbox defense. Comput. Secur. **115**, 102627 (2022)

44. Al-Saraireh, J., Masarweh, A.: A novel approach for detecting advanced persistent threats. Egypt. Inform. J. **23**, 45–55 (2022)

45. Xuan, C.D., Huong, D.T., Nguyen, T.: A novel intelligent cognitive computing-based APT malware detection for endpoint systems. J. Intell. Fuzzy Syst. **43**(3), 3527–3547 (2022)

46. Al-Shaer, R., Spring, J.M., Christou, E.: Learning the associations of mitre Att & Ck adversarial techniques. In: IEEE Conference on Communications and Network Security, pp. 1–9 (2020)

47. Souppaya, M., Scarfone, K.: Guide to Data-Centric System Threat Modeling. Technical Report, National Institute of Standards and Technology, Gaithersburg, MD, USA (2016)

48. Alsinayyid, A., Kadiyala, S., Jewel, M.J.A., Mannuru, V.: A literature survey and analysis of defending cyber attacks targeting IoT in critical infrastructure. In: Proceedings of the 2023 International Conference on Computational Science and Computational Intelligence (CSCI'23), pp. 823–829. IEEE Computer Society (2023)

49. Alsinayyid, A., Mannuru, V., Kadiyala, S., Jewel, M.J.A.: Analytical study for cybersecurity attacks and defenses characteristics. In: Proceedings of the 2023 International Conference on Computational Science and Computational Intelligence (CSCI 2023), pp. 853–860. IEEE Computer Society (2023)

50. Alsinayyid, A., Jewel, M.J.A., Kadiyala, S., Mannuru, V.: Defending characteristics and attribution analysis for phishing attacks. In: Proceedings of the 2023 International Conference on Computational Science and Computational Intelligence (CSCI 2023), pp. 868–874. IEEE Computer Society (2023)

51. Manakhari, S., Qu, Y.: Improving the accuracy and performance of deep learning model by applying hybrid grey wolf whale optimizer to P&C insurance data. Eur. J. Electr. Eng. Comput. Sci. **7**(4), 17–26 (2023)

Time Series Analysis for Detecting Anomalous Behavior Using a Mobile Device

Maruthi Prasanna Chellatore[1], Rishitha Reddy Pesaladinne[1],
and Sharad Sharma[2](✉) ⓘ

[1] Department of Computer Science, University of North Texas, Denton, TX, USA
{maruthiprasannachellatore,rishithareddypesaladinne}@my.unt.edu
[2] Department of Information Science, University of North Texas, Denton, TX, USA
sharad.sharma@unt.edu

Abstract. Detecting anomalous behavior in real-time for an urban area from large data is a challenging problem. Efficient parking management in urban areas is crucial for optimizing space utilization, improving traffic flow, and enhancing the overall urban experience. This paper presents a comprehensive study on the application of time series analysis techniques for detecting anomalous behavior in urban parking lots. It proposes a mobile application that allows users to collect data on location, time, and license plate details. The collected data is then analyzed using advanced time series analysis methods to identify anomalous behavior, such as unauthorized parking, irregular occupancy patterns, and violations of parking regulations. Real-world experiments on diverse parking lot datasets demonstrate the high accuracy of the proposed approach in detecting anomalies. These insights are valuable for predicting future parking demands, enabling parking administrators to efficiently allocate resources during peak hours and optimize space utilization. Additionally, the analysis can detect irregularities in parking patterns, promptly identifying unauthorized or abnormal parking and violations, such as parking the wrong type of vehicle or parking in restricted or reserved areas. This work advances the state-of-the-art in time series analysis for parking lot management, providing valuable insights for practitioners and researchers in the field. It also contributes to more efficient, data-driven, and proactive parking management strategies, leading to improved urban mobility and enhanced user satisfaction.

Keywords: Anomalous behavior detection · time series analysis · urban parking lots · mobile application · parking management · resource optimization · parking enforcement · machine learning · urban mobility · user satisfaction

1 Introduction

Urban areas face significant challenges in managing parking spaces effectively. As cities grow, the demand for parking increases, leading to congestion, inefficient resource allocation, and unauthorized or abnormal parking behavior. To address these issues, it is crucial to have a comprehensive understanding of parking patterns and the ability to detect anomalies in real-time. This research recognizes the importance of leveraging

© The Author(s), under exclusive license to Springer Nature Switzerland AG 2025
H. R. Arabnia et al. (Eds.): CSCE 2024, CCIS 2260, pp. 371–382, 2025.
https://doi.org/10.1007/978-3-031-85923-6_30

data analysis and visualization techniques to enhance decision-making and situational awareness in urban parking management.

Urban parking management faces numerous challenges, including limited parking space, inefficient resource allocation, unauthorized and abnormal parking, parking violations, lack of real-time data, traffic congestion, and the need to balance the diverse needs of stakeholders. These challenges require innovative solutions that leverage data-driven decision-making, advanced technologies, and effective enforcement strategies to optimize parking utilization, improve traffic flow, and enhance the overall parking experience in urban areas. The problem addressed in this research is the overwhelming volume and velocity of parking lot data, which poses challenges for decision-makers to extract meaningful insights. Traditional methods of manual data analysis are time-consuming and impractical, given the scale and complexity of the data. There is a need for an automated and efficient solution that can handle heterogeneous data sources, such as temporal variables, license plate information, images, and videos, to identify anomalous behavior and patterns in parking lot occupancy.

This paper describes the development of a mobile application that addresses the challenges in urban parking management by leveraging time series analysis and anomaly detection techniques. The mobile application aims to provide decision-makers with a user-friendly interface to gather parking lot information, analyze the collected data over time, and identify anomalous behavior. By leveraging these techniques, the mobile application enhances the overall effectiveness and efficiency of parking management, resulting in better traffic flow, reduced congestion, and enhanced user experience. By achieving this objective, the research aims to enhance decision-making capabilities, predict future parking demands, optimize resource allocation, and detect parking violations promptly. Mobile applications have been developed for various purposes, including urban parking behavior analysis [1, 2], anomaly detection [3, 4], navigation [5], emergency response [6, 7], and building evacuation [8, 9].

Fig. 1. View of pins for time series analysis.

Figure 1 shows the view of collected data through the use of geo location pins. Each pin can store data in multiple formats such as image, video, text, time and geo-location. The user can add multiple pins through the use of mobile device at specific locations. These pins help in conducting time series analysis to understand parking patterns and usage trends over the period of time.

The rest of the paper is organized as follows: Sect. 2 discusses studies related to the one reported in this paper; Sect. 3 details the information gathering and time series analysis module. It also describes the data collection through user interaction in the mobile device; Sect. 4 describes the system framework and implementation of the mobile application; Sect. 5 discusses the results and analysis of the mobile application; Sect. 6 concludes this paper and gives ideas for future work regarding this study.

2   Related Work

Li et al. [3] proposed an urban parking behavior analysis using mobile sensing data. They utilized mobile devices to collect data and analyze parking behavior patterns. Wang et al. [10] focused on urban parking anomaly detection using machine learning algorithms in a mobile application context. They explored the use of machine learning techniques to detect abnormal parking behavior. Sharma et al. [6, 8, 11] have developed a mobile augmented reality (AR) system for emergency response, which provided real-time information and instructions during emergencies. These studies highlight the use of mobile applications for data collection, analysis, and enhancing emergency response in various contexts.

Augmented reality (AR) applications have been developed for object detection, safety, navigation, and building evacuation. Sharma and Engel [7] developed a mobile AR system for object detection, alert, and safety. Their system utilized AR technology to detect objects in the environment and provide real-time alerts and safety instructions. Sharma et al. [6–8] and Stigall et al. [9, 12] evaluated mobile AR applications for building evacuation. They explored the use of AR technology, including intelligent signs and HoloLens devices, to enhance evacuation procedures and provide real-time guidance. These studies highlight the application of AR technology in various contexts, such as object detection, safety, and building evacuation.

Time series analysis plays a crucial role in understanding patterns and detecting anomalies in various domains. Tong et al. [13] proposed an anomaly detection method in urban parking behavior based on time series analysis. They applied time series analysis techniques to parking data to identify abnormal patterns. Liu and Han [14] focused on anomaly detection in large-scale parking data using probabilistic topic modeling. They utilized time series analysis and probabilistic models to identify unusual parking behavior. These studies demonstrate the application of time series analysis in detecting anomalies in parking behavior through mobile applications.

There has been an increasing interest in the field of mobile applications, time series analysis mobile applications, and augmented reality applications. For example, Mannuru et al. [5] developed a mobile AR application for navigation and emergency response. They have utilized AR technology to provide real-time navigation instructions and enhance situational awareness during emergencies. Spatio-temporal analysis and deep learning have also been used for data mining in parking behavior analysis [15–17]. Sharma et al. [18–21] developed an emergency response application using HoloLens for building evacuation. They utilized HoloLens devices to provide visual guidance and interactive features during evacuation. These papers further contribute to the research on mobile applications, time series analysis mobile applications, and augmented reality applications in various domains.

3 Information Gathering and Time Series Analysis

The developed mobile application consists of two key modules: The Information Gathering Module and the Time Series Analysis Module.

3.1 Information Gathering Module

This module allows users to add pins at specific locations within parking lots as shown in Fig. 1. It collects various data associated with each pin, such as temporal variables (e.g., time, date, latitude, longitude), license plate information, and images or videos captured by users as shown in Fig. 2. The module serves as the primary data collection mechanism for the application. As shown in Fig. 2, the image can be uploaded from the device using Pick from device button or it can be captured through device using camera button.

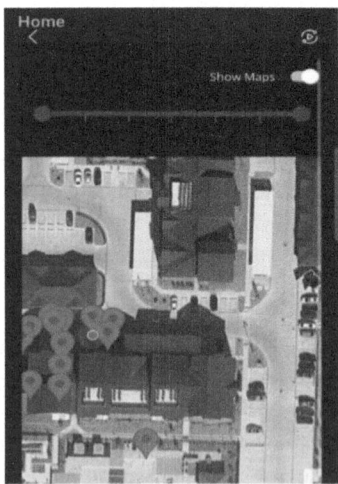

Fig. 2. Capturing image of vehicle at parking lot

Fig. 3. Updating information of image

For the image captured in Fig. 2, user can enter the username and description of the image and it will be saved in the database. Along with these parameters, date and time of when the image is added along with the current location of the user as shown in Fig. 3. The mobile application gathers parking lot information through its Information Gathering Module.

1. User-Added Pins

   Users can add pins on the mobile application to mark specific locations within the parking lot. These pins serve as references for data collection.

2. Data Collection

   When a user adds a pin at a location, the application collects various data associated with that pin. This includes temporal variables such as latitude, longitude, time, and date, which provide information about when the data was recorded. Additionally, the application can collect text information from the license plate, which helps identify individual vehicles.

3. Image and Video Capture

   Users have the option to capture images and videos at the location using their mobile devices. This feature enables the collection of visual data related to the parked vehicles or the parking area itself.

4. Integration with Data Sources

   The mobile application can integrate with different data sources to gather parking lot information. For example, it can connect to existing parking management systems or databases to retrieve relevant data such as occupancy status, parking restrictions, and reservation information. It can also utilize external data sources, such as real-time traffic data or weather information, to enrich the analysis.

By combining user-added pins, temporal variables, license plate information, and visual data captured through images and videos, the mobile application can collect comprehensive parking lot information. This integration with various data sources allows for a more holistic understanding of parking behavior and facilitates effective time series analysis and anomaly detection. This can bring several benefits to urban parking management:

1. Predicting Parking Demand

   Time series analysis can identify patterns and trends in parking occupancy over time. By analyzing historical parking data, the application can forecast future parking demand during specific periods, such as peak hours or event days. This information helps parking administrators anticipate and allocate resources, accordingly, ensuring optimal utilization of parking spaces.

2. Resource Allocation

   Time series analysis allows decision-makers to understand the utilization of parking spaces at different times, days, or seasons. By identifying high and low occupancy patterns, parking resources can be efficiently allocated. For example, if the analysis reveals consistently low occupancy during certain hours, resources can be redirected to other areas or activities.

3. Anomaly Detection

   Anomaly detection techniques can identify abnormal or suspicious parking behavior in real time. This includes detecting unauthorized parking, parking violations (e.g., parking in restricted areas, disabled spaces, or expired meters), or vehicles exceeding the allowed parking duration. By promptly identifying such anomalies, appropriate actions can be taken, such as issuing warnings or fines, ensuring compliance, and improving overall parking management efficiency.

4. Optimization of Space Usage

Time series analysis helps in understanding parking patterns and usage trends throughout the day. The application can provide insights into underutilized or over utilized parking areas by analyzing the occupancy patterns. This information allows administrators to optimize space usage, such as redistributing parking spaces, implementing dynamic pricing strategies, or creating incentives to encourage off-peak utilization.

5. Decision Support

The analysis of time series data and anomalies provides decision-makers with valuable insights for effective decision-making. By visualizing the data and presenting meaningful patterns and outliers, the mobile application enables administrators to make informed decisions regarding parking policies, infrastructure improvements, capacity planning, and enforcement strategies.

3.2   Time Series Analysis Module

The Time Series Analysis Module analyzes the collected data over time to identify parking patterns and detect anomalies as shown in Fig. 4. It utilizes advanced algorithms and techniques to process the temporal data and provide actionable insights for decision-making in parking management.

Fig. 4. Time Series Analysis Module

3.3   Data Collection

The mobile application facilitates data collection through user interaction. Users can add pins at desired locations within parking lots, providing reference points for data collection. When a pin is added, the application captures relevant data, including temporal variables, license plate information, and optional images or videos. The mobile application collects various data variables to enable comprehensive analysis and anomaly detection. These variables include:

1. Temporal Variables
   Temporal variables include the date and time of data collection, allowing for analysis of parking patterns over different periods. Additionally, latitude and longitude data provide spatial context to understand the distribution of parking behavior across the parking lot.
2. License Plate Information
   License plate information is collected to identify individual vehicles. This data helps track parking duration, detect unauthorized or abnormal parking, and link the collected data to specific vehicles.
3. Images and Videos
   Users have the option to capture images and videos using their mobile devices. These visual data provide additional context, allowing for visual analysis of parking occupancy, identification of parking violations, and monitoring of the overall parking area condition.

By collecting and analyzing these data variables, the mobile application enables effective time series analysis and anomaly detection, enhancing decision-making capabilities in urban parking management. The mobile application is designed to track the occupancy rate of parking lots over time. By utilizing the data collected through the Information Gathering Module, including temporal variables and license plate information, the application can analyze and monitor the occupancy status of parking lots at different time intervals. It processes the collected data to determine the occupancy status of the parking lot at specific time intervals. It can calculate the number of occupied parking spaces by analyzing the number of vehicles present during each time interval. The collected occupancy data is then analyzed using time series analysis techniques. This analysis helps identify occupancy patterns, trends, and fluctuations over different periods (e.g., hourly, daily, weekly). The mobile application can present the occupancy rate of the parking lot over time through visualizations such as graphs, charts, or heat maps. These visual representations provide a clear understanding of how the occupancy rate changes throughout the day, week, or other defined periods. The application can compare the current occupancy rate with historical data to identify any significant changes or anomalies. This helps in detecting abnormal or unexpected parking behavior. By tracking the occupancy rate of parking lots over time, the mobile application provides valuable insights into parking patterns, peak hours, and overall utilization of parking spaces. This information can assist in making informed decisions regarding resource allocation, parking capacity planning, and optimizing the parking experience for users.

4   System Framework and Implementation

The system architecture consists of multiple components that work together to provide a seamless mobile application experience. Figure 5 demonstrates how the user, devices, camera, and application functionalities are integrated. The user interacts with the application installed on either a phone or tablet and the application opens the map and the pins located in different places fetching them from the database. If the user wants to locate a pin and attach any image at the location, then they could click the image using a camera in the phone/tablet or pick it from the device.

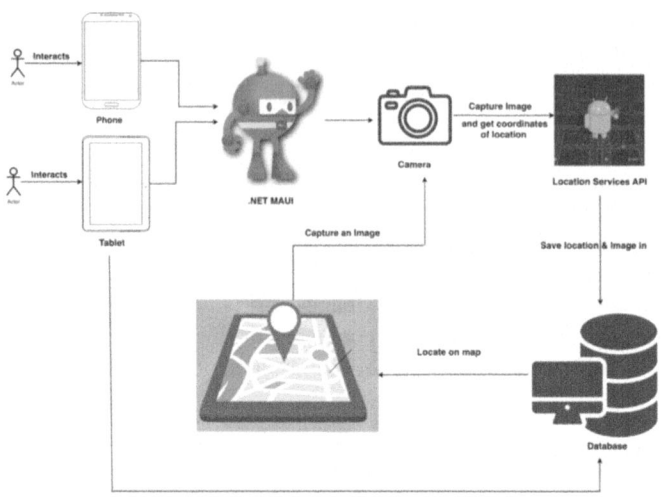

Fig. 5. System Framework diagram of the mobile application

The application layer is built using.NET Multi-platform App UI (MAUI), a framework that enables the development of cross-platform mobile applications using C# and XAML. It provides a robust user interface (UI) development environment, allowing developers to create visually appealing and responsive UI elements. The application layer acts as a bridge between the user and the underlying system components. One of the key features of the application is its integration with the Google Maps API, which offers comprehensive mapping and geolocation services. The Google Maps API enables the application to display maps, markers, and other relevant data to the user. It also provides functionalities such as geocoding (converting addresses to geographic coordinates) and reverse geocoding (obtaining address information from coordinates). By leveraging the Google Maps API, the application can deliver accurate and up-to-date location-based information to the users. The system architecture includes a local database component responsible for secure data storage. This database stores various types of data, including the pins representing different locations on the map and associated information. Additionally, the database stores any images captured by the user using the device's camera or selected from the device's storage. The captured or selected images are linked to the corresponding location pins, allowing users to attach visual content to specific places on the map.

The flow of data within the system architecture is as follows: when the user interacts with the application, the UI layer captures user input and triggers appropriate actions. For example, the user may choose to capture an image using the device's camera or select an image from the device's storage. The application layer handles these actions and securely stores the images in the local database, associating them with the relevant location pins. When the user opens the application, the data access layer retrieves the necessary information from the local database, including the pins and their associated images. This data is then displayed on the user interface, allowing the user to view the map, explore different locations, and access the attached images.

Overall, the system architecture provides a robust and intuitive mobile application experience. It leverages the capabilities of.NET MAUI, Google Maps API, device cameras, and local database storage to enable users to interact with the map, attach images to specific locations, and retrieve and display the collected data seamlessly.

5   Results and Analysis

The time series analysis conducted by the mobile application involves examining the occupancy rate of parking lots over various time intervals. It captures patterns and trends in parking behavior, such as daily or weekly fluctuations in occupancy. This analysis helps identify peak hours of parking demand, periods of low utilization, and recurring patterns that can be used to optimize resource allocation and improve operational efficiency. For example, it may reveal that parking lots experience higher occupancy rates during weekdays compared to weekends, allowing parking managers to adjust staffing or pricing accordingly.

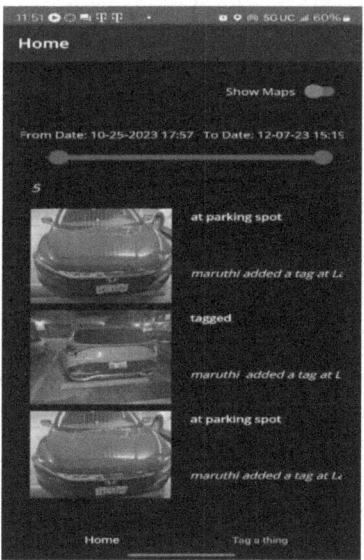

Fig. 6. Time Series Analysis in the Mobile Application

Figure 6 shows data extracted for time series analysis using the mobile device. The mobile application's anomaly detection algorithms play a crucial role in identifying and flagging anomalous behavior in parking lots. This includes instances of unauthorized parking, vehicles exceeding time limits, parking violations, or abnormal occupancy patterns. By promptly identifying such anomalies, parking managers can take appropriate actions, such as issuing warnings or fines, implementing stricter enforcement measures, or investigating potential security concerns. This helps maintain order, ensure compliance with parking regulations, and enhance overall parking lot security and safety. The mobile application extracts meaningful insights from the analyzed parking data, which can guide decision-making in parking management. These insights go beyond occupancy rates and anomalies and provide a deeper understanding of parking dynamics. For instance, the application may reveal the impact of external factors like nearby events or weather conditions on parking patterns. It can identify areas with consistently high or low occupancy, allowing for targeted interventions such as adjusting pricing or expanding parking capacity in high-demand areas. Additionally, the application's analysis can help identify potential inefficiencies in parking operations, such as underutilized spaces or bottlenecks in traffic flow, enabling parking managers to make data-driven improvements.

6 Conclusions

This paper highlights the capabilities and benefits of the developed mobile application for urban parking management. The application utilizes advanced data analysis techniques, anomaly detection, and predictive modeling to provide valuable insights and functionalities. It enables parking managers to predict future parking demands, allocate resources efficiently, optimize space usage, and detect irregularities and violations within parking facilities. By leveraging these features, the application enhances the overall parking experience, improves operational efficiency, and contributes to more sustainable and effective urban parking management. The developed mobile application holds significant importance in the realm of urban parking management. It addresses key challenges faced by parking managers, such as limited parking capacity, high demand fluctuations, inefficient resource allocation, and enforcement issues. By providing accurate predictions, optimizing resource allocation, and enhancing space utilization, the application helps alleviate parking congestion, reduce environmental impacts, and improve overall urban mobility.

The mobile application's integration with existing parking systems and infrastructure further enhances its value and feasibility. By leveraging the investments made in sensor technologies, payment systems, access control mechanisms, and enforcement systems, the application can seamlessly integrate into the existing parking ecosystem, ensuring compatibility and ease of implementation. Moreover, the mobile application's user-centric approach prioritizes the parking experience of individuals. Providing real-time information on parking availability, facilitating convenient payments, and promoting fair parking practices, enhances user satisfaction, reduces the time and effort spent searching for parking, and encourages the use of sustainable transportation options.

Overall, the developed mobile application represents a significant advancement in urban parking management. It leverages data-driven insights, advanced analytics, and seamless integration to optimize parking operations, improve resource allocation, and enhance the parking experience for both parking managers and users. With its potential to reduce congestion, improve efficiency, and contribute to a more sustainable urban environment, the mobile application holds immense importance in the field of urban planning and transportation management. In conclusion, the developed mobile application has the potential to revolutionize the way urban parking is managed. By leveraging advanced technologies, data analysis, and seamless integration, it offers valuable insights, improves operational efficiency, and enhances the overall parking experience. The application holds great promise for addressing the challenges associated with urban parking and can contribute to creating more sustainable, efficient, and user-friendly cities.

Acknowledgments. This work is funded in part by the Sub Award No. NSF00123–08 for NSF Award 2118285. The authors would also like to acknowledge the support of NSF Award 2319752, NSF award 2321539, and NSF Award 2321574.

Disclosure of Interests. The authors have no competing interests to declare that are relevant to the content of this article.

References

1. Wang, Y., Wang, Y., Chen, L., Li, J.: Urban parking behavior analysis using mobile sensing data. Sensors **20**(1), 32 (2020)
2. Li, Y., Xu, W., Zeng, L.: Urban parking behavior analysis using trajectory data. J. Transp. Eng. Part A: Syst. **144**(11), 04018075 (2018)
3. Li, Y., Xu, W., Zeng, L.: Anomaly detection for parking behavior using spatiotemporal data. In 2017 IEEE International Conference on Data Mining Workshops (ICDMW), pp. 1062–1067 (2017)
4. Chen, L., Wang, Y., Chen, X., Li, J.: Urban parking anomaly detection based on spatiotemporal analysis of parking data. ISPRS Int. J. Geo Inf. **7**(2), 74 (2018)
5. Mannuru, N.R., Kanumuru, M., Sharma, S.: Mobile AR application for navigation and emergency response. In: Proceedings of the IEEE International Conference on Computational Science and Computational Intelligence, (IEEE-CSCI-RTMC), Las Vegas, USA (2022)
6. Sharma, S.: Mobile augmented reality system for emergency response. In: Proceedings of the 21st IEEE/ACIS International Conference on Software Engineering, Management and Applications (SERA 2023), Orlando, USA (2023)
7. Sharma, S., Engel, D.: Mobile augmented reality system for object detection, alert, and safety. In: Proceedings of the IS&T International Symposium on Electronic Imaging (EI 2023) in the Engineering Reality of Virtual Reality Conference (2023)
8. Sharma, S., Stigall, J., Bodempudi, S.T.: Situational awareness-based augmented reality instructional (ARI) module for building evacuation. In: Proceedings of the 27th IEEE Conference on Virtual Reality and 3D User Interfaces, Training XR Workshop, https://doi.org/10.1109/VRW50115.2020.00020, Atlanta, GA, USA, pp. 70–78 (2020)
9. Stigall, J., Sharma, S.: Evaluation of mobile augmented reality application for building evacuation. In: Proceedings of ISCA 28th International Conference on Software Engineering and Data Engineering (SEDE 2019) in San Diego, CA, USA, vol. 64, pp. 109–118 (2019)
10. Wang, Y., Zhang, J., Huang, Y.: Urban parking anomaly detection using machine learning algorithms. J. Transp. Eng. Part A: Syst. **144**(12), 04018108 (2018)
11. Sharma, S., Jerripothula, S.: An indoor augmented reality mobile application for simulation of building evacuation. In: Proceedings of SPIE Conference on Engineering Reality of Virtual Reality, San Francisco, CA (2015)

12. Stigall, J., Sharma, S.: Mobile augmented reality application for building evacuation using intelligent signs. In: ISCA 26th International Conference on Software Engineering and Data Engineering, San Diego, CA (2017)
13. Tong, C., Li, J., Zhang, Q., Wang, X.: Anomaly detection in urban parking behavior based on time series analysis. In 2017 IEEE 3rd International Conference on Computer and Communications (ICCC), pp. 217–221 (2017)
14. Liu, Y., Han, J.: Anomaly detection in large-scale parking data using probabilistic topic modeling. IEEE Trans. Intell. Transp. Syst. **18**(10), 2707–2717 (2017)
15. Yu, J., Liu, X., Li, Y., Wang, J.: Parking anomaly detection based on spatiotemporal analysis and deep learning. Sensors **19**(20), 4374 (2019)
16. Wu, C., Wu, Q.: Anomalous behavior detection in urban parking lots using deep learning-based trajectory analysis. ISPRS Int. J. Geo Inf. **7**(11), 417 (2018)
17. Zhang, X., Wang, X., Hu, X., Li, L.: Anomaly detection in parking behavior based on spatiotemporal data mining. J. Traffic Transp. Eng. (English Ed.) **6**(5), 524–534 (2019)
18. Sharma, S., Bodempudi, S.T., Scribner, D., Grynovicki, J., Grazaitis, P.: Emergency response using HoloLens for building evacuation. In: Lecture Notes in Computer Science, vol. 11574, pp. 299–311 (2019)
19. Stigall, J., Bodempudi, S.T., Sharma, S., Scribner, D., Grynovicki, J., Grazaitis, P.: Use of Microsoft HoloLens in indoor evacuation. Int. J. Comput. Appl. **26**(1) (2019)
20. Sharma, S., Bodempudi, S.T., Scribner, D.: Identifying anomalous behavior in a building using HoloLens for emergency response. In: IS&T International Symposium on Electronic Imaging (EI 2020), in the Engineering Reality of Virtual Reality. Burlingame, California (2020). https://doi.org/10.2352/ISSN.2470-1173.2020.13.ERVR-224
21. Sharma, S, Bodempudi, S.T., Scribner, D., Grynovicki, J., Grazaitis, P.: Emergency response using HoloLens for building evacuation. In: Proceeding of 21st International Conference on Human-Computer Interaction. Orlando, Florida, USA, 26–31 July, HCII 2019, Lecture Notes in Computer Science, vol. 11574, pp. 299–311 (2019). https://doi.org/10.1007/978-3-030-21607-8_23. Online ISBN 978–3–030–21607–8

Enhancing Cybersecurity in Industrial Internet of Things: Machine Learning-Based Approaches for Cyber-Attack Detection in a Realworld Testbed Environment

Cayden Scott Cather[1], Eman Hammad[2], and Yuehua Wang[1(✉)]

[1] Computer Science Department, Texas A&M University-Commerce, Commerce, TX, USA
ccather@leomail.tamuc.edu, yuehua.wang@tamuc.edu
[2] Engineering Technology and Industrial Distribution, Texas A&M University, College Station, TX, USA
eman.hammad@tamu.edu

Abstract. The expansion of the Internet of Things (IoT) over the past decade has significantly changed how we interact with everyday appliances and industrial systems, from smart homes to the Industrial Internet of Things (IIoT). However, as cyberattacks become more frequent, sophisticated, and dynamic, IIoT systems are presenting new security challenges. There is a need for the timely availability of new efficient approaches and accessible/feasible testbeds to support new approach development and validation in real-world scenarios. In this paper, we present a novel security-oriented IIOT testbed that comprises a wide range of physical processes through diverse controllers and devices interacting with each other through various networking protocols. Additionally, we implement and test the performance of machine learning (ML) algorithms, including Random Forest, Decision Tree, Naive Bayes, K-nearest Neighbors, Logistic Regression, Multi-Layer Perceptron Classifier, Recurrent Neural Network, and Transformer for cyber-attack detection. Finally, we collect a new dataset and compare it with another IIoT-based dataset, CICIoT2023, revealing machine learning models' effectiveness in detecting various cyber-attacks and the feasibility and future work of the proposed testbed.

Keywords: IIoT · testbed · security · cyber-attacks · machine learning

1 Introduction

Cyberattacks on Industrial Internet of Things (IIoT) devices are experiencing a significant surge as these devices are increasingly more prevalent. IIoT refers

H. R. Arabnia et al. (Eds.): CSCE 2024, CCIS 2260, pp. 383–396, 2025.
https://doi.org/10.1007/978-3-031-85923-6_31

to technologies used in industrial environments to gather and share data. The systems of IIoT devices include four layers: the device layer, the network layer, the service layer, and the content layer. The device layer contains the hardware used in the system. Typical devices include sensors and physical machines. The network layer connects the devices with network buses and communication protocols, sending data collected by the device layer to the service layer. The service layer is the software that instructs the hardware and can display data to the user in a readable manner, as shown with the content layer. The content layer is the user interface (UI) devices (such as a screen) controlled by the user to oversee and control the hardware [1].

However, vulnerabilities at each layer are susceptible to exploitation by malicious users. It reported that there were over 1.5 billion reported security breaches between January and June 2023 [2]. IIoT devices are vulnerable to different types of cyberattacks, including response injections, command injections, Denial of Service (DoS), and reconnaissance (RECON) [3]. Response injection attacks manipulate a server's response to the client, causing incorrect behaviors in the control loop. The command injections are unauthorized commands executed in the system by an attacker. A DoS attack targets a system with high levels of traffic, intended to make it unable to perform its functions. RECON attacks are when an attacker gains critical information on a system to exploit its vulnerabilities.

To mitigate these vulnerabilities and enable cyber security, Machine Learning (ML) has emerged as a widely adopted effective technique for identifying and detecting prevalent cyber-attack activities and patterns. ML denotes the technology that can analyze a set of data and use its details to predict future data based on pattern recognition without explicit programming [4]. Simon uses the term "learning" to denote the alterations that a system makes to enhance its performance [5]. In [6], ML is used to study and analyze data from various devices and differentiate benign and negative activities in the IIoT systems. This ability improves the system's cybersecurity and minimizes downtime caused by attacks. However, ML can experience overfitting and drifting. Overfitting can cause a model to be unable to generalize to new data, and the model could become too customized to training data. Drifting occurs when the accuracy of the model decreases due to the new data substantially deviating from the data on which the model was originally trained.

While the security issues and vulnerabilities of IIoT devices have already been identified and tried to be mitigated in the field, limited efforts have been made to address emerging security challenges as cyberattacks become more prevalent, complex, and continually changing over time. Also, these attacks remain invisible and distributed, making traditional security measures such as intrusion detection and anti-virus programs less effective. Furthermore, we discovered that the current research was significantly limited by a lack of cost-effective, scalable, and feasible testbeds, as well as high-fidelity datasets in the IIoT domain, given that conducting security tests and validation in real-world IIoT systems can be hazardous and potentially disruptive. This also hinders researchers from developing and validating new security solutions before deploying them in the field.

In this paper, we aim to address the aforementioned challenges by proposing a new security-focused IIoT testbed that includes a variety of physical controllers and devices (like water pumps, smart cars, and a robotic arm) communicating via various networking protocols. To achieve high levels of fidelity and scalability, the testbed is developed with open-source software and cost-affordable IIoT hardware connected in real-world scenarios. To illustrate the capability of the testbed and support other research teams and educators who wish to duplicate our testbed and engage in real-world measurements and cybersecurity research, we implement and test the performance of ML algorithms in detecting cyber-attacks within a testbed incorporating IIoT devices. The ML algorithms are Random Forest (RF), Decision Tree (DT), Naive Bayes (NB), K-nearest neighbor (KNN), Logistic Regression (LR), Multiple-Layer Perceptron (MLP) Classifier, Recurrent Neural Network (RNN), and Transformer for cyber-attack detection. Finally, a new dataset is collected with four types of traffic: four different types of attacks and normal packets. The attack types are UDP Flood, SYN Flood, TCP Flood, and TCP Sequence Prediction. We then share the results based on the collected dataset and CICIoT2023 in terms of accuracy, precision, F1-Score, and specificity.

The rest of this paper is organized as follows. Section 2 gives a literature review on state-of-the-art research, highlighting the key features of existing ML algorithms, testbeds, and datasets for IIoT security. Section 3 presents the proposed IIoT testbed structure, system components, operations, functionalities, and different attacks studied in this work. The selected ML algorithms are also described in this section. Section 4 includes results and case studies, followed by the concluding lessons learned and future work in Sect. 5.

2   Literature Review

In this section, we briefly provide a description of existing IIoT testbed [3, 7–11] development along with threat models and machine-learning algorithms [3, 10, 12, 13] for cyber-attack detection.

IIoT Testbed: Few open IIoT testbeds have been developed to test new devices, protocols, networks, security vulnerabilities, and countermeasures due to their complexity and scalability. INFINITE (International Future Industrial Internet Testbed) [7] was built in 2017 by the Industrial Internet Consortium (IIC). It exploited big data to build virtual domains using software-defined networks. It became operational in Ireland in two phases. During phase one, three geographically scattered data centers were linked into a redesigned Dell network. Bluelight was a use case designed to improve pre-hospital emergency care during phase two. It [9] stated that the testbed could be applied to a wide variety of industries and sectors. Despite the fact that it is listed as being available to members of the Industrial Internet Consortium, the primary concern is how to access and use it to address security issues and mitigate potential risks with IIoT devices and systems due to the absence of technical specifics. Related use cases and applications have been largely under-explored.

Brown-IIoTbed [3,10] was developed by Al-Hawawreh and Sitnikova to address the lack of a standardized testbed for brownfield IIoT systems. A brownfield device is an old device that has outlived its expected lifecycle, often containing vulnerabilities against new types of attacks. The testbed was designed to run in a brownfield system using sensors, actuators, industrial devices, and open-source software. The STRIDE threat modeling method [14,15] was used to evaluate attacks and ML models. The STRIDE was proposed by Microsoft [15] to reason and find system threats by using data flow to ensure the system's authenticity, integrity, non-reputability, confidentiality, availability, and authorization.

Sair-IIoT testbed was introduced by Koroniotis et al. [11]. It was an airport cyber twins security-oriented IIoT testbed with several types of communication technologies like WiFi, Bluetooth low energy (BLE), ZigBee, and 5G. It consisted of 82 devices of 7 different types, such as gas detectors, water leak detectors, motion sensors, IP cameras, RFID readers, and drones. Even though the potential security threats in the smart airport systems were discussed in the survey [16], the authors failed to use the testbed to demonstrate security scenarios or adopt any ML-enabled cyber defense algorithms to protect the smart airport systems.

ML-Based Security Solutions: In [3,10], the ML algorithms included were random forest (RF), decision tree (J48), logistic regression (LR), k-nearest neighbor (KNN), and Naïve Bayes (NB). The algorithms were evaluated for their capability of detecting different attacks by observing network traffic. Types of attacks used were ARP spoofing, poisoning, Modbus DoS, and unprivileged MQTT subscribers. The outcome of the work was that RF was best at attack detection, and NB was the worst. The authors determined that the testbed successfully demonstrated the strength of ML algorithms in attack detection.

Jahromi et al. [12] introduce an advanced framework using ensemble deep learning for imbalanced datasets in industrial systems, with a two-stage process for attack detection and identification. The testbed utilizes a gas pipeline dataset and a Secure Water Treatment (SWaT) dataset. The gas pipeline dataset contained 274,628 observations, with 78.14% normal and 21.86% attack samples. The SWaT dataset contained 449,920 samples, with 87.9% normal and 12.1% attack samples. The framework used a deep representation-learning model and a decision tree for attack detection. When an attack was detected, ensemble one-versus-all Deep Neural Network (DNN) classifiers worked together for attack attribution. If an attack method was classified as unknown, further security analysis was performed. These two stages worked together to successfully identify and assign different attacks, whether previously known or unknown. The proposed framework outperformed the previous work. However, the framework lacked countermeasures against cyber threats.

In [13], the data imbalance problem was discussed. When some attack types are underrepresented in datasets, the accuracy of attack detection solutions degrades greatly. The authors proposed deploying an autoencoder, decision trees, and a supervised DNN, where Autoencoders can encode the features of data and help recognize the more unique patterns that less frequent attacks have, increasing their prediction ability. Trained on a SWaT (Secure Water Treatment) database, the model was found to be effective at identifying and discerning between types of attacks. It performed at 99.98% accuracy and outperformed existing frameworks.

These IIoT testbeds and studies collectively underscore the importance of high-fidelity testbeds with a focus on security to help identify and study vulnerabilities and threats, detect attacks, and test solutions for different layers. With the preliminary results of ML-based security solutions with collected IoT datasets in the literature, there is an urgent need for a flexible and accessible lab environment with open-source software, hardware, and real industrial IoT devices at low cost in real-world environments. Researchers, teachers, and students should easily use and extend it to investigate security issues and study and develop ML-based approaches. This study is being done to fulfill this need.

3 Design and Methodology

3.1 Testbed Design and Setup

Figure 1 illustrates the architecture of the testbed in the Cognitive Networked Sensing and Learning Lab (CNSL) at Texas A&M University-Commerce. In the CNSL, the testbed currently includes a server farm, routers, actors (programmable logic controllers, noted as PLCs), an industrial water pressure pump system, control buttons, and lights, and a robot arm [17] (in Fig. 2) connected by a software-defined network and controlled by software listed in Table 1. As a prototype, it can comprise physical systems like laptops and personal computers, as well as sensors, routers, smart devices, and any kind of PLCs and remote terminal units (RTUs).

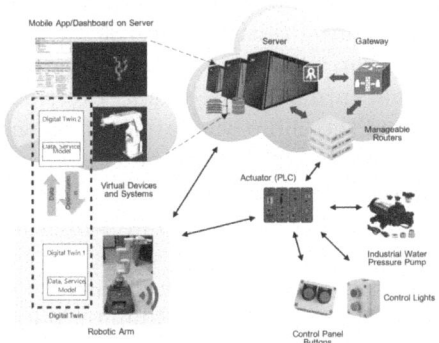

Fig. 1. Testbed Architecture

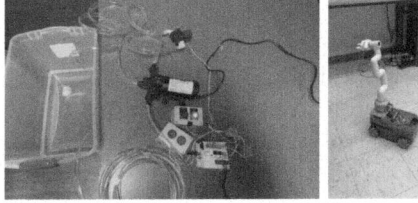

Fig. 2. Water Pump System and Robotic Arm

Table 1. Hardware and Software Table

Category	Tools	Description
Hardware	CLICK Power Supply	Powers the PLC
	CLICK Plus PLC	Stores and performs logic based on input/output
	Combo Modules C2-08DR-4VC, C2-14D2	Combines input and output channels into a single module
	Terminal Blocks	Provide safe connection of wires and PLC
	Electric Valve	Connects the PLC and the water pump
	Water Pump	Device used to test the output/results of the system
	Two Push-buttons	Provides input signals to the PLC
	Two lights	Server as output indicators
	MyCobot 280	Six-axis robotic arm system
Software	Python	Programming language
	Pycharm	IDE used for Python code
	RealVNC	Remotely access MyCobot280
	Elephant Robotics	MyCobot 280 software
	Click Programming	Software for PLC logic
	Hping3	Customize and send packets to the network

As a key component, the water pump system is introduced to enable automated control and monitoring of fluid flow within the testbed. This system incorporated a PLC and two control buttons that allow operators manually and system automatically to control the system and respond to attacks and alters, ensuring precise and efficient management. As shown in Fig. 2, the PLC is wired to a green and red push-button, a green and red light, and an electric valve. The electric valve switches on and off to control whether the water pump system is on or off. The PLC receives power directly from a power cord, stripped and wired directly to the PLC.

The logic functions based on the value assigned to the data register DS1, which serves as a switch to control the actions and connections between the push buttons, lights, and water pump. Once the push-buttons are pressed, they remain active until the other is pressed. If the electric valve is switched on, it provides electricity to the pump. For the DS1, if it is set to 1, pressing the green button activates the green light and turns on the pump, while pressing the red button activates the red light and turns off the pump. Pressing the green button would turn on the green light and turn off the pump when the DS1 was assigned the value of 2, and pressing the red button would turn on the red light. Pressing the green button, the red light was turned on, and the pump was turned on when the DS1 was assigned the value 3. Pressing the red button turned off the pump and lit the green light. Pressing the green button would turn on the red light and turn off the pump when the DS1 was assigned the value 4, and pressing the red button would turn on the green light and turn on the pump.

The robot arm, myCobot 280 [17] produced by Elephant Robotics is a six-axis collaborative robot. It operates with a Raspberry Pi and the Ubuntu Mate 20.04. With the use of its camera, the mobile robot MyAGV's algorithms can map its environment and instructions were followed for configuring the MyCobot arm and MyAGV. The robot arm will move as controlled using the script

myCobotCode if DS2 is equal to 1. The Modbus TCP protocol is used by the
script myCobotCode to communicate with the PLC and determine the DS2 status from the robot arm. This procedure was designed to enable industrial settings
where a task can only be completed with permission from another device.

To communicate with the PLC from the server via the Modbus TCP/IP
protocol, changeDS, a Python script, was created. Using the Modbus TCP port
and IP address, the function connect_to_plc() is to build a connection with the
PLCs. The function change_ds1_state() uses the write_single_register()
method of the ModbusClient object to write a value to the data register DS1.
For the data register DS2, the change_ds2_state() does the identical action.
Modbus addresses are assigned to each variable. For a given Modbus address,
the function display_coil_values() reads the coils' status and outputs the
data. The values of DS1 and DS2 are set according to the intended functionality
of the code. If DS2 is set to 1, the robot arm will move when the code in the
robot arm is run. The value of DS1 determines which of the above water pump
logic is run.

3.2   Machine Learning Algorithms

The machine learning algorithms we studied in this study include Decision Tree
(DT), K-Nearest Neighbor (KNN), Logistic Regression (LR), Multi-layer Perceptron (MLP) Classifier, Naive Bayes (NB), Random Forest (RF), Recurrent
Neural Network (RNN), and Transformer. The algorithms are outlined briefly
below.

- DT [18] is a decision tree-supported hierarchical learning method for classification and regression. It recursively partitions the data into subsets based
  on feature values, with each subset associated with a class value. In the tree,
  each node represents a decision based on its value. For the class, the method
  starts from the root node of the tree. Based on the comparison, the decision
  moves to the next node until it reaches the leaf node as the final node.
- KNN uses proximity to make classifications or predictions, where K denotes
  the number of closest points considered for classification via majority vote.
  Specifically, it predicts the class by looking at the nearest K points in the
  training set. If K = 3, the point is assigned to class A if two points are in
  class A and one is in class B.
- LR is a statistical model for binary classification. It determines the probability
  of an event by investigating the relationship between numerous variables and
  outcomes. A logistic function is used to determine probabilities ranging from
  0 to 1. Despite its simplicity, logistic regression may produce less accurate
  predictions when dealing with nonlinear interactions since it assumes a linear
  relationship between variables and class.
- MLP Classifier is a supervised learning algorithm that learns a non-linear
  function approximation with m (the number of dimensions) input features
  and a scalar output for classification and trains using backpropagation. More
  precisely, it trains using gradient descent, and the gradients are calculated

for the loss function with weights by propagating the error backward through the network to improve accuracy. It is quite useful when the dataset is large and the problem is a complex, non-linear one.

- NB is a Bayes' theorem-based algorithm that makes the "naive" assumption of conditional independence between each pair of features given the value of the class variable. It calculates the probability that a data point belongs to a classification based on the variables. Unlike logistic regression, it does not determine which features are most relevant for distinguishing between classes.
- RF [19] is a perturb-and-combine algorithm that generates multiple random decision trees by introducing randomness for classification and regression. Each tree functions independently, using randomly chosen factors to divide the nodes. For classification models, each tree provides a vote, with the majority class chosen as the final prediction. For regression models, the decision tree mean is employed for prediction.
- RNN is a class of neural networks used for time series or sequential data. In traditional neural networks, input and output data are separated. Alternatively, RNN uses the output from the previous step as input to feed the current step, making the data points sequences of data. The main feature of RNN is its hidden/memory state, which remembers information/past knowledge about a sequence. At each time step, the hidden state is updated to reflect changes in the network's knowledge of the past. RNN reduces the overall number of parameters and improves the efficiency and training efficiency of the model by sharing parameters among its many components.
- The Transformer [20] is a deep learning architecture developed by Google, based on the multi-head attention mechanism. It uses the encoder-decoder framework, but it is built for parallelization, resulting in faster training and inference times than RNN. In the Transformer, data is transformed into numerical representations called tokens, which subsequently transform them into vectors or tensors. The encoder uses these vectors as inputs to calculate attention scores. These vectors are used as inputs to the encoder to compute attention scores. The decoder takes the encoder's output and generates the target sequence. The attention mechanism enables the decoder to focus dynamically on different encoder outputs to enhance the model's performance.

4   Experiments and Evaluation

The testbed is successfully deployed and tested with connected wired and wireless devices. To demonstrate its feasibility and ML-based algorithms' performance for security testing, we generate network traffic (benign) and attacks (Negative communication/activities) achieved in a new dataset. Network traffic is collected over a time interval using Python scripts and Wireshark [21]. Originally, we saved it in Pcap files. It is then converted to CSV files for data processing and learning. Using Hping3, attack packets are generated to send personalized packets that are subsequently gathered and saved like regular network traffic. The attack packets are to attack the devices in the testbed based on network information such as IP addresses and ports. The Python script was run concurrently with the network traffic collection procedure to ensure that all network traffic was assigned the correct packet type. The TTL (time to live) of every attack packet is tailored to a particular variable specific to each kind of attack. The packets are randomized to imitate an organic test scenario prior to evaluation. To capture a broad range of packets, experiments, and data collection are conducted at different time periods throughout one month. Our dataset now includes approximately 650,000 packets.

Figure 3 shows the types and number of packets gathered in our dataset. Normal denotes the benign traffic (like application/communication data) where UDP(user datagram protocol), SYN (synchronize), TCP (transmission control protocol) flood, and TCP_sequence_prediction are four types of attacks.

- UDP_Flood attack is a DDoS (Distributed DoS) attack in which a server is overflowed by a high number of UDP packets. This overwhelming load hinders the server from responding correctly, leading legitimate users' requests to be denied and discarded over time.
- TCP_flood attack is also called TCP connection flood, where an attacker rapidly initiates multiple TCP communications to a target server, consuming its resources and impairing its ability to process legitimate requests. In this type of attack, the connection is established for each request from the attacker/client, making it difficult to distinguish legitimate and malicious communications.
- SYN_flood attack is to make a target server unavailable to legitimate traffic by sending a large number of SYN packets to establish connections and keep them open. The target drains its resources while waiting for responses that never arrive, compromising its capacity to fulfill legitimate requests.
- TCP_Sequence_Prediction is an attack against packets sent using TCP protocol. If successful, the attacker can predict the sequence number of the packets, allowing the attacker to gain access to the communication. This would give the attacker the ability to intercept communication and disguise malicious packets as legitimate ones.

To investigate more attack types and obtain deeper insight, the CICIOT2023 dataset [22] from the Canadian Institute for Cybersecurity (CIC) has been utilized to evaluate the performance of machine learning algorithms. This dataset contains real-time attacks in an IoT ecosystem with 105 devices and 33 different types of attacks. It also offers an authentic industrial setting for identifying attacks from six main groups: DDoS/DDoS, DDoS Fragmentation, Penetration, Malicious Traffic, RECON, and regular data. For simplicity, datasets 1 and 2 are used to refer to our dataset and the CICIOT2023. The accuracy, precision,

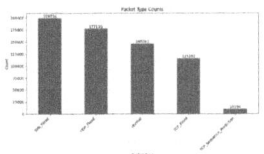

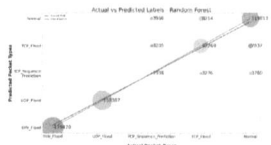

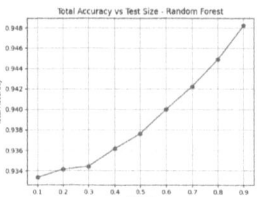

Fig. 3. Dataset Packets

Fig. 4. Interpolation for Data 2

Fig. 5. Interpolation for Data 2

Table 2. Performance metrics

Metric	Description
True Positive (TP)	Attack packet predicted as an attack packet
False Positive (FP)	Normal packet predicted as an attack packet
False Negative (FN)	Attack packet predicted as a normal packet
True Negative (TN)	Normal packet predicted as a normal packet
Accuracy (ACC)	$\frac{TP+TN}{TP+TN+FP+FN}$
Precision (P)	$\frac{TP}{TP+FP}$
Recall (R)	$\frac{TP}{TP+FN}$
Specificity (SP)	$\frac{TN}{TN+FP}$
F1-Score (F1)	$2 * \frac{Precision \cdot Recall}{Precision+Recall}$

Table 3. Performance of ML models with dataset 1(Testbed)

Models	Accuracy (%)	Precision (%)	Recall (%)	Specificity (%)	F1-Score (%)
Decision Tree (DT)	95.87	97.54	97.13	91.56	97.33
K-nearest neighbor (KNN)	95.71	97.89	96.55	92.82	97.21
Logistic Regression (LR)	94.82	95.49	97.94	84.08	96.7
Naive Bayes (NB)	92.49	91.38	99.71	67.61	95.36
Multiple-Layer Perceptron (MLP)	95.88	97.79	96.88	92.42	97.33
Random Forest (RF)	95.93	97.44	97.3	91.22	97.37
Recurrent Neural Network (RNN)	94.9	98.16	95.12	93.88	96.65
Transformer	95.5	97.66	96.51	92.03	97.08

recall, specificity, and F1-Score that are metrics defined in Table 2 are employed to evaluate the ML-based algorithm performance. Accuracy refers to the percentage of correct predictions for all classes, and precision presents the correctness of positive predictions for the target class. Recall is the proportion of true positive cases that are accurately identified as positive. Specificity refers to the percentage of normal situations that are appropriately identified as normal. F1-Score represents the harmonic mean of precision and recall.

Table 4. RF model prediction accuracy by packet type (Dataset 1)

Category	Accuracy (%)
Normal	91.22
SYN Flood	100
TCP Flood	88.93
TCP Sequence Prediction	21.8
UDP Flood	100
Total	94.82

Machine learning algorithms are evaluated with different train and test sizes to maximize the performance of the trained models in terms of the defined metrics. The test size ranges from 10% to 90% in increments of 10%. The test size with the highest accuracy is then used to calculate the accuracy of the trained model and that of other metrics. Tables 3 and Table 5 show the performance of the ML-trained models with datasets 1 and 2. All other figures and tables display a close look at the models' accuracy (ACC) in predicting the specific type of packet. For other metrics in Table 2, the models yield similar performance. These results are not included or discussed in detail due to their similarity and space constraints. More details, similar experimental data, and results can be found at [23].

Table 5. Performance of ML models with dataset 2 (CICIoT)

Models	Accuracy (%)	Precision (%)	Recall (%)	Specificity (%)	F1-Score (%)
Decision Tree (DT)	99.6	99.78	99.81	90.9	99.79
K-nearest neighbor (KNN)	99.15	99.74	99.39	89.2	99.56
Logistic Regression (LR)	98.97	99.79	99.15	91.43	99.47
Naive Bayes (NB)	91.73	99.96	91.57	98.51	95.58
Multiple-Layer Perceptron (MLP)	99.39	99.84	99.53	93.38	99.69
Random Forest (RF)	99.68	99.93	99.74	96.97	99.83
Recurrent Neural Network (RNN)	99.29	99.83	99.44	92.98	99.63
Transformer	99.24	99.85	99.37	93.71	99.61

As indicated in Table 3, the Random Forest (RF) model gets the highest overall accuracy (95.93%) and F1-Score (97.37%) across all models. Compared to other models, it also yields a better recall (97.3%), precision (97.44%), and average specificity (91.22%) in Table 4. Figure 4 shows the confusion matrix of the RF model. When misinterpreted, normal packets are most frequently thought to be TCP_floods. 35% of TCP_Sequence_Prediction packets are mistakenly categorized as TCP_flood packets, whereas 43.3% of packets are mistakenly classed as normal packets. The accuracy of the RF model with the test size is shown in Fig. 5. At the test size of 90%, it reaches its maximum accuracy of 94.82%. The accuracy ranged from 93.33% to 94.82% for all test sizes. We observe that as the test size increases, the accuracy of the RF model gets better, more stable, and more dependable.

With an accuracy of 95.87% and an F1-Score of 97.33%, the DT model comes in second with higher performance. NB model yields the best recall (99.71%) but is the worst in terms of other metrics, particularly specificity (67.61%). RNN is the most accurate in terms of accuracy (98.16%) and specificity (93.88%), but it has the lowest recall (95.12%). Overall, the models perform well; most of the scores are higher than 96%.

With Dataset 2, the models' performances are comparable. The DT model has resulted in the best recall, accuracy, and F1-Score. While precision is consistently high across all models, KNN yields the lowest specificity (89.2%) and precision (99.74%). The best accuracy (99.68%) and F1-Score (99.83%) are achieved by RF. NB produces the most diverse findings, with high precision (99.96%) and specificity (98.51%) but low accuracy (91.73%), recall (91.57%), and F1-Score (95.58%). The key distinction is found in specificity, where 13 out of 16 specificities range from 84% to 93%, corresponding to a 7% to 16% false positive rate. While other models do not show a substantial association between test size and accuracy, NB and RNN perform more accurately with smaller test sizes. This may indicate that the test size may have less of an effect on the accuracy of the models because of limited network topology and testing scenarios. Future tests and a variety of IIoT datasets would be used to confirm this.

When comparing the two datasets, Dataset 2 produced more accurate predictions, most likely due to its larger size and greater diversity of data. Of the eight models in Dataset 1, six of them identified SYN and UDP flood attacks with more than 98% accuracy. Only one model accurately detects TCP_flood attacks, which are frequently mistaken for regular or TCP_Sequence_Prediction packets. Normal packets are predicted accurately between 90% and 95% in six out of eight models. NB detects DoS/DDoS attacks with Dataset 2 only once, at 92.39%. In seven of the eight models, normal packets were accurately detected with an accuracy rate of greater than 90%. Overall, all ML models can efficiently identify attack packets.

5   Conclusion

This paper presented a new IIoT testbed to provide a flexible and accessible laboratory environment with open-source software, hardware, and real-industry internet-of-things devices at a lower cost for the exploration of disruptive cyber-attacks and ML-based approaches to enable novel cyberattack detection and countermeasure development and evaluation in a real-world environment.

We have demonstrated the testbed's usage and feasibility that operated in various real-world scenarios by implementing and analyzing the performance of ML models that were used for monitoring network traffic and detecting potential threats and attacks. The experimental results have shown that most ML models were able to detect attacks and identify their types. Six (6) out of eight (8) models can achieve higher accuracy. When the size of training samples is small, RNN and Transformer yield better performance than others. As it increases, the overall accuracy of each ML model trained with both the collected dataset and CICIoT2023 has not significantly improved. This would be further verified with additional experiments and various IIoT datasets in the future. We will also contribute to decreasing the rate of false positive prediction. We plan to further extend the testbed to a larger one by including more IIoT devices and studying to generate more types of attacks. This will offer a more realistic testing scenario that reflects an industrial environment. More ML algorithms will also be studied and evaluated to gain deeper insights and identify key attributes of various attacks.

This testbed is currently in use not only for research purposes but also for education and testing. It is easy and ready to duplicate and deploy in classrooms and laboratories, allowing security researchers and students to study and test security principles and methods, as well as their innovative ideas. In addition, more open-source operation and management tools would be available and shared in the community to solidify and expand it further.

Acknowledgment. This material is based upon work supported by the U.S. Department of Homeland Security under Grant Award Number, Award No18STCBT00001 through the Cross-Border Threat Screening and Supply Chain Defense Center of Excellence.

Disclaimer. The views and conclusions contained in this document are those of the authors and should not be interpreted as necessarily representing the official policies, either expressed or implied, of the U.S. Department of Homeland Security.

References

1. Hylving, L., Schultze, U.: Evolving the modular layered architecture in digital innovation: The case of the car's instrument cluster (2013)
2. Intersog, IoT security statistics: 6 facts, Intersog, vol. 6, February 2023
3. Al-Hawawreh, M., Moustafa, N.: Explainable deep learning for attack intelligence and combating cyber-physical attacks. Ad Hoc Networks **153**, 103–329 (2024)
4. Murphy, K.P.: Machine Learning: a Probabilistic Perspective. The MIT Press (2012)
5. Langley, P., Simon, H.A., Bradshaw, G.L.: Machine Learning. The MIT Press (1996)
6. Ratan, V.: Applying machine learning to IOT. Open Source For U, vol. 29, October 2018
7. INFINITE, Accessed 26 Jan 2024. https://hub.iiconsortium.org/infinite
8. Zhang, T., Xue, C., Wang, J., Yun, Z., Lin, N., Han, S.: A survey on industrial internet of things (iiot) testbeds for connectivity research," arXiv preprint arXiv:2404.17485 (2024)
9. Buckley, D., O'Sullivan, J., Fontaine, J.: Results, insights and best-practices from iic testbeds: Infinite testbed, Accessed 03 Oct 2023. https://www.iiconsortium.org/news-pdf/joi-articles/2017-Jan-Results-Insights-Best-Practices-from-INFINITE-Testbed.pdf

10. Al-Hawawreh, M., Sitnikova, E.: Developing a security testbed for industrial internet of things. IEEE Internet Things J. **8**(7), 5558–5573 (2020)
11. Koroniotis, N., Moustafa, N., Schiliro, F., Gauravaram, P., Janicke, H.: The sairiiot cyber testbed as a service: a novel cybertwins architecture in iiot-based smart airports. IEEE Trans. Intell. Transp. Syst. **24**(2), 2368–2381 (2021)
12. Jahromi, A.N., Karimipour, H., Dehghantanha, A., Choo, K.-K. R.: Toward detection and attribution of cyber-attacks in IoT-enabled cyber-physical systems. IEEE Internet Things J. **8**(17), 13 712-13 722 (2021)
13. Sravani, N., Valluri, S.P., Kosanam, C.S., Raj.: Toward detection and attribution of cyber-attacks in IoT-enabled cyber-physical systems, IEEE (2023)
14. Khan, R., McLaughlin, K., Laverty, D., Sezer, S.: Stride-based threat modeling for cyber-physical systems. In: 2017 IEEE PES Innovative Smart Grid Technologies Conference Europe (ISGT-Europe), pp. 1–6. IEEE (2017)
15. Kohnfelder, L., Garg, P.: The threats to our products, Microsoft Interface, Microsoft Corporation, vol. 33 (1999)
16. Koroniotis, N., Moustafa, N., Schiliro, F., Gauravaram, P., Janicke, H.: A holistic review of cybersecurity and reliability perspectives in smart airports. IEEE Access **8**, 209 802–209 834 (2020)
17. 6-axis Robot Arm KitmyCobot 6-DoF collaborative robot from elephant robotics, Accessed: 19 July 2023. https://shop.elephantrobotics.com/en-sg/collections/mycobot-280/products/holiday-mycobot-pi-raspberry-pipowered-6-dof-collaborative-robot
18. Gupta, B., Rawat, A., Jain, A., Arora, A., Dhami, N.: Analysis of various decision tree algorithms for classification in data mining. Int. J. Comput. Appl. **163**(8), 15–19 (2017)
19. Breiman, L.: Random forests. Mach. Learn. **45**(1), 5–32 (2001). Accessed 21 Feb 2024, ISSN: 1573-0565. https://doi.org/10.1023/A:1010933404324
20. Phuong, M., Hutter, M.: Formal algorithms for transformers, arXiv preprint arXiv:2207.09238 (2022)
21. Wireshark go deep: the worlds most popular network protocol analyzer, Accessed 12 Mar 2024. https://www.wireshark.org/
22. Neto, E.C.P., Dadkhah, S., Ferreira, R., Zohourian, A., Lu, R., Ghorbani, A.A.: Ciciot2023: a real-time dataset and benchmark for large-scale attacks in iot environment. Sensors **23**(13) (2023). Accessed: 05 Dec 2023, ISSN: 1424-8220. https://doi.org/10.3390/s23135941, https://www.mdpi.com/1424-8220/23/13/5941
23. Cather, C.S.: Toward cyber-attack detection for industrial internet of things systems using machine learning, Master's thesis, Commerce, TX, May 2024

Design of an Autonomous Mower and Embedded Microcontroller

Bassam Shaer[1]([✉]), Natalia DeJesus[2], Tyler Murray[1], and Malcolm Jones[1]

[1] ECE University of West Florida, Fort Walton Beach, Florida, USA
bshaer@uwf.edu
[2] ME Engineering Departments, University of West Florida, Fort Walton Beach, Florida, USA

Abstract. This paper presents the design and implementation of an intelligent embedded microcontroller in an autonomous mowing robot. The autonomous robot is able to maintain a residential lawn or commercial turf efficiently and within a set boundary. The robot will be designed with features that include: obstacle avoidance, self-containment to the area of operation, the ability to return to its docking station using its boundary wire direction sensors, and safety features for residential use. An emergency kill switch is included for emergency shutdown. The boundary wire system is designed to be connected to a standard household 120 V outlet, resulting in easy integration into the residence. This paper will describe the design, implementation, and results of each of these objectives.

Keywords: Intelligent · autonomous · mowing · robot · embedded · microcontroller

1 Introduction

When asked about their interpretation of the American dream, people might include owning a single-family home with a white picket fence, and a meticulously maintained and lush green lawn. When landlords, property management companies, and real estate agents advertise these same qualities may set their properties apart from the competition. We asked ourselves, what is the cost of this maintenance? On average, according to the Bureau of Labor and Statistics, Americans who participate in lawn maintenance as a primary activity spend 5.86 h on weekends alone maintaining their lawns [1]. Almost 6 h is a significant amount of a person's weekend, so many people outsource this to a lawn maintenance company. Our team found through research that a significant amount of money is spent in order to maintain a lawn. One source, Bankrate.com, gives homebuyers an estimation of maintenance costs, finding that the average American spends $1200–$2400 on lawn maintenance a year [2]. Our goal is to cut the amount of time and money spent on maintenance down drastically, freeing up the weekend and saving the consumer money over time.

The most applicable solution we were able to picture for solving this problem revolved around an autonomous robot. Most people have seen a Roomba and electric lawnmowers, but why don't we see more robots like this mowing residential lawns?

H. R. Arabnia et al. (Eds.): CSCE 2024, CCIS 2260, pp. 397–410, 2025.
https://doi.org/10.1007/978-3-031-85923-6_32

We researched what, if anything, was available on the market and found several units available for consumers already. Narrowing our search down to the top three we found; the WORX Landroid, Husqvarna Automower, and the GARDENA SILENO Minimower appear to be the closest products to what the team is trying to achieve. Each of these products has roughly an average of 4 of 5-star reviews online.

Looking first at the WORX Landroid, which comes in three model sizes made to maintain yards varying in size from an eighth to a half-acre. The appeal of this product as advertised is that it has an 8″ cutting deck, is compatible with their 20 V and 40 V battery line, is programmable to mow on certain days, can tackle 20-° slopes, and can detect the presence of rain in its operating environment all at a price point of $1158.82 for a quarter-acre maintaining model. Customer reviews for this machine average 3.7 out of 5 stars with 403 reviews, with the biggest complaints being build quality, lack of adequate length of wire for the boundary, and users experiencing issues with the boundary detection of this model and lack of GPS [8].

Second, the team has investigated the Husqvarna Automower 115H Lawn Mower. This model advertises for up to 0.4 acre and includes theft prevention, smartphone compatibility, an 8.7″ cutting deck, and an easy do-it-yourself setup. At a price point for this model (which is their lowest-end model) consumers are looking to pay roughly $1200. Though more expensive than the WORX's unit, this model is less of a consumer favorite coming in at 3.3 of 5 stars on Amazon with 111 reviews globally. Reviewer's biggest complaints about this model (outside of poor customer support which was the biggest) were that its stock wire mounting for the boundary cuts the boundary wires, it is advertised to work with an above-ground wire but it tends to cut its own boundary, and frequently requires manual intervention [4].

The final competitive comparison, which is the Amazon customer favorite, is the GARDENA SILENO Minimo. Some of the selling points for this model are that it can handle a 2700 square foot yard with up to a 19-° slope, it is Bluetooth compatible, it has a charging time of 60 min with a run time of 65 min, and AI technology that prevents it from repeating the same routes, and it is all weather. Over 6500 reviewers gave this unit an average rating of 4.1 out of 5 stars at its very competitive price point of $649.99. GARDENA does make a larger model for up to 16,200 square feet (0.37 acre) priced at $1399.99 with the same review rating overall. The biggest complaints against this mower from consumers are that it has a very low cutting height, slow speed, and lack of customer support revolving around its phone application [5].

To compete with the existing market and add innovation, we are focused on where predecessors have lacked in quality according to the reviews of similar products. We aim to design for higher slopes, include adjustable cutting heights, and make sure our robot does not have the same boundary-wire issues that plague the market. As an improvement where we see other products lacking, we want to have the addition of GPS to ours. The addition of GPS can solve two problems. First, the robot can use the location of the charging station and the GPS to get closer to the charging station before attempting to dock, which will save on battery life and prevent the consumer from having to manually reset the machine as often. Secondly, the addition of a GPS could help us to create a more reliable form of theft prevention for the unit. The rest of the paper is organized as follows. Section 2 discusses a brief system overview. Section 3 presents an overview of the technical approach. Section 4, presents the formal description of the testing approach. Section 5 presents the results of the work. Section 6 ends the paper with concluding remarks.

2   System Overview

This an autonomous mowing robot would have uses in both residential and commercial sectors. Residential consumers can utilize the time saved by the robot for other lawn maintenance activities like weeding, pruning or edging. The robot is intended to maintain the length of a lawn or commercial turf by operating more frequently than a standard walk behind mower. This ensures that the lawn will never grow faster than the unit's ability to maintain the area after the initial installation. Utilizing a simple boundary wire, the customer can establish a perimeter to be maintained. Commercial applications, such as sports fields, would also benefit from this product as groundskeepers could utilize the time saved frequently trimming the field to maintain other requirements.

The current design of the product operates under the assumption that the lawn or turf that the robot is maintaining has been pre-cut to four inches (or less) prior to the installation of the unit. The mower is not intended to be used to clear large overgrown patches of weeds or overgrown turf. Its primary purpose is to maintain the height of a previously trimmed lawn. External power to the charging dock is to be provided from a residence or building with a 120 V external outlet. The designed robot is not intended to be used for remote locations without access to residential outlets. A boundary wire will need to be installed prior to operation by the user. The Boundary wire must not be buried more than two inches away from the surface of the lawn. It is recommended that the boundary wire maintains at least four feet of straight path into the docking station (e.g. do not place the docking station one foot from a corner in which the robot will have to navigate while entering the docking station). It is also recommended that the docking station be placed in close proximity to the outlet providing power to the perimeter fencing generator.

Our team produced a fully automated robot capable of maintaining the height of both residential and commercial turf in a reliable manner. The robot utilizes a boundary wire for its containment system as well as various sensors for the detection of interference in order to safely and effectively operate. The goal is to come in at a lower cost and provide a more reliable product than those widely available now. A functional block diagram is shown in Fig. 1.

3 Technical Approach

3.1 Control Unit

Microcontroller. The ESP32 was utilized to control the mower. It was selected due to its ability to effectively control multiple sensors and its compatibility with circuit connectivity. Its programmable functions and interrupts are required for the integration of the robot's various components and systems [8].

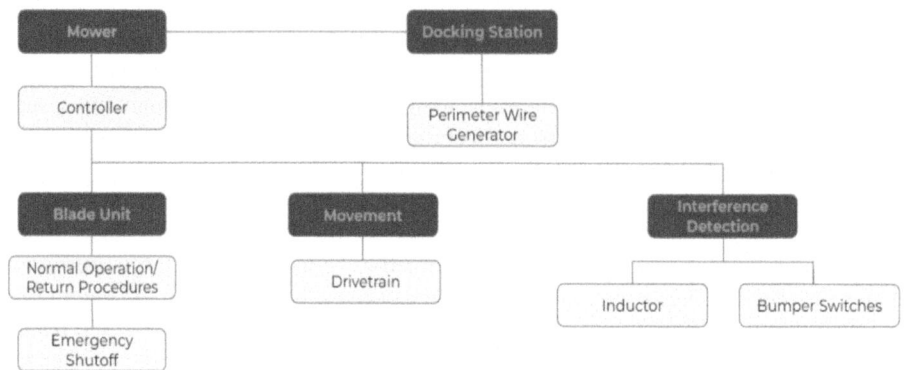

Fig. 1. Functional Block Diagram.

Interference Detection. The chassis of this robot includes a wooden bumper mounted on pistons to the front of the robot. The spring system of the pistons retracts in the event of object interference and depresses simple roller switches which return to the resting position once the object has been cleared. Two switches were utilized to ensure that contact from an obstacle while operating in the forward direction is accounted for. The bumper also acts as protection for the front of the wheels and motors to ensure no foliage would interfere with movement.

Boundary Detection. A boundary wire circuit is used to contain the robot within a fixed parameter. This is a 22-gauge wire which can be at the surface or buried beneath the ground. At both ends, the wire will be connected to a generator circuit on a PCB, which connects to the exterior outlet of a residence. The generator produces a 32–43 kHz square wave of around 50% duty cycle which produces a magnetic field that can be detected by the sensors (1 mH inductors), which are mounted on the bumper. This circuit provides an input to the GPIO pins of the ESP32 when the boundary wire is detected. The wire can be adapted to fit to any shaped yard. Figure 2 shows the schematic wire sensor circuit.

Battery Life. A 36V 10000 mAh lithium battery with a 30 A max discharge is used to power all components of the robot. Since the battery is stepped down using a golf cart transformer the max draw from the load is set to 12 V at 10 A and its run time was approximated with the calculations below.

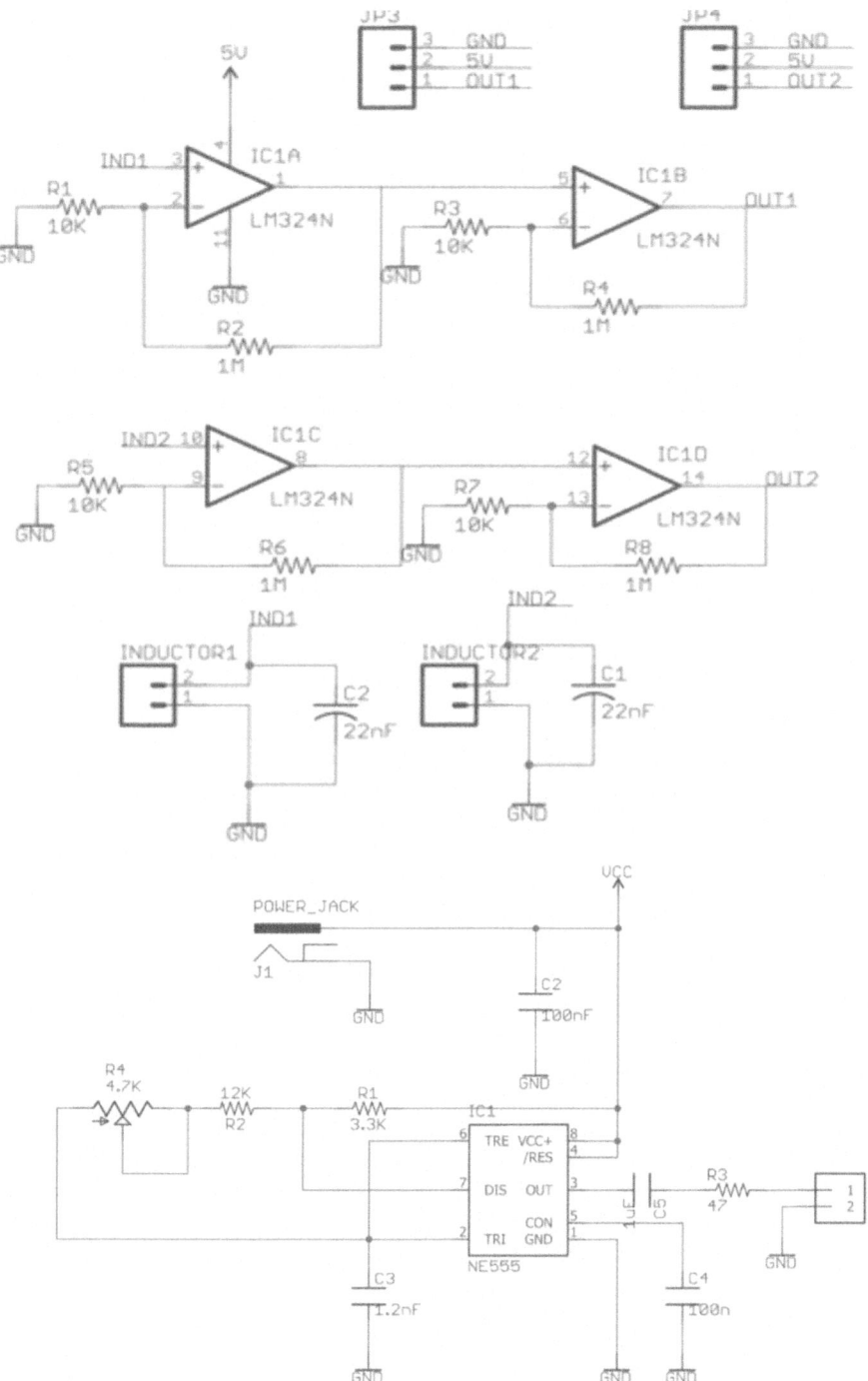

Fig. 2. Perimeter Wire Sensor Receiver Circuit Schematic [11].

Runtime is calculated using the equation below:

$$Runtime = \frac{Capacity}{Consumption} \tag{1}$$

The battery used is a 36V 10Ah. Converting to Watt hours:

$$Watt\,Hours = 36\,V * 10\,Ah \rightarrow 360\,Wh \tag{2}$$

$$Runtime = \frac{360\,Wh}{72\,W} \rightarrow Runtime = 5\,Hours \tag{3}$$

Initial design intent was for the mower to return to the docking station when low power was recognized from the battery, but from this data after testing it was determined that a run time limit would be set to a designated time and the mower would return to the docking station at the designated time.

Coding. We used the ArduinoIDE with ESP various libraries and C coding language to program the ESP32. We chose this based on our familiarization with the software, the finalized components selected, and our ability to develop the code required for the success of this project.

3.2 Robot Drivetrain

Driving Motors. Two high-torque 12 V (40000RPM) DC motors with pre-attached gearboxes were used to drive our two-wheel drive system. These motors, paired with gearboxes, have the specifications to transform the voltage applied by the battery to produce enough torque to consistently drive the robot over the lawn. Testing was done during assembly to ensure that the motors had the torque needed to drive the weight of the chassis and components from a full stop.

Each driving motor was independently controlled and were both set at 40% RPM, resulting in a 16000 unloaded RPM driving a 3.5in radius wheel. The total weight of the mower is 32 lbs. This weight is distributed amongst the two driving wheels and the caster at the rear. Center of gravity sits almost directly in the center of the chassis, evenly distributing the weight force between the front and rear wheels. This applies ~ 8 lbs. to each driving wheel and ~ 16 lbs. to the caster. From this calculation, the minimum required torque needed to drive the mower would have to be as shown below:

$$\tau = Fr = (8lb \cdot f) * (3.5in)$$
$$\therefore \tau_{minimum} = 28lb \cdot in = 2.3ft \cdot lb \tag{4}$$

Under load, it can be assumed that the RPM would be 60–80% of the unloaded RPM, this would be between 9600 and 12800 RPM. With the power provided in the data sheet as 45 W, the torque produced by the motor at 40% PWM would be as shown below

$$45\ W * \frac{0.00134\ HP}{1\ W} = 0.0603\ HP$$

$$\tau\,(ft.lb) = \frac{HP * 5252}{RPM} = \frac{0.0603\ HP * 5252}{11200\ RPM} = 0.03\,ft.lb \tag{5}$$

From the data sheet for the gearbox and motor, the gear ratio is 111.4:1, therefore the calculated torque output per motor is [11]:

$$\tau = 0.03ft.lb * 111.4 = 3.34ft.lb \tag{6}$$

Power. We utilized a 36 V lithium-ion electric bike rechargeable battery with a T-plug connector for easy integration with the charging port. This battery, paired with a 36 V to 12 V step-down transformer, was able to power all critical components of the mower. This includes the two driving motors as well as the blade motor. It is capable of lasting for the time it would take to mow a standard lawn multiple times before requiring charging. It is estimated that the battery would only have to be plugged in once weekly if the mower were to be run daily.

Speed Controller. The ESP32's GPIO pins were used to control the Pulse Width Modulation on the 6 V–30 V DC motor driver speed controller [9] used. Three total speed controllers are used for operation, two to control the driving motors and one for the blade motor. These require an input of 12 V and can handle a maximum current of 20 A.

3.3 Mower Deck/Frame

Blade Motor. DC 12–24 V 775 motor with a built-in 200 mm manganese blade was utilized as the main motor for cutting. The pre-attached blade simplified the assembly process when implementing. As mentioned above, a speed controller was used to regulate the voltage supplied. It is vital that independent circuitry is used to supply voltage to this motor, this is for the implementation of quick shut-off for emergency conditions.

Blade. The choice of manganese steel is ideal for mowing conditions because of its anti-wear properties. The blade chosen is designed to be integrated with the motor and has the ability to be exchanged with a larger blade if the need arises.

Frame. The main internal framing of the chassis also houses the blade motor in a stationary position. This is composed of steelworks slotted, zinc-plated steel pieces that can be joined together to create a durable, lightweight frame with the capability to easily connect to any other coverings or components. 3/8in. Thick plexiglass was used to line the base of this mower and to mount all of the circuitry components internally. The use of plexiglass is lightweight and durable to be able to mount and cut to size.

Bumper. The bumper system was fabricated out of 0.5in. Thick juniper wood, as it is a lightweight and durable material. The construction is simple, consisting of a flat front portion that is 24in. Length, as well as an overhanging top, right, and left side, all of which have a 1.75in. Depth. The inductor sensors are mounted on the lower right and left sides of the inside face.

Wheels. Two 7in × 1.5in, semi-pneumatic rubber tires were purchased for the use of the tires. The original rim was removed and a rim was designed and 3D printed to fit the tire and also have easy mounting with the driving motors used. The tread is vital for this application as the robot will be moving over grassy terrain, any slip of the wheel should be avoided.

Safety. Plexiglass was mounted on the chassis where the blade is exposed and acts as a layer of protection from the blade. This is easily mounted on an angled bracket which also aids in mounting the lid. This design is important for easy removal if there is any clogging or cleanup needed.

Cover. The cover was fiber glassed utilizing a jig of the dimensions required. Cheese-cloth was used in place of fiberglass cloth to save on weight and cost. Resin was applied to the cloth over the jig in order to shape the cover. The manufactured cover fit the designed chassis perfectly. This lightweight alternative is easily removable and protects the components from the elements. This also serves as protection for the consumer against any electronic components included inside. It is vital that these components are protected from any contact with water from the outside. In the event of mass production of this product a plastic cover could be designed from the fiberglass cover design to save more on manufacturing costs and weight.

Emergency Shutdown. A switch housed on the side of the chassis lid acts as a quick shutdown in need of emergency. This automatically cuts off all power from the battery, halting all operations immediately. This is also the switch to be used when charging to close the connection from the battery to the other components.

3.4   Docking Station

Energy Source. As discussed earlier, the battery used is already fitted with a T-plug to convert standard 120 V household outlets to recharge the battery. This connection will be used for simple manual charging.

Design. The docking station Fig. 3 itself consists of a dock that will serve as the base and primary platform for the robot to charge and park in its idle time. This structure is rectangular, measuring 37 × 44in. Leaving 6in on both sides for maneuvering room as the mower navigates inside of it. A bar is located on the lid and is lowered enough to depress the switch at the top of the mower which indicates that it has returned home. The open-ended concept allows for free drive-through capabilities if the mower was to get stuck. If this were to occur before the mower were on its return home routine, the depression of the top switch would not stop the mower and it would continue with normal operation.

Fig. 3. Docking Station.

4   Testing Approach

Iterative testing was performed on each component individually to ensure that they were functional, using bench supply when necessary. From initial testing, there was integration with controllers and the ESP32 with simple code to test component compatibility at a small scale. The 36V lithium battery was then integrated instead of the bench supply. Once the chassis structure was completed and the motors mounted, the drivetrain was the first to be tested. Once issues with the drivetrain were solved, the switches and sensors could be included. Final components such as the bumper and lid were mounted before manufacturing and testing the charging dock. All primary testing was done indoors on level ground and eventually brought onto the grass to be tweaked as needed. Finally, the blade and safety shields were added. These were done last to ensure that the mower was operating under the safest conditions.

Final testing and videos were taken on different lawns to ensure that the mower was compatible across the consumer base. As needed, adjustments were made to the hardware or software to result in a functional and efficient product. The basic principle for all of operation and the interference detection algorithms within the main program is shown in Fig. 4.

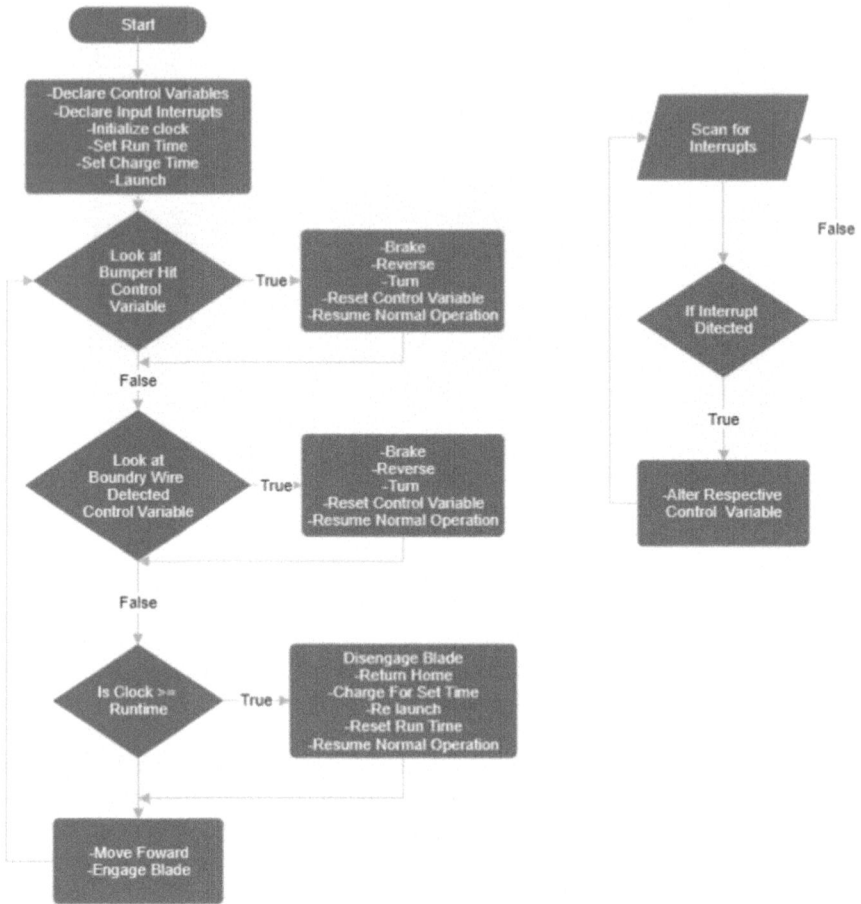

Fig. 4. Operation and the Interference Detection Algorithms.

5 Final Product/Project Results

During manufacturing and testing, some deliverables were adjusted to accommodate the functionality, safety, and reliability of the final product. These included small chassis design elements, removal of liquid detection, removal of the use of GPS navigation, and eliminating the use of contact charging at the dock. To obtain a fully functional robot without these elements there was the addition of a timer, adjustable bumper heights, manual charging, and an open-ended docking station.

The chassis design was manufactured using zinc-plated steel angles which were welded together to create a chassis designed to fit the components and mount the wheels.

The bumper system was simplified after manufacturing and testing to include only two contact switches. Two mounting shafts with springs were used to create a dynamic bumper with the capability to depress the switch and return to a resting position. The

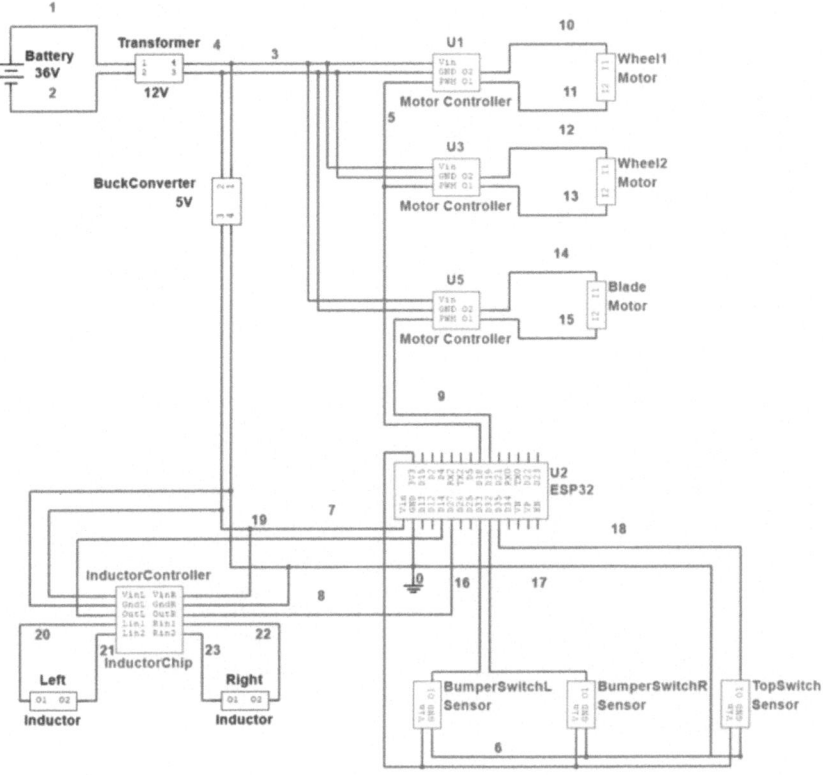

Fig. 5. Circuit Schematic.

Fig. 6. Top view of the Completed Circuit.

Fig. 7. Autonomous Mowing Robot.

juniper wood bumper was manufactured to have two individual height options, this is so that the height may be compatible with various grass lengths.

GPS usage was eliminated from this project due to its inaccuracies at small ranges. In order to navigate the lawn and back to the charging port, other methods were implemented as alternatives.

The initial design was to utilize analog voltage reading from the battery to detect battery levels, which when low would prompt the return home procedure. This procedure was altered when product testing and load calculation determined the battery run-time to be 5 h. With this information, the code was changed to integrate a timer so that power could be conserved to run only a set period of time and then docked at its station otherwise. Because of the extensive battery life, it was determined that contact charging was too large of a safety hazard and its implementation was unnecessary under the conditions. If needed, manual charging is as simple as plugging the battery externally.

The final design Figs. 5, 6, and 7 consists of an autonomous mower that can deploy from its docking station and freely roam the set boundary lawn while avoiding interference for a set period of time. Once the set period has passed, the robot will shut off the blade operation and navigate itself back to the entrance of the charging dock. Once detected that it is home, the mower will halt all operation and stay in its dock for a set period, or until the power is manually switched off.

6 Conclusions

At the conclusion of the project, the design objectives were met in the design of an autonomous mower that would remain within a set boundary and safely upkeep a residential or commercial lawn with the ability to return home for charging. The autonomous nature of the robot utilizes MEMS-based current sensors which detect the current field produced by the boundary wire encapsulating the yard; this ensures that the robot stays within bounds. For interference throughout the yard, the spring system bumper can be triggered when contact is made at any point on the front face and deter the mower appropriately. This mower will run for a set amount of time before navigating itself back to the docking station until ready to deploy again.

Future improvements to the design of this mower would be the addition of contact charging as initially suggested. Including this feature would allow for even less consumer participation and lead to a much more fluid overall process of the mower. Implementation of a more efficient pattern following is also a future improvement suggestion. Currently, the mower runs in a random pattern, with the expectation that it will cover the entirety of a lawn after a certain time while roaming. Including a trajectory for a rectangular or square lawn would be a first step to improving efficiency; even exploring patterns for abstractly shaped lawns could be added.

References

1. American Time Use Survey — 2015 Results (2016). https://www.bls.gov/news.release/pdf/atus.pdf
2. Dellinger, A.: What are the most common home maintenance costs? https://www.bankrate.com/homeownership/most-common-home-maintenance-costs/ Accessed 20 Apr 2023
3. Amazon.com: Worx Landroid M 20V Robotic Lawn Mower 1/4 Acre / 10,890 Sq. Ft Power ShareWR147 (Battery & Charger Included): Everything Else, www.amazon.com. https://www.amazon.com/WORX-WR147-Landroid-Robotic-Mower/dp/B097NJ37R7/ref=sr_1_3?crid=2XKLUJAZTMFJM&keywords=worx%2Blawn%2Bmower&qid=168219 5090&sprefix=WORX%2Caps%2C108&sr=8-3&ufe=app_do%3Aamzn1.fos.765d4786-5719-48b9-b588-eab9385652d5&th=1, Accessed 23 Apr 2023

4. "Amazon.com: Husqvarna Automower® 115H Robotic Lawn Mower (Bluetooth): Patio, Lawn & Garden, www.amazon.com. https://www.amazon.com/Husqvarna-Aut omower-115H-Robotic-Mower/dp/B07PGBSGXQ/ref=sr_1_2?crid=M60QRQ7ZP5YS& keywords=husqvarna+automower&qid=1682196192&sprefix=husqvarna+automowe% 2Caps%2C114&sr=8–2&ufe=app_do%3Aamzn1.fos.765d4786-5719-48b9-b588-eab938 5652d5, Accessed 23 Apr 2023

5. Amazon.com: GARDENA 15201-20 SILENO Minimo - Automatic Robotic Lawn Mower, with Bluetooth app and Boundary Wire, The quietest in its Class, for lawns up to 2700 Sq Ft, Made in Europe, Grey : Patio, Lawn & Garden," www.amazon.com. https://www.amazon. com/15201-20-Automatic-Bluetooth-Boundary-quietest/dp/B08LNQT5KW/ref=sr_1_2? crid=1IOH5SENPL8CQ&keywords=automatic%2Bmower&qid=1682194959&sprefix=aut omatic%2Bmower%2Caps%2C128&sr=8-2&ufe=app_do%3Aamzn1.fos.2b70bf2b-6730-4ccf-ab97-eb60747b8daf&th=1, Accessed 23 Apr 2023

6. Underwriters Laboratories, Electric Motor-Operated Hand-Held Tools, Transportable Tools and Lawn and Garden Machinery - Safety - Part 3-1: Particular Requirements For Transportable Table Saws, 04 February 2022

7. Underwriters Laboratories Inc. (UL), Lithium Batteries, 4 Jun 1999. https://www.mtixtl.com/ documents/UL1642.pdf, Accessed 17 Apr 2023

8. ESP32 Series Datasheet, vol. 4.2, Accessed 17 Apr 2022. https://www.espressif.com/sites/ default/files/documentation/esp32_datasheet_en.pdf

9. Amazon, 2020. Accessed 19 Apr 2023. https://www.amazon.com/dp/B07RQFN485?psc=1& ref=ppx_yo2ov_dt_b_product_detailspler-Isolation/dp/B0B8RL7PXM/ref=sr_1_51

10. Amazon, Accessed 23 Apr 2023. https://www.amazon.com/12-24V-Manganese-Mounting-Bracket-12V10000RPM/dp/B09Y484W4Q/ref=sr_1_3?crid=1D2UPRAQ6PSO2&key words=lawn%2Bmower%2Bblade%2Band%2Bdc%2Bmotor&qid=1681590577&sprefix= laqnmower%2Bblade%2Band%2Bdc%2Bmotor%2Caps%2C98&sr=8-3&th=1

11. DIY Perimeter wire generator and Sensor | RobotShop Community. 26 Sep 2023. Robot-Shop Community. https://community.robotshop.com/blog/show/diy-perimeter-wire-genera tor-and-sensorKidCars.tv Home (no date) FAQ - The Definitive 'Gearbox' thread. https://kid cars.tv/modifiedpowerwheels/viewtopic.php?t=103#google_vignette, Accessed 29 Nov 2023

A Low-Cost Automatic DEF Refueling Controller for Diesel Generators

Dania Mosuli and Hakduran Koc[✉]

College of Science and Engineering, University of Houston-Clear Lake, 2700, Bay Area Blvd, Houston, TX 77058, USA

{Almosulid5670,KocHakduran}@uhcl.edu

Abstract. This paper presents a design and implementation of a low-cost automatic controller for Diesel Exhaust Fluid (DEF) tanks. The controller monitors error codes from the generator's Engine Control Unit (ECU) and readings from a temperature and level sensors and refuels the generator's DEF tank when needed. The proposed controller presents a low-cost and easy to install solution for DEF refueling automation; eliminating cumbersome refueling process that requires constant user monitoring.

Keywords: Controller · TM4c123 · Diesel Exhaust Fluid (DEF) tank · generator · low cost · low power

1 Introduction

This project entails developing a control system for automatically switching a pump used to refill the Diesel Exhaust Fluid (DEF) tank in a diesel generator. The integration of DEF fluid into diesel generators is a relatively new development. While many general-purpose automatic controllers exist, they often come with a high cost and unnecessary features that may not align with the specific needs of the customer. Typically, diesel generators are located on-site with a DEF tote nearby and a pump. Currently, when the DEF level in the tank is low, the user manually turns on the pump and turns it off once the tank is full. To mitigate this issue, an automatic start controller can be implemented, providing a cost effective and customized solution for controlling the pump without unnecessary features.

To implement this controller, it must be connected to a temperature sensor to monitor the DEF temperature, ensuring that it remains above $-11\ °C$ (freezing point of DEF fluid), and a level sensor to verify that the external tote is not empty. Additionally, the controller needs to interface with the ECU of the generator to receive error codes via the Controller Area Network (CAN) bus. These error codes, specific to different manufacturers, inform the controller about the DEF tank's status, indicating whether it is running low or full. This paper proposes a low-cost controller designed solely for DEF fluid refueling; it requires minimal user setup and ensures automatic refueling

This work is supported in part by NSF Award 1928622.

H. R. Arabnia et al. (Eds.): CSCE 2024, CCIS 2260, pp. 411–415, 2025.
https://doi.org/10.1007/978-3-031-85923-6_33

for generators. The controller includes features such as auto baud rate detection, status updates over Wi-Fi, and the option to use either a built-in analog temperature sensor or an external digital temperature sensor.

2 Related Work

Several efforts have been made to create controllers for automating starting the generator and monitoring various parameters such as temperature, fuel level, and pressure. Obikoya et al. [1] devised a system equipped with sensors to monitor fuel tank temperature and level by transmitting status updates to users via SMS. Reza et al. [2] developed a microcontroller-driven system for monitoring and regulating water tank levels. Hemnandan et al. [3] introduced an embedded fuel control system for a diesel generator that notifies users if fuel level drops below critical limit. Since its introduction in 2007, the Diesel Exhaust Fluid (DEF) standard has been mandated by EPA diesel-powered machinery and vehicles [4]. Because of its recency, no prior work has addressed the implementation of an automatic DEF tank refueling system. Therefore, this study expands upon previous research on remote monitoring of generator parameters by incorporating the functionality of automatic refueling.

3 Overview

One of the functions of the ECU is to transmit error codes and status updates via a CAN bus port. When it detects any abnormalities, it generates error codes. These codes vary depending on the manufacturer and the model of the engine. This system requires continuous monitoring of the generator and proximity to the generator to refill the DEF tank promptly for uninterrupted engine operation. DEF fluids are often stored in nearby 330-gallon totes. The user must check the fluid level and ensure the temperature is above freezing before manually refueling, and then, manually switch on a pump. After refilling manually, the user must switch off the pump. This refueling process is cumbersome and requires constant user monitoring. Therefore, the proposed controller offers a low-cost, easy-to-install solution.

4 Design and Implementation

The controller was developed using the Texas Instruments Cortex M4 TM4C123 microprocessor [5]. This choice was made due to its integrated CAN module, ADC module, and UART module, as well as its numerous GPIOs, internal interrupts, and timers. For prototyping, a TM4C123-based development board from Texas Instruments was utilized and programmed using Code Composer Studio. Other circuit components include a voltage regulator, an LCD screen, a CAN transceiver, an ESP8266 Wi-Fi module, inputs for external sensors, an internal analog temperature sensor, and a single-coil relay. Figure 1 shows the block diagram of the circuit. The circuit is powered by the 12-V battery used to start the generator, requiring a voltage step-down regulator to provide 5 V and 3.3 V to the circuit's components.

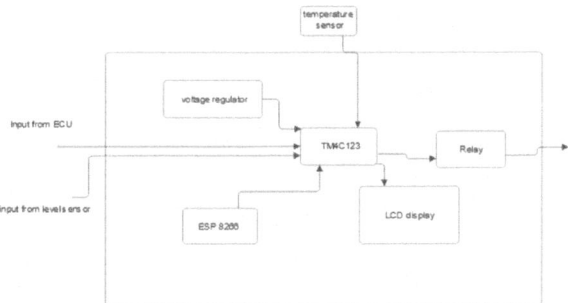

Fig. 1. Block diagram of the controller

To minimize heat dissipation, an L7805 voltage regulator was placed after the 12 V, followed by LD33V 3.3 V MOSFET regulators. This design represents an energy-efficient solution by relying on the 12-V battery used to start the generator, thereby removing the need for a dedicated power source. The circuit utilizes an LM35 analog temperature sensor, which is connected to the microcontroller's internal 12-bit ADC module for signal processing. The LM35 sensor is positioned outside the controller's housing and inside the tank. An external switch allows the user to choose between the LM35 and an external digital temperature sensor.

A 2 × 16 LCD screen is connected to the microcontroller through bit banging instead of I2C protocol, simplifying the hardware and design. The LCD screen is interfaced in 4-bit mode, reducing the required GPIOs from 8 to 4. The ESP8266 Wi-Fi module is integrated with the controller, enabling the user to monitor refueling cycles over time. It is connected to the microcontroller through UART. A solid-state relay is used in the design, with the controller's output connected to a BJT transistor and then to the relay's contacts to turn it on. When the GPIO output is set low, the relay is turned off, thus stopping the connected pump.

5 Firmware

The microprocessor was programmed using Texas Instrument's Code Composer Studio. A 16 MHz external oscillator was used to clock the microprocessor. After configuring the clock, the TM4C123 executes initialization functions to set up peripherals, including GPIO ports, the ADC module, CAN Handler, UART module, LCD, ESP8266 module, and other functions like sending AT commands to the ESP and checking error codes [5]. The schematic of the controller is shown in Fig. 2.

Once the program enters the main loop, it creates variables to store data from the sensors and the ECU. The ports are configured as inputs or outputs, followed by the execution of CAN and ADC functions to set up their routines. A function for automatically checking the CAN protocol's baud rate is implemented within the main loop. The remainder of the main loop handles the logic for controlling the relay, checking specific flags and sensor inputs to determine when to activate the relay. Simultaneously, it updates commands sent to the ESP8266 and the display on the LCD screen. When the

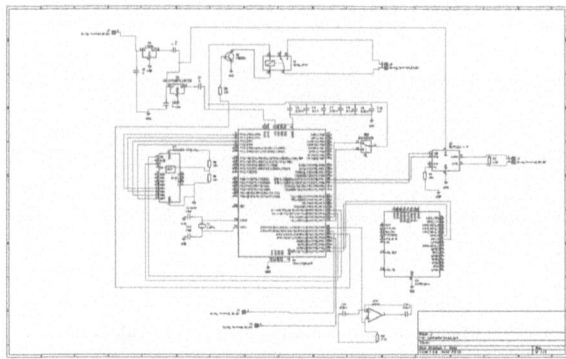

Fig. 2. Schematic of the controller.

tank is full, a code indicating this state is sent to the controller, allowing it to switch off the relay.

The ESP8266 module includes pre-installed firmware that enables it to interface with other microprocessors. The Wi-Fi module is connected to the Cortex M4, and communication between the two devices occurs through UART. The Cortex M4 sends AT commands to the ESP8266 to initialize it and to exchange data. The data is hosted on a server created on the ThingSpeak IoT platform.

6 Prototype and Testing

The prototype of the controller is shown in Fig. 3. The prototype was constructed on a breadboard using the TM4C123GH6PM development board by TI, which features the TM4C123 microprocessor. In order to verify the functionality of the design, an ATmega328P-based Arduino development board was employed alongside a CAN bus

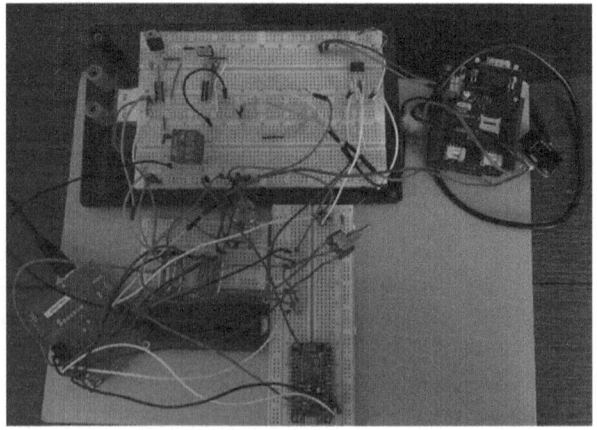

Fig. 3. Prototype of the controller

shield to emulate an ECU. The Arduino board simulated the generation of error codes, and based on the received feedback, the controller would toggle the switch accordingly.

7 Conclusion

This paper demonstrates the development and deployment of a cost-effective, low-power consumption, and easy-to-install DEF controller. In order to improve the functionality of the controller, a planned future work involves designing a user interface that enables users to customize settings and adjust temperature sensor limits.

References

1. Obikoya, G., Daniel, O., Dayo, O., Ogoo, A.: Monitoring and controlling fuel level of remote tanks using Aplicom 12 GSM module. ARPN J. Eng. Appl. Sci. **6**(1), 56–60 (2011)
2. Reza, S.M.K., Tariq, S.A.M., Reza, S.M.M.: Microcontroller based automated water level sensing and controlling: design and implementation issue. In: Proceedings of the World Congress on Engineering and Computer Science (WCECS) (2010)
3. Hemnandan, G.M., Gajanan, G., Anil, R.: Remote monitoring of fuel level for diesel generator set. In: National Conference on Electronic Technologies (2011)
4. Johnson, T.V.: Review of diesel emissions and control. Int. J. Engine Res. **10**(5), 275–285 (2009)
5. Texas Instruments, Tiva™ TM4C123GH6PM microcontroller, SPMS376E, https://www.ti.com/product/TM4C123GH6PM, Accessed 8 Apr 2024
6. Obikoya, G.D.: Design, Construction, and implementation of a remote fuel-level monitoring system. J. Wirel. Commun. Networking 76–85 (2014)

Author Index

H. R. Arabnia et al. (Eds.): CSCE 2024, CCIS 2260, pp. 417–418, 2025.
https://doi.org/10.1007/978-3-031-85923-6

The manufacturer's authorised representative in the EU is Springer
Nature Customer Service Centre GmbH, Europaplatz 3, 69115 Heidelberg,
Germany. If you have any concerns regarding our products, please
contact ProductSafety@springernature.com

Printed and bound by CPI Group (UK) Ltd, Croydon, CR0 4YY
27/04/2026
02097586-0015